The "Man Christ Jesus"

The "Man Christ Jesus"

The Humanity of Jesus in the Teaching of the Apostle Paul

STEPHEN O. STOUT

WIPF & STOCK · Eugene, Oregon

THE "MAN CHRIST JESUS"
The Humanity of Jesus in the Teaching of the Apostle Paul

Copyright © 2011 Stephen Oliver Stout. All rights reserved. Except for brief quotations in critical publications or reviews, no part of this book may be reproduced in any manner without prior written permission from the publisher. Write: Permissions, Wipf and Stock Publishers, 199 W. 8th Ave., Suite 3, Eugene, OR 97401.

Wipf & Stock
An Imprint of Wipf and Stock Publishers
199 W. 8th Ave., Suite 3
Eugene, OR 97401
www.wipfandstock.com

ISBN 13: 978-1-61097-287-1
Manufactured in the U.S.A.

Unless otherwise noted, the quotations from the English Bible are taken from the New American Standard Bible (NASB). Copyright © The Lockman Foundation 1960, 1962, 1963, 1968, 1971, 1972, 1973, 1975, 1977, 1988, 1995. Used by permission.

Unless otherwise noted, the quotations from the Greek NT are taken from the BibleWorks, v.8 database (BGT/BNT) of the United Bible Society 4th edition/ Nestle-Aland 27th edition of the *Greek New Testament*, edited by Barbara Aland, Kurt Aland, Johannes Karavidopoulos, Carlo M. Martini, and Bruce M. Metzger in cooperation with the Institute for New Testament Textual Research, Münster/Westphalia. Copyright © 1993 Deutsche Bibelgesellschaft, Stuttgart. Copyright © 1998–2008 *BibleWorks*, LLC. BibleWorks, v.8.

Citations from the Hebrew Bible are taken from the Groves-Wheeler Westminster Morphology and Lemma Database. Copyright © 2008 (release 4.10) by the Westminster Theological Seminary, and used by arrangement with Westminster Theological Seminary, Glenside, Pennsylvania. The Hebrew text has been corrected to the latest available facsimiles of Codex Leningradensis. Copyright © 1998–2008 BibleWorks, LLC.

Unless otherwise noted, the quotations from the Septuagint, the Greek Translation of the OT, are taken from the database of Rahlfs' Septuagint (Copyright © 1935 by the Württembergische Bibelanstalt/Deutsche Bibelgesellschaft, Stuttgart). Copyright © 1998–2008 BibleWorks, LLC.

Scripture quotations marked DBY are from The English Darby Bible 1884/1890, a literal translation by John Nelson Darby (1800-1882), ASCII version Copyright © 1988-1997 by the Online Bible Foundation and Woodside Fellowship of Ontario, Canada. Licensed from the Institute for Creation Research. Used by permission.

Scripture quotations marked ERV are from the English Revised Version (1885). The electronic text is Copyright © 2002 by Larry Nelson, Box 1681, Cathedral City, CA 92235. All rights reserved. Used by permission.

Scripture quotations marked ESV are from the Holy Bible, English Standard Version, copyright © 2001 by Crossway Bibles, a division of Good News Publishers. Used by permission. All rights reserved.

Scripture quotations marked HCSB are taken from the Holman Christian Standard Bible®. Copyright ©1999, 2000, 2002, 2003 by Holman Bible Publishers. Used by permission. Holman Christian Standard Bible®, Holman CSB®, and HCSB® are federally registered trademarks of Holman Bible Publishers.

Scripture quotations marked KJV, KJA, KJG are from the 1769 Blayney Edition of the 1611 King James Version of the English Bible. Copyright © 1988-1997 by the Online Bible Foundation and Woodside

Fellowship of Ontario, Canada. Licensed from the Institute for Creation Research. Used by permission. Scripture quotations marked NET are from *The NET Bible, Version 1.0*, Copyright © 2004, 2005 Biblical Studies Foundation. Used by permission in conformity with the stipulations listed at *www.netbible.org*.

Quotations designated NIV/NIB are from THE HOLY BIBLE: NEW INTERNATIONAL VERSION®. NIV®. Copyright © 1973, 1978, 1984 by International Bible Society, www.ibs.org. All rights reserved worldwide.

Quotations marked NRS are from the *New Revised Standard Version Bible*. Copyright © 1989, Division of Christian Education of the National Council of the Churches of Christ in the United States of America. Used by permission. All rights reserved.

Scripture quotations marked YLT are from The English Young's Literal Translation of the Holy Bible 1862/1887/1898, by J. N. Young. ASCII version Copyright © 1988-1997 by the Online Bible Foundation and Woodside Fellowship of Ontario, Canada. Licensed from the Institute for Creation Research. Used by permission.

All emphases in Scripture quotations have been added by the author.

Note on Style

This book follows the SBL *Handbook of Style* with a few exceptions: in contrast to SBL 4.3, distinction in gender will be observed in deference to biblical texts, particularly with regard to Divine Names. Also, in contrast to SBL 4.4.8, pronouns referring to Divine Names and Titles shall be capitalized, in conformity to the primary English version of use, the NASB, and in respect of the Father, Son, and Holy Spirit.

Contents

Acknowledgments ix
Foreword xi
Preface xiii
Abbreviations xvii

1 Introduction: Jesus and Paul, or, Jesus or Paul? / 1

2 The "Man Christ Jesus" in the Context of 1 Timothy 2:1–6 / 13

3 The "Man Christ Jesus" in the Epistles of Paul / 64

4 The "Man Christ Jesus" in the Presentation of Paul in the Acts of the Apostles / 143

5 The "Man Christ Jesus" in Association with His People / 193

6 Implications of The "Man Christ Jesus" in the Teaching of the Apostle Paul / 229

7 Conclusion: The "Man Christ Jesus" in the Teaching of Paul / 249

Appendix 1: A Complete Listing of the Preposition Σύν in the Pauline Epistles / 253
Appendix 2: A Synthesis of the Pauline References to Association With Christ / 267
Appendix 3: Similarities between the Johannine and Pauline Literature / 272
Scripture Index / 275
Author Index / 299
Subject Index / 302
Bibliography / 307

Acknowledgments

THIS BOOK IS DEDICATED to the memory of my friend Michael Lemmons (October 5, 1952—March 31, 1994), whom the Lord took home much too early, in my estimation, yet his diligence in study of the Word of God as a new and maturing believer continues to motivate me to handle accurately the word of truth (2 Tim 2:15).

It is also dedicated to my family, including my dear and patient wife Marlene; our children, Deirdre and Adam Mumpower; Danielle and Daniel Renstrom; and Lydia and David Poole; and our grandchildren, Brock, Macie and Jack Mumpower, and Bennett, Eden and Mercy Renstrom, plus any others God may provide to fill our quiver.

Special thanks is extended to the faculty and staff of Southeastern Baptist Theological Seminary for their biblical fidelity and scholarly excellence in my course of study; to my major professor in Biblical Theology, Dr. Andreas Köstenberger; to Dr. David Beck, who mentored me in New Testament studies; to Dr. Bruce Ware of Southern Baptist Theological Seminary, who offered many encouraging comments as my external reader; to the faculty of Carolina Evangelical Divinity School, Greensboro, N.C., who reduced my teaching schedule to pursue this project; to the Officers and Congregation of Shearer Presbyterian Church (PCA), Mooresville, N.C., who graciously paid my expenses and granted time away from pastoral duties to write this book; and, to Mrs. Lynn Haddock, who spent many tedious hours proofreading the first draft and making helpful suggestions for clarity of reading.

Supremely, this study is dedicated to the "Man Christ Jesus," who enabled me by His Spirit to pursue these studies in the teachings of His servant Paul. This book is presented for the edification of all those in association with the "Man Christ Jesus."

Foreword

STEPHEN STOUT'S *THE MAN Christ Jesus* is a brilliant contribution to the age-old question of the relationship between Jesus and Paul. Over the past century, a critical consensus increasingly coalesced that Paul had little if any interest in the earthly life of Jesus. One of the most influential voices in this regard was Rudolf Bultmann, who interpreted Paul's reference in 2 Corinthians 5:16, "So from now on we regard no one from an earthly point of view. Though we once regarded Christ in this way, we do so no longer," as suggesting that Paul adopted a disparaging stance toward historical Jesus material.

More recently, however, Oxford scholar David Wenham examined the question to a thorough examination in his work *Paul: Follower of Jesus or Founder of Christianity?* Wenham showed that Paul was far more interested in the earthly Jesus than had heretofore been surmised, particularly by German scholarship. In particular, Wenham unearthed several previously unrecognized or neglected allusions to Jesus' teaching in Paul's writings, such as the reference to mountain-moving faith in 1 Corinthians 13:2.

Stephen Stout, in the present revised version of his doctoral dissertation, builds on Wenham's important contribution and yet significantly goes beyond it. He shows with scrupulous care how Paul's coverage of Jesus' earthly life extends to virtually every major aspect of his career—from the cradle to the grave and beyond. Here is a work that has the potential of significantly altering the entire field of Jesus-and-Paul research. I am grateful to be able to commend this study to you for its meticulous scholarship, its sensible judgments, and its abiding results.

ANDREAS J. KÖSTENBERGER,
WAKE FOREST, NC, FEBRUARY 7, 2011

Preface

TITLE: THE MAN CHRIST JESUS

THIS BOOK IS A revision of my Ph.D. dissertation submitted to the Southeastern Baptist Theological Seminary in Wake Forest, N.C. in 2010, under the able mentorship of Dr. Andreas Köstenberger and Dr. David Beck, under the title "The 'Man Christ Jesus': The Humanity of Jesus in the Teaching of the Apostle Paul."[1] The dissertation studied 1 Timothy 2:5–6, "For there is one God, *and* one mediator also between God and men, *the* man Christ Jesus (ἄνθρωπος Χριστὸς Ἰησοῦς), who gave Himself as a ransom for all, the testimony *borne* at the proper time." For some years, my attention had been arrested by the intriguing description of Jesus as "The Man," for while orthodox Christianity affirms that Jesus is both God and man, my readings in Christology indicated that the humanity of Jesus often takes a distant back seat among fellow evangelicals in their appreciated efforts to defend the deity of Christ. Additional research in Pauline studies revealed a growing trend among popular critical scholars to divorce Paul from Jesus, as if the apostle had little or no use for the historical Jesus in his supposed rush to preach Him as a divine Savior. Such observations led me to ask of that phrase in 1 Tim 2:5, what does Paul teach about the "Man Christ Jesus" in his letters and sermons? That question produced my dissertation and now this book.

THESIS

The thesis of this work is that the Jesus preached by the apostle Paul is the same Jesus of history as portrayed in the four Gospels, so that Paul not only affirms the humanity of the "Man Christ Jesus" in his teachings and sermons, but he also develops his concept of salvation on the association of the Church with the historical events experienced by the "Man Christ Jesus." To prove this thesis, this book investigates the humanity of Jesus as presented in the signed epistles of Paul as well as in his sermons recorded in the Book of Acts and then develops how the apostle uses the historical events of the "Man Christ Jesus" in his theology of redemption. This work will show that the humanity of Jesus is far from being of little or no concern to Paul—as often asserted by modern scholarship in its supposition of 2 Cor 5:16[2]—but instead, the human Jesus of history actually serves as the foundation of

---

1. The title of this work necessarily adds the definite article to make for good reading in English, but the nominative phrase will be printed as the "Man Christ Jesus" in order to express what is written in Greek (ἄνθρωπος Χριστὸς Ἰησοῦς). This study shall argue that Paul intended this anarthrous expression as a technical designation.

2. 2 Cor 5:16 reads, "Therefore from now on we recognize no man according to the flesh; even though

Preface

the apostle's concept not only of his Christology, but also of his soteriology in the distinctly Pauline concept that the church is associated with the "Man Jesus Christ" in the historical acts of His life, death, burial, and resurrection.

RESEARCH METHODOLOGY

While this study interacts with the historical interpretation of Jesus according to Paul (especially in recent scholarship), it concentrates on all the canonical documents associated with the apostle, not only his thirteen signed epistles, but also the indirect testimony toward Paul in the Book of Acts. Thus, this study examines the entire corpus of evidence in order to present a comprehensive picture of the "Man Jesus Christ" according to Paul. From this data, the process identifies the linguistic similarities among the relevant Pauline passages in which allusions to the Jesus of history appear and organizes these verses into related categories. Further exegetical analysis of these texts reveals that the apostle employs a particular vocabulary of verbal compounds and prepositional phrases by which he describes the association of the church with Christ in the historical acts of salvation. Thus, while this study assumes a scholarly approach of an impartial manner required by historians, I attempt to appraise Paul's presentation of the human Jesus of history from his own perspective, asking—and hopefully, answering—what did Paul mean by his teaching?

CHAPTER SUMMARIES

Chapter 1 provides the thesis of this book, that the apostle Paul not only constantly refers to the "Man Christ Jesus" in his sermons and letters, but he also establishes the primary framework of salvation on the historical-redemptive association of the Church with the "Man Jesus Christ" and with His redemptive work accomplished in space-time historical events. A survey of the research into this topic shows that while critical scholarship posits a disparity between Jesus and Paul, evangelical scholarship assumes continuity from Jesus to Paul, yet it has not shown sufficiently how Paul implicitly establishes his gospel in general and his Christology in particular upon the space-time events enacted by the "Man Christ Jesus."

Chapter 2 concerns an exegetical study of the primary clause of this study, *ánthropos Christòs Iēsoûs* (ἄνθρωπος Χριστὸς Ἰησοῦς), as it appears in a liturgical context of 1 Timothy 2:5–6. In this soteriological description of Jesus as the one mediator between God and men and as the ransom given in the witness in His own time, this chapter explores why Christ Jesus is identified as a Man instead of the many other titles at Paul's disposal. The suggested answer is found in the OT appearances of the divine "Man," whose expectations are now fulfilled in the "proper (historical) times" of the mediatorial work of the "Man Christ Jesus" on behalf of God and humanity.

Chapter 3 includes a study of the "Man Christ Jesus" in Paul's letters, challenging the assertion of critical scholarship that Paul was a myth-maker who turned the simple Galilean peasant rabbi into a divine being. Instead, Paul provides the first written

---

we have known Christ according to the flesh, yet now we know *Him thus* no longer."

historical source of Jesus, and an investigation into his letters discovers that the human Jesus permeates the apostle's thinking in every part of his message. This chapter arranges Paul's view of the "Man Christ Jesus" according to the general order given in the Gospels: first, in his identity of the "Man Christ Jesus," addressing whether Paul intended to refer to the historical Jesus of Nazareth of the Gospel records. Second is the topic of the humanity of Jesus, demonstrating that Paul presents Jesus as a real flesh and blood man.[3] Third are those occasions when Paul refers to the ministry of Jesus,[4] and fourth are the instances when Paul cites the character of Jesus as a moral example.[5] Fifth are the allusions to the sufferings of Jesus,[6] and then sixth are the references to the events of Jesus' exaltation.[7] In all these areas, Paul agrees with the life of Jesus as presented in the Gospels although he does not describe Jesus in the setting of narrative biography.

The fourth chapter surveys the indirect testimony of Paul to the "Man Christ Jesus" as recorded in the Book of Acts, in Paul's conversion accounts (Acts 9:1–22; 22:1–16; 26:4–18); his first recorded sermon (Acts 13:16–41); and his missionary preaching (Acts 17:1–3; 17:18–31; 18:5; 19:1–7; 20:17–35). It is shown that Acts assumes that the Jesus whom Paul preaches as Lord and Savior is also the same as the Jesus of the Gospels.

The fifth chapter shows how Paul applies the historical events of the "Man Christ Jesus" to his message of salvation in the concept of the association of the Church with Christ. In distinction from Paul's well-known teaching on union in Christ, the apostle uses a consistent vocabulary involving the preposition *sún* to show the past association of the church with Jesus in His various historical events,[8] its present association with the

---

3. The verses under this topic find Paul presenting Jesus as a man (1 Cor 15:21, 47; Phil 2:8) of physical flesh (Rom 1:3; 8:3; 9:5; 2 Cor 5:16; 1 Tim 3:16; 1 Cor 10:16; 11:24, 27; Col 1:22; 2:9) and blood (Rom 3:25; 5:9; 1 Cor 10:16; 11:25; Eph 1:7; Col 1:20), who was an Israelite (Rom 9:5) born of a woman (Gal 4:4) with siblings (1 Cor 9:5; Gal 1:19) of impoverished means (2 Cor 8:9). His circumcision (Col 2:11), Abrahamic and Davidic lineage (Gal 3:16–17; Rom 1:3; 15:12; 2 Tim 2:8) and legal upbringing (Gal 4:4) prove Him to be a Jewish man.

4. These include: the ministry of Jesus to the Jews (Rom 15:18), beginning with His baptism (Rom 6:3; Col 2:12) and conducted by His preaching (Rom 16:25), evangelizing (Eph 2:7) and teaching on specific topics (Rom 14:14; 1 Cor 7:10; 9:14; 11:23–24, 1 Thess 4:15–5:2; 1 Tim 6:3), with the assistance of disciples (1 Cor 15:5; Gal 2:9) and vindication of angels (1 Tim 3:16).

5. These include: Rom 3:22, 26; 5:18; 1 Cor 11:1; 2 Cor 5:20; 10:1; Gal 2:16; 3:22; 15:3; Phil 1:8; 2:8; 3:19; 2 Thess 3:5; 1 Tim 1:15; and 1 Tim 3:16.

6. This section notes the Last Supper of Jesus (1 Cor 11:23–25); His betrayal (1 Cor 11:23); His deliverance for trial (Rom 4:25); His testimony (2 Tim 1:8); His condemnation under Pontius Pilate (1 Tim 6:13); His bodily injuries (Gal 6:17); His crucifixion (1 Cor 1:23; 2:2; 2 Cor 13:4); His crucifiers (1 Cor 2:8); His murder at the hands of Jewish leadership (1 Thess 2:15); His cross (1 Cor 1:18; Gal 3:1; 5:11; 6:12, 14; Eph 2:16; Phil 2:8; 3:18; Col 1:20); the nailing (Col 2:14); His death (Rom 5:6, 8, 10; 6:3, 5, 10; 8:34; 14:9, 15; 1 Cor 8:11; 11:26; 15:3; 2 Cor 4:10; 5:14–15; Gal 2:21; Phil 2:8; 3:10; Col 1:22; 1 Thess 4:14; 5:10; 2 Tim 2:11); His sacrifice as Passover (1 Cor 5:7); His giving as a ransom (1 Tim 2:6), and His burial in a tomb (Rom 6:4; 1 Cor 15:4; Col 2:12).

7. These include: His resurrection the third day (1 Cor 15:4); His raising from the dead (Rom 4:24–25; 6:4–5, 9; 7:4; 8:34; 10:9; 1 Cor 6:14;15:12–17; 2 Cor 4:14; 5:15; Eph 1:20; Col 2:12; 1 Thess 1:10, 4:14; 2 Tim 2:8); His appearances (1 Cor 9:1; 15:5–9); and His ascension (Rom 8:34; Eph 1:20; 1 Tim 3:16).

8. These include the following: that the Church was crucified with Christ (Rom 6:6; Gal 2:19); planted with Christ in His death (Rom 6:5, 8; Col 2:20); buried with Christ (Rom 6:4; Col 2:12); made alive with Christ (Eph 2:5; Col 2:13); raised with Christ (Eph 2:6; Col 2:12; 3:1); seated with Christ (Eph 2:6); and now

Preface

suffering of the "Man Christ Jesus," and its future association with the exaltation of the "Man Christ Jesus."[9] All these associations depend upon the "Man Christ Jesus" as a figure of human history.

The study concludes with some suggested theological implications, noting that Paul's order of salvation (*ordo salutis*) follows the historical order (*ordo historicis*), in that what the "Man Christ Jesus" did *for* His Church in human history (redemption) is imputed as if the Church did the same *with* Christ (association), resulting in the union of the Church *in* Christ (regeneration), producing what Christ works *in* the Church (sanctification). Thus, this book demonstrates that the foundation of Paul's gospel rests not only upon Jesus as the eternal Son of God but specifically upon Him as a man of history who brings salvation into human history in His life, death, and exaltation as the "Man Christ Jesus."

---

hidden with Christ (Col 3:3).

9. These include the following: that the Church shall live with Christ (Rom 6:8; 2 Cor 13:4; 1 Thess 5:10; 2 Tim 2:11), shall be with Christ (Phil 1:23; 1 Thess 4:17); shall appear with Christ (Col 3:4); shall be brought with Christ (1 Thess 4:14); shall reign with Christ (1 Cor 4:8; 2 Tim 2:12); shall be conformed with Christ (Rom 8:29; Phil 3:21); shall be glorified with Christ (Rom 8:17); shall be raised with Christ (2 Cor 4:14); shall be a fellow heir with Christ (Rom 8:17; Eph 3:6); and shall be given all things with Christ (Rom 8:32).

Abbreviations

BDAG *Greek-English Lexicon of the New Testament and Other Early Christian Literature.*

BDB *Hebrew-Aramaic and English Lexicon of the Old Testament.*

BDF *A Greek Grammar of the New Testament and Other Early Christian Literature.*

BW *Bible Works for Windows.* Copyright © 2008 Bible Works, and updates to Version 8.0.00.

BYZ *The New Testament in the Original Greek: Byzantine Textform (2005).* Public domain.

DLZ Delitzsch Hebrew New Testament (1877). Public domain.

DNTT *Dictionary of New Testament Theology.*

EDNT *Exegetical Dictionary of the New Testament*

ERV The English Revised Version (1885).

ESV The English Standard Version.

HB The Hebrew Bible.

HCSB The Holman Christian Standard Bible

KJV The King James Version of the English Bible.

LN *Greek-English Lexicon of the New Testament: Based on Semantic Domains.*

LXX The *Septuagint*, the Greek Translation of the OT.

MM *The Vocabulary of the Greek Testament: Illustrated from the Papyri and Other Non-Literary Sources*

MT Masoretic Text of the Hebrew Bible (see HB and OT).

NASB The New American Standard Bible

NET The NET Bible

NIV/NIB The New International Version of the Bible

NRS The *New Revised Standard Version Bible.*

NT The New Testament of the Christian Scriptures.

OT The Old Testament of the Hebrew Bible (HB).

TDNT *Theological Dictionary of the New Testament.*

Abbreviations

TLOT Theological Lexicon of the Old Testament.
YLT Young's Literal Translation of the Holy Bible

1

Introduction: Jesus and Paul, or, Jesus or Paul?

IN WHAT HAS TRADITIONALLY been considered one of the later epistles of the apostle Paul,[1] the aging evangelist reminds his disciple Timothy that the gospel message proclaims "God our Savior, who desires all men to be saved and to come to the knowledge of the truth" (1 Tim 2:3–4). The particular truth in Paul's mind follows in the next sentence: "For there is one God, and one mediator also between God and men, the man Christ Jesus, who gave Himself as a ransom for all, the testimony borne at the proper time" (1 Tim 2:5–6). Much has been written about the items of Paul's soteriology stated in this confession: his monotheism, his view of Jesus as mediator and ransom,[2] and the eschatological framework of the revelation of salvation.[3] Sometimes, however, the obvious can easily be overlooked, for what has not received much attention is the succinct identifying phrase, the "Man Christ Jesus" (*ánthropos Christòs Iēsoûs;* ἄνθρωπος Χριστὸς Ἰησοῦς). Here Paul is not referring to the heavenly Lord as he has done so earlier in the epistle (1 Tim 1:2, 12,

---

1. An unexpected defense of Pauline authorship of the Pastoral Epistles appeared from the otherwise quite critical scholar Robinson, *Redating the New Testament*, 67–85. Johnson, *The Writings of the New Testament: An Interpretation*, 423–31, examines the supposed reasons for denying Pauline authorship and frankly acknowledges that the Pastorals are written in Paul's name and "seek to communicate teaching which is recognizably Pauline" (ibid., 424). He calls for the Pastorals to be "restored to separate but equal stature within the Pauline collection" (ibid., 430). From a conservative perspective, Mounce, *Pastoral Epistles*, lxxxxiii–cxxix, ably defends Pauline authorship of 1 Timothy as he chronicles the concurrence of the church Fathers toward Pauline authorship and suggests that the large number of *hapax legomena* in this letter were necessitated due to the refutation of a new heresy. He also observes that the issue of authorship relates more to methodology than with the text itself. See also Porter, "Pauline Authorship and the Pastoral Epistles: Implications for Canon," 105–23, who calls for a "begrudging" acceptance of the Pastorals in formulating a full Pauline theology. This study follows his advice quite willingly in developing a total picture of Paul's thinking.

2. The allusion to the claim of Jesus ("The Son of Man did not come to be served, but to serve, and to give His life a ransom for many.") becomes quite evident when the two passages are compared:

Matt 20:28 || Mark 10:45	δοῦναι	τὴν ψυχὴν αὐτοῦ	λύτρον	ἀντὶ πολλῶν.
1 Tim 2:6	ὁ δοὺς	ἑαυτὸν	ἀντίλυτρον	ὑπὲρ πάντων.

3. Besides 1 Tim 2:6 and 1 Tim 6:13, this eschatological phrase καιροῖς ἰδίοις appears elsewhere only in Titus 1:3, that God promised eternal life "before the ages began but manifested it at the proper time (καιροῖς ἰδίοις)," although Luther gives it a much more personal translation, "zu seiner Zeit" ("in His time"), presumably referring to Jesus. This use of καιρός to express the appearance of Jesus in a pivotal, divinely appointed time is also found in Rom 3:26 ("for the demonstration, *I say*, of His righteousness at the present time") and Rom 5:6, "at the right time Christ died for the ungodly." See Ridderbos, *When the Time had Fully Come*, 44–60, where he argues that while the "times" are eschatological, they are also historical.

THE "MAN CHRIST JESUS"

14, 16, and possibly 1:17[4]) but rather to the earthly Jesus, proven by the ensuing reference in 1 Tim 2:6 to His death (presumed in the theological explanation of His giving as a ransom) and to His witness, a topic repeated at the close of this letter when Paul charges Timothy before "Christ Jesus, who testified the good confession before Pontius Pilate" (1 Tim 6:13). In both instances, Paul bases his arguments upon historical events in the life of Jesus that were familiar to Timothy, even though this epistle may have been written before the composition and circulation of any written Gospel records.[5]

Based upon this unique biblical phrase, the "Man Christ Jesus,"[6] it is the contention of this study that the apostle Paul not only affirms the humanity of the "Man Christ Jesus" in his teachings and sermons, but he also understands salvation as an association of the church with the historical events experienced by the "Man Christ Jesus." In order to defend this proposition, this work presents evidence that the "Man Christ Jesus" preached by Paul as the mediator of salvation between God and humanity is the same as the Jesus of history presented in the four Gospels—there is not "another Jesus" apart from the one Paul proclaimed (2 Cor 11:4).[7] The methodology used to prove this thesis follows an investigation of the humanity of Jesus as presented in the autographed epistles of Paul[8] as well as

---

4. In 1 Tim 1:2 and 1 Tim 1:12, "Christ Jesus our Lord;" 1 Tim 1:14, "the grace of our Lord overflowed for me with the faith and love that are in Christ Jesus;" and 1 Tim 1:16, "Jesus Christ might display His perfect patience as an example to those who were to believe in Him for eternal life." This writer is persuaded by the context of 1 Tim 1:17 ("Now to the King eternal, immortal, invisible, the only God, *be* honor and glory forever and ever. Amen.") that Paul also refers there to the ascended Jesus (see Mounce, *Pastoral Epistles*, 60).

5. Actually, Paul quotes Jesus in 1 Tim 5:18, "The worker is worthy of his wages," a statement recorded in Luke 10:7. It is uncertain, however, if Paul cites from a collection of Jesus' oral *logia* or if he refers to Luke's written gospel. Even Noack, "Teste Paulo: Paul as the Principal Witness to Jesus and the Primitive Christianity," 28, who assumes that Paul's information on Jesus is sparse and his sources incomplete, acknowledges that Paul is the earliest Christian writer so that the "Christian" understanding of Jesus starts with Paul.

6. The title of this work, "The Man Christ Jesus," necessarily adds the definite article to make for good reading in English, but the nominative phrase will be printed as the "Man Christ Jesus" in order to express what is written in Greek (ἄνθρωπος Χριστὸς Ἰησοῦς), an anarthrous expression that—it shall be argued—is intended as a technical designation. For this reason, the noun "Man" in this phrase shall be capitalized also.

7. *Contra* Stevens, *The Pauline Theology*, 206–8, who insists that although Paul was aware of the Jesus of history, he mentions only a "few historical facts incidentally" so that, "It is not the 'Christ of history' but the Christ of eternity to whom Paul traces back the work of salvation (2 Cor viii.9; cf. Phil 2:5 *sq.*)." This study shall argue that Paul shows the opposite, that salvation rests in the works of Jesus accomplished in human history.

8. The writer of this book is well aware that some may dismiss this study as unscholarly because it examines all thirteen of Paul's signed epistles as actually penned by Paul himself, so an appeal is extended to those who reject apostolic authorship to acknowledge that these letters certainly purport to be Pauline. See Wilder, *Pseudonymity, the New Testament, and Deception: An Inquiry into Intention and Reception*, 222–27, where he observes that the invocation of apostolic authority (1 Tim 1:1; 2:7; 5:21), the notice of an impending personal visit (1 Tim 3:14–15; 4:13), and the inclusion of insignificant personal details (1 Tim 5:23) means that someone went to a great deal of trouble to make the Pastorals appear to be genuinely Pauline. If that is the case, then such efforts make the claim of the forger, "I am telling the truth, I am not lying" (1 Tim 2:7) to be especially audacious—unless it is Paul himself making this claim; otherwise, the ethics of even non-deceptive pseudonymity (2 Thess 2:2) suggest that pseudonymous writings ought to be excluded from the canon (ibid., 255). If however, Paul did in fact author his signed epistles, then it would be remiss not to include all pertinent material in a study on Pauline Christology, as argued by Towner, "Christology in the Letters to Timothy and Titus," 220.

in his sermons recorded in the Book of Acts,[9] demonstrating that the humanity of Jesus is far from being of little or no concern to Paul—as often asserted by critical scholarship in its assumption that Paul discards the historical Jesus in 2 Cor 5:16.[10] Instead, the findings of this book will show how frequently the apostle refers to the Jesus of the Gospels, revealing that the human Jesus of history serves as the foundation not only of the apostle's Christology but also of his Soteriology in the distinctly Pauline concept that the church is associated with the "Man Christ Jesus" in the acts of His life, death, burial, resurrection, and ascension. Thus, this book supports the historical continuity between Jesus and Paul, as Michael Bird succinctly observes, "According to Paul, Christology is understanding the 'man Christ Jesus' (1 Tim 2:5) and the 'gospel of Christ. . . .'"[11]

The importance of such a study on the "Man Christ Jesus" remains pertinent, since writings continue to appear insisting that Paul was the originator of a divine Christ who has little or no connection to the historical, human Jesus;[12] thus, one must choose between Jesus or Paul—and invariably, the apostle is rejected. This perspective continues to resurface despite the efforts of conservative scholars to refute the contentions of the critics, as the Cambridge scholar Lightfoot divulged the fallacies of Baur in the late nineteenth century;[13] as Machen[14] and Rawlinson[15] corrected the comparative-religions intrusion of Wrede and Bousset upon Paul in the early twentieth century; as F. F. Bruce exposed

---

9. It is not within the scope of this study to explore the authenticity of the Pauline and Lukan corpora, since extensive studies on that topic currently exist; for example, see Köstenberger et al., *The Cradle, the Cross, and the Crown: An Introduction to the New Testament*. It is the opinion of this writer that the arguments supporting traditional authorship are convincing and can stand the tests of inquiry. That being the case, this study will assume the Pauline authorship of the thirteen letters bearing his signature, as well as the Lukan authenticity of the recorded sermons of Paul in the book of Acts. Furthermore, this study will also assume the apostolic authority of those writings as binding upon believers, written under the nomenclature of 2 Tim 3:16–17, that "All Scripture *is* given by inspiration of God, and *is* profitable for doctrine, for reproof, for correction, for instruction in righteousness, that the man of God may be complete, thoroughly equipped for every good work." In other words, this study will follow a textual approach within the traditional canon of the Bible.

10. 2 Corinthians 5:16 reads, "Therefore from now on we recognize no man according to the flesh; even though we have known Christ according to the flesh, yet now we know *Him thus* no longer." Bultmann, "The Significance of the Historical Jesus and the Theology of Paul," 241, often refers to this verse in support of his position that Paul is not interested in "Christ after the flesh," the historical Jesus, but only the proclaimed Christ who is the Lord.

11. Bird, *Introducing Paul: The Man, His Mission, and His Message*, 161. In support of this assertion, Bird also references Rom 15:19; 1 Cor 9:12; 2 Cor 2:13; 9:13; 10:14; Gal 1:7; Phil 1:27; 1 Thess 3:2.

12. As argued by Klausner, *From Jesus to Paul*; Lüdemann, *Paul, Apostle to the Gentiles: Studies in Christology*; Maccoby, *The Mythmaker: Paul And The Invention of Christianity*; Lüdemann, *Paul: The Founder of Christianity*; Kuhn, *Paul Knows Not Jesus*. A random internet search found such articles as these, showing the relevance of this issue: Danizier, "Paul vs. Jesus"; Wright, "Who Founded Christianity: Jesus or Paul?"; Jones, "Paul vs. Jesus: a List"; Nelson, "Yahshua (Jesus) and Judaism Versus Paul and Christianity"; Shriner, "The Apostle Paul Was A Deceiver!"; Zawadi, "What Did Paul Want To Know About Jesus?"; Zeoli, "Paul or Jesus?"; Brother Nazariah, "Yahshua or Paul? Essene Christianity Versus Paulinity: An Exposé and Call to Action"; Loflin, "The Apostle Paul Founder of Christianity."

13. Lightfoot, "St. Paul and the Three," in *The Epistle of St. Paul to the Galatians*, 292–374.

14. Machen, *The Origin of Paul's Religion*.

15. Rawlinson, *The New Testament Doctrine of the Christ: The Brampton Lectures for 1926*, 93–98.

THE "MAN CHRIST JESUS"

Bultmann's existential imposition on Paul;[16] and as Kim tackled Dunn's new perspectives on Paul at the turn of the twenty-first century.[17] One would have supposed that the reasoned arguments presented by A. M. Hunter to "liberal Protestantism" in demonstrating the unity between "The Lord and The Apostle" would have silenced all attacks,[18] but a new generation of critics has arisen, spearheaded by the bestselling novel of Pullmann[19] and the prolific writings of B. D. Ehrman, packaging the same faultfinding in new popular garb.[20]

For all their differences, critical scholars share the same basic rejection of the orthodox Christian belief that the miraculous occurred within human history, thus casting doubt on the doctrines of revelation, inspiration and canonicity in their claim to read the Bible like any other book.[21] Critical scholarship has insisted that since the supernatural cannot be verified scientifically, interpretation must call into question Paul's Damascus Road conversion, dismiss his claim to have received his gospel by divine revelation (Gal 1:12), and insist that his explanation of Jesus is an imposition of Hellenistic mythology[22] or Jewish apocalyptic legends.[23] Paul's teachings are viewed as no better than any other ancient source, and perhaps they may be worse.[24] In this sort of

---

16. Bruce, *Paul and Jesus*.

17. Kim, *Paul and the New Perspective: Second Thoughts on the Origin of Paul's Gospel*.

18. Hunter, *The Gospel according to Paul*, 77. He exposes "two fundamental mistakes of liberalism": first, it "denied the messianic element of Christ's person and work" and then it "sought to compare two incompatible things—the Jesus of the Gospel in *his* historical situation and the apostle's Christ in *his*" (italics original).

19. Pullman, *The Good Man Jesus and the Scoundrel Christ* (2010).

20. Ehrman, *Lost Christianities* (2003); *Misquoting Jesus* (2005); *Peter, Paul, and Mary Magdalene: The Followers of Jesus in History and Legend* (2006); *Jesus, Interrupted* (2009). Ehrman has popularized the opinions espoused in Walter Bauer's 1934 work, *Orthodoxy and Heresy in Earliest Christianity*, that no singular portrayal of the historical Jesus can be determined from the varied interpretations of His person in the first three centuries A.D. This view is aptly countered by Köstenberger and Kruger, *The Heresy of Orthodoxy* (2010).

21. Neill and Wright, *The Interpretation of the New Testament*, 33, calls this "the heart of the matter," that "all awkward questions were supposed to be stilled by the protection of inspiration." The classic study of Paul as interpreted by nineteenth century critical methods (mostly by German scholars) is that of Schweitzer, *Paul and His Interpreters: A Critical History* (1912). He is brutally frank in his assessment that critical scholars failed to find a Hellenized Paul in particular because they "became involved in the jungle of antinomies which they discover or imagine, and there perished miserably" (ibid., 240). Schweitzer found the solution in Paul's eschatology, developed in *Die Mystik des Apostels Paulus* (1931) and translated as *The Mysticism of Paul the Apostle* (1955).

22. Fee, *Pauline Christology: An Exegetical–Theological Study*, 10–15, surveys developments in this field in the twentieth century, noting the influences of Bousset, *Kyrios Christos: A History of the Belief in Christ from the Beginnings of Christianity to Irenaeus* as a "thoroughgoing advocate of a *religiongeschichtliche* ("history of religions") view of early Christian history" (ibid., 11). This same view was further promoted by Bultmann, "Die Bedeutung des geschichtlichen Jesus für die Theologie des Paulus" (220–46), who maintains that Jesus' preaching is irrelevant for Paul: the apostle centers not on the *Was* of Jesus as a *historische* person but the *Dass* of the *kerygma* (ibid., 241).

23. The idea that Paul understands Jesus as the Adam or Enoch figure of contemporary Jewish literature seems to be a growing trend in scholarship, now that it has been shown that Paul is thoroughly Jewish in his approach rather than one who synthesized Jesus with Greek or Persian mythology. For example, after noting the legendary ideas in *Ben Sirach, Wisdom of Solomon, Jubilees, The Life of Adam and Eve*, and other Second Temple Literature, Dunn writes that "Paul was entering into an already well-developed debate and that his own views were not uninfluenced by its earlier participants" (*The Theology of Paul the Apostle*, 90),

24. Kümmel, *The New Testament: The History of the Investigation of Its Problems*, 288–99, traces the views of

Introduction: Jesus and Paul, or, Jesus or Paul?

climate, it is no wonder that serious inquiry into Paul's view of Jesus has been sparse,[25] although a steady stream of studies into the relationship between Jesus and Paul has appeared over the past two centuries,[26] some arguing for continuity[27] but many contending

---

radical historical criticism toward Paul, so that Wrede, *Paulus*, 179, insisted that Jesus and Paul were so utterly different in their teachings that one must choose between one or the other. Wrede's view set the stage for the twentieth century discussions of Paul's Christology. In this vein, see Singer, *The Rival Philosophies of Jesus and of Paul* (1919), 80, who insists that Paul "never even troubled to inform himself what Jesus taught by consulting those who might have known," meaning that Paul is the one who conceived the idea of the "Christ."

25. Fee, *Pauline Christology*, 10, maintains that in the history of NT scholarship only one study can legitimately be called a "Pauline Christology," and that is the 1963 work of Kramer, *Christ, Lord, Son of God*—although Fee humbly omits his own 2007 monumental work. Fee adds to this the broader work of Cullmann, *The Christology of the New Testament*, who studies the titles of Jesus as focusing on "function" rather than "being" (ibid., 13). The dissolution of the *religionsgeschichtliche Schule* of Bousset and Bultmann was signaled by Hengel in his works, *The Son of God: The Origin of Christology and the History of Jewish-Hellenistic Religion*, and *Studies in Early Christology*, in which he demonstrates the Jewish roots of Paul's thinking. The next significant work is that of Dunn, *Christology in the Making: A New Testament Inquiry into the Origins of the Doctrine of the Incarnation* (2003), in which he advocates a modified adoptionist position of Paul's Christology. His view was answered by Kim, *Origin of Paul's Gospel* (2007), who maintains that Paul's Christology derives from his Damascus Road experience. Bauckham, *God Crucified: Monotheism and Christology in the New Testament*, argues that the church held from its inception that Christ shared in the divine identity of the one God of Israel, while Hurtado, *Lord Jesus Christ: Devotion to Jesus in Earliest Christianity* (2003), shows that the church maintained a high Christology from its beginning by ascribing worship to Jesus. While these works will be consulted regularly in this study, it is noted that their concern is the resolution of the tension between Paul's "first conviction, that there is only one God," with his identification of Christ as the divine Son of God (Fee, *Pauline Christology*, 7). This study shall approach the matter from another direction, showing how Paul views this same heavenly Person as also the "Man Christ Jesus." The tension between the humanity and deity of Jesus is latent in the text, created not so much by Paul, but by the human Jesus of Nazareth when He made Himself out to be God (John 10:33). The apparent conflict is resolved only by acknowledging that Paul preaches "Christ according to the flesh" who is also "God blessed forever" (Rom 9:5).

26. For a survey of works in German, see Regner, "*Paulus und Jesus*" (1977).

27. Matheson, "The Historical Christ of St. Paul" (1881), confirmed agreement of Paul with the Synoptics; Schmoller, "Die geschichtliche Person Jesu nach den paulinischen Schriften" (1894), answered B. Bauer, that Paul contributes to knowledge of Jesus; Resch, *Der Paulinismus und die Logia Jesu in ihrem gegenseitigen Verhaltnis untersucht* (1904) located hundreds of literary similarities between Paul and Jesus; Lloyd defended continuity in his 1901 article, "The Historic Christ in the Letters of Paul," as does Jülicher, *Paulus und Jesus* (1907); Feine's works, *Jesus Christus und Paulus* (1902) and *Paulus als Theologe* (1906), refuted Hellenistic influences on Paul but understands him within Jewish apocalyptic, while Heitmüller, "Zum Problem Paulus und Jesus" (1912) argued that Paul depends on Jesus but only as defined by Hellenistic Christianity; Kittel, "Jesus bei Paulus" (1912), found the historical Jesus in the foreground of Paul; Machen, "Jesus and Paul," observed that liberals created a liberal Jesus and then accused Paul of denying this Jesus; Knight asks, "Jesus or Paul? In Continuation of Gospels and Epistles" (1947), and Lattey studied "Quotations of Christ's Sayings in St. Paul's Epistles" (1949). Other defending continuity include: Duncan, "From Jesus to Paul" (1949); Ridderbos, *Paul and Jesus* (1950); Turlington, "The Apostle Paul and the Gospel History" (1951); Beare, "Jesus and Paul" (1959); Stanley, "Pauline Allusions to the Sayings of Jesus" (1961), and Jüngel, *Paulus und Jesus* (1967). Furnish, *Jesus According to Paul* (1994) explored what knowledge Paul had of Jesus; Barnes, *The Gospel: Did Paul and Jesus Agree?* (1994), compared their respective teachings and found them in general agreement; Wedderburn, *Paul and Jesus* (2004), contains essays on the relationship between Paul and Jesus, pro and con, while Still, *Jesus and Paul Reconnected* (2007) includes essays in defense of continuity, as does Murphy O-Connor, *Jesus and Paul: Parallel Lives* (2007). Of special note are the works by Wenham, *Paul: Follower of Jesus or Founder of Christianity?* (1995); *Paul and the Historical Jesus* (1998); *Paul and Jesus: The True Story* (2002); and, *Did St. Paul Get Jesus Right?* (2010). In sum, Bénétreau, "Jésus ou Paul? Qui et le fondateur du christianisme?" n. p., concludes his online article, "Deux suffisent pour la relation de Paul au

THE "MAN CHRIST JESUS"

for discontinuity.[28] In general, however, James Dunn notes that critical scholarship "maintains that Paul knew or cared little about the ministry of Jesus apart from His death and resurrection,"[29] following on the remark of Baur, that "the only question comes to be how the apostle Paul appears in his epistles to be so indifferent to the historical facts of the life of Jesus."[30]

While evangelical scholars have responded to defend the continuity between the teachings of Jesus and that of Paul,[31] many have conceded to the critical assertion that Paul shows at best only nominal interest in the historical Jesus, so that in-depth exploration of Paul's concept of the humanity of Jesus has been all but neglected.[32] Instead, it is the thesis

---

Jésus des évangiles, et nous privilégions: nouveauté dans la continuité."

28. Those generally arguing against continuity from Jesus to Paul are: F. C. Baur, *Paulus, der Apostel Jesu Christi* (1845), who raised the question why Paul seems "indifferent to the historical facts of the life of Jesus;" Paret, "Paulus und Jesus" (1858) maintained that apart from the *Geschichte* Jesus, the *Geschichte des Herrn* cannot be discerned; von Weizsäcker, *The Apostolic Age* (1894) insisted that Paul's theology derives from his own intuitions rather than the teachings of Jesus; Wendt, "Die Lehre des Paulus verglichen mit der Lehre Jesu," (1894) argued that Paul recast the teaching of Jesus in terms of salvation; Renan, *St. Paul* (1889) suggested that Paul transformed Jesus into the divine Christ; Strum, *Der Apostel Paulus und die evangelische Ueberlieferung* (1900), compared the "salvation words" of Jesus and Paul to demonstrate similarities while Goguel, *L'Apôtre Paul et Jésus-Christ* (1904), maintained that Paul's teaching differs fundamentally from Jesus' preaching; Wrede, however, in his work, *Paulus* (1907), contended that Paul identified Jesus with his pre-conversion idea of a divine Christ, making Paul the "second founder of Christianity;" Brückner, "Zum Theme Jesus und Paulus" (1906), concluded that Paul reveals no influence of Jesus on his Christology: their only commonality is found in Judaism; Weiss, *Paul and Jesus* (1909), insisted that Paul even witnessed the historical Jesus but was influenced only by His personality rather than His teaching; Meyer gave the choice, *Jesus or Paul?* (1909); Bousset, *Kyrios Christos* (1913) claimed to find the origin of Paul's Christology in Hellenistic mystery religions; Weinel, *Paulus* (1915), pioneered the history-of-religion method to support liberal theology; Deissmann, argued in *The Religion of Jesus and the Faith of Paul* (1923) and in *Paulus* (1925) that to the apostle, Jesus is not a historical figure but a present reality; Shirley Jackson Case, *Jesus: A New Biography* (1925) contended that Paul had no interest in the traditions of the life and teaching of Jesus; Bultmann, "Die Bedeutung des geschichtlichen Jesus für die Theologie des Paulus" (1928) insisted that Jesus' preaching is irrelevant for Paul; Windisch, "Paulus und Jesus" (1934), presented both Jesus and Paul as charismatic visionary "divine men;" and Klausner, *From Jesus to Paul* (1939) argued that Paul establishes Christianity on Hellenistic Judaism unlike the Palestinian Judaism of Jesus. Lindemann, "Paulus und die JesusTradition," 315–16, gives a bibliography of twentieth century works in German on this subject.

29. Dunn, "Jesus Tradition in Paul," 155. It seems that much of the critical field of scholarship still remains captivated by the "history of religions" views of Bultmann, *Theology of the New Testament*, 188, who maintained that Paul "barely shows traces of the influence of Palestinian tradition concerning the history and preaching of Jesus," but instead interprets Christ "in the categories of the Gnostic myth" (ibid., 298). Under such a scheme, there is no need to explore Paul's understanding of the humanity of Jesus.

30. F. C. Baur, *The Church History of the First Three Centuries*; cited by Meeks, ed., *The Writings of St. Paul*, 280. Once Baur pitted Paul against Peter in "Die Christuspartie in der corintheschen Gemeinde" (1831), it was inevitable that he would eventually question Paul's relationship to Jesus also.

31. In this group, one would include Machen, "Jesus and Paul," *Biblical and Theological Studies* (1912); Machen, *The Origin of Paul's Religion* (1921); Ridderbos, *Paul and Jesus: Origin and General Character of Paul's Preaching of Christ* (1950); Dungan, *The Sayings of Jesus in the Churches of Paul: The Use of the Synoptic Tradition in the Regulation of Early Church Life* (1971); Barnes, *The Gospel: Did Paul and Jesus Agree?* (1994); and more recent works by Wenham, *Paul and Jesus: The True Story* (2002); Wedderburn, *Paul and Jesus* (2004); and Still, ed., *Jesus and Paul Reconnected* (2007).

32. For example, Bruce, *Paul and Jesus*, 19, writes, "Paul is our earliest literary authority for the historical Jesus. True, he does not tell us much about the historical Jesus," so Bruce gives a paltry four paragraphs before

of this study that the apostle actually shows quite the opposite: he constantly refers to the historical "Man Christ Jesus" in his sermons and letters as the basis of his gospel message in that he presumes the actual life and events of Jesus of Nazareth.[33] An examination of these references will reveal that Paul is in complete agreement with the portrayal of Jesus found in the four Gospels, as he cites (by our count) seventy-one separate incidents from the life of Jesus, so that if the Gospels were unavailable, a skeletal biography of Jesus could be reconstructed strictly from the testimony of Paul, who, after all, is the earliest literary source of the historical Jesus.[34] This study will show that in referring to the human Jesus, Paul uses the common literary practice of allusion rather than employing extensive

---

admitting that "from the Pauline letters we should not know that Jesus habitually taught in parables, that He healed the sick or performed other messianic 'signs'; we should not know of His baptism or temptation, of His Galilean ministry, of the confession at Caesarea Philippi, or of the transfiguration . . . (ibid., 20–21)." This does not seem to be much to go on, and a survey of other evangelical scholars exhibits a similar resignation. Morris, *New Testament Theology,* 41–42, gives two paragraphs of Paul's historical interest in Jesus, with the admission, "It is true that in common with the epistolary tradition throughout the New Testament he (Paul) does not refer to many incidents in Jesus' earthly life." Ladd, *A Theology of the New Testament,* 378, comments on the "relative silence about Jesus" and concludes that "the facts of Jesus' earthly ministry, his teachings and mighty works, even his character and personality, were not a necessary part of the Pauline message of redemption." Guthrie, *New Testament Theology,* 225–26, devotes only three pages (out of 1064!) to Paul's view of the humanity of Jesus, stating that "it must be frankly admitted that Paul has more to say about the divine nature of Christ than about his humanity" and what references exist are "mostly incidental." While affirming that the centrality of Christ is the "theological vision" of the NT, Thielman, *Theology of the New Testament* (2005), 725, does not even address the historical connection between Jesus and Paul in his introductory chapter on Paul (ibid., 219–33). Even Ridderbos, from whom this writer learned the historical-redemptive framework of Pauline theology in his book *Paul: An Outline of His Theology* (1975), 65–68, nearly depreciates the earthly humanity of Jesus by his insistence upon Jesus as the exalted New Adam. All this indicates the need for a fuller investigation into Paul's view of the humanity of Jesus from an evangelical perspective.

33. This study understands "history" as what actually happened in human space and time, in the sense that Collinwood, *The Idea of History,* 9, defines historical research as inquiry into "actions of human beings that have been done in the past." He adds that the historical method "consists essentially of interpreting evidence," in the sense of asking, "What does this particular event mean?" (ibid., 10). Thus, this study examines the events of Jesus as mentioned by Paul and asks, what did those events mean for Paul in his applications to the churches to whom he wrote? This understanding contrasts to the application of existentialism to history by Fuchs, "The Theology of the New Testament and the Historical Jesus," 176, that Paul's view of faith actually "breaks the salvation-history scheme of promise-fulfillment" so that the important matter of NT theology is that it brings the historical Jesus into language (ibid., 190). Whatever Fuchs may mean by his comments, this study shall take Paul's statements of history at face value, not merely considering them as data for historical theology but rather providing an examination of the man Jesus who is the Source and Object of such study. See also the discussion, "What's Historical about Jesus?" in Johnson, *The Real Jesus,* 105–40, in which he reminds that the historical data of the NT was recorded from a faith perspective, a coloring distrusted by critical scholarship yet one that is brashly proclaimed by the NT. The reader must choose which approach provides the more credible results into the quest for Jesus.

34. This is the persuasive reminder of Akenson, *Saint Saul: A Skeleton Key to the Historical Jesus,* that Paul's letters pre-date the Gospels, which, he asserts, were all written after the destruction of Jerusalem in A. D. 70; however, Akenson rejects the historical record of Paul in Acts as well as half his epistles, leaving him with very truncated apostle with which to work. Furthermore, while he asserts that Paul probably did know and teach the stories and sayings of Jesus, when "moments of spiritual crisis loomed, . . . the entire earthly life of the historical Yeshua did not count. Only the post-earthly Christ did" (ibid., 173). This present study will challenge this statement directly and demonstrate that Paul rests his understanding of salvation initially on the historical Jesus who then became the "post-earthly" Lord by virtue of His resurrection and ascension.

citation—based upon the assumption that he shares the same knowledge of this Jesus with his original readers.

Yet it is apparent that Paul does not present a narrative biography of Jesus, a fact he states in another oft-discussed comment: "Even though we have known Christ according to the flesh, yet now we know *Him thus* no longer" (2 Cor 5:16). At first blush, Paul seems to indicate that to know only the Christ of the flesh (the historical Jesus) is insufficient, due to the obvious reason that He is no longer present in an earthly existence.[35] This deduction, however, overlooks the fact that had there been no historical Jesus, Paul would have no heavenly Lord to proclaim as Savior and Lord. Instead, the apostle makes the key historical events in the life of the "Man Christ Jesus" the foundation of his soteriology in that he associates the entire redeemed community with Christ in His life, death, burial, resurrection, and ascension.[36]

This association of the church with Christ in His historical works is a unique Pauline concept pervading his entire understanding of salvation, but it has been greatly neglected in theological studies, in part due to the imprecise translation of Pauline terminology in English versions and also because association with Christ is presumed to be identical to the well-known and oft-discussed teaching of union in Christ.[37] This study shall argue, however, that the mystical union in Christ more properly falls under the theological category of regeneration, whereas on the other hand, association with Christ roots in the historical realities of the earthly humanity of Jesus. Association thus relates to Paul's teaching on imputation with Christ as "the One Man" (Rom 5:15). This distinction shows that association with the historical Christ takes precedence soteriologically over union in Christ: there could be no participative union in Christ without the historical-redemptive

---

35. Machen, *Origin of Paul's Religion*, 131, observes that the prepositional phrase "according to the flesh" modifies the verb "we have known," not the direct object, "Christ," so that "(Paul) is not speaking of two different conceptions of Christ, but of two different ways of knowing Christ," one of His earthly career and the other of His heavenly status.

36. Dodd, *History and the Gospel*, 25–26, reminds that Christianity is a historical religion, meaning that its defining events happened in the course of human activity and that these incidents are preserved in the NT, which serves as "a record of the interest and meaning which they bore for those who took part in them." What makes the history of Christianity distinct is that it records unique supernatural events surrounding Jesus of Nazareth at every stage of His life—His conception, baptism, ministry, death, resurrection, and ascension. Yet Paul applies these same miraculous episodes to the experience of believers, linking together the acts of Jesus with those whom Paul describes as being baptized into His body (1 Cor 12:13). This study will explore how Christ and His people are linked historically by the concept of association.

37. Lohmeyer, "ΣΥΝ ΧΡΙΣΤΩ," *Festgabe für Adolph Deissmann* (1927), wrote his ground-breaking monograph on the topic of association with Christ but provides surprisingly little exegesis. Best, *One Body in Christ*, 44–45, gives a two-page overview of the pertinent texts. Schweizer, "Dying and Rising with Christ," calls his own article a "scanty summary" (ibid., 8), while Tannehill gives a fuller treatment in *Dying and Rising with Christ* but understands the concept eschatologically and sacramentally rather than historically (ibid., 39–43). Smedes, *Union with Christ: A Biblical View of the New Life in Jesus Christ*, 94–97, does not even list all the pertinent passages and explains "with Christ" dynamically rather than historically. While Douty, *Union with Christ*, 192–96, links the concept to the historical aspects of Christ's work, he gives no particular discussion to the "with Christ" idea in Paul, despite the title of his book; instead, he merges the concept into participative sanctification. It is generally assumed that Paul makes no differentiation between "in Christ" and "with Christ," but Harvey raises that possibility in his 1992 article, "The 'With Christ' Motif in Paul's Thought." This study picks up his challenge to show that the phrases display distinct soteriological emphases.

association with Christ, because the believer's union in Christ is the dynamic experience that rests on the reality of association with Christ—which in turn depends on the historical actualities of the life of Jesus.

Consequently, the thesis of this study is that the apostle Paul not only refers often to the historical Jesus—in contrast to the assertions of critical studies and resignations of conservative studies—but that he also establishes the primary framework of salvation on the historical-redemptive association of the church with the "Man Jesus Christ."[38] Thus the apostle displays a developed 'anthropological Christology' whereby he preaches Jesus not only as the heavenly Lord but also as the human Christ. Contrary to the assertions that Paul finds the center of his theology in the experience of his conversion, or in the mystical union in Christ, or even in the classical Protestant perspective of justification through faith in Christ (though not to diminish the importance of these and other aspects of Paul's teachings that could be added to the list),[39] it is the argument of this study that the center of Paul's theology—in his own words—is that "Christ is all and in all" (Col 2:11). While this Christ is now the ascended Lord who appeared to Paul, He was first known as the human Jesus who accomplished His redemptive work in space and time historical events. Had the "Man Christ Jesus" not acted in human history, Paul would have no gospel to proclaim, but now he preaches "Christ crucified" (1 Cor 1:23), a message about the historical actions of a man who lived "according to the flesh," but whom he then directly describes as "God blessed forever" (Rom 9:5).[40] It is this neglected aspect of Paul's use of the humanity of Jesus that this study shall explore, "since orthodox Christianity has historically had a tendency toward Apollonarianism, wherein one pays lip service to Christ's humanity but then emphasizes the deity in ways that often tend to negate the genuineness of the humanity."[41] Hopefully, the emphasis of this study on the humanity of Jesus will contribute to a fuller

---

38. Ridderbos, *Paul*, 39, surveys the twentieth century scholarship in Paul and states that the "growing consensus insofar that scholars are more and more finding in the point of departure for an adequate approach to the whole is in the *redemptive-historical, eschatological character of Paul's proclamation* (italics original). The governing motif of Paul's preaching is the saving activity of God in the advent and the work, particularly in the death and the resurrection, of Christ. This activity is on the one hand the fulfillment of the work of God in the history of the nation Israel, the fulfillment there also of the Scriptures; on the other hand, it reaches out to the ultimate consummation of the parousia of Christ and coming of the Kingdom of God."

39. Wright, *What Saint Paul Really Said*, 12–19, provides a succinct overview of the major Pauline scholars of the twentieth century (he lists Schweitzer, Bultmann, Davies, Käsemann, and Sanders), and then he summarizes the status of Pauline studies as the new century begins (ibid., 20–22). Amid the varieties of approaches to Paul, Wright states, "As we sharpen our scholarly lenses in order to bring Paul himself into focus, we begin to glimpse in the background a larger question of which he is a vital part. . . . Was Paul the true interpreter of Jesus?" (ibid., 22).

40. Romans 9:5 may well be the clearest affirmation of the deity of Christ in Paul's letters, as it reads, ". . . the Christ according to the flesh, who is over all, God blessed forever. Amen" (ὁ Χριστὸς τὸ κατὰ σάρκα, ὁ ὢ‡ν ἐπὶ πάντων θεὸς εὐλογητὸς εἰς τοὺς αἰῶνας, ἀμήν.). NET *Notes*, loc. cit. 14, comments that Rom 9:5 can be translated, "the Christ, who is over all, God blessed forever," or "the Messiah. God who is over all be blessed forever!" or "the Messiah who is over all. God be blessed forever!" It explains, "The translational difficulty here is not text-critical in nature, but is a problem of punctuation. Since the genre of these opening verses of Romans 9 is a lament, it is probably best to take this as an affirmation of Christ's deity (as the text renders it)." Even so, one should not overlook Paul's conspicuous assertion of the humanity of Jesus that He was "the Christ according to flesh."

41. Fee, *Pauline Christianity*, 513.

THE "MAN CHRIST JESUS"

picture of Paul's Christology, showing that the apostle not only preaches Jesus as the exalted and divine Lord—concepts for which he is well known—but he also teaches and assumes a highly developed humanity of the "Man Jesus Christ" as the one with whom the entire church is associated in the overall scheme of redemption.

While this study will interact with the historical interpretation of Jesus according to Paul (especially in recent scholarship),[42] a full-orbed understanding of Paul's view of the humanity of Jesus should concentrate on all the pertinent documents associated with the apostle, not only his thirteen signed epistles, but also the indirect testimony toward Paul in the book of Acts.[43] Thus, this study will take a canonical approach and weigh the entire corpus of evidence in this matter in order to present a comprehensive picture of the "Man Jesus Christ" according to Paul. To some, this limitation is a glaring deficiency, yet in the end, all that is known of Paul (other than post-biblical tradition) derives from this literary record. If a survey of the history of interpretation shows anything,[44] it is that studies wander into speculation on the evolution of Paul's theology. In actuality, what he presents in his letters arrives in fully developed form.[45] Even worse is the tendency of critical scholarship to impose upon Paul the very pagan notions he repudiates, whether derived from Greek mythology[46] or Jewish legends.[47] Thus, the best course of study takes the pertinent literature at face value rather than imagining what may or may not lie be-

---

42. Actually, the study of Pauline doctrine as a distinct discipline of Biblical Theology is fairly recent in terms of Christian scholarship. Schweitzer, *Paul and His Interpreters*, 9, traces its beginnings in 1824, when the Swiss theologian Leonhard Usteri, a pupil of Schleiermacher, published his *Entwicklung des Paulinischen Lehrbegriffs* (1824), a work "generally regarded as the starting-point of the purely historical study of Paulinism, the first attempt to give effect to the demands of Semler" to separate NT studies from dogmatic considerations by a "dispassionate, objective study of facts" (ibid., 6). Since 1824 Paul has been regularly subjected to nonbiblical philosophical impositions, as Schweitzer observes that Baur read Paul through Hegel's dialectical philosophy (ibid., 16), Holtzmann through Kantian idealism (ibid., 112), and Wrede through Comparative Religions ("religionschichtliche Methode," ibid., 175), even as Bultmann read Paul through Heidegger's existentialism. See also Macquarrie, *An Existentialist Theology: A Comparison of Heidegger and Bultmann* (1955). This study intends to understand Paul as explained by Paul himself and by the beloved physician Luke (Col 4:14), traditionally recognized as Paul's travelling companion.

43. A canonical approach implies boundaries of research, in contrast to the suggestion of Bella, *Challenges to New Testament Theology: An Attempt to Justify the Enterprise*, 22, who claims ". . . there is no need to exclude from 'theology' what Räisänen refers to as aspects of religion or branches in the study of religion: 'cult, rite, myth, community' including 'historical, psychological and social realities.'" Instead, this study limits itself to the Pauline witness as a corpus considered to be inspired by the church because of its apostolic origins.

44. For example, Fraser, *Jesus and Paul: Paul as Interpreter of Jesus from Harnack to Kümmel*, 11–32, surveys the debate toward the end of the twentieth century.

45. It seems to be an accepted notion of scholarship that Paul, like every other thinker, refines his opinions upon further reflection. Such a vacillating person is not the Paul one meets in the NT; in fact, he specifically denies such charges (2 Cor 1:17–19). This is not to say that Paul did not mature in his understanding of Jesus after his Damascus Road encounter, but the literary record in Acts and in Paul's Epistles reveals no trace whatsoever that he adjusted his Christology to changing circumstances.

46. As surmised by the *religionsgeschichte schule* of Bousset, Reitzenstein, and Bultmann.

47. For example, Cullmann, *Christology*, 166–81, while recognizing Paul's Jewish roots, tries to locate the origin of Paul's Christology in contemporary Jewish apocalyptic legends, such as a primal Adam.

hind the texts.[48] In this manner, what one finds is that Paul proclaims the Jesus of history through the lens of the OT Scriptures with one great historical reality: Jesus is now the resurrected Lord. Of necessity, Paul's post-resurrection perspective must be an advance on the pre-resurrection teachings of Jesus as recorded in the Gospels. Thus, Paul becomes the first (literary) explainer of that which Jesus anticipated, and the task of the interpreter is to determine precisely what Paul meant by his own explanations within the broader context of the canon of Scripture.

Such research, then, necessitates selection of the relevant passages in which allusions to the historical Jesus appear in Pauline contexts, identified by linguistic similarities and organized into related categories. Then, exegetical analysis of these passages will further limit the references to those including a particular Pauline concept this study shall describe as "association with Christ." It shall be demonstrated that Paul employs a distinctive vocabulary of word-compounds prefixed with the preposition *sún* (σύν) and prepositional phrases governed by *sún* (σύν) in which he associates the entire church with the "Man Christ Jesus."[49] These linguistic affinities total thirty instances in twenty-five passages by which Paul depicts the church as associated with (*sún*/σύν) Christ in His historical actions of salvation, primarily in His death and resurrection but also in His life and suffering.[50] Furthermore, while this study will assume a scholarly approach and an

---

48. Lüdemann, *Paul: The Founder of Christianity*, 71, reveals his reversed hermeneutic when he says of Paul's letter to Philemon, "It may well be that the real meaning of the letter is to be found not in what it says, but in what it omits and thereby suggests." Such a view bogs Lüdemann into a morass of meanings utterly foreign to the text and completely novel in Pauline studies, yet such an approach is what the back cover of his book describes as "painstaking historical research" and "brilliant exegesis."

49. Other terms such as "inter-relation, interchange, participation, partnership, inclusion, and alliance" were considered to describe this Pauline idea, but the term "association" was chosen as reflecting the basic meaning of the preposition Paul uses to convey this concept, σύν, which LN § 89.107 defines as "a marker of an associative relation, often involving joint participation in some activity."

50. Harvey surveys these distinctions in his important article, "The 'With Christ' Motif in Paul's Thought," 329–40. See also Appendix 2, "A Synthesis of the Pauline References to Association With Christ." All pertinent references include:

1. Fifteen words in eighteen appearances pre-fixed with the preposition σύν:

A. With past reference: crucified with Christ (Rom 6:6, συνεσταυρώθη); Gal 2:20 (Χριστῷ συνεσταύρωμαι); died with Christ (2 Tim 2:11, συναπεθάνομεν); planted with Christ in death (Rom 6:5, σύμφυτοι γεγόναμεν); buried with Christ (Rom 6:4, συνετάφημεν οὖν αὐτῷ; Col 2:12 (συνταφέντες αὐτῷ); made alive with Christ (Eph 2:5, συνεζωοποίησεν τῷ Χριστῷ); Col 2:13 (συνεζωοποίησεν ὑμᾶς σὺν αὐτῷ); raised with Christ (Eph 2:6, συνήγειρεν); Col 2:12 (συνηγέρθητε); Col 3:1 (συνηγέρθητε τῷ Χριστῷ); and, seated with Christ (Eph 2:6, συνεκάθισεν).

B. With present association: suffering with Christ (Rom 8:17, συμπάσχομεν); 2 Tim 1:8 (συγκακοπάθησον); 2 Tim 2:3 (συγκακοπάθησον).

C. With future reference: fellow-inheriting with Christ (Rom 8:17, συγκληρονόμοι δὲ Χριστου); living with Christ (Rom 6:8, συζήσομεν αὐτῷ); 2 Tim 2:11 (συζήσομεν); reigning with Christ (2 Tim 2:12, συμβασιλεύσομεν); conformed with Christ (Rom 8:29, συμμόρφους τῆς εἰκόνος τοῦ υἱοῦ αὐτοῦ); Phil 3:21, σύμμορφον); and, glorified with Christ (Rom 8:17, συνδοξασθῶμεν).

2. Twelve appearances in twelve verses of the preposition σύν when used in Paul's letters of Association with Christ:

A. With past reference: died with Christ (Rom 6:8, εἰ δὲ ἀπεθάνομεν σὺν Χριστω); Col 2:20 (Εἰ ἀπεθάνετε σὺν Χριστω); made alive with Christ (Col 2:13, συνεζωοποίησεν ὑμᾶς σὺν αὐτῷ); hidden with Christ (Col 3:3, κέκρυπται σὺν τῷ Χριστῷ ἐν τῷ θεῷ).

THE "MAN CHRIST JESUS"

impartial manner required by historians, it will conclude by suggesting several theological and pastoral implications arising from these findings, exploring how association with Christ places believers in association with one another in fellowship and ministry.

Amid this process, a reasonable observer will note that the apostle unabashedly attempts to persuade his readers to embrace his opinion of Jesus by uncompromisingly rejecting "another Jesus whom we have not preached" (2 Cor 11:4) and claiming there is but one foundation laid, the Jesus he proclaims (1 Cor 3:11). Whether a reader agrees with the apostle or not, one should approach his letters with the understanding that Paul fervently believes his interpretation of the "Man Christ Jesus" to be the correct one. It is therefore necessary to compare Paul's references to the humanity of Jesus with the portrayal of Jesus in the Gospels to determine if they present a unified depiction of the same person, especially whether the Jesus of Paul is genuinely human, as he claims Him to be. The quest of this study, then, is to examine thoroughly the stated assertions and numerous assumptions of Paul concerning the "Man Christ Jesus," following the advice of N. T. Wright, to "... explore a bit more how Paul himself suggests we read him. It is an attempt to study Paul in his own terms. It is trying to come to grips with what he really said."[51] In particular, this study shall explore how the apostle applies the humanity of Jesus to his gospel message in proclaiming that the one mediator between God and men is the "Man Christ Jesus" (1 Tim 2:5–6).

B. With future expectation: shall be raised with Christ (2 Cor 4:14, καὶ ἡμᾶς σὺν Ἰησοῦ ἐγερεῖ); shall live with Christ (2 Cor 13:4, ἀλλὰ ζήσομεν σὺν αὐτῷ); 1 Thess 5:10 (σὺν αὐτῷ ζήσωμεν); to be with Christ (Phil 1:23, σὺν Χριστῷ εἶναι); 1 Thess 4:17 (καὶ οὕτως πάντοτε σὺν κυρίῳ ἐσόμεθα); shall appear with Christ (Col 3:4, σὺν αὐτῷ); shall be brought with Christ (1 Thess 4:14, σὺν αὐτῷ); shall be given all things with Christ (Rom 8:32, σὺν αὐτῷ).

51. Wright, *What Saint Paul Really Said*, 23.

2

The "Man Christ Jesus" in the Context of 1 Timothy 2:1–6

INTRODUCTION

As my grandfather's diamond cufflinks are stored in the same jewelry box with ordinary tie clasps, so 1 Tim 2:5–6 appears as a theological gem amid some rather common instructions about church order. There, sandwiched between a discussion about types of prayer and women's apparel, Paul includes what this chapter will label as the "Christ-Creed," a statement confessing specific theological propositions about God, Jesus and salvation: "For there is one God, *and* one mediator also between God and men, *the* man Christ Jesus, who gave Himself as a ransom for all, the testimony *borne* at the proper time." Since this creed serves as the "text" for this study, it is important to examine it exegetically in order to determine the meaning of the phrase the "Man Christ Jesus" (*ánthropos Christòs Iēsoûs*; ἄνθρωπος Χριστὸς Ἰησοῦς), which serves as the title of this study.[1] Why would Paul describe Jesus this way, as "Man," when there are many other titles he could have used? What are the christological implications of this title? Such questions are the pursuits of this chapter.

THE CONTEXT OF 1 TIMOTHY 2:5–6

1 Timothy 2:5–6 stands as a particular unit within the larger context of the entire letter Paul writes to his co-worker Timothy with this stated purpose, "I write so that you may know how one ought to conduct himself in the household of God, which is the church of the living God" (1 Tim 3:15). Yet these ecclesiastical concerns of sound doctrine (1 Tim 1:10; 6:3), qualifications and oversight of officers (1 Tim 3:1–15; 5:17–25), pastoral ethics (1 Tim 4:11–16), and care of widows (1 Tim 5:1–16) are presented amid an opening emphasis on God as Savior (1 Tim 1:1; 2:3; 5:10),[2] a concept Paul also applies to "Christ Jesus

---

1. As noted in the Introduction, the anarthrous nominative phrase ἄνθρωπος Χριστὸς Ἰησοῦς will be translated in English as the "Man Christ Jesus" in order to express what is written in Greek.

2. Besides God our Savior (1 Tim 1:1; 2:3; 5:10), God is also named in 1 Timothy as God the Father (1 Tim 1:2); the Blessed God (1 Tim 1:4, 11); the only God (1 Tim 1:17); the One God (1 Tim 2:5); the living God (1 Tim 3:15; 4:10); and God as creator (1 Tim 4:3, 4). Other references to God include the mediator between God and men (1 Tim 2:5); the church of God (1 Tim 3:5); the household of God (1 Tim 3:15); the Word of God (1 Tim 3:5); before God (1 Tim 5:4, 21; 6:13); hope on God (1 Tim 5:5; 6:17); the name of God (1 Tim 6:1); and, "O man of God" (1 Tim 6:11).

THE "MAN CHRIST JESUS"

our Lord,"³ who "came into the world to save sinners" (1 Tim 1:15).⁴ While Lau rightly points out the "epiphany" of Christ's appearance as Savior is a theme of the Pastorals as a whole (1 Tim 6:13),⁵ it is this emphasis on both God and Christ as Savior that leads to the context of the second chapter of 1 Timothy. It begins with the admonition to pray for all those in authority, "in order that we (believers) may lead a tranquil and quiet life in all godliness and dignity" (1 Tim 2:1–2), and without using any connecting conjunctions, Paul evaluates this entire process in the next verse, "This is good and acceptable in the sight of God our Savior." The pronoun "this" (τοῦτο) presumably refers both to the admonition to pray as well as the resulting life of godliness and dignity,⁶ activities described by two nominative neuter singular adjectives, *kalòn* (καλὸν) and *apódekton* (ἀπόδεκτον). The first word defines the moral category of prayer and godliness by indicating that they are "good,"⁷ and the second adjective *apódekton* carries the idea of approval of conduct by an authority,⁸ who in this instance is God our Savior. While this precise prepositional phrase *enópion toū sotēros humōn theoū* (ἐνώπιον τοῦ σωτῆρος ἡμῶν θεοῦ) is unique to the Bible, the phrase "before God" (ἐνώπιον τοῦ θεοῦ) appears thirty-six times⁹ and is an indicator of Paul's concept of the immanence of God, that He is "not far from us" (Acts 17:27)¹⁰ but all life is lived "in His presence."¹¹ In 1 Tim 2:4 the particular aspect of God emphasized is that He is "Savior,"¹² a title that the Bible somewhat surprisingly applies to God only

---

3. Christ is mentioned by name or title eighteen times in 1 Timothy, as "Christ Jesus" (1 Tim 1:1, 1, 14, 15; 3:13; 4:6; 5:21; 6:13); "Jesus Christ" (1 Tim 1:16); "Christ Jesus our Lord" (1 Tim 1:2; 12); "our Lord" (1 Tim 1:14); "Lord of lords" (1 Tim 6:15); "our Lord Jesus Christ" (1 Tim 6:3, 14); "Christ" (1 Tim 5:11); and "Man Christ Jesus" (1 Tim 2:5). He is also discussed in several important christological statements (1 Tim 1:15–17; 2:5–6; 3:16; 6:13–16).

4. Philip Towner, "Christology in the Letters to Timothy and Titus," in *Contours of Christology in the New Testament*, 227–28, suggests that the "faithful saying" of 1 Tim 1:15 echoes the Johannine emphasis on Jesus "coming into the world" (John 9:39, 11:27; 12:46; 16:28; 17:18; 18:37) and the Lukan comment of the Son of Man coming to save sinners (Luke 19:10). Also, while 1 Tim 1:15 implies the preexistence of Christ, the "weight of the saying . . . is on the humanity of Jesus and its significance," so that "the fact of the Messiah's humanness, Paul insists, must remain central to an understanding of the gospel. . . . It is a salvation that is anchored in the humanity of God's Messiah—with that humanity actually making a difference 'for those who will believe for eternal life' (1 Tim 1:16; cf. 1:1)."

5. See Lau, *Manifest in Flesh: The Epiphany Christology of the Pastoral Epistles*, 279.

6. Wallace, *Greek Grammar*, 333, notes that the neuter singular of οὗτος is "used to refer both to an antecedent and a postcedent on a regular basis. . . ."

7. While the word καλός can denote attractiveness (as in "beautiful stones," Luke 21:5) or usefulness (as in "good fruit," Luke 3:9), Paul certainly intends for it to express here the moral quality of goodness (BDAG § 3900 2.b) reserved for God alone (Luke 18:19). If God deems a prayer to be good, it is also by consequence "acceptable or pleasing" (LN § 25.85) before Him.

8. BDAG § 904.

9. "Before God" appears at Exod 3:6; 22:7f.; Judg 21:2; 2 Sam 6:7; Ezra 7:19; Esth 10:3; Ps 55:14; 60:8; 67:4; Luke 1:19; 12:6; 16:15; Acts 4:19; 7:46; 10:31, 33; Rom 14:22; 1 Cor 1:29; 2 Cor 4:2; 7:12; Gal 1:20; 1 Tim 5:4, 21; 6:13; 2 Tim 2:14; 4:1; 1 Pet 3:4; Rev 3:2; 8:2, 4; 9:13; 11:16; 12:10; and 16:19.

10. BDAG § 2710. 3, understands the preposition ἐνώπιον to mean in the "opinion or judgment of God."

11. "Before Him," where the pronoun refers to God, is found in 1 Sam 3:18; 1 Kgs 17:1; 18:15; 2 Kgs 3:14; 5:16; Ezra 10:11; Ps 10:3; 18:6, 12; 22:29; 62:8; 68:4; 72:9, 14; 96:6; 100:2; 106:23; 142:2; Prov 20:23; Hos 6:2; Mal 3:16; Luke 1:17, 75; Rom 3:20; Heb 4:13; 13:20; and 1 John 3:22.

12. LN § 21.22 notes that σωτήρ is "derivative of σῴζω, 'to rescue, to save.'"

fourteen times,[13] although the idea that God saves is certainly one of the primary themes of the entire Scripture ("Whoever calls on the Name of the Lord shall be saved;" Joel 2:32; Acts 2:21; Rom 10:13). Even more specifically, God is "our" Savior, a pronoun defined by the broader context to mean all those have been rescued by God as Savior (1 Tim 1:1).

How is it that God becomes "our Savior"? This anticipated inquiry leads Paul to the nominative clause of 1 Tim 2:4, "who desires all men[14] to be saved and to come to the knowledge of the truth" (ὃς πάντας ἀνθρώπους θέλει σωθῆναι καὶ εἰς ἐπίγνωσιν ἀληθείας ἐλθεῖν). The initiative of salvation is credited to the desiring of God rather than to the willingness of men to be saved,[15] so that Paul views the scope of salvation as universal in the sense that the apostle becomes "all things to all men that I may by all means save some" (1 Cor 9:22).[16] A universal plan is not the same as a universal salvation, in that "all men" need to "come to the knowledge of the truth,"[17] a description of actual conversion. The content of this "knowledge of truth" necessary for salvation is defined in the next two verses, "For there is one God, *and* one mediator also between God and men, *the* man Christ Jesus, who gave Himself as a ransom for all, the testimony *borne* at the proper time" (1 Tim 2:5–6).

---

13. God as "Savior" appears in 2 Sam 22:3; Ps 106:21; Isa 43:3; 45:15, 21; Hos 13:4; Luke 1:47; 1 Tim 1:1; 2:3; 4:10; Titus 1:3; 2:10; 3:4; and Jude 1:25. See Werner Foerster, "σωτήρ," *TDNT* 7:1010–12.

14. The objects of God's saving are emphasized as "all men" (πάντας ἀνθρώπους), and Paul undoubtedly includes all humans—women as well as men—by this designation, but to translate πάντας ἀνθρώπους as "all people" (NET) removes the grammatical connection to the "Man Christ Jesus" in the next verse. Paul has already defined "all men" in 1 Tim 2:2 as "kings and all in authority," showing that he is using "all" to mean all types of people rather than all persons indiscriminately.

15. Paul uses the same verb θέλω in Rom 9:18, ἄρα οὖν ὃν θέλει ἐλεεῖ, ὃν δὲ θέλει σκληρύνει, where it clearly refers to God's sovereign desire, as it does also in Ps 115:3, "But our God is in the heavens; He does whatever He pleases" (ὁ δὲ θεὸς ἡμῶν ἐν τῷ οὐρανῷ ἄνω ἐν τοῖς οὐρανοῖς καὶ ἐν τῇ γῇ πάντα ὅσα ἠθέλησεν ἐποίησεν). This raises the question whether the desire of God is always determinative, so that He actually shall save "all men" universally. Such a view, however, would force a contradiction in Paul's own theology, as he indicates that those "who do not know God and . . . do not obey the gospel of our Lord Jesus . . . will pay the penalty of eternal destruction, away from the presence of the Lord and from the glory of His power" (2 Thess 1:8–9). Instead, Paul assumes that "all men" are in fact perishing and do not know the truth of salvation, but all these men may be saved through the one Mediator. In this sense, Paul's gospel is universalistic, in that he proclaims salvation universally to all (Acts 17:30, "God is now declaring to men that all everywhere should repent;" τοῖς ἀνθρώποις πάντας πανταχοῦ μετανοεῖν), based upon his understanding of God as "the Savior of all men, especially of believers" (1 Tim 4:10). Thus, in this particular context, θέλει should not be viewed as determinative but as desirative, as Paul may be echoing Ezek 18:23, where the same verb is found in God's question, "Do I have any pleasure (μὴ θελήσει θελήσω) in the death of the wicked rather than that he should turn from his ways and live?"

16. The Greek is indefinite, τοῖς πᾶσιν γέγονα πάντα, and in 1 Cor 9:22 it is better translated by the ESV, "I have become all things to all people."

17. This same expression is also found in 2 Tim 2:25; 3:7; Titus 1:1, as well as Heb 10:26. Paul places truth and faith in apposition to one another (1 Tim 3:8) and in opposition to myths (2 Tim 4:4; Titus 1:14), thereby indicating that the unsaved must learn certain propositional truths in order for them to experience salvation, which is defined in Eph 1:13 as "the message of truth, the gospel of your salvation" (τὸν λόγον τῆς ἀληθείας, τὸ εὐαγγέλιον τῆς σωτηρίας ὑμῶν).

THE "MAN CHRIST JESUS"

1 TIMOTHY 2:5–6 — A CREEDAL FORMULA?

The readers of the 27th *Nestle-Aland* Greek NT will notice immediately that 1 Tim 2:5–6 is printed in poetic format, as the pericope divides quite naturally into six stanzas of three words each,[18] with lines one and four rhyming in the final syllable (the words end in -ς) and lines three and six also rhyming in the final syllable (by the genitive plural suffix -ων). A final four-word, ten-syllable phrase—the longest of the entire structure—serves as an emphatic *conclusio* of the entire poem. A grammatical analysis displays the phrasing more succinctly:

εἷς γὰρ θεός	A.] *heis gàr theós* (4 syllables)
εἷς καὶ μεσίτης	B.] *heis kaì mesitēs* (5 syllables)
θεοῦ καὶ ἀνθρώπων	C.] *theoû kaì anthrópon* (6 syllables)
ἄνθρωπος Χριστὸς Ἰησοῦς	A'] *ánthropos Christòs Iēsoûs* (7 syllables)
ὁ δοὺς ἑαυτὸν	B'] *Hò doùs eautòn* (5 syllables)
ἀντίλυτρον ὑπὲρ πάντων	C'] *antílutron huper pánton* (8 syllables)
τὸ μαρτύριον καιροῖς ἰδίοις	*tò martúrion kairoîs idíois*

Since this poem could (and should!) be easily memorized, Mounce suggests that these two verses "may have been a creed, or part of a creed, known by Timothy and the Ephesian church, which Paul quotes in order to strengthen his argument."[19] This view is supported by the inclusion of other apparent creeds in this letter (as suggested by the same indented printing in *Nestle-Aland* of 1 Tim 3:16; 6:7–8, 11–12, 15–16), as Paul stresses to Timothy the importance of "sound doctrine" (1 Tim 4:6; 6:1) and "healthy teaching" (1 Tim 1:10; 4:13, 16; 5:17; 6:1, 3), in accord with "the faithful word" sayings (1 Tim 1:15; 3:1; 4:9).[20] Access to such doctrinal information is assumed by the author of these sayings, a fact that causes critics to relegate the Pastoral Epistles to a late first-century date of composition;[21] however, even the earlier letters of Paul refer to matters of mutual creedal instruction,[22] indicating that from its founding the church held to an established apos-

---

18. *Merriam-Webster's Collegiate Dictionary*, 11th ed., 1217, defines "stanza" as "a division of a poem consisting of a series of lines arranged in a usu. recurring pattern of meter and rhyme."

19. Mounce, *Pastoral Epistles*, 87; however, Dibelius and Conzelmann, *The Pastoral Epistles*, 41, deny that 1 Tim 2:5–6 is a "creedal formula" but describe it as a "liturgical piece," although what is a creed but a doctrinal formula used in liturgy?

20. See the discussion in Lau, *Manifest in Flesh*, 64–178.

21. For example, Ziesler, *Pauline Christianity*, 1, assumes that Paul's churches, being "far removed from Palestine and from the memories of the followers of Jesus, . . . probably knew very little of the oral teachings and words." It is most unreasonable to suppose that missionaries and converts would care so little for the teachings of the one they confessed as Lord, especially since the NT requires such information to be preached and learned.

22. Evidence of creedal instruction is found in the following passages: "The form of teaching to which you were committed" (Rom 6:17); "the teaching which you learned" (Rom 16:17); "hold firmly to the traditions, just as I delivered them to you" (1 Cor 11:2); "if any man is preaching to you a gospel contrary to that which you received, let him be accursed" (Gal 1:9); "the message of truth, the gospel of your salvation"

tolic *didachē* (Acts 2:42). Because 1 Tim 2:5–6 shares the linguistic markers common to creedal statements,[23] this reviewer is inclined to think that it also consists of one of these early creeds and shall therefore label it for the sake of reference, the "Christ-Creed."[24] By inserting this creed into his argument at this place, Paul is appealing to common confessional knowledge shared among his readership, which extends beyond only Timothy, as the instructions directed to "men in every place" in 1 Tim 2:8 assume.[25] The doctrinal formulas of "one God, one Mediator, the Man Christ Jesus, who gave Himself as a ransom for all" provide aspects of a foundational Christian confession essential to an informed belief leading to salvation. The specifics of this knowledge listed in this creed are not rooted in human religious experience but in divine activity of what God has accomplished through Jesus in His historical humanity in order to provide that all men may be saved and come to this particular knowledge of truth.

The First Stanza: εἷς γὰρ θεός

The first stanza states the theological foundation of saving knowledge, declared in the first exclamation of the Christ-Creed: "for one God!"[26] It is introduced by the postpositive coordinating conjunction, γάρ as a "marker of clarification,"[27] although it actually seems to be more of an inference from the previous statement of God's desire to save all people, showing what are the elements of saving knowledge of truth, the first being the oneness of God. While this statement rephrases the *Shema* of Deut 6:4 ("Hear, O Israel! The LORD

(Eph 1:13); "observe those who walk according to the pattern you have in us" (Phil 3:17); "established in your faith, just as you were instructed" (Col 2:7); "For you know what commandments we gave you by *the authority of* the Lord Jesus" (1 Thess 4:2); "hold to the traditions which you were taught, whether by word *of mouth* or by letter from us" (2 Thess 2:15).

23. Richard Longenecker, "Christological Materials in Early Christian Communities," 70, lists these literary indicators of an embedded creedal formula: (1) parallel structures; (2) presence of words or phrases not characteristic of the author; (3) preference for participles over finite verbs; and (4) an affirmation of the person or work of Christ. From this list, it is seen that 1 Tim 2:5–6 has (1) parallel structures; (2) words not characteristic of Paul ("mediator, ransom"); (3) no finite verbs but one participle, ὁ δοὺς; and (4) a very strong affirmation of both the person of Christ (the one mediator, the Man Christ Jesus) and His work ("who gave Himself as a ransom for all"). These markers indicate that the pericope is indeed a *homologia Iēsou*.

24. The comments of Stanley, *Arguing with Scripture*, 181–2, that Paul's appeal to the Jewish Scripture as a common basis of authority between himself and his readers would apply also to Paul's use of apostolic tradition.

25. Discourse Analysis has revealed many possible creedal formulae embedded in the NT. A pioneer work in this area was that of Carrington, *The Primitive Christian Catechism: A Study in the Epistles*, 42–43, in which he charts the literary parallels in Ephesians, Colossians, 1 Peter, 2 Peter, James, and Hebrews that suggest a shared catechism, as each follows the same pattern of new birth, *deponentes, virtues, subiecti, vigilate,* and *resistite*. Acts 2:42 notes that original disciples were "devoting themselves to the Apostles' teaching" (τῇ διδαχῇ τῶν ἀποστόλων), and it is reasonable to think that this *Didachē* very quickly took written form, as suggested in the lectures by C. H. Dodd in *The Apostolic Preaching and its Developments* (1950). See a response by Robinson, "The Most Primitive Christology of All?", 139–53.

26. Most English versions (including ESV, KJV, NIV) translate εἷς γὰρ θεός, "there is one God," although no demonstrative pronoun ("there") nor verb ("is") appear in the original text—nor, for that matter, is there any finite verb in the entire creed at all. The closest translation to the Greek appears to be the rendition in DBY, "For God is one," but even that rendering does not capture the abrupt nature of the phrase.

27. BDAG § 1599. 2.

THE "MAN CHRIST JESUS"

is our God, the LORD is one!"),[28] it establishes the monotheistic nature of Paul's theology (and indeed, of the Christian faith) as derived from what he calls the "old covenant" (2 Cor 3:14).[29] Fee observes, "First, whatever else is true about Paul,... he was an avid monotheist. On this point he is unyielding."[30] Even the terse word order here ("For one God!") suggests that Paul emphasizes not merely the singularity of one God (to the exclusion of all other gods), but the oneness of God as a unified being, consistent with His attributes.[31] Paul's point is that since there is but one God, He must—in order to be consistently unified within Himself—have one desire that all people be saved in one exclusive way, in accordance with the knowledge of truth through one Mediator. As Paul argues in Rom 3:30, all—Jew and Gentile alike—can be saved only through the one God.[32]

Of keen interest for this study, however, is how Paul insists that this one God is known through the one Mediator, the "Man Christ Jesus," whom the apostle places alongside the one God in honor and worship (as in 1 Cor 8:6, "for to us there is *but* one God, the Father, from whom are all things, and we *exist* for Him; and one Lord, Jesus Christ, by whom are all things, and we *exist* through Him").[33] Recent studies have explored the phenomenon (and apparent conundrum) that devoted worship of Jesus arose from within Jewish monotheism,[34] pondering how a "Pharisee of Pharisees" who maintains belief in

---

28. The LXX of Deut 6:4 reads, ἄκουε Ισραηλ κύριος ὁ θεὸς ἡμῶν κύριος εἷς ἐστιν. It is affirmed by Jesus in Mark 12:29 (ἄκουε, Ἰσραήλ, κύριος ὁ θεὸς ἡμῶν κύριος εἷς ἐστιν). See Richard Bauckham, *Jesus and the God of Israel: God Crucified and Other Studies on the New Testament's Christology of Divine Identity*, 1–17 and 107–126, on the unique identity of YHWH in Second Temple Judaism. Bauckham argues that early Jewish literature displays an "exclusive" monotheism of the "God Most High" (אֵל עֶלְיוֹן/ὁ θεὸς ὁ ὕψιστος) that "understands the uniqueness of the one God in terms of absolute difference in kind from all other reality" (ibid., 109).

29. Hurtado, "Paul's Christology," 186, notes that "Paul came to his Christian faith as a deeply religious Jew zealous for the distinguishing features of his Jewish traditions (e. g. Gal 1:13–14; Phil 3:4–6), among which a strong conviction about the uniqueness of the God of Israel (which we often refer to as 'monotheistic') was central. . . . The Christian Paul continued to assert an exclusivistic monotheistic stance, and it shaped and nourished his devotion to Christ (1 Cor 8:4–6)." Goguel, *Jesus the Nazarene: Myth or History?*, 162, suggests that Paul's point of view might be better styled "monolatry" since he acknowledges many "so-called gods" (1 Cor 8:5), but the apostle has already affirmed monotheism by asserting in 1 Cor 8:4, ". . . there is no such thing as an idol in the world, and that there is no God but one."

30. Fee, *Pauline Christology*, 7. See also Hagner, "Paul's Christology and Jewish Monotheism," 19–38.

31. This same word order appears in other Pauline examples: Rom 3:30, "Since God is one (εἷς ὁ θεὸς), He will justify the circumcised by faith and the uncircumcised through faith;" 1 Cor 8:6, "Yet for us there is *but* one God (εἷς θεὸς), the Father;" and Eph 4:6, "One God (εἷς θεὸς) and Father of all who is over all and through all and in all." The only grammatical exception is Gal 3:20, "Now a mediator is not for one *party only*; whereas God is *only* one" (ὁ δὲ θεὸς εἷς ἐστιν), but this phrase also emphasizes the oneness of God.

32. Mounce, *Pastorals*, 87.

33. N. T. Wright, *What Saint Paul Really Said*, 67, says of 1 Cor 8:6, "This verse is one of the genuinely revolutionary bits of theology ever written," in that the apostle places Jesus firmly in the middle of Jewish monotheism.

34. For example, see Hengel, *The Son of God: The Origin of Christology and the History of Jewish-Hellenistic Religion*; Newman et al., *The Jewish Roots of Christological Monotheism* (1990); Bauckham, *God Crucified* (1999); Hurtado, *Lord Jesus Christ* (2003); and Bauckham, *Jesus and the God of Israel* (2008), although in this important collection of essays, the author strangely omits 1 Tim 2:5 from his discussion.

the one God of Israel could also elevate the man Jesus to equal status.[35] Bird observes, "Paul is an advocate of what we should call *messianic monotheism*, that is, God is known through Jesus the Messiah, or Jesus is the one who reveals and manifests the person and work of God."[36] Whatever one may think of Paul's Christology, he does not view it as conflicting with his belief in the oneness of God.[37]

The Second Stanza: εἷς καὶ μεσίτης

The second stanza of the Christ-Creed introduces the one who mediates salvation with the legal designation, "and one mediator" (εἷς καὶ μεσίτης).[38] Whereas in matters of human arbitration both parties must agree to the same mediator in order to attain mutual compromise, in this case God has provided His one and only mediator to represent His singular interests and concerns. Here Paul insists that there is but one mediator, an exclusivity also claimed by Jesus Himself[39] and confirmed in the apostolic kerygma.[40] Towner calls this a striking paradox, that the "one God" signals universal access to salvation whereas "one mediator" narrows that access to a single means.[41] The logic, however, is inescapable: the major premise is "there is only one God;" the minor premise is that "He desires all people to be saved;" therefore, the one God provided one mediator to save all people. A God who would offer to mankind differing and even contradictory ways of salvation would be violating His own oneness, whereas the one God consistently recognizes only the one mediator, identified as the "Man Christ Jesus."

A mediator is one who negotiates between two parties to remove a disagreement or to reach a common goal, "one who is in the middle (μέσον),"[42] as Paul asks in 1 Cor 6:5, "*Is it so, that* there is not among you one wise man who will be able to decide between (*anà méson*/ ἀνὰ μέσον) his brethren?" As one who reconciles between conflicting parties, a mediator supposedly is neutral and not prejudiced toward either party. This mediator, however, is hardly neutral: He shares fully in humanity as the "Man," and it could be

---

35. Lau, *Manifest in Flesh*, 74, notes how Paul in 1 Cor 8:6 ". . . has modified the Jewish religion at its most essential point and redefined the *shema* christologically, indicating a dual referent in θεός and κύριος as well as acknowledging Christ's sharing of the Father's status and functions."

36. Bird, *Introducing Paul*, 125. Italics are in the original.

37. 1 Timothy 2:5 is a favorite proof-text employed by classic Unitarianism, as argued by Wright, *A Plain View of the Unitarian Christian Doctrine* (1815); and by Giles, *There is One God, and one Mediator between God and Men, the Man Christ Jesus* (1839). Trinitarian theology, however, reasons that that oneness of God does not militate against the Tri-unity of God (Matt 28:19; 2 Cor 13:14), noting that both concepts are taught in the NT. Fee, *Pauline Christology*, 481, comments on Paul's understanding of Christ as a preexistent person by observing, ". . . it is nearly impossible to account for such a Christ devotion by an avid monotheist unless his understanding of the one God now included the Son of God in the divine identity."

38. The insertion of an extra conjunction in the NAS, "*and* one mediator *also*" is unwarranted. The NIV translates the phrase more accurately, "and one mediator."

39. In John 14:6, "Jesus said to him, "I am the way, and the truth, and the life; no one comes to the Father, but through Me."

40. Peter declares in Acts 4:12, "And there is salvation in no one else; for there is no other name under heaven that has been given among men, by which we must be saved."

41. Towner, "Christology in the Letters to Timothy and Titus," 229.

42. BDAG § 4827. See also D. R. de Lacey, "Jesus as Mediator," 101–21.

THE "MAN CHRIST JESUS"

argued that implicit in this analogy is that the mediator also shares fully in deity—He certainly has a divine connection in His title as "Christ." While Heb 6:17 shows that God serves as His own mediator,[43] yet when Christ is called "the mediator of a new and better covenant,"[44] He is anything but neutral: He represents the interests of God and becomes the surety of His covenant of salvation.[45] Bernard suggests that Paul may have in mind here the "contrast between Moses as the μεσίτης for the Jews only, and the *Mediator of a new covenant* (Heb ix.15), whose mediation was for all mankind, Jew and Gentile alike."[46] Regardless, the concept of mediation is prevalent throughout the Bible, illustrated when Moses "stands between the Lord and You" (Israel; Deut 5:5), when Phineas interposed for the people (Ps 106:30), and when the priests "made atonement" for others (Lev 4:20).

Yet while the concept of mediation is common in Scripture, the actual word μεσίτης appears only seven times;[47] for this reason, Becker calls its only OT appearance (Job 9:33) an "inaccurate rendering" of the Hebrew מוֹכִיחַ, which, he claims, does not have the idea of arbitration but refers to one who "restores the infringed law by dealing with the guilty party."[48] Actually, it seems quite likely that Paul does in fact have in mind here the only LXX appearance of *mesítes* (μεσίτης), found in Job's complaint about God, "There is no umpire between us" (εἴθε ἦν ὁ μεσίτης ἡμῶν, Job 9:33). While the lexical indicator of the root word for מוֹכִיחַ is יָכַח (which BDB § 3927 defines as "to decide or judge"), Job surely seeks for a מוֹכִיחַ as "one who may lay his hand upon both" himself and God, in answer to his question, "But how can a man be in the right before God?" (Job 9:2). He despairs of any audience with God and laments, "For *He is* not a man (ἄνθρωπος) as I am that I may answer Him, that we may go to court together. There is no umpire between us (εἴθε ἦν ὁ μεσίτης ἡμῶν) who may lay his hand upon us both" (εἴθε ἦν ὁ μεσίτης ἡμῶν καὶ ἐλέγχων καὶ διακούων ἀνὰ μέσον ἀμφοτέρων, Job 9:32–33). Now, Paul provides an answer to Job's complaint: there is such a mediator—there is such a man (ἄνθρωπος) who can "lay his hand" upon both God and men—the "Man Christ Jesus."

---

43. "In the same way God, desiring even more to show to the heirs of the promise the unchangeableness of His purpose, interposed (ἐμεσίτευσεν) with an oath" (Heb 6:17).

44. Heb 8:6 reads, "But now He has obtained a more excellent ministry, by as much as He is also the *mediator of a better covenant*, which has been enacted on better promises" (νυν[ὶ] δὲ διαφορωτέρας τέτυχεν λειτουργίας, ὅσῳ καὶ κρείττονός ἐστιν διαθήκης μεσίτης, ἥτις ἐπὶ κρείττοσιν ἐπαγγελίαις νενομοθέτηται;); Heb 9:15 adds, "And for this reason He is the *mediator of a new covenant*, in order that since a death has taken place for the redemption of the transgressions that were committed under the first covenant, those who have been called may receive the promise of the eternal inheritance" (Καὶ διὰ τοῦτο διαθήκης καινῆς μεσίτης ἐστίν, ὅπως θανάτου γενομένου εἰς ἀπολύτρωσιν τῶν ἐπὶ τῇ πρώτῃ διαθήκῃ παραβάσεων τὴν ἐπαγγελίαν λάβωσιν οἱ κεκλημένοι τῆς αἰωνίου κληρονομίας); Heb 12:24 notes, "Jesus, *the mediator of a new covenant*, and to the sprinkled blood, which speaks better than *the blood* of Abel" (καὶ διαθήκης νέας μεσίτῃ Ἰησοῦ καὶ αἵματι ῥαντισμοῦ κρεῖττον λαλοῦντι παρὰ τὸν "Ἀβελ.). Italics added for emphasis.

45. As taught in Heb 7:22, "so much the more also Jesus has become the guarantee of a better covenant" (κατὰ τοσοῦτο [καὶ] κρείττονος διαθήκης γέγονεν ἔγγυος Ἰησοῦς).

46. Bernard, *The Pastoral Epistles*, 42.

47. The noun μεσίτης appears in Job 9:33; Gal 3:19, 20; 1 Tim 2:5; Heb 8:6; 9:15; 12:24.

48. Becker, "Covenant," *DNTT* 1:373.

The Third Stanza: θεοῦ καὶ ἀνθρώπων

For that matter, neither is Jesus neutral toward humanity. The third stanza of the Christ-Creed declares that He stands between God and men (θεοῦ καὶ ἀνθρώπων), although He actually represents both parties, so that the simple genitive "of" is the better translation, "one mediator *of* God and men."[49] While this mediator has been divinely appointed, His identity as mediator stands as "a man," because His primary interests are served on behalf of the salvation of humanity, the ones needing to be saved. Towner observes that "the thrust of the statement is to locate Jesus' mediatorship precisely in His humanity, with the phrase 'the *man* Christ Jesus' defining 'mediator.'"[50]

Evans suggests that this phrase echoes the *Testament of Dan* 6:2, "Draw near to God and to the angel which intercedes for you; for he is a mediator between God and humanity (μεσίτης θεοῦ καὶ ἀνθρώπων) for the peace of Israel, and he will stand against the kingdom of the enemy."[51] Admittedly, the phrase μεσίτης θεοῦ καὶ ἀνθρώπων is identical in both literary works, and the concept of a mediator representing both God and man is present in both contexts. The question is, would Paul identify the "Man Christ Jesus" with this interceding angel of *T. Dan* 6:2? If the Angel of the Lord in the OT is the pre-incarnate Jesus (as will be suggested later),[52] then it is not far-fetched to surmise that Paul might have *T. Dan* 6:2 in mind, but the connection is tenuous at best. At the least, both texts show that Paul and the author of *Testament of Dan* share the same concept of a mediator who stands between God and humanity, based upon OT themes.

Galatians 3:19–20 actually serves as a true Pauline parallel to this concept, as it is the only other passage in which Paul uses the noun μεσίτης. There he contrasts the Law with Promise and asks, "Why the Law then?"[53] He proceeds to answer his question, "It was added because of transgressions, having been ordained through angels by the agency of a mediator (μεσίτου), until the seed should come to whom the promise had been made."[54]

---

49. There is actually no preposition governing these two nouns. Most English versions provide the word "between," whereas Young's *Literal Translation* renders it, "one mediator of God and of men." Wallace, *Greek Grammar*, 136, notes, "A genitive substantive may *rarely* occur after certain nouns whose lexical nature requires a genitive. The genitive in such instances will not fit into one of the 'standard' genitive categories. The most common instances involve two genitives joined by καί with the meaning 'between.' This category is quite rare." The only other instances cited are Acts 23:7 (τοῦτο δὲ αὐτοῦ εἰπόντος ἐγένετο στάσις τῶν Φαρισαίων καὶ Σαδδουκαίων) and Rom 10:12 (οὐ γάρ ἐστιν διαστολὴ Ἰουδαίου τε καὶ Ἕλληνος). It could be argued that these nouns θεοῦ καὶ ἀνθρώπων in 1 Tim 2:5 are genitives of possession, that there is one mediator belonging equally to God and to humanity. In such a case, the Mediator not so much keeping adversarial opponents apart but positively representing the interests of both parties.

50. Towner, "Christology in the Letters to Timothy and Titus," 229.

51. Evans, *Ancient Texts for New Testament Studies*, 393. The Greek text of T. Dan 6:2 reads, ἐγγίζετε δὲ τῷ θεῷ καὶ τῷ ἀγγέλῳ τῷ παραιτουμένῳ ὑμᾶς· ὅτι οὗτός ἐστι μεσίτης θεοῦ καὶ ἀνθρώπων ἐπὶ τῆς εἰρήνης Ἰσραήλ, καὶ κατέναντι τῆς βασιλείας τοῦ ἐχθροῦ στήσεται. Lau, *Manifest in Flesh*, 79, suggests this passage "is not incompatible with the description of Christ as being the means by which God accomplished redemption in Christ."

52. See the following section, "God Appearing as Man."

53. This question (Τί οὖν ὁ νόμος;) has the idea of "why was the Law given" (NET) or, "what then was the purpose of the law"? (NIV).

54. The Greek text of Gal 3:19–20 reads, Τί οὖν ὁ νόμος; τῶν παραβάσεων χάριν προσετέθη, ἄχρις

THE "MAN CHRIST JESUS"

According to Moses' comment in Deut 32:2, the role of angels at the giving of the Law appears to be as attending dignitaries,[55] whereas Paul observes that the Law itself came "by the hand of a mediator" (ἐν χειρὶ μεσίτου), an apparent reference to Moses.[56] Now, Gal 3:19 tells how Moses as mediator of Law is superceded by the one to whom the Promise had been made, the coming Seed, already identified in Gal 3:16 as Christ, the Seed of Abraham.

Next, in Gal 3:20, an even closer linguistic parallel to 1 Tim 2:5 appears, as both verses mention "mediator" and the "one God"; however, the problem is that these verses seem to argue opposite conclusions: Gal 3:20 asserts the supremacy of the Promise over Law in that the Promise comes immediately from the one God whereas the Law came by the hand of a mediator. Conversely, in 1 Tim 2:5, Paul declares that salvation comes mediately from the one God through the one mediator between God and man, the "Man Christ Jesus." Has Paul contradicted himself, or has a pseudo-Paul slipped in his forging of this letter in the apostle's name?

The problem is compounded by the difficulties contained in Gal 3:20 itself:[57] Lightfoot mentions that the number of interpretations of this verse mounts up "to 250 or 300,"[58] but it appears that Paul is drawing out a general principle here, that "the mediator is not of one," meaning that any mediator—in this case, Moses—does not act on his own behalf but rather on behalf of at least two parties (in the Galatian context, God and Israel), just as Paul points out in 1 Tim 2:5, that Jesus serves as mediator of two parties, the one God and men.[59] However, in Gal 3:20, Paul asserts that since "God is one," He does not need another party to mediate for Him: He is the singular source of salvation and will Himself enact it. The reader of both passages would surely like to ask Paul, which is it? Does the one God *not* need a mediator (Gal 3:20), or does the one God *provide* a mediator (1 Tim 2:5)? Are these views hopelessly irreconcilable?

οὗ ἔλθῃ τὸ σπέρμα ᾧ ἐπήγγελται, διαταγεὶς δι' ἀγγέλων ἐν χειρὶ μεσίτου.

55. Deut 32:2 reads, "The LORD came from Sinai, And dawned on them from Seir; He shone forth from Mount Paran, And He came from the midst of ten thousand holy ones; At His right hand there was flashing lightning for them." Similar comments about angels delivering the law are made at Ps 68:17; Acts 7:52; and Heb 2:2.

56. Lightfoot, *Galatians*, 146, notes various rabbinical passages in which Moses is designated as μεσίτης, although he observes that Origen thought that Paul referred in Gal 3:19 to Christ and "carried a vast number of later commentators with him." Instead, Paul uses μεσίτης as a metonymy for Μωϋσῆς in this grammatical allusion to the prepositional phrase ἐν χειρὶ Μωυσῆ, which appears twenty-one times in the LXX (Lev 26:46; Num 4:37, 41, 45, 49; 9:23; 10:13; 15:23; 17:5; 33:1; 36:13; Josh 21:2; 22:9; Jda 3:4; Judg 3:4; 1 Kgs 8:56; 1 Chr 16:40; 2 Chr 33:8; Neh 9:14; 10:30; and Ps 76:21).

57. Gal 3:20 reads, "Now a mediator is not for one *party only*; whereas God is *only* one" (ὁ δὲ μεσίτης ἑνὸς οὐκ ἔστιν, ὁ δὲ θεὸς εἷς ἐστιν.).

58. Lightfoot, *Galatians*, 146, thankfully does not list all these interpretations. Eadie, *Galatians*, 269–74, gives a helpful overview of the historical comments on Gal 3:20 up until 1869 but rather oddly does not link the verse to 1 Tim 2:5 despite the common appearance of the same word μεσίτης.

59. BDAG § 4827 notes, "The sense of (Galatians 3) vs. 20, ὁ δὲ μ. ἑνὸς οὐκ ἔστιν, *an intermediary does not exist for one party alone*, is disputed. It prob. means that the activity of an intermediary implies the existence of more than one party, and hence may be unsatisfactory because it must result in a compromise. The presence of an intermediary would prevent attainment, without any impediment, of the purpose of the εἷς θεός in giving the law."

The solution to this apparent conflict is located in the respective contexts: in 1 Tim 2:5, Paul discusses the *process* of redemption by showing how Jesus as mediator reconciles the one God and men in one way, as the ransom, whereas in Gal 3:20, Paul explains the *source* of salvation, that it comes directly from the one God. Lightfoot found an agreement between these passages in his astute observation, that *God Himself serves directly as the Mediator*,[60] as Paul states in Gal 3:20 and as he implies in the title "Man Christ Jesus" in 1 Tim 2:5.[61]

The Fourth Stanza: ἄνθρωπος Χριστὸς Ἰησοῦς

The fourth stanza of the Christ-Creed now identifies the mediator as the "Man Christ Jesus" (ἄνθρωπος χριστὸς Ἰησοῦς). This is the fourth appearance of the noun ἄνθρωπος in this immediate context,[62] and it is a rather unusual description of Jesus, for it seems quite obvious that He was a man;[63] however, even in the apostolic period some may have denied the humanity of Jesus, as 2 John 1:7 warns, "Many deceivers have gone out into the world, those who do not acknowledge Jesus Christ *as* coming in the flesh."[64] Such docetic views became more widespread in the second century and were condemned by later Church Fathers, often by reference to this verse.[65] Still, one must wonder why Paul would modify "Christ Jesus" with this particular description of Him as, "Man."[66] This question necessitates a closer look at Paul's understanding of the humanity of Jesus.

---

60. Lightfoot, *Galatians*, 146, italics original. He adds, "It will be seen that St. Paul's argument here (in Galatians 3) rests in effect on our Lord's divinity as its foundation. Otherwise, He would have been a mediator in the same sense in which Moses was a mediator. In another and a higher sense St. Paul himself so speaks of our Lord (in 1 Tim ii.5)."

61. Witherington, "Jesus as the Alpha and Omega of New Testament Thought," 39, comments on "Christ as the one mediator between God and human beings. . . . But there is more emphasis here (in 1 Tim 2:5) on Jesus being both divine and human, and so standing at once on both sides of the fence in order to know, experience, and represent both sides of things."

62. See 1 Tim 2:1, ὑπὲρ πάντων ἀνθρώπων 1 Tim 2:4, πάντας ἀνθρώπους; 1 Tim 2:5, μεσίτης θεοῦ καὶ ἀνθρώπων, ἄνθρωπος χριστὸς Ἰησοῦς.

63. Fee, *Pauline Christology*, 430, ftnt. 39, keenly asks, "Why the point of Christ's being 'human,' one wonders, if there is not here a presupposition about his first of all being divine?"

64. See Streett, "They Went out from Us": The Identity of the Opponents in First John," 6–135, who surveys the views of those who claim that the opponents taught some type of gnostic docetism and finds them wanting; instead, Streett argues that the identifying mark of these opponents is not so much a denial of the humanity of Jesus but "their denial that Jesus is the Messiah" (ibid., 440). Streett may well be correct in his assessment; however, the argument of 1 John 4:2 ("every spirit that confesses that Jesus Christ has come in the flesh is from God") certainly presumes the appearance of Jesus as a Messiah of human flesh.

65. For example, Augustine, *Trin.*, 1.7.14. Irenaeus, *Adversus haereses* I.10.1, notes, "The Church, though dispersed throughout the whole world, even to the ends of the earth, has received from the Apostles and their disciples this faith: (She believes) . . . in one Christ Jesus, the Son of God, who became incarnate (τὸν σαρκωθέντα) for our salvation." There still seems to be a default docetism among modern evangelicals, as the full humanity of Jesus is ignored or worse, explained away, as if there would be something intrinsically evil about Jesus fully sharing in humanity—a trend this study hopes to expose and correct.

66. Fee, *Pauline Christology*, 429, correctly observes that the emphasis here is on the genuine humanity of Christ Jesus and "thus on the reality of his incarnation." However, in his desire to assert that Jesus was "truly (a) human being," Fee translates this clause, "Christ Jesus, himself human," obscuring the unusual Greek expression and missing the OT theme on the "Man" who is also Mediator and Ransom.

THE "MAN CHRIST JESUS"

Jesus as Man

The nominative ἄνθρωπος appears twenty times in the Pauline corpus,[67] and eight times it is modified by the preceding definite article,[68] but here in 1 Tim 2:5, ἄνθρωπος appears without the article when one might expect Paul to designate Jesus as "*The* Man." Wallace observes, "When a substantive is anarthrous, it may have one of three forces: indefinite, qualitative, or definite,"[69] and it might be supposed that ἄνθρωπος in "Man Christ Jesus" is qualitative,[70] that Paul stresses the essence of humanness in Jesus, as he does in Phil 2:8, where he states that Christ "emptied Himself, having been found in appearance as a man" (σχήματι εὑρεθεὶς ὡς ἄνθρωπος). Also, it could also be argued that Paul is using ἄνθρωπος to describe Jesus monadically, that He is a "one-of-a-kind Man." This study, however, suggests that Paul uses ἄνθρωπος in this phrase "Man Christ Jesus" as a particular OT title on the same footing as Χριστός, especially since he places both designations side by side as if defining one another, so that Man = Christ, and Christ = Man. What the Creed does is to unite two themes of the Hebrew Scriptures: the concept of Christ (מָשִׁיחַ, *mashiach*) with that of Man (אָדָם, *adam*).

Jesus as Man Compared and Contrasted to the First Man Adam

It would have been quite helpful if Paul had explained precisely what he meant by defining Jesus as "Man Christ," but since he did not do so, the modern reader must ask, Why would

---

67. The noun ἄνθρωπος appears in Rom 3:4, "Let God be found true, though every man *be found* a liar" (γινέσθω δὲ ὁ θεὸς ἀληθής, πᾶς δὲ ἄνθρωπος ψεύστης); Rom 6:6, "our old self was crucified with *Him*" (ὁ παλαιὸς ἡμῶν ἄνθρωπος συνεσταυρώθη); Rom 7:24, "Wretched man that I am!" (Ταλαίπωρος ἐγὼ ἄνθρωπος); Rom 10:5, "Moses writes that the man who practices the righteousness which is based on law shall live by that righteousness" (ὅτι ὁ ποιήσας αὐτὰ ἄνθρωπος ζήσεται ἐν αὐτοῖς); 1 Cor 2:14, "But a natural man does not accept the things of the Spirit of God" (ψυχικὸς δὲ ἄνθρωπος οὐ δέχεται τὰ τοῦ πνεύματος τοῦ θεοῦ); 1 Cor 4:1, "Let a man regard us in this manner" (οὕτως ἡμᾶς λογιζέσθω ἄνθρωπος); 1 Cor 6:18, "Every *other* sin that a man commits is outside the body" (πᾶν ἁμάρτημα ὃ ἐὰν ποιήσῃ ἄνθρωπος ἐκτὸς τοῦ σώματός ἐστιν); 1 Cor 11:28, "But let a man examine himself" (δοκιμαζέτω δὲ ἄνθρωπος ἑαυτὸν); 1 Cor 15:45, "The first man, Adam, became a living soul" (ἐγένετο ὁ πρῶτος ἄνθρωπος Ἀδὰμ εἰς ψυχὴν ζῶσαν); 1 Cor 15:47, "The first man is from the earth, earthy; the second man is from heaven" (ὁ πρῶτος ἄνθρωπος ἐκ γῆς χοϊκός, ὁ δεύτερος ἄνθρωπος ἐξ οὐρανοῦ); 2 Cor 4:16, "our outer man is decaying" (ὁ ἔξω ἡμῶν ἄνθρωπος διαφθείρεται); Gal 2:16, "knowing that a man is not justified by the works of the Law" (εἰδότες [δὲ] ὅτι οὐ δικαιοῦται ἄνθρωπος ἐξ ἔργων νόμου); Gal 6:1, "if a man is caught in any trespass" (ἐὰν καὶ προλημφθῇ ἄνθρωπος ἔν τινι παραπτώματι); Gal 6:7, "whatever a man sows, this he will also reap" (ὃ γὰρ ἐὰν σπείρῃ ἄνθρωπος, τοῦτο καὶ θερίσει); Eph 5:31, "For this cause a man shall leave his father and mother" (ἀντὶ τούτου καταλείψει ἄνθρωπος [τὸν] πατέρα καὶ [τὴν] μητέρα); Phil 2:7, "And being found in appearance as a man, He humbled Himself" (καὶ σχήματι εὑρεθεὶς ὡς ἄνθρωπος); 2 Thess 2:3, "the man of lawlessness" (ὁ ἄνθρωπος τῆς ἀνομίας); 1 Tim 2:5, "*the* man Christ Jesus" (ἄνθρωπος Χριστὸς Ἰησοῦς); 2 Tim 3:17, "the man of God" (ὁ τοῦ θεοῦ ἄνθρωπος). The BYZ text adds one more instance from Gal 3:12, "The man who practices them shall live by them" (Ὁ ποιήσας αὐτὰ ἄνθρωπος ζήσεται ἐν αὐτοῖς). This same quote of Lev 18:5 is found in Rom 10:5 and may derive from a different text of the LXX, or it may be the attempt of an early copyist to conform the two quotations.

68. In Romans 6:6; 10:5; 1 Cor 15:45, 47; 47; 2 Cor 4:16; 2 Thess 2:3; 2 Tim 3:17.

69. Wallace, *Greek Grammar,* 243.

70. Wallace, ibid., 244, defines a qualitative noun as one that "places the stress on quality, nature, or essence. It does not merely indicate membership in a class of which there are other members (such as an indefinite noun), nor does it stress individual identity (such as a definite noun)."

Paul combine these two nouns? It is tempting to credit his insight as being received along with other direct revelations (as he claims in Gal 1:13), but this study suggests that the Christ-Creed Paul uses instead has the dominical statement of Jesus in view, "For even the Son of Man did not come to be served, but to serve, and to give His life a ransom for many" (Mark 10:45).[71] If this is the case, then the common self-designation of Jesus as "the Son of Man" (ὁ υἱὸς τοῦ ἀνθρώπου/ בֶּן־הָאָדָם) seems to be a good starting place for the origin of Paul's idea of the "Man Christ Jesus."[72] "Son of Man" was the same title for Jesus that Paul had heard confessed by Stephen, "Behold, I see the heavens opened up and the Son of Man standing at the right hand of God" (Acts 7:56). He would no doubt deduce that this title was derived from the "Son of Man" who appears in Dan 7:13 (Aramaic: אֱנָשׁ כְּבַר),[73] and then he would follow this link further back to Ps 8:4 ("What is man, that Thou dost take thought of him? And the son of man (בֶּן־הָאָדָם; υἱὸς ἀνθρώπου), that Thou dost care for him?"). The Psalmist has Adam in view, but Paul applies it to Jesus by quoting Ps 8:6b in 1 Cor 15:25, "Thou hast put all things under His feet," showing he shared the same interpretive tradition with Luke 3:38 and Heb 2:6 of explaining Jesus as *ben Adam*.

This rather circuitous route reveals a pattern common in the apostolic church of tracing the Jesus' self-title of Son of Man back to the original man Adam and the expectation of his seed (Gen 4:25).[74] The biblical-theological connection between Jesus and Adam is quite pervasive in the NT, most notably in Paul's specific identification of Jesus as "the *eschatos Adam*" (1 Cor 15:45) who has brought in a "new creation" (2 Cor 5:21). Upon identifying Jesus as "son of Adam," Luke 4:1–13 reports the account of Jesus resisting the three temptations of Satan, clearly paralleling Gen 3:1–15 and Adam's fall to the three temptations of the serpent (who is identified in Rev 12:7 as "the serpent of old who is called the devil and Satan."). While Davies suggests that "the conception of Christ as the Second Adam was probably introduced into the church by Paul himself,"[75] it seems more likely that the source derives from Jesus' common designation of Himself as the "Son of Man (בֶּן־הָאָדָם)," thus raising the obvious question, how is Jesus the *Ben-Adam*? This linguistic connection of *Adam* (אָדָם) the individual and Adam as humanity (Gen 5:1–4) leads Barrett to remark, "Whenever in Paul we meet the word *man*, . . . we may suspect

---

71. See the following section on the fifth stanza of 1 Tim 2:5–6.

72. The DLZ Hebrew NT (1877) interestingly translates this phrase ἄνθρωπος Χριστὸς Ἰησοῦς in 1 Tim 2:5 by הוּא בֶן־אָדָם הַמָּשִׁיחַ יֵשׁוּעַ, "He (who is) Son of Man, the Messiah Jesus." One might have thought that the noun בֶן is an unnecessary addition, but the translator Franz Delitzsch apparently thought that this phrase evoked the entire "son of Man/Adam" connection.

73. Dan 7:13–14 reads, "I kept looking in the night visions, And behold, with the clouds of heaven One like a Son of Man was coming, . . . and to Him was given dominion, glory and a kingdom, that all the peoples, nations, and *men of every* language Might serve Him."

74. Gen 4:25 reads, "And Adam knew his wife again; and she bare a son, and called his name Seth: For God, *said she*, hath appointed me another seed instead of Abel, whom Cain slew" (KJV). Most recent English versions obscure the seed motif by translating זֶרַע / σπέρμα (Gen 4:25) by "offspring" (ESV, NAS) or "Child" (NET, NIV, RSV). See Ellis, *Paul's Use of the Old Testament*, 95–98.

75. Davies, *Paul and Rabbinic Judaism*, 44.

THE "MAN CHRIST JESUS"

that Adam is somewhere in the background, characteristically hiding himself, though now behind the Greek language."[76]

ADAM IN 1 TIMOTHY 2:13-14

Actually, Adam is quite visible in the foreground of 1 Tim 2:5-6, as Paul proceeds in 1 Tim 2:12-14 to illustrate his teaching on authority by use of the creation and the sin of Adam and Eve.[77] Also, Paul specifically makes this same typological connection of Adam to Jesus in Romans 5:12-21 (especially 5:14-15, "Adam, who is a type of Him who was to come, . . . the one Man Jesus Christ"), in 1 Cor 15:22 ("For as in Adam all die, so also in Christ all shall be made alive"), and in 1 Cor 15:45 ("So also it is written, 'The first man, Adam, became a living soul; the last Adam *became* a life-giving spirit'"),[78] using these two men as representatives of humanity. Also, when Paul refers to the exaltation of Jesus in 1 Cor 15:26-27, he does so in the language of Adam's original status with all things placed under his feet (quoting from Ps 110:1 and Ps 8:4-6); however, unlike Adam, who died after his self-exaltation, Jesus was exalted only after He was "made lower in death" (Rom 8:3; Gal 4:4-5; Phil 2:6-8). Ridderbos observes, "When (Paul) reflects upon the significance of Christ's redemption, he returns again and again to the beginning of history, especially in developing the parallel between Adam and Christ."[79] Luke 3:38 follows this same link in his genealogy of Jesus as "the *son* of Adam" (τοῦ ᾿Αδάμ/ בֶּן־אָדָם; the noun υἱός is assumed from Luke 3:23) and then next identifies Him as "Son of God" (τοῦ θεοῦ), introducing the intriguing paradox: what can it mean that Jesus as God's Son also appears in history as the son of Adam *par excellence*?

The background of Paul's Adam-Christology has been hotly debated, as Bultmann argued that Paul derived it from a Gnostic redeemer myth,[80] while Brandenberger maintained that Paul adopted the Adam mythology of Jewish-Gnostic prayers and speculation.[81] Others have noted the similarity that Paul shares with the Platonic idealism of Philo (*Leg. Allel.* 1.31f).[82] However, in 1 Cor 15:45 Paul cites his source when he quotes

---

76. Barrett, *From First Adam to Last: A Study in Pauline Theology*, 6.

77. "For it was Adam who was first created, *and* then Eve. And *it was* not Adam *who* was deceived, but the woman being quite deceived, fell into transgression" (1 Tim 2:13-14). See Schreiner, "An Interpretation of 1 Timothy 2:9-15: A Dialogue with Scholarship," pages 85-120 in *Women in the Church: A Fresh Analysis of 1 Timothy 2:9-15* (2005).

78. Dunn, *Christology in the Making*, 101-07, points out that the Adam narrative not only lies in the foreground of Rom 5:12-21; 1 Cor 15:21-22; and 15:45-50, but also in the background of Rom 1:18-25; 3:23; 7:7-11; 8:19-22; 1 Cor 11:7; 2 Cor 3:18; 11:3; Eph 4:24; and Col 3:10. He does not add 1 Tim 2:13-15 to the mix, as he doubts its Pauline authorship, although the appearance of the same motif in this passage strengthens the case for Paul as the author of this letter.

79. Ridderbos, *Paul and Jesus*, 121.

80. Bultmann, *Theology of the New Testament*, 1:174; Käsemann, *Romans*, 144, argues that the Pauline Adam-Christ analogy is "not even grasped, let alone solved" by efforts to find the source in pre- and extra-Christian Gnosticism, since the concepts are so different.

81. Brandenburger, *Adam und Christus*, 77-109. For examples, see in Charlesworth, ed., *The Old Testament Pseudepigrapha* (1983, 1985), *Apocalypse of Adam* (1:712-19); *Testament of Adam* (1:993-95); *Life of Adam and Eve* (2:258-95).

82. Rostron, *The Christology of St. Paul*, 60, leans toward this Philonic connection. See the discussion in

Gen 2:7, "So also it is written, 'The first man, Adam, became a living soul,'" and he alludes to it also in 1 Tim 2:13–14 ("For it was Adam who was first created, *and* then Eve. And *it was* not Adam *who* was deceived, but the woman being quite deceived, fell into transgression."). These citations to the initial creation of Adam, the subtle deception of Eve, and the subsequent disobedience of Adam make it apparent that Paul refers to the Adam of the Genesis narrative and views him as a figure of human history.[83] Kim submits a solution to the "hitherto unresolved problem of the origin of (Paul's) Adam-Christology:"

> The insight of Christ as εἰκών of God led Paul also to think of Christ in terms of Adam, because he is said to have been created in the image of God (Gen 1:26–27). Since Jesus Christ, who had been raised by God from the dead, appeared to him as the image of God on the Damascus Road, and His resurrection signaled the dawn of the eschaton, Paul began to perceive of Christ as the Adam of the eschaton, ὁ ἔσχατος Ἀδάμ (1 Cor 15:45), and to develop his distinctive (first) Adam-Last Adam typology (Rom 5:12–21; 1 Cor 15:21–22, 42–49; probably also Phil 2:6–11). . . . Christ as the Last Adam is conceived of as having restored the image and glory of God that the first Adam all but lost through his fall. So through his Adam-Christology Paul basically affirms Christ as the perfect human being and therefore also affirms Christ's humanity.[84]

Thus Paul clearly develops his literary and theological themes from a textual and historical perspective with both Adam and Jesus.[85]

While Barrett understands Adam as mythical and contends that Paul even views each individual man as Adam,[86] such a view disrupts Paul's analogy in 1 Cor 15:22 that both Adam and Christ were men who were the first of their respective humanities ("all in Adam; all in Christ"). Modern readers, heavily imbued with evolutionary assumptions, may find themselves embarrassed by the idea of an historical Adam and thus presume

---

Cullmann, *The Christology of the New Testament*, 148–150.

83. Bousset, *Kyrios Christos*, 178, sees behind Paul's use of Adam "the widespread Hellenistic myth of the Primal Man, only Paul transports this myth from the primeval age into the end time." It is true that legends about Adam abounded in Second Temple Jewish literature, but even these stories assumed a historical Adam, which Paul does also in his references. The analogy between the two men collapses if the transgression of Adam is not as historical as the obedience of Jesus. Whether the modern reader accepts Adam as historical or not, Paul surely understood Adam's creation and fall as occurring in real time and space, and he cannot be properly interpreted unless the reader acknowledges this perspective. Also, Paul apparently assumed a common acceptance of the Jewish Scripture with his readers (Rom 15:4; 1 Cor 9:10; 10:11) and that they possessed some competent understanding of those passages to which he refers. Thus, Stanley, *Arguing with Scripture*, 76, remarks, "In several places Paul refers to the Genesis creation story in a manner that presumes that the Corinthians were familiar with the story. Among the details that he mentions without explanation are that . . . the first man Adam was created out of dust . . . and death came into the world through Adam's sin."

84. Kim, *Paul and the New Perspective: Second Thoughts on the Origin of Paul's Gospel*, 172.

85 Kim, *Origins*, 167, refutes Bultmann by showing that Paul argues from "the OT-Jewish background, the early Christian kerygma, and Paul's personal experience of Christ, especially that on the Damascus Road" (ibid., 175).

86. Barrett, *From First Adam to Last*, 13, 20. Zielser, *Pauline Christianity*, 53, also allegorizes the analogy, asserting, "Paul is not just talking about two individuals, but about human beings as a whole." It seems clear, however, that Paul *is* talking about two individuals of history.

THE "MAN CHRIST JESUS"

that Paul rests his doctrine on a fundamental mistake,[87] but honest hermeneutics must resist the temptation to read Paul through secular lenses and instead–to be blunt–take him at his word, whether one thinks he is mistaken or not. When Paul writes about Adam, he assumes that he is the original figure of human history, as he is presented in Genesis 1–5;[88] otherwise, his comparisons with Christ as another man of history become sheer nonsense. While conceding that evolution and creationism are irreconcilable theories, this essay assumes the studies of others in refuting the former and defending the latter;[89] thus, it shall proceed as if the comparisons Paul draws between Adam and Christ are historically true, since this is the perception of the apostle. He presents the first man Adam as the first lord of original creation, but in his illegitimate desire to become like God, he sinned and became a slave to creation and subject to death. Jesus, by contrast, originally "existed in the form of God" yet became subject to fallen creation and still obeyed God, thus becoming Lord over creation. Adam's sin, therefore, is that he as man aspired to become like God through disobedience, resulting instead in the reign of death over all those "in Adam." Christ's obedience, to the contrary, consists in that He as "Man" became like men in order to die, so that all those "in Christ" would live in the reign of life.

ADAM AND CHRIST IN ROMANS 5:12–21

In this much studied pericope (Rom 5:12–19),[90] Paul draws what Bird describes as a *synkrisis* or comparison between these two men, Adam and Christ, who serve as types of one another:[91]

Verse	Adam	Christ
5:12	through one man sin entered	
5:14	death reigned from Adam until Moses	

---

87. Wiles, "Does Christology Rest on a Mistake?", 10–11, calls the orthodox understanding of creation, the fall of Adam, and Paul's analogy of Christ's redemption to these doctrines a mistake that confuses "the human historical story with the divine mythological story." Wiles hopes to rescue some semblance of the "specialness of Jesus" by imposing this Kantian-like distinction of the phenomenal and the noumenal upon the Bible, but he can only do so by destroying the historical foundation Paul so plainly establishes. Honesty requires that the reader take Paul at face value and then decide if his supernatural perspective accords with truth more truthfully than does a Darwinian assumption.

88. See Paul's theology of creation in Acts 17:25–26, where he speaks of God as one who "gives to all life and breath and all things; and He made from one (Adam), every nation of mankind to live on all the face of the earth."

89. See Morris, ed., *Scientific Creationism* (1985); Garner, *The New Creationism: Building Scientific Theory on a Biblical Foundation* (2009); and Thompson, *The Scientific Case for Creation* (2002).

90. See the studies by Brandenburger, *Adam und Christus* (1962); Barth, *Christ and Adam: Man and Humanity in Romans 5* (1957); Cullmann, *The Christology of the New Testament*, 166–181; Bultmann, "Adam and Christ according to Romans 5" (1969), 145–60; Wedderburn, *Adam and Christ: An Investigation into the Background of 1 Corinthians XV and Romans V 12–21* (1970); Quek, "Adam and Christ according to Paul," 67–79. For other works on Rom 5:12–21 written before 1980, see the Bibliography in Käsemann, *Romans*, 140.

91. Bird, *Introducing Paul*, 41.

The "Man Christ Jesus" in the Context of 1 Timothy 2:1–6

5:14	the offense of Adam, who is a type	of the coming One
5:15	by the trespass of the one many died	the grace of God and the gift by the grace of the one Man, Jesus Christ, abounded to the many
5:16	through the one having sinned …	
	judgment out of one unto condemnation	but the gift out of many … transgressions unto acquittal
5:17	by the transgression of the one	
	death reigned through the one	much more those who receive the abundance of grace and the gift of righteousness will reign in life through the One, Jesus Christ
5:18	through one trespass unto all men unto condemnation	through one righteous-act unto all men unto justification of life
5:19	through disobedience of the one man	through the obedience of the one
	many were made sinners	many shall be made just

In Rom 5:12, Paul introduces "one man" whom he identifies in Rom 5:14 as Adam, the one "through whom sin entered into the world," as evidenced by the reign of death spread upon all humanity even before Moses, whose Laws demanded death for disobedience (Rom 5:14). Yet Paul's concern is to establish a basic similarity between Adam and Christ by labeling Adam as a type[92] "of the Coming One" (Rom 5:15, Ἀδὰμ ὅς ἐστιν τύπος τοῦ μέλλοντος), a phrase which seems to be a variation of the Messianic title derived from Ps 118:26 ("Blessed is the one who comes [הַבָּא; LXX, ὁ ἐρχόμενος[93]] in the name of the

---

92. This reference to Adam as a "type" of Christ is an important key in Paul's hermeneutical approach to the OT, illustrated by his use of the word τύπος elsewhere in 1 Cor 10:6, "Now these things happened as examples (τύποι) for us, that we should not crave evil things, as they also craved." The latter reference is to the wilderness experience of Israel, whereby the particular historical events of the Red Sea crossing (1 Cor 10:1–2), the manna (1 Cor 10:3), the Rock (1 Cor 10:4), Israel's idolatry (1 Cor 10:7), immorality (1 Cor 10:8), and punishments (1 Cor 10:9–10), all happened as types to instruct the new Covenant community. Goppelt, *Tupos: The Typological Interpretation of the Old Testament in the New*, 6, shows that typology differs from allegory in that it gives "a historical understanding of revelation" by taking historical persons, actions, events, and institutions of the OT and applying Christological significance to them. Ellis, *Paul's Use of the Old Testament*, 127, adds. "NT typological exegesis is grounded firmly in the historical significance of the 'types.'" Critics may not like such a method and thus deny its reality, since typology assumes a predictive (miraculous) aspect—a "divine history" (ibid., 19, ftnt. 56)—that does not fit naturalistic assumptions. An honest critic, however, will admit that Paul plainly uses typological interpretation of the OT throughout his letters. One may disagree with the method, but the task to supply a better hermeneutic has proved fruitless, as Goppelt shows in his historical survey (*Tupos*, 6–15); instead, scholars have discovered a greater awareness of the typological method employed in the NT (ibid., 15–17). In particular, Paul understands that the historical person and work of Jesus fulfills the historical persons and works recorded in the Jewish Scripture.

93. This participial phrase ὁ ἐρχόμενος appears in Matt 3:11; 11:3; 21:9; 23:39; Mark 11:9; Luke 7:19–20; 13:35; 19:38; John 1:27; 3:31; 6:14; 10:2; 11:27; 12:13; Heb 10:37; 2 John 1:7; Rev 1:4, 8; and 4:8 (see the same idea also in 1 John 4:2 and 5:6), whereas in Rom 5:14 Paul uses the genitive participle τοῦ μέλλοντος. BDAG § 4798.3 defines the use of μέλλω in Rom 5:14, "The ptc. is used abs. in the mng. *(in the) future, to come*;" as

LORD."), a beatitude conveyed upon Jesus at His entry into Jerusalem (John 12:13). As a type, Adam portrays certain similarities with the coming Christ in His own historical timeframe—notably, both are the first men (Rom 5:12, 15) of their respective families so that their actions effected future generations, yet when Paul references the two men, the typology instead emphasizes a drastic contrast between them.[94] Adam's one action is described as a trespass (Rom 5:15), a sin (Rom 5:16), and a disobedience (Rom 5:19), and the outcome is a reign of death (Rom 5:14, 17) by which many died (Rom 5:15), bringing judgment unto condemnation (Rom 5:16, 18), because many were made sinners (Rom 5:19, ἁμαρτωλοὶ κατεστάθησαν). On the contrary, the one act of righteousness of "the one man Jesus Christ" (τοῦ ἑνὸς ἀνθρώπου Ἰησοῦ Χριστου)[95] is described as obedience (Rom 5:19) coming from the grace of God and the gift of grace (Rom 5:15, 17), leading to justification for all who receive this abundance of righteousness (Rom 5:16–18), as they shall be appointed as just (δίκαιοι κατασταθήσονται).[96]

While the act of Adam refers to his transgression (the noun παραπτώματα is used six times for dramatic effect, in Rom 5:15, 15, 16, 17, 18, 20) perpetrated in the Garden of Eden (Gen 3:6), Paul does not identify the one righteous act (δι' ἑνὸς δικαιώματος) of Christ. He may give a clue to his meaning by the startling statement that justification came "out of many transgressions" (ἐκ πολλῶν παραπτωμάτων, Rom 5:16), when earlier in Rom 4:25 he mentions the historical delivering up of Jesus to crucifixion "because of our transgressions" (διὰ τὰ παραπτώματα ἡμῶν).[97] Thus, the main point of comparison in this typology is that two men of history acted on behalf of others;[98] indeed, Paul's argu-

---

Paul writes of what is future from the perspective of OT typology. This same participial use is also applied to Jesus in Luke 24:21, "that He Himself is the one *about* to redeem Israel" (author's translation of ὅτι αὐτός ἐστιν ὁ μέλλων λυτροῦσθαι τὸν Ἰσραήλ·). Barrett, *From Adam to Christ,* 92, comments, "Relative to Adam, Christ is the 'Man to come', whether we think of the coming described in the gospels, or of his *parousia* in glory."

94. Quek, "Adam and Christ according to Paul," 72, notes, "In . . . Romans 5, attention shifts from the 'person' of each representative to their respective 'work or acts.'"

95. One may well wonder if there is more than a literary similarity to this designation of "the one man Jesus Christ" to the "one man" (εἷς ἄνθρωπος) who Caiaphas prophesied would die for the nation (John 11:49–50; 18:14). John certainly viewed this unwitting statement of the High Priest as a profound prophecy.

96. LN § 13.9 defines καθίστημι, "to cause a state to be." Paul uses this verb elsewhere only at Titus 1:5, "For this reason I left you in Crete, that you might set in order what remains, and appoint (καταστήσῃς) elders in every city as I directed you," but the usage is similar to Heb 7:28, "For the Law appoints (καθίστησιν) men as high priests who are weak, but the word of the oath, which came after the Law, *appoints* a Son, made perfect forever." The act of each respective "One Man" appointed humanity either to the state of being a sinner or of being just.

97. If Paul refers to the historical obedience of Jesus in His humanity, then the comment of Dunn, *Christology in the Making,* 108, is mistaken, when he insists that Christ's role as the last Adam does not begin "at (the) incarnation but at his resurrection." But Paul clearly has the act of the cross in view in Rom 5:12–21, not the resurrection. Also, Luke 3:38 takes the Adam analogy back to the progenesis of Jesus by titling Him as the "son of Adam, Son of God."

98. Bousset, *Kyrios Christos,* 178, makes an astounding twist of exegesis in stating, "Paul by calling Christ ἄνθρωπος in no way intended to indicate that the two men are bound together by the common essence of humanity." Why else would Paul describe both Adam and Jesus as "men" unless he was comparing their acts of humanity? Not surprisingly, having robbed Adam of humanity, Bousset insists that Paul's Christ-

ment is baseless if there are no historical men who performed these acts within real space and time.[99]

For purposes of this study, one should note that this description of "the One Man Jesus Christ" (Rom 5:15) acting "through one acquittal unto all men" (Rom 5:18) shares remarkable linguistic parallels to the Christ-Creed of 1 Tim 2:5–6, that the "Man Christ Jesus" is the "One mediator" for "all men." This emphasis upon the humanity of Jesus is quite striking, for Paul clearly wants to establish an affinity between Adam and Christ as men whose individual acts produced effects "unto all men" (εἰς πάντας ἀνθρώπους, Rom 5:12, 18). This prepositional phrase, to be sure, is a generic description encompassing all humans within each respective family, but the designation of "one Man" to both Adam (Rom 5:12) and Jesus (Rom 5:15) should not be generalized to mean, "one Person" (as translated by the NAB in both verses).[100] Since respective families originate from these two heads, the masculine nouns "man" and "men" ought to be retained in order to maintain the parallels between Paul's epistles, the symmetry in his vocabulary, and his meaning that the work of redemption is grounded in a specific historical act accomplished by "the one Man Jesus Christ."[101]

---

mysticism has no basis in the OT (ibid., 182)—certainly not in the way he understands Paul as borrowing his ideas from the suffering, dying, and rising god of Hellenistic mystery-religions (ibid., 188), especially the *Anthropos* of the first tractate of the Hermetic collection (ibid., 191). However, Yamauchi, *Pre-Christian Gnosticism*, 71, reviews the same data to show that Bousset was reading Gnosticism back into Paul when it is now clear that gnostic writings borrowed from the apostle. Bousset fell into the "parallelomania" trap warned by Sandmel, where if one religious doctrine appears remotely similar to another, it must involve wholesale borrowing. This way, Boussett makes Paul's entire theology rest on the pagan practices the apostle so vigorously renounces—even though Bousset acknowledges that Paul has merged myth with history in the "death of a real man" (ibid., 199).

99. Wrede, *Paulus*, 89, ftnt. 1, insists that Paul is not referring to a historical Jesus, but rather the 'obedience' of which Rom 5:19 speaks is that "of the heavenly being, who humbles himself to a life on earth, and even to the cross." Instead, the humanity of Jesus, as Paul conceives it, remains an "impalpable phantom" (ibid., 90). Wrede insists that for Paul, the historical, human Jesus is of no real concern: it is only the exalted Lord that is the center of his theology. While it is difficult to determine if Wrede thought that Paul even believed in the true humanity of Jesus, this study, to the contrary, insists that Paul refers to the fact of the historical Jesus who is now the exalted Lord.

100. Another tendency to de-humanize Rom 5:12–21 is found in Käsemann, *Romans*, 143, who writes, "Almost grotesque is the attempt, on the basis of the term *anthropos*, to emphasize the humanity of the person of Jesus, to develop something like an anthropology of Jesus and finally to speculate on its material priority over that of Adam and his successors." Yet, this seems precisely what Paul *is* emphasizing in the "one" act of both Adam and Christ as real men whose actions transcend individual consequences to effect profoundly all their successors. The reality of either condemnation or justification rests upon the historical actuality of acts performed by those who were actual men, thus necessitating that an anthropology of Jesus be recognized and developed.

101. Fee, *Pauline Christology* 517, observes, "The issue now, however, is not death itself but rather the cause of death, sin . . . (since) the emphasis throughout this passage is on the repeated use of ἄνθρωπος for both Adam and Christ whom Paul identifies in Rom 5:15 as 'the one Man' (τοῦ ἑνὸς ἀνθρώπου Ἰησοῦ Χριστου), a similar designation to 1 Tim 2:5 (ἄνθρωπος Χριστὸς Ἰησοῦς) and 1 Cor 15:45 (ὁ δεύτερος ἄνθρωπος ἐξ οὐρανοῦ)." He ponders on the thesis of this study, "What is the significance to the designation of Jesus as 'the One Man?'" (ibid.).

THE "MAN CHRIST JESUS"

ADAM AND CHRIST IN 1 CORINTHIANS 15:25-47

The next reference to the "Man Jesus" appears when Paul answers various questions asked by the Corinthian community about the resurrection of the dead.[102] He first lists appearances of the resurrection of Jesus (1 Cor 15:1-8), noting that "last of all, He appeared also to me" (1 Cor 15:8), no doubt referring to his Damascus Road experience (Acts 9:1-8). Since there were many witnesses to the resurrection of Jesus, Paul then asks, "How do some among you say that there is no resurrection of the dead?" (1 Cor 15:12), and he answers this question by noting the hopelessness if there is no resurrection (1 Cor 15:13-19). Such despair is not the case, as he announces, "But now Christ has been raised from the dead, the first fruits of those who are asleep" (1 Cor 15:20), and this link between Christ and His own introduces the parallel between Christ and Adam as progenitors of two humanities: "For since by a man *came* death, by a man also *came* the resurrection of the dead; for as in Adam all die, so also in Christ all shall be made alive" (1 Cor 15:21-22). The parallels and contrasts are plainly observed in the Greek text:

	Adam	*Christ*
1 Cor 15:21	ἐπειδὴ γὰρ δι' ἀνθρώπου θάνατος	καὶ δι' ἀνθρώπου ἀνάστασις νεκρῶν
1 Cor 15:22	ὥσπερ γὰρ ἐν τῷ Ἀδὰμ πάντες ἀποθνῄσκουσιν	οὕτως καὶ ἐν τῷ Χριστῷ πάντες ζῳοποιηθήσονται.

Fee claims that there is nothing earlier in the letter that prepares for the sudden mention of Adam in this passage;[103] however, the context speaks of the conquest of death by the resurrection of Christ (1 Cor 15:15-20), and this fact quite naturally leads to the question of the origin of death, to which Paul answers, "by a man *came* death" (1 Cor 15:21), an unmistakable reference to the entrance of death through the disobedience of Adam as recorded in Gen 2:17; 3:3-4; and 3:19. From that calamity, Paul draws the same contrast in 1 Cor 15:22 that he makes in Rom 5:12-21, that there are two historical heads of humanity, Adam and Christ. In Adam all die, since through this man came death (δι' ἀνθρώπου θάνατος), whereas "in Christ all shall be made alive," since through this Man came the resurrection of the dead (δι' ἀνθρώπου ἀνάστασις νεκρῶν).[104] In 1 Cor 15:21, Paul is quite abrupt in his language, eschewing verbs and definite articles but specifically including them in 1 Cor 15:22, "in the Adam all are dying; in the Christ all shall be made-alive (ζῳοποιηθήσονται)." While the contrasts are stark (Adam→ death→ all die; Christ → resurrection of the dead → all made alive), the common element is that both persons are described as ἄνθρωπος. Quek observes, "The analogous element (is) the twice-occur-

---

102. 1 Corinthians 15 is "next" in the sense of canonical order, since the Corinthian letters were composed before Romans was written. Besides the studies mentioned earlier, see Hultgren, "The Origin of Paul's Doctrine of the Two Adams in 1 Corinthians 15.45-49," 343-70.

103. Fee, *Pauline Christology*, 516.

104. As in Rom 5:18 (εἰς πάντας ἀνθρώπους) and 1 Tim 2:4 (πάντας ἀνθρώπους), Paul's universal "all" in 1 Cor 15:22 must be defined by the context: it is not an indiscriminate "all," leading to a universalistic salvation, but "all" who are either in Adam or "all" who are in Christ.

ring anarthrous prepositional phrase 'through man' (not through '*a* man'), (placed) in the emphatic first-position of the sentence, with reference being to Adam and Christ *as men*. While this is true of Adam, it does not describe Christ completely: the divine nature is left out of account without invalidating the Analogy."[105] While this observation is certainly true, it should not be overlooked that when Paul defines here the work of salvation in history, his appeal is not to the deity of Christ but to His humanity.

As Paul continues his argument, he places the reality of these two humanities, either all dying in Adam or all made alive in Christ, within the eschatological framework of the future of redemption (1 Cor 15:23–28). In 1 Cor 15:25, Paul references Ps 110:1b, "Sit at My right hand, Until I make Thine enemies a footstool for Thy feet" (κάθου ἐκ δεξιῶν μου ἕως ἂν θῶ τοὺς ἐχθρούς σου ὑποπόδιον τῶν ποδῶν σου) in the statement, "For He must reign until He has put all His enemies under His feet" (δεῖ γὰρ αὐτὸν βασιλεύειν ἄχρι οὗ θῇπάντας τοὺς ἐχθροὺς ὑπὸ τοὺς πόδας αὐτοῦ). Paul adapts Ps 110:1b to his context by changing the particles and subject of the verb from ἕως ἂν θῶ ("until I should place") to ἄχρι οὗ θῇ ("until which He should place," with God as the subject) and adding an implied emphasis, "*all* the enemies."[106] Then, in 1 Cor 15:27, Paul further defines his meaning of τίθημι by linking Ps 110:1 with Ps 8:6a, "Thou hast put all things under His feet" (πάντα ὑπέταξας ὑποκάτω τῶν ποδῶν αὐτοῦ), a reference to Adam's original mandate in Gen 1:26.[107] Dunn describes this connection as "one of the most fascinating transition points or points of development in earliest christology."[108] Ciampa and Rosner note this expansion: "If with Ps. 110 authority and domination is considered in relation to God's right hand, with Ps. 8 it is seen in relation to all of creation."[109] The point of contact for Paul is the word "all," by which he includes "death" as the final enemy to be subjected to Christ. One exception to this subjection is, of course, "the One who subjected all things to Him," so that when "all things are subjected to Him, then the Son Himself also will be subjected to the One who subjected all things to Him, that "God may be all in all" (1 Cor 15:28). By connecting Gen 1:26 with Ps 8:6 and Ps 110:1, Paul establishes that Jesus is the "last Adam" who completes what the first Adam failed to do and is therefore granted the divine mandate to rule over all things as God's vicegerent.[110]

---

105. Quek, "Adam and Christ According to Paul," 68.

106. See Martin Hengel, "Sit at My Right Hand! The Enthronement of Christ at the Right Hand of God and Psalm 110:1," pages 119–225 in *Studies in Early Christology*, especially 163–72, where he discusses Paul's "weaving together" of Ps 110:1 and Ps 8:7 in 1 Cor 15:24–28 (ibid., 165), as also seen in Eph 1:20–22 and 1 Pet 3:22.

107. "Then God said, 'Let Us make man in Our image, according to Our likeness; and let them rule over the fish of the sea and over the birds of the sky and over the cattle and over all the earth, and over every creeping thing that creeps on the earth'" (Gen 1:26).

108. Dunn, *Christology in the Making*, 108.

109. Ciampa and Rosner, "1 Corinthians," in the *Commentary on the New Testament Use of the Old Testament*, 745. Psalm 8:6 is also cited in Eph 1:22a (καὶ πάντα ὑπέταξεν ὑπὸ τοὺς πόδας αὐτοῦ) and Heb 2:8 (πάντα ὑπέταξας ὑποκάτω τῶν ποδῶν αὐτοῦ), and possibly echoed in 1 Pet 3:22 (ὑποταγέντων αὐτῷ ἀγγέλων καὶ ἐξουσιῶν καὶ δυνάμεων).

110. Kim, *Paul and the New Perspective*, 209, shows how these concepts combine.

THE "MAN CHRIST JESUS"

After giving several moral admonitions (1 Cor 15:29-34), Paul addresses a related question, "How are the dead raised? And with what kind of body do they come?" (1 Cor 15:35), and he answers by comparing heavenly and fleshly bodies (1 Cor 15:36-44). This comparison leads him to his Adam-Christ analogy again (1 Cor 15:45-49):

	Adam	*Christ*
1 Cor 15:45	ἐγένετο ὁ πρῶτος ἄνθρωπος Ἀδὰμ εἰς ψυχὴν ζῶσαν	ὁ ἔσχατος Ἀδὰμ εἰς πνεῦμα ζῳοποιοῦν
1 Cor 15:46	τὸ ψυχικόν	ἔπειτα τὸ πνευματικόν
1 Cor 15:47	ὁ πρῶτος ἄνθρωπος ἐκ γῆς χοϊκός	ὁ δεύτερος ἄνθρωπος ἐξ οὐρανοῦ
1 Cor 15:48	ὁ χοϊκός	ὁ ἐπουράνιος
1 Cor 15:49	τὴν εἰκόνα τοῦ χοϊκοῦ	τὴν εἰκόνα τοῦ ἐπουρανίου

In order to show the nature of the resurrection body, Paul contrasts the bodies of the leading men of two humanities, whom he identifies as "the first man Adam" and "the Last Adam / the Second Man," identified earlier in 1 Cor 15:22 as Christ.[111] As in Rom 5:12-21, the parallel here between the two men is primarily one of dissimilarity: they differ as object and subject, as Adam became a living soul whereas Christ makes alive in spirit (1 Cor 15:45);[112] they differ in historical order (Adam appears before Christ, 1 Cor 15:46); they differ in essential properties (Adam is "soulish" [ψυχικόν], whereas Christ is "spiritual" [πνευματικόν, 1 Cor 15:46]); they differ in location, as Adam is "the first man out of the dust" whereas Christ is "the second Man out of heaven" (1 Cor 15:47);[113] they differ in resulting communities, as Adam is "the earthy one, so also are those who are earthy,"[114] whereas Christ is "the heavenly one, so also are those who are heavenly" (1 Cor 15:48); and they differ in personal image, as Adam bears the image (εἰκόνα) of dust and Christ

---

111. Significantly, Paul's description of the first Adam avoids all the extraordinary features of rabbinic mythology, as noted by Davies, *Paul and Rabbinic Judaism*, 45-46.

112. The participle ζῳοποιοῦν (BDAG § 3398.1, "to cause to live, make alive, give life to.") is not used in the passive voice, as in 1 Peter 3:18, that Christ was "put to death in the flesh, but made alive (ζῳοποιηθεὶς) in the spirit"), but in the active voice, that He makes alive. Paul uses this verb elsewhere for God giving life to the dead (Rom 4:17) and to mortal bodies (Rom 8:11), although the reference to "making alive unto spirit" indicates that Paul refers to "being made alive" to the work of regeneration (Eph 2:5; Col 2:13).

113. Note the linguistic similarity of ὁ πρῶτος ἄνθρωπος to Job 15:7, where Eliphaz refers to the "first man" to be born (הֲרִאישׁוֹן אָדָם, πρῶτος ἀνθρώπων), an apparent reference to Adam.

114. Paul uses the adjective χοϊκός four times in this context (1 Cor 15:47, 48a, 48b, 49), which are the only usages of this word in the Bible, although LN § 2.16 notes that the domain of χοϊκός is "derivative of χοῦς 'dust,'" which is used fifty-four times in the BGT. "Dust," of course, pictures the mortality of earthly existence, as in Ps 103:14 ("For He Himself knows our frame; He is mindful that we are *but* dust") and Eccl 3:20 ("All came from the dust and all return to the dust"). Paul clearly references Gen 2:7, "Then the LORD God formed man of dust (χοῦς) from the ground," so that the NET renders the phrases in 1 Cor 15:47-49, "The first man is from the earth, made of dust; . . . like the one made of dust, so too are those made of dust; . . . as we have borne the image of the man of dust." This certainly captures the "dustiness" of Adam, "the dusty one," with the "heavenliness" of Christ, "the heavenly one."

The "Man Christ Jesus" in the Context of 1 Timothy 2:1–6

the image (εἰκόνα) of the heavenly (1 Cor 15:49).[115] Despite all these differences, there is one primary affinity shared between the two, as Paul describes both as ἄνθρωπος, leading Kim to observe, "The Adam-Christology basically affirms the humanity of Christ. . . ."[116] This significant point must not be overlooked amid all these contrasts, that Christ—even though viewed in His resurrection state—is still considered to be a "Man."

If so, how then can Christ be a "man out of heaven" (ἄνθρωπος ἐξ οὐρανοῦ)?[117] This description combines two seemingly opposite concepts: earthly humanity and a heavenly location, leading some to posit that Paul borrows from Philo's speculation of two Adams,[118] or that he understands Ἀδάμ as merely a metonymy for humanity, as (it is argued) the contrast is made with another mythical figure, the heavenly man.[119] Since the discovery of the Nag Hammadi fragments, it has been attractive to apply the Gnostic

---

115. BDAG § 2260.2 defines the use of εἰκών in 1 Cor 15:49 as "that which has the same form as someth. else (not a crafted object . . .), a *living* image." No doubt what lies behind this picture is Gen 1:26, "Then God said, "Let Us make man in Our image" (κατ᾿ εἰκόνα ἡμετέραν). Kim, *Origin of Paul's Gospel*, 266, ftnt. 3, argues that Paul "came to think of Christ in terms of Adam because he saw him as the image of God on the Damascus Road . . ." and tied that to Gen 1:26, "Then God said, "Let Us make man in Our image, according to Our likeness." Thus, Kim suggests that Paul found the Adam-Christ connection in "the exalted Christ in glory as the εἰκὼν τοῦ θεοῦ on the road to Damascus" (ibid., 193). This may well be, but Paul's analogy compares and contrasts two historical men, as repeated use of ἄνθρωπος indicates (1 Cor 15:21, 21, 47, 47). See also Schreiner, *Paul: Apostle of God's Glory in Christ*, Chapter 7, "Person Of Jesus Christ: Exaltation Of Christ For The Glory Of God."

116. Kim, *Origin of Paul's Gospel*, 266.

117. The BYZ text of 1 Cor 15:47b reads, ὁ δεύτερος ἄνθρωπος ὁ κύριος ἐξ οὐρανου, but Metzger, *Textual Commentary of the New Testament*, 501–02, comments, "The reading that best accounts for the origin of the others is ἄνθρωπος, supported by a strong combination of early and good witnesses representing several text-types (ℵ* B C D* G 33 1739* it[d, g 61] vg cop[bo] *al*). The insertion of ὁ κύριος (Marcion preferred κύριος as a substitute for ἄνθρωπος) is an obvious gloss added to explain the nature of "the man from heaven" (ℵ[c] A D[c] K P Ψ 81 104 614 1739[mg] *Byz Lect* syr[p, h, pal] goth arm *al*); if this were original, there is no reason why it should have been omitted. The singular reading of 𝔓46 (ἄνθρωπος πνευματικός) shows the influence of ver. 46, while the omission of ἄνθρωπος (cop[sa] Cyril) is merely a transcriptional accident." See also Creed, "The Heavenly Man," 113–36.

118. See the critique of this view in Dunn, *Christology in the Making*, 98–101. He points out some remarkable similarities between Paul and Philo, leading Evans, *Ancient Texts*, 171, to suggest, "Paul's typology may be assuming a distinction between the Adams of the two creation accounts that approximates Philo's exegesis." For example, Philo, *Leg. Alleg* 1.31, in discussing Adam, reads, "Now the heavenly man (οὐράνιος ἄνθρωπος), as being born in the image of God, has no participation in any corruptible or earth-like essence. But the earthly man (ὁ δὲ γήϊνος ἐκ σποράδος) is made of loose material, which he calls a lump of clay." However, Philo then taught that the first Adam did not fall but became the heavenly man and thus was not truly human; it was a second Adam, formed of dust, who fell because he was sensual (*Leg. Alleg* 1.53), meaning that Philo draws the opposite conclusion from Paul, who maintains that the first Adam of Gen 1:26 is the same Adam who sinned in Gen 3:6, and that Christ, even though originating "out of heaven," chronologically appears after Adam.

119. Barrett, *From First Adam to Last*, 90, insists that "Paul's story of the Redeemer and the redeemed does not simply contain a mythical element; it is mythical through and through," but then he struggles to explain why "Paul himself could afford to be content with a bare assertion of the realization in historical and personal terms, that is, in Jesus, of the eschatological myth of salvation" (ibid., 91). There is no solution to Barrett's dilemma, for if Adam is mythical, then the salvation in Jesus is mythical also, thus destroying Paul's analogy. What is apparent, however, is that Paul treats both Adam and Christ as if they are historical.

THE "MAN CHRIST JESUS"

myth of a pre-existent divine Man to Christ,[120] and while it is beyond the scope of this study to scrutinize the derivation of such an *Urmensch* (an "original man"), Dunn examines the current evidence and gives a "straightforward No to beginnings of a heavenly man redeemer figure speculation which may have influenced Paul."[121]

What then might Paul mean by describing Jesus as a "man out of heaven"? Pfleiderer argues that Paul refers to Christ in His pre-existence,[122] while Andrews maintains that Paul describes Christ in His post-resurrection state, as he would have seen Him as a "man out of heaven" in his Damascus Road experience.[123] Andrew's opinion may well be correct, but since Paul contrasts Jesus and Adam in this context (1 Cor 15:22, 45), it seems better to understand 1 Cor 15:47 as viewing Jesus incarnationally, since here Paul refers to the historical beginnings of both the first man Adam "from the earth" as well as the second man Jesus "from heaven," as indeed was the case in His conception (Luke 1:35). But beyond all this, since the apostle is relating Jesus to OT categories (by citing Ps 110:1; Hos 13:14; Ps 8:6; Gen 2:7), Barrett suggests that the apostle "is aware of another Old Testament passage which speaks of a man who comes from heaven—Dan 7:13, 'I saw in the night visions, and behold there came with the clouds of heaven like one unto a son of Man.' Paul understood this expression and knew that it meant a human figure, a man from heaven, a heavenly man...."[124] There may even be in 1 Cor 15:47 an echo to a claim of Jesus, since this unique expression ὁ δεύτερος ἄνθρωπος ἐξ οὐρανοῦ bears intriguing linguistic similarities to John 3:13, "And no one has ascended into heaven, but He who descended from heaven (ὁ ἐκ τοῦ οὐρανοῦ), *even* the Son of Man (ὁ υἱὸς τοῦ ἀνθρώπου)." Since the narrative in John 3 does not indicate any change of narrator from Jesus to the author, this statement appears to originate from Jesus Himself in His conversation with Nicodemus where He as the Son of Man out of heaven teaches the same concept employed by Paul. Both unite two opposite categories: first, "the (Son of) Man" suggests a human, earthly, and natural category, whereas the second category "out of heaven" speaks of a divine, celestial, and supernatural source—even implying the pre-existence of Jesus, although this concept is denied by Dunn.[125] These categories do not seem to be compatible, but they are clearly conjoined in the NT in the "Man-Christ." They indicate that Paul is not merely making literary comparisons but appealing to the two originators of their respective humanities, those of the "dusty one" and those of the "heavenly one" (1 Cor

---

120. Bultmann, *Theology of the New Testament*, 1:166.

121. Dunn, *Christology in the Making*, 123. Black, "The Pauline Doctrine of the Second Adam," 177, also concludes that "there is no unequivocal evidence pointing to the existence of such a conception (of a Gnostic heavenly man) in pre-Christian sources, particularly within Judaism."

122. Pfleiderer, *Paulinism: A Contribution to the History of Primitive Christian Theology*, 1:140.

123. Andrews, *The Meaning of Christ for Paul*, 96–97.

124. Barrett, *Paul: An Introduction to His Thought*, 112.

125. Ibid. Dunn claims that 1 Cor 15:45 views Jesus not in an incarnation state, but in His resurrection status, enabling him to deny Jesus' pre-existence. However, it is a *non sequitur* to insist that there is no hint of pre-existence in the expression, "a man from heaven" or in the title, "the heavenly one" (1 Cor 15:46). If Jesus was a mere mortal exalted to divine status, this raises a host of other theological problems beyond the scope of this particular study, as to why and how He alone among humanity acquired such a heavenly status. If, however, He pre-existed in heaven, this adaquately explains how He can be "a man from heaven."

15:47). If their offspring are actual—and they are, according to 1 Cor 15:48[126]—then the progenitors must also be real persons.

Kim suggests instead that when Paul mentions a man of heaven, he refers to his vision of the resurrected Christ on the road to Damascus.[127] His suggestion seems quite reasonable, especially since Paul has already mentioned that Christ appeared to him after His resurrection (1 Cor 15:8). At that time, He identified Himself as "Jesus of Nazareth" (Acts 22:8)—about as earthly and homely a place as one could imagine (John 1:46)—yet both Acts 9:3 and Acts 22:6 report that the derivation of the risen Lord was the same location Paul gives in 1 Cor 15:47, "out of heaven" (ἐκ τοῦ οὐρανοῦ). Furthermore, it should be noted in 1 Cor 15:45 that Paul does not appeal to his conversion experience for this explanation of Jesus but to the Genesis account, giving a scriptural argument for the differences between the natural body and the resurrection/ spiritual body by introducing this section with a quote from Gen 2:7, "So also it is written, 'The first man, Adam *became* a living soul.'" Paul provides some explanatory words to the text of the LXX (which reads, ἐγένετο ὁ ἄνθρωπος εἰς ψυχὴν ζῶσαν) by naming Adam and designating him as "first" (ἐγένετο ὁ πρῶτος ἄνθρωπος Ἀδὰμ εἰς ψυχὴν ζῶσαν), clarifying what is obvious in the Genesis account (that the first man of history was named Adam) while at the same time implying there is at least a second man.[128] Instead, Paul scans the scope of history all the way to "the last (ἔσχατος) Adam,"[129] a title leading some to argue that Paul is not concerned with historical categories at all, but only with eschatological concepts of salvation.

However, the saving implications are inherent within the historical parallels between Adam and Christ drawn by Paul: he notes that each is the first Man of his respective humanity, "all in Adam" and "all in Christ." Each one has a body appropriate to his location, either earthly or heavenly, and each body possesses respective corporeality, as shown in 1 Cor 15:40–44.[130] This observation raises the question why Paul would refer to Christ as "the second Man" (ὁ δεύτερος ἄνθρωπος) if he views Him in His resurrection state? Clearly Paul intends this designation as some sort of title, since he skips over numerous generations from Adam to Christ, yet this reference to "second Man" alerts the reader to stop at Gen 4:1 and consider the birth of the second man after Adam.[131] That would be Cain,

---

126. "As is the earthy, so also are those who are earthy; and as is the heavenly, so also are those who are heavenly" (1 Cor 15:48).

127. Kim, *Origin*, 193. More specifically, he ties the origin to Paul's understanding of Adam and Christ to the fact that he describes both in terms of εἰκὼν θεοῦ: Adam in 1 Cor 11:7 (based on Gen 1:26–27; 5:1; 9:6) and Christ in 2 Cor 4:4; Col 1:15 (see ibid.,193–205). This argument would be more compelling if Paul made this connection more than a literary echo, for he actually makes the analogy in Rom 5:12–14 and 1 Cor 15:47 on the basis of the humanity of each man rather than on the divine image.

128. While Paul refers to the creation of Adam's soul in 1 Cor 15:45, there is no parallel to the creation of Christ's soul—nor would there be, if He is pre-existent; however, the implication is that both had supernatural beginnings with regard to their humanity, Adam as the direct creation of God, and Jesus in a way not mentioned here but taught elsewhere as the Holy One conceived in the womb of the virgin Mary (Matt 1:20; Luke 1:35).

129. Scroggs, *The Last Adam: A Study in Pauline Anthropology* (1966).

130. Fee, *Pauline Christology*, 516, observes, "*Christ continues to have a body that is related to his life as a human being*" (his italics).

131. Since Stanley, *Arguing with Scripture*, 178, wonders if "Paul may have rendered some of his argu-

THE "MAN CHRIST JESUS"

who proves to be as opposite from Christ as imaginable,[132] yet he is the "man" of whom his mother Eve declared, "I have produced a man" (אִישׁ / ἄνθρωπος). This unique Hebrew sentence (קָנִיתִי אִישׁ אֶת־יְהוָה) raises translational difficulties, although the English versions almost always render the final two Hebrew words as a prepositional phrase, either, "I have gotten a man (child) with the help of the Lord" (NEB, NIV, RSV), or, "I have gained a man with/by the Lord" (NKJ, KJV; NET oddly renders Eve's exclamation, "I have created a man just as the LORD did!"), following the lead of the LXX (εἶπεν ἐκτησάμην ἄνθρωπον διὰ τοῦ θεοῦ). Yet אֶת is most commonly used in the MT of the Hebrew Bible as a marker of the accusative, so that a rather wooden translation reads, "I have acquired a man—the LORD." The weight of grammar supports this view, as in the vast majority of the 221 times אֶת־יְהוָה is found in the MT, it is used as the accusative object sign designating "the Lord."[133] Could Eve possibly mean that the "man" she births is also "the Lord'?

While this idea seems preposterous, the Pseudo-Jonathan Targum translates Eve's remark into Aramaic quite fascinatingly, קניתי לגבר ית מלאכא דייי ("I have acquired a man, the Angel of the Lord"), revealing an interpretive tradition linking the OT concepts of "Man" with the "Angel of the Lord." This view would mean that Eve announced (incorrectly, but at least hopefully) that her baby was the promised seed of Gen 3:15, a son who would bruise the serpent on the head. NET *Notes* calls this interpretation a "fanciful suggestion based on a questionable allegorical interpretation of Gen 3:15,"[134] but clearly Paul makes a typological application of Gen 3:15 in Rom 16:20, "The God of peace will soon crush Satan under your feet." Such hope in a Man who would conquer the serpent might also explain why Seth would name his son, "Enosh" (אֱנוֹשׁ = "Man"[135]) in further hope that a second Man would come to undo the calamity the first Man Adam had perpetrated (Gen 4:26). Now, Paul announces that this second Man has arrived in the "Man Christ Jesus."

Summary: Adam and Christ Contrasted

In summary, Paul presents both Adam and Christ as two historical men acting in human history, although each appeared in opposite circumstances: Adam in an original creation; Jesus in a world already marred by sin. Both Adam and Christ acted on behalf

---

ments incomprehensible, or at least obscure, to audience members who were unfamiliar to the characters or stories to which he refers," modern readers (who certainly comprise what Stanley considers to be a "minimal audience") must also wonder if by "second Man" Paul refers to Gen 4:1. However, any reader, ancient or modern, can correctly deduce that the "second Man" of biblical history was Cain, and that would lead to Gen 4:1 and the observation of the semantic similarities with 1 Cor 15:47.

132. Cain is mentioned three times by name in the NT—and never in a favorable way—in Heb 11:4 ("By faith Abel offered to God a better sacrifice than Cain."); in 1 John 3:11c–12 ("We should love one another; not as Cain, *who* was of the evil one, and slew his brother. And for what reason did he slay him? Because his deeds were evil, and his brother's were righteous."); and in Jude 11 ("Woe to them! For they have gone the way of Cain.").

133. The only exceptions where אֶת־יְהוָה is translated as a prepositional phrase, "with the Lord," are Num 20:13; 1 Sam 25:29; Isa 49:4. Hebrew is quite capable of using other prepositions to express, "with the Lord:" עִם־יְהוָה (Exod 34:28; 1 Sam 2:26; Ps 130:7) or אֶל־יְהוָה (Deut 3:23).

134. *NET Notes*, in *BibleWorks8*, loc. cit.

135. BDAG § 675.

The "Man Christ Jesus" in the Context of 1 Timothy 2:1–6

of all other men (εἰς πάντας ἀνθρώπους, Rom 5:18), but Adam disobeyed God, leading to death due to sin, whereas Christ obeyed, leading to life due to righteousness (Rom 5:19; 1 Cor 15:22). Both Adam and Christ reaped the consequences of their respective acts: Adam died whereas Christ lived. Finally, both affected their respective humanities: all in Adam die, but all in Christ shall live.[136] Despite these contrasts, what both individuals share in common is that each is "the one Man" (ὁ εἷς ἄνθρωπος), so that the upshot of the entire Adam-Christology is that "it basically affirms the humanity of Christ."[137] It is not merely that Adam and Christ serve as progenitors of their respective humanities, but Adam does so as the *protos anthropos* of dust whereas Christ does so as the *eschatos/deuteros anthropos* out of heaven. While Paul had been an eyewitness of this "Man out of heaven," his application of the word ἄνθρωπος to the "Man Jesus" comes more directly from a typological interpretation of the Jewish Scriptures. Moo observes, "The Old Testament ... furnished him with the necessary conceptual categories to develop the corporate dimensions of Christ's person. In a way quite foreign to most modern western thinking, the Old Testament views the nature and destiny of groups of people in terms of the actions of a key individual."[138] This recognition raises an important hermeneutical question: was Paul correct in finding in the OT an "anthropological soteriology" in which a Man (an *Adam*) would come and bring salvation? If so, how can such be reconciled with the declaration of Israel's Lord that "There is no savior besides Me"?[139] To find an answer, this study turns to the concept of "Man" as presented in the OT.

The Representative Man in the OT

The echo of Adam lingering in the context of 1 Timothy 2 indicates that Paul relies on the OT to establish his understanding of Jesus as the "Man" (in Hebrew, *adam* = "man") in a singular, covenantal sense, especially since the designation in 1 Tim 2:5, ἄνθρωπος Χριστὸς Ἰησοῦς ("Man Christ Jesus"), is unique in biblical literature and quite unusual as a description of any individual. One must wonder if Paul hints at something beyond the obvious that Jesus was of the masculine gender, raising the possibility that "Man" might also suggest another Old Covenant theme, particularly as it stands in apposition to the unmistakable OT concept of the Christ. Might Paul be using a messianic motif with the expression that would translate from Hebrew, "Adam-Messiah"?

The possibility is not as far-fetched as one might suspect, especially when one observes that the Christ-Messiah-Anointed One announced in the OT is also described as a "man" in 2 Sam 23:1, "David the son of Jesse declares, and the man (הַגֶּבֶר/ ἀνήρ)[140] who

---

136. Ridderbos, *Paul: An Outline of His Theology*, 60–61, declares, "Adam and Christ here (1 Cor 15:22) stand against each other as the two great figures at the entrance of two worlds, two aeons, two 'creations,' the old and the new; and in their actions and fate lies the decision for all who belong to them, because these are comprehended in them and thus are reckoned either to death or to life."

137. Kim, *Origins*, 266.

138. Moo, "The Christology of the Early Pauline Epistles," 176.

139. See Isa 43:11; 45:21; Hos 13:4; also Exod 15:2; Ps 3:8; Jonah 2:9.

140. BDAG § 1616 defines גֶּבֶר as "man as strong," since it is built upon the verb גָּבַר, "to be strong" (BDAG § 1615).

was raised on high declares, 'The *anointed* (מָשִׁיחַ/ χριστὸν) of the God of Jacob!'"[141] The OT provides extensive data for its anthropology, as the Hebrew word אָדָם (Gen 1:26) appears 555 times to express humanity in general,[142] and אִישׁ appears 2,187 times as defining man as male.[143] These words are translated in the LXX by ἄνθρωπος 1,657 times (beginning with Gen 1:26) and by ἀνήρ 1,584 times, a word that "signifies man as opposed to woman."[144] One might suppose that the LXX would translate אִישׁ by ἀνήρ and אָדָם by ἄνθρωπος (as in 2 Sam 7:14, "I will correct him with the rod of men [אֲנָשִׁים/ ἀνδρῶν] and the strokes of the sons of men" [אָדָם/ υἱῶν ἀνθρώπων]),[145] but in actuality there seems to be little consistency—the words are translated interchangeably; for example, both words first appear together in Gen 2:23–24, "The Man (הָאָדָם/ Αδαμ) said, 'This is now bone of my bones, and flesh of my flesh; She shall be called Woman, because she was taken out of Man' (מֵאִישׁ; ἐκ τοῦ ἀνδρὸς). For this cause a man (אִישׁ/ ἄνθρωπος) shall leave his father and his mother, and shall cleave to his wife; and they shall become one flesh." While אִישׁ/ ἀνήρ seems to distinguish a man from a woman, and אָדָם/ ἄνθρωπος may generally describe man as part of humanity, the following study reveals that both words are used to describe a most unexpected appearance of God as Man.

This extraordinary phenomenon is preceded by a repeated quest for a man who can represent others before God. In Gen 41:38, Pharaoh asks his servants, "Can we find a man like this (כָזֶה אִישׁ/ ἄνθρωπον τοιοῦτον), in whom is a divine spirit?" Pharaoh does not expect to find one, although that man is locked in his dungeon as the falsely accused Joseph, who proves to be such a man; in fact, the Genesis account says nothing detrimental about the character of Joseph, placing him alongside Daniel and Mordecai as worthy examples of true humanity. In Num 27:16, Moses prays that "the LORD, the God of the spirits of all flesh, appoint a man (אִישׁ/ ἄνθρωπον) over the congregation, who will go out and come in before them, and who will lead them out and bring them in, that the congregation of the LORD may not be like sheep which have no shepherd." Such a man is found in Joshua, a "man in whom is the Spirit" (אִישׁ אֲשֶׁר־רוּחַ בּוֹ/ ἄνθρωπον ὃς ἔχει πνεῦμα, Num 27:18), evidently qualifying him for this task. In similar fashion, "The LORD has sought out for Himself a man (אִישׁ/ ἄνθρωπον) after His own heart," and the LORD appointed David as this man to be ruler over His people (1 Sam 13:14). Conversely, when the Lord examined

---

141. Horbury, *Jewish Messianism and the Cult of Christ*, 34, summarizes, "Finally, the designation 'Son of man' is close to the use of various words signifying 'man' in pre-Danielic messianic oracles, including Num. 24.17; II Sam. 23.1 and Zech. 6.12, . . . and Ps. 80.18, which has *ben adam*."

142. BDAG § 135, defines אָדָם as "1. a man in general; 2. collectively, mankind; 3. proper name, Adam." Westermann, "אֲדָמָה," *TLOT* 1:42, states that אָדָם and אֱנוֹשׁ denote the category, "humanity as a whole, to which the individual belongs, humanity is defined by its origin, its creatureliness."

143. BDAG § 435, defines אִישׁ as "man with emphasis on sexual distinction and relation." Kühlewein, "אִישׁ," *TLOT* 1:99, states, "The word's basic meaning is 'man' (the mature male in contrast to the woman). This meaning establishes a natural semantic field in which man and woman stand in contrast." Thus every אִישׁ as a male would also be an אָדָם, whereas אָדָם could refer to humanity in general (Gen 5:2), as all אֱנוֹשׁ would include both men and women.

144. Oepke, "ἀνήρ," *TDNT* 1:361.

145. See also Isa 2:11, "The proud look of man (אָדָם/ἄνθρωπος) will be abased, and the loftiness of man (אֲנָשִׁים/ἀνθρώπων) will be humbled."

His people, "He saw that there was no man (אִישׁ/ ἀνήρ), and was astonished that there was no one to intercede" (Isa 59:16). Such a search was ordered of Jeremiah: "Roam to and fro through the streets of Jerusalem, and look now, and take note, and seek in her open squares, if you can find a man (אִישׁ/ ἄνδρα), if there is one who does justice, who seeks truth, Then I will pardon her" (Jer 5:1). Also the Lord reported to Ezekiel, "I searched for a man (אִישׁ/ ἄνδρα) among them who should build up the wall and stand in the gap before Me for the land, that I should not destroy it; but I found no one" (Ezek 22:30). To this end, the anthropology of the OT can be described as quite pessimistic, as reflected in the prayer of Solomon, "There is no man who does not sin" (2 Chr 6:36); thus, a godly man is extremely rare, if one can be found at all.

Yet amid this futile search, the OT tells of the Blessed Man (אַשְׁרֵי־הָאִישׁ/ μακάριος ἀνήρ) who is the ideal Man of God.[146] Such a Man of God is expected from the families of David[147] and Levi,[148] "a man whose Name is Branch" who shall build the Temple of the Lord;[149] however, such a Man shall be accosted by the sword,[150] for even though He is the Servant of the Lord, He shall be a man of sorrows.[151] Such a Man is the ideal expectation of the OT, and the culmination of this hope seems to be reflected in the coming of the Son of Man (Dan 7:13).

The Son of Man

This intriguing OT expression "son of man" (בֶּן־אָדָם/ υἱὸς ἀνθρώπου) is a title occurring 107 times in the OT (132 in the LXX, including the Apocrypha), of which ninety-three refer to the prophet Ezekiel and one to Daniel (Dan 8:17). Of the remaining instances, nine appear in parallel to אִישׁ[152] and do not seem to be messianically significant, leav-

---

146. אַשְׁרֵי־הָאִישׁ/ μακάριος ἀνήρ appears in Ps 1:1; 83:6; 112:1; 128:4; Jer 17:7; Isa 56:2. Variations include אַשְׁרֵי אָדָם/ μακάριος ἄνθρωπος (Ps 84:8, 12; 94:12; 127:5; Prov 3:13; 8:34); אַשְׁרֵי אָדָם/ μακάριος ἀνήρ (Ps 32:2; 84:5; Prov 28:14); אַשְׁרֵי הַגֶּבֶר/ μακάριος ἀνήρ (Ps 34:8; 40:4); and בָּרוּךְ הַגֶּבֶר/ εὐλογημένος ὁ ἄνθρωπος in Jer 17:7.

147. "Let Thy hand be upon the man of Thy right hand (ἐπ' ἄνδρα δεξιᾶς σου/ עַל־אִישׁ יְמִינֶךָ), upon the son of man whom Thou didst make strong for Thyself" (Ps 80:17).

148. "For thus says the LORD, 'David shall never lack a man (אִישׁ) to sit on the throne of the house of Israel; and the Levitical priests shall never lack a man (אִישׁ) before Me to offer burnt offerings, to burn grain offerings, and to prepare sacrifices continually'" (Jer 33:17–18).

149. "Then say to him, 'Thus says the LORD of hosts, "Behold, a man (הִנֵּה־אִישׁ/ ἀνήρ) whose name is Branch, for He will branch out from where He is; and He will build the temple of the LORD" (Zech 6:12). The Branch as a messianic motif is also found at Isa 4:2; 11:1; Jer 23:2; 33:15; and Zech 3:8.

150. Zechariah 13:7, "Awake, O sword, against My Shepherd, and against the man (עַל־גֶּבֶר/ ἄνδρα), My Associate," declares the LORD of hosts."

151. "He was despised and forsaken of men, A man of sorrows (אִישׁ מַכְאֹבוֹת/ ἄνθρωπος ἐν πληγῇ), and acquainted with grief" (Isa 53:3). The NT consistently understands this prophecy as referring to the suffering of Jesus (Acts 8:32–35; 1 Pet 2:22–24). Since Paul quotes from Isa 53:1 in Rom 10:16, referring to the hearing of the word of Christ, it is most probable he also understood the entire passage Messianically, meaning that he found the OT to announce the Servant of the Lord as a "Man."

152. These include Num 23:19, "God is not a man (אִישׁ) nor son of man (וּבֶן־אָדָם) that he should repent;" Job 25:6, "How much less man, *that* maggot, and the son of man, *that* worm!" (וּבֶן־אָדָם תּוֹלֵעָה אַף כִּי־אֱנוֹשׁ רִמָּה); Job 35:8, "Your wickedness is for a man (לְאִישׁ) like yourself, and your righteousness is for a son of man" (וּלְבֶן־אָדָם); Isa 51:12, "Who are you that you are afraid of man (מֵאֱנוֹשׁ) who dies,

THE "MAN CHRIST JESUS"

ing but four pertinent OT references: Ps 8:4–6;[153] Ps 80:17;[154] quite possibly Ps 144:3;[155] but especially Dan 7:13–14, when the prophet reports, "I kept looking in the night visions, and behold, with the clouds of heaven One like a Son of Man (כְּבַר אֱנָשׁ / ὡς υἱὸς ἀνθρώπου) was coming; and He came up to the Ancient of Days and was presented before Him; and to Him was given dominion, glory and a kingdom, that all the peoples, nations, and *men of every* language might serve Him; His dominion is an everlasting dominion which will not pass away; and His kingdom is one which will not be destroyed." Despite its infrequency in the OT, the title 'son of Man' represents the highest conceivable declaration of exaltation in Judaism," according to Cullmann.[156] Yet because the explanation given in Dan 7:18 that "the saints of the Highest One will receive the kingdom and possess the kingdom forever, for all ages to come," Mowinckel in his influential study *He That Cometh* insists that the OT expressions translated "son of man" (Hebrew: בֶּן־אָדָם; Aramaic: בַּר אֱנָשׁ, only at Dan 7:13) "mean no more than an individual of the human species, a human being,"[157] leading him to deny that the original context of Daniel 7 refers to an individual, personal Messiah of any sort;[158] however, the 'Son of Man' figure in Dan 7:13–14 is certainly presented as an individual, as indicated by use of the third personal masculine singular suffix "he/him." Even Mowinckel acknowledges that other Jewish sources make the connection between the Son of Man and a "heavenly man."[159] He

---

And of the son of man (וּמִבֶּן־אָדָם) who is made like grass?"; Isa 56:2, "How blessed is the man (אֱנוֹשׁ) who does this, And the son of man (וּבֶן־אָדָם) who takes hold of it;" Jer 49:18, 33; 50:40; and 51:43 are identical: "no one (אִישׁ) will live there, nor will a son of man (בֶּן־אָדָם) reside in it."

153. Psalm 8:4–6, "What is man, that Thou dost take thought of him? And the son of man (וּבֶן־אָדָם), that Thou dost care for him? Yet Thou hast made him a little lower than God, And dost crown him with glory and majesty! Thou dost make him to rule over the works of Thy hands; Thou hast put all things under his feet." Hebrews 2:6–10 applies this quote to Jesus as "son of Man (υἱὸς ἀνθρώπου) now crowned with glory because of His suffering of death" (Heb 2:9). Paul's quotation of Ps 8:6b (πάντα ὑπέταξας ὑποκάτω τῶν ποδῶν αὐτοῦ) in 1 Cor 15:27 (παντα γὰρ ὑπέταξεν ὑπὸ τοὺς πόδας αὐτοῦ) makes it clear that he shared the same interpretive understanding as the author of Hebrews (strengthening the argument that Paul might also be that author!), as both apply that Psalm to the ascension honor and rule of Christ—as the perfected *Anthropos*. Goppelt, *Tupos*, 163, observes this connection.

154. Psalm 80:17 prays, "Let Thy hand be upon the man (אִישׁ) of Thy right hand, upon the son of man (עַל־בֶּן־אָדָם) whom Thou didst make strong for Thyself." The context is clearly messianic, as seen in Ps 80:14–15, "O God *of* hosts, turn again now, we beseech Thee; Look down from heaven and see, and take care of this vine, Even the shoot which Thy right hand (יְמִינֶךָ) has planted, And on the son (בֵּן) whom Thou hast strengthened for Thyself." The LXX translates this instance of בֵּן as υἱὸν ἀνθρώπου, prompting Hengel, *Studies in Early Christology*, 169, to suggest that this is a "missing link" preparing the way for the connection to the son of Man in Daniel 7.

155. Psalm 144:3 asks, "O LORD, what is man (מָה־אָדָם), that Thou dost take knowledge of him? Or the son of man (בֶּן־אֱנוֹשׁ), that Thou dost think of him?"

156. Cullmann, *Christology of the New Testament*, 161.

157. Mowinckel, *He That Cometh*, 346.

158. Ibid., 350.

159. Ibid., 352. He refers to the Apocalypse of Enoch, the Ezra Apocalypse (2 Esdras), 2 Baruch, the Targums, and Philo, all which clearly build upon the Son of Man image from the book of Daniel (ibid., 353–57) as an eschatological, pre-existent heavenly being who is also regarded as the Messiah (ibid., 358–73). Bird, *Are You the One Who Is To Come?*, 89–91, tables the similarities between Daniel 7 and 2Q246, and notes a fascinating parallel in 4Q246 with the annunciation of Jesus (Luke 1:32–33).

observes that the Son of Man is also considered to be divine by possessing divine glory (Ps 8:5),[160] yet paradoxically "the striking fact (is) that the Son of Man is a pre-existent, heavenly being, but yet is called 'the Man.'"[161] Mowinckel sees this phenomenon as concurrent within Second Temple literature, which all seems derivative from the vision in Dan 7:13–14, despite Mowinckel's insistence that 'the Man' "did not originally have any connexion (sic) with the OT Messiah."[162] If not, when then did the concepts of "Christ" and "Son of Man" combine? The most obvious connection is established in the Gospels, when Jesus was placed under adjuration by the High Priest, to confess whether He was the Christ, the Son of God (Matt 26:64 || Mark 14:62), to which He answers, "You have said it *yourself*; nevertheless I tell you, hereafter you shall see the Son of Man sitting at the right hand of Power, and coming on the clouds of heaven," making obvious allusions to both Dan 7:13 and Ps 110:1.[163] Significantly, Stephen uses this same combination in Acts 7:56 when he cries out at his vision of Jesus, "I see the heavens opened up, and the Son of Man standing at the right hand of God," an exclamation heard by the attending Saul. As Moule suggests, "son of Man" is an ideal concept for the self-designation of Jesus, since in the OT it "constitutes the supremacy of Adam over the rest of nature," picturing Man in "suffering, vindication, and presentation before God."[164]

Thus, Hurtado observes, "It is clear when Jesus calls Himself 'the Man', *simpliciter*, he gives to this expression (ὁ υἱὸς τοῦ ἀνθρώπου) . . . specific meaning. 'The Man' (with a capital 'M') is not the same as any man."[165] A similar connection is made when Jesus asks His disciples, "Who do people say that the Son of Man is?" (Matt 16:13), to which Peter answers, "Thou art the Christ, the Son of the living God," a confession followed by Jesus' initial teaching that "the Son of Man must suffer many things" (Mark 8:31). Even Mowinckel acknowledges that Jesus' "use of the phrase proclaims boldly the original paradox, that he, who will one day come with the authority of God, is called 'the Man.'"[166] To

160. Mowinckel, *He That Cometh*, 374–75.

161. Ibid., 383.

162. Ibid., 420.

163. Hurtado, *Lord Jesus Christ*, 20, notes that the "primary function (of Son of Man) in the Gospels is as *a self-designation by Jesus*" (emphasis his). The reference to the "right hand" is an allusion to Ps 110:1, "The LORD says to my Lord: 'Sit at My right hand, Until I make Thine enemies a footstool for Thy feet,'" suggesting that the combination of Dan 7:13 and Ps 110:1 originates with Jesus.

164. Moule, *The Origin of Christology*, 14, 18. Bird, *Are You the One Who Is To Come?*, 78, notes that in the Gospels, the Son of Man tradition is generally stratified into three similar categories: "a present authoritative figure, a suffering figure, and a future eschatological figure."

165. Hurtado, *Lord Jesus Christ*, 347, observes this interesting grammatical difference between the OT and NT, as the phrase υἱὸς ἀνθρώπου is found 132 times in the LXX, and it is always anarthrous (υἱὸς/ υἱέ/ υἱὸν/ υἱῷ ἀνθρώπου), but of the eighty-eight times the title is found in the NT, it appears only four times anarthrously, in OT citations (Heb 2:6; Rev 1:13; 14:14) and in the quote of Jesus in John 5:27 (καὶ ἐξουσίαν ἔδωκεν αὐτῷ κρίσιν ποιεῖν, ὅτι υἱὸς ἀνθρώπου ἐστίν); otherwise, when used by Jesus, both nouns appear with the definite article, so that the indefinite υἱὸς ἀνθρώπου of the LXX becomes the specific ὁ υἱὸς τοῦ ἀνθρώπου of Jesus. Moule, *The Origin of Christology*, 13, argues for the significance of the definite article, that "behind the Greek, *ho huios tou anthrōpou*, must be some Aramaic expression that meant, unequivocally, not just 'Son of Man' but '*the* Son of Man' or '*that* Son of Man', and that this phrase was thus demonstrative because it expressly referred to Daniel's 'Son of Man.'"

166. Mowinckel, *He That Cometh*, 446.

THE "MAN CHRIST JESUS"

the original element of the exalted man Jesus adds his own "incomprehensible innovation in Jesus' view of Himself . . . that the Son of Man will be rejected, and will suffer and die before he comes in His glory with God's angels and sits down on the judgment seat."[167]

As the "Son of Adam" (Luke 3:38, בֶּן־אָדָם, DLZ), Jesus "acts as Adam was originally intended to act with the authority of God on earth; his authority is denied by men, but he will be vindicated by God."[168] Although the OT title lost its Hebraic peculiarity "son of" and becomes in Paul's writing, simply, the Man ("the Adam"), it becomes Paul's designation of Jesus not only as the "One Man" of the OT expectation, but also as the "man from heaven," echoing yet another fascinating OT concept, that of God appearing as man.

God Appearing As Man

Most intriguing are the OT narrative accounts when there is an appearance of a personage who is initially described as a man but then is subsequently identified as God. These appearances span across biblical history: the first is recorded in Genesis 18, when Abraham "lifted up his eyes and looked, behold, three men (שְׁלֹשָׁה אֲנָשִׁים / τρεῖς ἄνδρες) were standing opposite him" (Gen 18:2), yet the section is introduced as "when the Lord (יְהוָה) appeared to him" (Gen 18:1). One of the three "men" subsequently identifies Himself as the Lord (יְהוָה, Gen 18:14), and Abraham stands before יְהוָה interceding on behalf of Sodom and appealing to Him as the "Judge of all the earth" (Gen 18:22–25). Thus the one who arrives as Man departs as Yahweh (Gen 18:33).

A second account from the patriarchal period occurs in Gen 32:24 when "Jacob was left alone, and a man (אִישׁ/ ἄνθρωπος) wrestled with him until daybreak." This man informs Jacob that "you have striven with God," to which Jacob responds, "I have seen God (אֱלֹהִים) face to face" (Gen 32:30). The reader is left wondering, who is this wrestler against whom Jacob prevails yet who identifies Himself as God? How can a Man also be God—and yet be pinned by another man? The text leaves these questions unanswered.

The next appearance occurs at a critical moment in Israel's history, as the nation prepares to seize Jericho.[169] When Joshua reconnoitered the ancient city, "he lifted up his eyes and looked, and behold, a man (וְהִנֵּה־אִישׁ/ ἄνθρωπον) was standing opposite him with his sword drawn in his hand, and Joshua went to him and said to him, 'Are you for us or for our adversaries?' And he said, 'No, rather I indeed come now *as* captain of the host (שַׂר־צְבָא) of the LORD.' And Joshua fell on his face to the earth, and bowed down, and said to him, 'What has my lord (אֲדֹנִי) to say to his servant?'" (Josh 5:13–14). This worshipful response of Joshua and the ensuing command of the *sar-tzoboa* for Joshua to remove his sandals on this holy place are indications that the "Man" is actually the Lord God (אֲדֹנָי יְהוִה).

The next appearance of the Divine Man occurs in the period of the Judges, when Manoah's wife identifies the angel of the Lord as a man of God (אִישׁ הָאֱלֹהִים/ ἄνθρωπος θεοῦ, Judg 13:6).[170] After a second appearance of the angel of God, she again identifies him

---

167. Ibid., 448.

168. Marshall, *Origins of New Testament Christology*, 70.

169. Actually, earlier at the Red Sea Crossing, Moses sang, "The LORD is a man of battle" (מִלְחָמָה אִישׁ יְהוָה; Exod 15:3), but what Israelite would have understood this metaphor to be physical?

170. The מַלְאַךְ יְהוָה has already appeared in Gen 16:1–11; 22:1–15; Exod 3:2; Num 22:2–35; Judg

as a man (הָאִישׁ/ ὁ ἀνήρ, Judg 13:10), but after Manoah makes an offering to the angel, he exclaims to his wife, "We have seen God" (אֱלֹהִים/ θεὸν, Judg 13:22). The description of the Divine Angel as a man could be merely the language of appearance, but to Manoah's wife, the Angel who appeared at first to be a man is subsequently identified as God.[171]

There are three appearances of this Divine man in the visions seen by Ezekiel: in the first vision, the prophet sees "something resembling a throne, like lapis lazuli in appearance; and on that which resembled a throne, high up, *was* a figure with the appearance of a man" (כְּמַרְאֵה אָדָם/ ὡς εἶδος ἀνθρώπου; Ezek 1:26), whom he explains as "the appearance of the likeness of the glory of the LORD" (Ezek 1:28). This person sends Ezekiel to the sons of Israel "who have rebelled against me" (Ezek 2:3) and to whom he shall say, "Thus says the Lord God" (Ezek 2:4); thus, the one who appears as a man is actually the God of Israel. This same individual reappears in Ezek 8:2, when the prophet "looked, and behold, a likeness as the appearance of a man" (כְּמַרְאֵה־אִישׁ/ ἰδοὺ ὁμοίωμα ἀνδρός), who shows him the great abominations the house of Israel commits against "My sanctuary," so it obvious that the Man is also the Lord God. On a third occasion, Ezekiel "heard one speaking to me from the house, while a man (אִישׁ/ ὁ ἀνήρ) was standing beside me. And He said to me, "Son of man, *this is* the place of My throne and the place of the soles of My feet, where I will dwell among the sons of Israel forever" (Ezek 43:6-7). Again, the references to God's house and God's throne mean that this Man must be identified as Israel's God. Since the Torah mandates an earlier aversion to attributing to God any form whatsoever (Deut 4:12-16), this appearance of God as a man is quite startling, for Ezekiel's description borders on an idolatrous representation of God, yet it is clear that the prophet describes Israel's God as a man.

The final appearances of God as man appear in the Book of Daniel: the first appears in the exclamation of Nebuchadnezzar, "Look! I see four men (גֻּבְרִין/ ἄνδρας) loosed *and* walking *about* in the midst of the fire without harm, and the appearance of the fourth is like a son of *the* gods!" (לְבַר־אֱלָהִין; Dan 3:25). This fourth Man is not identified and vanishes from the narrative (and also from the furnace), but the LXX renders the Aramaic by ὁμοίωμα ἀγγέλου θεοῦ, apparently to conform it to prior appearances of the Angel of the Lord (Gen 16:10; Judg 13:6, et al.). The second appearance of a divine man (at least in part) occurred at Belshazzar's feast when "suddenly the fingers of a man's hand (יַד־אֱנָשׁ/ χειρὸς ἀνθρώπου) emerged and began writing opposite the lampstand on the plaster of the wall of the king's palace" (Dan 5:5). While critics credit this story to a mythical legend, the king is quite aware that he has witnessed a supernatural intervention, one that Daniel interprets as "the hand sent from him" (= God, Dan 5:24). How is it that God who is spirit can possess the fingers of a man? Again, the text leaves this question unanswered.

In Dan 8:1-14, after the prophet sees the vision of the Goats, he notes, "And it came about when I, Daniel, had seen the vision, that I sought to understand it; and behold, standing before me was one who looked like a man" (Dan 8:15, כְּמַרְאֵה־גָבֶר/ ὡς ὅρασις ἀνθρώπου). This person instructs the archangel Gabriel to give Daniel understanding of

---

2:1-4; 5:23; and 6:11-22; and this angel identifies Himself as the Lord.

171. See MacDonald, "Christology and 'The Angel of the Lord,'" 324-35. See also the discussion in Kim, *Origins,* 200-07.

THE "MAN CHRIST JESUS"

the vision, and although the man remains unidentified, the fact that he has authority over angels suggests His divinity. He appears to be the same man seen by Daniel in the Vision of the Conflict of Nations (Daniel 10–11), when the prophet states, "I lifted my eyes and looked, and behold, there was a certain man (אִישׁ־אֶחָד/ ἄνθρωπος) dressed in linen, whose waist was girded with *a belt of* pure gold of Uphaz" (Dan 10:5). This individual "having the likeness of the sons of men" (NKJ, כִּדְמוּת בְּנֵי אָדָם/ ὁμοίωσις υἱοῦ ἀνθρώπου; note the singular in the LXX) touched Daniel's lips so the prophet might speak (Dan 10:16), but the weakness of Daniel necessitated that "*this* one with human appearance (כְּמַרְאֵה אָדָם/ ὡς ὅρασις ἀνθρώπου) touched me again and strengthened me" (Dan 10:18). Daniel addresses this Man as "my lord" (אֲדֹנִי), which may be a title of respect (as in Dan 1:10), but it can also be an address to deity (as in Daniel's prayer in Dan 9:19); regardless, Kim rightly observes that "these passages in Daniel in which a divine or angelic figure is described as having the form or likeness of man should be compared with Dan 4:25 (sic) where an angelic figure is seen by Nebuchadnezzar as being 'like a son of the gods'...."[172] The actions of this Man (commanding, healing, and defending His people) favor his identification as Daniel's Lord God, meaning that at varying moments in OT history, God appears as Man.[173]

This brief survey reveals that from the earliest of Israel's patristic period (Genesis 19; 32), through the conquest (Joshua 5) and administration of the Judges (Judges 13), into the royal dynasty (Isaiah) to the exile (Ezekiel and Daniel) and on to the restoration (Zechariah 6; 13), the Hebrew Scriptures bear witness to the appearance of one described as a Man (or "like a man") yet who subsequently is identified as an Angel of the Lord or, even more surprisingly, as God. He appears as "a heavenly or divine being in human form."[174] What makes this phenomenon so surprising is the denial by God that He is a

---

172. Kim, *Origin*, 209. The reference should be corrected to Dan 3:25.

173. Note the similarity of language in Daniel 10 to the vision of John of the ascended Christ:

	Revelation 1:13–15	Daniel 10:5–6
Identity:	"one like a son of Man"	"A certain man"
Clothing:	"clothed in a robe reaching to the feet"	"dressed in linen,"
Belt:	"girded across His breast with a golden girdle."	"waist was girded with *a belt of* pure gold of Uphaz."
Head:	"And His head and His hair were white like white wool, like snow"	"His body also was like beryl, His face had the appearance of lightning,
Eyes:	"His *eyes were like a flame of fire;*"	"His eyes were like *flaming torches*,"
Feet:	"His *feet were like burnished bronze*, when it has been caused to glow in a furnace,"	"His arms and feet like the gleam of *polished bronze*"
Voice:	"His voice *was* like the sound of many waters."	"the sound of His words like the sound of a tumult."

The logical connection is that the Revelator sees the same individual as described by Daniel.

174. Mowinckel, *He That Cometh*, 352. Kuhlewein, אִישׁ, *TLOT* 1:102, observes, "In connection with pre-Israelite saga materials, Israel's most ancient period apparently had no misgivings about representing Yahweh as a man, who looks like other men, wanders the earth, eats, or fights (a similar concept may also be

man ("God is not a man, that He should lie, Nor a son of man, that He should repent," Num 23:19), as Moses reminds Israel that in God's appearance when "the LORD spoke to you from the midst of the fire, you heard the sound of words, but you saw no form—only a voice" (Deut 4:12). Since no form of God was seen, no image of God was allowed to be manufactured (Deut 4:15–16), yet this is said of Moses: "With him (Moses) I speak mouth to mouth, even openly, and not in dark sayings, and he beholds the form of the LORD" (Num 12:8). How can God not have the form of a man, yet appear in the form of a man? What seems to be contradictory is left unresolved in the OT: a heavenly being appears who at first is described as Man (ἄνθρωπος) but then is given unmistakable divine titles—so who is this God who appears as Man?

In 1 Tim 2:5, Paul provides the answer to this dilemma when he describes Jesus as "Man."[175] He is not at all doing what Dibelius suggests when he wonders if "the mention of ἄνθρωπος in this connection raises the question whether the cosmological myth of the redeemer is in the background."[176] For sure, the pagan Lystrans exclaimed of Paul and Barnabas, "The gods have become like men and have come down to us" (Acts 14:11), but the Apostles vehemently rejected any such adulation of themselves and surely would not apply any such polytheistic notions to Jesus. Instead, when Paul describes Jesus as "Man Christ," he echoes an OT concept of a divine mediator who is also described as "Man"—even more so, of Man who is subsequently identified as God (אֱלֹהִים, Gen 32:29). The confirmation of this interpretation comes when Paul defines the Man Jesus with the OT title of "Christ."

Jesus as Christ

In 1 Tim 2:5, Paul conjoins two distinct OT themes, the Man and the Messiah,[177] and unites them into one person, Jesus, designating Him as the Χριστὸς of Israel, by which His humanity is clearly established.[178] In his important study, Mowinckel defines the Messiah

---

found in Josh 5:13–15 and Ezek 8:2). A few post-exilic instances in connection with the prophetic view of the future describe the heavenly being sent to people (the prophets) as 'is; although these beings are not, in fact identical with God, they are also not always sharply distinguished from him" (citing Exod 12:12; Ezek 9:2; 40:3–5; 43:6; 47:3; Zech 1:8, 10; 2:5; Dan 10:5; 12:6). Kuhlewein does not separate angels from this divine figure, but full readings of the context generally do distinguish mere angels from God Himself.

175. Hays, *Echoes of Scripture in the Letters of Paul*, 23, proposes that Paul often uses "subliminal" intertextuality in his use of the OT, rather than employing a formal midrashic method.

176. Dibelius, *Pastorals*, 42.

177. See Chester, "Jewish Messianic Expectations and Mediatorial Figures and Pauline Christianity," in *Paulus und antike Judentum*, 17–89; Cullmann, *The Christology of the New Testament*, 111–36; Moule, *The Origin of Christology*, 31–35; Hengel, "Christos in Paul," in *Between Jesus and Paul: Studies in the Earliest History of Christianity*, 65–77; Hengel, "Jesus the Messiah of Israel," in *Studies in Early Christology*, 1–72; Fee, *Pauline Christology*, 530–85; Akenson, *Saint Saul: A Skeleton Key to the Historical Jesus*, 35–41.

178. The noun מָשִׁיחַ appears thirty-eight times in the OT (Lev 4:3, 5, 16; 6:15; 1 Sam 2:10, 35; 10:1; 12:3, 5; 16:6; 24:7, 11; 26:9, 11, 16, 23; 2 Sam 1:14, 16; 19:22; 22:51; 23:1; 1 Chr 16:22; 2 Chr 6:42; Ps 2:2; 18:51; 20:7; 28:8; 84:10; 89:39, 52; 105:15; 132:10, 17; Isa 45:1; Lam 4:20; Dan 9:25, 26; and Hab 3:13). It is applied to priests (Lev 4:3), prophets (Ps 105:15), but mostly to kings (1 Sam 2:10). In the LXX, Χριστὸς translates מָשִׁיחַ in Lev 4:3, 5, 16; 6:15; 1 Sam 2:10, 35; 12:3, 5; 16:6; 24:7, 11; 26:9, 11, 16, 23; 2 Sam 1:14, 16; 19:22; 22:51; 23:1; 1 Chr 16:22; 2 Chr 6:42; Ps 2:2; 18:51; 20:7; 28:8; 84:10; 89:39, 52; 105:15; 132:10, 17; Isa 45:1; Lam 4:20; Dan 9:25–26; and Hab 3:13. Conversely, *christos* translates other words in the LXX at Lev

THE "MAN CHRIST JESUS"

as *"the future, eschatological realization of the ideal of kingship"* of the Davidic kingdom,[179] though one who was a mortal man of David's line, though he may be called "David" in the sense that the nation of Israel is called "Jacob."[180] The cognate verbs in both Hebrew (מָשַׁח) and Greek (χρίω) carry the idea of smearing or anointing with fluid (usually olive oil),[181] although the words take on symbolic significance of anointing by the Spirit of God (1 Sam 16:13; Isa 61:1; Luke 4:18; Acts 10:38; 2 Cor 1:21–22). The "Anointed One" is a title assigned to Jesus from the outset of His ministry when "[Andrew] found first his own brother Simon, and said to him, 'We have found the Messiah' (which translated means Christ)" (John 1:41). Jesus claimed the title for Himself (for which he was condemned, Matt 26:63–64);[182] it was confessed by the Apostolic Church (Acts 2:36, "God has made Him both Lord and Christ—this Jesus whom you crucified.") and used by Paul as his most common designation of Jesus—not merely as another name for Jesus, as Ziesler contends,[183] but as a title of His royal-messianic significance.[184] While the OT pictures

---

21:10 ("oil of the Christ"); 21:12 ("anointing oil"); 2 Sam 2:5 (translates אֲדֹנֵיכֶם); 2 Sam 22:7 (translates the verb מָשִׁיחוֹ); and Amos 4:13 (God "reveals unto men His Christ," translating "reveals His plans."). See Grundmann, "χρίω, Χριστός, etc.," in *TDNT* 9:493–589. While Akenson, *Saint Saul*, 40, maintains that *"the concept of Messiah was only of peripheral interest to later Second Temple Judaism"* (italics his), it is plainly found in the OT and certainly becomes central in the NT.

179. Mowinckel, *He That Cometh*, 156, italics original. Bird, *Are You the One Who Is To Come?*, 36, notes two crucial elements in messianism: "(1) The sociological status of the messianic functionary is that of royalty; . . . (2) The temporal orientation of messianism is always toward the future, even though the sequence of events or the leadership paradigm may be drawn from Israel's sacred traditions about the past," noting especially 2 Sam 7:11–16; the royal Psalms 2, 72, 89, and 132, as well as Isa 9:6–7; 11:1–4; Jer 23:5–6; 33:17–22; Ezek 34:22–24; 37:24–25; Dan 2:44–45; 7:13; 9:24–27.

180. Ibid., 159.

181. BDAG § 5734. חשׁמ is generally translated by χρίω; BDAG § 7988 reports that the verb מָשַׁח appears in Gen 31:13; Exod 28:41; 29:2, 7, 36; 30:26, 30; 40:9ff., 13, 15; Lev 2:4; 6:13; 7:12, 36; 8:10ff.; 16:32; Num 3:3; 6:15; 7:1, 10, 84, 88; 35:25; Judg 9:8, 15; 1 Sam 9:16; 10:1; 15:1, 17; 16:3, 12f.; 2 Sam 1:21; 2:4, 7; 3:39; 5:3, 17; 12:7; 19:11; 1 Kgs 1:34, 39, 45; 5:15; 19:15f.; 2 Kgs 9:3, 6, 12; 11:12; 23:30; 1 Chr 11:3; 14:8; 29:22; 2 Chr 22:7; 23:11; Ps 45:8; 89:21; Isa 21:5; 61:1; Jer 22:14; Dan 9:24; Amos 6:6.

182. Marshall, *Origins of New Testament Christology*, 86, states, "There is little room for doubt that Jesus was put to death as one who was regarded as a pretender to Messiahship or kingship." Moule, *The Origin of Christology*, 32, suggests that Jesus shows reluctance in using the title for Himself, probably due to popular sentiment and nationalistic overtones of a "divinely appointed king," so when he claimed the title, he "did so only in a reinterpreted form" (ibid., 35). See also Hengel, "Jesus the Messiah of Israel," pages 15–32 in *Studies in Early Christology*, where he discusses the scholarly resistance toward any messianic consciousness in Jesus, calling a "completely unmessianic Jesus a fundamental error . . . both historically and theologically" (ibid., 32).

183. Ziesler, *Pauline Christianity*, 29, suggests that "Paul regularly uses the title as little more than a name, with no stress on its meaning." This is an irresponsible statement, for if "Christ" was an insignificant title, why should Paul use it at all—unless he had Christological reasons for doing so? In fact, Ziesler proceeds to show precisely why "Christ" was quite significant to Paul, as he uses it to show what type of messiah Jesus was—crucified and vindicated as a fulfillment figure (ibid., 30).

184. Hurtado, *Lord Jesus Christ*, 100. In Paul's signed letters, the word χριστός appears 403 times, eighty-nine times in the order of this verse (Χριστὸς Ἰησοῦς; four times in the nominative, five in the accusative, thirty in the genitive, and fifty in the dative) and eighty times in the inverted order, almost always (64 times) in the genitive, Ἰησοῦ Χριστοῦ; exceptions are three times in the dative (1 Thess 1:1; 2 Thess 1:1; 3:12); five times in the nominative (1 Cor 8:6; 2 Cor 13:5; Gal 3:1; Phil 2:11; 2 Thess 2:16); and six times in the accusative (Rom 13:14; 1 Cor 2:2; 2 Cor 4:5; Eph 6:24; Phil 3:20; 2 Tim 2:8).

the Messiah as anointed with supernatural qualities (Isa 61:1–2), He is first of all pictured as human, and so when "Paul speaks of Jesus' messianic character, there is stress on His humanity—that is, He was descended from David according to the flesh. The use of Christ for Jesus in Paul's letters, therefore should probably be seen as laying stress on the humanness of the Messiah."[185] Yet Paul preaches a Messiah of distinct and shocking novelty, a "Christ crucified" (Χριστὸν ἐσταυρωμένον; 1 Cor 1:23).[186]

The identity of Jesus as Messiah is patently obvious in the NT, but critical OT studies downplay references to Messianism,[187] a trend that Horbury challenges in his important work, *Jewish Messianism and the Cult of Christ*, as he asks how the OT came to offer "so much material which would be interpreted messianically in the Septuagint, the Targums, the Qumran texts and rabbinic literature? How did early Christian Christology, as represented in the NT, come to be so deeply imbued with messianic terms and concepts?"[188] Horbury answers his questions by showing that the OT is even organized along messianic lines[189] and that messianic prototypes are quite prevalent in the OT.[190] Likewise, Mowinckel refutes the idea that Messianism derived from non-Israelite mythology but instead shows its essential source was the royal ideology of the early monarchy as shown in Psalms 2 and 110.[191] As Horbury notes, even though the actual usage of מָשִׁיחַ is rare in the second Temple Jewish literature, it appears sufficiently to show that it stands for God's Messiah, as rooted in OT vocabulary (especially Dan 9:24–26[192]); thus, when the concept

---

185. Witherington, "Jesus as the Alpha and Omega of New Testament Thought," 38.

186. See the discussion by Hengel, "Jesus the Messiah of Israel," 41–58, in which he emphasizes, "... (We) cannot ignore that *the Messiah question runs through the Passion story of all the gospels like a red thread*" (45, his italics).

187. For example, Akenson, *Saint Saul,* 175, insists that "Messiah was only a peripheral concept in late Second Temple Judahism (sic)," but Paul moved it to the center of his belief system, making this "one of the definitive differences between Rabbinic Judaism and Christianity." However, see Horbury, "Jewish Messianism and Early Christianity," 3–13, who surveys the messianic expectation in such Second Temple Jewish works as *Psalms of Solomon, Sibylline Oracles, 1 Enoch, the Assumption of Moses, 2 Baruch,* and the *Eighteen Benedictions,* as well as the books of *Jubilees,* the *Testament of the Twelve Patriarchs,* the *Damascus Document,* plus the *Community Rules* of the Dead Sea Scrolls (1QS). These writings all confirm the contemporary Jewish expectation of a Messiah as chronicled in the Gospels.

188. Horbury, *Jewish Messianism and the Cult of Christ,* 2.

189. Ibid., 25–31, Horbury observes that the OT is edited Messianically, as it integrates these Davidic oracles: Jacob's prophecy of Judah (Genesis 49) → Balaam's oracles (Num 24:7, 17) → Hannah's prayer (1 Samuel 2) → David's songs (2 Samuel 22 = Psalm 18) → Isaiah's Davidic rule (Isaiah 7, 9, 11, 32, 55) → The Davidic Branch (in Jeremiah and Zechariah).

190. Ibid., 31–35. Messianic prototypes include Moses as king (Deut 33:5) who receives God's scepter (Exod 4:20); David (Psalms 18, 89, 78, 68, etc.); the Servant of Isaiah 53; the smitten shepherd of Zech 13:7; and the Son of Man (Dan 7:12).

191. Mowinckel, *He That Cometh,* 125–33, 159–62, 181–6.

192. Daniel 9:24–26 predicts, "Seventy weeks have been decreed for your people and your holy city, to finish the transgression, to make an end of sin, to make atonement for iniquity, to bring in everlasting righteousness, to seal up vision and prophecy, and to anoint the most holy *place* (וְלִמְשֹׁחַ קֹדֶשׁ קָדָשִׁים). So you are to know and discern *that* from the issuing of a decree to restore and rebuild Jerusalem until Messiah the Prince (עַד־מָשִׁיחַ נָגִיד) *there will be* seven weeks and sixty-two weeks; it will be built again, with plaza and moat, even in times of distress. Then after the sixty-two weeks the Messiah will be cut off (יִכָּרֵת מָשִׁיחַ) and have nothing, and the people of the prince who is to come will destroy the city and the sanctuary."

THE "MAN CHRIST JESUS"

of Messiah appears in the NT, it was part of common custom.[193] It is unquestionably Paul's belief that the Man Jesus was the promised Messiah of the OT, as affirmed in 1 Tim 2:5. His initial confession of Jesus is that "He is the Christ" (Acts 9:22, οὗτός ἐστιν ὁ χριστός), indicating that upon his conversion experience on the road to Damascus, Paul immediately combined his prior understanding of the Messiah with that of Jesus of Nazareth.[194]

A very significant observation for the purposes of this study is that the LXX (the OT of Paul's reading) links the Messiah with that of a "Man" in Num 24:7, 17, and Isa 19:20. This connection is noted by Towner, who comments, "In describing the mediator with this phrase (as Man), Paul also accesses the theme within developing messianism of 'a man to rule the nations' (Num 24:7, 17, LXX) and 'a man who will save us' (Isa 19:20)."[195] Towner notes how "several themes and ideas link these two OT discourses together and make the combination an attractive and clear interpretative framework for reflecting on the extent of Christ's work,"[196] most notably, that "the central actor in each drama is 'the man' (*anthropos*)."[197] This "Man" who shall come of the seed of Israel to rule the nations appears as a 'star rising out of Jacob' (Num 24:7) and then reverts to the more ordinary description of 'a man' (Num 24:17).[198] Also, the promise of the Lord to the Jews exiled in Egypt in Isa 19:20 records that "He will send them a Savior" (מוֹשִׁיעַ), yet the LXX does not

---

193. Horbury, *Jewish Messianism*, 12–13.

194. Goguel, *Jesus the Nazarene*, 186, suggests that Paul, as a rabbi before his Damascus Road experience, "already expected the arrival of a Savior who would rescue men from the dominion of sin and death and bring them into the Kingdom of the Spirit." By his conversion, Paul combined this doctrine of redemption "whose origins must be sought in Judaism with the historical episode of the life of Jesus" to produce his own unique theology (ibid., 187). This novel suggestion would be worthy of consideration, except Paul states in 1 Cor 15:1–3 that he had received the Gospel, that "Christ died for our sins according to the Scriptures," from prior tradition. In this case, it is more accurate to state that Paul's theology derives from Jesus' explanation of the OT (Luke 24:26–27, 44–47) handed down to him from his first mentors in Damascus.

195. Towner, "1–2 Timothy and Titus," 891–918. Numbers 24:7 LXX reads, "There shall come *a man* out of his seed, and he shall rule over many nations" (ἐξελεύσεται ἄνθρωπος ἐκ τοῦ σπέρματος αὐτοῦ καὶ κυριεύσει ἐθνῶν πολλῶν); Num 24:17 LXX reads, "I will point to him, but not now; I bless him, but he draws not near: a star shall rise out of Jacob, a *man* shall spring out of Israel" (δείξω αὐτῷ καὶ οὐχὶ νῦν μακαρίζω καὶ οὐκ ἐγγίζει ἀνατελεῖ ἄστρον ἐξ Ιακωβ καὶ ἀναστήσεται ἄνθρωπος ἐξ Ισραηλ); and Isa 19:20 LXX reads, "And it shall be for a sign to the Lord for ever in the land of Egypt: for they shall presently cry to the Lord by reason of them that afflict them, and he shall send them a *man* who shall save them; he shall judge and save them" (καὶ ἔσται εἰς σημεῖον εἰς τὸν αἰῶνα κυρίῳ ἐν χώρᾳ Αἰγύπτου ὅτι κεκράξονται πρὸς κύριον διὰ τοὺς θλίβοντας αὐτοὺς καὶ ἀποστελεῖ αὐτοῖς κύριος ἄνθρωπον ὃς σώσει αὐτοὺς κρίνων σώσει αὐτούς). Horbury, *Jewish Messianism*, 44, calls these oracles "enormously influential" in Second Temple Jewish thought.

196. Towner, "1–2 Timothy and Titus," 892, observes, "First, each text reports the content of a 'vision' (*horasis*). Second, whether incidental or not, Egypt and Exodus imagery figure in each discourse, and so do the Assyrians. . . . Third, and of obvious interest to Paul, each OT vision explores Israel's role in relation to 'the nations.' In Numbers, Balaam's third oracle casts Israel in the role, under the leadership of 'the man,' of subjugator or conqueror of the nations. . . ."

197. Ibid.

198. Towner, ibid., 892, also observes that "the MT of Num 24:7 lacks completely the first reference to 'a man'; at (Num) 24:17, where the prophecy of 'the star rising out of Jacob' does appear, it is subsequently described with the imagery of 'a rod' or 'sceptre,' likewise omitting any reference to a 'man.'" This means that the translators of the LXX have selected an interpretive concept of a Messianic "Man" to convey these Hebrew images.

translate this word by σωτήρ, as one might expect, but quite startlingly and significantly by ἄνθρωπον ὃς σώσει αὐτούς, a "man who shall save them."[199] This translation shows that *Anthropos* in certain OT contexts could serve as a synonym for *Messiah*—just as Paul modifies *Christos* by *Anthropos* in 1 Tim 2:5.[200] The Man of OT appearances is also The Christ of OT prophecy, and the apostle identifies this Man-Christ as the Jesus of history.

THE MAN CHRIST, JESUS

Paul now gives the ultimate identity of the Man he titles as the Christ—"Jesus."[201] The question arises, to which Jesus of history does Paul refer? The original *Yishuha* was the hero of Israel's Conquest and thus the name (translated 'Joshua') became fairly common in Jewish culture as a variation of יְהוֹשֻׁעַ (Exod 17:10; Matt 27:16; Col 4:1),[202] but the assumption is that the Ἰησοῦς to whom Paul refers is the same as the historical Jesus of Nazareth presented in the Gospel records. Watson states what is evident: "Any interpretation of the Gospels (or, for that matter, all the NT) that overlooks the obvious fact that the subject of the Gospels is the particular historical existence of Jesus of Nazareth, believed by Christians to be the Christ, the Son of God, is simply misinterpretation."[203] Here then in 1 Tim 2:5, the fourth stanza of the Christ-Creed identifies the historical Jesus of Nazareth with the OT designations as "Man Christ," emphasizing His work of mediation between God and men as being accomplished in His humanity, confirming further the primary thesis of this study.

---

199. It is indeed an interesting textual fact that the LXX translates מוֹשִׁיעַ ("Savior") by ἄνθρωπον in Isa 19:20, when the same word is translated by σωτῆρα in Jud 3:9, 15; Isa 45:15; and Isa 45:21; in fact, Isa 19:20 is the only place where the LXX translates מוֹשִׁיעַ by ἄνθρωπον. There is no textual evidence that the translators were using a now unknown Hebrew version that reads אָדָם or אִישׁ instead of מוֹשִׁיעַ. This supports the fascinating likelihood that ἄνθρωπον was understood by the LXX translators as a messianic designation, as the context indicates.

200. Towner, "1–2 Timothy and Titus," 893, asks, "But what is gained by describing the mediator in a way that recalls this background? First, Paul strengthens the argument for the universal gospel, based on the statement of God's will (2:4) and the *heis theos* ('God is one') formula (2:5), by depicting Christ, the mediator as fulfiller of the OT promise of 'a man.' Second, Paul in effect completes the development of the messianic 'man' theme by depicting the death of Christ as the means by which 'the man' takes up his rule and by transforming early OT imagery of subjugation salvation into the picture of salvation for the nations, via the gospel, in terms already emerging in Isaiah. . . . 'The man Christ Jesus' resumes and completes the messianic theme initiated in the Greek translation of Numbers and Isaiah."

201. Of the 212 times Paul refers to Jesus by His proper name, eighty-nine appear in this order "Christ Jesus;" seventy-nine/eighty in the order "Jesus Christ;" "Lord Jesus" another twenty-one times; "Jesus our Lord" ten times, and "Jesus" stands alone sixteen times (Rom 3:25; 8:11; 1 Cor 12:3; 2 Cor 4:5, 10, 10, 11, 11, 14; 11:4; Gal 6:17; Eph 4:21; Phil 2:10; 1 Thess 1:10; 4:14, 14).

202. Bauckham, *Jesus and the Eyewitnesses*, 67–92, "Palestinian Jewish Names," cites the work of Tal Ilan, *Lexicon of Jewish Names in Late Antiquity: Part I: Palestine 330 BCE—200 CE* (2002), who found that the name "Jesus/Joshua" was the sixth most common Jewish name in that time period.

203. Watson, "Toward a Literal Reading of the Gospels," 215. Goguel, *Jesus the Nazarene*, 178, adds, "Nothing, however, would be more erroneous than to consider the Pauline Christology as only a simple development of Jewish or Judeo-Hellenic premises. That which gives him his originality is the synthesis built up of these elements and the historical episode of the life and death of Jesus."

THE "MAN CHRIST JESUS"

The Fifth Stanza: ὁ δοὺς ἑαυτὸν

At this point, the Christ-Creed moves from the identity of the "Man Christ Jesus" to His saving work, by affirming that Jesus was the one "who gave Himself as a ransom for all." For the first time in the Christ-Creed, a verb appears, the aorist active nominative masculine singular participle ὁ δοὺς, which "snapshots" an action taken by Jesus,[204] giving rise to the obvious question: how did Jesus give Himself? Is it a philanthropic giving to those who ask (Matt 5:42)? Is it a giving of provisions to others, as He gave bread to His disciples (Matt 14:19)? The inclusion of the reflexive pronoun ἑαυτὸν answers the question, that it is a giving of Himself, but in what sense? Is it a giving of Himself to His divine mission (John 5:36)? It is certainly an example of His selfless love (John 13:15),[205] yet the consistent teaching of the NT is that Jesus gave Himself as a propitiatory sacrifice (Rom 3:25).[206] Behind the idea of propitiation (ἱλαστήριον) lies the "mercy seat" of the Tabernacle (Exod 25:17–22) upon which the High Priest sprinkled the sacrificial blood in order to "make atonement" (Lev 16:13–15),[207] a concept Paul clearly applies to the death of Jesus.[208] Although Käsemann admits that "the old view of the vicarious punishment of Christ (a view resting on Gal 3.13 and II Cor 5.21) is still maintained even today," he asserts, "the Pauline texts provide no basis for this."[209] Instead, he declares that "for Paul, salvation does not primarily mean the . . . forgiving (and) cancellation of former guilt" but rather the "possibility of new life."[210] Hengel, however, asks if the origin of the sotriological

---

204. Wallace, *Greek Grammar*, 554, likens the aorist tense to a "snapshot," and he quotes Fanning, *Verbal Aspect in New Testament Greek*, 97, that the aorist tense "presents an occurrence in summary, viewed as a whole from the outside, without regard for the internal make-up of the occurrence."

205. LN § 53.48, defines ἑαυτὸν δίδωμι as "an idiom, literally 'to give oneself,' to dedicate oneself to some activity in a completely willing manner, usually implying service on behalf of someone or something—'to give oneself to, to dedicate oneself to.'" The same idea is found in Jesus' claim, "I am the living bread that came down out of heaven; if anyone eats of this bread, he shall live forever; and the bread also which I shall give for the life of the world is My flesh" (καὶ ὁ ἄρτος δὲ ὃν ἐγὼ δώσω ἡ σάρξ μού ἐστιν ὑπὲρ τῆς τοῦ κόσμου ζωῆς," John 6:51).

206. Paul also uses the verb παραδίδωμι to describe how Jesus "delivered Himself up for me" (παραδόντος ἑαυτὸν ὑπὲρ ἐμοῦ, Gal 2:19) "because of our transgressions" (παρεδόθη διὰ τὰ παραπτώματα ἡμῶν, Rom 4:25, echoing Isa 53:12, διὰ τὰς ἁμαρτίας αὐτῶν παρεδόθη), and how He "gave Himself up for us, an offering and a sacrifice to God as a fragrant aroma" (παρέδωκεν ἑαυτὸν ὑπὲρ ἡμῶν προσφορὰν καὶ θυσίαν τῷ θεῷ εἰς ὀσμὴν εὐωδίας, Eph 5:2), as Christ gave Himself for the church (ἑαυτὸν παρέδωκεν ὑπὲρ αὐτῆς, Eph 5:25). While the verb may carry the legal overtones of "handing over to the custody" to another (BDAG § 5568 1. b) as well as the more sinister overtones of the handing over of Jesus in betrayal by Judas ('Ἰησοῦς ἐν τῇ νυκτὶ ᾗ παρεδίδετο, 1 Cor 11:23), yet ultimately it was God who "delivered His Son for us all" (ὑπὲρ ἡμῶν πάντων παρέδωκεν αὐτόν, Rom 8:32). It seems astounding that Käsemann, "The Saving Significance of the Death of Jesus in Paul," 43, would declare that "he (Paul) never definitely called Jesus' death a sacrifice," but then he denies that Paul authored Eph 5:2. The fact is, the sacrificial nature of Christ's giving permeates Paul's concept of the cross.

207. BDB § 4614, כָּפַר, "to cover over (fig.), pacify, make propitiation." See also Manson, "ἹΛΑΣΤΗ'ΡΙΟΝ," 4, where he likens Christ crucified to the mercy seat in the Holy of Holies.

208. See the carefully reasoned defense of the vicarious nature of ἱλαστήριον in Morris, *Apostolic Preaching of the Cross*, 144–213.

209. Käsemann, "Saving Significance," 43.

210. Ibid., 44. It seems unconscionable for this scholar to empty Paul's words of the obvious connections to the OT sacrificial system in order to impose an existential demythologizing upon the texts.

interpretation of the death of Jesus traces back to the primitive Jewish-Christian community and in essence back to the words and action of Jesus.²¹¹ Actually, Paul traces it through the tradition he had received (unquestionably from the Jerusalem community named in 1 Cor 15:5–7) back to its original source, the Scriptures,²¹² as κατὰ τὰς γραφὰς is a phrase found only here in 1 Cor 15:3–4. However, it also seems to echo the Upper Room experience when the risen Lord "opened the minds of the disciples to understand the Scriptures (τὰς γραφὰς), saying, 'Thus it is written, that the Christ should suffer and rise again from the dead the third day...'" (Luke 24:46–47). This connection means that the idea of a suffering and resurrected Messiah finds its source in the Jewish Scriptures (although neither Paul nor Jesus quote any specific passages in these references), not merely as a "righteous sufferer" (as in Ps 34:18–22), but as the Just One (Acts 22:14) who gives Himself in suffering "concerning sins" (Isa 53:10).²¹³

But this giving is neither an inanimate, impersonal sacrifice nor even the offering of a living animal, as it is in the OT; instead, the pronoun "himself" emphasizes the personal involvement of the "Man Christ Jesus" in the matter of salvation.²¹⁴ This self-giving of Christ is a repeated Pauline theme;²¹⁵ thus, here Paul refers to an historical action of Christ Jesus, no doubt referring to the crucifixion, for the death of the Man Jesus is a fact of history. It is a matter of record that He died on a Roman cross, yet Paul does not even use the word "death" here but instead describes it as a voluntary "giving."²¹⁶ This giving of the "Man Christ Jesus" is placed in the flow of redemptive history, as He gave Himself in a particular time (Passover) and place (Jerusalem), under Pontius Pilate (1 Tim 6:13).

The derivation of this creedal statement can be traced back to Jesus Himself as the source, according to His declaration of purpose in Matt 20:28 ‖ Mark 10:45, "The Son of Man did not come to be served, but to serve, and to give His life a ransom for many" (δοῦναι τὴν ψυχὴν αὐτοῦ λύτρον ἀντὶ πολλῶν). Mounce notes that "most commentators, using such terms as 'echo' (Spicq, Guthrie), 'free version' (Kelly) and 'reminiscence' (Lock),

---

211. Hengel, *The Atonement: Origins of the Doctrine in the New Testament*, 33.

212. In 1 Cor 15:3, the prepositional phrase, "ἐν πρώτοις" is generally translated as first in prominence (BDAG § 6397. 2), but the unusual plural structure, "in firsts," could be a reference to sequences, pointing toward the origin of the confession "at the first times" of the church.

213. The LXX renders Isa 53:10, ἐὰν δῶτε περὶ ἁμαρτίας ἡ ψυχὴ ὑμῶν ὄψεται σπέρμα ("If ye (pl) can give concerning sins, the soul of you [plural] shall see seed," LXE), but this stumbles badly over the Hebrew אִם־תָּשִׂים אָשָׁם נַפְשׁוֹ ("if he shall set his soul as guilt-offering"). It must have seemed impossible for the LXX translators to imagine that the Servant would become אָשָׁם (Lev 14:12–25), yet this is precisely what Isaiah wrote. Otherwise, Hengel, *The Atonement*, 57, correctly identifies Isaiah 53 as the only OT text that could have prompted the beginning of atonement through the Messiah's death, "as elsewhere the Old Testament tends to reject vicarious atonement or the death of a man for the sins of others."

214. BDAG § 2151 defines ἑαυτὸν as an "indicator of identity w. the pers. speaking or acting, *self.*"

215. The giving of Christ is observed in Gal 1:4; 2:20; Eph 5:2, 25; Phil 2:7–8 ("He emptied Himself, humbled Himself"); 1 Tim 2:6; Titus 2:14; see also Heb 7:27 ("He offered Himself," Heb 9:14, 25).

216. While the root meaning of δίδωμι is "to give," BDAG § 1961.10 lists the meaning in 1 Tim 2:6 as "to dedicate oneself for some purpose or cause, *give up, sacrifice*" (italics original). This particular definition leaves it unclear whether that sacrifice is Jesus' death or merely his dedication to his purpose, whatever that may be.

THE "MAN CHRIST JESUS"

agree this idea in some way goes back to the thought of Mark 10:45;"[217] however, Räisänen disagrees, remarking that the link between these passages is "not successful," although he provides no supporting argumentation.[218] Dibelius likewise asserts, "This verse is hardly a quotation from Mark 10:45, but rather a Hellenisticially colored variant of that word of Jesus,"[219] but neither does he give any evidence for his assertion. Instead, one is struck by the remarkable linguistic similarities between Mark 10:45 and 1 Tim 2:6,[220] even though the wording changes from ψυχὴν ("soul") to ἑαυτὸν ("self"), from λύτρον to ἀντίλυτρον, and from ἀντὶ πολλῶν ("for many") to ὑπὲρ πάντων ("for all"), although all these words are nearly synonymous.[221] Also, very similar terminology appears in the Eucharistic words when Jesus "had taken *some* bread *and* given thanks, He broke *it*, and gave *it* to them, saying, 'This is My body which is given for you (τοῦτό ἐστιν τὸ σῶμά μου τὸ ὑπὲρ ὑμῶν διδόμενον;'" Luke 22:19). This sacrificial giving of Jesus as the Suffering Messiah is the only explanation why one called Teacher would be honored as Lord within fifty days of His death. Hengel observes, "If Jesus had no messianic features at all, the origin of the Christian kerygma would remain completely inexplicable and mysterious;" instead, "the proclaimer became the proclaimed."[222] By this participial phrase of the Christ-Creed ὁ δοὺς ἑαυτὸν, then, Paul is reiterating the historical self-giving of Jesus that lies at the heart of the gospel proclamation (John 10:17), and now he proceeds to show how the "Man Christ Jesus" gave Himself—as a ransom for all.

The Sixth Stanza: ἀντίλυτρον ὑπὲρ πάντων

The designation of the "Man Christ Jesus" as a "ransom for all" introduces the concept of redemption confessed in the sixth stanza of the Christ-Creed, ἀντίλυτρον ὑπὲρ πάντων, which roots the saving work of Jesus firmly in historical soil as the act of a Redeemer who was "born as a man and was a man in the full sense of the word."[223] The idea of redemption is a fairly common biblical analogy to salvation (Ps 71:23; Luke 1:68, etc.), as the LXX generally translates the Hebrew גאל family of words by the nouns λύτρωσις[224]

---

217. Mounce, *Pastoral Epistles*, 89; Lau, *Manifest in Flesh*, 83–4, agrees, "We cannot dismiss *a priori* the probability that this christologically tradition, preserved in the logion of Mk. 10.45, could ultimately be traced back to Jesus Himself."

218. Räisänen, "The 'Hellenists': A Bridge between Jesus and Paul?", 183.

219. Dibelius, *Pastorals*, 43.

220. As noted in the introduction of this paper, the literary allusion in 1 Tim 2:6 to the claim of Jesus ("For even the Son of Man did not come to be served, but to serve, and to give His life a ransom for many.") is quite evident when the two passages are compared:

Matt 20:28 ‖ Mark 10:45	δοῦναι	τὴν ψυχὴν αὐτοῦ	λύτρον	ἀντὶ πολλῶν.
1 Tim 2:6	ὁ δοὺς	ἑαυτὸν	ἀντίλυτρον	ὑπὲρ πάντων.

221. Lau, *Manifest in Flesh*, 83, suggests that the changes are due to translation from Semitic idioms (as originally spoken in Aramaic by Jesus) to "more appropriate Hellenized" forms.

222. Hengel, *The Atonement*, 48.

223. Ridderbos, *Paul and Jesus*, 111.

224. The noun λύτρωσις appears in Lev 25:29, 48; Num 18:16; Jda 1:15; Jdg 1:15; Ps 48:9; 110:9; 129:7;

and ἀπολύτρωσις,[225] and the verb λυτρόομαι,[226] which, although appearing ninety-nine times in the LXX, is found only three times in the NT (Luke 24:21; Titus 2:14; 1 Pet 1:18), but each instance means "to release or set free with the implied analogy to the process of freeing a slave."[227] The one who pays the liberating price is a λυτρωτής (Lev 25:31; Ps 18:15; 77:35; Acts 7:35), and He does so by paying the λύτρον, "the means or instrument by which release or deliverance is made possible."[228] These words give Paul a working vocabulary for redemption (Rom 3:24; 8:23; 1 Cor 1:30; Eph 1:7, 14; 4:30; Col 1:14; Titus 2:14) and shows that his understanding of "ransom" stems back not into Greek religions nor Gnostic mythology[229] but deep into the OT. There the noun λύτρον appears twenty times[230] as a part of the Mosaic legislation of the price levied to free an object, such as property (Lev 25:24), houses (Lev 25:49), or one who had sold himself into slavery (Lev 25:48). Here in 1 Tim 2:6, however, is the only place where ἀντίλυτρον is used in the NT, although the cognate noun λύτρον appears twice, in the parallels of Matt 10:28 and Mark 10:45, each containing the same saying of Jesus previously noticed as influencing this Christ-Creed significantly.[231] Since the noun for "ransom" is used only three times in the NT, it is quite reasonable to link Paul's use to the saying of Jesus, fortifying the argument that Paul is delivering an apostolic *paradosis* as a *katechesis* (1 Cor 11:2).[232] Furthermore, in tracing this concept back to the original saying of Jesus, Riesner demonstrates how this ransom theology penetrates Paul's letters.[233]

Odes 9:68; Isa 63:4; Luke 1:68; 2:38; Heb 9:12.

225. The noun ἀπολύτρωσις appears in Dan 4:34; Luke 21:28; Rom 3:24; 8:23; 1 Cor 1:30; Eph 1:7, 14; 4:30; Col 1:14; Heb 9:15; 11:35.

226. The verb λυτρόομαι appears in Exod 6:6; 13:13, 15; 15:13; 34:20; Lev 19:20; 25:25, 30, 33, 48, 49, 54; 27:13, 15, 19, 20, 27, 28, 29, 31, 33; Num 18:15, 17; Deut 7:8; 9:26; 13:6; 15:15; 21:8; 24:18; 2 Sam 4:9; 7:23; 1 Kgs 1:29; 1 Chr 17:21; Neh 1:10; Esth 4:17; Ps 7:3; 24:22; 25:11; 30:6; 31:7; 33:23; 43:27; 48:8, 16; 54:19; 58:2; 68:19; 70:23; 71:14; 73:2; 76:16; 77:42; 102:4; 105:10; 106:2; 118:134, 154; 129:8; 135:24; 143:10; Prov 23:11; Isa 35:9; 41:14; 43:1, 14; 44:22, 23, 24; 51:11; 52:3; 62:12; 63:9; Jer 15:21; 27:34; 38:11; Lam 3:58; 5:8; Dan 3:88; 4:27; 6:28; Hos 7:13; 13:14; Mic 4:10; 6:4; Zeph 3:15; Zech 10:8.

227. LN § 37.128, "to set free, to liberate, to deliver, liberation, deliverance."

228. LN § 37.130.

229. For example, Bultmann, *Theology of the New Testament*, 1:167–79, asserts that the Johannine literature sets out to temper Paul's syncretism of Hellenistic mythology. Ensuing research in contemporary Jewish influences upon Paul—notably the OT—has disproved Bultmann's view.

230. The noun λύτρον appears in Exod 21:30; 30:12; Lev 19:20; 25:24, 26, 51, 52; 27:31; Num 3:12, 46, 48, 49, 51; 18:15; 35:31, 32; Prov 6:35; 13:8; Isa 45:13.

231. Except for the introductory conjunctions in Mark 10:45, it is identical to Matt 10:28, (καὶ γὰρ ὁ υἱὸς τοῦ ἀνθρώπου οὐκ ἦλθεν διακονηθῆναι, ἀλλὰ διακονῆσαι, καὶ δοῦναι τὴν ψυχὴν αὐτοῦ λύτρον ἀντὶ πολλῶν.

232. 1 Corinthians 11:1 exhorts, "Hold firmly to the traditions, just as I delivered them to you" (καθὼς παρέδωκα ὑμῖν, τὰς παραδόσεις κατέχετε).

233. In his important article, Riesner, "Back To The Historical *Jesus* Through *Paul* and His School (The Ransom Logion—Mark 10.45; Matthew 20.28)," 171–199, also notes echoes of the Ransom logion in Acts 20:28 and Acts 20:35, plus other possible connections in Col 1:13–14; 1 Tim 2:5–6; and the substance of it found in 1 Cor 9:19–23 and 1 Cor 10:33–11:1. He also suggests probable allusions to the ransom saying in 1 Cor 7:22–23; Phil 2:7; Rom 5:15; Gal 1:4, 10; 2:17, 20; 3:13; 4:5; Rom 15:8–9. He adds, "The Ransom logion may also have played a role in the dispute between Paul and Peter at Antioch (Gal 2:17–21) around (A.D.) 48 and apparently has shaped the pre-Pauline credal formula in 1 Cor 15:3–5 in the 30s. All this strengthens

THE "MAN CHRIST JESUS"

What does Paul mean that the "Man Christ Jesus" is a ransom? Morris argues convincingly that this family of words for redemption speaks not merely of 'deliverance,' but "both inside and outside the New Testament the payment of price is a necessary component of the redemption idea."[234] Although Dibelius alleges, "It is pointless to ask to whom the ransom is paid,"[235] it is actually a very important question, because the very concept of a ransom implies that someone holds people liable for their actions. While Origen taught that the ransom was paid to Satan as the one who captures humanity as hostage to sin,[236] the context of 1 Tim 2:6 pictures enmity between "God and men" who are liable to God, thus favoring the interpretation of Augustine, that the "Man Christ Jesus" offers Himself as the ransom to pay the debt owed for the release of sinners.[237] This meaning implies that "ransom" also carries a substitutionary concept, as Paul adjoins the prepositional prefix ἀντί to λύτρον in order to strengthen the idea of substitution, particularly when that same preposition modifies λύτρον in the Gospel parallels, λύτρον ἀντὶ πολλῶν.[238] Unquestionably, however, Paul affirms the substitutionary nature of this ransom-giving with the addition of the modifying prepositional phrase ὑπέρ πάντων.[239] This phrase serves as a reminder that the NT does not leave the historical events of the Man Jesus unexplained, as Watson points out;[240] indeed, it is a typical Pauline theme that Jesus gave Himself or died on behalf of something or someone else, as designated by the preposition

---

the trust in the authenticity of the Ransom logion" (ibid., 171).

234. Morris, *Apostolic Preaching of the Cross*, 61.

235. Dibelius, *Pastorals*, 43.

236. Origen, *Comm. Matt.* 16:8; see the comments in Kelly, *Early Christian Doctrines*, 185–6.

237. Augustine, *Confessions*, 10.68, quotes 1 Tim 2:5 to prove this point: "But the true Mediator, whom in Thy secret mercy Thou hast pointed out to the humble, and didst send, that by His example also they might learn the same humility—that 'Mediator between God and men, the man Christ Jesus,' appeared between mortal sinners and the immortal Just One—mortal with men, just with God; that because the reward of righteousness is life and peace, He might, by righteousness conjoined with God, cancel the death of justified sinners, which He willed to have in common with them." See the comments in Kelly, *Early Christian Doctrines*, 390–95.

238. Wallace, *Greek Grammar*, 388, observes, "Once ὑπέρ is even used with a form of λύτρον that has been strengthened by prefixing ἀντί, to it: 1 Tim 2:6. On this text, Davies ("Christ in Our Place," 89–90) points out that clearly the reference in I Timothy 2:6 which speaks of 'the man Christ Jesus, who gave himself as a ransom for all,' (ἀντίλυτρον ὑπὲρ πάντων) has a substitutionary meaning. The prefixed ἀντί- reinforces the idea of substitution already present in the λύτρον concept, and so even if the ὑπέρ were taken with the meaning 'for the benefit of,' the concept of substitution would be present in the text."

239. Moule, *Origin of Christology*, 111–13, notes the use of these prepositions on a "secular" level, that one may act—even die—"for the sake of another" (*huper*), as in John 13:37; 15:13; Rom 5:7; Rom 16:4; whereas it is quite less common that one may act—much less die—"in the place of, or instead" of another (*anti*). The "Christ-Creed" uncommonly employs both words in the phrase, ἀντίλυτρον ὑπὲρ πάντων.

240. Watson, "Toward a Literal Reading of the Gospels," 215–16.

ὑπέρ.²⁴¹ Thus, Paul writes that Christ gave Himself "for our sins;"²⁴² "for me;"²⁴³ "for us;"²⁴⁴ and, for the church.²⁴⁵ The same preposition ὑπέρ is used also with other verbs, to show that "Christ died for us,"²⁴⁶ that He was made sin "on our behalf" (ὑπὲρ ἡμῶν, 2 Cor 5:21), and that He became "a curse for us" (ὑπὲρ ἡμῶν, Gal 3:13).²⁴⁷

Where did Paul derive this idea that the death of Jesus was a substitution given on behalf of the sins of others? Nietzsche insists it came from Paul's hatred of Jesus by which he imposed a doctrine of atonement upon His crucifixion, as "he had no possible use for the life of the Saviour."²⁴⁸ Paul's explanation, however, is far afield from such ranting, as in his own words, he received it "from the Lord" in the historical event of the Last Supper when Jesus declared, "This is My body, which is for you" (ὑπὲρ ὑμῶν).²⁴⁹ This reference is more than a mere echo but a near quote of the Eucharistic words recorded in Luke

241. LN § 90.36 defines ὑπέρ with the genitive as "a marker of a participant who is benefited by an event or on whose behalf an event takes place—'for, on behalf of, for the sake of.'"

242. Galatians 1:4, τοῦ δόντος ἑαυτὸν ὑπὲρ τῶν ἁμαρτιῶν ἡμῶν; and 1 Cor 15:3, "For I delivered to you as of first importance what I also received, that Christ died for our sins (Χριστὸς ἀπέθανεν ὑπὲρ τῶν ἁμαρτιῶν ἡμῶν) according to the Scriptures." Käsemann, "Saving Significance," 39, identifies "Christ died for our sins" as one of the liturgical formulae as "already found in the oldest creedal tradition."

243. Galatians 2:20 reads, τοῦ ἀγαπήσαντός με καὶ παραδόντος ἑαυτὸν ὑπὲρ ἐμοῦ.

244. Ephesians 5:2 states, "Christ also loved you, and gave Himself up for us (παρέδωκεν ἑαυτὸν ὑπὲρ ἡμῶν), an offering and a sacrifice to God as a fragrant aroma;" and Titus 2:14, "who gave Himself for us" (ὃς ἔδωκεν ἑαυτὸν ὑπὲρ ἡμων).

245. Ephesians 5:25 teaches, "Christ also loved the church and gave Himself up for her" (ὁ Χριστὸς ἠγάπησεν τὴν ἐκκλησίαν καὶ ἑαυτὸν παρέδωκεν ὑπὲρ αὐτῆς). This cognate verb, παραδίδωμι, is defined by BDAG § 5568 1. b. "to *hand over, turn over, give up* a person," and it is used by Paul of Christ's giving also in Rom 4:24, "*He* who was delivered up because of our transgressions" (ὃς παρεδόθη διὰ τὰ παραπτώματα ἡμῶν), and Rom 8:32, "He who did not spare His own Son, but delivered Him up for us all" (ὑπὲρ ἡμῶν πάντων παρέδωκεν αὐτόν).

246. See Romans 5:6, "Christ died for the ungodly" (ὑπὲρ ἀσεβῶν); Rom 5:8, "Christ died for us" (Χριστὸς ὑπὲρ ἡμῶν ἀπέθανεν); Rom 14:15, "Do not destroy with your food him for whom Christ died" (μὴ τῷ βρώματί σου ἐκεῖνον ἀπόλλυε ὑπὲρ οὗ Χριστὸς ἀπέθανεν); and 1 Thess 5:10, "who died for us (ὑπὲρ ἡμῶν), that whether we are awake or asleep, we may live together with Him."

247. Outside the Pauline letters, ὑπέρ is used of Christ's work on behalf of others in Heb 2:9, "Jesus . . . by the grace of God . . . might taste death for everyone" (ὅπως χάριτι θεοῦ ὐ`πὲρ παντὸς γεύσηται θανάτου); Heb 10:12, "He, having offered one sacrifice for sins (ὑπὲρ ἁμαρτιῶν) for all time, sat down at the right hand of God;" 1 Pet 2:21, "Christ also suffered for you (ὑπὲρ ὑμῶν);" 1 Pet 3:18, "For Christ also died for sins once for all, *the* just for *the* unjust (δίκαιος ὑπὲρ ἀδίκων); and 1 John 3:16, "He laid down His life for us" (ὑπὲρ ἡμῶν).

248. Nietzsche, "The Jewish Dysangelist," 294–5.

249. Käsemann, "Saving Significance," 39, admits that the formula 'Christ died for our sins' "probably had its original place in the words used at the Lord's Table," but he is reluctant to trace it directly to Jesus, despite the specific claim of Paul in 1 Cor 11:23–24, "For I received from the Lord that which I also delivered to you, that the Lord Jesus in the night in which He was betrayed took bread; and when He had given thanks, He broke it, and said, "This is My body, which is for you; do this in remembrance of Me." The terminology of receiving and delivering suggests that Paul received this saying from apostolic tradition rather than by direct revelation, in accordance with the parallel in 1 Cor 15:1–5, "Now I make known to you, brethren, the gospel which I preached to you, which also you received, in which also you stand, by which also you are saved, if you hold fast the word which I preached to you, unless you believed in vain. For I delivered to you as of first importance what I also received, that Christ died for our sins according to the Scriptures, and that He was buried, and that He was raised on the third day according to the Scriptures, and that He appeared to Cephas. . . ." See Stephen O. Stout, "The New Testament Concept of Tradition," 105–37.

THE "MAN CHRIST JESUS"

22:19–20, "This is My body which is given for you (ὑπὲρ ὑμῶν); This cup which is poured out for you (ὑπὲρ ὑμῶν) is the new covenant in My blood."[250] This statement leads one to ask, where did Jesus derive the realization that He was giving His life in a sacrificial sense for others? The answer must be sought in the OT types of the sacrificial system, language Paul borrows in Eph 5:2 ("Christ also loved you, and gave Himself up for us [παρέδωκεν ἑαυτὸν ὑπὲρ ἡμῶν], an offering and a sacrifice to God as a fragrant aroma.") and also in 1 Cor 5:7, "For Christ our Passover also has been sacrificed." This sacrificial terminology echoes the substitutionary giving of the Lord's Suffering Servant as prophesied in Isa 52:13–53:12,[251] a passage often applied to Jesus in the NT.[252] Isaiah 53:9/10 may well lie in the background of 1 Tim 2:6, due to the affinities in vocabulary and concepts, "If he would render Himself *as* a guilt offering" (LXX, ἐὰν δῶτε περὶ ἁμαρτίας ἡ ψυχὴ ὑμῶν).[253] Another OT passage hovering in the horizon is Ps 49:7–8, "No man can by any means redeem *his* brother, or give to God a ransom for him, for the redemption of his soul is costly." The vocabulary in the ransom sayings of Jesus and Paul is similar enough to suggest the strong likelihood of allusion with this Psalm (ἀδελφὸς οὐ λυτροῦται λυτρώσεται ἄνθρωπος οὐ δώσει τῷ θεῷ ἐξίλασμα αὐτοῦ καὶ τὴν τιμὴν τῆς λυτρώσεως τῆς ψυχῆς αὐτοῦ) even though the conclusions are exact opposites: The Psalmist presumes that a substitutionary redemption by one man for another man is impossible because of the inestimable cost of the soul, yet Jesus claims to provide that amount by giving his soul as the ransom for all. Any Jew aware of Psalm 49 would be shocked at this apparent audacity, since Jesus implies that His soul is precious enough to ransom not only another brother but all others. Such pluck seemingly puts Jesus at odds with Psalm 49—unless Jesus is a man unlike all other men, one whose

---

250. The parallel in Mark 14:24 reads, "This is My blood of the covenant, which is poured out for many" (ὑπὲρ πολλῶν). Add to this the claims of Jesus in John 6:51, "I am the living bread that came down out of heaven; if anyone eats of this bread, he shall live forever; and the bread also which I shall give for the life of the world is My flesh" (ἡ σάρξ μού ἐστιν ὑπὲρ τῆς τοῦ κόσμου ζωῆς); and John 10:11, "I am the good shepherd; the good shepherd lays down His life for the sheep" (ὑπὲρ τῶν προβάτων).

251. Change to: Although the preposition ὑπέρ does not appear in this Servant Song, the LXX prefers the preposition δια, to express the same substitutionary idea: Isa 53:6, αὐτὸς δὲ ἐτραυματίσθη διὰ τὰς ἀνομίας ἡμῶν καὶ μεμαλάκισται διὰ τὰς ἁμαρτίας ἡμῶν; and Isa 53:12, διὰ τὰς ἁμαρτίας αὐτῶν παρεδόθη.

252. The 27th Edition of the Nestle-Aland *Novum Testamentum Graece*, "*Loci Citati vel Allegati: ex Vetere Testamento*," lists the following quotations (in *italics*) and allusions to the Servant Song of Isa 52:13–53:12 in the NT: 52:13 (John 3:14; Acts 3:13); 52:15 (Matt 13:16; *Rom 15:21*; 1 Cor 2:9); 53:1 (*John 12:38*; *Rom 10:16*); 53:3 (Mark 9:12; Phil 2:7); 53:4 (*Matt 8:17*; *1 Pet 2:24*; 1 John 3:5); 53:5 (Rom 4:25; 5:1; *1 Pet 2:24*); 53:6 (*1 Pet 2:25*); 53:7 (Matt 27:12; Mark 14:49; 61; John 1:29; *Acts 8:32*; Rev 5:6, 8); 53:8 (1 Cor 15:3); 53:9 (*1 Pet 2:22*, 1 John 3:5; *Rev 14:5*); 53:10 (Matt 20:28; Mark 10:45); 53:11 (Mark 14:24; Acts 3:13; Rom 5:17, 19; Phil 2:7; 1 John 3:5); 53:12 (Matt 12:29; 26:28; 27:38; Mark 15:27; Luke 11:22; *22:37*; 23:34; Rom 4:24; 1 Cor 15:3; Heb 9:28; *1 Pet 2:24*). Interestingly, the cross-references given at 1 Tim 2:6 cite Matt 20:28 but not Isa 53:10, which *Nestle-Aland* connects in the list above. One would think if 1 Tim 2:6 echoes Matt 20:28 that it would also echo Isa 53:10.

253. See Janowski and Stuhlmacher, *Suffering Servant: Isaiah 53 in Jewish and Christian Sources*. Note the grammatical and conceptual similarities between these passages:

Isa 53:10	ἐὰν δῶτε	ἡ ψυχὴ ὑμῶν		περὶ ἁμαρτίας
Matt 20:28 ‖ Mark 10:45	δοῦναι	τὴν ψυχὴν αὐτοῦ	λύτρον	ἀντὶ πολλῶν.
1 Tim 2:6	ὁ δοὺς	ἑαυτὸν	ἀντίλυτρον	ὑπὲρ πάντων.

The "Man Christ Jesus" in the Context of 1 Timothy 2:1-6

soul *is* precious enough to pay such a ransom. Paul confirms the claim of Jesus with this assessment, that the "Man Christ Jesus" actually gave Himself as that costly ransom for all because He is unique, the "one Mediator between God and men." The clause ἀντίλυτρον ὑπὲρ πάντων raises again the relationship of the One to the Many. The individual Jesus as the one Mediator gives Himself as one ransom, yet He does so on behalf of all, or more accurately, "for all." This precise prepositional phrase ὑπὲρ πάντων appears elsewhere only seven more times in the BGT (Dan 7:16; 2 Cor 5:14–15; Eph 5:20; Phil 1:4; 1:7; 1 Tim 2:1), and of those, only in 2 Cor 5:14–15 is it used soteriologically,[254] referring to those who benefit from Christ's death. The adjective πᾶς here is indefinite, since Paul does not specify who (or what) is the particular group to which "all" refers; however, one should properly assume he means the same as he did several sentences earlier, in 1 Tim 2:1, ὑπὲρ πάντων ἀνθρώπων.[255] In what sense, then, is Christ the ransom for all people? It is difficult to escape a universalistic effect of Christ's redemption if He is the actual ransom for all humans—not just that He made all people potentially savable through His ransom, but that He actually redeemed each individual because the ransom for their release has been paid. Such a view would create an irresolvable contradiction with Paul's teaching elsewhere, that some will finally be lost,[256] and that salvation comes only to all who believe (Rom 1:16; 3:22; 4:11; 10:4, 11; 1 Thess 1:7; 2 Thess 1:10), not merely to all regardless of faith and repentance. The solution appears in the grammatical and theological context that defines the "all" in 1 Tim 2:6, since Paul has defined "all men" in 1 Tim 2:1 as "kings and all in authority," meaning that the "all men" God desires to be saved (1 Tim 2:4) describe all sorts or types of people, not each person without discrimination. Regardless, Bird comments astutely, "While it may be possible to correlate the 'all/all men' with 'all believers', we should take seriously the representative function of Jesus as the Second Adam, who represents all humanity. Jesus is the representative of the whole human race and His death signifies that all human beings must undergo death. They can either enter death in the second Adam, who experiences death for them, or else can undergo death themselves."[257] It is certainly a primary concern in this last stanza of the Christ-Creed that the ransom for the redemption of all of humanity is the "Man Christ Jesus."

The Conclusio: τὸ μαρτύριον καιροῖς ἰδίοις

The Christ-Creed concludes with a statement of time, "the testimony *borne* at the proper time" (NAS).[258] Once again, Paul does not include a verb, so Young's *Literal NT* renders

---

254. 2 Cor 5:14–15 reads, "For the love of Christ controls us, having concluded this, that one died for all (ὑπὲρ πάντων ἀπέθανεν), therefore all died; and He died for all (ὑπὲρ πάντων ἀπέθανεν), that they who live should no longer live for themselves, but for Him who died and rose again on their behalf" (τῷ ὑπὲρ αὐτῶν ἀποθανόντι καὶ ἐγερθέντι). Here "all" contextually refers to believers, not to humanity in general.

255. In this chapter, Paul has already used πᾶς at 1 Tim 2:1 (twice), 2:2 (twice), 2:4, 2:6, plus πᾶς follows in 2:8 and 2:11.

256. See Acts 13:39; Rom 2:5, 8; 9:22; Eph 5:6; Col 3:6; 1 Thess 5:3; 2 Thess 1:9. The fact that some are lost rasies the question, how can one for whom the ransom is paid eventually be lost?

257. Bird, *Introducing Paul*, 103.

258. BDAG § 706.3 notes that ἀντί indicates "a process of intervention. Gen 44:33 shows how the sense 'in place of' can develop into *in behalf of, for* someone, so that ἀντί becomes ὑπέρ." Dibelius, *Pastorals*, 41,

the phrase, "the testimony in its own times," raising the questions, What testimony? What and whose times? The answers have led to this phrase being translated "proper times" (RSV), or "its own times" (ASV), or even, "His appointed time" (NET).[259]

The first question asks if "the witness" (τὸ μαρτύριον) could refer to Paul's own gospel witness, since he immediately follows with this statement, "And for this I was appointed a preacher and an apostle (I am telling the truth, I am not lying) as a teacher of the Gentiles in faith and truth" (1 Tim 2:7). If so, "the testimony of the proper times" is a concept parallel to 2 Thess 1:10, "our testimony to you was believed." But the phrase more naturally flows from the previous clause in 1 Tim 2:6, meaning that the Christ-Creed specifies a specific time frame for the giving of Christ as a Ransom; thus, it seems better to understand "the testimony of our Lord" (2 Tim 1:8) as referring to the time when Jesus "testified (μαρτυρήσαντος) the good confession before Pontius Pilate," an event Paul mentions toward the conclusion of this entire epistle (1 Tim 6:13). The reader should not think of his own hearing of the witness of Christ (as in 1 Cor 1:6) but rather to the particular moment when Jesus faithfully bore witness to the truth of His kingship (John 18:37) and His Sonship before unjust accusers (Matt 26:63–64).[260] Thus, what Paul refers to is an epoch in the history of salvation,[261] so that the Christ-Creed, then, places the aforementioned item of Christ's giving Himself within a particular moment of history, viewed as the fulfillment of the eschatological expectation predicted by the OT prophets.[262]

The next question asks whose or what times are the referents of the dative of time *kairois idíois* (καιροῖς ἰδίοις). The phrase seems simple enough, consisting of the plural noun "times,"[263] modified by the plural adjective, "theirs,"[264] but a translation difficulty arises because the antecedent noun τὸ μαρτύριον is singular, and the expression "the witness in their proper times" makes for a very awkward translation into English. To rectify this problem, most popular English versions render the original plural phrase as a

---

notes that "the extent of the quotation cannot be determined with certainty; does 'the testimony' still belong to the quotation or is it an elaboration of the writer?" The *Nestle-Aland* NT, however, prints this phrase as the *conclusio* of the Christ-Creed, since it clearly relates to the previous phrase.

259. It also seems strange that most popular English versions (ESV, NIV, RSV, NAS) translate the plural ("times") as singular.

260. NET, *loc. cit.*, notes: "This may allude to testimony about Christ's atoning work given by Paul and others (as v. 7 mentions). But it seems more likely to identify Christ's death itself as a testimony to God's gracious character (as vv. 3–4 describes). This testimony was planned from all eternity, but now has come to light at the time God intended, in the work of Christ." See 2 Tim 1:9–10 ("now has been revealed by the appearing of our Savior Christ Jesus"); Titus 2:11 ("For the grace of God has appeared, bringing salvation to all men"); and Titus 3:4 ("when the kindness of God our Savior and *His* love for mankind appeared") for similar ideas of the introduction of Jesus into human time and space.

261. Dibelius, *Pastorals*, 43.

262. Wright, *Paul in Fresh Perspective*, 154–161, shows that Jesus and Paul shared the same eschatological perspective of OT fulfillment of "creation, covenant, apocalyptic, and messianism" (ibid., 158). Vos, *The Pauline Eschatology*, 39, notes that in Paul's perspective, the coming age arrived in principle with the resurrection of Christ, so significant was that event.

263. BDAG § 3857.2, defines καιρός as "a defined period for an event."

264. BDAG § 3654.6 defines ἴδιος as "pert. to being distinctively characteristic of some entity, *belonging to/peculiar to an individual.*"

singular (RSV/ESV/NAS, "at the proper time;" NIV/NIB, "in its proper time"), as Wallace suggests, "at just the right moment."[265] To render this phrase in a singular form loses the plural integrity altogether, although the ASV attempts a compromise by translating the phrase "in its own times," and this rendition may be the best solution.

Clearly, the Christ-Creed uses *kairois idíois* as a descriptive technical phrase for eschatological epochs of divine activity. The identical phrase appears only three times in the Bible, here in 1 Tim 2:6; secondly in 1 Tim 6:14–15, "the appearing of our Lord Jesus Christ, which He will bring about at the proper time" (καιροῖς ἰδίοις); and thirdly in Titus 1:2–3, "God promised eternal life before the times of the ages but manifested His Word at the proper times" (καιροῖς ἰδίοις; author's translation). In each case, Paul announces some momentous changes in human history due to the intervention by Christ, meaning that the referents of *kairois idíois* in 1 Tim 2:6 are the life and times of the "Man Christ Jesus." This view agrees with the observations of BDAG that *idíois* in this verse belongs to "an individual,"[266] so that Tyndale's rendering, "at his tyme" may well capture what Paul intends here.

This use of *kairois* (καιρὸς) is certainly in keeping with Paul's usage of the right time of Christ's death (Rom 3:26; 5:6), in which he sees "the great turning point in the history of redemption, the intrusion of a new world aeon."[267] Hunter points out that this concept of 'inaugurated eschatology' is the primary point of fundamental continuity between Jesus and Paul, in that both preachers announced the fulfillment of the OT prophecies with the arrival of the reign of God in the Person of Jesus, with the major difference between them being the resurrection.[268] Historically, Jesus looked forward to what He called His *exodus* (Luke 9:31), whereas Paul looks back on Jesus' appearance as a past *epiphany* (2 Tim 1:10), as well as anticipating Jesus' future *epiphany* (1 Tim 6:14; 2 Tim 4:1, 8; Titus 4:8) and *parousia* (1 Cor 15:23; 1 Thess 2:19; 3:13; 4:15; 5:23; 2 Thess 2:1, 8). With the appearance of Jesus, a new epoch in history arrived "in His times," and this reference solidifies the historical appeal of the confession in the emphasis of Jesus Christ as "Man." Ridderbos notes that Paul's mention of Christ in time frames his message in terms of the history of salvation (*heilsgeschichte*): he looks back to the resurrection "as the highest point of the revelation of the divine mystery."[269] While the history of redemption has now progressed from the exaltation of the "Man Christ Jesus" in His ascension, Paul refers to the times when the historical Jesus ministered in Judea as the times of "His own witness."

Thus, Paul's "salvation history" is his way of placing the events of the life of Jesus (as well as the OT narratives of Adam, Abraham, David, et al.) as the outworking of the

---

265. Wallace, *Greek Grammar*, 157.

266. BDAG § 3654.6. Note how the adjective ἴδιος is used of personal possessions in 1 Timothy: it is translated "his own household" (1 Tim 3:4, 5; 5:4) "their own households" (1 Tim 3:12); "their own conscience" (1 Tim 4:2), "his own family (members)" (1 Tim 5:8); and "their own masters" (1 Tim 6:1).

267. Ridderbos, *Paul and Jesus*, 64. Paul uses the noun καιρὸς at Rom 3:26; 5:6; 8:18; 9:9; 11:5; 13:11; 1 Cor 4:5; 7:5, 29; 2 Cor 6:2; 8:14; Gal 4:10; 6:9, 10; Eph 1:10; 2:12; 5:16; 6:18; Col 4:5; 1 Thess 2:17; 5:1; 2 Thess 2:6; 1 Tim 2:6; 4:1; 6:15; 2 Tim 3:1; 4:3, 6; and Titus 1:3.

268. Hunter, *Gospel According to Paul*, 78–82.

269. Ridderbos, *Paul and Jesus*, 68.

THE "MAN CHRIST JESUS"

divine plan within human history: the great unveiling of God's mysteries "*has already come about* in and through the events concerning the Messiah, Jesus, particularly through His death and resurrection."[270] This historicity needs to be emphasized, for some want to distinguish "salvation history" from real, actual historical events,[271] whereas, for Paul, the "times" of Jesus, while theologically significant, are initially chronological days of human history. Ridderbos comments, "The basic attitude of Paul's gospel—if such can be spoken of—is dominated by the redemptive facts, by that which occurred in Christ. Therefore, any attempt to detach the connection between Paul's Christology and history is an attack upon the very heart of Paul's preaching."[272] Instead, Ridderbos adds, "It is this great redemptive-historical framework within which the whole of Paul's preaching must be understood and all of its subordinate parts receive their place and organically cohere."[273] This framework of salvation history is the approach of this study, that Paul's entire thinking assumes the historical reality of the person and work of Jesus.

This historical assumption is not merely Paul's presupposition, for the Gospels record that redemptive time was a matter of concern for Jesus: His opening message announced, "The time (ὁ καιρὸς) is fulfilled, and the kingdom of God is at hand; repent and believe in the gospel" (Mark 1:15). He replied to the sarcasm of His brothers, "My time (καιρὸς ὁ ἐμὸς) is not yet at hand, but your time is always opportune" (John 7:6). Jesus condenses this time even more when He announced at His entry into Jerusalem that the hour of His purpose had come (John 12:27), and John 17:1 defines this hour as the time in which the Son glorifies the Father. When the soldiers approached to arrest Jesus in the Garden, He declared, "The hour has come; behold, the Son of Man is being betrayed into the hands of sinners" (Mark 14:41). For Jesus, the hour of His times led Him to the moment of His betrayal and the sufferings to follow upon the cross—the same events that Paul interprets as when "He gave Himself as a ransom for all." Assuming that Paul refers to the witness of Jesus in His own proper times, the apostle then places the events of the Christ-Creed in their appropriate time frame, by inserting the redemptive occurrences within the historical events of the "Man Christ Jesus." To quote Ridderbos again, "Paul's Christology is a Christology of redemptive facts. Here lies the ground of the whole of his preaching, and it is with the historical reality of this event in the past as well as win the future, that both the apostolic kerygma and the faith of the church stand or fall (1 Cor 15:14, 19)."[274]

One cannot divorce Paul's understanding of the saving events enacted by Jesus from real space and time history. Since Paul emphasizes the humanity of Jesus when he reports that Christ "gave Himself as a ransom," it is apparent that he wants Timothy (and later readers) to consider reasons why the humanity of Jesus is an essential aspect of His saving work. The apostle assumes that his readers understand by his reference to Jesus he

---

270. Wright, *Paul in Fresh Perspective*, 52, italics original.

271. For example, it is difficult to tell whether Käsemann, "Justification and Salvation History in the Epistle to the Romans," 66–67, thinks that the biblical narratives tell mere stories or report actual history.

272. Ridderbos, *Paul and Jesus*, 68.

273. Hermann Ridderbos, *Paul: An Outline of His Theology*, 39.

274. Ibid., 49–50.

indicates that the one who is now the exalted Christ was also a "Man in His own times" within human history.

CHAPTER SUMMARY: THE "MAN CHRIST JESUS" IN THE CONTEXT OF 1 TIMOTHY 2:1-6

This chapter has conducted a rather extensive exegesis of the primary text of consideration, 1 Tim 2:5-6, in order to focus on the specific clause of interest, *ànthropos Christòs Iēsoūs* (ἄνθρωπος Χριστὸς Ἰησοῦς; 1 Tim 2:5), the "Man Christ Jesus." This designation appears as the fourth stanza of a "Christ-Creed" Paul inserts into this epistle to illustrate how God is our Savior who desires all men to be saved and come to the knowledge of truth (1 Tim 2:3-4). The content of this knowledge is the Christ-Creed itself: "One God and one mediator of God and men, Man Christ Jesus, the one having given Himself ransom on behalf of all, the witness in its times." Exegetical study reveals that the emphasis on the "Man Christ Jesus" reflects an OT particularity that God appeared as Man, so that "Man" became yet another title for the promised Redeemer, especially echoing the Son of Man in Daniel's vision (Dan 7:13). Thus, to Paul, Jesus is the fulfillment of the OT expectation of "the Man to Come," to use Barrett's translation of Rom 5:14, ὅς ἐστιν τύπος τοῦ μέλλοντος.[275] The apostle applies this theme in his epistles to his Adam-Christology, that Jesus appeared as the "one Man" (Rom 5:15, 19), "the last Adam" (1 Cor 15:45), and the "second Man from heaven" (1 Cor 15:47), who was "found in appearance as Man" (Phil 2:6).

Here in the Christ-Creed, this OT motif of Man is linked with another OT concept, that of the Christ, the Man whom God anointed as King—and then Paul ties both of these themes to the person of Jesus as a man of history in the "Man Christ Jesus." It is in His humanity that Jesus gave Himself as a ransom for all, as Towner notes, "The placement of *anthrōpos* designation between 'one mediator' and 'who gave Himself a ransom for all' seems intended to locate the mediating activity of Christ Jesus specifically in His humanity. What Jesus did to execute God's universal will to save, therefore He did as a human being in full solidarity with the human condition."[276] Jesus gave Himself as a ransom as a Man for men, a testimony He bore at the right moment in the history of redemption, showing that Paul anchors the life and work of the "Man Christ Jesus" firmly in human history.

So, in 1 Tim 2:5-6, Paul gives the broad scope of the redemptive giving of Jesus as Mediator on behalf of others, and that message is the core of his gospel, as summarized in another creedal statement, that "Christ died for our sins according to the Scriptures, and that He was buried, and that He was raised on the third day according to the Scriptures, and that He appeared . . ." (1 Cor 15:3-5). The crucified death and bodily resurrection of Jesus are the essential saving events that Paul preaches, but are these the only incidents in the life of Jesus he mentions? It is to this question that this study next turns, to see if other references to the "Man Christ Jesus" can be found scattered throughout Paul's letters.

---

275. Barrett, *From First Adam to Last*, 92.
276. Towner, "Christology in the Letters to Timothy and Titus," 230.

3

The "Man Christ Jesus" in the Epistles of Paul

It is a declared a *fait accompli* of critical scholarship that the apostle Paul has "very little to say about the life of Jesus"[1] and has meager or no interest in the historical life of Jesus.[2] Ziesler insists that Paul "betrays astonishingly little knowledge of or even interest in the traditions about Jesus" and calls this observation "one of the strangest and most puzzling areas of early Christian history."[3] More skeptical critics have labeled Paul as a "mythmaker" in his explanation of Jesus, as they claim he turned the simple Galilean peasant into a divine being.[4] Even conservative commentators seem embarrassed that Paul appears to care so little for the historical Jesus.[5]

---

1. Sanders, *Paul*, 23. As a minimalist, Sanders finds Paul citing Jesus only in 1 Thess 4:15–16, 1 Cor 7:10–11, and 1 Cor 11:23–25, asserting, "Of (Jesus') deeds Paul says nothing. . . ."

2. Wrede, *Paulus*, 89, contends, "The moral majesty of Jesus, his purity and piety, his ministry among his people, his manner as a prophet, the whole concrete ethical-religious content of his earthly life, signifies for Paul's Christology—nothing whatsoever." Ehrman, *The New Testament: A Historical Introduction*, 333, adds, "Paul scarcely says anything about the historical Jesus, that is, about the things Jesus said, did, and experienced between the time of his birth and the time of his death. You can see this for yourself by rereading Paul's letter and listing everything that he says about Jesus' life, up to and including his crucifixion. Part of the surprise is that you won't need an entire sheet of paper."

3. Ziesler, *Pauline Christianity*, 20. He claims that of the life of Jesus Paul tells only 1) that He was a Jew born of a woman under Jewish Law; 2) that He was of the line of David; 3) that His ministry was to Israel; and 4) that He had a meal with His disciples, including a betrayer, on the eve of His death.

4. This is argued by Maccoby, *The Mythmaker: Paul And The Invention Of Christianity*, and Lüdemann, *Paul: The Founder of Christianity*. One of the first systematic works to argue that Paul concocted a heavenly Christ was written by the English utilitarianist Jeremy Bentham, *Not Paul but Jesus* (1823). He challenged his readers in his introductory statement, "It rests with every professor of the religion of Jesus to settle within himself to which of the two religions, that of Jesus or that of Paul, he will adhere" (ibid., xvi). He proceeds to argue that Paul's conversion was improbable and discordant; and that Paul should be disbelieved in nearly every incident he mentions. Bentham concludes by declaring Paul's doctrines to be anti-apostolic and wondering if he was actually the Antichrist.

5. For example, Moo, "The Christology of the Early Pauline Epistles," 179, sums up what he calls Paul's rare concern for the earthly life of Jesus by finding only five incidents (that Jesus was human, that He was a Jew, that He was from the royal line of David, that He instituted a meal to commemorate His death, and that He sought to please others), two teachings (1 Cor 7:10 and 9:14), and a handful of verbal resemblances. Similarly, Dunn, *The Theology of Paul the Apostle*, 184, claims, "Had we possessed only Paul's letters, it would be impossible to say much about Jesus of Nazareth, let alone even attempt a life of Jesus." Dunn adds in *Jesus Remembered*, 143, "It is true, of course, that if we had nothing but Paul's letters to depend on for our knowledge of Jesus' Galilean and Judean mission we would know very little about him." This study will show this assessment to be far from accurate.

This issue requires closer examination in order to uncover if Paul was truly ignorant or indifferent to the traditions regarding Jesus.[6] This matter is quite crucial, for it must be asked if the apostle conflicts or concords with the Gospel accounts of the life and teachings of Jesus whenever he does make reference to the historical Jesus. Since Paul's letters provide what may well be the earliest extant written witness to any historical documentation of the life of Jesus,[7] one should perhaps reverse the question and ask if the Gospels conflict or concur with Paul. Either way, is there agreement or contradiction in the respective portrayals of Jesus between Paul and the Gospels?[8] This quest is the task that lies ahead of this chapter.

While a reader will quickly note that Paul does not develop the earthly ministry of Jesus in any great detail (his obvious emphasis centers on Jesus' death and resurrection), he will also observe that Paul certainly does refer to many specific events taken from the life of Jesus. These observations will be demonstrated later in this chapter, which shall examine a rather comprehensive and somewhat unexpected collection of information, due to the centuries of little-challenged criticism that Paul made scant reference to the historical Jesus in his haste to preach a divine Christ. Instead, one finds that critical scholars have made scant use of the historical Paul in their haste to prove he is either ignorant or dismissive of Jesus. Even listings of Paul's references to Jesus by evangelical scholars seldom agree *in toto*,[9] perhaps due to the begrudging acceptance of academic consensus that

---

6. Ehrman, *The New Testament*, 199, summarizes Paul's contributions as follows: "Jesus was born of a woman (Gal 4:4), that he was born as a Jew (Gal 4:4), that he had brothers (1 Cor 9:5), one of whom was named James (Gal 1:19), that he ministered among Jews (Rom 15:7), that he had twelve disciples (1 Cor 15:5), that he instituted the Lord's Supper (1 Cor 11:23–25), possibly that he was betrayed (1 Cor 11:23, assuming that the Greek term here means 'betrayed' rather than 'handed over' to death by God), and that he was crucified (1 Cor 2:2). In terms of Jesus' teachings, in addition to the words at the Last Supper (1 Cor 11:23–25), Paul may refer to two other sayings of Jesus, to the effect that believers should not get divorced (1 Cor 7:10–11) and that they should pay their preachers (1 Cor 9:14). Apart from these few references, Paul says almost nothing about the life and teachings of Jesus, even though he has a lot to say about the significance of Jesus' death and resurrection and his expected return in glory." A college student using this popular textbook would assume that Paul rather offhandedly refers to Jesus only nine times and quotes Him only twice. Instead, this study hopes to prove that the historical Jesus undergirds Paul's entire theology.

7. Of course, the dating of the books of the NT is quite speculative, since none of them provide a date of composition, so it is possible that one of the written Gospels preceded Paul's epistles; notwithstanding, this author finds himself attracted to the suggestion of the rather maverick and otherwise quite critical scholar Robinson, *Redating the New Testament*, 352, who places the completion of the entire NT before the destruction of the Temple in A.D. 70. He dates the Epistle of James to A.D. 47–8, before any of Paul's epistles, calling it "the first surviving finished document of the church" (ibid., 138–9). The Christology of James reflects the teachings of Jesus rather than giving details of His life, making it an important balance to Paul's allusions to the historical acts of Jesus.

8. Robinson, ibid., 352, also suggests that the Gospels of Matthew, Mark, and John could have been written before Paul penned his letters.

9. For example, compare these listings among scholars who are quite favorable toward Paul: In his excursus, "Summary of Information about Jesus in the Letters of Paul," Paul Barnett, *Jesus and the Logic of History*, 57–8, lists the following information as found in the Pauline corpus regarding Jesus: that He 1) was a descendant of Abraham the patriarch; 2) was a direct descendant of King David; 3) was born of a woman, suggesting Paul confirms the virginal conception of Jesus; 4) lived in poverty; 5) lived under Jewish law; 6) had a brother named James and other unnamed brothers; 7) that He lived a lifestyle of humility and meekness; 8) ministered primarily to Israel and Jews; 9) washed the feet of His disciples; 10) instituted a memorial

THE "MAN CHRIST JESUS"

Paul is not overly interested in the historical Jesus, so why bother to present a complete picture of the apostle's references to Jesus? Since some claim that the apostle is far more concerned that believers relate to Jesus as the risen Lord than as the earthly preacher, why should Paul afford any interest in the rabbi who trudged the dusty paths of Galilee? The fact is, however, that while Paul's well-known christological sections (in such passages as Romans 8, 1 Corinthians 15, Ephesians 1, Colossians 1) present the exalted Lord as the Life-giver of the church amid the current experiences of salvation, none of those passages deny the human Jesus; indeed, without "the Man Christ Jesus," Paul would have no risen Lord to proclaim.

Granted, Paul does not write about Jesus in the setting of narrative history;[10] instead, he scatters his references to Jesus throughout his letters without any indication of historical sequence (although they can be organized following the general pattern given in the Gospels, as this chapter shall do). Paul only cites a few specific instances from the life of Jesus to prove his points, making it appear that the apostle "underplays" the historical Jesus in his rush to transform Him into the resurrected Christ.[11] While Akenson agrees that Paul is the first literary source of the historical Jesus, he finds in Paul only thirteen allusions to the historical Jesus;[12] however, a closer reading discovers that the historical Jesus lies right on the surface of Paul's writings and permeates the apostle's thinking in every part of his message.[13] The apostle makes no pretences in his presentation of Jesus:

---

meal on the night He was betrayed; 11) was cruelly treated; 12) gave testimony before Pontius Pilate; 13) was killed by Jews of Judea, at Roman hands, on treasonable grounds; 14) was buried; and 15) was raised on the third day and seen alive on a number of occasions. Barnett expands his own list to nineteen items in *Paul: Missionary of Jesus*, 18–20. Johnson, *The Real Jesus: the Misguided Quest for the Historical Jesus and the Truth of the Traditional Gospels*, 119–20, gives a similar twelve-point summary. Dodd, *History and the Gospel*, 63–68, also gives an incomplete listing of the historical references of Jesus by Paul, although he is quite optimistic of their reliability and considers them representative of Paul's knowledge of Jesus. While these are admirable listings (and give interesting comparisons to Ehrman's findings in footnote 6), they nowhere exhaust the allusions to the historical Jesus found in Paul's writings, as shall be shown.

10. As reminded by Akenson, *Saint Saul: A Skeleton Key to the Historical Jesus*, 179.

11. Ibid., 201. Also, Furnish, "The Jesus-Paul Debate," 43–44, includes only twelve items of Jesus' life and three sayings from His teachings (1 Cor 7:10–11; 9:14; 11:23–25), plus another seven possible allusions. He lists these options: that Paul is a confirmer of Jesus, an interpreter of Jesus, or an innovator of Jesus, whether illegitimate (Wrede) or legitimate (ibid., 47–48).

12. Akenson, *Saint Saul*, 226–27. These include: the birth of Jesus; His Davidic ancestry; His brothers (one named Yacov/James); His twelve followers (one named Cephas, another named John); His comments on divorce; His mission to Israel; His call to support His laborers; His last meal; His betrayal; and His crucifixion/resurrection. Akenson concludes, "That is all: whatever other references to the historical Yeshua's biography and behavior exist in Saul's letters are either untagged or deeply encoded" (ibid., 227). Even so, Akenson finds Saul "to be much more trustworthy than anything that comes in a narrative that glorifies the earthly life of Yeshua, as do the Four Gospels" (ibid., 228).

13. Barnett, *Jesus and the Logic of History*, 42, argues that the letters of Paul are "the preferred point of historical entry to inquiry into Jesus as the earliest written sources about Christianity." Quite obviously—as Martin Hengel, *Between Jesus and Paul*, 178, notes—it would be impossible for Paul to proclaim Jesus as Lord without giving more information of what sort of man He was, and so Paul refers to the *paradosis* concerning Jesus (1 Cor 11:23–25, 15:1–3). Thus, one finds in 2 Corinthians a "biographical-theological sweep of Jesus' life" (Barnett, ibid., 48), yet Paul appeals to that which his readers knew about Jesus without filling in the details (ibid., 50). Barnett argues that the "logic of history" demands that the Risen Lord proclaimed by Paul is the same Jesus of Nazareth presented in the Gospels (ibid., 56–57).

he unabashedly persuades his readers of his opinion of Jesus by rejecting uncompromisingly "another Jesus whom we have not preached" (2 Cor 11:4), since there is but one foundation laid, that of the particular Jesus proclaimed by Paul (1 Cor 3:11). Whether the reader agrees with Paul or not, he should approach his letters with the realization that Paul fervently believes his interpretation of Jesus to be the correct one.[14] Thus, despite the insistence of some that historicity is not much of a concern to Paul,[15] it is apparent that the apostle refers to various events of the life of Jesus that he definitely assumes *are* historical. What then can be gleaned from Paul's letters regarding these assumptions of Jesus as the "Man Christ Jesus"?

THE IDENTITY OF THE "MAN CHRIST JESUS"

Depending on the textual variants, Paul mentions a man named Jesus between 213 and 216 times,[16] and Fee astutely observes that the "one unqualified reality that emerges in all of Paul's letters is that the name 'Jesus' always has as its primary referent the historical person Jesus of Nazareth. . . . Paul's use of the name in itself carries the assumption of Christ's genuine humanity."[17] While a translation of Matt 1:21 into Hebrew reveals a play on words in His birth announcement ("Jesus shall save;" יוֹשִׁיעַ יֵשׁוּעַ), Paul displays no conscious symbolism in the name; to the apostle, "Jesus" is the personal name of the one whom he designates another 188 times simply as "Christ."[18] This title is defined in John 4:25 as a translation of the Hebrew "Messiah (מָשִׁיחַ)," and even though the question remains whether Paul uses *christos* as a personal name or as a title for Jesus, Paul's dependence on the LXX indicates that he uses it primarily as a title, as the translation of the Hebrew "Messiah."[19] Suppose someone asked Paul, "Do you mean the historical Jesus when you

---

14. Beker, *The Triumph of God: the Essence of Paul's Thought*, 111, astutely observes that Paul claims in 2 Cor 4:1–2 that he is no innovator but a faithful translator of previous tradition.

15. Johnson, *Real Jesus*, 120, contends, "Not that these things really happened, but that Paul assumed the readers of his letters had already been taught that these things have happened. . . . These bits of information in Paul do not prove the historicity of the events, but they confirm the antiquity and ubiquity of the traditions concerning the events, in a period as much as two decades earlier than our earliest written Gospel." Johnson posits an unnecessary distinction between the actual events in the life of Jesus and what Paul's readers had been taught had happened in His life. Even so, this differentiation between history and tradition does not seem to be a problem for Johnson, who insists that the interpretive experience of Jesus' first followers gave rise to and continues the Christian movement (ibid., 135–36). His view, however, still disconnects the earliest interpretation of Jesus from the actual events of Jesus, for why would Paul bother to appeal to Jesus-traditions if they were not also Jesus-histories? Johnson insists that Paul refers to the Jesus story "not (as) the facts of his life but the meaning of his life" (ibid., 160), yet it is apparent that Paul appeals not merely to church traditions regarding Jesus' life, but the actual events of His life.

16. These statistics are according to the count in *BibleWorks 8*, depending on the BGT or BYZ texts.

17. Fee, *Pauline Christology*, 528.

18. Paul refers another seventy-nine times to "Jesus Christ," ninety times to "Christ Jesus," and twice to "Lord Christ." Paul labels Jesus as "Lord" 274 times in his letters, plus another twelve times in Acts (9:28; 16:31; 20:19, 21, 24, 35; 21:13; 22:10, 19; 23:11; 26:15; 28:31).

19. However, the LXX always uses χριστὸς to translate הַמָּשִׁיחַ (Lev 4:5, 16; 6:15; 1 Sam 24:6, 6, 11; 26:9, 11, 16, 23; 2 Sam 1:14, 16; 19:22; 23:1) or for מְשִׁיחוֹ (1 Sam 2:10, 35; 12:3, 5; 16:6; 2 Sam 22:51; 1 Chr 16:22; 2 Chr 6:42; Ps 2:2; 17:51; 19:7; 27:8; 84:9; 89:38, 51; 105:15; 132:10; 132:17; Isa 45:1; Lam 4:20; Dan 9:26, 27; Hab 3:13) or for שֶׁמֶן מִשְׁחַת (Lev 21:10, 12), but never as a personal name.

describe Him simply by the word *christos*?" one can imagine the apostle would respond with an incredulous stare as if to ask, "Who else would I intend?" He uses the name 'Jesus' and title 'Christ' quite interchangeably; for example, even when he speaks of knowing the historical Jesus, he states instead, "We have known *Christ* according to the flesh" (2 Cor 5:16), showing that both proper nouns refer to the same historical man.

According to the NT record, the confession of Jesus as the Christ did not originate with Paul. It was the title of Peter's notable confession (Matt 16:16), as well as the confession of Jesus that warranted His death sentence (Matt 26:63; Mark 14:61). Peter's initial sermon on Pentecost concluded, "Let all the house of Israel know for certain that God has made Him both Lord and Christ—this Jesus whom you crucified" (Acts 2:36). Despite the contention of Akenson that the Messiah was only a "peripheral concept in late Second Temple Judaism," he acknowledges that Paul moved the concept to the "centre of his belief-system" as describing a man who suffered as a sacrifice for the redemption of His people and had become a cosmic figure ready to return and judge the world.[20]

Akenson, however, insists that while Paul affirms the post-resurrection messiahship of Jesus, he simultaneously displaces the idea that 'Yeshua' of Nazareth acted as Messiah or claimed "Moshiahship" while on earth.[21] He makes the sweeping claim that Paul at no point suggests that 'Yeshua' ever declared Himself to be the Christ, or that 'Yeshua' Himself ever did anything to certify His 'Christship,' or that anyone ever heard or saw anything done by 'Yeshua' to claim Messiahship—all arguments blatantly denying the Gospel accounts.[22] The written fact is that Paul considered the historical Jesus to be the Christ from the moment of his initial confession in Damascus (Acts 9:22). The question must be raised, then, whenever Paul mentions Jesus, intending to mean the historical Jesus of Nazareth, does his portrayal agree with the Jesus presented in the Gospels?[23] This study will continue this quest with further comparisons.

---

20. Akenson, *Saint Saul*, 175.

21. Ibid., 176.

22. Ibid.

23. Bultmann, "The Significance of the Historical Jesus for the Theology of Paul," asks three questions: (1) "How far is Paul dependent on Jesus?" After a brief scan of Paul's references to Jesus, Bultmann asserts, "Jesus' teaching is—to all intent and purposes—irrelevant for Paul" (ibid., 223). Bultmann does not even consider that similarities in ethics between Jesus and Paul might be intentional. (2) Regarding the second question, "What is the relation of the theology of Paul to the proclamation of Jesus?", Bultmann traces the view of the Law as taught by both Jesus and Paul and finds that the difference is that Jesus looks forward to the future, whereas Paul looks back to the "turning point of the ages" (ibid., 233), the work of Christ (Gal 4:4). (3) Concerning his third question, "What is the significance of the historical person of Jesus for the theology of Paul?", Bultmann admits that Paul acknowledged the Jesus of history to be the Messiah, but then he makes a distinction between the content of the proclamation (the *Was*) from the fact that Christ is the One proclaimed (the *Dass*). This means that when Paul cites Jesus as a teacher, he is not appealing to the earthly Jesus, but to the exalted 'Lord'. "It is always the preexistent Christ who is the pattern. . . . Any evaluation of the 'personality of Jesus' is wrong and must be wrong for it would only be a knowing 'after the flesh.' . . ." Thus, "It is not the historical Jesus, but Jesus Christ, the Christ, preached, who is the Lord" (ibid., 239). This artificial separation between Jesus and the Christ is utterly unknown in the NT, and it smacks of philosophical doublespeak, as what seems to be crucial for Bultmann is not the actual historical life of Christ, but the preaching of that which becomes the "decisive question" (ibid., 242), so that "the new age is real in that Christ is being preached" (ibid., 243). This new age becomes present in "the exercise of the saying"

THE HUMANITY OF THE "MAN CHRIST JESUS"

The Gender of Jesus: Male

The noun ἄνθρωπος appears four times in the context of the primary passage of consideration, 1 Tim 2:1–5:[24] "I urge that entreaties . . . be made on behalf of all *men* (ὑπὲρ πάντων ἀνθρώπων); This is good and acceptable in the sight of God our Savior, who desires all *men* (πάντας ἀνθρώπους) to be saved . . . , for there is one God, one mediator also between God and *men* (ἀνθρώπων), *man* (ἄνθρωπος) Christ Jesus." The first three appearances are plural, referring to humanity in general, and so could be translated with the gender neutral, "people" (ESV); however, the literal rendering "men" (NASB) maintains continuity with the fourth (and only singular) ἄνθρωπος, which specifies a particular man, Christ Jesus. Even though the Greek text does not supply a definite article modifying ἄνθρωπος, Paul may be thinking of Jesus as the "Monadic Man"—one of a kind,[25] especially since the expression "Man Christ Jesus" is unique in biblical literature. Even so, the noun ἄνθρωπος surely emphasizes the common humanity of Jesus, so that the tendency of the gender-neutral translations (NET, NRS) is to render this noun ἄνθρωπος in 1 Tim 2:5 as "human."

(ibid., 244), so that the response of faith becomes "itself a part of the saving event, . . . itself revelation" (ibid., 245). Bultmann, then, wants to have a historical Jesus, but one who is accessible only through the kerygma, so ". . . when Paul says that the decisive saving of Christ is 'obedience and love,' he is not thinking of personality characteristics of the historical Jesus (Phil 2:6; 2 Cor 8:9; Rom 5:18; 15:1)—not actually what Jesus did, but these all speak of the preexistent Christ" (ibid., 246). Perhaps Bultmann thinks he answered his initial question of Paul's dependence upon the historical Jesus, but what he leaves is a convoluted rambling that makes no sense of Paul. See the critique of Bultmann's existentialist views by Ridderbos in *Paul and Jesus*, 17–27.

24. Of the 126 times the noun ἄνθρωπος appears in the Pauline letters, the apostle uses the vocative "O man," four times (Rom 2:1, 3; 9:20; 1 Tim 6:11); the anarthrous singular "man" forty times [Rom 1:23; 2:9; 3:4 ("every man"); 3:5 ("according to man"); 3:28; 5:12 ("through one man"); 7:24 ("wretched man"); 2:9; 14 ("natural man"); 3:3; 4:1; 6:18; 7:1, 26; 9:8; 11:28; 15:21a (Adam), 15:21b (Christ), 15:32; 2 Cor 12:2, 4; Gal 1:11, 12; 2:6, 16; 3:15a, 15b; 5:3; 6:1, 7; Eph 2:15 ("one new man"); 5:31; Phil 2:8; Col 1:28a, b, c; 1 Thess 4:8; 1 Tim 2:5; 2 Tim 3:17 ("the man of God"); Titus 3:10]; the articular singular ["the man" twenty times: Rom 4:6; 5:15b ("the one Man Jesus"); 5:19 ("the disobedience of the one man"); 6:6 ("the old man"); 7:1 ("law lords of the man"), 22 ("the inner man"); 10:5; 14:20; 1 Cor 2:11b, 11c; 15:45, 47a ("the first man"), 47b ("the second man"); 2 Cor 4:16 ("the outer man"); 12:3; Eph 3:16 ("the inner man"); 4:22 ("the old man"), 4:24 ("the new man"); Col 3:9 ("the old man"); 2 Thess 2:3 ("the man of lawlessness")]; the articular plural "men" eleven times [Rom 14:18 ("approved by the men"); 1 Cor 13:1; Eph 3:5; 4:8, 14; Col 2:8, 22; 2 Thess 3:2 ("the lawless men"); 1 Tim 6:9; 2 Tim 3:2; Titus 3:8]; and the anarthrous plural "the men" forty-nine times [Rom 1:18; 2:16, 29; 5:12 ("unto all men"), 18a, 18b ("unto all men"); 12:17; 1 ("before all men"); 12:18 ("with all men"); 1 Cor 1:25; 2:5, 11a; 3:21; 4:9; 7:7, 23; 14:2, 3; 15:19, 39; 2 Cor 3:2; 4:2; 5:11; 8:21; Gal 1:1, 10a, 10b, 10c; Eph 6:7; Phil 2:7; 4:5; Col 3:23; 1 Thess 2:4, 6, 13, 15; 1 Tim 2:1, 4; 2:5a; 4:10; 5:24; 6:5, 16 ("no-one of men"); 2 Tim 2:2 ("faithful men"); 3:8, 13 ("evil men"); Titus 1:14; 2:11; 3:2]. The apostle tends to use the plural to refer to lost humanity in general, making his anthropology rather pessimistic, but it is also evident that he can use the word "man" in a positive light, as in 1 Tim 2:5 when he ascribes humanity to the "Man Christ Jesus."

25. See the discussion on the "Absence of the Article" by Wallace, *Greek Grammar*, 248 where he notes that "a one-of-a-kind does not, of course, require the article to be definite." The anarthrous use of ἄνθρωπος here is hardly indefinite ("a man"), since Paul specifies which man he intends, "Christ Jesus." Furthermore, he has already mentioned "Χριστὸς Ἰησοῦς" seven times (1 Tim 1:1a, 1b, 2, 12, 14, 15, 16), always as a proper name not requiring the article. This study has previously argued that lying in the background of Paul's Christology of Jesus as "the Man" (Rom 5:17; 1 Cor 15:47) is the appearance of God as Man throughout OT history.

THE "MAN CHRIST JESUS"

Such a translation, however, is inadequate, because Jesus was not androgynous but a human of male gender. The NASB provides a better rendition, "*the* man Christ Jesus," using the common translation of the noun ἄνθρωπος, as in 1 Tim 6:11 ("O man of God," not "O human of God").[26]

Still, the word "man" is unexpected and seemingly redundant, for is it not obvious that Christ Jesus was human? Not necessarily, as 2 John 7 indicates that the humanity of Jesus already was being denied during the apostolic period.[27] Yet in 1 Tim 2:5, the emphasis is not upon Jesus as divine but upon Him as a human mediator,[28] as Paul pictures Jesus appealing to the one God on behalf of people not as a divine person, but as a man, since the one who needs defending is not the one God but all humanity. The Greek construction of this verse is terse, lacking any verbs, prepositions or definite articles ("for one God and one mediator of God and of men, man Christ Jesus"), all which must be supplied to make any English translation readable,[29] yet the brevity and order of the Greek text draws attention to the nominative phrases ("one God," "one mediator") and its defining appositional nominative phrase, "man Christ Jesus" (*ánthropos Christòs Iēsoûs*). The repetition of the nouns ἀνθρώπων ἄνθρωπος without any intervening words also arrests the attention of the reader to the affinity of Jesus as Man to all other men. By these grammatical devices, Paul clearly wants Timothy to notice the significance of each phrase with regard to Theology ("one God"), Soteriology ("one mediator of God and men"), and Christology ("Man Christ Jesus"), as each phrase accents the means of mediation given in the following participial phrase, "who gave Himself as a ransom for all," a reference to the substitutionary and atoning death of Christ.[30] What remains prominent in the entire section is the emphasis on the "Man Christ Jesus," accenting the mediating ministry of Jesus between God and men effected by a Man of human identity and human historicity ("testified in his tyme [sic]," Tyndale's translation).

Paul also emphasizes the humanity (and maleness) of Jesus in Rom 5:12–21, where he contrasts Christ and Adam as heads of their respective humanities, whereby "the one" (Adam) transgressed, leading to the death of many, whereas the gift of the grace of "the one Man Jesus Christ" (τοῦ ἑνὸς ἀνθρώπου Ἰησοῦ Χριστοῦ) abounded to many (Rom 5:15). Why does Paul add the appositional noun ἀνθρώπου when it seems obvious that

---

26. NET renders 1 Tim 6:11, "as a person dedicated to God," which is an interpretation rather than a translation.

27. 2 John 1:7, "For many deceivers have gone out into the world, those who do not acknowledge Jesus Christ *as* coming in the flesh." Streett, "'They Went out from Us': The Identity of the Opponents in First John," 414–38, examines this passage and argues that the identifying mark of these opponents is not so much a denial of the humanity of Jesus but "their denial that Jesus is the Messiah" (ibid., 440). Regardless, 2 John 1:7 presumes the appearance of Jesus as a Messiah of human flesh.

28. BDAG § 4927 defines a mediator as "one who mediates betw. (sic) two parties to remove a disagreement or reach a common goal."

29. YLT may come the closest to the Greek, "for one *is* God, one also *is* mediator of God and of men, the man Christ Jesus," but it does not make for very readable English.

30. Morris, *Apostolic Preaching of the Cross*, 51–52, points out the substitutionary nature of the phrase.

Jesus was a man? The same reasons given above on 1 Tim 2:5 apply here also, in that Paul explains how the work of salvation is effected by Jesus as Man.³¹

The same emphasis on Jesus' humanity appears in Paul's discussion of the resurrection in 1 Corinthians 15, where he declares of Jesus, "by a man (δι' ἀνθρώπου) also *came* the resurrection of the dead" (1 Cor 15:21), and when he contrasts Jesus and Adam in 1 Cor 15:46–47, "So also it is written, 'The first man, Adam, became a living soul.' The last Adam *became* a life-giving spirit. The first man is from the earth, earthy; the second man is from heaven" (ὁ πρῶτος ἄνθρωπος ἐκ γῆς χοϊκός, ὁ δεύτερος ἄνθρωπος ἐξ οὐρανοῦ). This observation gives quite a fascinating insight into Paul's "Christological anthropology," for in referring to Christ, Paul identifies his divine source as "the second man out of heaven," thus implying the pre-existence of Jesus,³² yet at the same time affirming His humanity by calling Him a "man." While Akenson argues from these verses that Paul did not believe in a physical resurrection but only in a spiritual experience of a cosmic nature,³³ he ignores what Paul writes elsewhere about the *sarkinos* nature of the resurrected Jesus (Phil 3:21; Col 2:9). Even in the 1 Corinthians 15 pericope, Paul emphasizes that the life-giving, heavenly experience comes from a *man*. By neglecting the larger context, Akenson has Paul affirming in 1 Cor 15:46 what he refutes in 1 Cor 15:12 ("Now if Christ is preached, that he has been raised from the dead, how do some among you say that there is no resurrection of the dead?"). Paul's argument would fail if Jesus had not been a man who was raised physically from the dead.

Another reference to Jesus as Man is found in the third strophe of the Christological hymn of Phil 2:5–11 (ἐν ὁμοιώματι ἀνθρώπων γενόμενος· καὶ σχήματι εὑρεθεὶς ὡς ἄνθρωπος),³⁴ which, after extensive literary examination, Martin translates, "Accepting a human-like guise, and appearing on earth as the Man."³⁵ While this description surely

---

31. Ridderbos, *Paul: An Outline of His Theology*, 62, notes that the creation by Christ of the church as the one new man (Eph 2:15; 4:15) and the use of the masculine pronoun in 2 Cor 5:14 ("For the love of Christ controls us, having concluded this, that one (εἷς) died for all, therefore all died') and in Gal 3:28 ("There is neither Jew nor Greek, there is neither slave nor free man, there is neither male nor female; for you are all one (εἷς) in Christ Jesus.") stress a personal relationship between Christ as His own, but these verses also assume the maleness of Jesus as the ancestral "father" who gives life to His people.

32. McCready, *He Came Down from Heaven: the Preexistence of Christ and the Christian Faith*, 70–104, gives a full-length defense of the orthodox position on this subject, although he rather oddly omits 1 Cor 15:47 from consideration as teaching Christ's preexistence. This verse begs the question, if Christ is a man who originated out of heaven, does this not presume His preexistence?

33. Akenson, *St. Saul*, 177–78.

34. Hooker, "Philippians 2:6–11," 157, calls the pericope "rhythmic prose" and points out the difficulty in distinguishing the original words from Paul's own comments. She finds the parallel in an Adam-Christ contrast with echoes of Gen 1:26 and in Adam's desire to be like God (Gen 3:5, 22) whereas Christ who was preexistent "in the form of God" made Himself nothing in order to become the Man that humanity was meant to be, also made in the form and likeness of God (ibid., 162).

35. Martin, *A Hymn of Christ: Philippians 2:5–11 in Recent Interpretation and in the Setting of Early Christian Worship*, 38. His rendition does not seem to be a particularly good translation of the participles γενόμενος and εὑρεθείς, especially since γενόμενος appears in the next verse (Phil 2:8), yet Martin does not even translate it at all, rendering the strophe, "He humbled Himself, in an obedience which went so far as to die." It would seem to make more sense to take translation hints from the way Paul uses the same two verbs in the next chapter (γενόμενος, Phil 3:6; εὑρεθῶ, Phil 3:9), so that a better rendering of Phil 2:7 might be,

THE "MAN CHRIST JESUS"

suggests the pre-existence of Christ[36] (although such an investigation falls beyond the scope of this particular study[37]), it seems clear that this strophe teaches that the humanity of Jesus began at His conception. Without expounding on the nature of Christ's humanity or explaining how He assumed a human nature, Paul simply states the historical fact: Jesus *became* man. Although it is quite likely Paul uses the participle γενόμενος to refer to the entire process of physical gestation (as he does in Gal 4:4, γενόμενον ἐκ γυναικός[38]), the nouns ὁμοίωμα and σχῆμα create a particular Christological problem, "whether Christ became Man completely and in the fullest sense, or whether he merely presented the picture of a Man, which appeared like a man, whereas in actual fact, he remained in the world as a divine being."[39] However, Paul's use elsewhere of ὁμοίωμα (Rom 1:23; 5:14; 6:5; 8:3) and σχῆμα (1 Cor 7:31) indicates that he is not describing a docetic Jesus who only seemed to resemble human form but one who actually appeared outwardly "as man;"[40] furthermore, the physical reality of Jesus as a human being is proven in Phil 2:8, in that "as a man, He humbled Himself . . . until (bodily) death."[41] Also, the subordinating conjunctional phrase, ὡς ἄνθρωπος may echo Hosea 6:7 ("like Adam;" ὡς ἄνθρωπος/ כְּאָדָם),[42] meaning that Jesus was found to be a man just as Adam was a man, and it may also echo the phrase ὡς υἱὸς ἀνθρώπου of Dan 7:13, even though it is not identical.[43] Hunter finds in

---

"having become in likeness of men, and having been found in appearance as Man. . . ."

36. Dunn, *Christology in the Making*, 114, calls preexistence a "presupposition" rather than a conclusion of Phil 2:6–11, and thus he contends that exegesis reveals no implication that Christ was preexistent. He interprets "existing in the form of God" as equality with Adam's original created glory, but the text states this is an equality with God, not with perfected humanity (surely Paul knew the difference between Adam and God!). Paul recounts his version of the incarnation: Jesus had always existed in the form of God, but in becoming man, He humbled Himself to obedience of death; now, therefore, He has been highly exalted–as the "Man Christ Jesus" who appeared to Paul from heaven. As resurrected Man, Jesus becomes the pattern for believers "to bear the image of the heavenly one" (1 Cor 15:49).

37. If Jesus was not preexistent but was the inception of a new creation, as the Last Adam, then how and when did He exist "in the form of God" (Phil 2:6–11)? Was He a sinless man who became deified? These are questions Dunn (*Christology in the Making*, 114–121) does not address but are discussed in detail by McCready, *He Came Down from Heaven: the Preexistence of Christ and the Christian Faith*.

38. The same verb is also used of the incarnation at John 1:14, ὁ λόγος σὰρξ ἐγένετο.

39. Martin, *A Hymn of Christ*, 201, quoting Michael, 'Zur Exegese von Phil. 2.5–11', 89–90, who also notes how ὁμοίωμα is used of the divine epiphanies reported in Ezek 1:26 (ὁμοίωμα ὡς εἶδος ἀνθρώπου) and Ezek 8:2 (ἰδοὺ ὁμοίωμα ἀνδρός).

40. BDAG § 7204 defines σχῆμα as "the generally recognized state or form in which someth. (sic) appears, *outward* appearance, *form, shape*."

41. Käsemann, "The Saving Significance of the Death of Jesus in Paul," 49, claims that "The hymn to Christ in Phil 2.6ff. contains no direct historical reminiscence. . . . The scantiness of Paul's Jesus tradition is surprising in general, but his silence here . . . is positively shocking. The theological interpretation drives out all historical information beyond the mere event of the crucifixion." One must wonder how Käsemann derives these insights from Phil 2:6–8, since the historical reminiscence of Jesus is explicit in Paul's appeal to Jesus as an example (Phil 2:5–6), His status as a servant (Phil 2:7), His appearance as a man (Phil 2:8a), and His humbling of Himself, all leading to His obedience to the death of the cross (Phil 2:8b). Rather than driving out the historical, the theological interpretation necessitates the historical actions of Jesus in His humanity.

42. As suggested by Martin, *A Hymn of Christ*, ibid., 207.

43. As argued by Lohmeyer, *Kyrios Jesus: Eine Untersuchung zu Philipper 2,5–11*, 94–95, and also noted

The "Man Christ Jesus" in the Epistles of Paul

these phrases not only allusions to the Son of Man figure but also to the Servant of Isaiah's prophecies,[44] that Jesus is not only "a human" but also "The Man" of OT expectation, whom Paul elsewhere describes as the "last Adam" (1 Cor 15:45), "the second Man out of heaven" (1 Cor 15:47), and "the one man Jesus Christ" (Rom 5:15).[45] All these links are grammatically feasible, but Paul's primary concern in using this Christ-hymn is to urge his readers to serve one another by imitating the very human example of Jesus.[46]

In thus describing Jesus as "Man," Paul agrees with the record of the Gospels that Mary and Joseph dedicated their first-born son "as it is written in the Law of the Lord, 'Every first-born *male* (ἄρσην)[47] that opens the womb shall be called holy to the Lord'" (Luke 2:23); that He was described by the Samaritan woman as "a *man* (ἄνθρωπον) who told me all the things" (John 4:29); and who describes Himself as "a *man* (ἄνθρωπον) who has told you the truth" (John 8:40). While it is true that Paul does not directly specify Jesus as male (ἀνὴρ), he certainly implies as much in his metaphor of 2 Cor 11:2 ("For I am jealous for you with a godly jealousy; for I betrothed you to one husband (ἑνὶ ἀνδρὶ), that to Christ I might present you *as* a pure virgin"). Even so, little should be made of this infrequency, although the apostle describes Jesus as ἄνθρωπος only five times (Rom 5:15; 1 Cor 15:21, 47; Phil 2:8; 1 Tim 2:5). One mention of Jesus' gender in Paul's epistles should be sufficient to prove that Jesus was indeed a man of male gender, yet these combined verses show that Paul taught "at one point (Jesus) had not been a human being but that when he did become one of us, he was fully and completely so."[48]

The Flesh of Jesus

Closely connected to the idea of Jesus as a Man is Paul's portrayal of Jesus as a Man "who was revealed in flesh" (1 Tim 3:16). Since Paul often uses "flesh" (σάρξ) in a derogatory manner, it may be unexpected that he describes Jesus as a man of flesh, but he does not hesitate from doing so several times to demonstrate the participation of Jesus in human

---

by Black, "The Son of Man Problem in Recent Research and Debate," 315.

44. Hunter, *Paul and His Predecessors*, 43.

45. *Christology in the Making*, 119, argues that the Adam-Christology lying behind Phil 2:6–11 requires that since Adam was not preexistent, "no implication that Christ was preexistent may be intended." This is using the humanity of Jesus to exclude any incarnational reality when that seems to be precisely what Paul is teaching as he moves from Christ existing in the form of God to that of being found in appearance as Man.

46. Hooker, "Philippians 2:6–11," 154, notes, "It seems nonsense to suggest that it (the reference to emptying etc.) is not the character of Jesus Himself. It is only the dogma that the Jesus of History and the Christ of Faith belong in separate compartments that leads to the belief that the appeal to a Christian character appropriate to those who are in Christ is not linked to the pattern as seen in Jesus himself."

47. BDAG § 1134.

48. Fee, *Pauline Christology*, 527.

weakness.[49] Not only does Paul affirm the incarnation in 1 Tim 3:16,[50] that Jesus was "revealed in the flesh (ἐν σαρκί),"[51] but in Rom 1:3, he describes Jesus as "His (God's) Son, born of a descendant of David according to the flesh (κατὰ σάρκα)." These verses affirm the Jewish ancestry of Jesus and His identity with David's family, the tribe of Judah (Ruth 4:12),[52] a fact he repeats in Rom 9:3–5, when he notes the origin of the Messiah from His "kinsmen according to the flesh (κατὰ σάρκα), . . . from whom is the Christ according to the flesh (κατὰ σάρκα)."[53] When these preceding references are compared to the wording of Gal 4:29 (where Ishmael is described as "born according to the flesh;" κατὰ σάρκα), they clearly manifest that Paul believed Jesus to be a man born according to the flesh as the "the seed of David,"[54] designating Him as springing from the royal family of Israel as David's heir.

49. Paul uses the word σάρξ ninety-one times, and BDAG § 6593 defines the noun as, "1. the material that covers the bones of a human or animal body (as in Rom 2:28; Gal 6:13); 2. the physical body as functioning entity a. as substance and living entity (as in Eph 5:29); b. as someth. with physical limitations, life here on earth (1 Cor 7:28); c. as an instrument of various actions or expressions (Rom 7:18; Gal 2:16); 3. one who is or becomes a physical being; 4. Human/ancestral connection (Rom 9:3, 5, 8; 11:14); 5. the outward side of life as determined by normal perspectives or standards. In Paul's thought the body is dominated by an immoral principle of flesh (as in Rom 7:5, 18, 25; 8:3a, 3c, 4, 5a, 5b, 6, 7, 8, 9, 12, 12, 13; 13:14, etc.), but he also uses flesh as a metonymy for a human being, although viewed in weakness (Rom 4:1; 1 Cor 1:29)."

50. Liddon, *The Divinity of Our Lord and Saviour Jesus Christ*, 306–7, affirms, "St. Paul insists with particular earnestness upon the truth of our Lord's real Humanity." Liddon's concern in this classic work is to defend the orthodox doctrine of the deity of Christ, so throughout his discussion of Paul's Christology (ibid., 306–59), he undercuts his own assertion by insisting Paul did not believe Jesus was a "mere man" (ibid., 313, 316), or "merely human" (ibid., 314) but that he had a "dignity more than human" (ibid., 333). Such an approach in exalting the Godhood of Jesus while depreciating His manhood is not atypical among evangelicals, who ought to give greater diligence in presenting both the humanity and the deity of Jesus.

51. The reading of the Majority Text of 1 Tim 3:16 is θεὸς ἐφανερώθη ἐν σαρκι, but according to Metzger, *A Textual Commentary on the Greek New Testament*, 574, "No uncial (in the first hand) earlier than the eighth or ninth century (Y) supports θεός; all ancient versions presuppose ὅς or ὅ; and no patristic writer prior to the last third of the fourth century testifies to the reading θεός. The reading θεός arose either (a) accidentally, through the misreading of OC as ΘC, or (b) deliberately, either to supply a substantive for the following six verbs, or, with less probability, to provide greater dogmatic precision."

52. Warfield, "The Christ that Paul Preached," 85, points out that by the phrase "according to the flesh," Paul "certainly has the whole of His humanity in mind—set in contrast to the divine titles that follow; thus, it belongs to the very essence of the conception of Christ as Paul preached Him, therefore that He was of two natures, human and divine" (ibid., 88).

53. The prepositional phrase κατὰ σάρκα ("according to the flesh") is peculiar to Paul in biblical literature, and he tends to use it in a derogatory manner, to refer to fallen sinful nature (Rom 8:4–5, 12–13; Gal 4:23), outward appearance (Eph 6:5; Col 3:22), or social status (1 Cor 1:26; 2 Cor 1:17; 5:16a; 10:2–3; 11:18), but he also uses it to describe one's nationality (Rom 9:3, "my kinsmen according to the flesh;" 1 Cor 10:18, "Israel according to the flesh"). BDAG § 6593.4 understands κατὰ σάρκα in Rom 9:5 to mean that "Christ is descended fr. the patriarchs and fr. David (τὸ) κατὰ σάρκα *according to the human side of his nature, as far as his physical descent is concerned*" (italics original).

54. Paul uses the identical phrase in 2 Tim 2:8, "Remember Jesus Christ, risen from the dead, descendant of David" (ἐκ σπέρματος Δαυίδ). This designation of Jesus as the Seed of David refers to the Davidic covenant, found in 1 Chr 17:7–14, especially v. 11, "I will set up *one of* your descendants (ἀναστήσω τὸ σπέρμα σου) after you, who shall be of your sons (the LXX translates אֲשֶׁר יִהְיֶה מִבָּנֶיךָ as ὃς ἔσται ἐκ τῆς κοιλίας σου, emphasizing the biological connection between David and his Seed). It is likely that Paul understood ἀναστήσω as fulfilled in the resurrection of Jesus, mentioned in the attending participial clause (τοῦ ὁρισθέντος υἱοῦ θεοῦ ἐν δυνάμει κατὰ πνεῦμα ἁγιωσύνης ἐξ ἀναστάσεως νεκρῶν, Ἰησοῦ Χριστοῦ

The flesh of Jesus also figures into His work of reconciliation, as noted in Col 1:22, "He has now reconciled (you) in His body of flesh by His death (ESV; ἀποκατήλλαξεν ἐν τῷ σώματι τῆς σαρκὸς αὐτοῦ διὰ τοῦ θανάτου) and in Eph 2:14, Christ "abolished in His flesh the enmity (τὴν ἔχθραν ἐν τῇ σαρκὶ αὐτοῦ), *which is* the Law of commandments *contained* in ordinances."[55] In accordance with his idea that σάρξ pictures humanity in weakness, Paul views the incarnation as "God sending His own Son in the likeness of sinful flesh" (ἐν ὁμοιώματι σαρκὸς ἁμαρτίας, Rom 8:3), by which "likeness" implies similarity but not exactness.[56] The similarity Jesus shares with humanity is in human flesh; the difference is in human sinfulness, as Heb 4:15 notes that Jesus was tempted "according to likeness without sin" (πεπειρασμένον δὲ κατὰ πάντα καθ' ὁμοιότητα χωρὶς ἁμαρτίας).

But how should Paul's comment in 2 Cor 5:16 be understood, "Therefore from now on we recognize no man according to the flesh; even though we have known Christ according to the flesh, yet now we know *Him thus* no longer," since it purportedly shows that Paul had no interest in the historical Jesus "according to the flesh"?[57] Heitmüller argues that Paul "quite decisively says here that the earthly Jesus, the human personality Jesus, has no meaning whatsoever for his religious life. . . . And that means the tradition about Jesus is also irrelevant."[58] Pfleiderer likewise contends that "this passage, in the first place, affirms once more that Paul had acquired his present Christian perception of Christ quite independently of any previous knowledge whatever of the historical Jesus. . . . The dogmatic teaching of Paul regarding Christ did not depend on the historical knowledge of Jesus."[59]

τοῦ κυρίου ἡμῶν, Rom 1:4).

55. Hebrews 10:20 links the "new and living way which He (Jesus) inaugurated for us through the veil, that is, His flesh."

56. BDAG § 5296. 3 notes, "In the light of what Paul says about Jesus in general it is prob. that he uses our word to bring out both that Jesus in his earthly career was similar to sinful humans and yet not totally like them." Witherington, "Jesus as the Alpha and Omega of New Testament Thought," 38–9, comments, "Probably the carefully worded phrase "in the likeness of sinful flesh" of Rom 8:3 is meant to indicate that Jesus did not look any different from any other human being, as well as to avoid saying that he was a sinner or was born with a sinful nature."

57. Longenecker, "A Realized Hope, a New Commitment, and a Developed Proclamation: Paul and Jesus," 19, includes the following "prominent scholars" who claimed that Paul's kerygmatic Christ displaced all interest in the historical Jesus: Baur, Weizsäcker, Wendt, Wrede, Heitmüller, Bultmann and Bornkamm. See the survey of interpretations of 2 Cor 5:16 in Fraser, *Jesus and Paul: Paul as Interpreter of Jesus from Harnack to Kümmel*, 47–62; and in Stanton, *Jesus of Nazareth in New Testament Preaching*, 89–93, who concludes, "2 Cor 5:16 cannot be used as an interpretive key to solve the question of Paul's understanding of Jesus of Nazareth, for that is not the question Paul is discussing here" (ibid., 93).

58. Heitmüller, "Zum Problem Paulus und Jesus," 320–37. Commenting on 2 Cor 5:16, Weinel, *St. Paul: The Man and His Work*, 314, insists, "Indeed Jesus can scarcely be said to have existed for him (Paul) as a human being." Likewise, Morgan, *The Religion and Theology of Paul*, 39, asserts that in 2 Cor 5:16 Paul "cuts himself loose from the historical basis as to render every hypothesis of dependence precarious if not untenable." Thus, in removing Paul's Christ from the Jesus of history, Morgan thinks he has found the solution for the worship of the modern church, but what he has done is severed Paul from Jesus in all but name only and left the church no Christ to worship at all.

59. Pfleiderer, *Paulinism: A Contribution to the History of Primitive Christian Theology*, 1:124. He insists that a hellenizing influence on Paul must have given him a prior "heavenly condition of Christ" (ibid., 130).

THE "MAN CHRIST JESUS"

In retrospect, these are astounding assertions. To treat Paul as if he had absolutely no prior knowledge of the historical Jesus before his Damascus Road encounter is to ignore the clear assertions in the apostle's own epistles (not to mention in the book of Acts) that he knew much about the historical Jesus—his initial opposition to "the Way" derived from the fact that he strenuously disagreed with Stephen's interpretation of Jesus as the Son of Man.[60] Even so, Fridricksen claims, "About Jesus of Nazareth Paul evinces little interest. He reports few of his sayings and admits freely that he had not known Jesus 'according to the flesh.'"[61] That such an interpretation reads far too much into this phrase is evident from Paul's sweeping assertion that "from now on we recognize no man according to the flesh" (2 Cor 5:16a). He obviously does not mean that believers belonging to the new community of Christ should never acknowledge another man's name, since Paul often addresses others by name in his letters (as in Rom 16:1–15). Bruce argues that Paul makes a contrast of perspective "between his former attitude to Christ . . . and his present attitude to Christ (as to the world in general) now that he is 'in Christ,'"[62] but it seems better to understand Paul's meaning as chronological, as he explains his meaning in the next verse, by stating that any social and cultural distinctions are now irrelevant because "if any man is in Christ, *he is* a new creature; the old things passed away; behold, new things have come" (2 Cor 5:17). One surely does not cease to be human through union in Christ, but in that new relationship, "fleshly" status no longer matters. As an illustration of the contrast between the old life and the new life, Paul cites the change that has now occurred to Jesus since His resurrection.[63] As a matter of fact (the first class conditional is introduced with εἰκαὶ, emphasizing a point of fact), "we have known (perfect active indicative) Christ according to the flesh, but now no longer we are knowing Him (present active indicative) in this manner," for the obvious reason that He is no longer present in the flesh but He has been seated in heaven.[64]

---

60. Andrews, *The Meaning of Christ for Paul*, 31, astutely observes, "Men do no persecute those of whom they know nothing."

61. Fredriksen, *From Jesus to Paul: The Origins of the New Testament Images of Jesus*, 174.

62. Bruce, *Paul and Jesus*, 24, suggests that Paul in 2 Cor 5:16 contrasts the way he used to think about the Messiah "which has been radically altered now that he has come to recognize the Messiah in Jesus" (ibid., 24). In his article, Bruce, "Further Thoughts on Paul's Autobiography: Galatians 1:11–2:14," 27, understands "after the flesh" as meaning, "from an unregenerate point of view."

63. See Fraser, *Jesus and Paul*, 46–60. He suggests that 2 Cor 5:16 refers to "the whole Christ," both pre- and post-resurrection (ibid., 58).

64. The word-order in Greek (ἐγνώκαμεν κατὰ σάρκα Χριστόν) is difficult to translate in good English, since "we have known according to the flesh Christ" is torturous reading. Most English versions, however, translate this sentence as if the prepositional phrase modifies "Christ," so that it reads "we have known Christ according to the flesh" (NASB, ASV, ESV, KJV). The NRS gives a paraphrastic rendering, "Even though we once knew Christ from a human point of view," but it captures the word-order. Kim, *Paul and the New Perspective: Second Thoughts on the Origin of Paul's Gospel*, 229, observes, "It is now commonly agreed that the phrase κατὰ σάρκα in (2 Cor) 5:16 is an adverbial phrase modifying the verbs in that verse and that Paul is here talking about knowing or estimating Christ according to the 'fleshly criterion' or from a 'fleshly' perspective." For this reason, Machen, *Origin of Paul's Religion*, 131, comments, "Paul says not, 'Even if we have known a Christ according to the flesh, we know such a Christ no longer,' but, 'Even if we have known Christ with a fleshly kind of knowledge, we know Him in such a way no longer.'" These remarks, while accurate, overlook that Paul assumes that at one time some did know Christ "according to the flesh," for

Despite Christ's current heavenly status, Paul is certainly not depreciating the humanity of Jesus; if anything, he affirms the historical "fleshliness" of Jesus, that He had once been known as one could know any other human. This fact raises the intriguing speculation suggested by Weiss[65] whether Paul may have actually known Jesus "according to flesh" and was a witness of his ministry—perhaps as one of the unnamed "lawyers" who posed entrapping questions.[66] What is certain is that after his conversion, Paul became

---

the plain reason that He was knowable as "the Christ according to the flesh" (Rom 9:5), as was "Abraham, our forefather according to the flesh" (Rom 4:1), "my kinsmen according to the flesh" (Rom 9:3), and "your masters according to the flesh" (Eph 6:5 and Col 3:22).

65. Weiss, *Paul and Jesus*, 47–48, insists from 2 Cor 5:16, that "here, the meaning must be that Paul had known Christ, as men know one another, that is, had seen Him with his eyes. Indeed, the expression implies more than this; it signifies the impression made not only by outward appearance, but by personality, the impression received by direct personal acquaintance."

66. The grammar of 2 Cor 5:16 can actually support the view that Paul had known Jesus. A search reveals two grammatically similar first class conditional sentences to 2 Cor 5:16, where the particle εἰ introduces an indicative form of γινώσκω in the protasis, followed by another indicative form of γινώσκω in the apodosis, expressing a circumstance of fact. The first appears in John 14:7, "If you had known Me, you would have known My Father also" [εἰ ἐγνώκατέ (perfect active indicative, 2pl) με, καὶ τὸν πατέρα μου γνώσεσθε (future middle indicative, 2pl)]. The BYZ text presents the sentence as a second class conditional by reading, Εἰ ἐγνώκειτέ με (pluperfect active indicative, 2pl), καὶ τὸν πατέρα μου ἐγνώκειτε ἄν (pluperfect active indicative), so that the BYZ reading significantly alters the meaning to a rebuke: if the disciples had known Jesus—but they did not—then they would have known the Father—whom they did not know either. A similar construction appears in 1 Cor 2:8 where the appearance of ἄν in the apodosis indicates this to be a second class conditional, assumed to be contrary to fact (Wallace, *Greek Grammar*, 694), "for if they had understood it—and they had not, then—they would not have crucified the Lord of glory" (ἣν οὐδεὶς τῶν ἀρχόντων τοῦ αἰῶνος τούτου ἔγνωκεν· εἰ γὰρ ἔγνωσαν, οὐκ ἂν τὸν κύριον τῆς δόξης ἐσταύρωσαν). The BGT reading in John 14:7, however, is much more positive: "If you had known me—and you have—then you shall know the Father—and you shall." Despite Philip's question in John 14:9, which might imply the disciples have not known Jesus, the BGT reading fits the context better, since the first class conditional in John 14:7 assumes that the disciples have in fact come to know Jesus, as he affirms in His prayer in John 17:7 and 17:25. Their knowledge of Jesus being the case, then they shall also certainly know the Father.

The second example appears in 1 Cor 8:2, in the context of things sacrificed to idols. In this matter, Paul notes, "We know that we all have knowledge" (1 Cor 8:1). The Christian understanding of this issue is readily available, but there is a danger in that "knowledge makes arrogant," and thus the situation must be balanced with "love edifies." This is because of an assumed truth: "If anyone supposes that he knows anything, he has not yet known as he ought to know" [εἴ τις δοκεῖ ἐγνωκέναι (perfect active infinitive; the BYZ reads the aorist active infinitive εἰδέναι) τι, οὔπω ἔγνω καθὼς δεῖ γνῶναι·]. Paul assumes there is someone in Corinth who supposes "he knows anything" (about this issue), yet in reality he does not know as he ought to know.

Applying these two similar patterns to 2 Cor 5:16, Paul uses the particle εἰ followed by ἐγνώκαμεν (perfect active indicative, 1pl) in the prostasis, and γινώσκομεν (present active indicative, 1pl) in the apodosis, showing the structure to be a first class conditional. Paul assumes to be true that "we" have known Christ according to the flesh, although "we" are not knowing Him any longer as such. He assumes that some of his readers have known Christ in the flesh, and the question is whether Paul includes himself in this group. Paul uses the 1st plural γινώσκω elsewhere only in 1 Cor 13:9 ("we know in part"), although he does use the 1st plural of οἶδα in Rom 2:2; 3:19; 7:1; 8:22, 26, 28; 1 Cor 2:12; 8:1, 4; 2 Cor 5:1, 16a; and 1 Tim 1:8. In each instance, it is likely that Paul includes himself as part of the "we." That being the case, when Paul writes, "even if we have known Christ according to the flesh" (2 Cor 5:16), if he intended to *exclude* himself from this group, he would have written, "if *others* have known Christ;" or, "if *they* have known Christ;" or, "if *anyone* has known Christ;" instead, by use of the first person plural, Paul may well be *including* himself as one who has known Christ this way. Ridderbos, *Paul and Jesus*, 42, argues the contrary, insisting if Paul had known Jesus "in all probability he would not have spoken of it in purely a hypothetical manner." Even if Ridderbos

self-depreciating about any first-hand experiences with Jesus (2 Cor 12:1–7), since "now we are no longer knowing" Him in this manner.[67] There is now no special status awarded to those who saw Jesus in the flesh, because prideful flesh would be tempted to boast, as some in Corinth bragged, "I am of Christ" (1 Cor 1:12). While the historical Jesus enacted reconciliation by His actions (2 Cor 5:19), it is now the ascended Christ into whom believers come into union (2 Cor 5:17).

It may seem obvious to a modern reader that Jesus was a man with corporeal flesh, but doceticism interpreted Jesus as a phantom merely appearing as human, an error eventually refuted by later church councils as unbiblical and unhistorical.[68] By describing Jesus as a Man in flesh, Paul agrees with the Gospels on the reality of the physical body of Jesus, that after His resurrection, He invited His disciples, "See My hands and My feet, that it is I Myself; touch Me and see, for a spirit does not have flesh and bones as you see that I have" (Luke 24:39). This physicality of Jesus is of no minor consequence to Paul, as he reports, the Father has now reconciled believers "by Christ's physical body" (Col 1:22 NIV). Without the physical body of the "Man Christ Jesus," there would be no reconciliation to God.

The Body of Jesus

The apostle also has an understanding of the corporeal body of Jesus; indeed, it lies at the heart of the Eucharist, as Paul asks, "Is not the bread which we break a sharing in the body of Christ?" (1 Cor 10:16).[69] In one of the rare occasions when he cites the *logia* of Jesus, Paul quotes the words of institution, "When He (Jesus) had given thanks, He broke it, and said, 'This is My body, which is for you; do this in remembrance of Me'" (1 Cor 11:24), and then he warns believers that unworthy partaking of the Supper would make the offender "guilty of the body and the blood of the Lord" (1 Cor 11:27). While it seems obvious that both Paul and Jesus refer to His physical body, it is equally apparent that eating a morsel of bread as a spiritual participation would be rendered nonsense unless the physical body of Jesus had been offered as a sacrifice—a fact to which Paul alludes in Col 1:22, "He has now reconciled you in His fleshly body (ἐν τῷ σώματι τῆς σαρκὸς αὐτοῦ) through death." Even more astonishing than the body of Jesus being offered as a sin-offering is Paul's proclamation that in Christ "all the fulness of Deity dwells in bodily form" (σωματικῶς; Col 2:9). These references to the body of Jesus show that Paul is in agreement with the Gospels, as when Jesus said of the woman identified as Mary in John 12:3, "For when she poured this perfume upon *My body*, she did it to prepare Me for burial" (Matt 26:12).

Also, while the Body of Christ is a well-known Pauline metaphor for the church (1 Cor 12:27), it is less recognized that Paul most likely derived his understanding from

---

is correct, Paul considers his pre-conversion knowledge of Jesus "according to the flesh" to be so mistaken that he completely repudiated his understanding as fallacious.

67. Machen, *Origin of Paul's Religion*, 54–56, *contra* Weiss, discusses 2 Cor 5:16 and concludes that "the passage is not so clear as to justify any certain conclusions about Paul's life in Palestine; it does not clearly imply any acquaintance of Paul with Jesus before the passion" (ibid., 56).

68. Kelly, *Early Christian Doctrines*, 141–42.

69. BDAG § 7216. 1 defines σῶμα as the human body, but it also recognizes the usage of "a unified group of people" (Rom 12:5; 1 Cor 10:17; 12:13, 27; Eph 1:23; 2:16; 4:4, 12, 16; 5:23, 30; Col 1:18, 24; 2:19; 3:15).

the cryptic statement of Jesus, "Destroy this temple, and in three days I will raise it up" (John 2:19), a remark John 2:21 explains, "He was speaking of the temple of His body." Where else would Paul make the connection between the church as the collective Body of Christ (Rom 12:5; Eph 4:12; 5:23) and the physical body of the believer as a temple of the Holy Spirit (1 Cor 6:19) if not to the physical, resurrected body of Jesus as now the new Temple of God? Once again, the doctrinal basis of Paul's teachings assumes the historical reality related to the "Man Christ Jesus," in this case, His physical body.

The Blood of Jesus

Physiologically, the human body is nourished throughout by the flow of blood, although in the normal course of conversation, one's blood would seem to be an odd subject to discuss.[70] Yet for Paul, the blood of Jesus stands as a vivid symbol of His violent death, offered as "a propitiation in His blood" (Rom 3:25) and pictured sacramentally in the sharing of the cup of the new covenant in the blood of Jesus (1 Cor 10:16; 11:25).[71] This sacrificial shedding of the blood of Jesus secures redemption (Eph 1:7) and brings sinners near to God (Eph 2:13), who has "made peace through the blood of His cross" (Col 1:20). As Goppelt observes,[72] the people of the New Covenant and the means of redemption are established in the Institution of the Lord's Supper, which uses the bread and wine to point to the body and blood of the Human Jesus, as the antitype of the Passover Lamb (1 Cor 5:7).[73] According to Paul and the Gospels (Matt 26:28; Mark 14:24; Luke 22:20; 1 Cor 11:25), it was Jesus Himself who poured out the cup with the explanation, "This cup . . . poured out for you is the new covenant in My blood" (τοῦτο τὸ ποτήριον ἡ καινὴ διαθήκη ἐν τῷ αἵματί μου τὸ ὑπὲρ ὑμῶν ἐκχυννόμενον, Luke 22:20), a phrase echoing Jer 31:31–34 (διαθήκην καινήν, בְּרִית חֲדָשָׁה) and Exod 24:8, "So Moses took the blood and sprinkled *it* on the people, and said, "Behold the blood of the covenant (τὸ αἷμα τῆς διαθήκης), which the LORD has made with you in accordance with all these words." Add to this also Zech 9:11, "As for you also, because of the blood of *My* covenant with you, I have set your prisoners free from the waterless pit" (καὶ σὺ ἐν αἵματι διαθήκης ἐξαπέστειλας δεσμίους σου ἐκ λάκκου οὐκ ἔχοντος ὕδωρ), and the redemptive significance of Christ's blood is plainly prefigured (see also Heb 9:20; 10:29).

Admittedly, Paul discusses the blood of Jesus in its sacrificial significance while a phlebotomist examines the material fluid coursing though the veins, yet in the search to discover Paul's meaning of the blood of Jesus, it can easily be overlooked that the apostle presumes Jesus to have been a real human who bled real blood when pierced with nails.

---

70. Actually such talk is not that unusual in the author's household, as his wife is an infusionist nurse, whose occupational discussion concerns the veins she penetrates with needles.

71. See Morris, *The Apostolic Preaching of the Cross*, 112–28, in which he argues that "blood" in the Hebrew Bible "signifies life violently taken rather than continued presence of life" (ibid., 121). He also argues (ibid., 144–213) that ἱλαστήριος refers to the removal of divine wrath and thus must be translated as "propitiation" rather than "expiation" (RSV), since it refers to the "mercy seat" (כַּפֹּרֶת) that covered the ark of the covenant (Exod 25:17) sprinkled by the sacrificial blood (Lev 16:15).

72. Goppelt, *Tupos: The Typological Interpretation of the Old Testament in the New*, 110.

73. Behm, "κλάω," *TDNT* 3:738–41.

THE "MAN CHRIST JESUS"

Thus, in his references to the blood of Jesus, Paul agrees with the Gospel record, that "one of the soldiers pierced His side with a spear, and immediately there came out blood and water" (John 19:34). If there is no forgiveness of sin without the shedding of blood (Heb 9:22), then of necessity there must be bleeding of physical blood. Thus, Paul once again bases a doctrinal teaching upon an incidental fact of history, that Jesus bled blood, an issue confirming the humanity of the "Man Christ Jesus."

Summary: Jesus as Human

When Paul describes Christ Jesus as a *man* (ἄνθρωπος Χριστὸς Ἰησοῦς), he implies that Jesus was a person of history who physically lived as a male human being who possessed a real physical body that was nourished by real circulating blood. Thus it cannot be claimed that the humanity of Jesus is inconsequential for Paul, since he writes in Rom 5:10, "We shall be saved by His life." While it can be argued that "His life" refers to the pneumatic participation with the ascended life of Jesus, yet even in 2 Cor 4:10–11, where Paul mentions that "the life of Jesus also may be manifested in our body, . . . for we who live are constantly being delivered over to death for Jesus' sake, that the life of Jesus also may be manifested in our mortal flesh," the present experience with the ascended life of Jesus presumes the historical life of Jesus as a man who lived in historical time and space.

THE YOUTH OF THE "MAN CHRIST JESUS"

It may also appear that Paul shows no concern for the childhood of Jesus, but in his letters, he alludes to a number of facts stated in the Gospels regarding Jesus' youth. These include His birth, His family, His ethnicity, His genealogy, His circumcision, and His legal upbringing as He lived out all of these circumstances in a life fraught with poverty.

The Birth of Jesus

It might seem pedantic to note that Paul believed Jesus was "born of a woman" (Gal 4:4), since birth by a mother is how all babies enter the world, but it should not escape the reader's notice that Paul asserts that the Son of God arrived on earth via natural childbirth: "When the fulness of the time came, God sent forth His Son, born of a woman." In Greek mythology, gods do not need human birth, and although some naturally-born men were later deified (such as the Emperor Nero), Jesus in any case does not fit this mold. Instead, He is the pre-existent the Son of God who became man by means of a natural nine-month gestation, resulting in birth of a human mother.

Still, one might ask why Paul does not mention the name of the mother of Jesus when the Gospels supply it as Mary.[74] Was Paul unaware of her name? Such ignorance

---

74. To be more precise, the mother of Jesus is identified as *Marias* (Μαρίας; Matt 1:16, 18; 2:11; Mark 6:3; Luke 1:41), although the people of His hometown knew her by her Hebrew name *Mariam* (Μαριάμ) by asking, "Is not His mother called Mary?" (Matt 13:55; Μαριάμ is used also at Luke 1:27, 30, 34, 38, 39, 46, 56; 2:5, 16, 19, 34; Acts 1:14), meaning that Mary was given the name of the sister of Moses (Exod 6:20; 15:20, 21; Num 12:1, 4, 5, 10, 15; 20:1; 26:59; Deut 24:9; 1 Chr 5:29; Mic 6:4). The Gospels are not shy about repeating that Jesus had a mother (Matt 2:13, 14, 20, 21; 12:46, 47; Mark 3:31, 32; Luke 2:33, 34, 48, 51; 8:19, 20; John 2:1, 3, 5, 12; 6:42; 19:25, 26, 27; Acts 1:14). While John's Gospel never identifies Mary by name, it

is most unlikely, since he knew the Jerusalem community of which Mary was a named member (Acts 1:14), and it would be quite normal for "James the Lord's brother" (Gal 1:19) to have introduced Paul to Mary. Even so, Paul's omission of Mary's name can be difficult to comprehend, leading Akenson to view the impersonal reference to Jesus being "born of a woman" as Paul disdaining any idea of Mary as the virgin mother.[75] It may well be, however, that the absence of her name is the apostle's way of protecting the privacy of Mary from the prying eyes and intimate questions of the curious. Furthermore, Paul's emphasis in Gal 4:4 is not upon the identity of Jesus' mother, but rather upon how God's Son was sent forth—originating out of a woman (γενόμενον ἐκ γυναικός),[76] as Paul does not use the customary verb for natural birth, γεννάω (as he does in Gal 4:23, Isaac "was born according to the flesh") but rather the verb γίνομαι.[77] He also utilizes γίνομαι in Rom 1:3 regarding the birth of Jesus as a descendant of David (γενομένου ἐκ σπέρματος Δαυὶδ κατὰ σάρκα)[78] and likewise in Phil 2:7 regarding the incarnation, that Christ was "made (γενόμενος) in the likeness of men."[79] By the selection of the verb γίνομαι rather than γεννάω, Paul not only avoids a word "which in its active form refers to the male act of begetting a child (as in Matthew 1 of the ancestors of Jesus),"[80] but it may well imply something different in the conception of Jesus from that of other babies. Instead of "refuting a doctrine too lurid in his view to grant a name,"[81] Paul actually leaves the door open for a virginal conception as well as allowing for the pre-existence of Jesus.

---

calls her "His mother," noting she was present at the first miracle of Jesus (John 2:1–12) and was "standing by the cross of Jesus" (John 19:25). Elizabeth provides the most stunning identification by calling Mary "the mother of my Lord" (ἡ μήτηρ τοῦ κυρίου μου, Luke 1:43).

75. Akenson, *Saint Saul: A Skeleton Key to the Historical Jesus*, 205.

76. Γίνομαι is one of the most common verbs in the Greek Bible, used +/- 2,893 times with a variety of meanings: BDAG § 5454 lists nine meanings, although the first listed is "what comes into existence . . . of persons (to) be born." It is used in conjunction with the birth of children in such places as Gen 4:18, 26; 10:21, 25; 21:5; 35:26; Job 15:7; etc., translating יָלַד, but that seems like an odd choice when γεννάω would seem more appropriate to describe birth (as in Matt 1:16, Ἰακὼβ δὲ ἐγέννησεν τὸν Ἰωσὴφ τὸν ἄνδρα Μαρίας, ἐξ ἧς ἐγεννήθη Ἰησοῦς ὁ λεγόμενος χριστός.).

77. While BDAG § 1646.1 defines γίνομαι in Gal 4:4, "to come into being through process of birth or natural production," Paul uses the same aorist middle accusative participle γενόμενον only once more in all his letters, in the next phrase, γενόμενον ὑπὸ νόμον. BDAG § 1646.9 defines this second usage, "to be closely related to someone or someth., *belong to*" (the law)." However, it is reasonable to assume Paul that uses γενόμενον in the same way in both phrases, so the best translation may be simply, "having been," as this alerts the reader to the historical reference of the existence of Jesus in His birth "of woman" and His upbringing "under Law."

78. Goguel, *Jesus the Nazarene: Myth or History?*, 138, ties Gal 4:4 to a phrase found in Job 11:2 (LXA), "Blessed *is* the short-lived offspring of woman" (γεννητὸς γυναικὸς); in Job 11:12, "a mortal born of woman (γεννητὸς γυναικὸς) *is* like an ass in the desert"; in Job 14:1, "Man, who is born of woman (γεννητὸς γυναικὸς), is short-lived and full of turmoil"; in Job 15:14, "For who, being a mortal, *is such* that he shall be blameless? or, *who that is* born of a woman (γεννητὸς γυναικός), that he should be just?"; and in Job 25:4, "How then can a man be just with God? Or how can he be clean who is born of woman (γεννητὸς γυναικός)?" It must be noted, however, that Paul uses a different verb in Gal 4:4, γίνομαι.

79. The same verb describes the incarnation in John 1:14 (ὁ λόγος σὰρξ ἐγένετο).

80. Wenham, *Paul and the Historical Jesus*, 16.

81. Akenson, *Saint Saul*, ibid., 180.

THE "MAN CHRIST JESUS"

Furthermore, why bother to mention that Jesus was born of a woman when it is self-evident that all babies are born of women—unless there was something unusual about this particular birth?[82] While Paul may be correcting docetic tendencies that denied Jesus had or needed a physical birth, it is quite possible that Paul in this context uses "woman" in echo of the prophecy of Gen 3:15, where the one who comes to bruise the head of the serpent is called the "seed of the woman" (γυναικὸς . . . τοῦ σπέρματος αὐτῆς)—a phrase surely implying the unusual nature of the Seed's conception (σπέρματος αὐτῆς) and which is used elsewhere only at Rev 12:17,[83] a context also discussing the Messiah's birth.[84] Whether or not this prophecy is echoed in Gal 4:4, Paul knew that Jesus had an earthly mother, meaning He had been born as a human baby,[85] another incidental fact confirming the humanity of the "Man Christ Jesus."

The Ethnicity of Jesus

When Paul lists the privileges of the Israelites, "from whom is the Christ according to the flesh" (Rom 9:5), he establishes the Jewish ethnicity of Jesus, a lineage also implied in Rom 15:8, "For I say that Christ has become a servant to the circumcision on behalf of the truth of God to confirm the promises *given* to the fathers." Paul does not mention the birthplace of Jesus in his letters (although he refers to His hometown of Nazareth in Acts 26:9), but he may hint at the dialect spoken by Jesus when he mentions the diminutive Aramaic form of *abba* (Gal 4:6; Rom 8:15–16), as prayed by Jesus in Mark 14:36. Clearly, Paul knew that Jesus was of Palestinian, Jewish ethnicity, yet another confirmation of the humanity of the "Man Christ Jesus."

The Genealogy of Jesus

Paul is neither ignorant nor uncaring about the Jewish lineage of Jesus, as he argues that Jesus is the fulfillment of the promises given by God to Israel's patriarch Abraham concerning his seed (Gal 3:16–17).[86] Also, Paul is aware of the connection of Jesus to the

---

82. Ehrman, *The New Testament*, rather flippantly notes, "Paul gives the following information (about Jesus). He says that Jesus was born of a woman (Gal 4:4; this is not a particularly useful datum; one wonders what the alternative may have been!)." Unwittingly, Ehrman raises a significant question: why else would Paul state the obvious, that Jesus was born of a woman, unless there *was* an alternative—that Jesus was born of a woman who was also a virgin, as recorded by Matt 1:25 and Luke 1:27.

83. In Rev 12:7, "the dragon (identified in v. 7 as Satan) was enraged with the woman (one who gives birth to a "male son, who is to rule all nations"), and went off to make war with the rest of her offspring (σπέρματος αὐτῆς), who keep the commandments of God and hold to the testimony of Jesus." The entire passage is packed with OT imagery and typology.

84. In addition, it should be noted that in a previous few verses (Gal 3:16, 19), Paul has just called Jesus the Seed (τὸ σπέρμα) of Abraham, another messianic title also signifying the true humanity of Jesus.

85. Barnett, *Paul: Missionary of Jesus*, 18–19, ftnt. 24, suggests that Gal 4:4–6 appears to be connected with the birth narratives in Luke's Gospel and asks, "Was Paul familiar with a source that Luke subsequently incorporated in his Gospel?" If Luke, who was a companion and "fellow-worker" of Paul (Col 4:14; 2 Tim 4:11; Phlm 24), was also the author of the third Gospel, as church tradition insists, then it is inconceivable that Paul would not have known from Luke about the virgin conception of Jesus.

86. Galatians 3:16–17 reads, "Now the promises were spoken to Abraham and to his seed. He does not say, 'And to seeds,' as *referring* to many, but *rather* to one, 'And to your seed,' that is, Christ." According to

Davidic lineage, as he describes Him as a "descendant of David according to the flesh" (ἐκ σπέρματος Δαυὶδ κατὰ σάρκα; Rom 1:3). This same idea is repeated in 2 Tim 2:8, "Jesus Christ, descendant of David" (ἐκ σπέρματος Δαυίδ), by which Paul confirms the record of Jesus' Jewish lineage recorded in Matt 1:6 and Luke 3:31, where David is listed in Jesus' geneologies. Although Fee maintains that Paul makes no point of Jesus' humanity ("It is simply the assumption inherent in the language itself"[87]), he overlooks the OT expectation that the Messiah would come physically as an offspring of David (2 Sam 7:14–15). By tracing Jesus through the genealogy of David, Paul insists that Jesus meets this Messianic qualification as the Seed of David.[88]

Also, in Rom 15:12, Paul interprets the Davidic lineage of Jesus as a fulfillment of OT prophecy, as he cites what Isaiah says about the father of David (Ruth 4:17), "There shall come the root of Jesse, and he who arises to rule over the Gentiles; in Him shall the Gentiles hope," a quote from the LXX of Isa 11:10.[89] (This same fact regarding the Davidic lineage of Jesus is affirmed by Paul in Acts 13:23,[90] in agreement with Matt 1:6, "to Jesse was born David the king.") Paul assumes the same tribal connection of Jesus drawn by the writer of Heb 7:14, "For it is evident that our Lord was descended from Judah," so that by calling Jesus the Seed of David, Paul presumes knowledge of the genealogical record of Jesus recorded in Matt 1:1–16 ("the genealogy of Jesus Christ, the son of David") and in Luke 3:23–38, where the lineage of Jesus is traced back through David (Luke 3:31) to "Adam the son of God" (Luke 3:38). In agreement, Paul clearly affirms the human genealogy of the "Man Christ Jesus."

The Family of Jesus

Paul is aware that several "brothers of the Lord" existed (1 Cor 9:5, οἱ ἀδελφοὶ τοῦ κυρίου), and he had personally met "James the Lord's brother" (Gal 1:19, Ἰάκωβον τὸν ἀδελφὸν τοῦ κυρίου). This family connection is confirmed in Acts 1:14 ("Mary the mother of Jesus, and His brothers") and especially in Matt 13:55 ∥ Mark 6:3, where Jesus is identified as "the carpenter, the son of Mary and brother of James and Joses and Judas and Simon." Whereas

---

Archer and Chirichigno, *Old Testament Quotations in the New Testament*, 5, "From Gen 13:15 there is only a single phrase וּלְזַרְעֲךָ ("and to your seed") that has been adopted by Gal 3:16, where the messianic fulfillment is found in the person of Christ Himself, as *the* 'seed' *par excellence*, of Abraham."

87. Fee, *Pauline Christology*, 528.

88. Duling, "The Promises of David and Their Entrance into Christianity—Nailing Down a Likely Hypothesis," 55–77, recognizes that the NT applies "Son of God" to Jesus in terms of the Davidic covenant in 2 Sam 7:12–13, but he does so without affirming Jesus to be the Son of David (ibid., 68), an inconsistency Kim, *Origin of Paul's Gospel*, ftnt. 3, 109–10 describes charitably as "curious."

89. Paul's quote (ἔσται ἡ ῥίζα τοῦ Ἰεσσαὶ καὶ ὁ ἀνιστάμενος ἄρχειν ἐθνῶν, ἐπ' αὐτῷ ἔθνη ἐλπιοῦσιν) is an abbreviation of LXX translation of Isa 11:10, καὶ ἔσται ἐν τῇ ἡμέρᾳ ἐκείνῃ ἡ ῥίζα τοῦ Ιεσσαι καὶ ὁ ἀνιστάμενος ἄρχειν ἐθνῶν ἐπ' αὐτῷ ἔθνη ἐλπιοῦσιν. Paul apparently understands ὁ ἀνιστάμενος as the arising of Jesus in resurrection, as he uses the verb that way in 1 Thess 4:14, "if we believe that Jesus died and rose again" (ἀνέστη). See the discussion by Seifrid, "Romans," 690.

90. Acts 13:23, "From the offspring (σπέρματος) of this man (David), according to promise, God has brought to Israel a Savior, Jesus."

THE "MAN CHRIST JESUS"

the Gospels refer to Jesus as "son of Joseph" (Luke 3:23; John 1:45, 6:42),[91] Paul does not mention any earthly father of Jesus, much less name Joseph, although the existence of His brothers implies they also shared a common father (Jesus by adoption and the other sons presumably by birth, despite the Roman Catholic dogma that the brothers of Jesus are not subsequent children of the Virgin Mary but sons of "the other Mary" of Matt 27:56[92]). The absence of Joseph in Paul's letters, however, does not imply ignorance, since Joseph is not mentioned outside the nativity narratives except for John 6:42.[93] Other than this paternal omission, Paul knew that this "Man Christ Jesus" was born of a mother and had several brothers—as recorded in the Gospel narratives.

The Religion of Jesus, Judaism

It is obvious that Paul knew the man Jesus to be a Jew, although he never specifically calls Him such; however, in titling "the Man Jesus" as "Christ" 371 times, Paul identifies Jesus as the Messiah of Israel,[94] a concept derived from the Hebrew Bible (Ps 2:2; Isa 61:1; Dan 9:25–26). When the apostle identifies with his own ethnic people, he describes the Israelites as those "from whom is the Christ according to the flesh" (ἐξ ὧν ὁ Χριστὸς τὸ κατὰ σάρκα, Rom 9:4–5), affirming the Jewish roots of Jesus. This is, of course, the united testimony of the Gospels, as when the Samaritan woman quizzed Jesus, "You, being a Jew?" (John 4:9).[95] That Paul knew Jesus to be Jewish is yet another fact confirming the humanity of the "Man Christ Jesus."

The Circumcision of Jesus

In Col 2:11, Paul refers to "the circumcision of Christ" as being the instrument whereby believers are "circumcised with a circumcision made without hands." While his concern is the dynamic, regenerating effect of the "removal of the body of the flesh" by association with Christ, Paul's reference in this context to several other historical events of Jesus (including His baptism, crucifixion, and resurrection) suggests that he also refers to the physical circumcision of Jesus, as recorded in Luke 2:21 ("at the end of eight days, when He was circumcised," ESV). This act further verifies the Jewish heritage of Jesus and the devotion of His parents in presenting Him to receive the sign of the Abrahamic Covenant

---

91. The community assumption was that Jesus was "the son of the carpenter" Joseph (Matt 13:55; Mark 6:3; Luke 4:22; John 6:42). Even with Luke's emphasis on Mary's virgin conception of Jesus, he is not averse to calling Joseph the father of Jesus (Luke 2:33), although he qualifies that relationship by noting "Jesus was supposedly—ὡς ἐνομίζετο–the son of Joseph" (Luke 3:23). It is apparent that Joseph raised Jesus as if he was his own son.

92. *Catechism of the Catholic Church* § 499–500. In its effort to preserve Mary as *Aeiparthenos* ("the ever-virgin"), the Roman Catholic Church must explain away the obvious implications of Matt 13:35, lessening the true humanity of Jesus as a man with brothers and sisters.

93. In retrospect, Paul's omission of the personal name Joseph becomes a very wise choice—imagine the consternation of his readers had he specified Joseph as the father of Jesus while neglecting to name His mother.

94. John 1:41 helpfully explains the translation of the Hebrew מָשִׁיחַ with Χριστός.

95. The Jewish roots of Jesus are mentioned also in Matt 2:6, 21; 10:6; 15:24; 27:42; Mark 15:32; Luke 1:68; 2:32, 34; 7:9; 24:21; John 1:49; 12:13; Acts 1:6.

(Gen 17:11). This incidental remark not only verifies the male gender of the "Man Christ Jesus" but also confirms His infancy and subsequent childhood, as presented in Luke's Gospel (2:21–52), as a child raised within a pious Jewish family.

The Legal Upbringing of Jesus

In Gal 4:4, Paul notes that Jesus was "made under the law," a reference to His legal upbringing under the Law of Moses, as also reported in Luke 2:22, "When the days for their purification according to the law of Moses were completed, (Mary and Joseph) brought Him up to Jerusalem to present Him to the Lord;" in Luke 2:27, "the parents brought in the child Jesus, to carry out for Him the custom of the Law;" and in Luke 2:39, "they performed (for Him) everything according to the Law of the Lord." This historical reference to the upbringing of Jesus in the Torah is quite pertinent to Paul's understanding of humanity held in custody "under law" (Gal 3:23), for that necessitated Jesus "having come out of woman, having come under law" into order to identify with humans who are also "under law" (Gal 4:5, 21). While Jesus had some well-publicized disagreements with the Jewish leadership over the application of the Mosaic Law, His attitude toward the Law itself is quite strict ("Do not think that I came to abolish the Law or the Prophets; I did not come to abolish, but to fulfill," Matt 5:17). He did, however, condense the "whole Law and Prophets" to two primary OT commands (Matt 22:37–40), to love God (Deut 6:5) and to love one's neighbor as oneself (Lev 19:18). Wenham suggests that this may be what Paul has in mind in Gal 6:2 by "the law of Christ," since he has just quoted from Lev 19:18, "For the whole Law is fulfilled in one word, in the *statement*, 'You shall love your neighbor as yourself'" (Gal 5:14).[96] Wenham further proposes that this connection is strengthened when one asks what is *the* law of Christ, and what naturally comes to mind is the "new commandment" of Jesus to "love one another as I have loved you" (John 13:34).[97] By these references in his letters, Paul knew that Jesus was a Man who obeyed the regulations of the Law of Moses (Rom 5:19–20), and he used this knowledge in his application of the Law to the church.

The Poverty of Jesus

Paul was aware of the socio-economic situation of Jesus that he describes this way: "For you know the grace of our Lord Jesus Christ, yet for your sake He became poor,[98] that you through His poverty might become rich" (2 Cor 8:9). This remark presupposes that Paul knew that Jesus lived in poverty; otherwise, his chiastic analogy of Jesus becoming poor and believers becoming rich holds little weight.[99] The contrast lies between the heavenly wealth that Jesus exchanged for the earthly poverty He experienced as the "Man Christ

---

96. Wenham, *Paul and Jesus*, 74.
97. Ibid., 75.
98. BDAG § 6421 translates πτωχεύω, "to be or become poor as a beggar."
99. Stanton, *Jesus of Nazareth in New Testament Preaching*, 107, undercuts his own point that Paul uses the character of Jesus as an example but "is not appealing to the literal poverty of Jesus." That seems to be precisely what Paul *is* doing here, for if Jesus had not been poor, this analogy would have been quite disingenuous.

THE "MAN CHRIST JESUS"

Jesus," confirming the Gospel record that His parents gave the offering of the poor when they dedicated their son (Luke 2:23–24).[100] Jesus Himself claimed that He had no place to lay His head (Matt 8:20; Luke 9:58), and His ministry was dependent on the charities of others (Luke 8:2–3). At His death, His total possessions divided by the soldiers included only His outer garments and tunic. But it is not just Paul who knew the poverty of Jesus: he states that his readers in Corinth also share that same knowledge: they too knew how poor Jesus had been, a fact Paul had presumably taught them in an earlier visit. While few would cite poverty as a credential (Ghandi comes to mind), Paul uses the poverty of Jesus to illustrate the incarnational emptying of Jesus and as an impetus to encourage the Corinthians to complete the offering for the "support of the saints" (2 Cor 8:4).

Summary: The Youth of Jesus

Paul contradicts nothing of the Gospel records about the childhood and youth of Jesus but confirms what information is given there. Had no Gospel accounts ever existed, one would learn from Paul that Jesus was a Jew born of a woman of the descent of Abraham and David (thus of the tribe of Judah) and was raised in the piety of the Torah by a poor family consisting of several brothers. If Paul proclaimed only the kerygmatic Lord with no interest in the historical Jesus, as Bultmann declared,[101] this information would be superfluous; as it is, Paul weaves these details of historical information into his doctrinal presentations of the incarnation (Gal 4:4), fulfillment of Messianic prophecy (Rom 1:3; 9:4–5; 15:8, 12; 2 Tim 2:8), his apostolic credentials (Gal 1:19) and liberties (1 Cor 9:1), regeneration (Col 2:11), and as an incentive for charity (2 Cor 8:9). These historical references to the youth of Jesus reveal that the apostle could and would use incidental facts about the "Man Christ Jesus" to bolster his doctrinal arguments.

THE MINISTRY OF THE "MAN CHRIST JESUS"

A reader of Paul's letters searches in vain for a narrative outline of the ministry of Christ, although his sermon recorded in Acts 13:23–31 (to be examined in the next chapter) provides a Pauline summary of Jesus' ministry. This epistolary absence leads such a critic as Akenson to contend that for Paul, the historical Jesus is "barely visible," that he is even "openly contemptuous of certain beliefs about the historical Jesus . . . circulating throughout the web of Yeshua followers," so that at times he "consciously diminishes the figure of the historical Yeshua" and possesses "a casual attitude toward the mundane facts about the historical Yeshua, an attitude that these are of secondary importance because, actually they were mundane."[102] This section refutes these charges by examining the references in Paul's letters to events that happened during the ministry of Jesus, including His baptism, His call to twelve disciples, His ministry among the Jews, His status as the Lord's Servant,

---

100. NET *Notes* at Luke 2:24 comment that the text quotes from Lev 12:8 and 5:11. "The offering of *a pair of doves or two young pigeons*, instead of a lamb, speaks of the humble roots of Jesus' family—they apparently could not afford the expense of a lamb" (ibid., loc. cit.).

101. Bultmann, "The Significance of the Historical Jesus for the Theology of Paul," 239.

102. Akenson, *Saint Saul*, 173.

The "Man Christ Jesus" in the Epistles of Paul

His transfiguration, plus citations and allusions to the teaching, preaching, and evangelistic ministry of Jesus.

The Baptism of Jesus

Twice Paul mentions the baptism of Jesus; first, in Rom 6:3 ("Do you not know that all of us who have been baptized into Christ Jesus have been baptized into His death?") and then in Col 2:12 ("having been buried with Him in baptism"), yet it is not uncommon for commentaries to discuss the significance of baptism and not once consider that Paul is assuming the historical baptism of Jesus as the prototype of all Christian baptisms.[103] While located outside of his letters in Acts 13:24–25 and Acts 19:4, Paul's comments concerning John the Baptist confirm that Paul was aware that the ministry of Jesus proceeded from John's earlier ministry. Had Jesus not been baptized by John "to fulfill all righteousness," there would be no pattern of baptism for later converts to follow; thus, Paul uses the incident of the baptism of Jesus as a part of his doctrine of association with Christ, applying this historical event to an aspect of salvation effected by the "Man Christ Jesus."

The Disciples of Jesus

Paul knows that Jesus was accompanied by a group of believers he labels as Apostles, in agreement with the Gospels (Matt 10:2; Mark 6:30; Luke 6:13; 22:14); more exactly, "Paul knows not just of the Apostles in general, but also specifically of the twelve (1 Cor 15:5)."[104] Paul numbers himself along with "the rest of the Apostles" (1 Cor 9:5), although he recognizes those in Jerusalem who were "Apostles before me" (Gal 1:17). Within that group, he recognizes the leadership of Peter as one of the three "pillars" of the church along with James and John (Gal 2:9),[105] a possible allusion to the choice by Jesus of three Apostles to His inner circle (Matt 17:1; Mark 14:33; Luke 9:28).[106] It needs to be noted that Paul not only refers to Peter by His Christ-given name Πέτρος (Matt 16:18) but more frequently by his Aramaic name כֵּיפָא (Κηφᾶς; 1 Cor 1:12; 3:22; 9:5; 15:5; Gal 1:18; 2:7–9, 11, 14) in what may be a deliberate allusion to Jesus' play on Peter's name as the "rock."[107]

---

103. Wenham, *Paul: Follower of Jesus or Founder of Christianity?*, 346, observes that both Jesus and Paul view baptism as a ritual performed with water (Eph 5:26), that it is associated with the being baptized with the Spirit (1 Cor 12:13), and that it involves a declaration of sonship (Gal 3:26–27).

104. Wenham, *Paul: Follower of Jesus or Founder of Christianity?*, 200.

105. Since Baur, it has been common to suppose Paul is being somewhat sarcastic in calling James, Cephas, and John "pillars," especially when he remarks about "those of high reputation—what they were makes no difference to me" (Gal 2:6). Paul's point, however, is that his Apostleship rests on equal footing with the Jerusalem Apostles, "for He who effectually worked for Peter in *his* Apostleship to the circumcised effectually worked for me also to the Gentiles" (Gal 2:8). Whatever Paul's tone may have been in Gal 2:6—and it can be understood as declarative rather than cynical—the upshot is that all parties shared the right hand of fellowship, a symbol of goodwill and agreement (Gal 2:9).

106. The Apostle James mentioned in Gal 2:9 must be James, the Lord's brother (Gal 1:19), since James the brother of John had been executed by Herod Agrippa I some years earlier (Acts 12:2). Even at that time, Peter recognized the Lord's brother James as the leader (the "pastor?") of the Jerusalem church (Acts 12:17).

107. BDAG § 5898, "Πέτρος (ὁ πέτρος = 'stone')"; BDAG § 4234, "Κηφᾶς, ᾶ, ὁ (כֵּיפָא 'rock') Aram.

THE "MAN CHRIST JESUS"

Wenham notes what he calls the "enormous" parallels between Jesus' call of Peter (Matt 16:16–20) and Paul's record of his own call (Gal 1:15–16) by his use of the same phrases, "revealing the Son" by God and not by "flesh and blood."[108] Wenham also suggests the possibility that when Paul recognizes Peter's entrustment of the gospel to the circumcision (Gal 2:7; the passive voice of πεπίστευμαι indicates a divine commission, as in Titus 1:3—who else commissioned Peter if not Jesus?), he is aware of Jesus' instruction to Peter as one of the twelve to go "to the lost sheep of the house of Israel" (Matt 10:6).[109] Also, Paul refers to another disciple named John as a pillar of the Jerusalem church (Gal 2:9), and presumably he refers to John the Apostle, as both writers present the "Man Christ Jesus" being accompanied by His disciples.[110]

The Ministry of Jesus to the Jews

It is incorrect to assert that Paul never refers to the ministry of Jesus to the Jewish people when he certainly does so in Rom 15:8, "Christ has become[111] a servant to the circumcision on behalf of the truth of God to confirm the promises *given* to the fathers." This comment appears in the context concerning the weaker/stronger brother conflicts disturbing the church in Rome, and as a solution, Paul points to the example of Christ in not pleasing Himself for the good of his neighbor (Rom 15:3). The apostle reminds his readers of God's purpose in creating one worshipping community (Rom 15:6), as Christ accepted both Jews and Gentiles (Rom 15:7)—and the historical proof of that acceptance is that "Christ has become a servant to the circumcision on behalf of the truth of God to confirm the promises *given* to the fathers, and for the Gentiles to glorify God for His mercy; as it is written, 'Therefore I will give praise to Thee among the Gentiles, and I will sing to Thy name'" (Rom 15:8–9). This comment indicates that Paul knew the saying of Jesus, "I was sent only to the lost sheep of the house of Israel" (Matt 15:24), a statement of purpose uttered in conversation with the Gentile woman whom He then helped with the "crumbs which fall from the master's table" (Matt 15:27). Thus, Paul was aware that the primary focus of Jesus' ministry was devoted to the Jewish people while the Gentiles anxiously awaited His blessings, precisely the way presented in the Gospels.

For concerns of this study, it important to see how Paul has embedded a reference to the past public ministry of Jesus to the Jewish people into his argument as a stimulus for present Christian unity. If Paul had been ignorant of or unconcerned for any such earthly ministry of Jesus, he would have no reason to use such an argument; as it is, Paul once

---

surname of Simon."

108. Wenham, *Paul: Follower of Jesus,* 201–02.

109. Wenham, *Paul and Jesus,* 70.

110. See Appendix 3, "Similarities Between The Johannine And Pauline Literature."

111. This is the only appearance in Paul's letters of the perfect passive infinitive γεγενῆσθαι, "to have become." Here in Rom 15:8 it is used in indirect discourse as the object of the verb λέγω, so the remainder of the verse is a substantive clause indicating it is a quotation from the apostle, as if Paul says the same sort of statement as part of this particular teaching (Wallace, *Greek Grammar,* 603). Also, the perfect tense points to the past time when Jesus began and continued his ministry (ibid., 573–4, on the definition of the perfect tense as describing an act with abiding results.).

again assumes that his readers in Rome share his knowledge of the ministry of Jesus in Galilee and Judea some thirty years earlier, so he could use it as an historical 'sealer' of his ideas on church unity. By showing how Jesus surrendered His freedoms in order to serve the Jews in bondage to legal scruples, Paul finds an appropriate example for the weaker/stronger brother controversy in Rome in the ministry of the "Man Christ Jesus."

The Status of Jesus as Servant

In this same context, Paul states in Rom 15:8 that "Christ has become a servant (διάκονον) to the circumcision," combining in Jesus two apparently contradictory concepts; first, that He is the Anointed One, the Messiah of Israel—arguably the highest position attributed to any man—and secondly, this Christ has become a servant—the lowest position of social status. This is not an isolated concept, but it also part of the traditional Christ-hymn Paul cites in Phil 2:7, that Jesus took the form of a servant (μορφὴν δούλου λαβών). While Paul is quite eager to call himself a servant (δοῦλος) of Christ (Rom 1:1; Gal 1:10; Phil 1:1; Titus 1:1) or his minister (διάκονος, 1 Cor 3:5; 2 Cor 3:6; 11:23; Col 1:23),[112] to designate One whom Paul confesses to be Lord of all as a servant—and especially as a slave—would seem to be a quite demeaning. Where would Paul find the idea that Jesus took the form of a servant? Stanton suggests that עַבְדִּי of Isa 53:11 hovers in the background ("By His knowledge the Righteous One, My Servant, will justify the many."), so that δοῦλος points to the "portrait of the obedient righteous man of Judaism of which Isaiah 53 is the supreme example."[113] Yet, more to the point, the identification must derive from Jesus Himself, who not only commended servant status of His disciples,[114] but He presented Himself as the penultimate example of service: "For even the Son of Man did not come to be served, but to serve" (Matt 20:28 || Mark 10:45). Whether Paul cites another early creed or hymn in this section of Philippians, as many think,[115] he certainly shows knowledge of Jesus as Servant—a very condescending title to give to one who is his Lord—unless, of course, the concept originated with the "Man Christ Jesus" Himself.

The Transfiguration of Jesus

One of most significant events of the ministry of Jesus occurred when He was transfigured (μετεμορφώθη) before His disciples on the mountain (Matt 17:1–8; Mark 9:1–8; Luke 9:28–36), at which time the Father repeated the words uttered at His baptism, "This is My beloved Son, with whom I am well-pleased; listen to Him!" (Matt 17:5). Certainly, Paul cannot claim to be either an eye-witness or an ear-witness to the Transfiguration in the manner Peter later verifies his participation in this experience and rejects any manipula-

---

112. The noun διάκονος is broadly used of an agent or assistant who acts at the behest of a superior (BDAG § 1858) while δοῦλος more specifically defines a slave under another's total control (BDAG § 2089).

113. Stanton, *Jesus of Nazareth in New Testament Preaching*, 105.

114. Jesus commends servanthood in Matt 23:11 ("Whoever wishes to become great among you shall be your servant. But the greatest among you shall be your servant"); in Mark 9:35 ("If anyone wants to be first, he shall be last of all, and servant of all" and Mark 10:44, "Whoever wishes to become great among you shall be your servant; and whoever wishes to be first among you shall be slave of all."

115. See the careful investigation of Phil 2:7 in Martin, *A Hymn of Christ*, loc. cit.

tion by "cleverly devised tales" (2 Pet 1:16–19). Even so, Paul's use of the unusual word μεταμορφόω in 2 Cor 3:18 may suggest that he has the Transfiguration in mind when he writes, "But we all, with unveiled face beholding as in a mirror the glory of the Lord, are being transformed (μεταμορφούμεθα) into the same image from glory to glory, just as from the Lord, the Spirit" (2 Cor 3:18).[116] This connection is strengthened when the physical transformation of Jesus is described in language similar to the appearance of Jesus to Paul on the Damascus Road; for example, Matt 17:2 reports that "His face shone *like the sun*" (ἔλαμψεν ὡς ὁ ἥλιος) and "His garments became as white *as light*" (τὸ φῶς). When Paul saw the Risen Lord, he uses these same words, "I saw on the way *a light* (φῶς) from heaven, brighter than *the sun*, shining all around me" (περιλάμψαν με, Acts 26:13). He also recounted seeing "the glory of the light" (τῆς δόξης τοῦ φωτὸς, Acts 22:11), a phrase suggesting Jesus' "appearance in glory" (ὀφθέντες ἐν δόξῃ, Luke 9:31). While these grammatical similarities may be nothing more than coincidental, it is possible to argue they are intentional, since they both describe a heavenly appearance of the same person, the "Man Christ Jesus."

The Teachings of Jesus

An area of great difficulty in Paul's letters arises due to the scarcity of references to the teachings of Jesus. Shaw insists that the reason for this dearth is that the two men had nothing in common, claiming, "There is not one word of Pauline Christianity in the characteristic utterances of Jesus."[117] Kim notes that when one moves from the Gospels to the Pauline letters, one is "struck by the virtual absence of quotations or sayings of Jesus."[118] Furthermore, Paul's emphasis on the Gospel message centering on the death and resurrection of Jesus as the primary saving events differs quite considerably from Jesus' preaching of the Kingdom, so one must wonder about this seeming disparity.[119] Still, in 1 Tim 6:3, Paul cautions his disciple to beware of those who "do not agree with sound words, those of our Lord Jesus Christ." He assumes that Timothy would know the content and location of the *logia* of grace that fell from Jesus' lips, causing audiences to marvel (Luke 4:22). It should be remembered that Paul could not quote the Gospels in his letters since he wrote before their completion. This means that any reference to Jesus' teachings had to

---

116. Barnett, *Paul: Missionary of Jesus*, 19, points out that the unusual verb μεταμορφόω appears only in the account of Jesus' physical transfiguration (Matt 17:2 and Mark 9:2) and in Paul's expectation of the believer's spiritual transformation (Rom 12:2 and 2 Cor 3:18).

117. Shaw, "The Monstrous Imposition upon Jesus," 299.

118. Kim, "Jesus, Sayings of," 474. Even Köstenberger, "Diversity and Unity in the New Testament," 146, makes this surprising admission, "Without involving Jesus and Paul in actual contradictions, we should lay more stress on the discontinuity between these two pivotal figures, primarily owing to the different stages in salvation history they inhabited and to the different roles they had to fulfill as a result." This could be better stated that one should lay more stress on the advancement and explanation of ideas from Jesus to Paul.

119. However, Wenham, *Paul: Follower of Jesus or Founder of Christianity?*, 34–103, shows that Paul is clearly familiar with the concept of the Kingdom (mentioned in Rom 14:17; 1 Cor 4:20; 6:9–10; 15:24, 50; Gal 5:21; Eph 5:5; Col 1:13; 4:11; 1 Thess 2:12; 2 Thess 1:5; 2 Tim 4:1, 18; plus Pauline comments in Acts 14:22, 19:8, 20:25, 28:23 and 31.).

come from earlier tradition,[120] of which many individuals had previously undertaken to compile, according to Luke 1:1. Despite this vast resource available to Paul, Furnish as a minimalist maintains that the apostle clearly cites Jesus' teaching only on three occasions (1 Cor 7:10; 9:14; 11:23–25),[121] while at the other extreme, Resch as a maximalist counts well over a thousand allusions to Jesus' teaching in Paul's epistles![122] Kim, as a "moderatist," suggests thirty-one possible quotes and echoes of sayings of Jesus by Paul,[123] illustrating how remarkable it is that competent scholars can vary so dramatically in this matter. Not surprisingly, those who maintain continuity between Jesus and Paul find more similarities, while those who posit discontinuity find fewer.[124] Since Hays has demonstrated that the NT frequently echoes the OT without designating a particular passage,[125] this study suggests that Paul does the same with the *logia* of Jesus, which John 21:25 implies was such a far larger pool of information that even "the world itself would not contain the books which were written–" vindicating Resch as closer to the correct estimate.

More recent studies in tracing the Jesus-traditions throughout Paul's letters, an approach taken by David Wenham,[126] have proven to be quite beneficial. F. F. Bruce also contributed by observing the ethical similarities of Rom 12:1–15 with the Sermon on the Mount, showing "how thoroughly imbued the apostle was with his Master's teaching" so that "even where he (Paul) does not quote actual sayings of Jesus, he shows himself well acquainted with the substance of many of them."[127] After citing several probable allusions to Jesus' teaching, Dunn calls the claim "much disputed . . . that Paul was not interested in

---

120. As noted by Thompson, *Clothed with Christ: The Example and Teaching of Jesus in Romans 12.1–15.13*, 71.

121. Furnish, *Jesus According to Paul*, 40–65. Ehrman, *The New Testament*, 333, even narrows the quotes of Jesus to one, as he is not sure about 1 Cor 7:10 and 9:14. He does, however, find similar sayings on paying taxes (Rom 13:7 with Mark 12:17) and loving ones neighbor (Gal 5:14 with Matt 22:39–40), yet he adds, "Paul gives no indication that he knows that Jesus himself spoke these words" (ibid.).

122. Resch, *Der Paulinismus und die Logia Jesu in ihrem gegenseitigen Verhaltnis untersucht* (1904). In the course of this research, it was noted that Resch is frequently mentioned by scholars but usually dismissed out of hand, probably because he claimed to find a number of unknown sayings of Jesus in Paul's letters and elsewhere; however, his linguistic comparisons between Paul and the rest of the NT are painstakingly thorough and remain the standard by which all subsequent studies should be measured.

123. Kim, "Jesus, Sayings of," 481.

124. See other studies on Paul's use of Jesus' teaching: Addley, "The Sayings of Jesus in the Epistles of Paul" (1971); Dungan, *The Sayings of Jesus in the Churches of Paul: The Use of the Synoptic Tradition in the Regulation of Early Church Life* (1971); Wenham, ed., *The Jesus Tradition outside the Gospels* (1984); Calvert, "An Examination of the Criteria for Distinguishing the Authentic Words of Jesus," 209–19; Gerhardsson, *Memory and Manuscript: Oral Tradition in Rabbinic Judaism and Early Christianity* with *Tradition and Transmission in Early Christianity* (1998), 288–323; Lindemann, "Paulus und die JesusTradition" (2008), 281–316; Neirynck, "Paul and the Sayings of Jesus" (1986), 265–321; Stanley, "Pauline Allusions to the Sayings of Jesus," 26–39; Stuhlmacher, "Jesustradition im Römerbrief: Eine Skizze?", 240–50; Walter, "Paul and the Early Christian Jesus-Tradition," 51–80.

125. Hays, *Echoes of Scripture in the Letters of Paul* (1989).

126. See Wenham, *Paul: Follower of Jesus or Founder of Christianity?*, as well as his earlier edited work, *The Jesus Tradition Outside the Gospels* (1984).

127. Bruce, *Paul Apostle of the Heart Set Free*, 96. He notes in *Paul and Jesus* the agreement of Paul and Jesus on justification by grace (ibid., 56–61), on the Father and the Spirit (ibid., 61), and on salvation history (ibid., 62–67). See also Bedard, "Paul and the Historical Jesus: A Case Study in First Corinthians," 9–22.

THE "MAN CHRIST JESUS"

Jesus' pre-passion ministry . . . ,"[128] although he asks the pertinent question, if Paul knew the Jesus-traditions, why did he not identify them as such?[129] Paul seems to provide his own reason for not citing Jesus more often, when he distinguishes his teaching from that of Jesus, stating, "I give instructions, not I, but the Lord, . . . but to the rest I say, not the Lord'" (1 Cor 7:10, 12); in other words, if Jesus had spoken on an issue, there was no need for Paul to mention that fact, assuming that his readers had some general knowledge of that tradition. Also, it should be noted that Paul only cites a saying of Jesus in particular situations that both shared in common, thus accounting for the infrequent quotations, since Paul addresses far more pastoral and ethical issues among his Gentile converts than Jesus did among his Jewish listeners, who would have shared with Him a common knowledge of the OT. Jesus had no occasion to discuss the merits of Gentile circumcision, table fellowship with Gentiles, foods offered to idols, or the rampant immorality among the Roman and Greek world, matters that occupy Paul quite extensively.[130] Paul obviously cannot cite Jesus on matters He never discussed. Imagine the railings of Paul's critics if the apostle had concluded his arguments with supposed quotes from Jesus that were not verified in the Gospels! Paul could then be legitimately charged with invoking the name of Jesus in support of his own teachings, an indictment of pseudonymity in the least, although Paul emphatically denies all such dishonesty (Rom 9:1; 2 Cor 11:31; Gal 1:20; 1 Tim 2:7).[131] Taken in canonical order, then, this study shall distinguish the specific references made by Paul to Jesus' teachings from the more likely allusions, based on linguistic and contextual similarities.

Specified References to the Teachings of Jesus

In this examination, "the first step should be to consider those places where Paul cites sayings of Jesus *explicitly*"[132] by using statements collaborated in the Gospels. Although the apostle claims "that the things which I write to you are the Lord's commandment"

---

128. Dunn, *The Theology of Paul*, 651, lists these echoes of the Jesus-Tradition in Paul: (1) that Jesus preached the gospel; (2) that Jesus preached the kingdom, and Paul preached its arrival in the Spirit (Rom 14:17); (3) that Jesus shared table fellowship with sinners; (4) that believers practice the same "abba" prayer with Jesus (Rom 8:15–17; Gal 4:6–5); and (5) that there are echoes to Jesus' ministry below the surface, such as Christ being used as a moral example (Rom 15:1–5; 1 Cor 11:12; Rom 6:17, the "type of teaching").

129. Ibid., 652.

130. Bird, *Introducing Paul*, 144, suggests that the paucity of references to what Jesus taught "is explainable on the ground that the issues Paul encountered, such as circumcision, criteria of Apostleship, and how to facilitate Jew-Gentile fellowship did not feature much as part of Jesus' teaching in Galilee and Judea."

131. Wilder, *Pseudonymity, the New Testament, and Deception: An Inquiry into Intention and Reception*, 146, finds that "where a work was known to be pseudonymous, the early church rejected and excluded it from the writings they recognized as normative."

132. Dungan, *The Sayings of Jesus in the Churches of Paul*, xxx. Beyond the citations in Paul's letters and the Damascus Road conversation, Acts 18:9–10 cites a direct revelation from Jesus to Paul ("And the Lord said to Paul in the night by a vision, 'Do not be afraid *any longer*, but go on speaking and do not be silent; for I am with you, and no man will attack you in order to harm you, for I have many people in this city.'"), plus Paul cites an otherwise unprovenanced saying of Jesus in Acts 20:35, "Remember the words of the Lord Jesus, that He Himself said, 'It is more blessed to give than to receive.'" Paul also quotes a direct revelation from Jesus in 2 Cor 12:9, "And He said to me, 'My grace is sufficient for you, for power is perfected in weakness.'"

The "Man Christ Jesus" in the Epistles of Paul

(1 Cor 14:37), Paul specifically refers to such sayings of Jesus at least six times, in Rom 14:14; 1 Cor 7:10; 9:14; 1 Tim 5:18; 1 Cor 11:23–25; and 1 Thess 4:15.[133]

The first occurs in Rom 14:14, when Paul asserts, "I know and am convinced in the Lord Jesus that nothing is unclean in itself." Thompson declares, "A dominical echo is virtually certain,"[134] because the preposition ἐν can sometimes have the instrumental meaning (as in Rom 15:19),[135] so that Paul could mean, "I am convinced *by* the Lord Jesus;" that is, by His teaching as recorded in Mark 7:19 (|| Matt 15:11) when "He declared all foods clean." The likelihood of a reference to Jesus surely fits the context in Romans 14 where Paul is discussing table fellowship among Jewish and Gentile believers. Also, Paul assumes the same declaration of Jesus toward food in Col 2:21–22, where he discusses how food perishes "in accordance with the commandments and teachings of men," echoing a similar indictment of Jesus, "But in vain do they worship Me, teaching as doctrines the precepts of men" (Mark 7:7, quoting from Isa 29:13).

In 1 Cor 7:10, Paul plainly quotes Jesus: "But to the married I give instructions, not I, *but the Lord*, that the wife should not leave (μὴ χωρισθῆναι) her husband," echoing the saying of Jesus, "What therefore God has joined together, let no man separate" (μὴ χωριζέτω, Mark 10:9), with a clarification in Mark 10:12, "If she herself divorces her husband and marries another man, she is committing adultery." Dunn thinks Paul cites this saying because He is going *beyond* (his italics) what Jesus taught on divorce,[136] but Paul carefully distinguishes his own counsel from the more authoritative teaching of Jesus in 1 Cor 7:12, "I say, not the Lord." Akenson insists that Paul is correcting a "*halachah* of Yeshua," which was far stricter than Paul allowed,[137] but Dodd rightly notes, "That Paul did not confuse his spiritual revelations with the tradition is clear from his discussion on the ethics of sex in 1 Corinthians vii."[138] In fact, Dungan argues that Paul seems to allude to the entire Synoptic account (Matt 19:10–12; Mark 10:11–12; Luke 16:18) within this context,[139] indicating that Paul was using a larger Jesus-tradition that also goes back to the original teachings of Jesus. Longenecker observes by this reference in 1 Cor 7:10 that Paul not only knew of a collection of Jesus' sayings but also his Gentiles converts knew it well enough to know what it contained (when Paul quotes Jesus) and what it did not contain, "where He goes beyond the recorded teaching of Jesus and attempts to contextualize the Christian gospel with respect to the problems faced by his converts."[140]

---

133. Dungan, ibid., xxxii, limits his inquiry to only two sayings (1 Cor 7:10 and 9:14), but this study recognizes that Paul makes a specific appeal to Jesus in the other four passages.

134. Thompson, *Clothed with Christ*, 199.

135. Romans 15:18–19 reads, "Christ has accomplished . . . by word and deed, in the power of signs and wonders, in the power of the Spirit" (ἐν δυνάμει σημείων καὶ τεράτων, ἐν δυνάμει πνεύματος).

136. Dunn, *Theology of Paul*, 562.

137. Akenson, *Saint Saul*, 182, calls what Paul does in 1 Cor 7:10–11 a subversion of the teaching of Jesus, feeling that "he is himself a more skilled teacher of the written and oral Torah than is Yeshua." If so, surely the Corinthian community would have called his hand and rejected his arrogant presumption.

138. Dodd, *History and the Gospel*, 57.

139. Dungan, *The Sayings of Jesus in the Churches of Paul*, 132.

140. Longenecker, "Christological Materials in Early Christian Communities," 65.

THE "MAN CHRIST JESUS"

Next, in support of his own apostleship, Paul cites Jesus directly in 1 Cor 9:14, "So also the Lord directed those who proclaim the gospel to get their living from the gospel." This comment paraphrases the saying of Jesus, "The worker is worthy of his support" (ἄξιος γὰρ ὁ ἐργάτης τῆς τροφῆς αὐτοῦ, Matt 10:10 ‖ Luke 10:7), which appears in the context of the sending out of the twelve (Τούτους τοὺς δώδεκα ἀπέστειλεν ὁ Ἰησοῦς, Matt 10:5) and the seventy (Luke 10:1).[141] Dunn claims—without any explanation—that Paul quotes Jesus because he *disregards* what Jesus commanded,[142] but Bruce notes that Paul is not ignoring Jesus; rather, he is choosing to forgo a privilege Christ extends to his workers to accept payment for his ministry, that he might offer the gospel without charge, so as not to make full use of his authority in the gospel (1 Cor 9:18).[143]

Quite significantly, Paul later quotes this same saying of Jesus in 1 Tim 5:18 without citing his source yet calling it "Scripture" and prefacing it in parallel with Deut 25:4 (οὐ φιμώσεις βοῦν ἀλοῶντα), "For the Scripture says, "You shall not muzzle the ox while He is threshing" (Paul changes the word order to βοῦν ἀλοῶντα οὐ φιμώσεις). To this OT quote Paul then adds, "The laborer is worthy of his wages" (ἄξιος ὁ ἐργάτης τοῦ μισθοῦ αὐτοῦ). This saying is a verbatim quotation of Luke 10:7 (ἄξιος γὰρ ὁ ἐργάτης τοῦ μισθοῦ αὐτοῦ), suggesting that Paul was referencing a *written* collection of sayings of Jesus which Luke later employed in his Gospel, as he stated in his preface (Luke 1:1–4).

The next citation of Jesus' teaching appears in 1 Cor 11:23–25, when Paul confirms, "For I received from the Lord that which I also delivered to you, that the Lord Jesus in the night in which He was betrayed took bread; and when He had given thanks, He broke it, and said, 'This is My body, which is for you; do this in remembrance of Me.' In the same way *He took* the cup also, after supper, saying, 'This cup is the new covenant in My blood; do this, as often as you drink *it*, in remembrance of Me.'" Although Maccoby and Wilson think that Paul is the "inventor and creator of the Eucharist,"[144] the terminology makes it clear that Paul echoes the words of Jesus—not via a direct revelation from the Risen Lord, as Watson argues[145]—but as recorded in Matt 26:26–28 and Mark 14:22–24, although "what Paul cites is almost verbatim with what appears in Luke's Gospel" in Luke 22:17–20.[146] It is apparent that Paul is not meaning by "received from the Lord" that his knowledge came by way of special revelation (as in Gal 1:12) but rather as information

---

141. Wenham, *Paul and Jesus*, 157, notes the likelihood that Paul refers to Jesus' teaching in that both contexts concern support of those who proclaim the gospel with the specific right to food and drink. Wenham, *Paul: Follower of Jesus or Founder of Christianity?*, 199, finds at least eleven items in Paul's letters that are also located in the mission discourses of Jesus.

142. Dunn, *Theology of Paul*, 653.

143. Bruce, *Paul and Jesus*, 73.

144. Maccoby, *The Mythmaker*, 113; also Wilson, *Paul*, 165–66. It is incredible that Paul could invent such a crucial doctrine as Christ's sacrificial death and foist it upon the apostolic church with apparent full acceptance and nary an objection until the fourth century by the Ebionites, as reported by Epiphanius of Salamis, *Panarion*, 30.

145. Watson, "'I Received from the Lord . . . :' Paul, Jesus and the Last Supper," 123. Watson does not adequately answer why Paul would use the terminology of receiving and delivering tradition if this saying was given to him by direct revelation.

146. Fee, *Pauline Christology*, 526.

transmitted through oral or written tradition, as the terminology of "receiving/delivering tradition" verifies (1 Cor 11:2; 15:1-3; 1 Thess 2:13; 4:1; 2 Thess 2:15; 3:6).[147] This process would indicate that the historical Jesus is the ultimate source of this saying in 1 Cor 11:23- 25.[148] The importance of this quote indicates that Paul is not the inventor of a sacrificial theology overlaid on Jesus' death, but that he received what had been originated by Jesus Himself and had been practiced from the beginning by the apostolic community in the *klasis,* the "breaking of the bread" (Acts 2:42; 20:7).

In 1 Thess 4:15, Paul remarks, "For this we say to you *by the word of the Lord*, that we who are alive, and remain until the coming of the Lord, shall not precede those who have fallen asleep." As no specific quote on this subject can be located in the Gospels, we can rightly ask, where did Paul discover this information on the return of Jesus? May he have received it by direct revelation, or may he be citing an unwritten *agraphon* (like the saying in Acts 20:35)? More likely, he is making implications from a common source of Jesus' teachings about His return, of which there is a large amount included in the Gospels.[149] What Akenson calls but an "indirect reference" actually finds many direct grammatical similarities in the teachings of Jesus,[150] especially in the Olivet Discourse.[151] Clearly, Paul does not invent sayings of Jesus. Instead, he appeals here to the authority of Jesus on eschatological doctrine in this particular issue by explaining what happens to those living at the *parousia* of the Lord. Behind his appeal lays the same issue to which Jesus spoke in Matt 24:39-40, that at the *parousia* of the Son of Man, "There shall be two men in the field; one will be taken, and one will be left."[152] From the fact that the living shall be taken

---

147. See Stephen O. Stout, "The New Testament Concept of Tradition," 49–104.

148. Ibid., 43. Machen, *Origin of Paul's Religion,* 148, understands "I received from the Lord," not as direct revelation, but in the manner Paul uses the same verb in 1 Cor 15:3, where it refers to ordinary information obtained from eyewitnesses. Machen asks, "Why should the risen Christ give to His Apostle detailed information which could be obtained perfectly well by ordinary inquiry from the eyewitnesses?"

149. See Kim, "The Jesus Tradition in I Thess 4.13–5:11," 225–42; and Longenecker, "Christological Materials in Early Christian Communities," 55–60, who points out, "Futuristic eschatology in these passages functions much as it does in the Old Testament—that is, as a prophetic summons to a seriousness of purpose, a life lived in holiness and justice, and a watchful expectation that awaits God's future actions. The only real difference in the NT eschatological passages is that the prophetic call is christologically oriented, with a focus on the parousia or 'coming' of Christ."

150. Akenson, *Saint Saul,* 220.

151. There are quite remarkable points of agreement and even identical vocabulary shared by 1 Thess 4:15-17 and the various eschatological sayings of Jesus: "the coming of the Lord" → Matt 24:27, "just as the lightning comes from the east, and flashes even to the west, so shall the *coming* of the Son of Man be; "from heaven"→ Matt 24:30 (ESV), "Then will appear in *heaven* the sign of the Son of Man;" the dead as sleeping → John 11:13; "Now Jesus had spoken of His death, but they thought that He was speaking of literal sleep;" "with a shout"→ Matt 25:6, "But at midnight there was a *shout*, 'Behold, the bridegroom!';" "the voice of the archangel" → Matt 25:31, "And He will send forth His *angels*;" "But when the Son of Man comes in His glory, and all the *angels* with Him;" "the trumpet"→ Matt 24:31, "And He will send forth His angels with a great *trumpet*;" the resurrection of dead ones → Matt 22:31; living believers on earth snatched up → Matt 24:30-31, "the Son of Man shall send forth His angels with a great trumpet to gather His elect;" Christ coming in *clouds* → Matt 24:30, "they will see the Son of Man coming on the *clouds* of the sky with power and great glory;" and, a meeting with the Lord → Matt 25:6, "Come out to *meet* him." See the discussion in Wenham, *Paul: Follower of Jesus or Founder of Christianity?,* 307–11.

152. Wenham, *Paul: Follower of Jesus or Founder of Christianity?,* 332–33.

THE "MAN CHRIST JESUS"

at the Lord's coming to be united with those who have "fallen asleep," Paul makes the implication that believers who have died must already be with the Lord.

These six references indicate that Paul not only knew various sayings of Jesus, but he cited them in ways that implied the larger contexts of the statements as eventually written in the Gospels. Dungan concludes his study, "Paul's concrete application of these traditional sayings of the Lord in the context of his churches fits almost perfectly into a general pattern of similar interpretation and application of the same sayings in the church of his day, as typified by the three Synoptic editors."[153]

Linguistic Similarities to the Teachings of Jesus

Having established a pattern of Paul's references to Jesus' teachings that imply the broader context, one begins to note numerous similarities in Paul's vocabulary with the teachings of Jesus. While these likenesses may be nothing more than grammatical coincidences, a number of them bear a striking resemblance in doctrinal affinity as well. Following, then, is a compilation and brief discussion of the more obvious allusions and echoes to the teachings of Jesus as found in Paul's letters, listed generally in canonical order:[154]

One such echo is the unexpected appearance of the Aramaic word *abba* (אבא) in Rom 8:15 ("you have received a spirit of adoption as sons by which we cry out, 'Abba! Father!'") and in Gal 4:6 ("because you are sons, God has sent forth the Spirit of His Son into our hearts, crying, 'Abba! Father!'"), which Paul helpfully translates for his readers.[155] This term of endearment for "father" is the cry of a son for his "papa," and it hardly seems reverent as a title for God, yet that is precisely how Paul uses it. The only other appearance of ἀββά in the NT is found in Mark 14:36, when Jesus was agonizing in the Garden of Gethsemane and was crying out, "Abba! Father!" Paul's use of ἀββά leads Wenham to observe, "It is easy for us to miss the oddness of Paul writing in Greek to Greek-speaking readers and describing the Christian cry as 'Abba' (in Aramaic). But the obvious explanation is that the cry goes back to Jesus, for whom Aramaic was almost certainly His first language, and that it became a specially treasured part of the Christian tradition."[156]

---

153. Dungan, *The Sayings of Jesus in the Churches of Paul*, 141.

154. Thompson, *Clothed with Christ*, 30, defines allusions as "statements which are intended to remind an audience of a tradition they are presumed to know as dominical; clear examples by this definition are 1 Cor 7.10 and 9.14. 'Echo' or 'reminiscence'... refer to cases where the influence of a dominical tradition upon Paul seems evident, but where it remains uncertain whether he was conscious of the influence at the time of dictating." Thompson gives the following criteria for evaluating allusions and echoes: (a) verbal agreement; (b) conceptual agreement; (c) formal agreement (Rom 16:19 and Matt 10:16); (d) the place of the Gospel saying in the tradition; (e) common motivation; (f) dissimilarity to Greco-Roman and Jewish traditions; (g) presence of dominical indicators (Rom 14:14); (h) presence of tradition indicators (1 Cor 6:9); (i) presence of other dominical echoes or word clusters in the immediate context; (j) likelihood the author knew the saying; and (k) exegetical value. A full study of such echoes is far beyond the purposes of this study: for a thorough treatment, one should consult Resch, *Der Paulinismus und die Logia Jesu*.

155. BDAG § 6, "ἀββα (accented ἀββά in W-H. and N.25; others ἀββᾶ; Aram. אבא vocative form, orig. a term of endearment, later used as a title and personal name; rarely used in ref. to God), *father*."

156. Wenham, *Paul and the Historical Jesus*, 5. He further elaborates in *Paul: Follower of Jesus or Founder of Christianity?*, 278–79, how the inclusion of the same words "abba, flesh as weak, spirit" in Rom 8:16 suggest also parallels to the Gethsemane experience.

The "Man Christ Jesus" in the Epistles of Paul

Machen points out how the commonality of *abba* between Jesus and Paul shows that both share the same concept of God as Father in such an endearing manner, which is quite a coincidence, unless Paul was consciously alluding to the words of Jesus.

One who is familiar with the teachings of Jesus will immediately notice similarities throughout Paul's entire discussion in Romans 12–15. Michael Thompson in his careful study of this section shows how it echoes the teachings of Jesus from the Sermon on the Mount in particular (Matthew 5–7), as well as the Sermon on the Plain (Luke 6:20–49) and the Olivet Discourse (Matthew 24–25).[157] For example, Paul's admonishment in Rom 12:14, "Bless those who persecute you; bless and curse," certainly parallels Jesus' commands, "Bless those who curse you; pray for those who mistreat you" (Luke 6:28 || Matt 5:44). The same can be said for Rom 12:17, "Never pay back evil for evil to anyone" (μὴ δενὶ κακὸν ἀντὶ κακοῦ ἀποδιδόντες), which reflects the saying of Jesus in Matt 5:39, "I say to you, do not resist him who is evil" (ἐγὼ δὲ λέγω ὑμῖν μὴ ἀντιστῆναι τῷ πονηρῷ)." Even clearer is the dependence of Rom 12:18, "If possible, so far as it depends on you, be at peace with all men" (μετὰ πάντων ἀνθρώπων εἰρηνεύοντες·) with Mark 9:50, "Be at peace with one another" (καὶ εἰρηνεύετε ἐν ἀλλήλοις). When Rom 12:19–21 ("Do not be overcome by evil, but overcome evil with good;" μὴ νικῶ ὑπὸ τοῦ κακοῦ ἀλλὰ νίκα ἐν τῷ ἀγαθῷ τὸ κακόν) is compared to Jesus' sayings in Luke 6:27 ("Love your enemies, do good to those who hate you") and Luke 6:35 ("But love your enemies, and do good"), more echoes surface.

In the thirteenth chapter of Romans, Paul commands, "Render to all what is due them" (ἀπόδοτε πᾶσιν τὰς ὀφειλάς, 13:7), and Bruce calls this Paul's "generalization of Jesus answer in Mark 12:17, "Render to Caesar the things that are Caesar's, and to God the things that are God's" (τὰ Καίσαρος ἀπόδοτε Καίσαρι καὶ τὰ τοῦ θεοῦ τῷ θεῷ).[158]

In Rom 13:9 ("If there is any other commandment, it is summed up in this saying, 'You shall love your neighbor as yourself.'"), Paul summarizes the Decalogue (Deut 5:17–21) exactly as Jesus did when he also quoted Lev 19:18, "You shall love your neighbor as yourself; on these two commandments depend the whole Law and the Prophets" (refer also to Matt 19:18–19; 22:39–40; Mark 10:19; 12:31; Luke 18:20). Because Rom 13:9 lacks any specific appeal to Jesus or any dominical indicators, Thompson claims that the "allusion here at best is only a possibility,"[159] but the teaching is certainly identical.[160] Similarities are also observed between Rom 13:11–14 and Mark 13:33–37 in the matter of spiritual slumber in face of the Lord's coming,[161] and Paul's warnings against judging

---

157. Thompson, *Clothed with Christ: The Example and Teaching of Jesus in Romans 12.1–15.13.*

158. Bruce, *Paul,* 109. Thompson, *Clothed with Christ,* 119, says of Rom 13:7, "A dominical echo is probable; an allusion, possible at best."

159. Thompson, *Clothed with Christ,* 139.

160. Ellis, *Paul's Use of the Old Testament,* 88. The same idea re-appears in Gal 5:14, "For the whole Law is fulfilled in one word, in the *statement,* 'You shall love your neighbor as yourself.'" This explanation seems to be the meaning of "the law of Christ" Paul mentions in Gal 6:2 and 1 Cor 9:21.

161. Romans 13:11, "It is already the hour for you to awaken from sleep; for now salvation is nearer to us than when we believed;" and Mark 13:35–36, "You do not know when the master of the house is coming, whether in the evening, at midnight, at cockcrowing, or in the morning–lest He come suddenly and find you asleep."

(Rom 14:4, 10, 13; Μηκέτι οὖν ἀλλήλους κρίνωμεν) reflect the same command of Jesus in Luke 6:37, "Do not judge and you will not be judged" (μὴ κρίνετε, καὶ οὐ μὴ κριθῆτε). Both Jesus and Paul share the same condemnation of "stumbling-blocks" who cause offences (Rom 14:13, τὸ μὴ τιθέναι πρόσκομμα τῷ ἀδελφῷ ἢ σκάνδαλον, with Matt 18:6; Mark 9:42; Luke 17:2), leading Thompson to surmise, "Paul has probably been influenced by the teaching of Jesus, but he has not drawn attention to the origin of the thought."[162] Actually, the apostle does draw attention to the source of these moral precepts when he states in the next verse, Rom 14:14, "I know and am convinced *in the Lord Jesus* that nothing is unclean in itself" (italics added). By this assertion, Paul cites the authority of his ethical instruction: it is the kingdom preaching of Jesus, as he reminds his readers in Rom 14:17 that "the kingdom of God is not eating and drinking, but righteousness and peace and joy in the Holy Spirit." The apostle thereby emphasizes the same spiritual essence of the kingdom as taught by Jesus, "If I cast out demons by the Spirit of God, then the kingdom of God has come upon you" (Matt 12:28) and from his answer to Nicodemus, "Truly, truly, I say to you, unless one is born of water and the Spirit, he cannot enter into the kingdom of God" (John 3:5). Thompson recognizes this significance by claiming, "Here Paul's decisive criterion corresponds to an emphasis of the historical Jesus."[163]

What Thompson claims for these allusions and echoes in Romans 12–15, that "the cumulative effect . . . favors the conclusion that dominical teachings significantly influenced Paul,"[164] may be extended to all his letters. Thus, Wenham notes the verbal parallels between 1 Corinthians 1–2 with the prayer of Jesus found in Matt 11:25–27.[165] He also observes that Paul's reminder in 1 Cor 4:5 that "the Lord will bring to light the things hidden in the darkness and disclose the motives of *men's* hearts"[166] sounds much like the warning of Jesus, recorded in Mark 4:22, "For nothing is hidden, except to be revealed."[167] Also, Walter finds what he calls a "nest" of Jesus' sayings in 1 Cor 4:11–13. There in Paul's cry of deprivation, "To this present hour we are both hungry and thirsty" (ἄχρι τῆς ἄρτι ὥρας καὶ πεινῶμεν καὶ διψῶμεν, 1 Cor 4:11) one can hear the Lord's beatitude, "Blessed are those who hunger and thirst for righteousness" (Matt 5:6, μακάριοι οἱ πεινῶντες καὶ διψῶντες τὴν δικαιοσύνην).[168] Paul's portrayal of ministry-suffering in 1 Cor 4:12b–13 ("We toil, working with our own hands; when we are reviled, we bless; when we are persecuted, we endure; when we are slandered, we try to conciliate; we have become as the scum of the world, the dregs of all things, *even* until now.") reflects the description of ministry-suffering in the words of Jesus, "Blessed are you when men hate you, and ostra-

---

162. Thompson, *Clothed with Christ*, 184.

163. Ibid., 207.

164. Ibid., 238.

165. Wenham, *Paul: Follower of Jesus?*, 130–31.

166. The Greek text reads, ὃς καὶ φωτίσει τὰ κρυπτὰ τοῦ σκότους καὶ φανερώσει τὰς βουλὰς τῶν καρδιῶν, and it is essentially repeated in 1 Cor 14:25, that "the secrets of his heart are disclosed" (τὰ κρυπτὰ τῆς καρδίας αὐτοῦ φανερὰ γίνεται).

167. The Greek text of Mark 4:22 reads, οὐ γάρ ἐστιν κρυπτὸν ἐὰν μὴ ἵνα φανερωθῇ which is identical in Matt 10:26 ‖ Luke 8:17.

168. Walter, "Paul and the Early Christian Jesus-Tradition," 56.

cize you, and cast insults at you, and spurn your name as evil, for the sake of the Son of Man. "Be glad in that day, and leap *for joy*, for behold, your reward is great in heaven; for in the same way their fathers used to treat the prophets" (Luke 6:22–23).

Also, in 1 Cor 6:16 and Eph 5:31, Paul quotes Gen 2:24 ("The two will become one flesh;" οἱ δύο εἰς σάρκα μίαν) and applies it exactly as Jesus does in Matt 19:5 ‖ Mark 10:7–8. When Paul understands Exod 17:6 typologically ("They were drinking from a spiritual rock which followed them; and the rock was Christ, " 1 Cor 10:4), he may have in mind the comparison Jesus makes of Himself as "living water" from whom one should drink (John 4:10; 6:37), especially since Jesus also applies aspects of the Exodus to Himself (John 6:31).[169] The principle Paul writes in 1 Cor 10:27, "If one of the unbelievers invites you, and you wish to go, eat anything that is set before you" (πᾶν τὸ παρατιθέμενον ὑμῖν ἐσθίετε) appears to be a quotation of the command of Jesus, "And whatever city you enter, and they receive you, eat what is set before you" (ἐσθίετε τὰ παρατιθέμενα ὑμῖν, Luke 10:27). If Paul is quoting Jesus' instruction to the seventy, he shows how "he is generalizing from a particular occasion to a recurring situation."[170]

Three possible allusions to Jesus' sayings surface in 1 Cor 13:2–3. First, when Paul writes, "If I have all faith, so as to remove mountains, but do not have love, I am nothing," one hears an echo of the words of Jesus, "If you have faith as a mustard seed, you shall say to this mountain, 'Move from here to there,' and it shall move" (Matt 17:20; also 21:21); secondly, when Paul claims in 1 Cor 13:2, "If I know all mysteries," an echo of Matt 13:11 is heard: "To you it has been granted to know the mysteries of the kingdom of heaven;" and thirdly, when Paul states in 1 Cor 13:3, "If I give away all my possessions," one hears the commands of Jesus to the young ruler, "If you wish to be complete, go *and* sell your possessions and give to *the* poor" (Matt 19:21).[171]

In 2 Cor 1:17–18, Paul attests, "As God is faithful, our word to you is not yes and no," alluding no doubt to the command of Jesus, "But let your statement be, 'Yes, yes' *or* 'No, no'; and anything beyond these is of evil" (Matt 5:37). Even though Jesus probably uttered this order in Aramaic while Paul wrote it in Greek, Wenham comments, "The verbal similarity between these sayings is sufficiently striking to alert us to the possibility of some connection between them."[172] Later in 2 Cor 13:1, Paul quotes from Deut 19:15, "Every fact is to be confirmed by the testimony of two or three witnesses," citing it exactly as Jesus does in Matt 18:16, "But if he does not listen *to you*, take one or two more with you, so that by the mouth of two or three witnesses every fact may be confirmed," showing

---

169. Ellis, *Paul's Use of the Old Testament*, 88, notes the elements to the Exodus typology in applications made by Jesus (John 6:31), just as Paul interprets the same events in 1 Cor 10:1–10.

170. Bruce, *Paul and Jesus*, 71.

171. Goguel, *Jesus the Nazarene*, 153–55, suggests that 1 Cor 13:3a, "If I give all my possessions to feed *the poor*," echoes Luke 12:23, "For life is more than food, and the body than clothing."

172. Wenham, *Paul: Follower of Jesus?*, 27. Note the comparison in Greek:

| 2 Cor 1:18 | οὐκ ἔστιν | ὁ λόγος ἡμῶν | ὁ πρὸς ὑμᾶς | ναὶ καὶ οὔ. |
| Matt 5:37 | ἔστω δὲ | ὁ λόγος ὑμῶν | | ναὶ ναί, οὒ οὔ· |

THE "MAN CHRIST JESUS"

that the two men agreed precisely on matters of legal proceedings.[173] An identical agreement on another principle from the Torah is noted in how both Paul and Jesus interpret Lev 18:5, "So you shall keep My statutes and My judgments, by which a man may live if he does them" (καὶ ποιήσετε αὐτά ἃ ποιήσας ἄνθρωπος ζήσεται ἐν αὐτοῖς). In Gal 3:12, Paul quotes this verse, "However, the Law is not of faith; on the contrary, 'He who practices them shall live by them'" (ὁ ποιήσας αὐτὰ ζήσεται ἐν αὐτοῖς), and in Luke 10:28, Jesus agrees with the lawyer's answers on what to do to inherit eternal life by keeping the Great Commandment, as "He said to him, 'You have answered correctly; do this, and you will live'" (τοῦτο ποίει καὶ ζήσῃ).[174] This same agreement on OT texts is seen in Eph 6:2-3, where Paul cites the fifth commandment ("Honor your father and mother") and applies it exactly as Jesus does (Matt 15:4 || Mark 7:16). While these similarities could demonstrate a sharing of common rabbinical interpretation, the agreement on such fundamental points seems to be more than mere coincidence.

Although criticism is leveled at Paul for ignoring the parables of Jesus, Wenham suggests that Paul's repeated illustration of the Word of God as seed bearing fruit and being received (Col 1:5-6; 1 Thess 1:6) echoes the parable of the sower (Mark 4:1-20).[175] Also, Paul's imprecation in 1 Thess 2:16, "But wrath has come upon them (the Jews) to the utmost," seems to be an echo of Jesus' prophecy in Luke 21:23, of "wrath upon the (Jewish) people." Then, in 1 Thess 5:2, Paul reminds his readers, "You yourselves know full well that the day of the Lord will come just like a thief," a simile which seems to be a sure echo of Jesus' saying in Matt 24:43, "But be sure of this, that if the head of the house had known at what time of the night the thief was coming, he would have been on the alert and would not have allowed his house to be broken into."[176] In 1 Thess 5:3, Paul likens the sudden destruction at the Lord's return to birth pangs, an identical illustration used

---

173. The wording in all three accounts is nearly identical:

2 Cor 13:1	ἐπὶ στόματος	δύο μαρτύρων	καὶ τριῶν	σταθήσεται	πᾶν ῥῆμα
Deut 19:15	ἐπὶ στόματος	δύο μαρτύρων	καὶ ἐπὶ στόματος τριῶν μαρτύρων	σταθήσεται	πᾶν ῥῆμα
Matt 18:16	ἐπὶ στόματος	δύο μαρτύρων	ἢ τριῶν	σταθῇ	πᾶν ῥῆμα.

Paul also alludes to Deut 19:15 in 1 Tim 5:19, "Do not receive an accusation against an elder except on the basis of two or three witnesses" (κατὰ πρεσβυτέρου κατηγορίαν μὴ παραδέχου, ἐκτὸς εἰ μὴ ἐπὶ δύο ἢ τριῶν μαρτύρων). Goguel, *Jesus the Nazarene*, 153–55, also finds an allusion to Matt 18:20 in 1 Cor 5:4, when Paul summons the assembling of the church to hear discipline cases.

174. While Jesus requires strict obedience to the Law (as with the rich ruler, Matt 19:17-19), it ought to be noted that Paul does also ("for not the hearers of the Law are just before God, but the doers of the Law will be justified," Rom 2:13). The problem both Jesus and Paul recognize is that humanity does not and cannot fulfill the Law (Matt 23:23; Rom 2:12), and the resolution given by both is that God provides forgiveness in the death of the Son (Matt 26:28; Eph 1:7).

175. Wenham, *Paul: Follower of Jesus?* 86–90.

176. Wenham, *Paul and Jesus*, 97, notes how unlikely it would be for any Christian to have compared Jesus to a thief, making it all the more likely that the only one to have done so was Jesus Himself. Also, how would the Thessalonians know very accurately (ἀκριβῶς) this saying, unless it was part of a well-known Jesus-tradition previously taught to them by Paul?

by Jesus (Matt 24:8, "But all these things are *merely* the beginning of birth pangs").[177] For this reason, believers must "not sleep (μὴ καθεύδωμεν) as others do, but let us be alert (γρηγορῶμεν)," where 1 Thess 5:6 uses the identical language found in the Parable of the Virgins, who fell asleep (ἐκάθευδον), leading Jesus to admonish believers to be on the alert (γρηγορεῖτε) for His return (Matt 25:5, 13). Not only is the vocabulary the same, but it appears in the same context of the Lord's return, showing that Paul gives complete agreement on the eschatological teachings of Jesus.[178]

Along with these more obvious echoes and allusions,[179] Paul often asks his readers, "Do you not know?" with the implication that indeed they do know or ought to know. By his question, Paul refers to some previous information he had taught them, as he inquires, "Do you not remember that while I was still with you, I was telling you these things?" (2 Thess 2:5). To be sure, some of these questions appeal to matters of common knowledge[180] while others take the readers back to knowledge acquired from the OT.[181] But often, Paul will ask, "do you not know" issues bearing resemblance to sayings of Jesus, including a question on baptism (Rom 6:3, "Do you not know that all of us who have been baptized into Christ Jesus have been baptized into His death?") that echoes Jesus' prediction to James and John, "You shall be baptized with the baptism with which I am baptized" (Mark 10:39c). Also, Paul's questions on the body as God's temple (1 Cor 3:16, "Do you not know that you are a temple of God, and *that* the Spirit of God dwells in you?" and 1 Cor 6:19, "Do you not know that your body is a temple of the Holy Spirit who is in you?") assumes that the Corinthians knew of Jesus' likening of His body to Herod's Temple ("Destroy this temple, and in three days I will raise it up. . . . But He was speaking of the temple of His body" John 2:19, 21). This same comparison may also lie behind the

---

177. Wenham, Paul: *Follower of Jesus?* 106–7, notes the grammatical likenesses in 1 Thess 5:3 ("While they are saying, "Peace and safety!" then destruction will come upon them suddenly like birth pangs upon a woman with child; and they shall not escape.") to teachings of Jesus: The adjective αἰφνίδιος is found elsewhere only in Luke 21:34, "that day come on you *suddenly* like a trap;" the end travails are likened to birth pangs in Matt 24:8, "But all these things are *merely* the beginning of birth pangs;" the verb ἐφίστημι is also used in Luke 21:34, "that day *come on* you suddenly like a trap;" and, the verb ἐκφεύγω is common to both: the lost shall not escape (ἐκφύγωσιν), but the saved should pray to escape (ἐκφυγεῖν, Luke 21:34).

178. Ibid., 307–11.

179. Goguel, *Jesus the Nazarene*, 153–55, also adds these to the list of allusions by comparing 1 Thess 4:8 with Luke 10:16; Gal 4:17 with Matt 23:13; and Gal 6:2 with Mark 9:33. Actually, the list continues to expand the more one compares Paul's epistles with the Gospels, thereby favoring the research of Resch, *Der Paulinismus und die Logia Jesu*.

180. As Paul assumes in Romans 6:16, "Do you not know that when you present yourselves to someone *as* slaves for obedience, you are slaves of the one whom you obey, either of sin resulting in death, or of obedience resulting in righteousness?"; Rom 7:1, "Or do you not know, brethren (for I am speaking to those who know the law), that the law has jurisdiction over a person as long as he lives?"; 1 Cor 5:6, "Do you not know that a little leaven leavens the whole lump *of dough*?"; 1 Cor 9:24, "Do you not know that those who run in a race all run, but *only* one receives the prize?"

181. As Paul alludes in Romans 11:2, "Or do you not know what the Scripture says in *the passage about* Elijah, how he pleads with God against Israel?" (quoting 1 Kgs 19:10); 1 Cor 6:16, "Or do you not know that the one who joins himself to a harlot is one body *with her*? For He says, 'The two will become one flesh'" (quoting Gen 2:24); 1 Cor 9:13, "Do you not know that those who perform sacred services eat the *food of the* temple?" (an allusion to Lev 6:26, "The priest who offers it for sin shall eat it. It shall be eaten in a holy place, in the court of the tent of meeting.").

THE "MAN CHRIST JESUS"

question of 1 Cor 6:15, "Do you not know that your bodies are members of Christ?"[182] Furthermore, there is similarity in the way both Paul and Jesus use the term "leaven" to indicate an evil influence.[183] In the question of Paul, "Do you not know that saints will judge the world?" (1 Cor 6:2) one hears an echo of Jesus' prediction in Luke 22:30, "You will sit on thrones judging the twelve tribes of Israel" (also Matt 19:28)–a saying which in turn may echo the judging role by the saints found in Dan 7:22.[184] Finally, when Paul asks, "Do you not know that the unrighteous shall not inherit the kingdom of God?" (1 Cor 6:9), he may well be referring to a similar teaching of Jesus regarding righteousness as a requirement to inherit God's kingdom.[185]

If Paul was referencing Jesus, would his original readers recognize echoes of Jesus' teaching? Stanley thinks not: he contends that only an educated few would have had the ability to read Paul's letters at all, much less be able to assess his handling of an embedded allusion, so that the original listeners would have their understanding of the text "entirely shaped by the interpretive comments (if any) offered in the letter itself" or by explanations given to the listeners by whomever read the epistle to them.[186] In this scenario, the idea of any sort of "reader-response" would be greatly minimized, to say the least. Stanley's opinion, however, flies in the face of Paul's explicit statement in 2 Cor 1:13, "For we write nothing else to you than what you read and understand, and I hope you will understand until the end." Concerning this issue, Bockmuehl observes, "Not only does the New Testament imply a certain kind of reader, but in fact the shape of its own texts elicits at least the outline of a certain kind of reading."[187] Paul expects a proper "reading-response," even when he does not specifically cite the source of a question or command, as when he solemnly reminds the young believers in Thessalonica, "You know what com-

---

182. Ellis, *Paul's Use of the Old Testament*, 90–91, shows that Paul's understanding of the temple not only echoes Jesus but Isa 61:1 as well. Kim, *Paul and the New Perspective*, 271, also links this temple reference to Christ's body with the eucharistic sayings of Jesus quoted by Paul in 1 Cor 11:23–24.

183. Compare Mark 8:15 ("And He was giving orders to them, saying, 'Watch out! Beware of the leaven of the Pharisees and the leaven of Herod.'") with 1 Cor 5:6, "Your boasting is not good. Do you not know that a little leaven leavens the whole lump *of dough*?"

184. Paul's next question in 1 Cor 6:3, "Do you not know that we shall judge angels?" is more obscure, since Jesus did not speak directly to this matter, although he does predict that "eternal fire (is) prepared for the devil and his angels" (Matt 25:41). Perhaps Paul took this saying of the believer's authority in judgment over humanity and extended that authority over the angelic realm as well.

185. As in Matt 5:20, "For I say to you, that unless your righteousness surpasses *that* of the scribes and Pharisees, you shall not enter the kingdom of heaven;" and Matt 25:34, "Then the King will say to those on His right, 'Come, you who are blessed of My Father, inherit the kingdom prepared for you from the foundation of the world.'"

186. Stanley, "'Pearls before Swine': Did Paul's Audiences Understand His Biblical Quotations," 129–30. The title of Stanley's article tips his hand to his answer because it is an echo from Matt 7:6, "Do not throw your pearls before swine, lest they trample them under their feet, and turn and tear you to pieces." Stanley implies that Paul's audience consisted of illiterate "swine" who would have no appreciation of Paul's literary skills and would tear up his epistles—hardly the response any author would want from his readers. Ironically, Stanley assumes his own informed readers would pick up on this biblical echo, but he does not afford the same insight to Paul's original readers; however, even if those first readers were ignorant of the original source, Jesus' metaphor is perfectly understandable.

187. Bockmuehl, *Seeing the Word*, 108.

mandments we gave you by through the Lord Jesus" (διὰ τοῦ κυρίου Ἰησοῦ; 1 Thess 4:2). What commandments would these be if not specific instructions of Jesus in moral and doctrinal matters, as the context of 1 Thessalonians 4 exhibits?

Summary: Paul and the Teachings of Jesus

While it remains a tenuous matter to locate certain echoes of Jesus' teachings within the epistles of Paul,[188] linguistic similarities seem to be more than mere literary coincidences,[189] particularly when Paul specifically cites a saying of the Lord;[190] however, Paul's method often parallels the manner in which he cites the OT—by way of paraphrase or allusion—a "re-presenting in his own language."[191] Fee notes, ". . . those (quotes) that do appear are sufficient evidence that there is a much deeper pool of Jesus tradition from which Paul could cite if he had been so inclined."[192] Still, one must wonder why Paul did not conclude more than a few controversies with a direct quotation from Jesus, especially when he demands agreement with the "sound words of our Lord Jesus Christ" (1 Tim 6:3). Ehrman suggests these options: "1. Paul knew a large number of traditions about Jesus but never spoke of them in his surviving letters because he had no occasion to do so. . . . 2. Paul knew more traditions of Jesus but considered them irrelevant to his mission. . . . 3. Paul didn't mention more about Jesus' words and deeds because he didn't know very much more."[193] Ehrman leaves his readers to resolve this dilemma (he seems to favor the third

---

188. Wenham, *Paul: Follower of Jesus?*, 30, suggests that the best that can be said is, "There is a possible echo of a saying of Jesus here, but the evidence is quite inconclusive." In his pamphlet, *Paul and the Historical Jesus* (1998), Wenham makes the following suggestions in assessing parallels between Jesus and Paul: If there are linguistic parallels that are particularly striking; if the parallels are substantial and not just verbal; if there is no obvious image from common Jewish background; if Paul makes reference to earlier tradition, "this supports the view that the direction of dependence is from Jesus to Paul, not *vice versa*" (ibid., 19). So why did Paul not cite Jesus more often? Wenham answers, (1) "The sheer quantity of echoes and allusions to the stories and sayings of Jesus that we have identified makes it clear that traditions of Jesus were extremely influential in the earliest days of the church" (ibid., 20); (2) The failure of Paul to identify explicitly the Jesus-traditions he uses as coming from Jesus is because "they were extremely well-known, indeed foundational to Paul and his readers" (ibid., 20); (3) "There is important evidence that Paul did pass on traditions of Jesus to his converts, notably in 1 Corinthians 11 and 15" (ibid., 21); (4) In those passages, "Paul highlights those Jesus-traditions because the Corinthians had particular problems" in those areas (ibid., 21); and, (5) "For Paul the death and resurrection of Jesus were of primary importance to him, putting other things about Jesus in the shade" (ibid., 21). In addition, writing material was expensive in Paul's day, leading him to "short-hand" his comments, and time was of the essence to answer specific questions and problems of each congregation, causing him to be quite selective in the information he cites.

189. See Allison, "The Pauline Epistles and the Synoptic Gospels: The Pattern of the Parallels," 1–32.

190. For example, Lüdemann, *Paul: The Founder of Christianity*, 199–208, lists six quotations (1 Cor 7:10–11; 9:14; 14:37; 2 Cor 12:9; 1 Thess 1:8; Acts 20:35) and eighteen possible allusions (Rom 12:14, 17a, 21b; 13:7; 8–10, 14:10a, 13, 14; 1 Thess 4:8, 4:9b; 13–14; 15–17; 5:2, 3, 6, 13b, 15, 16). After doubting that any of these provide sufficient evidence of being actual sayings from Jesus, he inconsistently (but quite correctly) admits that these "make it certain that Paul was familiar with traditions about Jesus' teachings" (ibid., 208).

191. Kim, *Paul and the New Perspective*, 275. See also the findings of Earl Ellis, *Paul's Use of the Old Testament*, 86–92.

192. Fee, *Pauline Christology*, 526.

193. Ehrman, *The New Testament*, 333–35. Ziesler, *Pauline Christianity*, 22, lists only two options: that either Paul did not know the Jesus-traditions in any detail, or he had no interest in them. Meyer, *Jesus or Paul?* (1909), claims that Jesus and Paul differ on the nature of Jesus' death (ibid., 79), on their views of God (ibid.,

THE "MAN CHRIST JESUS"

option), but he omits a fourth option, that Paul's writings *assume* a common knowledge of Jesus' teaching shared between himself and his readers, as indicated by the many literary similarities observed between his letters and the Gospels.[194] Ehrman, however, intends for his readers to doubt any continuity between the two men,[195] although it becomes apparent that any presentation of Jesus (from either the Gospels or Paul) not fitting Ehrman's notion of Jesus as an Apocalyptic Prophet is summarily dismissed.[196] Ehrman has concocted a truncated Jesus at the expense of the whole picture, since he rejects any *logia* he suspects of reflecting later Christian dogma; thus, Ehrman eliminates Jesus' claims in John's Gospel, as well as Synoptic sayings where Jesus considered Himself to be the Son of Man (Mark 8:31) or when he called for belief in Himself (Matt 18:6), not to mention the high Christology of Paul. To deny these teachings of either Jesus or Paul is to force an irreconcilable division between them, leading to the futile quests for the so-called historical Jesus and the historical Paul. Instead, these two historical figures exist only as men conjoined by the NT.

It seems apparent, then, that Paul does not quote the historical teachings of Jesus more often because he assumes that his readers already possess some basic knowledge of those teachings: this is implied in his instruction to "hold firmly to the traditions, just as I delivered them to you" (1 Cor 11:2) and to "remember Jesus Christ, risen from the dead, seed of David, according to my gospel" (2 Tim 2:8). The format of this information was originally delivered in oral form (preaching), but Luke reports that much written historical information about Jesus was circulating when he researched the sources in composing his Gospel (Luke 1:1–4). Likewise, it is reasonable to presume that Paul also used written catechisms (the *tupos* of *didachē*, Rom 6:17) to teach his converts the *logia*

---

80), and on the indwelling Christ from the earthly Jesus (ibid., 81–82). Unlike Ehrman, who suspects Paul of being a disingenuous re-creator of Jesus, Meyer sees Paul's remake of Jesus as an improvement toward true religious freedom (ibid., 116), although he fears that Paul's approach may block many from the "childlike piety of Jesus" (ibid., 120).

194. Ehrman, *The New Testament*, 335. Even Ehrman acknowledges these similarities between Jesus and Paul: "They both subscribed for example to the belief in the one God who had created the world, who made a covenant with his people Israel, and who revealed his will through the Jewish Scriptures. Moreover, they were both apocalypticists who thought they were living at the end of time and that God was soon going to intervene in history by sending a cosmic redeemer from heaven to overthrow the forces of evil that plague the world."

195. Ehrman, ibid., 336, lists "some of the differences" between Jesus and the apostle: Jesus thought that the coming judge is the Son of Man (someone other than himself), whereas Paul believes the judge is Jesus himself; to escape judgment, one must keep the Law as Jesus interpreted it, whereas Paul taught that one escapes judgment by believing in the death and resurrection of Jesus, not by relying on the Law; that Jesus taught faith involves trusting God to bring His future kingdom, whereas Paul taught that faith involves believing in the past death and resurrection of Jesus; that Jesus taught his importance lies in his proclamation of the coming of the end and his correct interpretation of the Law, while Paul saw Jesus' importance in his death and resurrection; and, that Jesus taught that the end of the age began in the lives of those who implemented his teachings, whereas to Paul, the end of the age began with the defeat of the power of sin at the cross of Christ.

196. Ehrman, *Jesus: Apocalyptic Prophet of the New Millennium*, 79. If one compares the list of what Ehrman thinks Paul knew about Jesus (he includes the same list in *The New Testament*, 333) and what can be genuinely derived about Jesus from the Gospels, one finds there is not much difference (ibid., 98–100). Even so, Ehrman selects from his own meager collection to concoct his apocalyptic Jesus.

of Jesus. Besides, a natural curiosity about Jesus among early hearers (Acts 17:19) dictates that the primitive church would provide catechetical resources (ἡ διδαχή τῶν ἀποστόλων, Acts 2:42) to inform inquirers of the life and teachings of Jesus. Paul intimates as much in 2 Thess 2:5 when he asks his converts, "With regard to the coming of our Lord Jesus Christ, and our gathering together to Him, . . . do you not remember that while I was still with you, I was telling you these things?" This evidence leads Dunn to suggest that the church community assumed the traditions of Jesus and that the allusions would have been recognized without specific citation: "The allusions reinforce the authority of the teachings of Jesus."[197] In this vein, Kim suggests that "the early church treated the Jesus tradition *separately* as a unique and sacred tradition,"[198] as evidenced by the existence of four separate Gospels that are followed by the Pauline epistles in the canonical order for good reason: the editors of the canon expected the Gospels to be read first and then explained by Paul.[199] Since the words of Jesus were already held in authoritative esteem, Paul need only refer to them by way of allusion, unless there was a particular reason for citing them specifically; one way or another, Paul indicates repeatedly that he relies upon the teachings of the "Man Christ Jesus."

The Preaching of Jesus

As is his custom to conclude his letters with a benediction, Paul closes Romans, "Now to Him who is able to establish you according to my gospel and the preaching of Jesus Christ . . . ," where the infinitive στηρίξαι is modified by the preposition κατὰ, which governs two nouns, τὸ εὐαγγέλιόν μου και τὸ κήρυγμα Ἰησοῦ Χριστοῦ (Rom 16:25). It may seem a bit presumptuous for Paul to describe the gospel as his own, but he does so also in Rom 2:16 and 2 Tim 2:8, where he stresses his apostolic understanding of the gospel as the correct interpretation, as he also does in Gal 1:8 ("But even though we, or an angel from heaven, should preach to you a gospel contrary to that which we have preached to you, let him be accursed."). Of interest for this study is the second part of the prepositional phrase in Rom 16:25, τὸ κήρυγμα Ἰησοῦ Χριστοῦ, whether this phrase should be understood as an objective genitive ("the proclamation *of* Jesus Christ," NIV) or as a subjective genitive, the preaching proclaimed *by* Jesus. In support of the latter is the parallel with τὸ εὐαγγέλιόν μου, which is certainly not an objective genitive (the gospel is surely not about Paul!), but rather the gospel preached by Paul. Also, in the biblical literature, whenever the noun κήρυγμα is followed by a possessive, it is always a subjective genitive (except for the disputed reading in Mark 16:8, κήρυγμα τῆς αἰωνίου σωτηρίας), describing the activity of preaching.[200] In Rom 16:25, then,

---

197. Dunn, *Theology of Paul*, 652.

198. Kim, *Paul and the New Perspective*, 287, italics original.

199. Trobisch, *The First Edition of the New Testament*, 38, shows while the books of the NT appear in differing sequences among the manuscript evidence, the variations appear within the fourfold-organization of Gospels, Acts, Epistles, and Revelation.

200. The noun κήρυγμα appears twelve times in the BGT (2 Chr 30:5; Prov 9:3; Jonah 3:2; Matt 12:41; Mark 16:8; Luke 11:32; Rom 16:25; 1 Cor 1:21; 2:4; 15:14; 2 Tim 4:17; Titus 1:3). In 2 Tim 4:17 and Titus 1:3, Paul uses it to refer to the content being preached, the *kerygma*; however, when κήρυγμα is followed by

THE "MAN CHRIST JESUS"

Paul states that his readers are established according to the content of his gospel *and* the content preached by Jesus, meaning—as a logical consequence—that Paul knew Jesus had been a preacher. This realization, of course, agrees with the initial introduction of Jesus' public ministry, "From that time Jesus began to preach (κηρύσσειν) and say, 'Repent, for the kingdom of heaven is at hand'" (Matt 4:17). He even stated that preaching was one of his divine missions, when He said to his disciples, "Let us go somewhere else to the towns nearby, in order that I may preach (κηρύξω) there also; for that is what I came out for" (Mark 1:38).[201] So, while Jesus was surely the primary object of Paul's gospel ("We preach Christ crucified," 1 Cor 1:23), in the context of Rom 16:25, it is also the message preached by Jesus—His doctrine—that establishes believers in the faith. How else would Paul's readers be established in the preaching of Jesus unless they had been previously informed of its content and knew how to access His preaching—by referring to "that form of teaching to which you were committed"? (Rom 6:17). Thus, by this reference to the "preaching of Jesus," Paul knew that the "Man Christ Jesus" had been a preacher of the Word of God.

The Evangelizing Ministry of Jesus

In Eph 2:17, Paul combines Isa 57:19 (when YHWH says, "Peace, peace to him who is far and to him who is near") with Isa 52:7 ("How lovely on the mountains are the feet of him who brings good news, who announces peace;" πόδες εὐαγγελιζομένου ἀκοὴν εἰρήνης ὡς εὐαγγελιζόμενος ἀγαθά) to comment, "He came and preached peace (εὐηγγελίσατο εἰρήνην) to you who were far away, and peace to those who were near." Paul previously specified the subject of the one who "evangelized" as Christ Jesus (Eph 2:13),[202] clarifying the identity of the evangelist of peace who declares in Isa 61:1 that "the LORD has anointed me to 'evangelize' to the afflicted" (με εὐαγγελίσασθαι πτωχοῖς). Quite significantly, Jesus applies this same text to Himself in His first recorded sermon, as reported in Luke 4:18, "The Spirit of the Lord is upon Me, because He anointed Me 'to evangelize' (εὐαγγελίσασθαι) to the poor." Now, in Eph 2:17, Paul applies this same evangelizing ministry to "Christ Jesus," the Anointed One, clearly referring to the historical coming (ἐλθών[203]) of Jesus and His activity of evangelizing when He offered peace to Israel (Luke 19:42) and promised His own peace to believers (John 14:27; 16:33) in His proclamation

---

a genitive in Matt 12:41 || Luke 11:32 (τὸ κήρυγμα Ἰωνᾶ), it is not the "preaching about Jonah," but Jonah's preaching; in 1 Cor 2:4 (καὶ ὁ λόγος μου καὶ τὸ κήρυγμά μου), it is not the preaching "about me (Paul)," but Paul's preaching; and in 1 Cor 15:14 (εἰ δὲ Χριστὸς οὐκ ἐγήγερται, κενὸν ἄρα [καὶ] τὸ κήρυγμα ἡμῶν), it is not the "preaching about us," but "our preaching."

201. When used of Jesus, the verb κηρύσσειν describes his preaching activity (Matt 4:17; 9:35; 11:1; Mark 1:14, 38, 39, 45; Luke 4:44; 8:1; 20:1) and does so by explaining his preaching as a messianic sign in fulfillment of Isa 61:1 (Matt 11:5; Luke 4:18–19, 43; Luke 7:22; 16:18).

202. BDAG § 3197.2 defines this use of εὐαγγελίζω, "to proclaim the divine message of salvation, *proclaim the gospel.*" The word transliterates into English as *evangelizo*, and thus means, "to evangelize."

203. BDAG § 3143 1. b. α. notes that ἔρχομαι is used of Jesus as Messiah (Luke 3:16; John 4:25; 7:27, 31) in fulfillment of Ps 118:26, announcing Him as ὁ ἐρχόμενος (Matt 11:3; Luke 7:19; Heb 10:37) or ὁ ἐρχόμενος ἐν ὀνόματι κυρίου (Matt 21:9; 23:39; Mark 11:9; Luke 13:35; 19:38; John 12:13). In John 6:14; 11:27 and 26:28, the verb has incarnational overtones, "of Jesus having come heaven-sent to the earth."

of the εὐαγγέλιον of the kingdom.²⁰⁴ This "evangel" evangelized by Jesus (Matt 4:23; 19:35; 24:14; Luke 7:22; 16:16) is a definite point of similarity with the "evangel" evangelized by Paul (Rom 1:15; 15:19–20; 1 Cor 15:1; 2 Cor 10:16; etc.), even though the content preached by each one has a different emphasis. Paul evangelizes the Son Himself (Gal 1:16), while Jesus evangelized the arrival of the Kingdom of God (Luke 4:43), although He expects that "the gospel of the kingdom will be preached in the whole world" (Matt 24:14; 26:13). The book of Acts assumes that this is the same gospel preached by the inaugural church (Acts 8:25, 40; 14:7, 15, 21; 15:7; 16:10; 20:24), although it complements the "evangelizing the good news about the kingdom of God" with "the name of Jesus Christ" (Acts 8:12)—or even more personally, "evangelizing the Lord Jesus" (Acts 11:20). Even so, the "kingdom" remains a topic in Paul's preaching (Acts 19:8; 20:25; 28:23, 31), as references to the kingdom are widespread throughout his letters.²⁰⁵ Thus, when Paul asks the Corinthians, "Do you not know that the unrighteous shall not inherit the kingdom of God?" (1 Cor 6:9; also in Gal 5:21), his question "implies that they should know because . . . they had been specifically taught about the Kingdom of God."²⁰⁶ Once again, Paul assumes continuity with the "Man Christ Jesus" in that both evangelize the good news that God's Kingdom has arrived in the Person of Christ, bringing peace with God.

The Identity of Jesus as the Stone of Ps 118:22

In Rom 9:30–32, Paul cites a reason why Israel has not attained unto righteousness—because that nation largely pursued it by works rather than by faith. In this pursuit, Israel stumbled over the "stone of stumbling, just as it is written, 'Behold, I lay in Zion a stone of stumbling and a rock of offense, and he who believes in Him will not be disappointed'" (Rom 9:33). At first glance, this quotation appears to come from Isa 28:16,²⁰⁷ but upon closer examination one observes that Paul has conflated that verse with Isa 8:14.²⁰⁸ It is apparent that Paul applies this stone metaphor to Jesus as the one whom Israel stumbled over, but where would Paul derive this stone motif?

It appears that he makes an important intersection with Jesus, for Matt 21:42 records that Jesus applies the stone motif to Himself when He asked His opponents, "Did you never read in the Scriptures, 'The stone (λίθον) which the builders rejected, this became the chief corner *stone*' (κεφαλὴν γωνίας)?" Here Jesus quotes Ps 118:22, applying this

---

204. BDAG § 3198 defines εὐαγγέλιον, "God's good news to humans." Thus, the evangelist (εὐαγγελιστής) evangelizes (εὐαγγελίζω) the evangel (εὐαγγέλιον).

205. Paul mentions the Kingdom at Rom 14:17; 1 Cor 4:20; 6:9–10; 15:24; 50; Gal 5:21; Eph 5:5; Col 1:13; 4:11; 1 Thess 2:12; 2 Thess 1:5; 2 Tim 4:1, 18.

206. Wenham, *Paul and Jesus: The True Story*, 68.

207. Isaiah 28:16 reads, "Therefore thus says the Lord God, "Behold, I am laying in Zion a stone, a tested stone, A costly cornerstone *for* the foundation, firmly placed. He who believes *in it* will not be disturbed" (ἰδοὺ ἐγὼ ἐμβαλῶ εἰς τὰ θεμέλια Σιων λίθον πολυτελῆ ἐκλεκτὸν ἀκρογωνιαῖον ἔντιμον εἰς τὰ θεμέλια αὐτῆς καὶ ὁ πιστεύων ἐπ' αὐτῷ οὐ μὴ καταισχυνθῇ). A comparison with Rom 9:33 underlines the differences: ἰδοὺ τίθημι ἐν Σιὼν λίθον προσκόμματος καὶ πέτραν σκανδάλου, καὶ ὁ πιστεύων ἐπ' αὐτῷ οὐ καταισχυνθήσεται.

208 Isaiah 8:14 reads, "Then He shall become a sanctuary; But to both the houses of Israel, <u>a stone to strike and a rock to stumble over</u>, And a snare and a trap for the inhabitants of Jerusalem."

THE "MAN CHRIST JESUS"

typology to Himself as the rejected stone who becomes the Cornerstone for the "gate of the Lord" (118:19–20). Paul picks up this messianic motif in Eph 2:20, that the church has been "been built upon the foundation of the Apostles and prophets, Christ Jesus Himself being the corner *stone.*"[209] Furthermore, in Luke's account of the same event, Jesus adds this warning, "Everyone who falls on that stone (τὸν λίθον) will be broken to pieces; but on whomever it falls, it will scatter him like dust" (Luke 20:18), a statement not only echoing Isa 8:14—the same verse Paul cites in Rom 9:33—but also the apocalyptic vision of Dan 2:34–35, where a stone (λίθος) cut without hands crushed the great statue of gold and scattered it as chaff.[210] Significantly, Peter also employs this same OT imagery in his sermon in Acts 4:11 when he describes "Jesus Christ the Nazarene, who you crucified, who God raised from the dead—He is the stone which was rejected by you, the builders, *but* which became the very corner *stone*." Peter also uses this same concept in his first epistle, "But for those who disbelieve, 'The stone which the builders rejected, This became the very corner *stone*,' and, 'A stone of stumbling and a rock of offense'; for they stumble because they are disobedient to the word, and to this *doom* they were also appointed (1 Pet 2:7–8).

It is apparent, then, that when Paul identifies Jesus with the Stone of OT typology, he shares a messianic theme not only preached by the primitive church, but one that originated with the "Man Christ Jesus," revealing his agreement with both the teaching of Jesus and that of the primitive church.

The Angelic Assistance of Jesus

As a Pharisee, Paul acknowledged the existence of angels (Acts 23:8), was a recipient of angelic ministering (Acts 27:23–24), and mentioned angels throughout his letters.[211] Paul includes angels in the christological confession in 1 Tim 3:16, "Great is the mystery of godliness: . . . He (Jesus) was beheld by angels (ὤφθη ἀγγέλοις)."[212] This comment shows that Paul was aware of traditions now recorded in the Gospels, that angels superintended the ministry of Jesus: in His conception (Matt 1:20; Luke 1:26), His birth (Luke 2:13), His temptation (Matt 4:11), His anguish (Luke 22:43), and His resurrection (Matt 28:2).

---

209. In Eph 2:20, Paul uses ἀκρογωνιαῖος, a *hapax legomenon* that BDAG § 292 suggests is the capstone, which is very similar to the "head of the corner" (κεφαλὴν γωνίας).

210. These connections are observed by Earl Ellis, *Paul's Use of the Old Testament*, 87.

211. Paul mentions angels at Rom 8:38; 1 Cor 4:9; 6:3; 11:10; 13:1; 2 Cor 11:14; 12:7; Gal 1:8, 3:19; 4:14; Col 2:18; 2 Thess 1:7; 1 Tim 3:16; 5:21.

212. The creed echoes Luke 22:43, "an angel appeared to Him" (ὤφθη αὐτῷ ἄγγελος). There are three basic approaches to 1 Tim 3:16, according to Mounce, *Pastoral Epistles*, 215–18. First, it is viewed as a continuous chronology of the earthly ministry of Jesus (Alford, Barrett); secondly, as two chiastic stanzas, lines 1–3 of Christ's life and 4–6 of the world's reception of Him (Lock); and thirdly, as three parallel stanzas of two lines each, giving a theological progression of salvation (Spicq, Gundry, Towner). Mounce favors the second, yet the first is the least complicated, as the hymn places the life of Christ in general historical sequence, moving from His incarnation ("revealed in the flesh"), to His baptism ("vindicated in the Spirit"); His temptation ("beheld by angels," Matt 4:11); His preaching ministry ("proclaimed among the nations"), with resulting belief ("believed on in the world"), and finally, His ascension ("taken up in glory"). Within this historical context, the reference to angels refers to their spectating of the earthly ministry of Jesus, that "angels came and ministered to Him" (Matt 4:11).

While critics might disparage the supernatural report of angels, Paul finds in this confession that Jesus was "beheld by angels" yet another confirmation of the ministry of the "Man Christ Jesus."

What about the Miracles of Jesus?

It is puzzling, however, that Paul does not mention the miracles attributed to Jesus by the Gospels, although it seems quite impossible that Paul never heard about Jesus' miracles (especially since Peter affirmed them in the first Christian sermon, Acts 2:22); in fact, Paul confirms his own apostolic credentials by "signs and wonders" that Christ accomplished through him (Rom 15:18–19; also 2 Cor 12:12), showing that he knew the Risen Lord continues to perform miracles. Kim asks, "Does not the fact that he regards miracles as a sign of an apostle, as the representative and revealer of Jesus Christ, imply that he knows that Jesus demonstrated the salvation of the kingdom of God though his miracles?"[213] For that matter, Paul downplays miracles in his own evangelistic preaching (1 Cor 1:22–23, "For indeed Jews ask for signs, and Greeks search for wisdom; but we preach Christ crucified, to Jews a stumbling block, and to Gentiles foolishness.") in the same way Jesus upbraided His listeners for their misunderstanding of His signs ("Unless you see signs and wonders, you will not believe," John 4:48).[214] A faith trusting in miracles is misdirected—belief should rest on the Sign-Giver, and for this reason both Jesus and Paul minimize the importance of miraculous signs (1 Cor 2:5). Neither Jesus nor Paul emphasize themselves as wonder-workers even though their miracles confirmed their respective ministries as truly Spirit-anointed, even if such works did little to engender true saving faith.[215]

Thus, to conclude from Paul's omission of Jesus' miracles that he disbelieved in the miraculous or was ignorant of their occurrence is an inference from silence. To the contrary, Paul stated unequivocally that a marvelous miracle happened to Jesus when He was "declared the Son of God with power by the resurrection from the dead" (Rom 1:4). Paul knew Jesus to be "the power of God" (1 Cor 1:24), implying His supernatural credentials as one who "shall raise us up through His power" (1 Cor 6:14) just as He had raised the dead during His ministry (Matt 11:5; Mark 1:31; Luke 7:14–15; John 11:43). It is, then, a reasonable deduction to conclude that Paul believed that Jesus performed miracles, although it did not serve the purposes of his letters to mention the miraculous ministry of Jesus. After all, the apostle does not teach that sinners are saved by believing that Jesus wrought miracles, but by believing that God raised Him from the dead (Rom 10:9). It is the resurrection that is the ultimate miracle of the "Man Christ Jesus."

---

213. Kim, *Paul and the New Perspective*, 282.

214. Moule, *Origins of Christology*, 147, notes that even Jesus for the most part tried to conceal His miracles.

215. For example, there is no indication that Paul's miraculous blinding of Elymas the magician (Acts 13:11) and His exorcism of the slave girl (Acts 16:18) led to the conversions of these individuals.

THE "MAN CHRIST JESUS"

Summary to the Ministry of Jesus

While it is readily admitted that Paul's letters lack the specific details of Jesus' earthly ministry, the Pauline allusions to the ministry of the historical Jesus agree completely with the record as documented in the Gospels. It should be recognized that the genre of Paul's correspondence is not narrative biography purporting to present the works of a great man. Instead, Paul uses specific incidents from the ministry of Jesus when appropriate to illustrate and fortify his doctrines; otherwise, Paul emphasizes the crucified and resurrected Christ, the one he had seen on the Damascus Road. In other words, Paul writes about the Jesus who appeared to him but he yields to apostolic tradition in matters where he is neither an eyewitness nor an ear-witness of Jesus' earthly ministry, deferring to those who had seen Him and heard His instructions on such topics as the Eucharist and His *parousia*. Since Paul had no first-hand knowledge of the teachings and miracles of Jesus, this accounts for his rare references to them except by appeal to common tradition. On the other hand, the traditional authors of the Gospels were either first-hand witnesses (Matthew and John) or had access of those who were eyewitnesses of Jesus (Mark; Luke 1:1–4) in their task to present more of a biological narrative of Jesus. The Evangelists are the story-tellers of Jesus, whereas Paul is an explainer of Jesus, for his task is to define the significance of the historical ministry of the "Man Christ Jesus."

THE CHARACTER OF THE "MAN CHRIST JESUS"

Yet Paul is not merely interested in the events of Jesus' ministry, but he also draws attention to His character as well. This is not to say that Paul presents a personality profile of Jesus, leading Stanton to observe, "We know nothing about the personality of Jesus in the modern sense of His psychological makeup."[216] This lack, however, has not prevented psychological analyses of Jesus, but these have proven to be fruitless endeavors, because the Gospel writers of the NT are far more concerned with the actions and words of Jesus than revealing His personality. His character, however, is a point of interest to the Evangelists, as it is for Paul, for in his letters he often appeals to the character of Jesus—showing the type of man He was. This appeal is patently clear when Paul makes this breathtaking command: "Be imitators of me, just as I also am of Christ" (1 Cor 11:1).[217] Even if Paul had not known Christ "according to the flesh," he had encountered Him personally and learned of His character through the "traditions" he had received and delivered (1 Cor 11:2). In these ways, Paul presents himself as an example *par excellance* of the behavioral model of Jesus,[218] leading Dodd to comment, "Further, Paul has a definite conception of the

---

216. Stanton, *Jesus of Nazareth in the Preaching of the New Testament*, 189.

217. The same idea of imitation of Christ is found in Phil 2:5–11; 1 Thess 1:6; and implied in Rom 13:14; 15:1–6; 2 Cor 3:18; and Phil 1:21. It is not the exalted Christ who is to be imitated, but the earthly One, for the whole idea of *Imitatio Christi presupposes information about Jesus*. Bird, "The Purpose and Preservation of the Jesus Tradition: Moderate Evidence for a Conserving Force in its Transmission," 178, notes, "The early Christians may have preserved elements of the Jesus tradition by imitating Jesus. One observes in the NT that the example of Jesus is a constituent element of ethics for the believing community (e.g., Rom 13:14; 1 Cor 11:1; Phil 2:5–11; Heb 2:18–3:2; 12:3–4; 1 Pet 2:21)."

218. Weiss, *Paul and Jesus*, 117, observes, "It is unnecessary to point out that Paul could never have laid

character of Christ. Not only does he emphasize His righteousness and obedience (which might be taken as general or conventional), but also he notes as His outstanding traits of character gentleness, forbearance, humility, and a complete absence of self-seeking. These traits are expressly held up for the imitation of Christians."[219] Each of these indicators presupposes that Paul had learned much about the character of Jesus in order to imitate His virtues himself, and throughout his letters, he presents the virtues of Jesus as exemplary behavior to emulate, as this section shall show.[220]

"The Meekness and Gentleness of Christ"

We begin with a seemingly incidental remark when Paul urges the Corinthians through "the meekness and gentleness of Christ" (διὰ τῆς πραΰτητος[221] καὶ ἐπιεικείας[222] τοῦ Χριστοῦ, 2 Cor 10:1), an analogy that would be senseless if his readers did not have some knowledge that Jesus had been meek and gentle—just as He claimed in Matt 11:29, "I am gentle (πραΰς) and humble in heart," a saying that Paul may well have in mind in this exhortation. Paul's reference to the meek and gentle character of Jesus, however, is made in passing: he is not discussing some fine point of Christology. He just happens to use these virtues of Jesus in an ethical appeal to his readers, and in so doing, he assumes that they have some previous awareness of the character of Jesus. Barclay draws an inference from this observation, noting,

> There must have been instruction in the actual historical life of Jesus. There is a phrase in one of Paul's letters which makes this to all intents and purposes certain. In appealing to the Corinthians Paul writes: 'I, Paul, myself entreat you by the meekness and gentleness of Christ' (2 Cor 10:1). It is perfectly plain that such an appeal is meaningless unless the Corinthians were aware of actual incidents and events in the life of Jesus in which this meekness and gentleness was demonstrated. This appeal would be totally ineffective unless it was made to people who knew that life in which the meekness and gentleness were clear for all to see.[223]

Barclay's important insight applies to all of Paul's allusions to the historical Jesus, that they presuppose a pool of knowledge about Jesus shared in common between the

---

down this principle (in 1 Cor 11:1), if he had not possessed a clear picture of the moral character of Jesus." See also Kim, "*Imitatio Christi* (1 Corinthians 11:1): How Paul Imitates Jesus Christ in Dealing with Idol Food (1 Corinthians 8–10)," 193–226.

219. Dodd, *History and the Gospel*, 65.

220. Because these virtues do not appear in a systematic manner in Paul's letters but generally as illustrations of particular principles, they are also arranged in a rather arbitrary order in this section of the study. Whenever possible, an attempt is made to place these particular virtues in the order they appear in the Gospels.

221. BDAG § 6133 defines πραΰτης simply as "meekness," mentioned by Paul as a Christian virtue in Gal 5:23; 6:1; Eph 4:2; Col 3:12; 2 Tim 2:25; Titus 3:2. How would meekness be identified as a Christian virtue unless it had been modeled by Jesus?

222. BDAG § 2949 defines ἐπιείκεια variously as "clemency, gentleness, graciousness, courtesy, indulgence, tolerance." It is used elsewhere in the NT only in the flattery of Tertullus to Felix, "But, that I may not weary you any further, I beg you to grant us, by your *kindness*, a brief hearing" (Acts 24:4).

223. Barclay, "A Comparison of Paul's Missionary Preaching and Preaching to the Church," 168–69.

THE "MAN CHRIST JESUS"

apostle and his readers, knowledge that not only included the saving acts of the death and resurrection of Jesus but also various incidental details of His life. In this case, how would the Corinthians know that Jesus had been meek and gentle unless Paul had previously informed them of His character so that he could now use that information as a catalyst for Christlike behavior? Thus, this reference to the meekness and gentleness of Jesus is part of "Paul's whole method of preaching (that) involved a background knowledge of the life of Jesus,"[224] including information on the ethical character of the "Man Christ Jesus."

"The Compassion of Christ Jesus"

One of the first character traits of Jesus mentioned in the Gospels appears in Mark 1:41, which notes He was "moved with compassion" (σπλαγχνισθείς). The Apostle Paul uses this same virtue in Phil 1:8, when he tells his readers, "For God is my witness, how I long for all of you with the compassion of Christ Jesus" (NRS; ἐν σπλάγχνοις Χριστοῦ Ἰησοῦ).[225] Paul may refer here to his own affections motivated by his relationship in Christ, as he does in Phil 2:1, "If there is any encouragement in Christ, . . . if any affection (σπλάγχνα) and compassion." If so, one might expect him to follow ἐν σπλάγχνοις with the dative, ἐν Χριστῷ, referring to affections that flow out of union in Christ. However, the grammatical construction in Phil 1:8 follows ἐν σπλάγχνοις with the genitive Χριστοῦ Ἰησου, which could be objective, referring to Paul's affections directed toward Christ, but that does not fit the context, since Paul is describing his longing toward the Philippians. It seems better, then, to understand the genitive as subjective, referring to Christ's personal and intimate affections for the Philippians.

The larger question, however, is how Paul knew that Christ Jesus was an affectionate person, and that information must have come from the Jesus-histories later included in the Gospels, as when Matt 9:36 reports, "And seeing the multitudes, (Jesus) felt compassion (ἐσπλαγχνίσθη) for them" (the same concept appears in Matt 15:32 || Mark 8:2; also Matt 9:36, 14; 20:34, || Mark 1:41; 6:34; || Luke 7:13). Knowing this quality of Jesus, Paul could compare his own care for the Philippians with the same sort of affections both he and his readers knew to be in the "Man Christ Jesus."

"The Love in Christ Jesus"

Closely associated with compassion is the character virtue of the love of Christ, exhibited when Jesus conversed with the rich young ruler and "felt a love for him" (ἠγάπησεν αὐτὸν, Mark 10:21). Paul constantly mentions the love of Christ in his letters, and some of those references describe the dynamic, existential quality of Christ's love (Rom 8:35; 2 Cor 5:14; Eph 3:19; 6:23). Yet a more subjective content to that love seems to be present in Paul's exhortation in 2 Tim 1:13, "Retain the standard (ὑποτύπωσις) of sound words which you have heard from me, in the faith and love which are in Christ Jesus" (ἐν πίστει καὶ ἀγάπῃ τῇ ἐν χριστῷ Ἰησου). Here Paul uses his teaching as providing the prototypical

---

224. Ibid.

225. BDAG § 6772 defines σπλάγχνον as "the *viscera*," which in the ancient world served as the seat of emotions and is extended "by metonymy of the feeling itself of affection."

behavioral standard,[226] but only as defined by the faith and love observed in Christ Jesus. A very similar grammatical parallel is found in 1 Tim 1:13–14, when Paul recounts his pre-conversion hostility, when "formerly I was a blasphemer, persecutor, and insolent opponent. But I received mercy because I had acted ignorantly in unbelief, and the grace of our Lord overflowed for me with the faith and love that are in Christ Jesus" (μετὰ πίστεως καὶ ἀγάπης τῆς ἐν Χριστῷ Ἰησοῦ, English translation from the ESV). One might suppose that Paul would define the love of Christ by his conversion experience on the Damascus Road, yet when he cites an example of this faith and love in the next verse (1 Tim 1:15), it is couched in one of the "faithful word" sayings that "Christ Jesus came into the world to save sinners, among whom I am foremost *of all.*"[227] Thus, when Paul defines Christ's love, he points not to a heavenly encounter (whether his own or the sinner's conversion) but to events of human history related to the saving purpose of Christ; for example, even in Paul's amazed exclamation that "the Son of God . . . loved me," it is displayed in that "He delivered Himself up for me" (Gal 2:20), referring to Christ's deliverance "for our trespasses" at the cross (Rom 4:25 ESV). In Eph 5:2, Paul presents this same pattern to believers, who are to "walk in love, just as Christ also loved you, and gave Himself up for us," an example given specifically to husbands, who are to love their wives "as Christ also loved the church and gave Himself up for her" (Eph 5:25). Christ's example holds weight only if Paul refers to the voluntary giving of a historical man in human time and space as an expression of love.

Surely, then, Paul agrees with the Gospel records that Jesus was a loving man, who "loved His own who were in the world, (and) He loved them to the end" (John 13:1; see also Mark 10:21; John 11:3, 5, 36; 13:23, 34; 14:21; 15:9–10, 12; 19:26; 20:2; 21:7, 20). While the Risen Christ continues to love His own with a dynamic love, when Paul invokes the benediction of "our Lord Jesus Christ Himself," it is as a Man who has loved us (ὁ ἀγαπήσας ἡμᾶς) in a specific point moment of human history, exhibited by His sacrificial death (2 Thess 2:16).

"Christ Jesus came into the world to save sinners"

As noted above, Paul states the loving purpose of Jesus this way, "It is a trustworthy statement, deserving full acceptance, that Christ Jesus came into the world to save sinners" (1 Tim 1:15; Χριστὸς Ἰησοῦς ἦλθεν εἰς τὸν κόσμον ἁμαρτωλοὺς σῶσαι).[228] This creedal

---

226. As BDAG § 7649 defines ὑποτύπωσις.

227. The Pastoral Epistles contain five of these statements introduced by πιστὸς ὁ λόγος (1 Tim 1:15; 3:1; 4:9; 2 Tim 2:11–12; Titus 3:8), and each one cites a traditional creedal concept as pre-Pauline in origin.

228. Paul includes five of these "faithful sayings" in the Pastoral epistles, identified by the expression, πιστὸς ὁ λόγος, which is roughly translated, "Faithful (is) the word." Besides this one in 1 Tim 1:15, the others are: 1 Tim 3:1 ("It is a trustworthy statement: if any man aspires to the office of overseer, it is a fine work he desires *to do.*"); 1 Tim 4:9 ("It is a trustworthy statement deserving full acceptance;" this probably referring to the previous sentence, "godliness is profitable for all things, since it holds promise for the present life and *also* for the *life* to come"); 2 Tim 2:11–13 ("It is a trustworthy statement: For if we died with Him, we shall also live with Him; If we endure, we shall also reign with Him; If we deny Him, He also will deny us; If we are faithless, He remains faithful; for He cannot deny Himself."); Titus 3:8 ("This is a trustworthy statement; and concerning these things I want you to speak confidently, so that those who have believed God

THE "MAN CHRIST JESUS"

statement implies the pre-existence of Jesus (He came into the world from a previous existence), His incarnational coming (He entered into the physical world as a man), and His soteriological purpose (He came to save sinners). Amid all the opinions of the purpose and identity of the historical Jesus, how did Paul arrive at this saving purpose of Christ Jesus? Why should his view be accepted to the exclusion of all others?

The answer is that this "faithful saying" echoes a saying of Jesus, "For the Son of Man came to seek and to save that which was lost" (Luke 19:10, ESV).[229] He repeats the same basic idea in John 12:47, "I did not come (ἦλθον) to judge the world, but to save the world" (ἀλλ' ἵνα σώσω τὸν κόσμον). Both Jesus and Paul even describe the unsaved with the same interchangeable terms: "sinners," the "lost/perishing" and "the world" (Matt 9:13; 2 Cor 4:3; 1 Cor 1:21), and both are in precise agreement on the purpose for Christ's coming into the world with a saving aspiration. Either this resemblance is a profound coincidence, or Paul relies upon the original teachings of Jesus as codified in this "Faithful Saying" and inscribed throughout his letters as confirming the saving purpose the "Man Christ Jesus."

"The Steadfastness of Christ"

In accord with His purpose, Jesus "resolutely set His face to go to Jerusalem" (Luke 9:51), and it is for such Christ-like endurance that Paul prays, "May the Lord direct your hearts into the love of God and into the steadfastness of Christ" (εἰς τὴν ὑπομονὴν τοῦ Χριστοῦ, 2 Thess 3:5).[230] This is a prayer for a heart experience of these spiritual realities, which are best understood as subjective genitives, God's love and Christ's steadfastness. While ὑπομονή appears often in Paul's letters,[231] this prepositional structure is unique in canonical Scripture, giving us pause to ask, how would Paul know that Jesus had a steadfast character? The writer to the Hebrews specifies this steadfastness by noting, that Jesus "endured the cross, despising the shame" (Heb 12:2), and even if Paul does not have the endurance of the cross in mind (although that would not be unusual), he certainly assumes that his readers have some idea of what it meant that the "Man Christ Jesus" was steadfast in character as a figure of history.

---

may be careful to engage in good deeds. These things are good and profitable for men."). All of these faithful sayings appear to be catechetical expressions Paul embeds either in whole or in part. He may have received them from original catechisms of the church (Acts 2:42) which in turn derived from sayings of Jesus.

229. Compare 1 Tim 1:15, Χριστὸς Ἰησοῦς ἦλθεν εἰς τὸν κόσμον ἁμαρτωλοὺς σῶσαι, with Luke 19:10, ἦλθενγὰρ ὁ υἱὸς τοῦ ἀνθρώπου ζητῆσαι καὶ σῶσαι τὸ ἀπολωλός.

230. LN § 25.174 ὑπομονή, ῆς f: "capacity to continue to bear up under difficult circumstances- 'endurance, being able to endure.'"

231. In Paul's letters, the noun ὑπομονή appears in Rom 2:7; 5:3–4; 8:25; 15:4–5; 2 Cor 1:6; 6:4; 12:12; Col 1:11; 1 Thess 1:3; 2 Thess 1:4; 3:5; 1 Tim 6:11; 2 Tim 3:10; Titus 2:2; and the verb ὑπομένω appears in Rom 12:12; 1 Cor 13:7; 2 Tim 2:10, 12.

The "Man Christ Jesus" in the Epistles of Paul

"He Humbled Himself"

Paul certainly does have the cross in mind when he cites his 'Christ-Hymn' in Phil 2:5–11,[232] where his primary point is not to teach an orthodox understanding of the Person of Christ—although the hymn certainly does that—but rather to illustrate what sort of humble thinking the participants of the church ought to have among themselves. Paul prefaces the hymn, "Have this attitude in yourselves which was also in Christ Jesus" (Phil 2:5), in that He "humbled Himself" (ἐταπείνωσεν ἑαυτὸν, Phil 2:8).[233] In this statement, Paul encompasses the entire life of Jesus as a humbling of Himself, "becoming obedient to the point of death, even death on a cross."

Where did Paul learn about this humble attitude of Jesus, since he does not cite any first-hand knowledge of this virtue? It might be argued that Paul is merely making deductions from the "Son of Man" vision in Dan 7:13–14, because that seems to be hovering in the background, but there is nothing in Daniel's account about any humbling of that apocalyptic figure. Instead, this Christ-hymn is incarnational, reflecting historical tradition that Paul would have learned from those who were eyewitnesses of Jesus and had told him of His humble attitude that led Him to the cross. They may have also informed him of the saying of Jesus now recorded in Matt 11:29, "I am gentle and humble in heart" (πραΰς εἰμι καὶ ταπεινὸς τῇ καρδίᾳ), but even if that were not so, Paul certainly agrees with that assessment in Phil 2:8 when he uses the same virtue to encourage his readers to display the same example of humbleness. Thus, Paul's knowledge of the humbleness of Jesus must have come not only as he reflected on the cross as a voluntary humiliation by Jesus but also from Christ-histories recounting the humble character of the "Man Christ Jesus."

"He Became Obedient"

The Christ-hymn of Phil 2:8 further notes that the evidence of Jesus' humbling of Himself is that "He became obedient to the point of death, even death on a cross." Obedience and submission to proper authority are characteristics promoted often by Paul,[234] virtues he views as crucial to salvation as the "obedience of faith" (Rom 1:5; 16:26).[235] In fact, Paul blames the entire loss of humanity on the disobedience of "the one man" Adam, "as through the one man's disobedience the many were made sinners" (Rom 5:19a), but then he credits the salvation of mankind to Christ's obedience, "so through the obedience of the One the many will be made righteous" (Rom 5:19b). The display of Jesus' obedience is the "one act of righteousness" that brought "justification of life to all men" (Rom 5:18), undoubtedly referring to His obedience unto the death of the cross (Phil 2:8), yet the implication is that He lived obediently throughout His lifetime as well.

---

232. The reader is again referred to Martin, *A Hymn of Christ*. See also Fee, "Philippians 2:5–11: Hymn or Exalted Pauline Prose?", 29–46.

233. BDAG § 7258 shows that the basic idea of ταπεινόω is "to make low;" but when used of persons, it means to "lose prestige or status, *humble, humiliate, abase.*"

234. The concept of obedience is found in Rom 13:1, 5; 1 Cor 7:15; 14:34; 16:16; Eph 5:21, 24; 6:1, 5; Phil 2:12; Col 3:18, 22; 2 Thess 3:14; 1 Tim 2:11; 3:4; Titus 2:5, 9; 3:1; Philm 21.

235. See also Rom 6:16–17; 10:16; 15:18; 16:19; 1 Cor 7:15; 2 Thess 1:8.

THE "MAN CHRIST JESUS"

This is certainly how the Gospels present the character of Jesus, as Luke 2:51 comments that as a boy, Jesus "continued in subjection" to Mary and Joseph. More significantly, John 8:29 records this saying of Jesus, "He who sent Me is with Me; He has not left Me alone, for I always do the things that are pleasing to Him." Such a claim for absolute obedience to God is quite remarkable, indicating that Jesus was either deluded about His own failures (as Solomon observes in 1 Kgs 8:46, "There is no man who does not sin."), presumptuously proud (like the rich young ruler boasting of the Law, "I have kept all these things from my youth up," Mark 10:20), or in fact habitually obedient to the Father. This third option is the impression given by the Gospels, culminating in Jesus' prayer in the Garden of Gethsemane, "Not as I will, but as you will" (Matt 26:39 ESV).

How did Paul come to know that Jesus' life was characterized by obedience? It could have been a reasonable deduction that as a pious Jew, Jesus obeyed the Law of God consistently, for even Paul as a Pharisee boasted that he was blameless according to the Law (Phil 3:6). Instead, it is Jesus' higher allegiance to the plan of the Father in being obedient to the cross that brings life to many. It should not be overlooked that Paul assumes the reality of Christ's obedience lived out in human history as that which serves as the basis of salvation: if Jesus had not been obedient, Paul's foundation of justification collapses. But since Jesus was obedient on behalf of others, now the apostle calls on believers to take "every thought captive to the obedience of Christ" (εἰς τὴν ὑπακοὴν τοῦ Χριστοῦ, 2 Cor 10:4) in order to emulate this same virtue of the "Man Christ Jesus."

"One Act of Righteousness"

Righteousness as demonstrated in Christ's obedience is one of the most important character traits identified by Paul (Rom 5:17–19), as he states, "the doers of the Law will be justified" (Rom 2:13) but "the unrighteous shall not inherit the kingdom of God" (1 Cor 6:9).[236] The ultimate standard for Paul is the "righteousness of God" (Rom 1:17; 3:5, 21–22; 10:3; 2 Cor 5:21) revealed in His Law, which Paul describes as "holy and righteous and good" (Rom 7:12). Thus, the one declared to be justified by the righteous God is the one who is just—the one who fulfills the righteous requirements of the Law (Rom 8:4).

Paul finds such a Man in Jesus, whom he describes as "righteousness from God" (1 Cor 1:30), through whom also by "one act of righteousness there resulted justification of life to all men" (Rom 5:18). In context, this act refers to the "obedience of the One" (Rom 5:19), previously argued as referring to "obedience unto the death of cross" (Phil 2:8); however, all acts of Jesus must also have been deemed righteous in order for Him to qualify for the supreme act of righteousness of His obedience to death.

It should not be overlooked that Paul had to have some prior knowledge of the righteous character of Jesus in order to teach that Jesus had lived according to the standard

---

236. It is not evident to the English reader that the Greek words for righteousness, justice, justification, judgment, etc, are all related to the same root δικ-. The BGT counts that Paul uses these related words some 152 times in his letters, and other than the place-name Λαοδικεία (Col 2:1; 4:13, 16), all concern the idea of righteousness or lack thereof. Packer, *Apostolic Preaching of the Cross*, 252, defines the basic concept of these words as "something in conformity with some standard of right. The righteous man is one who is adjudged right by such a standard, and righteousness indicates a state of having attained to the standard in question."

of the Law of God, which is Paul's definition of righteousness (Rom 2:13; 10:5; Phil 3:6). What makes his declaration all the more remarkable is that Paul, when he was Saul the Pharisee, would have considered Jesus of Nazareth to be most unrighteous; for, after all, He had been condemned on a charge of blasphemy against the Law of Moses (Matt 26:65). Paul's "converted" knowledge of Jesus as a man of righteous character, then, had to have come not only through his Damascus Road encounter with Jesus of Nazareth, but also from eyewitnesses who observed the actual practices of His life and confessed Him as "the Righteous One" (Acts 3:14). It is significant to note that "the Righteous One" was the title Saul heard Stephen confess of Jesus (Acts 7:52), and it was one of the initial epithets given to Jesus by Ananias at Saul's baptism (Acts 22:14). How could the Crucified One in reality be the Righteous One? Only in fulfillment of the messianic prophecy of Isa 53:11, "By His knowledge the Righteous One, My Servant, will justify the many (δικαιῶσαι δίκαιον)—as He will bear their iniquities."

Of course, all this emphasis on righteousness agrees with the same standard of justice taught by Jesus from the time of His baptism when He compelled John to baptize Him, "for in this way it is fitting for us to fulfill all righteousness" (Matt 3:15). Jesus described His judgment as just (John 5:30), and as the one who seeks the glory of the Father who sent Him, "there is no unrighteousness in Him" (John 7:18). Even Pilate's wife described the condemned Jesus as "that righteous one" (Matt 27:19), just as the centurion declared of Jesus after witnessing His suffering, "Certainly this was a righteous Man!" (ὄντως ὁ ἄνθρωπος οὗτος δίκαιος ἦν, Luke 23:47).

It is no understatement, then, to insist that Paul's entire concept of salvation rests in this righteous act of Jesus given on behalf of "those who receive the abundance of grace and of the gift of righteousness" (Rom 5:17). If the righteousness of Jesus is merely a mythical legend, then Paul's teaching of the justification of sinners by faith in Jesus as the Christ holds no substance whatsoever—it too is a mythical promise. To the contrary, Paul's entire presumption in his contrast between the transgression of Adam and the righteousness of "Man Christ Jesus" is that these were events that transpired in human history and demonstrated the character of two men of history.

"The Faith of Jesus Christ"

This righteousness of God comes to believers through another virtue of Jesus commended by Paul, and that is the "faith of Jesus" (πίστεως Ἰησοῦ, Rom 3:22), although this phrase is usually translated as a dative, "faith *in* Christ." Such rendition leads Wallace to comment, "Arguably the most debated group of texts involves the expression πίστις Χριστοῦ: should it be translated 'faith *in* Christ' (objective gen.) or 'the faith/faithfulness *of* Christ' (subjective gen.)?"[237] Both translations are certainly possible, but significantly, when the

---

237. Wallace, *Greek Grammar*, 114–16. The Pauline references (KJV) are: Rom 3:22, "*the righteousness of God which is by <u>faith of Jesus Christ</u>* (διὰ πίστεως Ἰησοῦ Χριστοῦ) unto all and upon all them that believe" (εἰς πάντας τοὺς πιστεύοντας); Rom 3:26; "that he might be just, and the justifier of him <u>which believeth in Jesus</u>" (τὸν ἐκ πίστεως Ἰησου); Gal 2:16, "Knowing that a man is not justified by the works of the law, but by <u>the faith of Jesus Christ</u> (διὰ πίστεως Ἰησοῦ Χριστου), even we have believed in Jesus Christ (ἡμεῖς εἰς Χριστὸν Ἰησοῦν ἐπιστεύσαμεν), that we might be justified by <u>the faith of Christ</u>" (ἐκ πίστεως Χριστου), and

THE "MAN CHRIST JESUS"

noun πίστις is elsewhere followed by a genitive in Pauline literature, it is translated as the faith *of* another, not faith *in* that individual.[238] Thus, it seems more consistent to translate πίστεως Ἰησοῦ as faith *of* Christ rather than faith *in* Christ, since it is recognized that πίστις can describe the subjective characteristic of faithfulness, just as the NASB translates πίστιν τοῦ θεοῦ by "faithfulness of God" (Rom 3:3).[239] Why not be consistent and translate πίστεως Ἰησοῦ (Rom 3:22) as "the faithfulness of Jesus" as well?[240]

The apparent fear is that "faithfulness of Christ" would somehow detract from justification by faith, but an examination of the pertinent texts shows that Paul distinguishes between Christ's faithfulness as the basis for believing from the act of the believer's faith in Christ—both ideas of faith *in* Christ and faith *of* Christ are included as distinct issues.[241] So, while Bousset insists, "Paul does not proclaim the faith of Jesus, but faith in Jesus,"[242] it is precisely the faithfulness of Christ that Paul proclaims by use of the genitive, πίστεως Ἰησοῦ Χριστοῦ. Wallace observes, "The faith/ faithfulness of Christ is not a denial of faith *in* Christ as a Pauline concept (since the idea is expressed in many of the same contexts, only with the verb πιστεύω rather than with the noun), but it implies that

---

not by the works of the law: for by the works of the law shall no flesh be justified;" Gal 2:20, "I live by the *faith of the Son of God*" (ἐν πίστει ζῶ τῇ τοῦ υἱοῦ τοῦ θεοῦ);" Gal 3:22, "the promise by *faith of Jesus Christ*" (ἐκ πίστεως Ἰησοῦ Χριστοῦ) might be given to them that believe" (τοῖς πιστεύουσιν); Eph 3:12, "In whom we have boldness and access with confidence by *the faith of him*" (διὰ τῆς πίστεως αὐτοῦ); Phil 3:9, "not having mine own righteousness, which is of the law (μὴ ἔχων ἐμὴν δικαιοσύνην τὴν ἐκ νόμου), but that which is through *the faith of Christ*" (ἀλλὰ τὴν διὰ πίστεως Χριστοῦ), the righteousness which is of God by faith" (τὴν ἐκ θεοῦ δικαιοσύνην ἐπὶ τῇ πίστει). The KJV is the only English version that translates the phrase as a subjective genitive (although the NET has more recently done so), but as noted here, even the KJV is not consistent. See similar genitive constructions in Acts 3:16 ("faith through Him"); Jas 2:1 ("the faith of our Lord Jesus Christ of glory"); and Rev 14:12 (the ones keeping . . . the faith of Jesus") .

238. As in Rom 3:3, "the faithfulness of God" (τὴν πίστιν τοῦ θεοῦ); Rom 4:5, λογίζεται ἡ πίστις αὐτοῦ εἰς δικαιοσύνην is not, "faith *in* him is reckoned unto righteousness," but "his faith is reckoned as righteousness"; πίστεως τοῦ πατρὸς ἡμῶν Ἀβραάμ (Rom 4:15) is surely not "faith in Abraham," but "the faith of Abraham"; πίστεως ἀνυποκρίτου is a "sincere faith," not "faith in sincerity" (1 Tim 1:5); πιστοῦ λόγου is "faithful word," not "faith in the word" (Titus 1:9); πίστεώς σου is "your faith," not "faith in you" (Phlm 1:6; also Rom 1:8; 1 Cor 2:5; 2 Thess 1:3). The closest to an objective genitive might be in Phil 1:27, συναθλοῦντες τῇ πίστει τοῦ εὐαγγελίου ("striving for the faith in the gospel"), yet even the NASB translates this phrase as a subjective genitive, "striving together for the faith *of* the gospel." It seems odd that the only construction of "faith" followed by a genitive translated regularly as "faith in" is πίστεως Ἰησοῦ.

239. In fact, BDAG § 5941 1a. gives as the first definition of πίστις, "the state of being someone in whom confidence can be placed, *faithfulness, reliability, fidelity, commitment*," citing Rom 3:3, but then it defines all the phrases πίστις Ἰησοῦ Χριστοῦ as objective genitives, "faith in Christ," although it notes the "distinction with similar prepositional phrases clearly meaning *faith in Christ*."

240. A reasoned defense of this position is argued by Robinson, "Faith of Jesus Christ'—a New Testament Debate," 71–81. See also the articles on this topic in Bird and Sprinkle, eds., *The Faith of Jesus Christ: Exegetical, Biblical, and Theological Studies* (2010).

241. Paul uses a variety of prepositional phrases to express faith in Christ. BDAG § 5941.2b lists πίστις εἰς Χριστὸν (Acts 20:21; 24:24; 26:18; Col 2:5); πίστις ἐν Χριστῷ (Gal 3:26; Eph 1:15; Col 1:4; 1 Tim 3:13; 2 Tim 3:15); διὰ πίστεως ἐν τῷ αὐτοῦ αἵματι (Rom 3:25); πίστις ἣν ἔχεις πρὸς τ. κύριον Ἰησοῦν (Phlm 5); πίστις διὰ τοῦ κυρίου ἡμῶν Ἰ. Χριστοῦ (Acts 20:21). One should ask if he might intend any distinctions in meaning between them, and if so, how might these differ from πίστεως Ἰησου?

242. Bousset, *Kyrios Christos*, 155.

The "Man Christ Jesus" in the Epistles of Paul

the object of faith is a worthy object, for He Himself is faithful."[243] By the phrase "faith of Christ," Paul refers to the historical conduct of Jesus, that He was a faithful Man, as Heb 3:6 reports, "Christ *was* faithful as a Son" and that "He remains faithful" (2 Tim 2:13). As Jesus commends the faith of others (Matt 8:10; 9:2, 22, 29; 15:28) and was Himself a man who trusted God (Matt 27:43), so too is Paul impressed with the faithfulness of the "Man Christ Jesus."[244]

"Christ Did Not Please Himself"

In the context of the weaker-stronger brother controversy, Paul's solution is that believers are not to "please ourselves" but to "please one's neighbor for his good" (Rom 15:1–2). The reason given for this counsel is that "even Christ did not please Himself, but as it is written, 'The reproaches of those who reproached Thee fell upon Me'" (Rom 15:3). Paul makes an obvious reference to the earthly life of Jesus, illustrating it with this quote from Ps 69:9, showing that Paul knew of the selfless example of Jesus, in accordance with the astounding claim of Jesus, "I always do the things that are pleasing to Him" (John 8:29). Even though the concept of pleasing is positive in John's Gospel but negative in Romans, both verses concern not only the same Person (Jesus) but also the use of the same root word (ὁ Χριστὸς οὐχ ἑαυτῷ ἤρεσεν; ἐγὼ τὰ ἀρεστὰ αὐτῷ ποιῶ πάντοτε). Paul then presents Christ as the pattern believers are to follow by denying themselves for the sake of others (Rom 15:1).

Also, by quoting from Ps 69:9, Paul may have in mind the episode of the first cleansing of the Temple, when the disciples saw a fulfilling of this same Psalm ("His disciples remembered that it was written, 'Zeal for Thy house will consume me,'" John 2:17), leading to the first public reproach of Jesus by those Jews who demanded, "What sign do You show to us, seeing that You do these things?" (John 2:18). As Lord of the Temple, Jesus did not deserve such a reproach, but in His constant self-denial, He continued to bear the insults of others, even though these were reproaches ultimately aimed at the God who had sent His Son. Jesus would eventually be vindicated from these reproaches by His resurrection from the dead, which is a possible meaning of the second article of faith in the Christ-confession of 1 Tim 3:16, "by common confession great is the mystery of godliness: . . . He was vindicated in the Spirit" (ἐδικαιώθη ἐν πνεύματι). This rendering is an unusual translation of the verb δικαιόω, which is usually translated, "to justify." One must wonder, then, did Jesus need justification? Apparently He did, in the sense of being declared to be just in the sight of God. If πνεῦμα here refers to the Holy Spirit,[245] then this "justification" could refer to the anointing of Jesus by the Holy Spirit at His baptism, or to His continual enabling by the Spirit throughout His ministry (Luke 4:1, 14; Matt 12:28;

---

243. Wallace, *Greek Grammar*, 116.

244. Hooker, *From Adam to Christ: Essays on Paul*, 180, observes that in all the pertinent passages that Paul is concerned "not simply with 'life in Christ,' but with the activity of the earthly Jesus," although she mingles the concepts by adding that each context also stresses "the importance of participation in Christ."

245. The phrase ἐν πνεύματι usually means "in the Holy Spirit" in Paul's letters (Rom 2:29; 8:9; 9:1; 14:17; 15:16; 1 Cor 12:3; 14:16; 2 Cor 6:6; Gal 6:1; Eph 2:22; 3:5; 5:18; 6:18; Col 1:8; 1 Thess. 1:5).

THE "MAN CHRIST JESUS"

Acts 10:38), but eventually it refers to His ultimate declaration as the Son of God "with power by the resurrection from the dead, according to the Spirit of holiness" (Rom 1:4).

Regardless of the precise event in view, Paul had knowledge that Jesus had been "justified" in the sense that God declared Him to be His Son (Matt 3:17; 17:5; John 12:28), and this identity was made manifest in the selfless example of Jesus that Paul cites as one who did not please Himself but His Father. Surely this lesson was not lost on his readers in Rome, any more than it would be missed by modern Christians who have read the Gospels—that Paul believed the "Man Christ Jesus" presented a selfless example to emulate.

"He Knew No Sin"

In 2 Cor 5:20–21, Paul writes, "We beg you on behalf of Christ, be reconciled to God. He made Him who knew no sin *to be* sin on our behalf, that we might become the righteousness of God in Him." The pertinent clause is τὸν μὴ γνόντα ἁμαρτίαν ὑπὲρ ἡμῶν ἁμαρτίαν ἐποίησεν, which may well be the most astounding assertion ever made by one writer about another individual. The subject of ἐποίησεν ("he made") is implied from the previous verse, referring to God, and it is quite startling that this God—who is described here by the attribute of righteousness—"made . . . sin," when He is the one of whom Paul asks, "There is no injustice with God, is there? May it never be!" (Rom 9:14). A righteous God is incapable of "making sin" (as "it is impossible for God to lie," Heb 6:18), yet this righteous God went even beyond that: He made sin of the One who did not know sin! In context, this one who "knew not sin" refers to Christ, to whom Paul attributes sinlessness, since "to know" here must mean more than "to have come to the knowledge of something,"[246] for surely Jesus knew what sin was: He often preached against it! The point here is that He did not experience or practice sin. In 2 Cor 5:21, then, Paul confirms his earlier typology in 1 Cor 5:7 when he described Jesus as "our Passover Lamb who had to be unblemished and spotless to be an appropriate sacrificial offering to God."[247] Peter uses the same type by describing the blood of Christ as of a lamb "unblemished and spotless" (1 Pet 1:19) and by presenting the suffering of Jesus as an example to follow, in that He "made no sin" (ἁμαρτίαν οὐκ ἐποίησεν; 1 Pet 2:22). Couple these claims with the description of Heb 4:15 that Jesus was "without sin" (χωρὶς ἁμαρτίας) and with the declaration of 1 John 3:5, "In Him there is no sin" (ἁμαρτία ἐν αὐτῷ οὐκ ἔστιν), and there is a united testimony among NT writers that Jesus was sinless.

Because of this notable description that Jesus "knew no sin," Fee describes 2 Cor 5:21 as the one text in Paul's letters "that explicitly puts Christ's humanity outside the framework of what is common to all other human beings,"[248] which is the fact that "all have sinned" (Rom 3:23). How did Paul know that Jesus had never committed a sin? Since he wrote of Jesus' testimony before Pilate (1 Tim 6:13), it is a fair assumption that Paul also knew Pilate's declarations that he found no guilt in Jesus (Luke 23:4, 14, 22; John 18:38; 19:4, 6), meaning that Jesus was crucified unjustly as an innocent man. Even so, legal in-

---

246. As BDAG § 1647.6a lists this usage of γινώσκω in 2 Cor 5:21.
247. Witherington, "Jesus as the Alpha and Omega of New Testament Thought," 39.
248. Fee, *Pauline Christology*, 529.

nocence is a far cry from sinlessness, so it seems equally certain that Paul also knew of the shocking question of Jesus, "Which one of you convicts Me of sin?" (John 8:46). Such a challenge invites inquiry, and Paul must have known of the futile search by the Sanhedrin to find violations of the Law (sins) by which to condemn Jesus. When they found a charge that stuck, it was not for sinful conduct but His own claim to be the Son of God (Luke 22:70–71), an avowal implying sinlessness.

Thus, what Paul declares about the "Man Christ Jesus" in 2 Cor 5:21 is that He was sinless. How else would Paul know this information unless he also knew the Christ-histories originating with Jesus Himself, as one who referred to Himself in this manner, that "there is no unrighteousness in Him" (John 7:18)?

Summary to the Character of Jesus

This overview of the character of the "Man Christ Jesus" in Paul's letters verifies the observation of Machen, "Thus the paucity of references in the Pauline Epistles as to the teaching and example of Jesus has sometimes been exaggerated. The Epistles attest considerable knowledge of the details of Jesus' life, and warm appreciation of His character."[249] Stanton also notes, "Paul's references to the character of Jesus cannot merely be references to the pre-existent Christ. Where does this rich portrait come from? As it cannot be attributed simply to traditional Jewish beliefs or to Christological reflections of a dogmatic kind, it must have been deeply influenced by Paul's knowledge of the earthly Jesus."[250] Otherwise, Paul could not call upon his readers in 1 Cor 11:1, "Be imitators of me, just as I also am of Christ" unless he assumed that he was also correctly imitating the example of Jesus, not merely in His exaltation state, but also in His earthly character, having received such information though delivered traditions (1 Cor 11:2).

Also, each of these virtues mentioned above presumes that knowledge of the character of Jesus must have been commonly shared as part of the traditions Paul impressed among his converts as the *summum bonum* of character development.[251] To write about the compassion, love, purpose, steadfastness, humbleness, obedience, righteousness, faithfulness, and selflessness of Jesus—in short, His sinlessness—implies that the readers had some knowledge of those virtues. It is therefore incorrect to make a distinction between applications of the life of Jesus from the actualities of the events of Jesus, as Johnson insists Paul does by applying the "mind of Christ" to practical humbleness in Phil 2:1–8. While he acknowledges that Paul applies the example of Jesus in humbling Himself, so "that Christians should have the same outlook and behavior as Jesus,"[252] Johnson contends that Paul does not employ facts from the Jesus-tradition but rather uses only patterns of Jesus' obedience, even though he concedes that these patterns are the same as those given

---

249. Machen, *Origin of Paul's Religion*, 151.

250. Stanton, *Jesus of Nazareth in New Testament Preaching*, 109.

251. One cannot help but note the similarity with these character qualities of Jesus with the virtues Paul commends in 2 Tim 3:10–11, "But you followed my teaching, conduct, purpose, faith, patience, love, perseverance, persecutions, *and* sufferings" and 1 Tim 4:12, "Let no one look down on your youthfulness, but *rather* in speech, conduct, love, faith *and* purity, show yourself an example of those who believe."

252. Johnson, *Real Jesus*, 161.

THE "MAN CHRIST JESUS"

in the Gospels and are memories of the real Jesus.[253] The fact is, however, that Paul's applications of Jesus' character rest upon historical precedence, that Jesus actually was a man of such character. There could be no applications if the events did not happen, and the events would not have happened if Jesus had not been a man of impeccable godly character.

Thus, Paul's allusions to the character of Jesus agree completely with the portrayal of Jesus given in the Gospels: both describe the same man. In this matter, Bruce summarizes, "Paul's chief argument in his ethical instruction is the example of Jesus himself. And the character of Jesus as Paul understands it is consistent with the character of Jesus as portrayed in the Gospels."[254]

THE SUFFERINGS OF THE "MAN CHRIST JESUS"

Just as the Gospels devote a significant percentage of their narratives to the last week of Jesus' life, leading up to His crucifixion,[255] so Paul likewise devotes most of His references to the historical Jesus to His suffering, crucifixion, and death, which he explains as the substitutionary sacrifice for the sins of His people. Yet Fee observes, the excruciating death by crucifixion does not begin for Paul as theology but "as *history*, where a truly human Jesus died as the Jewish messiah."[256] Paul is well aware of the physical sufferings of Jesus, since he likens his present sufferings to the fact that "the sufferings of Christ (τὰ παθήματα τοῦ Χριστοῦ) are ours in abundance" (2 Cor 1:5). He tells the Colossians, "I do my share on behalf of His body (which is the church) in filling up that which is lacking in Christ's afflictions" (τῶν θλίψεων τοῦ Χριστοῦ, Col 1:24). While these references speak of a continuing dynamic of Christ's sufferings in the experiences of the church, they would make no sense had Jesus not physically suffered. Likewise, when Paul writes of his own participation in Christ's sufferings, he places it in the historical context of His death (Phil 3:10, "that I may know Him, and the power of His resurrection and the fellowship of His sufferings (κοινωνίαν [τῶν] παθημάτων αὐτοῦ), being conformed to His death."). Thus, references scattered throughout his letters indicate that Paul sets before the eyes of his readers "Jesus Christ publicly portrayed *as* crucified" (Gal 3:1),[257] although the use of the plural, "sufferings," indicates that Paul refers to afflictions of Jesus beyond just that of the cross, as this section will now explore:

---

253. Ibid., 162. One must wonder how patterns of character can be derived and emulated apart from descriptive reports of that character.

254. Bruce, *Paul*, 96.

255. Matthew gives seven chapters out of 28 to the events of the crucifixion; Mark gives five chapters out of 16; Luke gives four and a half chapters out of 24, and John gives nine out of 21.

256. Fee, *Pauline Christology*, 529, his italics.

257. See the summary by Weiss, *Paul and Jesus*, 20. He writes, "In fact the picture of the Crucified must have stood before his mind in more than mere outline: colour, features, and expression must have been manifest to him, or he could never have 'evidently set it forth before the eyes' of the Galatians (Gal 3:1). This expression indisputably presupposes a vivid, sympathetic, and realistic description of the event and not merely an impressive proclamation of the fact."

The "Man Christ Jesus" in the Epistles of Paul

"Christ Our Passover"

When Paul gives a theological interpretation of the death of Jesus, "Christ our Passover has been sacrificed" (1 Cor 5:7), he "connects the death of Jesus to the Passover celebration of the Jews" on the fourteenth day of Nisan.[258] Paul was aware that Jesus ate this Passover "in the night He was betrayed" (1 Cor 11:23), agreeing with the record of the Gospels, that the arrest of Jesus happened on the evening after He partook of the *pascha* meal with His disciples, on the eve of the Passover Day (Matt 26:19; Mark 14:16; Luke 22:15). "John, however, specifies in addition that this was not only the day of preparation of the Sabbath, but also the day of preparation of the Passover, so that the Sabbath on the following day was the Passover (cf. John 19:34)."[259] Thus, Paul had knowledge of the particular day of the sufferings of the "Man Christ Jesus," that He was condemned on the morning of a Passover that preceded a Sabbath.

"The Night He Was Betrayed"

Paul had also "received from the Lord" through the traditions of Christ-histories the information that when Jesus shared in a Passover meal "in the night in which He was betrayed" (1 Cor 11:23), He inaugurated the Lord's Supper (1 Cor 11:20).[260] This primary ordinance of the liturgy of the church proclaims the historical fact of the Lord's death "until He comes" (1 Cor 11:26). Thus, Paul was well aware that the "Man Christ Jesus" originated the liturgy of the Eucharist in a particular meal on a particular night, just as the Gospels present this information (Matt 26:26–28; Mark 14:22–24; Luke 22:19–20).[261]

The significance of this statement is profound, for it shows that Paul understood the typological application of the bread and wine of the Passover liturgy to the body and blood of Jesus originated with Jesus Himself.[262] This connection means that Jesus taught the sacrificial nature of His death before His crucifixion:[263] it is not an interpretation superimposed on His death by Paul many years later and codified in the creedal statement

---

258. Johnson, *Real Jesus*, 119.

259. NET *Notes, loc. cit.* in *Bibleworks8* under John 19:14.

260. See Stout, "The New Testament Concept of Tradition," 124–30, for support of the view that Paul did not receive this particular information of the Lord's Supper as direct revelation from the exalted Lord, but rather he relied on the passed-on tradition originating in the practice of the *Urgemeinde* in Jerusalem (Acts 2:42, 46), who in turn received its knowledge directly from the historical Jesus on Passover eve in the Upper Room.

261. Surprisingly, the classic study of Jeremias, *The Eucharistic Words of Jesus*, 111–13, devotes a rather short discussion to 1 Cor 11:23–25 as providing an independent tradition of the Lord's Supper (ibid., 101–105). While Jeremias finds that Paul's account displays the most "greacizing" of the forms (ibid., 185–86), he asserts that all the accounts "go back therefore to a common eucharistic tradition lying behind . . . (the) texts" (ibid., 86). Thus he determines, "We have every reason to conclude that the common core of the tradition of the account of the Lord's Supper—what Jesus said at the Last Supper—is preserved to us in an essentially reliable form" (ibid., 203).

262. "When He had given thanks, He broke it, and said, 'This is My body, which is for you (ὑπὲρ ὑμῶν); do this in remembrance of Me.' In the same way *He took* the cup also, after supper, saying, 'This cup is the new covenant in My blood; do this, as often as you drink *it*, in remembrance of Me'" (1 Cor 11:24–25).

263. This insight is credited to Ben Witherington III, in a lecture heard by the author on 1 Cor 11:17–34, delivered in Charlotte, N.C. on Oct 12, 2009 at a seminar on the Lord's Supper.

THE "MAN CHRIST JESUS"

of 1 Cor 11:23–25.[264] Instead, the "Man Christ Jesus" is the source of the substitutionary explanation of His own death, that "the Son of Man . . . came to give His life a ransom for many" (ἀντὶ πολλῶν; Mark 10:45).

"The Lord Jesus Was Betrayed"

Paul also knew that on this same Passover eve that Jesus was betrayed, as he writes, "the Lord Jesus in the night in which He was betrayed took bread" (1 Cor 11:23), implying that Paul not only knew of the event, but also that the betrayer came from within the ranks of Jesus' disciples, as implied by this use of παραδίδωμι to describe the act of Judas.[265] Ehrman, however, insists that that "in every other instance that Paul uses *paradidomi* with reference to Jesus, it refers to the act of God, who 'handed Jesus over' to death for the sake of others," so that "there is no reference in any of Paul's letters to Judas Iscariot or to his act of betrayal."[266] Ehrman is correct that Paul uses this verb to describe divine handing over (in Rom 4:25; 8:32; Gal 2:20; Eph 5:2, 25), yet he neglects to mention that Paul also uses the same word earlier in 1 Cor 11:23 for "delivering" information he had received "from the Lord"—through the means of apostolic tradition originating with Jesus (1 Cor 11:2; 15:3). This usage not only reminds us that words have different meaning in different contexts, but it also shows that "the chain of historical tradition which Paul received goes back unbroken to the words of Jesus himself."[267] Inserted in this tradition is a historical detail of that inaugural Eucharist, that it happened "in the night He was betrayed," a matter that was also a topic of shocked conversation at the moment of the sharing of the cup during that meal (Luke 22:21–22). Paul's mention of this betrayal suggests that he

---

264. Those who maintain this opinion on the whole do not seem to be aware of the audacious hoax perpetrated by Paul if it is true he invented the atoning death of Jesus. Not only would Paul have to put fraudulent words into the mouth of Jesus but he would also implicate the entire apostolate in the conspiracy as well, since he claims to have received these quotations from the Lord presumably through those who were with Him at the Last Supper. Surely if Jesus made no such interpretation of the Passover as applying to His body and blood, these eyewitness disciples would have called Paul's hand and exposed him as a fraud. As it is, by citing prior tradition in 1 Cor 11:2, 23; 15:3, Paul invites the Corinthians to confirm his sources.

265. The verb παραδίδωμι is used of Judas' betrayal in Matt 26:16; 21, 23, 24, 25, 46, 48; 27:3; Mark 14:11, 18, 21, 42, 44; Luke 22:4, 6, 21, 22, 48; John 13:2; 11; 21; 18:2; 5. LN § 37.111 defines παραδίδωμι in this usage as "to deliver a person into the control of someone else, involving either the handing over of a presumably guilty person for punishment by authorities or the handing over of an individual to an enemy who will presumably take undue advantage of the victim—'to hand over, to turn over to, to betray.'"

266. Ehrman, *The Lost Gospel of Judas Iscariot: A New Look at Betrayer and Betrayed*, 16. Ehrman has a uncanny knack of taking what seems obvious—that Paul refers to Judas' betrayal—and making it seem sinister on the part of the NT writers; for example, he asserts that Paul did not know about Judas and his betrayal because he writes in 1 Cor 15:5 that Jesus appeared to the Twelve, so, "How could he have appeared to all of them if Judas was no longer among their number?" This is completely disingenuous, since the "Twelve" is a title for the Apostolate, regardless of the number of members actually part of it (Acts 6:2). Proof of this is that John 20:24 describes Thomas as "one of the Twelve" when he saw the risen Jesus even though Judas was at that time presumably dead, leaving the group with eleven, yet it is still called "the Twelve." Ehrman is masterful at driving wedges between the NT writers by assuming that their perspective is mistaken at the least and sinister at worst. Not surprisingly, then, he turns the NT portrayal of Judas as a betrayer on its head and concludes that the *Gospel of Judas* may well be correct in presenting Judas as "the greatest of all the Apostles" (ibid., 180).

267. Ladd, "Revelation and Tradition in Paul," 226.

presumably knew the name of the betrayer as well but chose not to identify Him, perhaps as a warning to his disruptive readers in Corinth whose conduct bordered perilously close to a betrayal of Christ in another way (1 Cor 11:29–30). Thus, in this little detail, Paul agrees with the record of the Gospels, that the "Man Christ Jesus" was betrayed by one of His own disciples, Judas (Matt 26:25; Mark 14:10; Luke 22:48; John 18:2).

"The Jews Killed the Lord Jesus"

The idea of betrayal implies a sinister conspiracy (one who is betrayed is handed over to an enemy by an ally), and in 1 Thess 2:15 Paul implicates "the Jews . . . who killed the Lord Jesus." On the surface, this comment seems to be very anti-Semitic, until it is remembered that Paul himself was Jewish, as was Jesus. Certainly not every Jew was complicit in the murder of Jesus, so Paul must be using this indictment in the sense that he tells the leading Jews in Rome that he had been "delivered prisoner from Jerusalem into the hands of the Romans" (Acts 28:17). In that instance, "the Romans" serves as a synecdoche of the whole nation for only one part, in this instance, for Caesar, as shown in Paul's appeal to the emperor (Act 25:11). Applying this same figure of speech to "the Jews," the reference would be to the Jewish authorities of the Sanhedrin who determined to "kill Jesus," just as the Gospels report (Matt 26:4; Mark 14:1; John 11:53), even describing His murder with the same verb Paul uses in 1 Thess 2:15, ἀποκτείνω.[268] While Johnson concedes somewhat to critical arguments, he notes, "If 1 Thessalonians 2:14–16 is authentic and not an interpolation as some scholars hold, then Paul also involves the Jews of Judea directly in the death of Jesus."[269] Actually, there is no textual evidence that this pericope is inauthentic or interpolated,[270] and it certainly agrees with the Gospel records and the reports in Acts of Jewish opposition to Jesus and the Gospel. Paul himself admits that he was involved in this opposition when he states, "I used to persecute the church of God beyond measure, and tried to destroy it" (Gal 1:13). So, it is no surprise for Paul to implicate the contemporary Jewish leaders in the death of Jesus. Indeed, it is quite possible that Paul as Saul the Pharisee himself may have been part of that conspiracy to crucify the "Man Christ Jesus."

"Jesus Was Delivered for our Transgressions"

Paul also knew that this complicity led to the binding of Jesus over to trial, because he states in Rom 4:25, "Jesus . . . was delivered up because of our transgressions." At times, the verb παραδίδωμι is translated "taken into custody" (Matt 4:12), and it particularly conveys this idea when the Sanhedrin delivered Jesus over to the authority of Pilate (Matt

---

268. LN § 20.61 explains ἀποκτείνω or ἀποκτέννω "to cause someone's death, normally by violent means, with or without intent and with or without legal justification—'to kill.'"

269. Johnson, *Real Jesus,* 120.

270. The argument is put forth that 1 Thess 2:15 does not sound very Pauline, but it should be noted that Paul does not diminish the complicity of human agents in the injustice of Jesus' death anymore than Peter does in Acts 2:23 when he accuses his own Jewish countrymen, "this *Man*, delivered up by the predetermined plan and foreknowledge of God, you nailed to a cross by the hands of godless men and put *Him* to death."

THE "MAN CHRIST JESUS"

26:2; 27:2, 18; Mark 15:1; Luke 24:7, 20; John 18:30, 35; Acts 3:13).[271] Gavanta, however, points out that the use of παραδίδωμι in Rom 8:32 ("He who did not spare His own Son, but <u>delivered</u> Him up for us all") points instead to the "*role Paul ascribes to God*" (italics original) in the death of Jesus.[272] This observation is theologically accurate, as it shows the allusion to the binding of Isaac, the *Aqedah* of Gen 22:9, lying behind Rom 8:32. Also Rom 4:25 echoes the delivering of the Suffering Servant, whom "the Lord delivered for our sins" (κύριος παρέδωκεν αὐτὸν ταῖς ἁμαρτίαις ἡμῶν, Isa 53:6; διὰ τὰς ἁμαρτίας αὐτῶν παρεδόθη, Isa 53:12). Jesus seems to have this prophecy in mind when He announces to the Twelve, "All things which are written through the prophets about the Son of Man will be accomplished, for he will be delivered (παραδοθήσεται) to the Gentiles . . ." (Luke 18:31–32). Thus, the prophetic fulfillment of the Servant being delivered for sins would require a legal arraignment as well, so that the theological application Paul makes in Rom 4:25 and Rom 8:32 would have no bearing unless there had been a historical delivering of Jesus for trial. For Paul to refer to the prophetic deliverance of Jesus assumes that he also knew of the handing over of the "Man Christ Jesus" to the authority of Rome for adjudication of the charges brought against Him by the Sanhedrin—just as reported in the Gospels.

"The Testimony of our Lord"

In a context where he mentions his own legal troubles and incarceration, Paul asks Timothy, "Do not be ashamed of the testimony of our Lord or of me His prisoner" (2 Tim 1:8). The word "witness" (μαρτύριον) can of course be used of "Christian preaching and the gospel in general,"[273] as it is used in Acts 4:33 and 2 Thess 1:10,[274] but in 2 Tim 1:8, the context suggests a legal testimony given in a courtroom. Paul parallels his own witness (presumably to Roman authorities) to that of Jesus, indicating that he knew of the testimony given by Jesus to the Sanhedrin—even though it resulted in His condemnation (Matt 26:65–66)—as well as His response to Pilate's inquiry, "For this I have been born, and for this I have come into the world, to bear witness (μαρτυρήσω) to the truth" (John 18:37).[275] Paul also alludes to this testimony in the Christ-Creed, when "the "Man Christ Jesus" gave Himself as a ransom for all, the testimony (τὸ μαρτύριον) *borne* at the proper time" (1 Tim 2:6). These references show once again how Paul uses a historical episode in the life of Jesus to undergird his own teaching and testimony.

---

271. LN §57.77 defines παραδίδωμι, "to hand over to or to convey something to someone, particularly a right or an authority—'to give over, to hand over."

272. Gaventa, "Interpreting the Death of Jesus Apocalyptically: Reconsidering Romans 8:32," 127.

273. BDAG § 4723. 1b.

274. Acts 4:33; "with great power the apostles were giving witness to the resurrection of the Lord Jesus;" 2 Thess 1:10, "our testimony to you was believed."

275. The concept of witness-bearing is a common theme in the Gospel of John (1:7–8, 15, 32, 34; 2:25; 3:11, 26, 28, 32, 33; 4:39, 44; 5:31–34, 36–37, 39; 7:7; 8:13–14, 17, 18; 10:25; 12:17; 13:21; 15:26–27; 18: 23, 37; 19:35; 21:24), usually referring to the witness borne by Jesus of Himself.

The "Man Christ Jesus" in the Epistles of Paul

"Christ Jesus Testified Before Pontius Pilate"

Furthermore, Paul knew the identity of the Roman procurator who had heard the testimony of Jesus, as he charged Timothy "in the presence of Christ Jesus, who testified the good confession before Pontius Pilate" (1 Tim 6:13). As a Pharisee living in Jerusalem, Paul would certainly know the name the Roman representative over Judea, whom he also names in his sermon in Pisidian Antioch, "And though they found no ground for *putting Him to* death, they asked Pilate that He be executed" (Acts 13:28). This agrees with Peter's earlier accusation of the Sanhedrin, of "Jesus, *the one* whom you delivered up, and disowned in the presence of Pilate, when he had decided to release Him (Acts 3:13; also 4:27). In another explanation of this event, Paul states in 1 Cor 2:8, "If the rulers of this age had understood, they would not have crucified the Lord of glory," hinting at the consternation Pilate felt when he inquired of Jesus, "Where are you from?" (John 19:9).[276] Despite his better judgment, Pilate conceded to the threatening violence of the Jewish mob and handed Jesus over for crucifixion.

The reference to Pilate in 1 Tim 6:13 shows that Paul was well aware of these Christ-histories; in fact, he supplies the full name of "Pontius Pilate," just as Luke 3:1 does in dating the ministry of Jesus "when Pontius Pilate was governor of Judea."[277] These citations make it certain that no other procurator would be confused with Pilate, whose execution of Jesus came despite His testimony of innocence (His "good confession"). This unjust condemnation is also implied when Paul describes Jesus' crucifixion as "one act of righteousness . . . and obedience" (Rom 5:18–19), hardly the language one would use of a condemned felon. By this implication, Paul agrees with the Gospel records, that Pilate found no basis for executing Jesus (Luke 23:4, 14, 22; John 18:38; 19:4, 6; as well as Acts 13:28), but his concern is not merely historical accuracy. Instead, he finds an impetus to charge Timothy "to keep the commandment without stain or reproach" from the good confession of the "Man Christ Jesus" when He "suffered under Pontius Pilate."[278]

---

276. Gaventa, "Interpreting the Death of Jesus Apocalyptically," 138, understands "rulers of this age" primarily as cosmic, demonic forces which "may include those human beings in Jerusalem who made certain decisions and carried out certain actions against Jesus of Nazareth, although it is more likely that those residents of Jerusalem are but pawns in the control of the real 'rulers.'" While Paul describes Satan as "the ruler of the authority of the air" (Eph 2:2), the context in 1 Cor 2:6–8, where the expression "rulers of this age" is used twice, seems to refer to human rulers, not just "anti-god powers" (ibid., 139).

277. The historical fact of the rule of Pontius Pilate is also confirmed by Josephus, *Jewish Wars* 2.9.2–4 and *Antiquities* 18.3.1.

278. It is of interest to historical theology that Pilate's infamy was guaranteed by his inclusion in the Apostle's Creed, that Jesus "suffered under Pontius Pilate." The Creed places the suffering of Jesus firmly into a historical context (Pilate served in Judea from A. D. 26–36) and also implicates the governor in a gross injustice. This would be an important apologetic for the early church, for no Roman could imagine that a Savior would suffer the indignity of crucifixion, and certainly not under Roman law! However, by the repeated reference to Pilate, the early church found support for the injustice perpetrated on Jesus in the official Roman court records.

THE "MAN CHRIST JESUS"

The Reproaches that Fell on Jesus

It has been previously noted that the first sentence in Rom 15:3, "For even Christ did not please Himself," shows that Paul knew of the selfless example of Jesus. Paul, however, cites a specific incident from the sufferings of Jesus in the second sentence, "but as it is written, 'The reproaches of those who reproached Thee fell upon Me'" This quotation comes from Ps 69:9, "For zeal for Thy house has consumed me, and the reproaches of those who reproach Thee have fallen on me," which is also quoted in John 2:17 in the context of Jesus' first cleansing of the Temple, when Jesus' disciples later remembered that it was written, "Zeal for Thy house will consume me." This allusion to Ps 69:9 "suggests that Jesus underwent abuse and humiliation,"[279] especially as Paul employs the same verb ὀνειδίζω as used by the Gospels regarding the insults cast at Jesus by the thieves who were crucified with Him (Matt 27:44; Mark 15:32).[280] Again, Paul uses an example from the suffering of Jesus to support an ethical injunction that would otherwise have no bearing if the "Man Christ Jesus" had not endured similar taunts from His accusers.

"The Brand Marks of Jesus"

In Gal 6:17, Paul states, "From now on let no one cause trouble for me, for I bear on my body the brand-marks of Jesus (τὰ στίγματα τοῦ Ἰησοῦ)." While these *stigmata* are sometimes understood as symbolic marks of Paul's identification with Jesus,[281] there is little reason to doubt he refers to the physical scars on His body as the result of His many beatings and lashings for the cause of Christ (2 Cor 11:23–25). Yet Paul does not write of marks *for* Jesus, but τὰ στίγματα τοῦ Ἰησοῦ, a phrase that can be understood as a subjective genitive describing the brand-marks that belong to Christ. Wenham observes, "It may well be that Paul's rather obscure comments about His own body bearing the marks (the *stigmata*, in Greek) of Jesus in (Gal) 6:17 allude to the marks of flogging and crucifixion of Jesus."[282] In this case, Paul's reference would agree with the Gospel accounts of Jesus' predictions of His scourging (Matt 20:19; Mark 10:34; Luke 18:33) and its fulfillment (John 19:1), plus the other physical tortures He suffered (the crown of thorns, John 19:2; the blows to His head, John 18:23; 19:3; and the other beatings, Luke 22:63). Again, Paul refers to a historical reality in the torture of Jesus as a parallel for his own suffering, an allusion that is valid only if the "Man Christ Jesus" actually suffered from such bodily injuries.

"Jesus Christ Crucified"

From a cursory reading of Paul's letters, one concurs with Dunn's observation that it is self-evident that the "centre of gravity of Paul's theology . . . lies in the death and resurrec-

---

279. Johnson, *The Real Jesus*, 120.

280. BDAG § 5316.1, defines ὀνειδίζω "to find fault in a way that demeans the other, *reproach, revile, mock, heap insults* upon as a way of shaming."

281. BDAG § 6830, defines στίγμα as a mark such as a brand a master tattoos on a slave.

282. Wenham, *Paul and Jesus: The True Story*, 62.

tion of Jesus.[283] Paul knew that the manner of Jesus' death was by crucifixion,[284] and he vividly placed before the eyes of his readers "Jesus Christ publicly portrayed *as* crucified" (Gal 3:1).[285] He includes a nest of references to the crucifixion in his discussion on the unity of the gospel as the "word of the cross" (1 Cor 1:18) by which "we preach Christ crucified" (1 Cor 1:23); therefore, Paul determines to "know nothing among you except Jesus Christ, and Him crucified" (1 Cor 2:2). Whereas a crucified Messiah had been the original scandal for the prosecutor Saul, now as the converted Paul, he sees the crucifixion in such different light that had the rulers of this age understood, "they would not have crucified the Lord of glory" (1 Cor 2:8). Also, in 2 Cor 13:4, Paul notes that Jesus was "crucified because of weakness," a likely allusion to the shame and humiliation of the cross described in the Gospels, or as Goguel suggests, "the exhaustion he passed through before expiring."[286]

Paul also knows that the instrument of crucifixion was a cross, which he mentions often in his letters (1 Cor 1:17–18; Gal 5:11; 6:12, 14; Eph 2:16; Phil 2:8; 3:18; Col 1:20; 2:14), even calling the gospel the "word of the cross."[287] While the σταυρός itself was usually a wooden stake driven in the ground upon which the Romans often tied their victim to a crossbeam,[288] Paul incidentally notes that Jesus was crucified by nailing[289] at some elevation, as he comments in Acts 13:29, "They took Him 'down' from the cross." When Paul mentions that God has nailed the debts against us to the cross (Col 2:15), Wenham suggests there might be an allusion to "Pilate writing the accusation that stood against Jesus and attaching it to the cross."[290] To be sure, the cross became the means of Jesus' death (Phil 2:8) in a violent display of exsanguination when "the blood of His cross" was shed (Col 1:20). Even so, Paul is far more concerned with the significance of "the cross of our Lord Jesus Christ" (Gal 6:14) as God's means of reconciliation (Eph 2:16) and peace-making (Col 1:20) than as an instrument of execution.

These references by Paul agree with the record of the Gospels, that Jesus was crucified (Matt 27:35; Mark 15:27; Luke 23:33; John 19:18) by being nailed (John 20:25) to a

---

283. Dunn, *Theology of Paul*, 208.

284. The classic scholarly work on crucifixion is that of Hengel, *Crucifixion: In the Ancient World and the Folly of the Message of the Cross* (1977).

285. BDAG § 6176.2 defines the verb προγράφω "to set forth for public notice," as Paul portrayed the crucifixion of Jesus so vividly that it was as if the Galatians were eyewitnesses to the event. The language raises the intriguing possibility that Paul presented his own eyewitness recollection of the crucifixion—something entirely feasible since he was studying in Jerusalem at that time, according to his testimony in Acts 22:3.

286. Goguel, *Jesus the Nazarene*, 148.

287. Paul insists in 1 Cor 1:17–18, "Christ did not send me to baptize but to preach the gospel, not in cleverness of speech, that the cross of Christ should not be made void. For the word of the cross is to those who are perishing foolishness, but to us who are being saved it is the power of God."

288. Schneider, "σταυρός," *TDNT* 7:572, "The cross was a vertical, pointed stake . . . or it consisted of an upright with a cross-beam above it (T, *crux commissa*), or it consisted of two intersecting beams of equal length (†, *crux immissa*)."

289. BDAG § 6296 defines προσηλόω, "*Nail* the condemned man *fast* to the pyre, a verb related to the noun ἧλος (BDAG § 3432, a nail)."

290. Wenham, *Paul: Follower of Jesus or Founder of Christianity?*, 365.

THE "MAN CHRIST JESUS"

cross (Matt 27:32; John 19:17). Thus, it may seem rather pedantic to ask, how did Paul know about the crucifixion? As the prosecutor Saul, he had heard about the crucifixion from the preaching of the Jerusalem Apostles (Acts 2:36; 4:10), but there may be no other historical fact so prominently self-evident in both Paul's letters and the Gospels than that of the crucifixion of the "Man Christ Jesus."

"Christ Jesus is He Who Died"

It is by way of the cross that Jesus met His death (Phil 2:8), revealing that Paul not only knew the means but the fact of Jesus' death. There is no question that the death of Jesus is critical to Paul's understanding of salvation. He mentions it specifically at least twenty-three times plus assumes or references it other times besides, that "Christ Jesus is He who died" (Rom 8:34).[291] The death of Jesus is so pervasive in Paul's letters, that Bousset contends, "In fact, in the entire earthly manner of existence of Jesus, it is only the death that actually interests (Paul)."[292] This assertion is what one might charitably call a scholarly overstatement, since the previous listing of Paul's references to the historical Jesus is quite extensive. Even so, Bousset is correct that Paul's greatest interest lies in the historical death of Jesus because of the saving significance he places upon it. It must not be overlooked, however, that had Jesus not actually died in human time and space, Paul's soteriology would be rendered null and void. It is the giving of the "Man Christ Jesus" in death that becomes the ransom for humanity.

"Christ Was Buried"

In 1 Cor 15:4, Paul states the tradition he had received, "that Christ was buried." The verb θάπτω does not indicate which method of burial was used, although in his speech in Acts 13:29, Paul reports that Jesus was taken down from the cross and laid in a tomb (ἔθηκαν εἰς μνημεῖον).[293] He then agrees with the Gospel records, that "they laid Him in a tomb cut into the rock, where no one had ever lain" (Matt 27:59–60; Mark 15:46; Luke 23:53; John 19:38–42), as predicted by Jesus in His anointing by Mary (Matt 26:12; Mark 14:8; John 12:7). The fact that Paul moves directly from the burial to the appearing of Christ does not mean he was ignorant of an empty tomb or a bodily resurrection. Bruce notes, "It is implied that the raising . . . was the reversal of burying, and this points to the motif of the empty tomb,"[294] for it assumes a physical resurrection.

---

291. Paul uses these various phrases: "Christ died" (Rom 5:6, 8, 10; 6:3, 5, 10); "Christ Jesus is He who died" (Rom 8:34); "For to this end Christ died" (Rom 14:9); "for whom Christ died" (Rom 14:15); "the brother for whose sake Christ died" (1 Cor 8:11); "you proclaim the Lord's death" (1 Cor 11:26); "Christ died" (1 Cor 15:3); "always carrying about in the body the dying of Jesus" (2 Cor 4:10); "one died for all, and He died for all, that they who live should no longer live for themselves, but for Him who died" (2 Cor 5:14–15); "Christ died" (Gal 2:21); "He humbled Himself by becoming obedient to the point of death" (Phil 2:8); "being conformed to His death" (Phil 3:10); "He has now reconciled you in His fleshly body through death" (Col 1:22); "we believe that Jesus died" (1 Thess 4:14); "Christ who died" (1 Thess 5:10); "For if we died with Him, we shall also live with Him" (2 Tim 2:11).

292. Bousset, *Kyrios Christos*, 208–09.

293. LN § 7.75, defines μνημεῖον as "a construction for the burial of the dead—'grave, tomb.'

294. Bruce, *Paul and Jesus*, 47.

The "Man Christ Jesus" in the Epistles of Paul

While the burial of Jesus seems to be a mere matter of historical interest, Paul uses the entombment of Jesus as an aspect of the believer's association with Jesus, according to Paul's thought in Rom 6:4, "we have been buried with Him" and in Col 2:12, "having been buried with Him in baptism." The fact remains, however, that had there been no actual burial of Jesus, there would be no reality to the association of the believer in that burial. So, once again, Paul somewhat incidentally uses a unique historical occurrence of the "Man Christ Jesus" to support a doctrinal implication, the explanation of which will be explored in greater depth in Chapter 5.

Summary to the Sufferings of Jesus

This section has shown that all of Paul's allusions to the suffering of Jesus agree with the Gospel records: that Jesus shared a last Supper with His disciples on the Passover eve; that He was betrayed (ostensibly by one of His disciples); that there was Jewish complicity in handing Him over to Pontius Pilate for trial; and that despite the good testimony of Jesus, He was delivered for crucifixion on a cross after enduring beatings and taunting. All these events led to His physical death and the entombment of His body. While Paul omits many of the details found in the Gospel narratives, he certainly adds no new information or legendary material but rather he repeatedly uses historical information to affirm the sufferings of the "Man Christ Jesus."

THE EXALTATION OF THE "MAN CHRIST JESUS"

To this point in our study, we have seen how Paul describes Jesus as an individual man who lived in human space and time. Hints at the supernatural have been incidental (such as the attendance of angels and the possibility of miracles), but with the mention of the exaltation of Jesus by God, Paul enters into a supernatural realm deemed to be impossible by critics both modern and ancient (Acts 17:32, "Now when they heard of the resurrection of the dead, some *began* to sneer"). Yet Paul makes no distinction of identity between Jesus, the man of history, and Jesus, the exalted Christ. In this section, we explore Paul's understanding of the "Man Christ Jesus" who is also the resurrected Lord, who appeared to His disciples, and who ascended into heaven.

"Christ Was Raised From The Dead"

Dunn accurately identifies "the centre of gravity of Paul's theology . . . in the death and resurrection of Jesus,"[295] gauged not merely from the numerous times Paul mentions these events but primarily from the weight he places on them as savingly significant. In actuality, Paul uses the specific word resurrection (ἀνάστασις) of Jesus only three times (Rom 1:4; 6:5; Phil 3:10)[296] as he tends to use that term to refer to the more general resurrection of all the dead (1 Cor 15:12, 13, 21, 42; Phil 3:11; 2 Tim 2:18).[297] When he discusses the raising of Jesus

---

295. Dunn, *Theology of Paul*, 208.

296. Romans 1:4, "He was declared the Son of God with power by the resurrection from the dead; Rom 6:5, "we shall be also *in the likeness* of His resurrection;" Phil 3:10, "the power of His resurrection."

297. Paul also refers to the resurrection of the dead in Acts 17:18, 32; 23:6, 8; 24:15, 21, 23. In 1 Cor

THE "MAN CHRIST JESUS"

from the dead, he prefers to use the verb ἐγείρω in the passive voice with the Father as the implied agent[298] or in the active voice with God the Father as the stated agent.[299] Paul also uses the verb ἀνίστημι of Christ's resurrection in 1 Thess 4:14 ("Jesus . . . rose again," ἀνέστη) as well as in his speeches in Acts 13:34, 17:3 and 17:31.[300]

Generally, Paul mentions the resurrection of Christ as a corollary of some other aspect of salvation, whether imputation of righteousness (Rom 4:24), justification (Rom 4:25), regeneration (Rom 6:4; Col 2:12), union in Christ (Rom 7:4), conversion (Rom 10:9), ethical behavior (2 Cor 5:15; 1 Thess 1:10), or the believer's future resurrection (Rom 8:11; 1 Cor 6:14; 2 Cor 4:14; 15:12–20; 1 Thess 4:14). Supremely, however the resurrection of Jesus is His vindication by the Father of His Sonship, Messiahship and Lordship (Rom 1:4; 6:9; 8:34; 1 Cor 15:4; Gal 1:1; Eph 1:20; 2 Tim 2:8). Clearly, without the historical resurrection of Jesus, Paul would have no gospel to preach, as he makes clear in 1 Cor 15:14, "if Christ has not been raised, then our preaching is vain, your faith also is vain."

15:12–24, Paul reasons from the general to the specific in this manner: that since there will be a resurrection of all the dead at the end of the age, then Christ is the first of what will inevitably follow. See Vos, *Pauline Eschatology*, 136–225.

298. The verb ἐγείρω in the passive voice is found at Rom 4:25, "He was raised (ἠγέρθη) because of our justification;" Rom 6:4, "as Christ was raised from the dead (ἠγέρθη Χριστὸς ἐκ νεκρῶν) through the glory of the Father;" Rom 6:9, "Christ, having been raised from the dead (Χριστὸς ἐγερθεὶς ἐκ νεκρῶν), is never to die again;" Rom 7:4, "to Him who was raised from the dead (τῷ ἐκ νεκρῶν ἐγερθέντι);" Rom 8:34, "Christ Jesus who was raised (ἐγερθείς);" 1 Cor 15: 4, "He was raised (ἐγήγερται) on the third day according to the Scriptures;" 1 Cor 15:12, "Christ is preached, that He has been raised from the dead (ἐκ νεκρῶν ἐγήγερται);" 1 Cor 15:13, "But if there is no resurrection of the dead, not even Christ has been raised (οὐδὲ Χριστὸς ἐγήγερται);" 1 Cor 15:14, "if Christ has not been raised (εἰ δὲ Χριστὸς οὐκ ἐγήγερται), then our preaching is vain;" 1 Cor 15:16, "For if the dead are not raised, not even Christ has been raised (ἐγήγερται);" 1 Cor 15:17, "if Christ has not been raised (Χριστὸς οὐκ ἐγήγερται), your faith is worthless;" 1 Cor 15:20, "But now Christ has been raised from the dead (Χριστὸς ἐγήγερται ἐκ νεκρῶν);" 2 Cor 5:15, "Him who died and rose again" (ἐγερθέντι); 2 Tim 2:8, "Remember Jesus Christ, risen from the dead (ἐγηγερμένον ἐκ νεκρῶν)."

299. The verb ἐγείρω in the active voice is found at Rom 4:25, "for our sake also, to whom it will be reckoned, as those who believe in Him who raised (τὸν ἐγείραντα) Jesus our Lord from the dead;" Rom 8:11, "He who raised Christ Jesus from the dead (ὁ ἐγείρας Χριστὸν ἐκ νεκρῶν) will also give life to your mortal bodies through His Spirit who indwells you;" Rom 10:9, "God raised Him from the dead (ὁ θεὸς αὐτὸν ἤγειρεν ἐκ νεκρῶν);" 1 Cor 6:14, "God has not only raised the Lord (ὁ θεὸς καὶ τὸν κύριον ἤγειρεν);" 1 Cor 15:15, "Moreover we are even found *to be* false witnesses of God, because we witnessed against God that He raised Christ (ἤγειρεν), whom He did not raise (ἤγειρεν), if in fact the dead are not raised;" 2 Cor 4:14, "He who raised the Lord Jesus (ὁ ἐγείρας τὸν κύριον Ἰησοῦν);" Gal 1:1, "Paul, an Apostle . . . through Jesus Christ, and God the Father, who raised Him from the dead (θεοῦ πατρὸς τοῦ ἐγείραντος αὐτὸν ἐκ νεκρῶν);" Eph 1:20, "which He brought about in Christ, when He raised Him from the dead (ἐγείρας αὐτὸν ἐκ νεκρῶν);" Col 2:12, "God, who raised Him from the dead (τοῦ ἐγείραντος αὐτὸν ἐκ νεκρῶν);" 1 Thess 1:10, "His Son, whom He raised from the dead (ἤγειρεν ἐκ [τῶν] νεκρῶν)." Romans 8:11 is unique in that Paul credits the raising of Jesus to "the Spirit of Him who raised Jesus from the dead (τὸ πνεῦμα τοῦ ἐγείραντος τὸν Ἰησοῦν ἐκ νεκρῶν)."

300. Acts 13:34, "He raised Him up from the dead (ἀνέστησεν αὐτὸν ἐκ νεκρῶν), no more to return to decay;" Acts 17:3, "explaining and giving evidence that the Christ had to suffer and rise again from the dead (ὅτι τὸν χριστὸν ἔδει παθεῖν καὶ ἀναστῆναι ἐκ νεκρῶν);" Acts 17:31, "He has fixed a day in which He will judge the world in righteousness through a Man whom He has appointed, having furnished proof to all men by raising Him from the dead (ἀναστήσας αὐτὸν ἐκ νεκρῶν)." BDAG § 670 defines ἀνίστημι initially as "to cause to stand or be erect, *raise, erect, raise up*," and thus, "to come back to life from the dead, *rise up, come back from the dead*."

The "Man Christ Jesus" in the Epistles of Paul

So while Akenson insists that Paul teaches a "spiritually-raised Christ, but not a physically resurrected Yeshua,"[301] the contextual vocabulary Paul uses for resurrection and raising from the dead demonstrates that he refers to the restoration of the body: this fact is patently clear in the contrast of Phil 3:21, "The Lord Jesus Christ will transform the body of our humble state into conformity with the body of His glory." Certainly the nature of the resurrection body differs from that of the earthly, mortal body, in that it is imperishable (as Paul teaches in 1 Cor 15:40–44), but the body of Jesus which "died and was buried" is the same body that was "raised the third day" (1 Cor 15:4). Furthermore, as will be explored in the next chapter, the resurrected Christ that Paul encountered identifies Himself as Jesus the Nazarene (Acts 22:8), one who was most surely a physical man.

All these Pauline statements agree with the Gospel records, that the body of Jesus buried in the tomb of Joseph came up missing on the third day after the crucifixion, and that Jesus was seen in this same body as raised from the dead (Matt 28:6–7; Mark 16:6; Luke 24:6, 34; John 21:14). For Paul to use the resurrection of Jesus to bolster his doctrinal teachings without the historical resurrection of Jesus would be absurd: all these tenets would rest merely upon Paul's imagination and collapse without any basis in reality. Conversely, Paul truly believed that God raised Jesus from the dead, not just because Jesus appeared to Him on the Damascus Road, but because He had previously appeared to over five hundred others as well (1 Cor 15:6). Thus, Paul's teaching is utterly dependant upon the historical resurrection of the "Man Christ Jesus" occurring "on the third day, according to the Scriptures" (1 Cor 15:4).

"He Was Raised on the Third Day"

Paul was also aware of a Christ-history giving the time of the resurrection of Jesus, that "He was raised *on the third day* (ἐγήγερται τῇ ἡμέρᾳ τῇ τρίτῃ) according to the Scriptures" (1 Cor 15:4), that is, on the third day after the crucifixion. Paul previously located that event to a Passover during the administration of Pontius Pilate, while this reference limits Jesus' resurrection to a particular day of the week. Bruce suggests that the Scriptures alluded to in 1 Cor 15:4 might include Hos 6:2 ("He will revive us after two days; He will raise us up on the third day [ἐν τῇ ἡμέρᾳ τῇ τρίτῃ ἀναστησόμεθα] that we may live before Him."), although he prefers an allusion to Lev 23:11, 15, 16, which date the waving of the sheaf on the "day after the Passover."[302] Since the NT borrows this Hebrew terminology of the "first of the Sabbaths" to designate "the first day of the week," it would seem that the early church understood "third day" as falling upon the day after the Sabbath.[303]

---

301. Akenson, *St. Saul*, 177.

302. Bruce, *Paul and Jesus*, 48. The English translation of the phrase מִמָּחֳרַת הַשַּׁבָּת is "from the morning of the Sabbath," but the LXX translates it as τῇ ἐπαύριον τῆς πρώτης, "on the morning of the first" (Lev 23:11), meaning the morning after the Sabbath Day.

303. "The first of the Sabbaths" is the day of Jesus' resurrection appearances in Matt 28:1 (εἰς μίαν σαββάτων); Mark 16:2 (καὶ λίαν πρωῒ τῇ μιᾷ τῶν σαββάτων); Luke 24:1 (Τῇ δὲ μιᾷ τῶν σαββάτων); John 20:1 (Τῇ δὲ μιᾷ τῶν σαββάτων); and John 20:19 (τῇ μιᾷ σαββάτων). It also refers to the day of gathered worship in Acts 20:7 (Ἐν δὲ τῇ μιᾷ τῶν σαββάτων) and presumably also in 1 Cor 16:2 (μίαν σαββάτου).

THE "MAN CHRIST JESUS"

Certainly the reference in 1 Cor 15:4 to the third day reflects the saying of Jesus that He would be raised up on the third day (Matt 16:21; 17:23; 20:19; 27:64; Luke 13:32; 24:7, 21, 46), a fact confirmed by Peter in Acts 10:40, "God raised Him up on the third day." Once again, had there been no actual resurrection on "the third day," Paul's specification of this incident would be useless at least and deceptive at worst. As it is, by mentioning the third day in 1 Cor 15:4, Paul not only confirms the fulfillment of Scripture and the testimony of the Jerusalem Apostles, but he also shows knowledge of the prediction by the "Man Christ Jesus" that "on the third day He will be raised up" (Matt 20:19).

"Christ Appeared"

In 1 Cor 9:1, Paul asks the question, "Have I not seen Jesus our Lord?"[304], and he answers it affirmatively in 1 Cor 15:5–8 by including himself in a list of those who had also seen the resurrected Lord, "He appeared to Cephas, then to the twelve. After that He appeared to more than five hundred brethren at one time, most of whom remain until now, but some have fallen asleep; then He appeared to James, then to all the Apostles." Paul does not claim that this is an exhaustive list, nor could it be, as each Gospel provides additional appearances of the resurrected Christ, such as those to Mary Magdalene, the other ladies, the Emmaus disciples, and the seven disciples at the Sea of Galilee.[305] Now we learn only from Paul that Jesus also appeared to "more than five hundred at one time" (in Galilee?) and to James. His list centers on the foundational authorities of the new church, to which he adds himself, "Last of all, as it were to one untimely born, He appeared to me also" (1 Cor 15:8), a reference to his Damascus Road experience, which will be examined in the next chapter.

Despite Paul's insistence that he is an eyewitness of the Risen Jesus, his claim has not prevented critics from denying the resurrection of Christ entirely, although a more common explanation is to insist that Paul does not teach a physical resurrection anyway, since he speaks of the "spiritual body" and Christ becoming a "life giving spirit" (1 Cor 15:44–45). Thus, Christ's appearance to Paul is explained as a visionary experience, not as a physical resurrection, as Akenson contends, "Crucially, Saul never suggests that he had seen Yeshua in the flesh before the crucifixion and he does not now claim to have seen

---

304. In 1 Cor 9:1, Paul asks four questions, each negated by οὐ, "Am I not free? Am I not an apostle? Have I not seen Jesus our Lord? Are you not my work in the Lord?" Robertson, *Grammar of the Greek New Testament*, 1157, observes that "in interrogative (independent) sentences οὐ always expects the answer 'yes.' . . . The use of a negative in the question seems naturally to expect the answer 'yes,' since the negative is challenged by the question." Thus, each of the four questions requires an affirmative answer: Yes, Paul is free; he is an apostle, he has seen the Lord, and the Corinthians are his work. In the third question, Paul even uses the intensive οὐχί (a strengthened form of οὐ; BDAG §5447) as if to emphasize the reality of his vision of the risen Lord.

305. A combined list from all the sources indicates these reported appearances of the resurrected Jesus: (1) To Mary Magdelene (John 20:11–18); (2) to the other women (Matt 28:9); (3) to the Emmaus Road disciples (Luke 24:13–34); (4) to Simon Peter/Cephas (Luke 24:33; 1 Cor 15:5a); (5) to the ten disciples (Luke 24: 36; John 20:19–25); (6) to the eleven disciples (John 20:26–31; same as the Twelve of 1 Cor 15:5b?); (7) to the seven disciples at the Sea of Galilee (John 21:1–25); (8) to the Eleven at the mountain in Galilee (Matt 28:16); (9) to "more than five hundred brethren at one time" (1 Cor 15:6); (10) to James (1 Cor 15:7a); (11) to "all the apostles" (1 Cor 15:7b); (12) to the apostles at the Ascension (Acts 1:1–11); (13) to Paul on the Damascus Road (Acts 9:3–6; 1 Cor 15:8).

a physically resurrected Yeshua, but instead a glorified Christ."[306] What then does Paul mean when he asks, "Have I not seen the Lord Jesus?" By "the Lord Jesus," does Paul mean a heavenly apparition rather than a physical person?

Much of the debate hinges on the meaning of the aorist passive ὤφθη used of the resurrection appearances of Jesus (Luke 24:34; Acts 13:31; 1 Cor 15:5, 6, 7, 8), whether it necessitates a visionary experience or if it may also describe a physical appearance.[307] While ὤφθη describes the appearance of Jesus to Paul (Acts 9:17; 1 Cor 15:8), it is also used of angelic appearances (Luke 1:11; 22:43; Acts 7:30) and even of theophanies (Acts 7:2). These accounts report that there was an objective appearance of a supernatural person who was actually seen by a human, as the Lord appeared to Abram (Gen 17:1), Isaac (Gen 26:2), Jacob (Gen 35:9), Moses (Exod 3:2), Gideon (Judg 6:12), David (2 Chr 3:1), and Solomon (1 Kgs 3:5), whether by a dream, through a vision, or in person. In each case, however, the emphasis is not upon the *manner* of the appearance but on the *person* who appears. The nature of the one who is seen must be determined by other factors, and the analogy between the raising of the "mortal bodies" of believers with that of the Father raising Jesus from the dead (Rom 8:10–11) makes the argument that it is the physical body of Jesus that was raised and transformed into a "spiritual body." Since His body no longer shares in the "flesh and blood" of the old realm (1 Cor 15:50), it has been transformed to dwell in the kingdom of God as imperishable and immortal (1 Cor 15:53).[308] So, whatever may be the precise nature of the resurrection body of Jesus—which is the original prototype until the general resurrection of the dead—it began as a perishable, mortal, "dusty" body that expired physically on a cross and was buried, but now that same body has been supernaturally changed to be imperishable, powerful, and spiritual.

It is in this transformed body that Jesus appeared after His resurrection, as Paul confirms in Acts 13:31, "For many days (Jesus) appeared to those who came up with Him from Galilee to Jerusalem, the very ones who are now His witnesses to the people." The Gospels consistently report that the body of Jesus buried in the tomb of Joseph was missing on the morning after the Sabbath (Matt 28:6; Mark 16:6; Luke 24:3, 24), but it turned out that Jesus was truly risen and began appearing to His disciples (Luke 24:34, 39), not as an apparition in a vision, but in corporeality, as "flesh and bones" (Matt 28:9; Luke 24:39; John 20:20, 27; 21:12). Thus, Paul's reference to the "spiritual body" of Jesus must describes the sphere of the body rather than its corporeal nature, as being fitted for life in the coming age, meaning that Paul's use of ὤφθη concurs with the Gospel accounts, that the historical facts to which Paul refers are the objective resurrection appearances of the "Man Christ Jesus" to His disciples after His crucifixion and burial—in the same physical body, albeit now "the body of His glory" (Phil 3:21).

---

306. Akenson, *St. Saul*, 168.

307. The indicative verb ὤφθη is the aorist passive of ὁράω, defined by BDAG § 5358.1.d. to "become visible, appear."

308. Vos, *Pauline Eschatology*, 167, declares, "Paul means to characterize the resurrection-state as the state in which the Pneuma rules." He argues, "The whole tenor of the argument (for such it actually is) compels us to think of the resurrection as the moment at which τὸ πνευματικόν entered" (1 Cor 15:46)."

THE "MAN CHRIST JESUS"

"He Was Taken Up In Glory"

In 1 Cor 15:8, Paul separates himself from the others to whom Christ appeared, admitting, "Last of all, as it were to one untimely born, He appeared to me also." Perhaps Paul sensed the untimeliness of his experience, because unlike all the other appearances, his encounter happened after the ascension of Jesus to heaven, as recorded in Acts 1:9 ("He was lifted up while they were looking on, and a cloud received Him out of their sight."). Still, Paul shows knowledge of the event of the ascension in that he alludes to it in Eph 4:8–10,[309] and he includes the ascension as an article of faith in the Christ-Confession of 1 Tim 3:16, "By common confession great is the mystery of godliness: He was . . . taken up in glory (ἀνελήμφθη ἐν δόξῃ)."[310] Also, when Paul refers to Jesus being seated at the right hand of God (Rom 8:34; Eph 1:20; Col 3:1),[311] he assumes the ascension, as he does in 1 Cor 15:25, "For He must reign until He has put all His enemies under His feet," where he alludes to Ps 110:1 ("The LORD says to my Lord: 'Sit at My right hand [κάθου ἐκ δεξιῶν μου], until I make Thine enemies a footstool for Thy feet.'").

So, Paul clearly has a Christology of ascension,[312] but is it true, then, as Käsemann asserts, that Paul "proclaims the ascension as a pure article of faith, without any narrative accomplishment at all"?[313] How would Paul answer, should one ask him if there had been an actual event when Jesus physically ascended into heaven from a geographical place (the Mount of Olives located east of Jerusalem), on a particular day (forty days after the resurrection), and attended by numerous eyewitnesses, as recorded in Acts 1:9–12?[314] Käsemann even thinks that the one who builds his faith on these reports as historical

---

309. Ephesians 4:8–10 reads, "Therefore it says, "When He ascended (ἀναβὰς) on high, He led captive a host of captives, and He gave gifts to men." (Now this *expression*, "He ascended," what does it mean except that He also had descended into the lower parts of the earth? He who descended is Himself also He who ascended (ὁ ἀναβὰς) far above all the heavens, that He might fill all things.)"

310. BDAG § 507, defines ἀναλαμβάνω, "to lift up and carry away." It describes the ascension also in Acts 1:2, 11, 22.

311. Romans 8:34 reads, "Who is the one who condemns? Christ Jesus is He who died, yes, rather who was raised, who is at the right hand of God (ὃς καί ἐστιν ἐν δεξιᾷ τοῦ θεοῦ), who also intercedes for us;" Eph 1:20, "which He brought about in Christ, when He raised Him from the dead, and seated Him at His right hand in the heavenly *places*" (καθίσας ἐν δεξιᾷ αὐτοῦ ἐν τοῖς ἐπουρανίοις);" Col 3:1 "If then you have been raised up with Christ, keep seeking the things above, where Christ is, seated at the right hand of God (ὁ Χριστός ἐστιν ἐν δεξιᾷ τοῦ θεοῦ καθήμενος).

312. Inexplicably, Moo, "The Christology of the Early Pauline Epistles," 184, claims, "Paul never refers to Jesus' ascension," although Paul certainly exalts the ascended Christ, which assumes the historical event.

313. Käsemann, "Saving Significance," 49.

314. Acts 1:9–12 describes the ascension with the verb ἀναφέρω, which BDAG § 580.1 defines as "to cause to move from a lower position to a higher." The ascension is depicted as a "taking up" in Acts 1:2, "until the day when He was taken up (ἀνελήμφθη);" in Acts 1:9, "And when He had spoken these things, while they beheld, He was taken up (καὶ ἀνεφέρετο εἰς τὸν οὐρανόν) and a cloud received Him out of their sight;" in Acts 1:11, "This Jesus, who has been taken up (ὁ ἀναλημφθεὶς) from you into heaven, will come in just the same way as you have watched Him go into heaven;" and in Acts 1:22, "beginning with the baptism of John, until the day that He was taken up from us (ἀνελήμφθη)." The account in Acts 1 is an expansion of the brief notation in Luke 24:51, "And it came to pass, while He blessed them, He was parted from them, and carried up into heaven (καὶ ἀνεφέρετο εἰς τὸν οὐρανόν)." The ascension is also recorded in the disputed ending of Mark 16:19, "So then, after the Lord had spoken to them, He was received up into heaven (ἀνελήμφθη εἰς τὸν οὐρανὸν), and sat down at the right hand of God."

fact is bound to fall into an "uncertainty of salvation, since historical recollection is no longer able to say what really happened."³¹⁵ For this reason, he maintains that redemption is found only in the act of preaching of the cross, not in the act of the crucifixion.³¹⁶ After all, it is quite a stretch for modern readers to believe that a man physically ascended into heaven (wherever that is) apart from any supporting mechanism (such as an aircraft), so it seems quite reasonable to dismiss the ascension as a religious myth.

Such assumption is reasonable only if one discards the supernatural perspective of the NT, which certainly presents the ascension of Jesus as a historical fact—even though the witnesses could scarcely believe their own eyes when Jesus was taken up from them and received out of their sight into a cloud (Acts 1:9). Yet, just as Jesus predicted His resurrection, so He had also foreseen His own ascension (John 3:13; 6:62; 20:17):³¹⁷ to deny one is to reject the other, since they are both supernaturally caused yet both occurred in human history.

Thus, Käsemann is quite correct that Paul has a christological conception of the ascension: in 1 Cor 15:25, the apostle views it as the fulfillment of Ps 110:1, "The LORD said to my Lord, 'Sit at my Right Hand,'" by which God coronated David's "lord" to the place of highest position, with His enemies made a footstool for His feet.³¹⁸ Paul links this verse with Ps 8:6, "Thou dost make him to rule over the works of Thy hands; Thou hast put all things under His feet," so that the sitting at the right hand symbolizes the sovereign rule of Jesus as Lord over all, as Paul displays in Eph 1:20–22.³¹⁹ This interpretation was shared by the Jerusalem apostolate, as demonstrated in the early sermons of Peter;"³²⁰ indeed, the

---

315. Käsemann, "Saving Significance," 50.

316. Ibid.

317. Jesus mentions His ascension in John 3:13, "And no one has ascended (ἀναβέβηκεν) into heaven, but He who descended from heaven, *even* the Son of Man;" in John 6:62, "*What* then if you should behold the Son of Man ascending (ἀναβαίνοντα) where He was before?"; and in John 20:17, "Jesus said to her, 'Stop clinging to Me, for I have not yet ascended (ἀναβέβηκα) to the Father; but go to My brethren, and say to them, I ascend (ἀναβαίνω) to My Father and your Father, and My God and your God.'"

318. Paul assumes the ascension, as he does when he echoes Ps 110:1, "The LORD says to my Lord: 'Sit at My right hand, Until I make Thine enemies a footstool for Thy feet' (κάθου ἐκ δεξιῶν μου ἕως ἂν θῶ τοὺς ἐχθρούς σου ὑποπόδιον τῶν ποδῶν σου)" in 1 Cor 15:25, "For He must reign until He has put all His enemies under His feet (δεῖ γὰρ αὐτὸν βασιλεύειν ἄχρι οὗ θῇ πάντας τοὺς ἐχθροὺς ὑπὸ τοὺς πόδας αὐτοῦ)." See Hengel, "'Sit at My Right Hand!' The Enthronement of Christ at the Right Hand of God and Psalm 110:1,"163–65. He also notes the possible link to Ps 80:18, "Let Thy hand be upon the man of Thy right hand (ἄνδρα δεξιᾶς σου), upon the son of man whom Thou didst make strong for Thyself." Although this verse is not quoted *expressis verbis* in the NT, it does contain the same important theme of this "man of Thy right hand" who is also described in Ps 80:15 as "the son whom Thou hast strengthened for Thyself," translated in the LXX as υἱὸν ἀνθρώπου (ibid., 168–69). Hengel notes, "One should not deny that Paul took the terms ἔσχατος Ἀδὰμ and ἄνθρωπος ἐξ οὐρανοῦ in 1 Cor 15:45, 47 from the tradition of the son of man. The titles which were from the beginning regularly used by him were only κύριος or the son of (God). On the basis of Ps. 2; 8; 89 and 110 (perhaps also 80:16–18), these titles were from earliest times interchangeable" (ibid., 170).

319. Ephesians 1:20–22 reads, "which He brought about in Christ, when He raised Him from the dead, and seated Him at His right hand in the heavenly *places*" (καθίσας ἐν δεξιᾷ αὐτοῦ ἐν τοῖς ἐπουρανίοις), far above all rule and authority and power and dominion, and every name that is named, not only in this age, but also in the one to come. And He put all things in subjection under His feet."

320. Acts 2:33 reads, "Jesus . . . having been exalted to the right hand of God (τῇ δεξιᾷ οὖν τοῦ θεοῦ ὑψωθείς) . . . for it was not David who ascended into heaven, but he Himself says: 'The Lord said to my Lord,

THE "MAN CHRIST JESUS"

first OT application of Jesus known to have been heard by Paul (as Saul the Pharisee) was the "right hand" Christology of the testimony of Stephen in Acts 7:55–56, when he proclaimed the vision of "Jesus standing at the right hand of God."[321]

The source of this interpretation, according to the Synoptics, traces back to the question of Jesus to the Pharisees, "What do you think about the Christ, whose son is He?" When they answered, "The Son of David," he asks a second question concerning Ps 110:1, "Then how does David in the Spirit call Him 'Lord,' saying, 'The Lord said to my LORD, "Sit at My right hand (κάθου ἐκ δεξιῶν μου), until I put Thine enemies beneath Thy feet?"'" (Matt 22:44 || Mark 12:46 || Luke 20:42). He leaves his query unanswered but certainly implies that He is referring to Himself. This identity becomes quite plain when He responded to the adjuration by the High Priest at His trial before the Sanhedrin, "Hereafter you shall see the Son of Man sitting at the right hand of Power" (καθήμενον ἐκ δεξιῶν τῆς δυνάμεως, Matt 26:64 || Mark 14:62 || Luke 22:69). Thus, when Paul uses this same right-hand imagery to express the exaltation of Christ, he continues an interpretive tradition of Ps 110:1 that flows through Jesus to the early church and on through the rest of the NT.[322] Even so, when Paul mentions the ascension, he cites it as a practical application of the heavenly ministry of Christ as one who makes intercession on behalf of His people (Rom 8:34). Likewise, Paul attaches an ethical impetus of the ascension to the command in Col 3:1, "If then you have been raised up with Christ, keep seeking the things above, where Christ is, seated at the right hand of God (ὁ Χριστός ἐστιν ἐν δεξιᾷ τοῦ θεοῦ καθήμενος)." These applications of the ascension would be futile had there been no actual event when Jesus was lifted up into heaven, and Paul plainly accepts the historicity of the ascension when he places it in a firm historical sequence: that the "Man Christ Jesus" died, that He was raised, and that He is now at the right hand of God (Rom 8:34).

"Sit at My right hand;" Acts 5:31 reads, "He is the one whom God exalted to His right hand as a Prince and a Savior (ὕψωσεν τῇ δεξιᾷ αὐτοῦ)."

321. Acts 7:55–56 reads, "But being full of the Holy Spirit, (Stephen) gazed intently into heaven and saw the glory of God, and Jesus standing at the right hand of God (Ἰησοῦν ἑστῶτα ἐκ δεξιῶν τοῦ θεοῦ); and he said, 'Behold, I see the heavens opened up and the Son of Man standing at the right hand of God' (τὸν υἱὸν τοῦ ἀνθρώπου ἐκ δεξιῶν ἑστῶτα τοῦ θεοῦ)." Hengel, "Sit at My Right Hand!", 170, notes, "One could with all caution ask whether the 'standing' is not the ruling or judging gesture of the formulation of Ps. 8:7 (κατέστησας . . . ὑπέταξας ὑποκάτω τῶν ποδῶν αὐτοῦ) instead of the 'sitting' of Ps. 110:1."

322. The influence of Ps 110:1 is also echoed in Heb 1:3, "When He had made purification of sins, He sat down at the right hand of the Majesty on high (ἐκάθισεν ἐν δεξιᾷ τῆς μεγαλωσύνης ἐν ὑψηλοῖς);" in Heb 8:1, "We have such a high priest, who has taken His seat at the right hand of the throne of the Majesty in the heavens (ἐκάθισεν ἐν δεξιᾷ τοῦ θρόνου τῆς μεγαλωσύνης ἐν τοῖς οὐρανοῖς);" in Heb 10:12, "He, having offered one sacrifice for sins for all time, sat down at the right hand of God (ἐκάθισεν ἐν δεξιᾷ τοῦ θεοῦ);" in Heb 12:2, "Jesus, the author and perfecter of faith, who for the joy set before Him endured the cross, despising the shame, and has sat down at the right hand of the throne of God (ἐν δεξιᾷ τε τοῦ θρόνου τοῦ θεοῦ κεκάθικεν);" and in 1 Pet 3:22, "Christ . . . who is at the right hand of God, having gone into heaven (πορευθεὶς εἰς οὐρανόν)." The motif continues in Rev 5:7, when Jesus as the Root of David took the scroll "out of the right hand of Him who sat on the throne," which then becomes the throne of the Lamb (Rev 22:3).

The "Man Christ Jesus" in the Epistles of Paul

Summary to the Exaltation of Jesus

Undoubtedly, the Christ to which Paul refers most frequently is the exalted Lord, for the primary reason that this is the Jesus with whom the church fellowships in the present age: it knows Him no longer according to the flesh (2 Cor 5:16) but according to the power of His resurrection (Phil 3:10). Even so, this same exalted Lord is also the Man Christ Jesus who was raised from the dead on the third day, who appeared to His disciples, and who has now ascended to the right hand of God. The main difference is location, brought about by the supernatural exertion of God the Father in transforming the mortal body of Jesus into one that is now imperishable. Still, it is crucial to note that for Paul, the one who is now the heavenly Lord was at a particular time in history also the earthly Jesus, the same one whom Paul longs to share in the "fellowship of His sufferings, being conformed to His death" (Phil 3:10). Thus, in Paul's thought there is no discontinuity and certainly no change of identity between "our Lord Jesus Christ" and the "Man Christ Jesus." To Paul, there is but one Jesus: the one once "born of a woman" now sits exalted at the right hand of God.

CHAPTER SUMMARY: THE "MAN CHRIST JESUS" IN THE LETTERS OF PAUL

For the reader who assumes that Paul shows little interest in the historical Jesus—as claimed by critical scholarship—this listing of Paul's references to that same Jesus is not only an unexpected compilation, but quite startling in its breadth. Throughout his epistles, Paul alludes to the following facts about Jesus: His true humanity, including real physicality; His natural birth; His Jewish ethnicity; His Davidic descent; His family relationships of mother and brothers; His circumcision and Torah upbringing; and His impoverished condition. From Jesus' ministry Paul includes His baptism, His gathering of disciples (including the Twelve), His teaching (at least six specified but many more referenced by allusion), His preaching and evangelizing among the Jews, His status as servant, His transfiguration, His OT interpretations (such as the motifs of the Stone and the Right Hand), and His assistance by angels. Paul knew the character of Jesus to be compassionate, loving, purposeful, steadfast, humble, obedient, righteous, faithful, selfless and sinless. He also knew of the sufferings of Jesus during a Passover after a final supper with His disciples, one of whom betrayed Him to Jewish authorities. He was arraigned before the Roman procurator Pontius Pilate and was condemned despite His good confession, after which He was taunted, tortured, and then crucified by nailing to a cross. This torment led to His physical death and burial; however, on the third day after this suffering, He was exalted in resurrection, appeared to His disciples and many other witnesses, and then ascended to heaven.[323]

---

323. After surveying all the evidence of what Paul knew regarding the man Jesus, Wenham, *Paul: Follower of Jesus or Founder of Christianity?*, rates as highly probable the following: Paul knew of the Last Supper; of Christ's resurrection; of Jesus' teaching on divorce, payment to preachers, and His return; of His ethical teaching; of His declaring foods clean; and of His reference to God as Abba (ibid., 381–83). Wenham also rates as probable Paul's knowledge of Jesus' baptism, His commissioning of Peter, His preaching on the Kingdom, His revealing mysteries, His woe against those who persecute the prophets, and His positive

THE "MAN CHRIST JESUS"

While lacking any chronological scheme upon which to organize these events and omitting most of the specific teachings of Jesus, the basic framework given by Paul is still quite comprehensive when compared with the life of Jesus as presented in the Gospels. Machen observes, "Thus the incidental character of Paul's references to the life and teaching of Jesus shows clearly that Paul knew far more than he has seen fit in the Epistles to tell. The references make the impression of being detached bits taken from a larger whole."[324] Even so, this compilation shows clearly that the historical Jesus is of great concern to Paul; after all, there would be no heavenly Lord had there been no earthly teacher.[325] These many echoes of the Jesus of history give greater significance to the contrast Paul makes in Rom 5:10, "for if while we were enemies, we were reconciled to God through the death of His Son, much more, having been reconciled, we shall be saved by His life" (ἐν τῇ ζωῇ αὐτοῦ), for it was in His earthly life that Jesus reversed the ruin of the first man Adam, as Paul goes on to show in Rom 5:12–21.

The question remains, however, why Paul does not settle debates more frequently by quoting the teachings of Jesus or by referring to His earthly example? The simplest and most reasonable answer is that Paul uses a rather common literary device in discussing Jesus, and that is historical allusion. He presumes that his readers share with him a common pool of information about the life and teachings of Jesus,[326] and for the sake of brevity, he proceeds in his epistles on the assumption that his readers already know some basic facts about the historical Jesus; in other words, they have heard or read the early *paradosis* of the life and deeds of Jesus, now preserved in the Gospel records. This assumption is verified by his brief but repeated references to the historical Jesus:[327] he assumes that his readers possess this basic knowledge, and there is no sense in covering the same ground when more pressing matters are at hand; namely, how new converts should believe in Jesus as the crucified and resurrected Savior and live in the reality of Him of the ascended and returning Lord.[328] As Hays shows that the larger OT context hovers in the

---

attitude toward sinners (ibid., 384–85). Wenham also considers many other facts as plausible, including Jesus' birth, His temptation, His beatitudes and parables, and His anguish in Gethsemane (ibid.). Although the evidence is impressive, much of it depends on literary affinities due to the simple fact that Paul alludes to many of these events and teachings rather than specifically mentioning them.

324. Machen, *Origin of Paul's Religion*, 152.

325. Rostron, *The Christology of St. Paul*, 189, observes, "We have seen how the really human nature of Christ is demanded by the conception which St. Paul formed of Him as Messiah, as Second Adam, and as redeemer. As the Saviour of the House of David, He was born of a human mother. As the Head of a new Humanity, of a Redeemed Race, He was the Perfect Man, the Second Adam, in Whom as the Author of their salvation and the Strength and Stay of their Lives, the new creation lived."

326. This same reading dynamic is true for every successive generation of readers. One reads Paul on the assumption that he refers to the same Jesus presented in the Gospels and simply fills in the Pauline gaps by making reference to the Gospels.

327. Dodd, *History and the Gospel*, 68, notes, "The Pauline testimony therefore, is all of a piece. He attests the character of Jesus, something of His life and death, and something of His teaching; and he assigns Him His place in history as a crucified messiah. This testimony is of utmost importance, since we know that Paul came into the church (which he already knew before his conversion) within seven years (probably less) from the Crucifixion. . . ."

328. Machen, *Origin of Paul's Religion*, 167, "The details of Jesus' earthly ministry no doubt had an important place in the thinking of Paul. But they were important, not as an end in themselves, but as a means to an

background of Paul's theology when he concerns himself with a quotation or allusion,[329] so he also argues that the apostle writes from the same basis with regard to the teaching and life of Jesus—he has an implicit narrative of Jesus in mind.[330] Only in this case, Paul has no Gospels to quote, as they had not yet been written. He must appeal to the Jesus-traditions, rarely by direct quotation, and sometimes by allusion, but frequently in echoes, taking for granted (rightly or wrongly) that his readers share the same common pool of information, as he chides in 2 Thess 2:5, "Do you not remember that while I was still with you, I was telling you these things?"

The overwhelming fact is that Paul refers to Jesus Christ more than anyone else in his letters except for God, and the natural assumption is that he refers to the same Jesus as portrayed in the Gospels, even though presumably he wrote before the completion of the Gospels.[331] His sources then must of necessity be apostolic tradition rather than the completed Gospels, and he readily admits this dependency in his letters (1 Cor 11:2, 23-25; 15:3-4, 2 Thess 2:15). Because of this, direct quotes of Jesus are few and far between in Paul's writings, whereas certain events in the life of Jesus clearly dominant Paul's gospel—notably His death and resurrection of Jesus—but one should not rush to the conclusion that other incidents are of no concern to Paul. Close scrutiny of the texts has revealed that Paul mentions dozens of Christ-events throughout his writings, as elucidated in this chapter. He need only refer to an event one time (i.e. that Jesus had brothers) to show that he accepted its historicity, and once Paul's connection is established to the "Man Christ Jesus," the reader begins to see allusions and echoes to Jesus surfacing throughout Paul's letters.[332] These are not literary coincidences nor are they imaginary illusions, but they are so integrated into Paul's thinking as to be second nature to the apostle, woven into his letters by use of paraphrase and application.[333] Thus when he writes, "Be imitators of me, just as I also am of Christ" (1 Cor 11:1), he is not giving audacious spiritual advice but providing himself as an accurate example of the historical Jesus. By remembering Paul

---

end. They revealed the character of Jesus. They showed why He was worthy to be trusted." This brings His death and resurrection to the forefront, for redemption is not found in following the teachings of Jesus nor imitating the character of Jesus, but rather in believing His redemptive acts as Christ crucified and risen again.

329. Hays, *Echoes of Scripture in the Letters of Paul* (1989).

330. Hays, *The Faith of Jesus Christ: The Substructure of Galatians 3:1—4:11*, 139-91.

331. One can assume that Paul had the same access to the circulating oral and written traditions of Jesus that were used by Luke when he researched for the writing of his Gospel (Luke 1:1-4). If Luke is the unnamed travel-companion of Paul in the "We" sections of Acts (as is traditionally believed), then he accompanied Paul to Jerusalem (Acts 21:17) and sailed to Rome with him (Acts 27:1), meaning he could have used the time of Paul's Caesarean imprisonment to research and write his Gospel—and share his notes with Paul.

332. This is the argument of Resch, *Der Paulinismus und die Logia Jesu*, a 1904 work that may gain a fresh appraisal by scholarship now that it is available online and has been reprinted by Kessinger, even if in the original German. His meticulous research deserves more than a passing nod in Pauline studies, much less a condescending dismissal.

333. Wenham, *Paul: Follower of Jesus or Founder of Christianity?*, 393, notes that "one particular feature of Paul's periphrastic use of Jesus-tradition is that he picks up ideas from the stories and sayings of Jesus without reproducing the stories themselves. . . . He is, we might say, 'deparabolizing' the parables (and other stories), replacing the storytelling technique of Jesus and the Gospels with less colorful theological discourse."

THE "MAN CHRIST JESUS"

in all things, his readers can hold fast to the Jesus-traditions just as Paul delivered them (καθὼς παρέδωκα ὑμῖν, τὰς παραδόσεις κατέχετε, 1 Cor 11:2).

Clearly, Paul believes there is a one-to-one correspondence between his teachings and the person of Jesus. He sees himself as a precise reflection of Jesus in his own life and doctrine, as demonstrated in the extensive references, allusions, and echoes of Jesus scattered throughout his letters, taught so that his readers may become "obedient from the heart to that form of teaching to which you were committed" (παρεδόθητε τύπον διδαχῆς, Rom 6:17). Rather than ignoring or remaking the historical Jesus, "Paul turns out to be a most important witness to the historical Jesus."[334] He is certainly the first literary witness to the historical Jesus, as his letters provide the first historical record of His life and teaching, as Goguel astutely observed, "Far from contradicting the historical personality of Jesus, the Pauline Christology would be incomprehensible if it had not made the historical facts its starting point."[335] Paul's letters, then, presume his own preaching of the "Man Christ Jesus," and for this reason samples of Paul's preaching of the "Man Christ Jesus" are preserved in the first history of the early church, the book of Acts, to which this study now turns.

---

334. Wenham, *Paul and the Historical Jesus*, 24.
335. Goguel, *Jesus the Nazarene: Myth or History?*, 148.

4

The "Man Christ Jesus" in the Presentation of Paul in the Acts of the Apostles

A SECONDARY SOURCE THAT links the historical Jesus with the historical Paul exists in the NT, and that is the Acts of Apostles. Notwithstanding the dismissal of Acts by critical scholarship,[1] this study accepts the traditional evaluation of Acts as authored by Luke (also the writer of the third gospel) and confirms Luke's authorship by comparing the respective prologues found in Luke 1:1–4[2] and Acts 1:1–3.[3] As one who claims to be a careful historian, Luke provides the answers to the intriguing questions raised in the letters

---

1. Although the author of Acts claims to give accurate information, so that Theophilus, the original reader, "might know the exact truth about the things you have been taught" (Luke 1:1), critical scholarship has long dismissed Acts as a credible historical source; for example, Ehrman, *Peter, Paul and Mary Magdalene: The Followers of Jesus in History and Legend*, 96, declares, "... some of the accounts of Acts are as much the stuff of legend as historically verifiable reports." Ehrman insists that the inconsistencies are demonstrated by the disparities between Paul's letters and Acts, but in actuality these are exegetical matters, not historical issues, although Ehrman assumes the accounts cannot be reconciled. Likewise, Fredriksen, *From Jesus to Paul: The Origins of the New Testament Images of Jesus*, 53, summarily dismisses Acts because (she claims) it dates long after the destruction of Jerusalem (although there is not a hint of the city's destruction in the book); because it contradicts Paul's own statements (presumably in Galatians 1–2), and because Paul's speeches are free compositions, telling us more about Luke than about Paul. By cutting away Paul's letters from the historical context given in Acts, modern readers find themselves at the mercy of critical scholars who pontificate which parts are fact and which are legend. In contrast, see Barnett, *Paul: Missionary of Jesus*, 209–10, who notes, "Luke knew Paul at *first-hand*; he did not merely know *about* him, and write about him from a distance, as Plutarch did about Cicero.... The implications of this Luke-Paul nexus for historical analysis are considerable. It means, first, that Luke's narrative about Paul must be regarded as reliable; Paul was Luke's direct (oral) source. Paul's letters and the book of Acts form the basis for establishing a chronological sequence for Paul's mission. In consequence, secondly, we are able to plot the time and place Paul wrote (many) of his letters to the churches" (italics in original).

2. Higgins, "The Preface to Luke and the Kerygma in Acts," 82, insists that the Lukan preface shows that "Acts is an essential part of the confirmation Luke is able to provide, because so much of it, and not only in the *preaching* of the church leaders, is a witnessing to the truth of the *historia Jesu* which Theophilus has learned and which is now recorded afresh in the former treatise."

3. Critics are hard-pressed to refute the classic work of Ramsey, *St. Paul the Traveler and Roman Citizen*, which ably defended Lukan authorship of Acts in this first-hand study published in 1897. Sherwin-White, *Roman Society and Roman Law in the New Testament* (1963), chided critical scholars who rejected the veracity of Acts when he compared Acts with contemporary Roman historians and concluded, "For Acts the confirmation of historicity is overwhelming" (ibid., 188). Hengel and Schwemer, *Paul: Between Damascus and Antioch, the Unknown Years*, 6–11, also support Lukan authorship, acknowledging, "Basically, we do not know what we owe to Luke. Not only our knowledge of Jesus' preaching and its historical order, but also the dates of Paul's life largely go back to him.... (Acts) helps us build a bridge... 'between Jesus and Paul'" (ibid., 11).

THE "MAN CHRIST JESUS"

of Paul:[4] who is this Christian evangelist named Paul who apparently had no first-hand knowledge of Jesus?[5] How did he acquire the apostolic authority he claims?[6] Introduced in Acts 7:58 as a hostile prosecutor of those who follow this new Way (Acts 9:2), Saul the Pharisee—more familiarly identified by Acts 13:9 as Paul the apostle[7]—becomes the main character in Acts, mentioned by name 150 times, more than anyone else in the book.[8] This fact alone is quite remarkable, because undoubtedly the most important person in Acts is Jesus, yet He is named but sixty-nine times and exits the narrative in Acts 1:9 at His ascension, re-appearing only twice afterwards—once to Stephen at his stoning (Acts 7:55) and lastly to Saul on the Road to Damascus (Acts 9:5), and both times from heaven. Despite these brief appearances of the main character, Luke advances his concern in writing this book as "all that Jesus began to do" (Acts 1:1). Thus, Acts reports how

---

4. Hengel, *Acts and the History of Earliest Christianity*, 36, describes Acts as a "historical monograph," without which "it would be almost impossible to put Paul and his work in a chronological and geographical setting" (ibid., 38). Also, Blaiklock, "The Acts of the Apostles as a Document of First Century History," 47–54, shows how Acts fits what is known of the first-century Roman world, giving the historical context for the life of Paul.

5. Lüdemann, *Opposition to Paul in Jewish Christianity*, 5, however, operates on the assumption that F. C. Baur in his essays on Acts "destroyed the assumption that Acts had been composed by a companion of Paul (a church tradition that had enjoyed unqualified trust in the scholarly work [sic] on Acts prior to Baur)" so that "the theology of the Apostle to the Gentiles must be reconstructed solely on the basis of his letters." When Baur subsequently noted that Acts tends to portray Paul in a Petrine manner and Peter in a Pauline manner, he refused to correct his views and assumed that "Acts was the product of a Paulinist who wanted to present a Judaizing portrait of Paul and . . . minimize the differences between Paul and Peter as insignificant" (ibid., 6). The possibility that there *were* few differences between the two apostles is not a consideration for either Baur or Lüdemann, although Lüdemann concedes that Lightfoot's historical research defending the historicity of Acts (J. B. Lightfoot, "St. Paul and the Three," Dissertation III in *The Epistle of St. Paul to the Galatians*, 292–374) would be quite persuasive except for his theological approach; in other words, the only legitimate challenges to Baur's views could come from those who "abandoned a supernaturalistic perspective" (ibid., 11), meaning that the miraculous element in Acts (including Paul's conversion) must be summarily dismissed in the interest of pure exegesis. This study, however, shall exegete Acts on the assumption of its historical reliability, even of supernatural events.

6. These questions are addressed by Bruce, "Is the Paul of Acts the Real Paul?", who shows the agreement between the Paul of Acts and the Paul of the Epistles in matters of biographical information (ibid., 285–93), in affinities of ministry to the Jew first, then to the Gentiles (ibid., 293–98); and in the substance of doctrine in his speeches and epistles (ibid., 299–304). Bruce concludes, "Yes; he is the real Paul, seen in retrospect through the eyes of a friend and admirer, whose own religious experience was different from Paul's and who wrote for another public and purpose than Paul had in view when writing his letters" (ibid., 305). See also Porter, *The Paul of Acts: Essays in Literary Criticism, Rhetoric, and Theology* (1999); and Köstenberger, "Diversity and Unity in the New Testament," 150, for additional reasons uniting Paul in Acts with Paul in his letters.

7. Since Paul does not mention the name 'Saul' in his letters, Buitenwerf, "Acts 9:1–25; Narrative History Based on the Letters of Paul," 82–84, suggests that Luke gave Paul this Jewish name to emphasize his Jewish roots. Buitenwerf does not seem to consider that 'Saul' might actually be Paul's given Jewish name. Apparently, the silence of Paul means ignorance of Saul, but this is a *non sequitur*, since 'Barnabas' is a Christian name given to Joseph of Cyprus (Acts 4:36), but Paul only identifies him as Barnabas (1 Cor 9:6; Gal 2:1, 9, 13). Did Luke then also invent Barnabas' earlier Jewish name since Paul never mentions it? It is far less complicated to accept the record given by Luke at face value rather than to force contradictions on the texts.

8. Hengel, *Between Jesus and Paul: Studies in the Earliest History of Christianity*, 2, suggests that Acts should be titled, "From Jesus to Paul," since its "central and positive interest (is) in the person and missionary work of Paul. He is the real goal of the work."

the ascended Lord intervened within the history of the early church,[9] and one his most significant works was the apprehension of the Pharisee Saul (to use Paul's image from Phil 3:12). That event changed him dramatically and instantly from being a hostile opponent against "the Name" (as Jesus was being proclaimed by His Jerusalem followers, Acts 4:16, 41; 26:9) into an ardent adherent of Jesus as the Christ and a devoted worshipper Him as the Son of God (Acts 9:20, 22). Since the record of the case claims that the Christology of Saul originated in his life-changing experience on the road to Damascus,[10] the question must be asked if the Ascended Christ of Paul's vision is also the same person as the "the Man Christ Jesus" of the Gospels and of Paul's letters.

THE MAN CHRIST JESUS OF SAUL'S CONVERSION

There may be no conversion account more famous, more studied, more vilified or more praised than that of Saul the zealous Pharisee when he was transformed into Paul the apostle of Jesus.[11] There is no question that something profound happened to Saul as he traveled from Jerusalem to Damascus. In his own words, he claimed that the risen Christ "appeared to me" (1 Cor 15:8), so that he received his gospel "through a revelation of Jesus Christ" (Gal 1:12). These claims lead one to ask, who is this Jesus that Paul claimed to encounter on the road to Damascus? When Machen contends, "The heavenly Christ of Paul was also the Christ of those who had walked and talked with Jesus of Nazareth,"[12] can his assertion be supported from the available facts?

---

9. Buitenwerf, "Acts 9:1–25," 62, reflects a critical perspective, that Acts "contains too many miracle stories and divine interventions to be considered ancient historiography, but on the other hand it contains too many facts and details to be a novel." He labels this mixture of fact and fiction as "mimetic historiography," leading one to wonder why the report of a miracle renders a work nonhistorical and how the historical facts are to be distinguished from fancy. In his article, Buitenwerf makes numerous attempts to do this, but he provides no criteria other than his own subjective speculation.

10. See the argument in Hurtado, *Lord Jesus Christ: Devotion to Jesus in Earliest*, 64–77, on experience as the original source of Christ-devotion. While the power of experience is very real, the NT credits the origin of the Christian movement not merely to subjective religious experiences but to objective appearances of the resurrected Jesus (Acts 1:22; 2:32; 3:15; 5:32; 10:39–41; 13:31).

11. See the survey in Hurtado, "Convert, Apostate, or Apostle to the Nations? The Conversion of Paul in Recent Scholarship," 273–84. Maccoby, *The Mythmaker: Paul and the Invention of Christianity*, 50–61, argues that Paul was not a Pharisee at all, despite his claim in Phil 3:5, alleging that Paul's interpretation of the OT differs radically from Pharisaic/Rabbinic writings; however, Maccoby takes Pharisaic ideas from the later Misnah and Talmud, compiled after the destruction of Jerusalem in A. D. 70, and reads them anachronistically back upon Paul. Actually, though, the greater difference is that the rabbis read the OT as yet to be fulfilled, whereas Rabbi Saul began to read the OT as finding fulfillment in the person of Jesus of Nazareth. Quite naturally then, Paul's interpretation of the OT would be quite different from that of the rabbinic writings.

12. Machen, *Origin of Paul's Religion*, 135. The meticulous research and careful reasoning of Machen makes his work first published in 1921 an abiding classic in the field of Pauline studies.

THE "MAN CHRIST JESUS"

The Jesus Saul Knew about Before His Conversion

When Saul is first introduced, he appears as a threatening antagonist against fellow Jews who followed Jesus (Acts 8:1–3; 9:1–2).[13] What did he find so offensive in their allegiance to Jesus that he deemed them worthy of death? Dunn argues that Saul was offended by these Jews who offered the gospel of Messiah Jesus to Gentiles,[14] yet Acts indicates that the animosity of the Sanhedrin was aggravated by the preaching of the apostles that Jesus was the Christ of OT prophecy (Acts 3:13–20; 4:2, 10–12; 5:30–32, 42) and by the perception that His death and resurrection would destroy Jewish distinctives (Acts 6:13–14).[15] The

---

13. Acts 8:1, 3 reads, "Saul was in hearty agreement with putting (Stephen) to death. And on that day a great persecution arose against the church in Jerusalem; and they were all scattered throughout the regions of Judea and Samaria, except the apostles.... But Saul *began* ravaging the church, entering house after house; and dragging off men and women, he would put them in prison;" Acts 9:1–2 adds, "Now Saul, still breathing threats and murder against the disciples of the Lord, went to the high priest, and asked for letters from him to the synagogues at Damascus, so that if he found any belonging to the Way, both men and women, he might bring them bound to Jerusalem." Paul adds his own perspective to this in Acts 22:4–5 ("And I persecuted this Way to the death, binding and putting both men and women into prisons, as also the high priest and all the Council of the elders can testify. From them I also received letters to the brethren, and started off for Damascus in order to bring even those who were there to Jerusalem as prisoners to be punished.") and in Acts 26:9–12 ("So then, I thought to myself that I had to do many things hostile to the name of Jesus of Nazareth. And this is just what I did in Jerusalem not only did I lock up many of the saints in prisons, having received authority from the chief priests, but also when they were being put to death I cast my vote against them. And as I punished them often in all the synagogues, I tried to force them to blaspheme and being furiously enraged at them, I kept pursuing them even to foreign cities. While thus engaged as I was journeying to Damascus with the authority and commission of the chief priests."). Paul often writes of his persecuting activities (1 Cor 15:9; Gal 1:13–14, 23; Phil 3:6; 1 Tim 1:13), driven by his zeal for the law, leading Dupont, "The Conversion of Paul and Its Influence on His Understanding of Salvation by Faith," 185, to observe, "His conduct makes it clear that Christianity seemed to him to be apostasy in regard to the law, and the Christian faith to be a denial of his ideal of the strict observance of the law's requirements." This traditional view is challenged by Dunn, *The New Perspective on Paul: Collected Essays*, but critiqued by Westerholm, *Perspectives Old and New on Paul* (2003). While this debate on the "New Perspectives on Paul" lies beyond the scope of this study, suffice it to say that this reviewer is convinced by the arguments of Dupont ("The Conversion of Paul," 194) that the essential issues in Paul's conversion are the "realization of salvation in the person of the risen Christ" and a repudiation of the Pharisaic soteriology of "a salvation which may be secured by observance of the law."

14. Dunn, *Theology of Paul*, 352. His opinion, however, overlooks that Acts 10 reports that the messianic believers did not preach to Gentiles until some time *after* Saul's conversion. Gager, *Reinventing Paul*, 26–27, argues on similar lines, that since Paul made Gentile inclusion a center of his thinking after the Damascus Road experience, this must have been his preoccupation spurring him to oppose the Way before his experience. The 'conversion' of Saul, then, was more a mammoth change of attitude toward Gentiles than a recognition of Jesus as the Messiah. Gager puts the proverbial cart before the horse, since Paul's subsequent ministry to Gentiles flows out of his commission from Jesus to "bear His name before the Gentiles and kings and the sons of Israel." This means that the initial issue in Saul's conversion was the proper identification of the Name of Jesus.

15. These charges were filed against Stephen before the Sanhedrin: "This man incessantly speaks against this holy place, and the Law; for we have heard him say that this Nazarene, Jesus, will destroy this place and alter the customs which Moses handed down to us" (Acts 6:13–14). These accusations indicate that the initial source of conflict between the Sanhedrin and the new messianic movement concerned whether "the Way" of salvation came through observance of the liturgy (what Paul later calls "works of law") or through faith in the name of Jesus the Nazarene—an issue ignited by the healing of lame man at the Beautiful Gate of the Temple (Acts 3:16). Already the adherents of this new Way were described as "the ones believing" "in the Lord" (Acts 2:44; 4:4, 32; 5:14), so that "even a great many of the priests were becoming obedient to the faith" (τῇ πίστει, Acts 6:7), no doubt much to the consternation of the Sanhedrin. Dupont, "The Conversion

culmination of this Jewish anger erupted in the stoning of Stephen upon his confession of Jesus as "the Son of Man standing at the right hand of God" (Acts 7:56). This is the exact confession made by Jesus that led directly to His condemnation by the High Priest (Matt 26:64–65), so when Saul heard this same profession from Stephen, he approved of his stoning and acquired documents from the chief priests to bind all who called upon the name of Jesus (Acts 9:14), perhaps based upon the legal precedence of the execution of Jesus. It is not unreasonable to surmise that Saul adamantly refused to accept Stephen's consideration that anyone who had hung on a tree could be "the Righteous One" of OT prophecy (Acts 7:52) because Deut 21:23 announces that "he who is hanged (upon a tree) is accursed of God."[16]

As a persecutor of the followers of the Way of Jesus,[17] Saul would have made it his business to learn much more about the "heresies" of Jesus of Nazareth in order to prosecute His disciples before the Sanhedrin (Acts 6:14).[18] He would have known, at the very least, that the followers of Jesus believed that Jesus was the "Righteous One" of OT prophecy (this title in Acts 7:52 derives from Isa 53:11) who had been crucified but was now proclaimed as being resurrected.[19] Having attended to the cloaks of those who stoned

---

of Paul," 185, notes that Saul as a prosecutor "sought to uproot Christ's religion because he had a conviction that it was incompatible with the religion of the law and with the place he accorded to the law in the plan of salvation." If Jesus was perceived as destroying the Temple, the Law, and the Mosaic customs, Saul had to oppose of followers of "this Nazarene, Jesus," vigorously.

16. Bird, *Introducing Paul: The Man, His Mission, and His Message*, 32–33, lists these reasons for Saul's persecution of the church: (1) its scandalous belief in a *crucified* Messiah; (2) its incorporation of Jesus into religious devotion reserved for Yahweh; and (3) its view of the Torah threatening the integrity of the boundaries separating Jews from Gentiles. Acts does not give evidence of this third reason until well after Saul's conversion (Acts 11:19–21). Paul's stated reason strictly concerned the identity of Jesus ("I thought to myself that I had to do many things hostile to the name of Jesus of Nazareth," Acts 26:9).

17. Wilson, *Paul: the Mind of the Apostle*, 55, suggests that Acts 9:17 indicates that Saul was an employee of the Temple police and thus may have been involved in the arrest of Jesus. Wilson even argues that "in some sense Paul was the Ur-author of the Passion story in Mark." On the other hand, Maccoby, *The Mythmaker*, 59, argues that Saul's connection with the Sadducee High Priest shows he could not have been a Pharisee. Maccoby does not account for the fact that hardening attitudes against the Nazarenes united political enemies as it had done so earlier against the Nazarene (Matt 16:1).

18. Hengel, *Acts and the History of Earliest Christianity*, 83, notes, "Even as a prosecutor, he (Saul) must have become acquainted with the basic features of the tradition about Jesus and the theology of the church in controversies and legal hearings." The contention of Hahn, *The Titles of Jesus in Christology: Their History in Early Christianity*, and Heitmüller, "Zum Problem Paulus und Jesus," 320–37, that before Saul's conversion there was a Jewish Palestinian church, a Hellenistic Jewish church, and a Hellenistic Gentile church, simply finds no support in the text of Acts. The internal difficulties disturbing the apostolic church appear to stem from a language difference (Acts 6:1) whereas it was united behind a Christology distinctly drawn from the OT.

19. Kim, *Origin of Paul's Gospel*, 105, asks, "At the time of Paul's conversion, what did the early Christians mean when they proclaimed Jesus of Nazareth as the Messiah, the Lord, and the Son of God?" The primary source is Acts 1–7, which records that Jesus is called "the Holy One" (Acts 2:27; 3:14; 4:30), the Lord (Acts 1:6, 21; 2:34, 36), the Christ (Acts 2:36, 38; 3:6, 18, 20; 4:10, 26; 5:42), God's servant (Acts 3:13, 26; 4:30), the Righteous One (Acts 3:14; 7:52), the Prince of life (Acts 3:15), the Prophet like Moses (Acts 3:22), the Stone (Acts 4:11), Prince (Acts 5:31), Savior (Acts 5:31), and the Son of Man (Acts 7:56). Jesus was proclaimed as one who suffered (Acts 3:18), was crucified (Acts 5:30) but was raised again (Acts 2:31–32; 3:15), ascended (Acts 2:33) and is returning (Acts 3:20). He is addressed in prayer, a clear indication of His deity (Acts 1:24–25). While this Christology may lack the cosmic dimensions found in Col 1:15–21 (although Acts 2:33; 5:31; and 7:55–56 locate Christ at the right of God, a cosmic location), there is no indication of an evolving

Stephen, Saul had heard the declaration of Stephen, "Behold, I see the heavens opened, and the Son of Man standing at the right hand of God" (Acts 7:56)—the same confession Jesus had made of himself before the Sanhedrin ("From now on the Son of Man shall be seated at the right hand of the power of God," Luke 22:69). Saul heard the dying prayer of Stephen, "Lord Jesus, receive my spirit!" (Acts 7:59), a plea remarkably similar to the dying prayer of Jesus (Luke 23:46),[20] yet now Stephen directed it to Jesus as One who possesses authority to admit the dying into presence of God.[21] Saul's consent to Stephen's execution demonstrated that he understood the claim of the Christian *kerygma*, that Jesus of Nazareth was believed to be the Messiah—but this was an opinion Saul would not tolerate among his fellow Jews.[22]

Furthermore, it is not impossible that Saul may have seen and heard Jesus "according to the flesh" (2 Cor 5:16) while he was studying in Jerusalem under Gamaliel.[23] Nor is it farfetched to suppose that Saul could have been one of the "lawyers" who baited Jesus with legal technicalities (Matt 22:35; Luke 10:25).[24] He may well have heard the

---

Christology: the same Jesus is proclaimed in Acts as He is in the Epistles.

20. It is most likely that Paul was the primary source of Luke's information for Stephen's lengthy defense, as he was both an eye-and ear-witness of it (Acts 7:58). While Stephen's martyrdom is clearly modeled on the passion of Jesus, Stanton, *Jesus of Nazareth in New Testament Preaching*, 36, astutely observes that "Luke has not turned the passion narrative (of Jesus) into an account of a martyrdom (like Stephen)." No one ever grants atoning significance to Stephen's death in the way the entire NT does to the death of Jesus.

21. Maccoby, *The Mythmaker*, 72, is quite aware that Luke designs the Stephen-episode to provide a link between Paul and Jesus, although Maccoby claims Luke can only do so by using many "unhistorical features" such as creating the similarity with the trial of Jesus as a rhetorical device and "falsifying" the original political charge in both trials to that of blasphemy (ibid., 78). This is, of course, not at all how Luke presents the stoning of Stephen; instead, Maccoby gives a classic case of dismissing a text if it does not fit one's theory, which in his case is to deny any continuity between Jesus and Paul.

22. The relationship of Saul to his own contemporary Judaism is, of course, the topic of the bellwether work by Sanders, *Paul and Palestinian Judaism: A Comparison of Patterns of Religion* (1977), who builds on the previous work of Davies, *Paul and Rabbinic Judaism* (1967). Sanders, ibid., 542, purports that "*Paul presents an essentially different type of religiousness* (in Judaism) *from any found in Palestinian Jewish literature*" (italics in original), leading Räisänen in his work *Paul and the Law* (1986) to wonder if Paul distorted contemporary Judaism. Since Paul is only one of two Pharisees to leave behind any extant literature on first-century Judaism (the other is Josephus), one might instead wonder if Räisänen has distorted Paul, since it would make no sense for the apostle to describe his own former religion inaccurately, particularly when he engaged in debate with Jewish antagonists (as he does so in Romans 2:17–3:8).

23. Paul states he had been "brought up in Jerusalem under Galmaliel" (Acts 22:3) from his youth (Acts 26:4), but Bultmann, "The Significance of the Historical Jesus for the Theology of Paul," 223, dismisses the accounts of Saul's upbringing in Jerusalem and his studies with Gamaliel as legendary because Paul writes in Gal 1:22, "I was not known by sight to the churches of Christ in Judea." It should be noted in that verse that Paul is not referring to his Jewish compatriots in Jerusalem; instead, he states that the churches in the outlying area of Judea would not have recognized "his face," although they certainly knew his persecuting reputation (Gal 1:23). Barnett, *Paul: Missionary of Jesus*, 27, suggests that Paul had come to Jerusalem in his early teens, circa A. D. 17, making it all but certain that his time there overlapped the visits of Jesus. Chilton and Neusner, "Paul and Gamaliel," 1–43, also show that in the theological systems between these two men, "the particulars and the consequent topical interests attain cogency precisely where, in Judaism, they should."

24. Such a scenario raises the intriguing possibility that Paul was a first-hand source for the Gospels' information of the Sanhedrin's internal scheming against Jesus.

pronouncement of Pontius Pilate, "Behold the man!" (ἰδοὺ ὁ ἄνθρωπος, John 19:5),[25] and he may have witnessed the crucifixion of Jesus, since he was later able to set before the eyes of the Galatians "Jesus Christ as publicly portrayed as crucified" (Gal 3:1).[26] It within the realm of possibility that Saul was one of those from Cilicia (a province in Asia Minor where Paul's birthplace of Tarsus was located) who had disputed about Jesus with Stephen in the Synagogue of the Freedmen (Acts 6:9). What is certain is that by the time Saul witnessed the stoning of Stephen (Acts 7:58), he zealously opposed the doctrine taught by this young deacon and understood that his deductions about Jesus would spell an end to Temple-centered Judaism.[27]

Thus, by the time Saul set off for Damascus to extradite those "disciples of the Lord" who were "belonging to the Way" (Acts 9:1–2), he would have learned as an official prosecutor that the original followers had formed a rather remarkable Christology from its inception. They were already confessing Jesus the Nazarene (Acts 2:22; 3:6; 4:10; 6:14) as a man crucified, resurrected, ascended, and returning, and even praying to Him as the "heart-knower" (Acts 1:24). His followers honored Jesus with the OT titles of Lord (Acts 1:6, 21; 2:36; 4:33; 7:59–60; 8:16; 9:1), Holy One (Acts 2:27; 4:30), David's fruit (Acts 2:30), the Christ (Acts 2:31, 36; 3:6, 18a, 18b, 20; 4:10, 26; 5:42; 8:5, 12), the Servant (Acts 3:13; 4:27, 30), the Just One (Acts 3:14; 7:52), the Prince of life (Acts 3:15; 5:31), a Prophet like Moses (Acts 3:22; 7:37), Savior (Acts 5:31), the Corner Stone (Acts 4:11), and the Son of Man (Acts 7:56).[28] While it is probable that Saul as a Pharisee might have believed that

25. If one thinks it is far-fetched to hear Pilate's pronouncement in the wording of 1 Tim 2:5, the "Man Christ Jesus," it should be noted that the only Pauline reference to Pilate appears later in that same epistle ("Christ Jesus, who testified the good confession before Pontius Pilate," 1 Tim 6:13). When Pilate presents Jesus, "Behold the Man (ἰδοὺ ὁ ἄνθρωπος, John 19:5)," he may well have unknowingly echoed the unwitting prediction of Caiaphas when he prophesied the death of "one man" (εἷς ἄνθρωπος) for the nation (John 11:50). The literary connections between these three statements are quite intriguing.

26. Weiss, *Paul and Jesus*, 37, 94, consistently argues that Saul was personally and profoundly influenced as an eyewitness to the force of Jesus' personality. To Weiss, this means that Paul's conversion was determined by "psychological conditions" (ibid., 29) already existing in Paul's mind, namely "a lofty supernatural figure in divine glory" (ibid., 30) coupled with previous knowledge of Jesus (ibid., 31). To Weiss, there was no objective appearance of Jesus to Paul: it was a psychological vision, rising from "deep and permanent impressions which the man Jesus made upon his disciples during His lifetime" (ibid., 31), so that their profound faith enabled them to experience the resurrection (ibid., 32). Even if Saul had seen and heard Jesus before His crucifixion, this is certainly not how Acts or Paul describes the Damascus Road experience.

27. The question arises whether Paul was influenced by Stephen's address (Acts 7). Hengel, *Between Jesus and Paul*, 29, claims that "we owe a real bridge between Jesus and Paul to those almost unknown Jewish Christian 'Hellenists' of the group around Stephen and the first Greek-speaking community in Jerusalem they founded." Räisänen, however ("The 'Hellenists': A Bridge Between Jesus and Paul?", 149–202), questions whether such a separate "community" existed, although he concedes the existence of Greek-speaking Jewish converts, as Acts presents (ibid., 159). Any influence on Saul was initially negative, implied in the accusation that Stephen's message reflected how "this Nazarene, Jesus, will destroy this place and alter the customs which Moses handed down to us" (Acts 6:14). Hengel, ibid., 22, shows how this language reflects the original charges against Jesus (Matt 26:61) in which the actual sayings of Jesus (John 2:19) were misquoted. Since Paul was an eyewitness of Stephen's death, and thus an ear-witness of his message, he would have great cause to investigate what had been taught by the historical Jesus in order to refute it. See also Cousins, "Stephen and Paul," 157–62.

28. For studies on Palestinian Christianity prior to the destruction of Jerusalem in A. D. 70, see Longenecker, *The Christology of Early Jewish Christianity* (1970); and Longenecker, "Christological Materials

THE "MAN CHRIST JESUS"

these titles rightly applied to the promised Messiah,[29] he certainly would not have applied them—as the primitive church did—to "the Name of Jesus" (Acts 2:21, 38; 3:6, 16; 4:10, 12, 17–18; 5:28, 40–41; 8:12, 16), particularly since His name had already been interchanged with the Name of יְהֹוָה (Acts 2:21, 28).[30] Furthermore, Saul would have learned that these same titles had been addressed to Jesus by others without His correction, or, even more significantly, applied by Jesus to himself, thereby making him the originator of this practice.[31] No other reason accounts for Saul's vehement opposition toward these fellow Jews unless he knew their views and heard their preaching in the Name of Jesus. Thus, the paramount issue for Saul was christological—his threats were directed against Jews who identified Jesus of Nazareth as the promised Messiah who was once crucified but is now enthroned at the right hand of God as the Son of Man. It is the identification of this man Jesus as the Christ that Saul so zealously opposed.

The Jesus Saul Encountered on the Damascus Road

When Saul arrived in Damascus, however, his status had remarkably changed from antagonist to proponent, as he proclaimed, "This Jesus is the Christ" (Acts 9:22). What happened to Saul on the road to Damascus is recorded three times in Acts[32] (9:1–22; 22:1–16;

---

in Early Christian Communities," 47–78. Other studies include: Rawlinson, *The New Testament Doctrine of the Christ*, 31–52; Taylor, *The Person of Christ in New Testament Teaching*, 24–31; 190–222; and Danielou, *The Theology of Jewish Christianity* (1977).

29. While Paul describes Jesus by many of these same titles after his conversion, he never uses "Son of Man," a title credited often to the Messiah in Jewish apocalyptic literature (such as 1 Enoch 46:2–4; 48:2; 60:10; 62:5, 7, 9, 14; 63:11; 69:26–27, 29; 70:1; 71:14, 17). While Paul later taught a "Man-Christ" Christology based on OT typology, Machen, *Origin of Paul's Religion*, 192, comments. "It is evident, therefore, that the Pauline Christology was not derived from the particular apocalypses that are still extant." He adds, "The Messiah of the Jewish apocalypses is not great enough to have been the basis of the Pauline Christ" (ibid., 204).

30. Longenecker, *Christology of Early Jewish Christianity*, 45, notes, "Just as 'the name' was a pious Jewish surrogate for God, so for early Jewish Christians it became a designation for Jesus, the Lord's Christ."

31. The Gospels use these titles of Jesus: Lord (John 13:13; Luke 20:44), Holy One (John 6:69), David's son (Matt 22:43–44), the Christ (Matt 23:10), the Servant (Matt 20:28), the Just One (Matt 10:41; 27:19; Luke 23:47), the Way, the Truth, the Life (John 14:6), a Prophet (Matt 10:41; 13:57; 21:11; Luke 7:16; 13:33; John 4:19; 7:40), Savior (Luke 2:11; John 4:32), the Stone/Corner Stone (Matt 21:42, 44), and especially, the Son of Man (Matt 26:64). Since Jesus uses some of these of himself, Marshall, *Origins of New Testament Christology*, 43–58, answers his own question, "Did Jesus have a Christology?" with the statement, "The Messianic titles which appear in the Gospels need to be reassessed in the light of the fact that Jesus did know himself to be the Messiah" (ibid., 57). This issue is examined in detail by Bird, *Are You the One Who Is To Come? The Historical Jesus and the Messianic Question* (2009), who argues that "Jesus spoke of himself as the Son of Man from Daniel, as an eschatological figure with a messianic function as the representative of Israel" (ibid., 79).

32. A comparison of the three accounts of Paul's conversion (Acts 9; 22; 26) reveals the following (the particular elements of each passage are underlined):

	9:1–22	22:1–16	26:4–18
Setting:	Paul as persecutor and zealot of Judaism (Acts 9:1–2)	(Acts 22:3–5; see also Gal 1:13–14; Phil 3:3–5; and 1 Cor 15:8–10)	(Acts 26:9–12)

The "Man Christ Jesus" in the Presentation of Paul in the Acts of the Apostles

Event:	"suddenly a light from heaven flashed around him" (Acts 9:3; Gal 1:15–17a)	"And it came about that as I was on my way, approaching Damascus about noontime, a _very bright_ light suddenly flashed from heaven all around me" (Acts 22:6)	"at midday, O King, I saw on the way a light from heaven, _brighter than the sun, shining_ all around me _and those who were journeying with me_." (Acts 26:13)
Effect:	"and he fell to the ground" (Acts 9:4a)	"and I fell to the ground" (Acts 22:7a)	"And when _we had all fallen_ to the ground" (Acts 26:14)
Voice:	"(he) heard a voice saying to him, "Saul, Saul, why are you persecuting Me?" (Acts 9:4b)	"and (I) heard a voice saying to me, 'Saul, Saul, why are you persecuting Me?'" (Acts 22:7)	"I heard a voice saying to me _in the Hebrew dialect_, 'Saul, Saul, why are you persecuting Me? _It is hard for you to kick against the goads_.'" (Acts 26:14)
Paul's First Question:	"And he said, "Who art Thou, Lord?"" (Acts 9:5)	"And I answered, 'Who art Thou, Lord?'" (Acts 22:8)	"And I said, 'Who art Thou, Lord?'" (Acts 26:15)
Answer:	"And He said, "I am Jesus whom you are persecuting." (Acts 9:5b)	"And He said to me, 'I am Jesus _the Nazarene_, whom you are persecuting.'" (Acts 22:8)	"And _the Lord said_, 'I am Jesus whom you are persecuting.'" (Acts 26:15)
Paul's 2nd Question:		"And I said, 'What shall I do, Lord?'" (Acts 22:10)	
Command:	"but rise, and enter the city, and it shall be told you what you must do." (Acts 9:6)	"And the Lord said to me, 'Arise and go on _into Damascus_ and there you will be told of _all that has been appointed for you to do_.' (Acts 22:10)	'But arise, and _stand on your feet_." (Acts 26:16)
Companions	"And the men who traveled with him stood speechless, _hearing the voice_ (ἀκούοντες μὲν τῆς φωνῆς = "sound," LN § 14.74), but _seeing no one_." (Acts 9:7)	"And those who were with me _beheld the light_, to be sure, but _did not understand the voice_ [δὲ φωνὴν (= "voice," LN § 33.103) οὐκ ἤκουσαν τοῦ λαλοῦντός μοι] of the One who was speaking to me." (Acts 22:9)	
Condition:	"And Saul got up from the ground, and though his eyes were open, he could see nothing; leading him by the hand, they brought him into Damascus. _And he was three days without sight, and neither ate nor drank_" (Acts 9:8–9)	"But since I could not see _because of the brightness of that light_ I was led by the hand by those who were with me, and came into Damascus." (Acts 22:11)	

26:4–18); the first is narrated by Luke and the other two are told by Paul himself,[33] with the third given as a legal defense.[34] In his testimony, Paul later explains what occurred: "He—the risen Christ—appeared to me" (1 Cor 15:8).[35] Despite those who deny the reality of the supernatural, an honest appraisal of the record will conclude that the explanation given in both Acts and Paul's letters is that Saul's abrupt about-face from prosecutor to proclaimer is due to a miraculous intervention, based on his later claim, "Have I not seen Jesus our Lord?" (1 Cor 9:1).[36]

The Light and Voice from Heaven

By his own confession, Saul's knowledge of Jesus as recorded in Acts was determined by his conversion experience on the Damascus Road. Granted, Paul does not use the word "conversion" (ἐπιστροφή) to describe what happened to him: Wilson is quite correct in arguing that Paul did not convert "from" Judaism "to" Christianity, because Paul considered himself to be a Jew to his dying day.[37] It is certain, however, that Paul as Saul changed in his viewpoint of Jesus, from considering Him as a blasphemous pretender to being the promised Messiah, and it is in this sense that this study refers to Saul's encounter as a "conversion."[38] When Paul reports, "I saw on the way a light from heaven, brighter than the sun, shining all around me . . . and heard a voice saying to me in the Hebrew dialect, 'Saul, Saul, why are you persecuting Me?'", he describes an objective experience that begs to be explained.[39] The proconsul Festus later expresses one explanation: Saul was insane (Acts 26:24); after all, the materialist assumes that sane people do not see heavenly lights and hear extra-terrestrial voices. Paul politely rejects this explanation by stating, "I am

---

33. Ramsey, *St. Paul the Traveler and Roman Citizen*, 42, notes that "the subjective touch in Acts 8:1, 'Saul was consenting unto his death,' is a clear indication that Luke's authority was Paul himself. The phrase is a confession of inward feeling, not a historian's account of action; and the words are Paul's own (Acts 22:2)."

34. Ehrman, *Peter, Paul, and Mary Magdalene*, 96–97, assumes these three accounts are hopelessly contradictory (did Paul's companions hear a voice but see no one, as reported in Acts 9:7, or did they see the light but not hear the voice, as Acts 22:9 reports?), accusing Luke of recreating his story depending on the audience. Such a view, however, makes Luke to be a very incompetent author by leaving his finished work in such a convoluted form. The fact that the three testimonies are hard to reconcile (but not impossible) shows that Luke was honest enough to report the accounts as they were delivered in each instance, with the difficulties left intact.

35. Hengel, *Paul Between Damascus and Antioch*, 39, comments that Paul regards the "splendour of light, which makes itself known as the 'Lord' and is recognized by him as such. Nowhere is there any thought this could have been an illusion."

36. Despite Paul's specific claim to have "seen the Lord," Maccoby, *Mythmaker*, 89, insists that Paul "did not, apparently, see the face and form of Jesus, but only the bright light."

37. Wilson, *Paul*, 61. Paul confirms his Jewish heritage in Acts 22:3; Rom 9:3; 11:1; 2 Cor 11:22; Phil 3:5.

38. Gager, *Reinventing Paul*, 22–27, argues that there was no "Christianity" in existence to which Saul could convert; however, he acknowledges that Paul later uses conversion language, such as considering his Jewish credentials "rubbish" in order to gain Christ (Phil 3:8–9). If "conversion" is not Paul's chosen word, he does call his experience a "revelation" (Gal 1:16), an "appointment" (Acts 22:10, 14; 26:16; 1 Tim 2:7; 2 Tim 1:11) and a display of mercy (1 Tim 1:13).

39. Wilson, *Paul*, 70, makes the intriguing suggestion that Saul had been a Temple guard responsible for the arrest of Jesus leading to His crucifixion, making this question of Jesus, "Why are you persecuting me," really quite personal.

not out of my mind, most excellent Festus, but I utter words of sober truth" (Acts 26:25). Indeed, the logical arguments in his letters are not the ramblings of a mad man; therefore, this insanity charge is rarely invoked, although Shaw suggests that Saul's vision was the flash of a great idea that he could start a religion based on his own "delirious terrors" of sin and death.[40] Klausner admits to the reality of Saul's experience by agreeing that he saw a "heavenly vision" (οὐράνιος ὀπτασία, Acts 26:19) and heard some sounds, but he credits all the post-resurrection appearances of Jesus to "psychological phenomenon found among dreamers and visionaries," such as the Kabbalists.[41] Nietzsche calls Paul's experience an "instantaneous flash of enlightenment" by which Paul became the "inventor of Christianity,"[42] but Paul is emphatic in his later explanation that his experience was not an ecstatic mystical feeling; instead, he asks rhetorically, "Have I not seen Jesus our Lord?" (1 Cor 9:1). Although Luke shapes his narrative in "the literary pattern of punishment and repentance" as found in other Jewish literature,[43] Ananias later delivers the reason for this encounter as the divine choice of Saul as an "elect vessel" by God Himself (Acts 9:15).

Saul's experience was not a solitary dream such as that experienced by Joseph (Matt 1:20), nor was it the appearance of an angel (as recorded in Acts 5:19–20), nor was it similar to the vision Paul later received in Corinth (Acts 16:9). Rather, Paul describes his Damascus Road experience as a heavenly vision (τῇ οὐρανίῳ ὀπτασίᾳ), where the word *optasia* may imply a different sort of revelation from the other visions in Acts, which describes them with the word ὅραμα.[44] The Damascus Road vision was an objective visual and auditory event that occurred in broad daylight in a geographical locale (a public highway) and was witnessed by others who could verify to the fact that something quite extraordinary happened—something more than a lightning strike or a clap of thunder, but real enough to leave Saul temporarily blinded as a result. Granted, those accompanying Saul "saw no one,"[45] but then, the resurrected Lord appeared "not to all the people, but to witnesses who were chosen beforehand by God" (Acts 10:41), as Ananias later explained to Saul, "The God of our fathers has appointed you to know His will, and to see the Righteous One, and to hear an utterance from His mouth" (Acts 22:14). Thus, Saul's experience was not merely a subjective impression in his mind: it was an objective, sensual

---

40. Shaw, "The Monstrous Imposition upon Jesus," 297. Interestingly, he acknowledges "that the chronicler of the Acts of the Apostles sees nothing of the significance of this" (of Saul's prior desire to start a new religion). In other words, Shaw's theory is not found in the text: it is a monstrous imposition upon Paul.

41. Klausner, *From Jesus to Paul*, 324. He thinks that the great light seen by Paul was a result of an epileptic seizure such as experienced by mystics like Dostoevsky (ibid., 326). In that moment, "the new idea of Jesus as a suffering Messiah flashed into the brain of Paul . . ." (ibid., 329). This author has witnessed epileptic seizures, and the victims usually remember nothing about them, much less receive from them life-changing insights.

42. Nietzsche, "The First Christian," 290–1.

43. Buitenwerf, "Acts 9:1–25. Narrative History Based on the Letters of Paul," 70. He notes similar themes in Gen 22:1–2; 31:11–13; 46:2–4, and *Joseph and Aseneth* 14, but we must insist that Luke is not merely "recreating history" (ibid., 85) for the sake of a good story, but he is recounting a true story.

44. BDAG § 5355, defines ὅραμα, "in our lit. of extraordinary visions, whether the pers. who has the vision be asleep or awake." It is used in Acts 7:31; 9:10, 12; 10:3, 17, 19; 11:5; 12:9; 16:9–10; 18:9.

45. The masculine singular μηδένα is not "no thing," but "no one" (Acts 10:28; 24:23).

THE "MAN CHRIST JESUS"

(by sight and sound) experience he later explains as an appearance of the risen Lord in the same manner as He had previously appeared to the other apostles (1 Cor 15:7-8).[46]

As previously noted in Chapter 2, the literary similarities describing the vision seen by Saul and that seen by Ezekiel are striking: the OT prophet reports seeing "a figure with the appearance of a man" (ἀνθρώπου) whom he identifies as "the appearance of the likeness of the glory of the LORD" (Ezek 1:28), while Paul uses similar terminology in Acts 22:11 to describe "the glory of that light."[47] The likeness of this "Man" identifies Himself to Ezekiel as the Lord God against whom Israel had rebelled (Ezek 2:3), so in both visions the deity of such a person is immediately obvious: who else could appear from heaven in a blazing display reminiscent of divine glory if not a divine personage?[48] It is certainly possible that there is an intentional analogy between the two visions—particularly if both reveal the same heavenly Person![49] Paul even later describes Jesus in divine terms as "the Lord of the glory" (1 Cor 2:8), yet he also makes Jesus the "model of eschatological humanity"[50] when he identifies man as "the image and glory of God" (1 Cor 11:7, an allusion to Adam in Gen 1:26) and then titles Jesus as the "last Adam" and the "second Man from heaven" (1 Cor 15:45, 47). It is Jesus as this Man of glory who becomes the ultimate focus of the believer's glorification, as "we all, with unveiled face beholding as in a mirror the glory of the Lord, are being transformed into the same image from glory to glory, just as from the Lord, the Spirit" (2 Cor 3:18).

Since Saul's life was immediately transformed by this vision, modern psychology and popular preaching have used his experience as an archetype of religious conversion,[51] even though the text of Acts indicates that his experience was unique: it is not at all like

---

46. Akenson, *Saint Saul*, 173, adamantly argues that Saul encountered "a spiritually raised Christ, but not a physically resurrected Yeshua," so the humanity of 'Yeshua' disappears and a spiritual Christ emerges. Besides misunderstanding the corporeal nature of the resurrection body, Akenson cannot explain why Saul has any need to mention the historical Jesus at all—which Saul most certainly does.

47. There are also some remarkable similarities in the visions of the ascended Christ by both Saul and John (Rev 1:11-18). Both men are interrupted by the spoken voice (φωνή) of Christ (Acts 9:4, 7; 22:9, 14; 26:14; compare Rev 1:12, 15), by a light shining as the sun (Acts 26:13; compare Rev 1:16), and by the *ego eimi* identification of Jesus (Acts 9:5; 22:8; 26:15; compare Rev 1:17). Both men have similar reactions to their respective visions by falling before Christ (Acts 9:4; 22:7; compare Rev 1:17).

48. See the discussion of this divine epiphany in Kim, *Origin of Paul's Gospel*, 205-07, and in Kim, *Paul and the New Perspective: Second Thoughts on the Origin of Paul's Gospel*, 165-192.

49. Quite interestingly, it is the Jewish interpreter Segal, *Paul the Convert: the Apostolate and Apostasy of Saul the Pharisee*, 8-11, who observes this connection with Ezekiel's chariot vision, so that Saul saw the *Kavod YHWH* (τῆς δόξης τοῦ φωτὸς, Acts 22:11), which he later describes in 2 Cor 3:16-4:6 in terms of divine glory. Segal attributes Saul's vision to a *Merkabah* (מֶרְכָּבָה, "Chariot") experience of Jewish mysticism in which God was seen as a divine man (ibid., 40-52). A careful comparison, however, shows that visions recorded in 1 Enoch and the Ascension of Isaiah, for example, are nothing like Saul's experience: in Jewish mystical literature, the worshipper is raised heavenward, whereas Saul remains quite earthbound while the light and voice descended from heaven. Segal overlooks the obvious: the mystic is seeking a divine encounter, whereas Saul most certainly was not.

50. Thrall, "The Origin of Pauline Christology," 309.

51. Corley, "Interpreting Paul's Conversion—Then and Now," 1. He traces the influence of William James, *Varieties of Religious Experience*, on sudden conversions like Saul's. See also Cutton, *The Psychological Phenomena of Christianity* (1908); and Segal, "Paul's Conversion; Psychological Study," in *Paul the Convert*, 285-300.

any of the other conversions described in Acts, which are the results of the preaching of the gospel and not the effects of a divine appearance.[52] A careful exegetical study of Paul's conversion will show it does *not* exhibit the symptoms of a classic religious conversion, such as sensory deprivation, overstimulation, emotional crisis, or cultural expectation of "Jewish mystical apocalypticism."[53] Also, Saul shows no indication of absolution for a tormented conscience;[54] in fact, the opposite is the case, as he later describes himself as once "becoming blameless according to righteousness that is in law" (Phil 3:6 YLT), leading him to "breathe threats and murder against the disciples of the Lord."[55] Thus, the sudden appearance of the blinding light and the interrogation of the heavenly voice were not met with thankful relief from a "wretched man" experience—a dubious in-reading of Romans 7:24 into Paul's conversion, where if anything, Paul wrestles with the awakened, regenerated conscience of a believer.[56] Instead, the goads against which Paul was kicking on this Damascus Road encounter were the proddings of a master's rod, not the pangs of a guilty conscience.[57] Paul's experience was not a humble surrender of a penitent to a benevolent patron, but a sovereign mandate of a conqueror to a hostile enemy: "It shall

---

52. See the accounts of conversions in Acts 7:12, 35–36; 10:44–48; 13:48; 14:9; 16:14, 31–32; 17:3–4, 11–12, 32–24; 18:26–28; 19:4–5.

53. Segal, *Paul the Convert*, 295. Lüdemann, *Paul: The Founder of Christianity*, 189–90, explains Saul's conversion in terms of "depth-psychology" of an "emotional maelstrom" whereby he transformed the "humble and self-sacrificing Jesus" into a "mythic Christ-Redeemer." Such psychoanalysis seems to be quite an odd answer to Paul's rhetorical question, "Have I not seen Jesus our Lord?" (1 Cor 9:1).

54. Stendahl, "The Apostle Paul and the Introspective Conscience of the West," 78–96, notes that the introspective conversion view stems from Augustine's *Confessions* and Luther's *Bondage of the Will*, whereas Paul shows instead a rather "robust" conscience—"there was no indication that he had any difficulty fulfilling the law" (ibid., 80). Saul the Pharisee reveals no burden of conscience concerning personal shortcomings that he would label sins (ibid., 82), militating against a psychological explanation of Paul's Damascus Road experience. Paul's struggles of conscience with the Law (Rom 7:7–25) make more sense as post-conversional experiences, although Gundry, "The Moral Frustration of Paul Before His Conversion," 228–45, argues for a pre-conversion struggle against sexual lust; and Rostron, *The Christology of St. Paul*, 21–22, also finds in this passage a "subjective preparation in process in the heart before the objective appearance of the risen Christ." This reviewer, however, is still convinced that Paul describes a post-conversional experience in Rom 7:7–25. His state of mind on the road to Damascus was seething with threats and murder against the disciples of the Lord (Acts 9:1), hardly the sort of remorse that might lead a broken man to repentance.

55. Paul's experience becomes the source of his understanding that he was called by divine grace (Gal 1:15), not by self-righteousness or religious zeal.

56. Käsemann, "Justification and Salvation History in the Epistle to the Romans," 60–78, insists that Saul sometime before his conversion discovered he was a "wretched man" before the Law. This view, however, seems to be an eisegetical imposition to explain Romans 7 as Paul's commentary on his conversion, as Maccoby does in *The Mythmaker*, 90–4. Paul's later reflections on his pre-conversion status (Gal 1:13–14) reveal self-righteous pride rather than a troubled conscience, and the accounts in Acts present an unexpected interruption of Saul's misguided zeal by an encounter with the sovereign Lord.

57. Picirilli, *Paul the Apostle*, 43, understands Jesus' comment in Acts 26:14, "It is hard for you to kick against the goads," as describing the "inner prodding" of Saul's conscience; thus, Picirilli sees Saul's intense persecution as a resistance against divine conviction. However, since a "goad" refers to a pointed stick used by the master to prod a balking animal (BDAG § 4195.2), the Lord's metaphor implies a stubborn resistance toward the divine will, not an inward conviction of conscience. Paul is not kicking against himself, but against the Risen Lord.

THE "MAN CHRIST JESUS"

be told you what you must do" (Acts 9:6).[58] To be sure, Saul was utterly humbled, as his will was subdued to the sovereign choice of the Ascended Lord in a demonstration of the Augustinian understanding of conversion.[59] Yet when the apostle later holds out his conversion as an example of divine mercy (1 Tim 1:16), he does not present his experience as a norm for conversion but his conduct as a model of Christlike deportment (1 Cor 11:1). Indeed, Paul's encounter cannot be the standard for subsequent conversions because it is also his call to be an apostle, qualifying him for apostolic service by making him an eyewitness of the resurrected Lord (Gal 1:15-16; Acts 1:22).[60]

Paul's Question, "Who are you, Lord?"

When the heavenly voice demanded, "Saul, Saul, why are you persecuting Me?," the stunned prosecutor instinctively recognized that only a divine Person could interrupt his life in such a supernatural manner; thus, he responds to the celestial question with an inquiry of divine identity, "Who art Thou, *Lord*?" (Acts 9:4-5; 22:8, 10; 26:15). Granted, his use of κύριε could be nothing more than a polite acknowledgement of a superior person ("sir," as in John 20:15), but the vocative κύριε in Acts is always addressed to Jesus as one of supreme—even Divine—authority.[61] This connection, however, has been questioned in critical circles since the 1913 publication of Bousset's *Kyrios Christos*, which contends that the designation of Jesus as "Lord" was a product of Hellenistic syncretism Paul derived from the Damascus messianic community.[62] If so, this would make the pious Jewish disciple Ananias the most likely originator of this designation, judging from his visionary conversation with "the Lord" (so identified five times in Acts 9:10-16). However, the imposition of a pagan, polytheistic title upon Jesus by a monotheistic Jew described as "devout by the standard of the Law, and well spoken of by all the Jews who lived there" (Acts 22:12) stretches credulity to a breaking point, especially since Paul later emphatically asserts that Jesus is one Lord (εἷς κύριος Ἰησοῦς Χριστὸς) to the exclusion of many other "so-called" lords (1 Cor 8:5-6). Bousset can maintain his view only by denying the specific OT applications in the inaugural Christian sermon of Peter (Acts 2:34-36), whereby he interprets Joel 2:32 (πᾶς ὃς ἂν ἐπικαλέσηται τὸ ὄνομα κυρίου σωθήσεται,

---

58. Machen, *Origin of Paul's Religion*, 60-68, also refuted the psychologizing of Saul's conversion decades before Stendahl's famous address cited above, noting that Saul was well acquainted with many facts about Jesus, but they had only filled him with hatred. At the appearance of the Person of Jesus on the road to Damascus, Saul's hatred was transformed into love.

59. Corley, "Interpreting Paul's Conversion—Then and Now," 6-7.

60. Bruce, *Paul: Apostle of the Heart Set Free*, 74-75, notes that the vision also included verbal communication by which Paul was not only converted but commissioned, in accordance with the experiences of Isaiah (Isa 6:1-9) and Ezekiel (Ezek 1:4-3:11).

61. See the use of κύριε in Acts 1:6, 24; 4:9; 7:59-60; 9:5, 10, 13; 10:4, 14; 11:8; 22:8, 10, 19; 26:15. As Paul later says that Jesus spoke "in the Hebrew dialect" (= Aramaic; Acts 26:14), it is reasonable to assume that Saul answered in the same language, מָן אֲנַת מֹרִי. This raises the same question whether Saul intended *mari* as a term of honor or of deity. Since Paul later transliterates the Aramaic *maranatha* (מָרַן אֲתָא, 1 Cor 16:22) into Greek, μαράνα θά (or Μαρὰν ἀθά, BYZ), Moule, *Origins of Christology*, 149, wryly observes, "But all the same, you do not call upon a dead Rabbi to 'come' (*marana tha*); and since it is demonstrably possible for *mar* to signify also a divine or transcendent being, it appears that in this context it must have done so."

62. Bousset, *Kyrios Christos*, Chapter 4, "Paulus," 125-86, 142-44, in the German edition.

Acts 2:21) and Ps 110:1 as designating Jesus as κύριος.[63] Furthermore, it is the record of Acts 1–8 that the original church titled Jesus as Lord from the outset (Acts 1:6, 21) and directed its first recorded prayer to Him as "Lord heart-knower of all" (κύριε καρδιογνῶ στα πάντων, Acts 1:24).[64] Such usage would be a logical deduction from the application of κύριος made by Jesus in His own questions on the relationship of David's Son to David's Lord in Psalm 110:1.[65] Wenham notes, "The subtle thrust of Jesus' question is a claim on Jesus' part to be not only Son of David but also David's Lord."[66] In such a case, the originator of Jesus as the Lord is Jesus himself, as He notes, "You call Me Teacher and Lord; and you are right, for *so* I am" (John 13:13).

This much, then, should be obvious from Saul's Damascus Road confrontation, that he immediately realized the one who spoke to him from the brilliant light could only be a person of divine origin. This realization would indicate that Saul's address to this heavenly speaker as κύριε must be more than a title of respect to a superior but rather a title of worship to a deity.[67] The identity of that person is pointedly confirmed to Paul three days later by Ananias, "The Lord sent me—Jesus, the one having appeared to you on the way which you were coming" (Acts 9:17, author's translation of ὁ κύριος ἀπέσταλκέν με, Ἰησοῦς ὁ ὀφθείς σοι ἐν τῇ ὁδῷ ᾗ ἤρχου). Thus, when Saul instinctively acknowledges Jesus as "Lord" on the road to Damascus (and identifies Him as ὁ κύριος in his later testimonies in Acts 22:10 and 26:15), this initial response establishes his subsequent (and frequent) references to Jesus as Lord,[68] thereby indicating that Paul met his own initial requirements for salvation: first, by confessing Jesus as Lord and second, by believing that God raised Him from the dead (Rom 10:9). To be sure, from that moment on, Paul equated Jesus with divinity by describing Him as the Lord "by whom are all things" (1 Cor 8:6).

The Identity of the Lord

The concern of Saul's question, "Who are you, Lord?" is not a conflict with his own psyche but a matter of the identity of the one who has revealed himself from heaven. The idea that Paul's conversion from Pharisee to apostle was the result of a conflicted self is an imposition of modern psychologizing completely absent from the text.[69] Saul the Pharisee

---

63. Bousset's views are examined extensively and refuted decisively by Vos, "The Kyrios Christos Controversy," 21–89.

64. Also, Machen, *Origin of Paul's Religion*, 300, observes that Paul's use of the Aramaic μαράνα θά (1 Cor 16:22) "pushes the use of the title 'Lord' back to the primitive Christian community."

65. Mark 12:35–37 reads, "How *is it that* the scribes say that the Christ is the son of David? David himself said in the Holy Spirit, 'The Lord said to my LORD, "Sit at My right hand, Until I put Thine enemies beneath Thy feet." David himself calls Him 'Lord'; and *so* in what sense is He his son?" See the observations on this saying in Marshall, *Origins of New Testament Christology*, 107.

66. Wenham, *Paul and the Historical Jesus*, 7.

67. Kim, *Origin*, 223–33, shows how Paul later explained this vision in terms of OT theophanies in Gal 1:16; 1 Cor 2:8; 15:47–49; Col 1:15; 2:9; and especially 2 Cor 3:1–4:6.

68. Besides the twelve times Paul describes Jesus as "Lord" in the book of Acts (9:28; 16:31; 20:19, 21, 24, 35; 21:13; 22:10, 19; 23:11; 26:15; 28:31), he titles Jesus as Lord +/- 265 times in his letters. See the brief but concise study by Chrisope, *Jesus is Lord* (1982).

69. Maccoby, *The Mythmaker*, 96–7, argues that Saul's turmoil was produced not by guilt stemming from legalism—a traditional Protestant explanation—but by his inability to reconcile his Hellenistic concepts

THE "MAN CHRIST JESUS"

betrays no doubt in his zeal to rid Judaism of the troublesome heretics of this new Way: the light and sound experience catches Saul completely by surprise. The essential question is this: who did Paul think he had encountered? The second account of Saul's testimony leaves no doubt as to the identity of the person in his encounter, as the heavenly apparition introduces Himself most unexpectedly by name and hometown, "Jesus the Nazarene" (Acts 22:8), thereby making no separation between the earthly Jesus from the heavenly Lord. It had to be stunning to Saul's Pharisaic realizations that the speaker identified himself not only as "Jesus whom you are persecuting" (Acts 9:5), but more specifically, "Jesus the Nazarene" (Ἰησοῦς ὁ Ναζωραῖος). There could be no mistaking the identity of this heavenly Speaker, since Saul had heard the previous charges lodged against Stephen that "this Jesus the Nazarene (Ἰησοῦς ὁ Ναζωραῖος οὗτος) would destroy the Temple and the customs of Moses" (Acts 6:13). Surely as a resident of Jerusalem, Saul would have known that "Jesus the Nazarene" (Ἰησοῦς ὁ Ναζωραῖος) was the exact appellation that Pilate had placarded from the cross with the treasonous and offensive title, "The King of the Jews" (ὁ βασιλεὺς τῶν Ἰουδαίων, John 19:19). Could this voice speaking from a heavenly vision belong to this same man, this Jesus of Nazareth?[70] Such information must have been absolutely astounding to this zealous Pharisee. Could it be that this heavenly Speaker was the same historical Jesus who His followers insisted had been resurrected from the dead? Furthermore, in the answer to Saul's question, "Who are you, Lord?" had he heard an echo of the divine Name? After all, the response of Jesus (ἐγώ εἰμι) echoes OT replies of the divine "I Am" (אָנֹכִי), as in Exod 3:6, 14, and Isa 43:25 (ἐγώ εἰμι ἐγώ εἰμι ‖ אָנֹכִי אָנֹכִי). Had God Himself spoken to him?

Yet Saul had to wait three days in unsighted darkness, pondering the meaning of this crisis encounter and waiting on a promised "someone" to come and tell him what to do next (Acts 22:10). Notwithstanding the novel suggestion of Brenton that Paul was tricked by a Jesus who faked His own death,[71] Saul's mind had to recall similar experiences from his reading of the Jewish Scriptures, such as the appearance of the Captain of the Hosts to Joshua (Josh 5:13–15), the epiphany of Wonderful to Manoah (Judges 13:15–22), the appearance of the thrice-holy Lord to Isaiah (Isa 6:1–13), the accompaniment of One

---

with the monotheism of Judaism. The fact that there is absolutely nothing in either Acts or Paul's epistles to support Maccoby's claim that Saul converted from paganism does not deter him from crediting Saul's conversion to "extreme mental turmoil and near breakdown" (ibid., 100).

70. Kim, *Origin*, 31, asserts, "Many of Paul's references and allusions to his conversion and call on the Damascus Road (1 Cor 9:1; 15:5–10; Gal 1:13–17; Phil 3:4–11; 2 Cor 3:4–4:6; 5:16–21; cf. also Acts 22:3–16; 26:4–18) stand in the polemical context of defending his gospel and Apostleship. However, not only these but also the rest of his allusions to the Damascus event make it clear that his gospel and Apostleship are grounded solely in the Christophany on the Damascus Road and that he understands himself solely in the light of it. The Damascus event is the basis both of his theology and his existence as an Apostle." This study would add that Paul's Christology derives originally from this event as well, since he was confronted by a Divine personage who identified himself as Jesus the Nazarene, a historical Man—thus, the "Man Christ Jesus."

71. Brenton, *Paul* (2006). His thesis is that Saul was tricked into conversion when Jesus *actually* appeared to him, not as a resurrected Lord but as a man who had been rescued from death by James, Peter, and Mary Magdalene. Paul did not learn of this ruse until Peter confessed it to him when they were about to be executed by Nero. One must wonder how Jesus pretended to die and where He hid from His followers for the remainder of His life.

"like a son of the gods" with the three Hebrew lads (Dan 3:24–26), and especially the One coming "upon the clouds of heaven as a Son of Man" (Dan 7:13).[72] Since the Scriptures record such theophanies throughout Jewish history, Saul could not dismiss that such might have happened also to him.[73] Furthermore, the appearances of God in light and sound from heaven echoed previous divine encounters recorded in OT history, including the burning bush episode of Moses (Exod 3:2–4) and the fire on Mt. Sinai (Exod 19:18–20).[74] Confirmation of the identity of this Lord was about to come to Saul from a rather unlikely source, one whom he had intended to extradite back to Jerusalem, Ananias.

The Jesus Proclaimed by Ananias

An overlooked player in Saul's conversion and instruction is a "certain disciple at Damascus, named Ananias," who became the messenger of Saul's commission from Jesus (yet he is completely absent from the narrative in the third account). As Saul was interrupted by the Voice and Light from heaven, likewise without warning Ananias was also abruptly beckoned by "the Lord," and the text assumes that this Lord mentioned five times in this visionary conversation (Acts 9:10, 10, 11, 13, 15) is the same "Lord" who appeared earlier to Saul (Acts 9:5). Although this Lord remains unnamed throughout this conversation, Ananias instinctively realizes he is speaking with the same One who identified Himself previously to Saul as "Jesus whom you are persecuting" (Acts 9:5). Any doubt is removed when Ananias specifically identifies Him as "the Lord Jesus" in Acts 9:17. While Bousset argued that the title of κύριος was applied to Jesus by the Damascus fellowship under Hellenistic influences,[75] the impossibility of such an occurrence is implied in the description of Ananias as "a man who was devout by the standard of the Law, and well spoken of by all the Jews who lived there" (Acts 22:12). Such comments would never be made of a Jew who brought pagan influences into the synagogue; besides, the text presumes that the position and title of κύριος had already been applied to Jesus as the original confession of the church (Acts 1:21; 2:36; 7:59; 8:16) on the basis of OT prophecy (Acts 2:34, quoting Ps 110:1).

72. Kim, *Origin*, 251, notes, "Paul's Damascus experience must have led him immediately to Dan 7:13 because he saw a heavenly figure 'like a son of man' just as Daniel did. It must also have led him to understand that with the self-designation 'the Son of Man', which he in all likelihood had already known, Jesus referred to himself as the Son of God who appeared to Daniel כְּבַר אֱנָשׁ, as he later describes this experience as God revealing 'His Son' (Gal 1:16)."

73. Significantly, the Jewish writer Segal, "Paul's Jewish Presuppositions," 170, comments on what he calls "Paul's mysticism," observing, "To me this suggests that Paul has received a theophany of the human figure of the Lord *YHWH*, the so-called angel of the Lord."

74. Hengel, *Paul Between Damascus and Antioch*, 39, connects the "bright light from heaven" to the "pattern of an Old Testament epiphany," by which Paul saw Jesus as the "Lord of glory" (1 Cor 2:8), so that "the divine δόξα of the Exalted One corresponds to the blinding light of the vision. This indicates the contemporary Jewish apocalyptic notion of God stamped by the Old Testament: the hymn I Tim 6.16 uses the phrase 'God, who dwells in unapproachable light' (φῶς οἰκῶν ἀπρόσιτον) is in good Jewish style." Grammatically, the subject of "the one dwelling in unapproachable light" is κύριος τῶν κυριευόντων, and contextually, this refers to τοῦ κυρίου ἡμῶν Ἰησοῦ Χριστοῦ of the previous verse (1 Tim 6:14), suggesting that Paul has in mind the Damascus Road Christophany, in which he equates the "unseeable" glory of God (Exod 33:20; John 1:18) with the glory of the exalted Jesus. This is a remarkable confession from one who earlier wrote in this same letter (1 Tim 2:5) that there is but one God, for in 1 Tim 6:14 he credits divine "honor and eternal dominion" to Jesus as the one "who alone possesses immortality."

75. Note the entire argument of Bousset, *Kyrios Christos*, 125–86.

THE "MAN CHRIST JESUS"

Also, Luke frames his conversation between the Lord and Ananias in a manner that Jewish readers would recognize as echoing similar epiphanies to their patriarchs and prophets, because the dialogue is initiated when "the Lord said to him in a vision, 'Ananias.' And he said, 'Behold, *here am* I, Lord'" (ἰδοὺ ἐγώ, κύριε, translated in DLZ as הִנֵּנִי אֲדֹנִי), a reply that is identical to the response of Abraham,[76] Jacob,[77] Moses,[78] and Samuel.[79] Luke evidently wants his readers to understand that the speaker of this vision is equivalent to the Lord of the OT.

Also, Ananias explains his understanding of Jesus and His "Way" (Acts 9:2) in OT concepts when he describes the disciples of Jesus as "saints" for the first of many times in the NT (the next are found in Acts 9:32 and 9:41), although this title had been previously applied to the Jewish people of God (Ps 16:3; 34:9; Matt 27:52), most notably in the description of the saints of the Son of Man in Daniel's vision of the Four Great Beasts (Dan 7:18–27). Indeed, Paul's portrayal of believers as "saints" during his defense before King Agrippa (Acts 26:10) echoes Ananias' description of God's people and perhaps suggests that Paul derived this initial understanding of the people of Jesus from Ananias.[80] Another OT theme applied to Jesus appears when Ananias identifies Saul as one who has authority to bind all who "call upon Thy name" (Acts 9:14). This same motif appears in the OT for calling on the name of Israel's God,[81] yet it had significantly appeared in Peter's sermon when he quoted Joel 2:32[82] and applied it to Jesus (Acts 2:21). Not coincidentally, this same connection is made by Paul in Romans 10:13, where he repeats what he first heard from Ananias, telling him to be "calling on His name" (Acts 22:16). All these references indicate that the Name of God had been ascribed to Jesus from the outset, and the special *rôle* of Ananias was to deliver the commission to Saul that he shall become the one to bear this Name before Gentiles, Kings, and Israel (Acts 9:15).

Indeed, Dunn contends that the entire Damascus Road event was not so much a conversion of conduct as a change of Paul's commission to be an apostle of Jesus to the Gentiles.[83] It is evident, however, from Paul's later testimony (Gal 1:13–16; Phil 3:3–6;

---

76. "God tested Abraham, and said to him, 'Abraham!' And he said, 'Here I am'" (ἰδοὺ ἐγώ, הִנֵּנִי, Gen 22:1); "The angel of the LORD called to him from heaven, and said, 'Abraham, Abraham!' And he said, 'Here I am'" (ἰδοὺ ἐγώ, הִנֵּנִי, Gen 22:11).

77. "Then the angel of God said to me in the dream, 'Jacob,' and I said, 'Here I am'" (הִנֵּנִי, Gen 31:11); "God spoke to Israel in visions of the night and said, 'Jacob, Jacob.' And he said, 'Here I am'" (הִנֵּנִי, Gen 46:2).

78. "God called to him from the midst of the bush, and said, 'Moses, Moses!' And he said, 'Here I am'" (הִנֵּנִי, Exod 3:4).

79. "The LORD called Samuel; and he said, 'Here I am'" (ἰδοὺ ἐγώ, הִנֵּנִי, 1 Sam 3:4).

80. Paul describes Christian believers as "saints" forty times (Rom 1:7; 8:27; 12:13; 15:25–26, 31; 16:2, 15; 1 Cor 1:2; 6:1–2; 14:33; 16:1, 15; 2 Cor 1:1; 8:4; 9:1, 12; 13:13; Eph 1:1, 15, 18; 2:19; 3:8, 18; 4:12; 5:3; 6:18; Phil 1:1; 4:21–22; Col 1:2, 4, 12, 26; 1 Thess 3:13; 2 Thess 1:10; 1 Tim 5:10; Phlm 1:5, 7).

81. וַאֲנִי אֶקְרָא בְשֵׁם־יְהוָה, 1 Kgs 18:24; Isa 12:4; 41:24; 65:1; Zeph 3:9; Zech 13:9.

82. וְהָיָה כֹּל אֲשֶׁר־יִקְרָא בְשֵׁם; πᾶς ὃς ἂν ἐπικαλέσηται τὸ ὄνομα κυρίου σωθήσεται. Kim, *Origin*, 253, also notes that the question of Jesus, 'Why are you persecuting me?' would lead Paul to "recognize the unity of Christ with His people: to persecute the followers of Jesus is to persecute him."

83. Dunn, *Theology of Paul*, 346–47. Gager, *Reinventing Paul*, 54, follows Dunn by asserting that "not only Gentiles formed the center of both the conversion experience itself (Gal 1.16) and its consequences (Paul as apostle to the Gentiles), but that in some sense Gentiles must have been an underlying factor lead-

1 Tim 1:12–15), that both aspects are present:[84] Paul is converted by Jesus whom he had persecuted, who then commissions him to be His missionary.[85] Characteristically, Luke repeats the account, giving the first in the words of the risen Lord;[86] the second[87] in the words of Ananias to Saul; and the third in the testimony of Paul as quoting Jesus.[88] Each of these enumerations builds upon the information supplied by the prior accounts, so that the differences among them are due to the particular perspectives specific to each situation and audience.[89] Of great significance to Saul is that he not only learns insights regarding Jesus from Ananias, but that he also hears from Ananias quotations from Jesus that would become formative in the Christology found in Paul's later letters. For example, Paul learned from Ananias (if he had not surmised it already) the sovereignty of Jesus who had chosen him as His own vessel, a metaphor Paul later uses at Rom 9:21–23, 2 Cor 4:7, and 2 Tim 2:20–21. The authority of Jesus is implied in His Name that Saul is to bear to kings, not by a show of force but in suffering (παθεῖν, Act 9:16) on behalf of that Name in a manner similar to that of the suffering of Jesus as a Passover sacrifice (τὸ πάσχα ἡμῶν ἐτύθη Χριστός, 1 Cor 5:7). Also, Ananias places Saul's entire experience in the context of Israel's covenant God and history,[90] and he applies to Jesus the OT title of the Righteous

---

ing to the conversion." It seems, however, that the center of Saul's conversion is his change toward Jesus of Nazareth, who then commissions Saul to go to the Gentiles.

84. Köstenberger and O'Brien, *Salvation to the Ends of the Earth: A Biblical Theology of Mission*, 161–201, discusses Paul's conversion as also his commissioning as a missionary of Jesus and how he understood his calling and message as an apostle to the Gentiles.

85. Barrett, *Paul: Missionary of Jesus*, 59–70, charts the "before and after pattern" of Paul's autobiographical comments in his letters by showing how the "Damascus event" had changed him. Also Buitenwerf, "Acts 9:1–25," 64–66, notes that Saul's blindness implies divine punishment for his sins against the church, making his fasting and baptism reflections of true repentance and as marks of a conversion.

86. Acts 9:15–16 reports, "But the Lord said to him (Ananias), 'Go, for he is a chosen instrument of Mine, to bear My name before the Gentiles and kings and the sons of Israel for I will show him how much he must suffer for My name's sake.'"

87. Acts 22:14–15 quotes Ananias, "The God of our fathers has appointed you to know His will, and to see the Righteous One, and to hear an utterance from His mouth. For you will be a witness for Him to all men of what you have seen and heard."

88. Paul says in his testimony in Acts 26:15–18, "The Lord said, 'I am Jesus whom you are persecuting. But arise, and stand on your feet; for this purpose I have appeared to you, to appoint you a minister and a witness not only to the things which you have seen, but also to the things in which I will appear to you, delivering you from the *Jewish* people and from the Gentiles, to whom I am sending you, to open their eyes so that they may turn from darkness to light and from the dominion of Satan to God, in order that they may receive forgiveness of sins and an inheritance among those who have been sanctified by faith in Me.'"

89. Although Ananias is not named in the third account, the reader assumes his participation from the two prior narratives. One might also wonder why the additional information in the third account is absent from the previous two narratives and even suspect Paul of embellishment, but it makes little sense for Paul to lie (essentially) in his defense before a king or for Luke to invent wording that witnesses of this public hearing could later refute. This study assumes that both Paul and Luke are telling the truth in this third account, meaning that this longest version of the commission came via special revelation from the risen Lord communicated to Paul at the same time as Ananias' visit. Because Luke omits some details in each account does not mean he is lying when he includes those matters in subsequent reports. Had Luke been composing rather than reporting, he would have made sure all three accounts read the same way; as it is, the differences attest to the genuineness of each testimony.

90. In Acts 22:14, Ananias uses the designation, "God of our fathers" (ὁ θεὸς τῶν πατέρων ὑμῶν), which

THE "MAN CHRIST JESUS"

One (τὸν δίκαιον, Acts 22:14), already ascribed to Jesus by Stephen (Acts 7:52) and Peter (Acts 3:14), yet surely echoing the description of the Suffering Servant of Isa 53:11 as the "Righteous One" (δίκαιον, צַדִּיק; it is also used of the Messianic king in Zech 9:9).[91] There seems little doubt that the language of Isa 53:11 ("by His knowledge the Righteous One, My Servant, will justify the many;" בְּדַעְתּוֹ יַצְדִּיק צַדִּיק עַבְדִּי לָרַבִּים) plays prominently in Paul's later discussion of the obedience of Jesus as the One Man who brings righteousness and justification (Rom 5:15–19).

All of these themes combine when Ananias greets his prospective persecutor with a remarkable embrace, "Brother Saul, the Lord Jesus appeared to you on the road" (Acts 9:17). Saul would learn from Ananias about Jesus as Healer when his mentor laid hands upon him to regain his sight just as Jesus laid hands upon a blind man to heal him (Mark 8:23–25). From Ananias, Saul would also learn about Jesus as the Filler of the Holy Spirit, whom He had poured forth at Pentecost (Acts 2:4, 33); now Saul also becomes a recipient of the filling of the Spirit in fulfillment of this OT prophecy (Isa 44:3; Ezek 36:26–27; 37:14; Zech 12:10), a topic that will become a centerpiece of Paul's pneumatology (Rom 5:5; 15:13; 2 Cor 1:22; 6:16; Gal 4:6; Eph 5:18; Titus 3:5). He would also learn from Ananias a new significance for water baptism as a ordinance of the washing away of his sins (βάπτισαι καὶ ἀπόλουσαι τὰς ἁμαρτίας σου, Acts 22:16), still another theme that appears later in Paul's writing (ἀπελούσασθε, 1 Cor 6:11).[92]

Thus, the Christology of Ananias is remarkable not for its innovation, but that it displays the same understanding of Jesus as previously applied to Him by the Jerusalem church, using the same OT themes, titles, and terminology.[93] This "Lord Jesus" proclaimed by Ananias is the same Lord who appeared to Saul, although it is fair to assume that Saul learned more about this new Lord not only through the healing and baptism administered through Ananias, but especially in the commission delivered to him by this humble disciple of Damascus. Thus, Saul is certainly not the founder of a Damascus-Hellenistic Christology in contrast to a Jerusalem-Jewish Christology—as Lüdemann insists—[94] because Ananias plainly shows he is in complete conformity to the same Christ Jesus as the one he confirmed to Saul.

---

is found in the LXX at Gen 43:23; 46:3; Exod 3:13, 15, 16; 4:5; Deut 1:11, 21; 4:1; 6:3; 12:1; 27:3; Josh 1:11; 1 Chr 12:18; 2 Chr 20:6; 36:15; 1 Esd 1:48; Ezra 7:27; Jdt 10:8; Tob 8:5; Tbs 8:5; Odes 7:26; 8:52; 12:1; 14:34; Ezek 28:26; Dan 3:26, 52; Dat 2:23; 3:26, 52. These "fathers" are specified in Acts 3:13, 5:30, and 7:32 as "The God of Abraham, Isaac, and Jacob, the God of our fathers."

91. Longenecker, *Christology of Early Jewish Christianity*, 46–47, notes that canonical Jewish Christian materials employ δίκαιος "not only as an attribute of Jesus but also in substantival adjective form as a Christological title." He connects this title to the "righteous Branch" of Jer 23:5 and Jer 33:15, and to the just King of Zech 9:9.

92. Insisting that Paul sought and received no instruction after his revelation, Maccoby, *The Mythmaker*, 105–06, claims that Luke invented the Ananias story to perpetuate the myth that Paul agreed with the Jerusalem apostles. Such warrantless speculation spends inordinate time searching for spurious motives that are completely absent from the texts when read at face value.

93. Akenson, *St. Saul*, 172, posits continued friction between Paul and the Jerusalem church, but Luke gives no evidence of such, even in the disputations of the Council in Acts 15, when the Jerusalem Apostolate agreed with Paul's message to Gentiles. Even then, the issue is not the identity of Jesus but the relationship of the Law to Gentile believers.

94. Lüdemann, *Paul: The Founder of Christianity*, 214–15.

The "Man Christ Jesus" in the Presentation of Paul in the Acts of the Apostles

The Jesus Saul Confessed After His Conversion

The Book of Acts reports that once Saul was baptized and aligned himself with the other messianic disciples at Damascus, he immediately began to declare that the Jesus is "the Son of God" (Acts 9:20) and that "Jesus is the Christ" (Acts 9:22; confirmed in Gal 1:17b). Both of these statements serve as primary confessions of later NT Christology,[95] and they raise the question: what did Paul mean by applying these titles "Son of God" and "Christ" to the Man Jesus?

"He is the Son of God" (Acts 9:20)

Other than the disputed reading in Acts 8:37,[96] Paul's confession of Jesus, "He is the Son of God" (Acts 9:20), is the first post-ascension confession of Jesus as Son of God to appear in Christianity. For that matter, besides Paul's later explanation of Ps 2:7 in Acts 13:33 (discussed later in this chapter), this is the only appearance of ὁ υἱὸς τοῦ θεοῦ in the book of Acts, lending support to the veracity of this saying as a genuine Pauline confession, since the Sonship of Jesus is not a prominent motif in Acts.[97] For that matter, Jesus as God's "Son" is not used as a frequent title in Paul's letters either,[98] making his initial

---

95. See John 20:31; Rom 1:4; 1 Cor 1:9; 2 Cor 1:19; Gal 2:20; 1 John 3:23; 2 John 9.

96. Acts 8:37 reads, "And Philip said, 'If you believe with all your heart, you may.' And he answered and said, 'I believe that Jesus Christ is the Son of God'" Metzger, *Textual Commentary on the New Testament*, 315, comments, "Ver. 37 is a Western addition, not found in 𝔓⁴⁵, ⁷⁴ ℵ A B C 33 81 614 vg syr^{p, h} cop^{sa, bo} eth, but is read, with many minor variations, by E, many minuscules, it^{gig, h} vg^{mss} syr^{h with *} cop^{G67} arm. There is no reason why scribes should have omitted the material, if it had originally stood in the text. It should be noted too that τὸν Ἰησοῦν Χριστόν is not a Lukan expression. The formula πιστεύω . . . Χριστόν was doubtless used by the early church in baptismal ceremonies, and may have been written in the margin of a copy of Acts. Its insertion into the text seems to have been due to the feeling that Philip would not have baptized the Ethiopian without securing a confession of faith, which needed to be expressed in the narrative. Although the earliest known New Testament manuscript that contains the words dates from the sixth century (ms. E), the tradition of the Ethiopian's confession of faith in Christ was current as early as the latter part of the second century, for Irenaeus quotes part of it (*Against Heresies*, III.xii:8)." The eunuch's confession is certainly apostolic, even if this particular text is not.

97. Those who would suppose that Luke did not think much of this title "Son of God" overlook the fact that he applies it to Jesus in pivotal historical events: at the virgin conception (Luke 1:32, 35); at the baptism of Jesus (Luke 3:22); in the final designation in Jesus' genealogy (Luke 3:38); at the temptations of Jesus (Luke 4:3, 9); in His confrontation with demons (Luke 4:41); by the divine declaration on the Mount of Transfiguration (Luke 9:35); in the knowledge given to the Son (Luke 10:22); and at the confession of Jesus before the Sanhedrin (Luke 22:70). Hengel, *Paul Between Damascus and Antioch*, 46, asks, "Is it mere coincidence that in Acts 9:20, as in Gal 1.16, the messianic title 'Son of God' appears, a title which is not very frequent in Luke and Paul—and which for Luke in Acts is very pointed?"

98. Paul titles Jesus as "Son" in Rom 1:3–4, 9; 5:10; 8:3, 19, 29, 32; 1 Cor 1:9; 15:28; 2 Cor 1:19; Gal 1:16; 2:20; 4:4, 6; Eph 4:13; Col 1:13; 1 Thess 1:10. One should refrain, however, from assuming that the concept is unimportant to Paul simply because he mentions it less than twenty times: theology is not a matter of statistics but of significance, and the Sonship of Jesus is clearly a significant confession of Paul's varied Christology as shown in his list of references to God as the Father of Jesus, also implying His Sonship (Rom 1:7; 8:15–17; 1 Cor 1:3; 8:6; 2 Cor 1:2–3; 11:31; Gal 1:1, 3, 5; Eph 1:2, 3, 17; 2:18; 3:14–15; 4:6; 5:20; 6:23; Phil 1:2; 2:11; 4:20; Col 1:3; 3:17; 1 Thess 1:1; 2 Thess 1:1–2; 1 Tim 1:2; 2 Tim 1:2; Titus 1:4; Phlm 3). Hurtado, *Lord Jesus Christ*, 107, suggests Paul may not use "Son" often for fear that his converts might liken Jesus to pagan sons of gods, but Paul shows no such reticence in describing Jesus as Lord, which was also used as a pagan title. It remains an unanswerable question why Paul does not employ "Son of God" more often, so the proper question to ask is why he uses a particular title in any given context.

THE "MAN CHRIST JESUS"

response highly notable. How then did the newly converted Saul come to this deduction, "Jesus is the Son of God?" Was this identification the result of divine illumination, thereby making Paul the first to receive this designation (as implied in the accustomed translation of Gal 1:16, "God revealed His Son in me"[99]), or is Paul customarily repeating what was a previously accepted confession of the primitive church?

The sudden and unexplained appearance of Saul's immediate declaration of Jesus as "the Son of God" favors the latter, since it presumes that the confession had already found consent in the Damascus church, derived approvingly from the apostolic community in Jerusalem and from there back to Jesus Himself, as reported frequently in the Gospels (e.g. John 10:36).[100] This explanation refutes the notion that the phrase "Son of God" was borrowed from a Gnostic myth of a divine dying and rising redeemer that Paul imposed upon Jesus in order to deify Him, even though the concept carries with it the idea of pre-existent deity.[101] Commenting on the title 'Son of God,' Kim observes, "For through his seeing the exalted and enthroned Jesus Paul could have received the confirmation of the veracity of the confession on the one hand *and* other factors that led him to deepen the primitive Son-Christology and affirm the Son's pre-existence and sending in the world on the other, so that the Son-Christology became an essential part of his testimony to the Damascus Road experience."[102] While Kim notes Paul's later high Christology suggests the personification of Wisdom in the Jewish literature (Prov 8:22–31; Sir 24:3–12; Wis 10:17; 11:4),[103] the close connection Acts 9:20–22 makes between "Son of God" and "Christ"

---

99. The Greek of Gal 1:16 reads, ἀποκαλύψαι τὸν υἱὸν αὐτοῦ ἐν ἐμοί, which could be taken as an intensely inward illumination rather than an external revelation, although it is evident that Paul has in mind his Damascus Road experience. He certainly emphasizes the personal nature of his calling rather than relying upon any consent given by the apostles (Gal 1:17), and that may account for the intensive phrase (ἐν ἐμοί), although Paul uses the same phrase in 1 Cor 14:11 (ὁ λαλῶν ἐν ἐμοὶ βάρβαρος) where he clearly designates another speaking *to* him, not *in* him. This usage justifies the ESV translation of Gal 1:16, "He revealed His Son *to* me."

100. Fee, *Pauline Christology*, 553, observes, that "Paul's understanding of Christ as the preexistent Son very likely had its origin within the community that preceded him." Actually, the most logical source of the title is Jesus Himself, as He often referred to Himself as "the Son" (Matt 11:27; John 5:21). Saul's initial confession either presumes this prior use or that Saul for some inexplicable reason invented (or borrowed from Gnostic mythology) a new category subsequently embraced wholeheartedly by the rest of the NT. Ridderbos, *Paul and Jesus: Origin and General Character of Paul's Preaching of Christ*, 91, calls this latter scenario "historically unexplainable." Moule, *Origin of Christology*, 22–23, identifies this confession of Jesus as the Son of God "the crux of Christology."

101. This is the insistence of the *religionsgeschichtliche Schule* of Bousset, Reitzenstein, Bultmann, and more recently, Maccoby, but it is refuted by Hengel, *The Son of God, The Origin of Christology and the History of Jewish-Hellenistic Religion*, 33, who states, "In reality there is no Gnostic redeemer myth in the sources which can be demonstrated chronologically to be pre-Christian." Klausner, however, *From Jesus to Paul*, 466, while admitting that all of Paul's teachings came from authentic Judaism, insists his understanding was influenced unconsciously by Hellenistic coloring. Nevertheless, in his letters Paul pointedly rejects paganistic practices in favor of biblical ideas, making it quite unthinkable that he would apply pagan mythology to his foundational understanding of Jesus.

102. Kim, *Origin*, 112.

103. Kim, ibid., 115–16, points out that Paul shows an extensive Wisdom-Christology in 1 Cor 10:1–4; Rom 10:6–8; 1 Cor 1:24, 30; 2 Cor 4:4; Col 1:15; 2:3; Phil 2:7. While this observation is correct, it is questionable that Wisdom plays a part in Luke's theology of the Son, since he ties the Son of God not so much to

shows a new understanding of OT Messianic themes, since the concepts are rarely linked in Jewish thought[104] as they are throughout the NT.[105] This combination not only helps one term to define the other, but it presupposes another explanation of these OT titles often linked together in Paul's later writings, that "Son" and "Christ" find their identity and definition in Jesus.[106]

For example, this conjunction of Son of God and Christ appears in the adjuration of Jesus by the High Priest, "You tell us whether You are the *Christ*, the *Son* of God" (Matt 26:63).[107] This connection is quite intriguing, because the exact expression, "the Son of God" does not appear in the OT, although Marshall points out that the OT refers to three types of persons as "sons of God:" angels (Deut 32:8; Job 1:6; 2:1; 38:7), Israel as the firstborn son of the Lord (Exod 4:22–23; Hos 11:1), and the Davidic kings (2 Sam 7:14; Ps 2:7; 72:1; 89:27).[108] The cry of David to YHWH, "Thou art my Father, My God" (Ps 89:26), establishes this father-son relationship between God and His anointed king as the firstborn (בְּכוֹר || πρωτότοκος), as YHWH declares of David's son, "I will be a father to him, and he will be a son to Me" (2 Sam 7:14 || 1 Chr 17:13), a relationship also applied to Solomon (1 Chr 22:10; 28:6). The Davidic King as God's Son appears pointedly in Ps 2:7 in the decree of יְהוָה ("He said to Me, 'Thou art My Son, Today I have begotten Thee.'") and in the command to the kings of the earth, "Kiss the Son, or he will become angry" (Ps 2:12 ESV). Jesus himself asks of this Psalm, "What do you think about the Christ, whose son is He?" (Matt 22:42). The Gospels supply the answer with the startling announcement of Mark 1:1, "The beginning of the gospel of Jesus *Christ*, the *Son* of God."

---

a divine origin, but to Jesus as also "the son of Adam" (Luke 3:38), raising the question, how can a son of Adam also be the Son of God? Paul addresses this issue in 1 Cor 15:22 and 1 Cor 15:45, verses discussed in the previous chapter.

104. Akenson, *Saint Saul*, 42–43, is quite adamant that "in none of the texts known at present is there indicated an identity *at the time of the Second Temple* of the concept of Messiah and of Son of God, Son of Man, and of the coming Kingdom of God" (italics original), with the exception of the *Aramaic Apocalypse* 2.1 (4Q246) which mentions one "who will be called son of God, and they will call him son of the most high" (ibid., 264, ftnt. 37). Since the NT regularly unites the concepts of Christ and Son, it ought to be admitted that this combination is a distinctly Christian understanding, attributed to Jesus by his own use of these terms.

105. "Simon Peter answered and said, "Thou art the *Christ*, the *Son* of the living God" (Matt 16:16); "And demons also were coming out of many, crying out and saying, 'You are the *Son* of God!' And rebuking them, He would not allow them to speak, because they knew Him to be the *Christ*" (Luke 4:41); "(Mary) said to Him, 'Yes, Lord; I have believed that You are the *Christ*, the *Son* of God'" (John 11:27); "these have been written that you may believe that Jesus is the *Christ*, the *Son* of God" (John 20:31); "(He) was declared the *Son* of God . . . Jesus *Christ* our Lord" (Rom 1:4); "For the *Son* of God, *Christ* Jesus . . . was preached among you by us" (2 Cor 1:19); "*Christ* was faithful as a *Son* over His house" (Heb 3:6); "our fellowship is with the Father, and with His *Son* Jesus *Christ*" (1 John 1:3); "we believe in the name of His *Son* Jesus *Christ*" (1 John 3:23); "we are in Him who is true, in His *Son* Jesus *Christ*" (1 John 5:20).

106. Kim, *Origin*, 119, notes "that the ideas of Jesus' pre-existence and mediatorship in creation appear with the titles 'Christ' (1 Cor 8:6; 10:4; 2 Cor 8:9; Phil 2:6) and 'Lord' (1 Cor 8:6; 2 Cor 8:9) as well as 'Son' (Col 1:13ff.)."

107. Fee, *Pauline Christology*, 552, observes that "the evidence from Paul himself indicates that the origin of the *language* 'Son of God' is to be found in a Jewish messianism that traces its roots back to the Davidic covenant" (italics in original).

108. Marshall, *Origins of New Testament Christology*, 112.

THE "MAN CHRIST JESUS"

Even though these titles define one another, they may also stand apart from each other,[109] showing that each has a distinct nuance, with "Son" implying an obvious relationship to "the Father." This observation is confirmed by the verbal declaration of God, "This is My Son," uttered at the baptism of Jesus (Matt 3:17; Mark 1:11; Luke 3:22; John 3:34) and reiterated at the mount of His transfiguration (Matt 17:5; Mark 9:7; Luke 9:35), although it was challenged by Satan (Matt 4:3, 6) and parodied by demons (Matt 8:29). Despite what critics may deny, Jesus describes His relationship to God as a son to His father (Matt 11:27; John 5:19–27), and "Son of God" is a title conferred upon Him by the amazed disciples (John 1:49; Matt 14:33), reaching the climax in Peter's confession, "Thou art the Christ, the Son of the living God" (Matt 16:16). That these statements do not support an adoptionist sonship is affirmed by the natal announcement (Luke 1:32, 35)[110] and verified by the resurrection of the Son (Rom 1:3–4).[111] If these incidents are historically true (as 1 John 5:20 insists, "We know that the Son of God has come."), then Saul's confession is not an anomaly—certainly it is not his innovation to Christology—but it is an expected response of new faith practiced by the church from its inception.

It is impossible to know how fully developed Saul's Christology was at the moment of his initial confession of Jesus as "the Son of God;" however, what is clear is that Paul equates the Man Jesus with this OT royal title so that "the Son of God who was revealed to Paul on the Damascus Road (becomes) the content of his gospel."[112] Zielser's comment, "It is impossible to be dogmatic about when Paul sees Christ as becoming the Son" is thus a misnomer,[113] because in his initial confession, Paul "immediately" declares that the Man Jesus is also the Son of God: He could not "become" what He always had been. What is remarkable is that for Saul to confess Jesus as Son of God expresses "the total opposite of what he had thought of Jesus prior to his conversion."[114]

"This One is the Christ" (Acts 9:22)

As if expecting his readers to understand the connection between Son and Christ as quite normal, Luke reports that Saul immediately coupled his confession of Jesus as the Son of God (Acts 9:20) with his complementary declaration that Jesus is also the Christ (Acts 9:22). These confessions occurred while Saul remained in Damascus "many days" (Acts 9:23), as "he kept increasing in strength and confounding the Jews . . . by proving that this One—this Man Jesus whom he already confessed as Son of God—is the Christ" (Acts 9:22).[115] It is important to note that this confession is not a novel innovation of

---

109. As in Matt 11:27, "No one knows the Son, except the Father; nor does anyone know the Father, except the Son, and anyone to whom the Son wills to reveal *Him*"; and Matt 23:10, "One is your Leader, *that is*, Christ."

110. The angel announces to Mary of her baby, "He will be called the Son of the Most High; . . . the holy offspring shall be called the Son of God" (Luke 1:32, 35).

111. Marshall, *Origins*, 120, "May it not be the case that the early church regarded the resurrection as a confirmation of an already-existent status rather than as the conferring of a new status?"

112. Kim, *Origin*, 136.

113. Ziesler, *Pauline Christianity*, 43.

114. Hurtado, *Lord Jesus Christ*, 108.

115. The grammatical construction of Acts 9:22 (συμβιβάζων ὅτι οὗτός ἐστιν ὁ χριστός) is actually

Saul and should not be understood as if no one had previously conceived of Jesus as the Christ until the moment of Saul's affirmation, as contended by Akenson, who insists that to Saul it is only the resurrected Jesus who is the Messiah, not the earthly Jesus.[116] Peter, however, argued this precise point in his inaugural sermon, that the resurrection of Jesus proved Him to be the Messiah (Acts 2:31–36). Both Peter and Paul clearly refer to "Jesus of Nazareth" as the Christ (Acts 4:10, 22:8), so that the primary formulations of Christology found in Paul's letters appear at this initial stage of his new faith: the Man Jesus possesses a divine relationship as the Son of God and a prophetic fulfillment as the Messiah of Israel, as Paul links together these two OT themes.

This study has previously examined Paul's application of Χριστός (= מָשִׁיחַ) to Jesus, noting that while some in critical scholarship understand the title as little more than a *cognomen* for Jesus, it is by far the most common title Paul applies to Jesus.[117] Since Jesus discourages the use of the title to himself publicly (although not privately, Matt 16:20; 23:10; John 17:3),[118] Hengel ponders why it became the most associated title for Jesus in such a relatively short time. He suggests that the historical basis of the title can be found in the crucifixion of Jesus as a messianic pretender (Mark 15:32),[119] yet the irony is that the crucifixion actually verifies Jesus as the Messiah, albeit one who was crucified (1 Cor 1:23; 2:2; Gal 3:1) yet now resurrected (1 Cor 15:20). The linking together of Jesus as the Christ forever joins a particular interpretation of the Messiah with the Man Jesus as crucified and resurrected.

Eventually, as Kim argues, all of Paul's theological method flows from his conversion experience, that by "*seeing Jesus' claim (and the early church's kerygma) confirmed by the Damascus revelation, he interpreted the revelation in the light of the Jesus tradition as well*

---

a quotation, although no English versions render it thus, "proving, 'This is the Christ'" (Young's *Literal Translation* comes the closest, "proving that this is the Christ."). The title "the Christ" is applied to Jesus twenty-five times in Acts: in Peter's Sermon at Pentecost (Acts 2:31, 36, 38); in the healing of the lame man (Acts 3:6, 18, 19); in Peter's defense (Acts 4:10, 26); in the preaching of the apostles (Acts 5:42), by Philip (Acts 8:5, 12), by Saul (Acts 9:22); in Peter's healing of Aeneas (Acts 9:34); in Peter's preaching to Cornelius (Acts 10:36, 48; 11:17); at the Jerusalem Council (Acts 15:26); in Paul's command to the demoniac (Acts 16:18); in Paul's missionary preaching (Acts 17:3; 18:5); in the preaching of Apollos (Acts 18:28); in Paul's defenses (Acts 24:24; 26:23); and in his closing ministry (Acts 28:31). "Christ" refers especially of Jesus as the fulfillment of the OT expectation of the Messiah.

116. Akenson, *Saint Saul*, 176. He claims that while Saul's immediate confession affirms the post-resurrection Christship of Jesus, it is "simultaneously displacing the idea that Yeshua of Nazareth acted or claimed messiahship while on earth." One must wonder how a confession establishing Yeshua as Messiah at the same time displaces Him from that position.

117. While Paul mentions the name "Jesus" 213 times in his signed letters and designates Him as "Lord" +/- 265 times, Paul uses Χριστὸς 382 times. Add to this the seven times he uses Χριστὸς in Acts (9:22; 16:18; 17:3; 18:5; 24:24; 26:23; 28:31), and it is by far the most common title he applies to Jesus. Kramer, *Christ, Lord, Son of God*, 19–44; 133–150, conducts extensive analysis in Paul's choice of words but his findings seem inconclusive since he understands "Christ" as a proper name from the beginning (ibid., 219). This begs the question why the early church would assign this OT Messianic title to Jesus in the first place if "Christ" was little more than a nickname.

118. Hengel, "Christos in Paul," in *Between Jesus and Paul*, 66.

119. Ibid., 77.

THE "MAN CHRIST JESUS"

as the Scriptures and vice versa."[120] Since Jesus appeared to Saul as the resurrected Lord, it is to be expected that the apostle would emphasize this aspect of Christology in his letters, but certainly not to the exclusion of the earthly Jesus: these two aspects are united in Paul's confession that Jesus (the Man) is the Son of God, the Christ. As Andrews observes, "The very beginning of Paul's career as a Christian was founded upon the identity of Christ with the human Jesus."[121]

Summary: The Jesus of Saul's Conversion

There is no question whatsoever that the author of the three accounts of Saul's conversion intended for the readers to understand that the heavenly Person who appeared to Saul was not only the ascended Lord, but also the historical, earthly, Jesus of Nazareth. The text of Acts indicates that the resurrected Christ spoke from heaven, yet His geographical address of Nazareth unmistakably identifies the speaker as the historical Jesus of whom Saul would have possessed considerable information he had deemed to be blameworthy—particularly, that this Jesus had been condemned by the Sanhedrin as a blasphemer of Jahve's Name and crucified by the Romans as a pretender to Caesar's throne. The true identity of Jesus is confirmed to Saul by Ananias, when he tells him that "the Lord appeared to me—Jesus, the one having appeared to you on the road which you were coming" (Acts 9:17, author's translation), in an experience by which he defines the choice of Saul "to see the Righteous One and to hear a sound out of His mouth" (Acts 22:14).[122]

By the time of his public confession, Saul had come to realize that the heavenly personage whom he addressed as κύριε with presumed divine indications, was none other than the historical Jesus. The one whom he had so bitterly opposed as a crucified Messiah was now unquestionably raised from the dead—a fact confirmed by this appearance. Although Paul does not give the details of his Damascus Road experience in his letters, he writes of the event this way, that it was a "revelation of Jesus Christ" (Gal 1:12) who appeared to him in an "objective, external event"[123] that transformed his estimation of Jesus from a false prophet to the Christ, the Lord, and the Son of God (Gal 1:16).[124] While skeptical readers may doubt the reality of this experience or dismiss it by means of some

---

120. Kim, *Paul and the New Perspective, Second Thoughts on the Origin of Paul's Gospel*, 206, italics original. In his opening chapter, Kim takes to task the views of Dunn in his *Theology of Paul*, 346–89, in which Dunn asserts that Paul's Damascus Road experience was more a matter of his commissioning to preach to Gentiles than a conversion of thought about Jesus. Kim insists—and rightly so—that both conversion and commission are involved in Saul's encounter.

121. Andrews, *The Meaning of Christ for Paul*, 36.

122. Ridderbos, *Paul and Jesus*, 46, remarks, "*In this encounter with the person of the exalted Christ is to be found the starting point of Paul's apostolic preaching, as well as the real significance of his conversion, and it is this confrontation to which he appeals again and again to justify his preaching of Christ*" (italics in original).

123. Kim, *Origin*, 56.

124. See a similar listing in Richard Longenecker, "A Realized Hope, a New Commitment, and a Developed Proclamation: Paul and Jesus," 25, to which he adds "Christ's appearance to (Paul) had a revolutionary effect on his life, so that he came to consider 'everything (particularly his past Jewish credentials and accomplishments) a loss compared to the surpassing greatness of knowing Christ Jesus my Lord' and to focus only on 'knowing Christ' with all that such a consuming passion involved (Phil 3:7–11)."

natural explanation, the paramount question remains: who did Paul claim to see that day? His answer is univocal: he saw the "Man Christ Jesus" in a glorified, heavenly state. Critics may not accept this explanation, yet the text does not allow any postmodern distinction between Jesus the Man of Nazareth and Christ the Lord of heaven: the Man Jesus is one and the same as the Lord Christ. His location has changed from earth to heaven because of His ascension, but Paul insists he saw the same Man who had been identified by His crucifixion placard, "Jesus the Nazarene" (John 19:19). The implications of this appearance were staggering and utterly transforming for Saul, when he realized that the one who had once been a historical Man is now a heavenly Person, providing the derivation of a Divine-Man who becomes the center of Paul's entire theological system.

THE MAN CHRIST JESUS OF PAUL'S JERUSALEM PREACHING (ACTS 9:26–29)

In his subsequent return to Jerusalem, Saul was at first shunned by the disciples until Barnabas brought him to the apostles with the validation "how he had seen the Lord on the road and that He had talked to him, and how at Damascus he had spoken out boldly in the name of Jesus" (Acts 9:26–27). The reader correctly assumes that "the Lord" referred to by Barnabas is the same earthly Jesus addressed by those apostles before His ascension (Acts 1:6), for in their estimation, the heavenly Lord is one and the same as the historical Jesus they had accompanied "all the time that the Lord Jesus went in and out among us" (Acts 1:21). Now Saul is numbered with these same men, as Luke pictures him "with them (μετ' αὐτῶν) moving about freely in Jerusalem, speaking out boldly in the name of the Lord" (Acts 9:28). It is implicit here that the Jesus preached by Saul in Jerusalem is exactly the same person as the Jesus of the Jerusalem church. Had there been a difference, Saul would never have been accepted by the apostolic community,[125] but instead, he unites with the apostles in the same ministry espousing the same message based on the Name of Jesus, a theme to become prominent in Pauline epistles.[126]

There exists, however, some significant difficulties reconciling the account in Acts 9:26–29 with Paul's recollections of the same episode in Galatians 1 and 2;[127] in-

---

125. Hunter, *Paul and His Predecessors*, 89, states, "The effect of Paul's conversion was not so much to give Paul a new theory about Christ as to convince him of the truth of the claims already made by Christians. The Crucified, he now realized, was indeed the exalted messiah and Lord. Stephen and others had been right." This unity between Paul and the Jerusalem apostles disproves the contention of Maccoby, *The Mythmaker*, 139–55, that Paul was in conflict with the original apostles as initial leaders of the sect of the Nazarenes, and that later Christianity suppressed the understanding of Jesus by Jewish Christianity, which Maccoby claims to be the more authentic strain of the historical Jesus. That there was tension between the Jewish believers and the increasing number of Gentile believers is readily admitted in the NT, but to drive a wedge of "hardly veiled contempt" (ibid., 146) between Paul and the apostles terribly misreads the resolutions reached in Acts 15:19–29 and Gal 2:6–10. Maccoby turns Paul's confrontation of Peter on its head and makes Paul the deceptive villain by breaking with the authentic link to the historical Jesus in favor of his own revealed Christ (ibid., 150–51). Maccoby wants the original apostles to remain exclusively Old Covenant Jews, overlooking that their confession of Jesus as Messiah required New Covenant changes.

126. Paul mentions the "Name of Jesus" in Rom 1:5; 10:13; 1 Cor 1:2, 10; 5:4; 6:11; 2 Cor 9:2; Eph 5:20; Phil 2:9–10; 4:3; Col 3:17; 2 Thess 1:12; 3:6; 2 Tim 2:19.

127. While the issue of the chronologies of Acts and Galatians is beyond the scope of this study, see the

deed, Fitzmyer writes, "The correlation of the Pauline and Lucan data about the visits to Jerusalem after the conversion is the most difficult aspect of any reconstruction of Paul's life."[128] There is an apparent difference in chronology,[129] which is resolved in the way Luke condenses time by using the phrase "many days" to express an indefinite period of time.[130] Also, there is a difference in reporting Paul's reception upon his return to Jerusalem,[131] but this difficulty is easily resolved as Gal 1:23 gives the eventual settling of the initial suspicion against Paul reflected in Acts. More serious, however, is the difficulty in audience, as Paul insists that after his conversion, "I did not immediately consult with flesh and blood, nor did I go up to Jerusalem to those who were apostles before me" (Gal 1:16–17a). Three years later, he "went up to Jerusalem to become acquainted with Cephas, and stayed with him fifteen days. But I did not see any other of the apostles except James, the Lord's brother" (Gal 1:18–19). This sequence is hard to square with Acts 9:27–28, that "Barnabas took hold of him (Paul) and brought him to the apostles," and he began "with them moving about freely in Jerusalem, speaking out boldly in the name of the Lord." While this report sounds as if Paul ministered with far more than two apostles, Luke does not specify them as "the Twelve," as he does in Acts 6:2. His purpose is to show that both Paul and the Jerusalem apostles preached the same gospel "in the name of the Lord"—which is the same point Paul makes in Gal 2:7–9, even though each targeted a different audience.[132] Paul stresses that he was not dependant upon the authorization of

---

suggested framework in Witherington, *The Paul Quest: The Renewed Search for the Jew of Tarsus*, 304–31. Also Riesner, *Paul's Early Period: Chronology, Mission Strategy, Theology*, 3–28, notes how twentieth century scholarship generally abandoned Acts as historically reliable and "yielded little in the way of even moderately unified results" (ibid., 25). When discussing Paul's escape from Damascus, Riesner shows his approach in this statement: "Although much in our reconstruction remains hypothetical, it at least seems possible to make both the Pauline and Lukan accounts historically comprehensible" (ibid., 89). Since what we actually have in hand are these respective texts, both ought to be examined in light of the other in an effort to recreate the historical circumstances.

128. Fitzmyer, *Paul and His Theology: A Brief Sketch*, 12.

129. Acts 9:23 simply states, "when many days had elapsed," Paul had to flee Damascus (Acts 9:25) and seemingly left immediately for Jerusalem, whereas in Gal 1:16–17, he states he "did not go up to Jerusalem" after his conversion but "went away to Arabia, and returned once more to Damascus; then three years later I went up to Jerusalem."

130. Luke evidently uses the phrase ἡμέραι ἱκαναί to describe an indefinite period of time Paul remained in Damascus (Acts 9:23). He also uses this phrase at Acts 9:43; 18:18; and 27:7 to cover an indefinite period, showing it is shorter than "a long time" (ἱκανὸν χρόνον, Acts 14:3), but longer than a few days (ἡμέρας τινάς, Acts 10:48), even extending over several months (Acts 18:18). Since Luke does not mention Paul's excursion to Arabia, a reconstructed chronology reveals that Paul after his conversion stayed in Damascus for "many days" (Acts 9:23). He next went to Arabia and returned back to Damascus (Gal 1:17), from which he had to escape due to threats on his life (Acts 9:23; he verifies this episode in 2 Cor 11:22–23). He then traveled back to Jerusalem (Acts 9:26) after a three-year absence for a fifteen day visit (Gal 1:18). To be fair to Luke, he does not specify a time but simply states, "When Paul came to Jerusalem" (Acts 9:26).

131. Acts 9:26 reports that when Paul finally returned to the Jerusalem and tried to associate with the disciples, he found that memories of his past persecution (Acts 9:1–2) were still fresh in their minds, "for all were afraid of him, not believing him to be a disciple," whereas Paul says in Gal 1:23 that "all were glorifying God because of me." Acts 9:26 gives the initial response of suspicion whereas Paul provides the eventual outcome when the fears were allayed.

132. Ridderbos, *Paul and Jesus*, 48, notes that Paul's contact with the original church is "firmly established on the basis of repeated and unanimous witness of Acts (Cf. 7:58; 8:1, 3; 9:1, 13, 21; 22:3ff.; 26:4ff.)."

the Jerusalem Apostolate for his credentials, but rather he had received his own first-hand commission from the same Jesus, albeit in His ascended glory (Gal 1:12).[133]

This claim creates yet another difficulty, for while Paul denies receiving his gospel from men (οὐδὲ ... παρέλαβον, Gal 1:12) yet he also asserts that he did receive (ὃ καὶ παρέλαβον, 1 Cor 15:3) certain facts from prior tradition (1 Cor 11:23; 15:1–5).[134] Either Paul carelessly contradicts himself, or he senses no conflict between these two sources.[135] On one hand, he received his gospel commission immediately from the risen Lord, but on the other hand, he received the historical details about Jesus through apostolic tradition: it is not a matter of either/or, but both/and.[136] Thus, the facts of the earthly life of Jesus came to him through the account of eyewitnesses, of whom there were more than five hundred (1 Cor 15:6). Presumably he learned the historical traditions through word of mouth, but they may well have come via written sources, as indicated by the literary similarities noted in the comparison of 1 Tim 2:5–6 to Mark 10:45.[137] While Paul's favorable mention of tradition (2 Thess 2:15; 3:6) can be most unsettling to a Protestant reader because of

---

There is nothing in his epistles in conflict with this, not even Galatians 1:22, to which an appeal is often made. . . . Paul's spiritual origin in Palestinian Judaism is established by Paul himself in such passages as Philippians 3:5 ("circumcised the eighth day, of the nation of Israel, of the tribe of Benjamin, a Hebrew of Hebrews; as to the Law, a Pharisee") and 2 Corinthians 11:22 ("Are they Hebrews? So am I. Are they Israelites? So am I. Are they descendants of Abraham? So am I.")."

133. Wenham, *Paul and Jesus: The True Story*, 22–5, gives a brief but helpful reconciliation of Acts 9 and Galatians 1–2.

134. Bird, "The Purpose and Preservation of the Jesus Tradition: Moderate Evidence for a Conserving Force in Its Transmission," 17, notes, "The verb παραδίδωμι in the NT (and similarly in rabbinic and Greco-Roman literature) is a technical term for the transmission of traditions. It refers to the fact of the handing on of the traditions but does not say how or in what setting they were transmitted. Second, the traditions were passed καθὼς παρέδοσαν ἡμῖν ("just as they were delivered to us"), which implies a consciousness of the possibility of false transmission."

135. Hengel, *Paul Between Damascus and Antioch*, 44, observes, "However, even if he (Paul) did not receive his gospel and his apostleship through human beings, but above all 'through a revelation of Jesus Christ', he does have important traditions which he received from others, like I Cor 15:1–7, where in connection with the message that he proclaimed in Corinth he himself emphasizes what he had 'already received' (ὃ καὶ παρέλαβον), and despite the 'received from the Lord' (παρέλαβον ἀπὸ τοῦ κυρίου), the report of Jesus' last night and the Lord's Supper which he instituted (I Cor 11.23–25) of course presupposes concrete historical tradition which rests on the living memory of participants. Moreover, a statement like I Cor 15:11 ("Whether then *it was* I or they, so we preach and so you believed;" wording added.) with its emphasis on the basic agreement in the preaching of the eyewitnesses to the resurrection mentioned earlier is only possible on the basis of a common tradition which was communicated to Paul by third parties. . . ."

136. See Stanton, "Paul's Gospel" in *The Cambridge Companion to St. Paul*, 174, where he notes that in 1 Cor 15:1–3, "Paul acknowledges that the central themes of the gospel he had passed on to the Corinthians were transmitted to him by his Christian predecessors," as he "uses two verbs for the transmission and reception of the gospel (*paradidōmi* and *paralambanō*) which recall the semi-technical terminology used for the careful transmission of teaching from one generation of Jewish teachers to another." Machen, *Origin of Paul's Religion*, 145, wisely notes, that "The Epistle to the Galatians must always be interpreted in the light of 1 Cor xv. 1–11." See also Stout, "The New Testament Concept of Tradition."

137. See Lau, *Manifest in Flesh: The Epiphany Christology of the Pastoral Epistles*, 56–61, on Paul's varied use of prior Christological tradition, where he maintains that Paul "has essentially accepted traditional formulae and used existing material rather than creating new ones" (ibid., 58), but he also enlarges on the explication of redemptive significance within the same apostolic tradition.

THE "MAN CHRIST JESUS"

the historical polemic against Roman Catholic tradition,[138] he obviously means by tradition those authoritative teachings delivered from the apostolic community, who in turn derived their traditions from Jesus, meaning that "the gospel as tradition relates to historical facts."[139] Yet Paul cites not merely historical information acquired from tradition (that Christ died), but also the apostolic interpretation of the historical events, that "Christ died *for our sins according to the Scriptures*" (1 Cor 15:3, italics added for emphasis). Ridderbos observes, "The question on what does Paul base his preaching of Jesus as the Christ is answered by Paul's epistles and the book of Acts. The answer is twofold: first, on the *revelation* which he personally experienced, and second, on the *tradition* known already to the established church."[140] This tradition incorporated not only the OT Scriptures as a source, but also the OT as interpreted by Jesus (Luke 24:44), who becomes the fountain-head of the pool of Paul's Christology. Hatch suggested that these teachings were gathered very early into written "Testimony Books," as he noted blocks of OT quotations agreeing with parallel NT passages rather than with the LXX versions.[141] This same idea was furthered by Harris in his work *Testimonies*,[142] which Dodd calls the "starting point of modern study of the Old Testament in the New,"[143] although Dodd argued that these collections were primarily oral *testimonia* of the "doctrine of the apostles" (Acts 2:32) based upon these collected OT quotations.[144] Regardless of method, Saul as a new convert certainly received from Ananias some sort of remedial instruction in the traditions concerning Jesus.

This indication implies that Paul's understanding of the "Man Christ Jesus" was not fully derived from the Damascus Road revelation, but it also relied upon apostolic tradition he learned from other sources. It is not insignificant that while Paul's conversion is singularly unique, his immediate contact with "the Way"[145] in Damascus (Acts 9:2) shows that he was dependant upon the church from the outset, through the healing and commis-

---

138. For example, *The Westminster Confession of Faith* 1.6, states, "The whole counsel of God, concerning all things necessary for His own glory, man's salvation, faith and life, is either expressly set down in Scripture, or by good and necessary consequence may be deduced from Scripture: unto which nothing at any time is to be added, whether by new revelations of the Spirit, or traditions of men." Not surprisingly, the Roman Catholic scholar Fitzmyer, *Paul and His Theology*, 32, correctly points out Paul's dependence on the apostolic traditions of the early church—"its kerygma, liturgy, hymns, confessional formulas, theological terminology, and parenesis."

139. Bruce, *Paul and Jesus*, 41. See also Dodd, *History and The Gospel*, 55, where he notes, "In the NT . . . the tradition is always vital and its historical character indispensable."

140. Ridderbos, *Paul and Jesus*, 43; italics original.

141. Hatch, "On Composite Quotations from the Septuagint," in *Essays in Biblical Greek*, 203–4.

142. Harris, *Testimonies* (1916, 1920).

143. Dodd, *According to the Scriptures: the Sub-Structure of New Testament Theology* (1953), 25.

144. Ibid., 126. Dodd does not dismiss the possibility of written prooftexts, for it seems quite natural and normal that these OT testimonies would soon be written down, as it is evident that the early church was literate from the outset, proven not only in its use of the OT, but also in its written correspondence (Acts 15:23).

145. Luke refrains from calling this group the "church" in Acts 9. This may suggest that the messianic disciples in Damascus at this stage were still Jewish believers meeting within the synagogues, not in distinct Christian churches. See Hengel, *Paul Between Damascus and Antioch*, 81.

sioning given by Ananias, his baptism into the Messianic community,[146] and his interaction with those disciples for several days afterwards (Acts 9:17–19).[147] Most naturally, the new convert would be full of questions about the ministry of the one whose name he has called upon in baptism (Acts 22:16), as Hengel notes, "To do this, he must have known some basic facts about this Lord."[148] Since Paul makes no appeal to any knowledge of Jesus according to the flesh (other than the tantalizing reference in 2 Cor 5:16), he had to rely upon eyewitness tradition for information of the events before his conversion, just as he reports in 1 Corinthians 11 and 15.[149] Yet Paul's letters clearly reveal his knowledge of Jesus as a historical figure, and such data must have been derived, not from direct revelations, but from testimonies of first-hand witnesses.[150] Certainly, when Barnabas introduced Saul to the apostles upon his return to Jerusalem (Acts 9:27), it would be quite natural for this newly-converted Pharisee to inquire of these friends of Jesus—Cephas in particular, according to Gal 1:18—about their first-hand accounts of the activities and teachings of the everyday Jesus.[151] As Bruce notes, "But with the revelation on the Damascus Road came the knowledge that the crucified Jesus had been raised from the dead and was now exalted as Lord. Here was incentive enough to know as much about him as could be known, and there were disciples in Jerusalem who could supply this knowledge."[152]

---

146. Barnett, *Paul: Missionary of Jesus*, 74, states, "My contention is that Paul's subsequent and frequent proclamation of Jesus as the Son of God in Damascus . . . had its beginnings in his baptismal instruction in Damascus (cf. 1 Thess 1:9–10; 2 Cor 1:19)."

147. Hunter, *Paul and His Predecessors*, 13, asks, "What is Paul's debt to the Christianity which existed before and alongside him? How much of the common apostolic Christianity current, say between A. D. 30 and 50, can we detect with some certainty in Paul's epistles?" He answers by showing the following evidences: (1) a derived *paradosis* received from the primitive Palestinian church (1 Cor 15:1–7; 11:23–25), as shown in Paul's acceptance of baptism as the initial ritual to enter the messianic movement (Acts 9:18), assuming some sort of catechizing; (2) various creedal formulae (Rom 1:3–5; "the word of the faith" in Rom 10:8–9; Rom 4:24–25; the triad of faith, hope and love of 1 Cor 13:13; Hunter later adds Rom 3:24–25); (3) hymns (Eph 5:14; Phil 2:6–12; Col 1:15–20); (4) "Words of the Lord" (1 Cor 7:10; 9:14; 11:23–25; 1 Thess 4:15; Acts 20:35; also "tacit use of sayings of Jesus in his exhortations" (ibid., 51) in Rom 12:14, 17, 21; 13:7, 8–10; 14:3, 14, 17; plus echoes of Jesus' teachings in 1 Thessalonians 4–5; Rom 16:19; 1 Cor 13:2; Phil 4:6; Rom 8:15; Col 3:13; 2 Thess 3:3; (5) Paraenetic/Catechetical Tradition (1 Thess 4:1; 2 Thess 3:6; Rom 6:17); (6) OT interpretive methods; (7) a shared view of Baptism and the Lord's Supper; (8) a shared view of Jesus as the Christ and Lord (Aramaic *maran*, 2 Cor 16:22), as pre-existent son of Man (1 Cor 15:27 → Ps 8:6; ibid., 86), as Stone, and as Son of God (Acts 13:33 → Ps 2:7); (9) a shared view on the Holy Spirit; and (10) a shared eschatology (the resurrection of Jesus, His parousia, judgment, and final resurrection).

148. Hengel, *Paul Between Damascus and Antioch*, 43.

149. See Stout, "The New Testament Concept of Tradition," 108–137.

150. Paul's insistence in Gal 1:11–17 that he did not receive his gospel from consulting "flesh and blood" nor from the apostles in Jerusalem speaks more of his apostolic authority rather than specific information about Jesus. Ridderbos, *Paul and Jesus*, 47–48, cautions that "one may not separate the statements in Galatians 1:11–12 from their context and purposes."

151. Bruce, *Paul and Jesus*, 84, notes that "the purpose of Paul's going to Jerusalem on this occasion (was) . . . not merely to make his acquaintance (with Cephas) but to inquire of him (for this is the force of the verb *hisorēsai* which he uses)." The importance of Peter as a bridge between Jesus and Paul is explored by Bockmuehl, "Peter Between Jesus and Paul: The 'Third Quest' and the 'New Perspective' on the First Disciple," 101, who notes that Peter harbors "unrealized potential" in this endeavor.

152. Bruce, "Further Thoughts on Paul's Autobiography: Galatians 1:11–2:14," 26.

THE "MAN CHRIST JESUS"

Quite naturally, as a new convert, Saul would inquire about the life of Jesus. He would want to know answers to such questions as, where He had be been born? Were there any unusual circumstances of His birth? Where He was raised? Who were His relatives? How had He ministered? What were His teachings? Allusions and echoes to this information sprinkle throughout Paul's letters, as noted in the previous chapter, showing that far from being inconsequential to his doctrine, he weaves many of these historical details into his understanding of salvation through the "Man Christ Jesus." In the observation of Stanton, "There is plenty of evidence which, taken cumulatively, indicates that the early church was interested in the life and character of Jesus, and that the primary (though not the only) *Sitz im Leben* of that interest was the missionary preaching of the church,"[153] to which this study now turns in examining the preaching of Paul with regard to the "Man Christ Jesus."

Thus, we can deduce that Paul's Christology crystallized within a few days of his Damascus Road experience, as he embraced what was implied in "the name of Jesus" he began to proclaim. Kim suggests three primary lines of identification in Paul's perception of Jesus: as "the Christ, the Lord, and the Son of God," concepts that appear in the text of Acts 9 and then re-appear in Rom 1:3–4.[154] Kim's thesis is that "the ideas of the pre-existence, mediatorship in creation, and sending and giving up of the Son of God are a Pauline contribution (sic) and they are grounded ultimately in Paul's Damascus experience."[155] However, since these concepts are found in the OT as they relate to the Messiah and as they are taught by Jesus in the Gospels, it might be better to suggest that Paul was the first (after Jesus) to formulate these concepts, as Kim aptly demonstrates.[156]

The concern of this present study, however, addresses a neglected aspect of Paul's Damascus Road experience, that the Jesus who appeared to him was not only the Christ, the Lord, and the Son of God—all titles indicating His deity—but He was also Jesus, a man "of Nazareth." It is the thesis of this study that this same historical Jesus does not fade from Paul's thought but rather becomes so interwoven with his message that the saving significance of Jesus becomes inseparably bound with His humanity—in the events of His life, suffering, crucifixion, burial, resurrection, and ascension, all experienced by Jesus not in the realm of His deity as such, but in the events of His humanity, lived out in historical time and space. Thus, Paul realized from the moment of his conversion that a direct continuity existed between the historical Jesus of Nazareth and the ascended Son of God. Machen asks, "How then did Paul come to identify his heavenly Messiah with Jesus

---

153. Stanton, *Jesus of Nazareth in New Testament Preaching*, 9. By "preaching" he refers not to the activity but to "the content of the message proclaimed" (ibid., 10).

154. Kim, *Origin*, 106.

155. Ibid., 114.

156. Ibid., 114–131, where Kim unites the OT concept of divine wisdom with the Pauline concept of Jesus as the pre-existent, wisdom of God (1 Cor 1:24; 1:30; Col 2:3). Also, see pages 136–159, where he ties Paul's designation of Christ as the "image of God" (1 Cor 15:49; 2 Cor 3:18; Col 1:15; 3:9–10) with Gen 1:26–27. He argues quite persuasively that Paul derived his understanding of the divine Jesus from his Damascus Road experience, drawn from deductions of a bright light from heaven—which he later describes in Acts 22:11 as "the glory of that light," suggesting the OT Shekinah glory of God—and a speaking voice from a celestial Being. Who else could such a person be if not God?

of Nazareth?" He answers, "It could only have been through the strange experience with Him he had near Damascus."[157]

Therefore, the entire picture of Paul's Christology presented in his epistles emerges from his initial rendezvous with the "Man Christ Jesus." Paul's understanding began first with the historical Jesus the Nazarene who appeared to him on the Damascus Road and spoke to him from heaven as the resurrected Lord. It is not as though Paul worked from a divine Christ to a historical man; instead, Paul's understanding of Jesus began with His humanity. Paul must have reasoned, how is it that Jesus the Nazarene—so recently crucified as a common criminal—could occupy the place of Lordship in heaven? There is but one answer: that Paul's concept of Jesus as Lord, Son of God, and Christ began with his encounter with the historical Man (albeit ascended), Jesus the Nazarene.[158] This finding is the opposite of Klausner's view, as he holds that "the more Jesus became spiritual and heavenly, and the less he became earthly, actual, historical, the more it was possible for Paul to claim 'apostleship' for himself on the basis of the vision he had seen on the road to Damascus."[159] Instead, Paul assumes that the historical Man has now become the Ascended Man, confirming Jesus of Nazareth to be the Lord, the Son of God, and the Christ.[160]

In this one dynamic event, then, Saul changed his opinion of Jesus as a menace to Judaism and instead recognized Him as the Lord, the Son of God, and the Messiah of Israel. This conversion (what else would it be?) put him in agreement with the initial Christian confessions of Peter,[161] Martha,[162] Thomas,[163] the Centurion,[164] and the Beloved Disciple.[165] Such an abrupt change of personality, belief, and conviction is incomprehensible to many observers, both ancient (Acts 9:21) and modern, but reverses in attitudes toward Jesus are commonly recorded in testimonies of converts who once vehemently opposed Jesus yet overnight took that same knowledge of Him and confessed Him as Savior

---

157. Machen, *Origin*, 205.

158. Rostron, *The Christology of St. Paul*, 55, notes, "So it is rather on the human side that we find Jesus Christ fulfilling the highest conceptions of the Messiah that Jewish prophecy or Apocalypse had expressed.... We can thus see that, however else St. Paul thought of Christ, He was in his eyes truly human, His life was really lived on this earth."

159. Klausner, *From Jesus to Paul*, 442.

160. The historical reality of the resurrection of Jesus remains the crux of Paul's Christology. Lüdemann, *Paul: The Founder of Christianity*, 230–31, denies the physical resurrection of Jesus, but contends that Paul deceived himself into believing it, so that he grossly distorted the religion of Jesus. Despite this distortion, Lüdemann claims, "Except for (Paul), we never would have heard about Jesus." Thus, Lüdemann leaves the modern reader with a deceived Paul and an unknown Jesus. In such a case, is it any wonder he feels that "most of today's Christians do not take Christianity seriously anyway and have already departed from Paul" (ibid., 240)?

161. In Matt 16:16, "Simon Peter answered and said, 'Thou art the Christ, the Son of the living God.'"

162. In John 11:27, Martha replies, "Yes, Lord; I have believed that You are the Christ, the Son of God, *even* He who comes into the world."

163. In John 20:28, "Thomas answered and said to Him, 'My Lord and my God!'"

164. In Mark 15:39, "when the centurion, who was standing right in front of Him, saw the way He breathed His last, he said, 'Truly this man was the Son of God!'"

165. John 20:31 reports, "These have been written that you may believe that Jesus is the Christ, the Son of God."

THE "MAN CHRIST JESUS"

(C. S. Lewis comes to mind).[166] Clearly then, from the moment of the Damascus Road encounter, Paul's knowledge of Jesus abruptly reverses itself from antagonist to advocate, as the heavenly voice identifies himself as "Jesus the Nazarene, who you are persecuting" (Acts 22:8). Thus, the inception of Paul's Christology was entirely formed at his conversion, not by the experience itself, as Segal contends,[167] but by the one who appeared and spoke to him.

The Man Christ Jesus of Paul's Preaching at Pisidian Antioch (Acts 13:16–41)

For Saul's safety, the apostles spirited him away to his hometown of Tarsus, contributing to his absence from the narrative until Barnabas again sought him out, this time to help with the new church in Antioch (Acts 11:25–26). The Holy Spirit eventually directed the prophets-teachers of this congregation to commission Barnabas and Saul for a mission to Pisidian Antioch, from which Luke transcribes the first recorded sermon of Saul (Acts 13:16–41),[168] who by this time has become known as Paul (Acts 13:9).[169] It is likely that Luke gives this sermon as a sample of what Paul normally preached in his synagogue evangelism,[170] and it is organized chronologically, following a biblical-redemptive framework.[171] The sermon begins with an overview of Israel's history (Acts 13:17–22), leading

---

166. Lewis, *Surprised by Joy: the Shape of my Early Life* (1956). This fact lies behind the famous prologue of George Littleton in his classic letter to Gilbert West, *Observations on the Conversion and Apostleship of St. Paul* (1805), 3, in which he reminds his friend of "the late conversation we had together upon the subject of Christianity" when "I thought the conversion and Apostleship of St. Paul alone, duly considered, was of itself a demonstration sufficient to prove Christianity to be a divine revelation." He gives the options, that either Paul was an imposter, an enthusiast of "over-heated imagination," someone deceived by others, or, "what he declared to have been the cause of his conversion, and to have happened in consequence of it, did all really happen; and therefore the Christian religion is a divine revelation" (ibid., 10–11).

167. Segal, *Paul the Convert*, 69, states, "Paul's conversion experience and his mystical ascension form the basis of his theology." Segal confuses the Damascus Road event with Paul's Paradise revelation of 2 Cor 12:1–5, since Paul was never taken up anywhere in the former experience: he stayed earthbound the entire time, as Acts 9:4 reports, "he fell to the ground."

168. Ehrman, *Peter, Paul, and Mary Magdalene*, 143, insists this account cannot record a genuine Pauline sermon because in his letters Paul (1) never takes his gospel to the Jews in the synagogue; (2) because Paul never recounts the events of Jewish history; (3) because "there is nothing in Paul's own writings to indicate that Jesus' earthly life was of primary (or any) importance to him;" and (4) because Paul's view of Christ's death as providing atonement for sins and Luke's view that Christ's death leading to forgiveness of sins are "not the same thing." This listing is very disingenuous, since (1) Paul does not write that he never preached in synagogues; (2) he certainly recounts Jewish history in Romans 4, 1 Cor 10:1–10, and Gal 3–4; (3) he often gives principal interest to the events of Jesus life, even if primarily by assumed reference; and (4) the conclusion of Paul's sermon (Acts 13:38–39) shows specific parallels to his writings (such as Rom 3:24–26). Ehrman violates his own admission that neither Acts nor the Epistles contain everything Paul said or did—much is left to implications of the facts. For support of the authenticity of these sermons, see Bruce, *The Speeches in the Acts of the Apostles* (1942); and Bruce, "The Speeches in Acts Thirty Years After," 53–68.

169. Maccoby, *The Mythmaker*, 96, ftnt, 4, thinks that the apostle took the name of the proconsul of Cyprus, Sergius Paulus, mentioned two verses earlier in Acts 13:7. This is an interesting suggestion but nothing more than speculation, especially since Paul never refers to his Hebrew name (שָׁאוּל) nor explains his Greek name in his letters.

170. This synagogue strategy of Paul is noted in Acts 13:5, 14; 14:1; 17:1, 10, 17; 18:4, 19; 19:8.

171. Ziesler, *Pauline Christianity*, 134, expresses the common critical attitude that "Paul's speeches in Acts may well reflect Lukan rather than Paul's distinctive ideas," because they contain "nothing about the

to the reign of King David, from whose offspring God promised to Israel a Savior, whom Paul promptly identifies as Jesus (σωτῆρα Ἰησοῦν, Acts 13:23), who now becomes the primary focus of this sermon.

The hearers (and subsequent readers) of Paul's message learn about the Man Jesus, that He was a descendant of David (Acts 13:23, "From the offspring of this man, according to promise, God has brought to Israel a Savior, Jesus"), meaning that He was a Jew of the tribe of Judah and born into a royal heritage, implying that He fulfilled the kingdom expectation of the Davidic Covenant. This relationship establishes Jesus as the Seed of David, to whom God promises, "I will give you the holy *and* sure *blessings* of David" (Acts 13:34, quoting from Isa 55:3).[172] Paul also likens the historical appearance of Jesus to the arrival of a royal heir (πρὸ προσώπου τῆς εἰσόδου αὐτοῦ; Acts 13:24, which also echoes Mal 3:2, "Who can endure the day of His coming [εἰσόδου αὐτοῦ]?"), and he places Jesus' coming in the historical setting of the proclamation by John the Baptizer, as Paul quotes the prophecy of John about "One (who is) coming after me the sandals of whose feet I am not worthy to untie" (Acts 13:24). This important statement in which John denies he is the Messiah (as some may have presumed of him) is later included in all four Gospels (Matt 3:11; Mark 1:7; Luke 3:16; John 1:27), but probably it had been reported to Paul by those who had heard it first-hand from John himself. Its inclusion here shows that Paul was aware of the baptism of Jesus and understood it as the historical inception of His ministry and as an indication of His Messianic credentials.

Paul then skips from the beginning of Jesus' ministry to its end, as he recounts details of His death, commencing with the indictment of "those who live in Jerusalem, and their rulers, recognizing neither Him nor the utterances of the prophets which are read every Sabbath, fulfilled *these* by condemning *Him*" (Acts 13:27). This condemnation happened in accordance with prophecy and was interpreted by Jesus in the same way ("all things which are written about Me in the Law of Moses and the Prophets and the Psalms must be fulfilled," Luke 24:44). Again, Paul agrees with the Gospel accounts that the Jewish leaders "found no ground for *putting Him to* death" (at least, no legitimate grounds) but still "asked Pilate that He be executed" (Acts 13:28), agreeing with John 18:31 that the Sanhedrin lacked legal authority to put anyone to death. Although the Roman government eventually becomes involved in this conspiracy, Paul omits Pilate's concession to the outcry for Jesus' death despite his better judgment. Even so, Paul sees this injustice as fulfillment of prophecy when he adds, "when they had carried out all that was written concerning Him, they took Him down from the cross" (literally, a tree, ξύλον), confirming the manner of Jesus' death, by crucifixion (Acts 13:29). Then, in agreement with Luke

---

new being in Christ." Zielser overlooks that the preaching in Acts is primarily evangelistic, addressed to unbelievers, whereas the Epistles are didactic, addressed to believers, thus accounting for differences in subject matter.

172. Paul's quotation (δώσω ὑμῖν τὰ ὅσια Δαυὶδ τὰ πιστά, Acts 13:34) abbreviates the LXX of Isa 55:3 (διαθήσομαι ὑμῖν διαθήκην αἰώνιον τὰ ὅσια Δαυὶδ τὰ πιστά), which translates חַסְדֵי דָוִד הַנֶּאֱמָנִים וְאֶכְרְתָה לָכֶם בְּרִית עוֹלָם. Archer and Chirichigno, *Old Testament Quotations in the New Testament*, 254, comment, "If we reckon the Acts 13:34 quote as beginning with ὑμῖν rather than with δώσω (which differs from the אֶכְרְתָה of the MT, which takes בְּרִית as *object*, to which חַסְדֵי דָוִד is an epexegetic appositive), then apart from that the MT = LXX = NT."

THE "MAN CHRIST JESUS"

23:55, Paul mentions the verification of His death, in that "they laid Him in a tomb," a fact he corroborates in 1 Cor 15:4 ("He was buried").

So far, all these historical facts could be confirmed by common knowledge, as well as through court documents, should one be disposed to access them.[173] What Paul announces next is the divine correction of this injustice, when "God raised Him from the dead" (Acts 13:30), a fact confirmed by His appearance for many days "to those who came up with Him from Galilee to Jerusalem, the very ones who are now His witnesses to the people" (Acts 13:31). This incidental reference to Galilee is important from a historical perspective because it agrees with the Gospel record that the people considered Jesus to be "the prophet from Nazareth in Galilee" (Matt 21:11). Next, Paul strings together four OT passages that he applies to the resurrection of Jesus: first, from "the second Psalm, 'Thou art My Son; today I have begotten Thee'" (Acts 13:33);[174] then, from Isa 55:3, "I will give you the holy *and* sure *blessings* of David" (Acts 13:34); thirdly from Ps 16:10 ("Thou wilt not allow Thy Holy One to undergo decay" (Acts 13:35); and lastly, from 1 Kgs 2:10, that David "fell asleep and was laid among his fathers" (Acts 13:36). Significantly, Paul verifies the resurrection of Jesus by reference to the same prophecy in Ps 16:10 employed by Peter in his Pentecost sermon (Acts 2:27), that the physical body of the Messiah would not undergo decay. Paul then concludes his sermon with an invitation of sorts,[175] couched in typical Pauline terminology found in his letters and then closing with a warning from Hab 1:5.[176]

Thus, in his first recorded sermon, Paul mentions these facts about the historical Jesus: that He was a Jew from Galilee of the royal lineage of David and ministered after the proclamation of John the Baptist until His condemnation by the Jerusalem leadership, who asked for Him to be executed by Pilate, a sentence carried out by crucifixion and burial—but God raised Him from the dead, and He appeared in Jerusalem for many days afterwards in a display of the physical resurrection. In this brief presentation (presumably condensed by Luke), Paul agrees with the testimony of the Gospels concerning the

---

173. Barclay, "A Comparison of Paul's Missionary Preaching and Preaching to the Church," 168, observes that Acts 13:27–31 "*is intelligible to us because we already know the story. . . .* It implies the whole story of the life, the trial and death of Jesus. It implies the story of the death and resurrection of Jesus" (italics original).

174. The royal sonship of the Messiah is based on the cry of David to YHWH, "Thou art my Father, My God" (Ps 89:26), establishing a father-son relationship between God and His anointed king as the firstborn (בְּכוֹר ‖ πρωτότοκος), as YHWH declares of David's son, "I will be a father to him, and he will be a son to Me" (2 Sam 7:14 ‖ 1 Chr 17:13), a status first applied to Solomon (1 Chr 22:10; 28:6). The Davidic King as God's Son appears pointedly in the second Psalm in the decree of the Lord ("He said to Me, 'Thou art My Son, Today I have begotten Thee,'" Ps 2:7) and in the command to the kings of the earth, "Kiss the Son, or he will become angry" (Ps 2:12 ESV). Jesus himself asks of this Psalm, "What do you think about the Christ, whose son is He?" (Matt 22:42). An interesting connection with the Epistle to the Hebrews is also noted by Paul's quotation of Psalm 2:7 in Acts 13:33, "Thou art My Son; today I have begotten Thee," cited also in Heb 1:5 and 5:5. All three incidences use Ps 2:7 to show how the resurrection of the Messiah verifies His Sonship.

175. Acts 13:38–39, "Therefore let it be known to you, brethren, that through Him forgiveness of sins is proclaimed to you, and through Him everyone who believes is freed (δικαιωθῆναι) from all things, from which you could not be freed through the Law of Moses."

176. Acts 13:40–41, "Take heed therefore, so that the thing spoken of in the Prophets may not come upon *you*: 'Behold, you scoffers, and marvel, and perish; For I am accomplishing a work in your days, A work which you will never believe, though someone should describe it to you.'"

historical Jesus in every detail he mentions.[177] As with most evangelistic sermons, it omits far more of the historical facts of Jesus' life than it includes (its basic theme is that Jesus fulfills the Davidic Covenant, so the events and prooftexts support that theme), but an omission cannot be interpreted as ignorance or denial by the preacher. Far from it, Paul's purpose in this sermon was to establish enough of the life of Jesus (notably His death and resurrection) to validate his proclamation that Jesus is one who brings forgiveness of sins and justification (Acts 13:38–39), themes he develops more fully in his epistles.[178] In other words, everything the apostle presents in this sermon about the "Man Christ Jesus" is in accordance with both the earlier historical records of Jesus' life and the later explanations by Paul in his letters.[179]

THE MAN CHRIST JESUS OF PAUL'S PREACHING IN THESSALONICA (ACTS 17:1–3)

Paul's next reference to the historical Jesus appears in a brief explanation to the synagogue at Thessalonica (Acts 17:1–3).[180] Here, Paul reasons in a classic syllogistic argument: his major premise is that the OT Scriptures[181] present these identifiers of the Messiah–that

---

177. See Resch, *Der Paulinismus und die Logia Jesu in ihrem gegenseitigen Verhältnis untersucht*, 122–26, in which he relies upon his earlier book, *Die Logia Jesu nach dem griechischen und hebräischen Text wiederhergesestellt: ein Versuch* (1898). Resch finds twenty-two allusions to Gospel sayings in Acts 13:23–46 (13:23 → Matt 15:22; Acts 13:24a → Matt 11:13; Luke 7:27; Acts 13:24b → Matt 3:1; Acts 13:25a → Luke 3:16; Acts 13:25b → Matt 3:11; Acts 13:27 → Luke 23:24; Acts 13:28 → Luke 23:4, 22; Acts 13:28b → Matt 27:23; Acts 13:29a → Luke 22:37; Acts 13:29b → Luke 23:53; Acts 13:30 → Luke 24:6; Acts 13:31 → Luke 23:55; 24:50; Acts 13:38a → Matt 26:28; Acts 13:38b → Luke 16:15; Acts 13:39 → Luke 18:14; 7:50; Acts 13:46a → Mark 7:27; Acts 13:46b → Matt 10:13; Acts 13:46c → Matt 21:43).

178. This reference to justification apart from the Law of Moses seems to appear from nowhere, leading Gager to claim that Paul redirects his remarks not to the Jews of the synagogue but to the visiting, God-fearing Jews (*Reinventing Paul*, 51, 68, 77). He maintains this because he is convinced that Paul preaches one way of salvation for Jews (by Law) and another for Gentiles (by faith in Jesus). Gager's view collapses with Paul's introduction addressed to both "Men of Israel, and you who fear God" (Acts 13:16). If anything, when Paul gives his invitation, it is specifically addressed to "you men, brethren," presumably intending his Jewish brethren, whom he reminds, "you (Jews in particular) could not be justified through the Law of Moses" (Acts 13:39). Also, Acts 6:13 reports that the Law had become a volatile issue between the "Way" and the Synagogue from the time of Stephen's ministry. Luke assumes that his readers would understand that since that time, Paul had done a lot of thinking about the proper place of the Law.

179. Köstenberger, "Diversity and Unity in the New Testament," 146, notes that ". . . during Paul's ministry, the OT-promised Messiah still had to be demonstrated. This could be accomplished not by quoting Jesus' words but by furnishing proof that the events in Jesus' life, especially His crucifixion and resurrection, fit the pattern laid out in the OT. Thus the OT, not Jesus, was Paul's primary theological source."

180. Acts 17:1–3 reads, "Now when they had traveled through Amphipolis and Apollonia, they came to Thessalonica, where there was a synagogue of the Jews. And according to Paul's custom, he went to them, and for three Sabbaths reasoned with them from the Scriptures, explaining and giving evidence that the Christ had to suffer and rise again from the dead, and *saying*, 'This Jesus whom I am proclaiming to you is the Christ.'"

181. While Stanley, *Arguing with Scripture: The Rhetoric of Quotations in the Letters of Paul*, 60, doubts that "many of the people in Paul's congregations knew the Jewish Scriptures well enough to evaluate his handling of the biblical texts" (something quite true of modern readers!), Acts 17:11 notes how those in the synagogue of Berea "received the word with great eagerness, examining the Scriptures daily, *to see* whether these things were so," indicating not only an accessibility to the OT but also a proficient level of literacy leading to faith among Jews and "a number of prominent Greek women and men." Stanley's view of "reader-response"

THE "MAN CHRIST JESUS"

He must suffer and rise out of the dead.¹⁸² His minor premise is unstated here, but it is assumed from Paul's earlier message in Acts 13, that Jesus suffered and rose from the dead; therefore, the deduction based on the historical fulfillment of these prophecies declares, "This Jesus whom I am proclaiming to you is the Christ" (οὗτός ἐστιν ὁ χριστὸς [ὁ] Ἰησοῦς).¹⁸³ The argument would crumble if Jesus had not actually (a) lived, (b) suffered,¹⁸⁴ and (c) risen again from the dead. A comparable usage is found in Acts 18:5 when Paul was "solemnly testifying to the Jews (in Corinth) that Jesus was the Christ" (εἶναι τὸν χριστὸν Ἰησοῦν). These similar deductions lie at the heart of Paul's saving message and rest on the assumption that Jesus lived, suffered, died and rose from the dead in the context of history. All these points of Paul's preaching raise the question, where did Paul derive his particular hermeneutic of the OT Scriptures as being fulfilled in Jesus if not in the pattern of interpretation developed by Jesus himself¹⁸⁵ and received by Paul from apostolic tradition?¹⁸⁶

---

requires a dynamic interplay between the author, the text (in this case, an OT quotation), and the reader (ibid., 32), yet the further he examines Paul's methods, the more he realizes that "Paul made a serious effort to frame his quotations so that individuals with a relatively low level of biblical literacy could grasp the rhetorical point of his quotations" (ibid., 55). The hermeneutical issue is not how Paul's readers understood Paul's arguments (he is often misunderstood), but what Paul intended to mean by his rhetorical use of the OT.

182. Marshall, "The Resurrection in the Acts of the Apostle," 98, observes from Acts 17:3, "This indicates that one main purpose of the preaching of the resurrection was to make the apologetic points that the Messiah expected by the Jews would do certain things prophesied in the Old Testament, that Jesus had done these things, and that therefore He was the Christ."

183. It is outside the scope of this study to explore Paul's other source for the life of Jesus, the OT Scripture, as he reads it in light of the suffering and resurrection of Jesus—just as explained by Jesus to His disciples (Luke 24:26, 46). Thus, Paul frequently reasons from the Scriptures, explaining and giving evidence that the Christ had to suffer and rise again from the dead, and saying, "This Jesus whom I am proclaiming to you is the Christ" (Acts 17:3). Granted, his interpretation of OT Scripture is admittedly christocentric, lending itself to distinctly Messianic explanations based on the suffering and resurrection of Jesus (1 Cor 15:3–5). See the discussion on Paul's use of the OT in Ridderbos, *Paul and Jesus,* 59–61, plus the full study by Ellis, *Paul's Use of the Old Testament* (1957).

184. The use of the verb πάσχω owes more to the use of it by Jesus than to the OT, since it is not used in the LXX regarding the Messiah's suffering (Πάσχω is found in Esth 9:26; Ezek 16:5; Amos 6:6; Zech 11:5; 2 Macc 6:30; 7:18; 9:28; 4 Macc 4:25; 9:8; 10:10; 14:9; Wis 12:27; 18:1, 11; 19:13; Sir 38:16; Ep Jer 1:33). In the Gospels, Jesus uses πάσχω to describe His death as one of suffering (Matt 16:21 || Mark 8:31 || Luke 9:22, Matt 17:12; Mark 9:12; Luke 17:25; 22:15; 24:26; 24:46). The apostle Peter picks up this usage in Acts 3:18; 1 Pet 2:21, 23; 3:18 (inexplicably translated by the NASB "Christ *died* for sins"); and 1 Pet 4:1, as does the writer to the Hebrews (Heb 2:18; 5:8; 9:26; 13:12).

185. Resch, *Der Paulinismus,* 124, notes the grammatical affinity of Acts 17:3 (χριστὸν καὶ ἀναστῆναι ἐκ νεκρῶν) to Luke 24:26 (οὐχὶ ταῦτα ἔδει παθεῖν τὸν χριστὸν καὶ εἰσελθεῖν εἰς τὴν δόξαν αὐτοῦ;).

186. Dodd, *According to the Scriptures,* 110, observes, "The New Testament itself avers that it was Jesus Christ himself who first directed the minds of his followers to certain parts of the scriptures as those in which they might find illumination upon the meaning of His mission and destiny," citing Luke 24:25–27 and Luke 24:44–45.

THE MAN CHRIST JESUS OF PAUL'S PREACHING
AT THE AREOPAGUS (ACTS 17:31)

The next reference of Paul to the historical Jesus appears in his address to the Areopagus (Acts 17:18–31), occasioned because Paul was proclaiming "Jesus and the resurrection" (τὸν Ἰησοῦν καὶ τὴν ἀνάστασιν)—which the philosophers assumed were two novel deities (Acts 17:18).[187] Paul concludes his remarks on the nature of the one true God with a startling assertion that this God is "now declaring to men that all everywhere should repent, because He has fixed a day in which He will judge the world in righteousness through a Man whom He has appointed, having furnished proof to all men by raising Him from the dead" (Acts 17:30–31). One might assume that this reference to Jesus (notably unnamed in the entire message up until this point) and His historical resurrection caused Paul's address to fail (Acts 17:32),[188] but it must be noted that others were attracted to the concept of a resurrected Man who becomes God's furnished proof (Acts 17:34).[189] It is noteworthy that when Paul preaches Jesus to this sophisticated audience, he does not appeal to His divinity—as one might expect, in opposition to the numerous gods honored by the Athenians—but instead, the apostle firmly plants his concept of salvation in a space-time Man appointed by God (ἐν ἀνδρὶ ᾧ ὥρισεν). This is certainly Christology understood from "the ground up," for Paul presents Jesus as a man, but one now divinely designated as risen from the dead and ready to judge the world. Thus, in this declaration to the Athenians, Paul succinctly encapsulates the whole work and purpose of the "Man Christ Jesus."

THE MAN CHRIST JESUS OF PAUL'S WITNESS
TO JOHN'S DISCIPLES (ACTS 19:4)

The next reference to the historical Jesus appears in Acts 19, when Paul met some disciples and discovered that they had received the baptism of John the Baptizer yet did not know the reality to which it pointed, the Holy Spirit (Acts 19:3). Paul's response to these men presumes the historical account recorded in the Gospels (Matt 3:11; Luke 3:16; John 1:15), as he said, "John baptized with the baptism of repentance, telling the people to believe in Him who was coming after Him, that is, in Jesus" (εἰς τὸν ἐρχόμενον μετ' αὐτὸν ἵνα πιστεύσωσιν, τοῦτ' ἔστιν εἰς τὸν Ἰησοῦν, Acts 19:4). This study has previously established that "The Coming One" was a messianic title based on Dan 7:13 ("And behold,

---

187. See the classic essay by Stonehouse, "The Areopagus Address," pages 1–40 in *Paul Before the Areopagus and Other New Testament Studies* (1957), in which he refutes the *religionsgeschechtliche Methode* of Norden and Dibelius and shows that Paul preaches to this pagan audience from a Christian theistic viewpoint.

188. Such a failure is suggested by Ramsey, *St. Paul the Traveler and Roman Citizen*, 194, who writes, "It would appear that Paul was disappointed and perhaps disillusioned by his experience in Athens. He felt that he had gone at least as far as was right in the way of presenting his doctrine in a form suited to the current philosophy, and the result had been little more than nothing. When he went on from Athens to Corinth, he no longer spoke in the philosophic style."

189. Luke's comment in Acts 17:34 indicates that Paul's address was not at all an evangelistic failure, as "some men joined him and believed, among whom also were Dionysius the Areopagite and a woman named Damaris and others with them." Most evangelists would be delighted with such results.

THE "MAN CHRIST JESUS"

with the clouds of heaven One like a Son of Man was coming.") that was applied to Jesus during His ministry (Luke 7:20; see also John 4:25); now Paul announces the fulfillment of the Coming One in the Jesus of history. While Paul does not mention John the Baptizer in his epistles, the theology that one receives the Holy Spirit upon believing certainly concurs with his doctrine in Eph 1:13, "in Him you also, when you heard the word of truth, the gospel of your salvation, and believed in Him, were sealed with the promised Holy Spirit" (ESV). The significance is that, once again, Paul frames his message in terms of the historical appearance of the "Man Christ Jesus" as announced by John the Baptizer.

THE MAN CHRIST JESUS OF PAUL'S PREACHING AT MILETUS (ACTS 20:17–35)

The next account in which Paul mentions the humanity of Jesus comes in his address to the Ephesian elders at Miletus (Acts 20:17–35). Because Paul is defending his own ministry and not presenting an evangelistic or exhortatory message, this rather lengthy message includes only four references to Jesus. The first two apply to Him in His ascended position as "our Lord Jesus Christ" who is the object of faith (Acts 20:21) and as the one who appointed Paul to "the ministry which I received from the Lord Jesus" (Acts 20:24), a reference to his Damascus Road commission.

The third reference contains one of the most fascinating comments relating to all of Christology, as Paul affirms both the humanity and deity of Jesus in the passing remark of Acts 20:28, when he mentions that God purchased the church "with His own blood"—an argument which makes sense only if Jesus as God existed as a corporeal man with blood coursing through His veins. Of equal importance is that this verse is the clearest reference in Acts to the vicarious suffering of Jesus, thus raising the question, how did Paul connect the risen Lord with the saving significance of His death? While Paul's epistles are replete with references to the death of Christ as a substitutionary sacrifice for others,[190] the only mention in Acts to suffering is found in Jesus' prophecy of how much Paul must suffer for the sake of Christ's Name (Acts 9:16).[191] Even in the third account of Paul's commission, when Jesus himself outlines the future ministry and message of Paul,[192] nothing is said about the death of Jesus for others as an appeal for conversion.[193] Certainly the motifs of

---

190. For example, see Rom 3:25; 5:8; 1 Cor 6:20; 7:23; 15:3–4; Gal 1:4; 3:13; 4:5; Eph 5:1–2; 1 Thess 5:10; Titus 2:14.

191. In fact, the idea of Christ suffering for Paul—or for anyone else—is conspicuously absent from the theology of Acts. Since Acts 20:28 is one of the few references to Christ's death as a purchasing sacrifice—a prominent Pauline theme—this indicates the genuineness of Paul's address as being his own words and not those of Luke.

192. Paul will be sent to both Jews and Gentiles "to open their eyes so that they may turn from darkness to light and from the dominion of Satan to God, in order that they may receive forgiveness of sins and an inheritance among those who have been sanctified by faith in Me" (Acts 26:18).

193. It should be observed, however, that in his gospel invitations Paul does not appeal to the death of Jesus for the lost; for example, Paul's clearest conversion verse makes no mention of Christ's vicarious death but instead declares, "If you confess with your mouth Jesus *as* Lord, and believe in your heart that God raised Him from the dead, you shall be saved" (Rom 10:9). Rather, Paul always applies the death of Christ to those who are already believers ("While we were yet sinners, Christ died for us," Rom 5:8). Perhaps modern

forgiveness, inheritance, sanctification, and faith included in that commission do relate directly to Paul's understanding of salvation, but in Acts they are not specifically linked to Christ's death, causing Ehrman to claim that Paul and Luke hold disagreeing concepts of salvation.[194] Granted, the idea of atonement is sparse in the book of Acts (although it is clearly stated here in Acts 20:28, "the church of God which He purchased with His own blood," and it is implied in the earlier echoes to Deut 21:23 of Jesus "hanging on a tree"[195]), but one must ask if Luke would teach that the death of Christ is only a "gross miscarriage of justice" for which people should be "overcome by remorse and ask for forgiveness"?[196] This understanding overlooks that Luke's theological concern is to show how Christ's death and resurrection fulfills OT prophecy, whereas Paul's letters provide the atoning significance of those events, although he disclaims originality for such an idea; instead, he states that he received the earlier tradition that "Christ died for our sins according to the Scriptures" from prior sources (1 Cor 15:3).

A better source for a vicarious understanding of Christ's death can be traced to Ananias' direction to Paul to "arise and be baptized and wash away your sins, calling on His Name" (Acts 22:16). These actions signified to Paul the atoning aspects of salvation he later incorporates in his letters (baptism as a death to sin in Rom 6:3; washing away of sin in 1 Cor 6:11; calling on His Name in repentance in Rom 10:12–14 and 1 Cor 1:20).[197] Still, one must wonder how Paul—and before him, the apostolic church—arrived at the propitiatory nature of Christ's death, unless the concept came from the interpretation Jesus placed upon His death when He declared during the Last Supper, "This is My body which is given for you; This cup which is poured out for you is the new covenant in My blood" (Luke 22:19–20). Significantly, Paul relies on earlier tradition of these same eucharistic words in his doctrine of Christ's substitutionary death (1 Cor 11:23–24), leading Hengel to suggest that the sayings and symbolic actions of the original Eucharist serve as the ultimate source of Christ's death "for our sins," although the idea can be traced back even earlier to Jesus' statement, that He came "to give His life a ransom for many" (Mark 10:45).[198]

The fourth reference to the historical Jesus appears when Paul appeals to the *verbi Domini* by reminding the elders of "the words of the Lord Jesus, that He himself said, 'It is more blessed to give than to receive'" (Acts 20:35). This precise quote is not recorded in

---

evangelism needs to re-assess its message to become more biblical.

194. Ehrman, *Peter, Paul and Mary Magdalene*, 143–44, insists that Paul's view of salvation—Christ's death as an atonement—and Luke's view of Christ's death leading to forgiveness of sins, are "not the same things," so that "in Paul's way of looking at salvation, Christ had to be sacrificed to pay the debt of others; in Luke's way of looking at it, God forgives the debt without requiring a sacrifice." This seems to be yet another example of a scholarly "either/or" rather than a more reasonable approach of "both/and."

195. The "tree" is mentioned in Acts 5:30; 10:39; 13:29, although in each verse the NASB translates ξύλον as "cross," dropping the connection to Deut 21:23. The ESV has restored the image by translating each instance as "tree."

196. Ehrman, *Peter, Paul and Mary Magdalene*, 144. Ehrman fail to show why anyone apart from the direct perpetrators of the crucifixion should feel remorse for the death of Jesus. If there is nothing vicarious about the death of Jesus, there would be no personal guilt arising from His death.

197. Kim, *Origin*, 304, notes that "it is generally agreed that in Paul faith and baptism belong together with regard to justification and salvation, each referring to the other."

198. Hengel, *Paul Between Damascus and Antioch*, 99.

THE "MAN CHRIST JESUS"

the Gospels,[199] but even the Evangelists admit that Jesus did (and presumably said) many others signs than what are written (John 20:30; 21:25; Acts 1:1), so it appears that Paul appeals to one such saying from a recognized collection of the *logia* of Jesus, which he later mentions in 1 Tim 6:3 and 2 Tim 1:13.[200] While these *logia* of Jesus were originally transmitted orally, it is reasonable to assume they were soon written down for the sake of accuracy and preservation—and Paul reminds the elders of their knowledge of these familiar words of Jesus.[201] So, in this sermon at Miletus, Paul easily moves from the exalted Jesus to the earthly Jesus without any transition, for He is one and same person, whether viewed in His heavenly exaltation or His earthly location. What is important for this study is to note that Paul refers in this message to the "Man Christ Jesus" not only in His death but also in His teaching.

THE MAN CHRIST JESUS OF PAUL'S REPEATED TESTIMONIES (ACTS 21–26)

A substantial part of Acts 21–26 includes the testimonies of Paul delivered before various groups, including (1) his conversion testimony spoken to the crowd on the temple steps in Jerusalem (Acts 21:40–22:21); (2) his defense given to the Sanhedrin in Jerusalem (Acts 23:1–6); (3) his hearing delivered before the procurator Felix at Caesarea (Acts 24:10–21), and (4) his conversion testimony presented two years later before King Agrippa, also at Caesarea (Acts 26:2–23). These last three testimonies appear in the setting of legal hearings in which Paul turns the charges against him into a referendum on the resurrection from the dead.[202] More specifically, he applies this general truth to the particular resurrection of Jesus, so that when Festus explains the case to Agrippa, he reduced it to "some points of disagreement with him about their own religion and about a certain dead man, Jesus, whom Paul asserted to be alive" (Acts 25:19). The obvious should not be overlooked in this matter perplexing the Roman procurator: Paul was referring to a specific man Jesus as one who had died in space-time history but whom Paul now affirmed to be living again.

The Christology of Paul's conversion testimonies has been examined earlier in this chapter, noting how each account differs somewhat in detail, as to be expected when one retells the story of his or her conversion. For example, when Paul asks his question of Acts 9:5 ("Who art Thou, Lord?"), the answer of Jesus specifies his hometown, "I am Jesus *the Nazarene*" (Acts 22:8). Paul adds this same element in Acts 26:9, "I thought to

---

199. Echoes of this saying can be found in the Gospel records in Matt 5:42 ("Give to him who asks of you."); Matt 10:8 ("Freely you received, freely give."); Matt 19:21 ("Give to *the* poor."); Luke 6:38 ("Give, and it will be given to you."); Luke 11:41 ("But give that which is within as charity."); Luke 12:33 ("Sell your possessions and give to charity.").

200. 1 Tim 6:3, "If anyone advocates a different doctrine, and does not agree with sound words, those of our Lord Jesus Christ;" 2 Tim 1:13, "Retain the standard of sound words which you have heard from me, in the faith and love which are in Christ Jesus."

201. Bruce Longenecker, "Good News to the Poor: Jesus, Paul and Jerusalem," 51, notes that Paul's "speech in character" shows precise agreement between Jesus and Paul in the care of the poor.

202. Note his declarations: Acts 23:6, "I am on trial for the hope and resurrection of the dead!"; Acts 24:21 "For the resurrection of the dead I am on trial before you today"; Acts 24:15, "There shall certainly be a resurrection of both the righteous and the wicked."

myself that I had to do many things hostile to the name of Jesus of Nazareth." Perhaps this item of geography is included because Paul's audience in Caesarea needed more specific identification of the particular Jesus not necessary in the first account.[203] Regardless, this reference certainly agrees with the report of the Gospels that the hometown of Jesus was Nazareth of Galilee.[204] Another added detail concerns the language of Jesus, as Paul notes, "I heard a voice saying to me in the Hebrew dialect" (λέγουσαν πρός με τῇ Ἑβραΐδι διαλέκτῳ, Acts 26:14), a bit of information that might have intrigued Agrippa as the king of Judea, but it certainly adds a touch of humanity to one who speaks from heaven.

Other than these references to the hometown and dialect of Jesus, these testimonies contribute no additional information concerning "the name of the Lord Jesus" (Acts 21:13), nor do they reveal any development of Paul's Christology from his original confession in Acts 9; in fact, Paul explicitly disclaims to King Agrippa any personal originality, "stating nothing but what the Prophets and Moses said was going to take place; that the Christ was to suffer, *and* that by reason of *His* resurrection from the dead He should be the first to proclaim light both to the *Jewish* people and to the Gentiles" (Acts 26:22–23). However, when Paul quotes his commission from Jesus that others "may receive forgiveness of sins and an inheritance among those who have been sanctified by faith in Me" (κλῆρον ἐν τοῖς ἡγιασμένοις πίστει τῇ εἰς ἐμέ, Acts 26:18), he mentions soteriological concepts anticipated in his later teachings on forgiveness, inheritance, holiness and faith,[205] as well as echoing a phrase found often in Jesus' teachings as recorded in John's Gospel, belief "into" Jesus.[206] Although the issue in these testimonies concerns the resurrected Christ, it is quite implicit that Paul deems this Christ to be one and the same as Jesus, a man of Nazareth.

THE MAN JESUS OF PAUL'S SHIPBOARD ADDRESS (ACTS 27:18)

While Paul sails to Rome, he delivers two short addresses to the beleaguered passengers as their ship is driven toward an unknown island, the first being a prophecy of impending shipwreck (Acts 27:21–26) and the second an encouragement of certain preservation (Acts 27:33–34). Neither address contributes any new thought to Paul's Christology, although the second contains a possible allusion to a saying of Jesus when Paul encourages the famished people to partake of food. He reminds his audience of the promise revealed

---

203. The Greek is Ἰησοῦς ὁ Ναζωραῖος, which differs from Peter's description of Ἰησοῦν τὸν ἀπὸ Ναζαρέθ (Acts 10:38). It may be that Paul emphasizes the connection to the Nazarite vow of Numbers 6 echoed in Matt 2:22, that Jesus "resided in a city called Nazareth, that what was spoken through the prophets might be fulfilled, 'He shall be called a Nazarene'" (Ναζωραῖος κληθήσεται, Matt 2:23).

204. Nazareth as Jesus' hometown is mentioned in Matt 1:23; 21:11; 26:71; Mark 1:24; 10:47; 16:6; Luke 1:26; 2:29, 51; 4:16, 34; 18:37; 24:19; John 1:45–46; 18:5, 7; 19:19.

205. See Paul's comments on forgiveness (Eph 1:7; Col 1:14), inheritance (Rom 4:13, 14; 8:17; 1 Cor 6:9, 10; 15:50; Gal 3:18, 29; 4:1, 7, 30; 5:21; Eph 1:11, 14, 18; 5:5; Col 1:12; 3:24; Titus 3:7), and sanctification (Rom 6:19, 22; 1 Cor 1:2; 30; 6:11; 7:14; 2 Cor 1:12; 7:1; Eph 4:24; 5:26; 1 Thess 3:13; 4:3, 4, 7; 5:23; 2 Thess 2:13; 1 Tim 4:5; 2 Tim 2:21). His emphasis on faith (142 times) and believing (54 times) is quite extensive and renowned.

206. See "believing into" (πιστεύω εἰς) in John 1:12; 2:11, 23; 3:15–16, 18, 36; 4:39; 6:29, 35, 40, 47; 7:5, 31, 38–39, 48; 8:30; 9:35–36; 11:25–26, 45, 48; 12:11, 36–37, 42, 44, 46; 14:1, 12; 16:9; 1 John 5:10, 13.

THE "MAN CHRIST JESUS"

earlier to him by an angel, that none of them shall be lost (Acts 27:22); now he adds even more specifically, "for not a hair from the head of any of you shall perish" (οὐδενὸς γὰρ ὑμῶν θρὶξ ἀπὸ τῆς κεφαλῆς ἀπολεῖται Acts 27:34). Fascinatingly, this statement is a near quote of a saying of Jesus recorded in Luke 21:18, "Yet not a hair of your head will perish" (καὶ θρὶξ ἐκ τῆς κεφαλῆς ὑμῶν οὐ μὴ ἀπόληται). While the proverbial nature of the saying is fairly common to humanity in general,[207] this particular reference seems too specific to be coincidental, especially since the context of the teaching of Jesus concerns His disciples giving testimony amid persecution (Luke 21:12–17), which is the very reason Paul's life is endangered on this sea-voyage. Instead, Paul takes a saying of Jesus addressed to His disciples and applies it to pagans who will heed His message; thus, he changes the verb ἀπόλλυμι from the aorist subjunctive to the future indicative to make it conform to the prophecy he had received. As in Acts 20:35, this saying shows how the apostle skillfully employs teachings and illustrations of the Man Jesus to enhance his message.

THE MAN JESUS IN PAUL'S PREACHING IN ROME (ACTS 28:23, 31)

Luke reports that when Paul arrived in Rome, he had an initial meeting with the Jewish leaders in which he outlined his legal situation (Acts 28:17–20); and then at a later date, "they came to him at his lodging in large numbers; and he was explaining to them by solemnly testifying about the kingdom of God, and trying to persuade them concerning Jesus (περὶ τοῦ Ἰησοῦ), from both the Law of Moses and from the Prophets, from morning until evening" (Acts 28:23). His tactics with a Jewish audience remain the same: to show that the man Jesus fulfills the types and prophecies of the OT. Some Jews are persuaded but many more do not believe, leading Paul to announce that salvation has been sent to the Gentiles. On that note, the book of Acts concludes with the remark that Paul "stayed two full years in his own rented quarters, and was welcoming all who came to him, preaching the kingdom of God, and teaching concerning the Lord Jesus Christ with all openness, unhindered" (Acts 28:30–31). One would surmise that Luke completed his work before there was any resolution on Paul's case before the Roman government; but even if not, Paul's Christology at the end of Acts is the same as at his conversion, with the "Man Christ Jesus" attributed the titles of Lord and Messiah.

CHAPTER SUMMARY: THE MAN JESUS OF PAUL'S PREACHING IN ACTS

In summary, an ordinary reading of the book of Acts shows that the Jesus proclaimed by Paul is unquestionably understood as being the same Man Jesus as presented in the

---

207. Similar expressions are found in 1 Sam 14:45, "As the LORD lives, there shall not one hair of his head fall to the ground;" 2 Sam 14:11, "As the LORD lives, not one hair of your son shall fall to the ground;" Ps 40:12, "My iniquities have overtaken me, so that I am not able to see; they are more numerous than the hairs of my head;" Ps 69:4, "Those who hate me without a cause are more than the hairs of my head."

The "Man Christ Jesus" in the Presentation of Paul in the Acts of the Apostles

Gospel records.²⁰⁸ Acts also records that Paul mentions Jesus by His name fifteen times,²⁰⁹ and others discuss what Paul preaches about this same Jesus another nine times.²¹⁰ In every instance, the historical Jesus of the Gospel records is certainly intended as the referent, so that even the evil spirit answers the sons of Sceva, "I recognize Jesus, and I know about Paul, but who are you?" (Acts 19:15).

This study has observed, however, that Paul in Acts includes several historical details about Jesus not found in his letters: these include his hometown, Nazareth in Galilee (Acts 22:8; 26:9), His language (that Jesus spoke to Paul "in the Hebrew dialect," Acts 26:14), and His coming as signaled by the prophecy of John the Baptizer (Acts 13:24–25; 19:4), yet it has been suggested that Paul had no necessary compulsion to mention these matters in his epistles. Also, Paul refers to some teachings of Jesus not found in either the Gospels (Acts 20:35) or in his letters (Acts 27:34), but it has been argued that the inclusion of new

---

208. For all the supernatural characteristics of Jesus presented in the Gospels, the Four Evangelists also present Jesus as a man (as if it needs to be stated): in the confession of John: [John 1:30, "This is He on behalf of whom I said, 'After me comes a _man_ (ἀνήρ) who has a higher rank than I, for He existed before me;'"]; in public comments about Jesus [John 4:29, "Come, see a _man_ (ἄνθρωπον) who told me all the things that I _have_ done; this is not the Christ, is it?"; John 7:46, "The officers answered, 'Never did a _man_ speak the way this man speaks (οὐδέποτε ἐλάλησεν οὕτως ἄνθρωπος);'" John 9:16, "Therefore some of the Pharisees were saying, 'This _man_ (ὁ ἄνθρωπος) is not from God, because He does not keep the Sabbath.' But others were saying, 'How can a _man_ (ἄνθρωπος) who is a sinner perform such signs?' And there was a division among them;" John 10:33, "The Jews answered Him, 'For a good work we do not stone You, but for blasphemy; and because You, being a _man_ (ἄνθρωπος ὤν), make Yourself out _to be_ God.'"]; in the Debate of the Sanhedrin [John 11:47, "Therefore the chief priests and the Pharisees convened a council, and were saying, 'What are we doing? For this _man_ (οὗτος ὁ ἄνθρωπος) is performing many signs;'" John 11:50 (also John 18:14), "nor do you take into account that it is expedient for you that one _man_ (εἷς ἄνθρωπος) should die for the people, and that the whole nation should not perish.")]; in Peter's denial of Jesus as the _man_ [Matt 27:72, 74; Mark 14:71, "And again he denied _it_ with an oath, 'I do not know the _man_'" (οὐκ οἶδα τὸν ἄνθρωπον); John 18:17, "The slave-girl therefore who kept the door said to Peter, 'You are not also _one_ of this _man's_ disciples (εἶ τοῦ ἀνθρώπου τούτου;), are you?'"]; in the declaration of Pilate [Luke 23:4, "And Pilate said to the chief priests and the multitudes, 'I find no guilt in this _man_'" (οὐδὲν εὑρίσκω αἴτιον ἐν τῷ ἀνθρώπῳ τούτῳ); Luke 23:6, "But when Pilate heard it, he asked whether the _man_ was a Galilean" (εἰ ὁ ἄνθρωπος Γαλιλαῖός ἐστιν); Luke 23:14, "You brought this _man_ (τὸν ἄνθρωπον τοῦτον) to me as one who incites the people to rebellion, and behold, having examined Him before you, I have found no guilt in this _man_ (ἐν τῷ ἀνθρώπῳ τούτῳ) regarding the charges which you make against Him;" John 18:29, "Pilate therefore went out to them, and said, 'What accusation do you bring against this _man_?'" (τίνα κατηγορίαν φέρετε [κατὰ] τοῦ ἀνθρώπου τούτου;); John 19:5, "Jesus therefore came out, wearing the crown of thorns and the purple robe. And _Pilate_ said to them, 'Behold, the _Man_!'" (ἰδοὺ ὁ ἄνθρωπος)]; in the confession of the centurion [Mark 15:39, "And when the centurion, who was standing right in front of Him, saw the way He breathed His last, he said, 'Truly this _man_ was the Son of God!'" (ἀληθῶς οὗτος ὁ ἄνθρωπος υἱὸς θεοῦ ἦν); Luke 23:47, "Now when the centurion saw what had happened, he _began_ praising God, saying, 'Certainly this _man_ was innocent'" (ὄντως ὁ ἄνθρωπος οὗτος δίκαιος ἦν)]; in post-crucifixion comments [Luke 24:19 (ESV), "And they said to him, "Concerning Jesus of Nazareth, a _man_ who was a prophet (ὃς ἐγένετο ἀνὴρ προφήτης) mighty in deed and word before God and all the people.'"]; and, in Peter's Pentecost Sermon [Acts 2:22, "Men of Israel, listen to these words: Jesus the Nazarene, a _man_ (ἄνδρα) attested to you by God with miracles and wonders and signs which God performed through Him in your midst."]. The most notable is the statement of Jesus about himself, "But as it is, you are seeking to kill Me, a _man_ (ἄνθρωπον) who has told you the truth, which I heard from God" (John 8:40).

209. In Acts 9:20, 27; 13:23, 33; 16:18, 31; 17:3, "This Jesus whom I am proclaiming to you is the Christ"; Acts 18:5; 19:4; 20:21, 24, 35; 21:13; 22:8; 29:9.

210. See Acts 17:7, 18; 19:13, 15; 24:24; 25:19; 26:15; 28:23, 31.

THE "MAN CHRIST JESUS"

material does not insinuate creative innovation to fit a particular situation. It is quite evident that Jesus said and did much more than what is included in the Gospels (John 21:25), just as Paul had access to more information than he needed or had occasion to use in his letters (for example, see 1 Thess 4:2). Paul's silence of a situation or teaching of Jesus should not be taken as ignorance or disagreement.

Also, a comparison of Acts and Paul's Epistles, while raising some difficulties, shows that these two literary bodies are not contradictory, despite Ehrman's insistence,[211] but rather they are complementary of one another. It is important to observe that the Jesus of the book of Acts is also the Jesus of the letters of Paul: the apostle understood Jesus to be a biological man (Acts 17:30 → Rom 5:15) with human blood in His veins (Acts 20:28; Rom 3:23) and a Jew of Davidic lineage (Acts 13:23 → Rom 1:3). While Acts records that Paul said little of the character of Jesus (other than quoting the words of Ananias in which he described Jesus as "the Righteous One," Acts 22:14 → 2 Tim 4:8), both the Paul of Acts and the Paul of his letters stress the suffering of Jesus in fulfillment of Messianic prophecy (Acts 26:22–23 → 1 Cor 15:3–4); His deliverance unto trial (Acts 13:3 → Rom 4:24–25); His condemnation under Pontius Pilate despite His innocence (Acts 13:28 → 1 Tim 6:13); His murder at the hands of Jewish leadership (Acts 13:27 → 1 Thess 2:14), culminating in His death on a tree (Acts 13:29 → Gal 3:13); and His burial in a tomb (Acts 13:29 →1 Cor 15:4). This injustice was divinely overcome, however, in the bodily resurrection and appearances of Jesus to those who continue His witness (Acts 13:30, 33; 17:31→ 1 Cor 15:4–7) by declaring Jesus to be Son of God (Acts 9:20 → Rom 1:4), Lord (Acts 16:31 → Rom 10:9), Christ (Acts 9:22 → 2 Tim 2:8), and Savior (Acts 13:23 → Titus 2:13). In other words, the person of Jesus preached by Paul in Acts is precisely the same as the person of Jesus written about by Paul in his epistles.

A COMPOSITE OF THE "MAN CHRIST JESUS" IN PAUL'S PREACHING AND TEACHING

This concurrence means that Paul is no innovator of history but a presenter of the historical record. Therefore, while the Christology of Jesus in Acts is not as comprehensive as that of Paul's Epistles (and neither bodies of literature are as extensive in this matter as that of the Gospels), a composite picture of the historical Jesus derived from Paul's letters and his sermons in Acts reveals the following information about the "Man Christ Jesus:"

---

211. Ehrman, *Peter, Paul, and Mary Magdalene*, 99, argues that the Paul of Acts does not act like the Paul of his letters, and "if all you had available was the book of Acts, you would not know some of the most important teachings of Paul." Ehrman ignores his own statement that the NT writings are occasional and not systematic (ibid., 95), just as it is not the purpose of Acts to explain everything Paul taught but rather to give a general chronology providing historical backgrounds for many of his letters. Ehrman, however, thinks modern readers should reject Acts as a *bona fide* "repository of historically accurate information" of initial Church history (ibid., 99), leaving one with a myriad of speculative stories lacking any canonical unity—like the same apocryphal works rejected by the church because they contained the sort of legendary material Ehrman insists is found in Acts. The modern reader then must decide whether to follow Ehrman into utter uncertainty, or to trust that Luke wrote for his readers to know the exact truth (Luke 1:4). The difference between these two historians cannot be more accentuated.

The "Man Christ Jesus" in the Presentation of Paul in the Acts of the Apostles

1. His Name, Jesus (+/- 215 times in his epistles);
2. His Title, the Christ (+/- 382 times in his epistles);
3. His gender, a man (Acts 17:30; Rom 5:15; 1 Cor 15:21, 47–48; Phil 2:8; 1 Tim 2:5);
4. His physical body of flesh (Rom 1:3; 8:3; 9:5; 1 Cor 10:16; 11:24, 27; 2 Cor 5:16; Col 1:22; 2:9; 1 Tim 3:16);
5. His blood (Acts 20:28; Rom 3:25; 5:9; 1 Cor 10:16; 11:25; Eph 1:7; 2:13; Col 1:20);
6. His birth, as One "born of a woman" (Gal 4:4);
7. His several brothers (1 Cor 9:5);
8. His brother named James (Gal 1:19);
9. His nationality, an Israelite (Rom 9:5);
10. His Abrahamic lineage (as the Seed of Abraham, Gal 3:17);
11. His Davidic lineage (Acts 13:23; Rom 1:3; 15:12; 2 Tim 2:8);
12. His legal upbringing as "made under the law" (Gal 4:4);
13. His circumcision (Col 2:11);
14. His language, Hebrew/Aramaic (Acts 26:14);
15. His hometown, Nazareth in Galilee (Acts 13:33; 26:9);
16. His interaction with John the Baptist (Acts 13:24–25; 19:4);
17. His baptism (Rom 6:3; Col 2:12);
18. His ministry to the Jews (Romans 15:8);
19. His status as a servant (Phil 2:7);
20. His twelve disciples (1 Cor 15:7);
21. His disciple named Cephas (1 Cor 15:7);
22. His disciple named John (Gal 2:9);
23. His preaching (Rom 16:25);
24. His evangelizing ministry (Eph 2:7);
25. His words and doctrine (1 Tim 6:3);
26. His teaching on giving (Acts 21:13);
27. His teaching on foods (Rom 14:14);
28. His teaching on marriage (1 Cor 7:10);
29. His teaching on ministerial remuneration (1 Cor 9:14);
30. His teaching on the Eucharist (1 Cor 11:23–25);
31. His teaching on love (Gal 2:20);
32. His teaching on the end times (1 Thess 4:14; 5:2),

THE "MAN CHRIST JESUS"

33. Numerous echoes to other teachings (i.e. Rom 12–14);
34. His transfiguration (2 Cor 3:28; with Mark 9:2 || Matt 17:2);
35. His identity as the Cornerstone (Eph 2:20);
36. His fulfillment as "a stone of stumbling and a rock of offense" (Rom 9:33);
37. His assistance by angels (1 Tim 3:16);
38. His compassion (Phil 1:8);
39. His meekness (2 Cor 10:1);
40. His gentleness (2 Cor 10:1);
41. His humbleness (Phil 2:8);
42. His patience (2 Thess 3:5);
43. His poverty (2 Cor 8:9);
44. His grace (2 Cor 8:9);
45. His love (Rom 8:35; 2 Cor 5:14);
46. His obedience (Rom 5:19; Phil 2:8);
47. His "knowing no sin" (2 Cor 5:21);
48. His righteousness (Rom 5:18);
49. His purpose, to save sinners (1 Tim 1:15);
50. His faith (or faithfulness, Rom 3:22, 26; Gal 2:16; 3:22; Phil 3:19);
51. His selfless example (Rom 15:3a);
52. His Last Supper, with His explanation of His death as sacrificial and substitutionary (1 Cor 11:23–24);
53. His betrayal on that same night (1 Cor 11:23);
54. His deliverance for trial before the Jewish leaders (Acts 13:27; Rom 4:24–25);
55. His testimony and good confession (1 Tim 6:13; 2 Tim 2:8);
56. His condemnation under Pontius Pilate (Acts 13:28; 1 Tim 6:13);
57. His legal innocence (Acts 13:28);
58. His bearing of reproaches (Rom 15:3b);
59. His bodily injuries (Gal 6:17);
60. His sufferings (Acts 17:3; 2 Cor 1:5; Col 1:24);
61. His murder at the hands of Jewish leadership (Acts 13:27; 1 Cor 2:8; 1 Thess 2:15);
62. The fact of His crucifixion (1 Cor 1:23; 2:2; 2 Cor 4:10; 13:4; Gal 3:1);
63. His crucifixion by nailing (Col 2:14);
64. His crucifixion on a cross (Acts 13:29; Gal 6:14; Phil 2:8);

65. His cross fashioned from a tree (Acts 13:39; Gal 3:13);

66. His physical death (Rom 14:9; 1 Cor 15:3);

67. His sacrifice as Passover (suggesting the time of year, 1 Cor 5:7);

68. His burial in a tomb (Acts 13:29; Rom 6:4; 1 Cor 15:4; Col 2:12);

69. His bodily resurrection (Acts 13:30; 17:31; Rom 10:9; 1 Cor 6:14; 2 Cor 5:14; 1 Thess 1:10; 4:14; 2 Tim 2:8);

70. His resurrection appearances (Acts 13:31; 1 Cor 9:1; 15:5–7);

71. His bodily ascension (Rom 8:34; Eph 1:20; 1 Tim 3:16).

This list provides a rather impressive catalogue of separate facts about the life and character of the historical Jesus, many of which are alluded to several times in Paul's letters.[212] Should no other written record of Jesus exist, this list would provide a reasonably significant biography of Jesus from which one could construct a skeletal outline of His life, even though it lacks a chronological timeline. The evidence in this list surely refutes the notion that Paul was disinterested in the historical Jesus at the expense of the exalted Lord.[213] Also, it should embolden evangelical scholars who have assumed that Paul has little to say about the historical Jesus, when it is quite obvious that his sermons and letters are replete with references to the Nazarene, occasionally by way of specific citation but more often by means of historical allusion to shared knowledge with his readers.

Certainly there are major omissions in this information, as Paul says nothing specifically about the miracles or parables of Jesus,[214] nor does he provide a detailed chronology by which one may organize these scattered references—although his sermon in Acts 13:14–41 follows a broad historical outline of the ministry of Jesus and furnishes an important framework for Paul's epistolary referrals to Jesus. Furthermore, it should be acknowledged that the specifics of Jesus' ministry lie outside the scope of his letters, which were not written in the genre of biographical Gospels; however, it likewise should be admitted that Paul clearly assumes his readers are familiar with certain details of the life of Jesus to some extent; otherwise, his comments would be nonsensical to his original readers. When it suits his purpose to illustrate a doctrine—and that is often—Paul

---

212. It was noted in Chapter 3 that other scholars have compiled similar lists of Paul's allusions to the historical Jesus, but few have included more than a dozen or so entries and even then most did not agree with one another. This list is based on all the data gathered from Acts and Paul's epistles, and it has been compiled by this author in an effort to present a complete inventory. Future researchers are encouraged to locate additional items in order to make this index exhaustive.

213. Sanders, *Paul*, 80–1, notes that, "Liberal Christians have generally tried to redefine true divinity so as not to interfere with humanity, which is for them more important. Conservatives often give only lip service to true humanity in order to preserve divinity. They may propose, for example, one should not study the historical Jesus by using the ordinary methods of criticism, since he was not an ordinary person." Sanders does not specify which conservatives advocate this method, nor is this reviewer aware of any evangelical scholars who reject historical research. Both the Jesus and Paul of history will emerge from the proper application of historical research of the literary evidence available in the NT.

214. Although Wenham, *Paul: Follower of Jesus or Founder of Christianity?* (1995), argues quite persuasively that Paul's letters contain many literary echoes of the parables of Jesus.

presents the example of the historical Jesus with some reference to His life or character, showing how important the humanity of Jesus was to his Gospel message.

Yet for Paul, to know Christ only according to the flesh would be an empty historical curiosity (2 Cor 5:16), because if all a person knew about Jesus were the events of His life, he would be left with many pertinent questions, such as, how does the knowledge of the life, death, resurrection, and ascension of Jesus, acted out during the reign of Tiberius Caesar and under the high priesthood of Annas and Caiaphas (Luke 3:1–2), relate to believers living beyond those times and events? How does His redemption accomplished "under Pontius Pilate" (in the words of the Apostle's Creed) apply to those existing at the present moment? Since Jesus has ascended back into heaven, how does He minister to believers today? How do the present-day followers of the risen Lord relate to the ministry of Jesus of Nazareth when He walked about the provinces of Galilee and Judea? How does what Jesus said and did with His first disciples apply to those disciples now living two millennia from that time and far from those locations?

After all, other than a few precious moments of privacy (Matt 14:13) and the lonely hours of His suffering when His disciples forsook Him (Matt 26:56), Jesus always seemed to have followers with Him. While at times He sought for some solitary moments to pray (Mark 1:35), He was otherwise accompanied by His twelve disciples whom He called to "be with Him" (Mark 3:14). In addition to the large crowds that surrounded Him constantly, Jesus was joined by many other followers, a fact Paul mentions in his synagogue sermon, that "for many days (Jesus) appeared to those who *came up with Him* from Galilee to Jerusalem" (Acts 13:31). This verb (συναναβᾶσιν[215]) carries no intrinsic christological significance: it merely describes a geographical movement of ascending from the lower valleys of Galilee to the mountainous regions of Jerusalem. Interestingly, the same word συναναβαίνω is used only once more in the NT, and that is in Mark 15:41, when it describes the same action of these same followers, identified as the ladies who witnessed the crucifixion of Jesus, that "when He was in Galilee, they used to follow Him and minister to Him; and *there were* many other women who had *come up with* Him (συναναβᾶσιν αὐτῷ) to Jerusalem." There was evidently such a deep desire among many to associate with Jesus during His ministry that they left everything to follow Him (Mark 10:28). This association is particularly true of His hand-picked disciples, so when Jesus "*began* going about from one city and village to another, proclaiming and preaching the kingdom of God," Luke 8:1 adds, "and the twelve were with Him." This same mention of association is also noted "when the hour had come He reclined *at the table* (of the Last Supper), and the apostles (were) with Him" (Luke 22:14).

It is in this association of God's people with Christ that Paul finds a concept to show how the church relates to the saving events of the historical life, death, resurrection and ascension of Jesus. The apostle teaches in his letters that Jesus as the one Mediator not only gave Himself as a ransom for all, but also the entire church is (divinely) considered to be associated with Christ in His saving works—as if every believer was present with Him in those events. It is to this association with the "Man Christ Jesus" that this study now directs its attention.

---

215. BDAG § 7020, συναναβαίνω, "to go up with."

5

The "Man Christ Jesus" in Association with His People

INTRODUCTION: ONE ASSOCIATED WITH MANY

HAVING NOW ESTABLISHED THAT Paul not only quotes the Jesus of history on occasion, but far more frequently alludes to His teaching, His ministry, and the events of His life—and assumes that his (original) readers possessed a common knowledge of and agreement with such information—this study now directs its attention to the apostle's application of these historical allusions of the "Man Christ Jesus" to the central focus of Paul's gospel; *viz.*, that these historical acts of Jesus secure salvation for "all who call upon the name of the Lord" (Rom 10:13).[1]

What one finds is that Paul's viewpoint assumes a divine perspective, that God considers all believers to be associated with Christ in the historical events which secure their salvation, not as passive bystanders but as active participants in those events; namely, they have been crucified with Christ (Rom 6:6), have died with Him (Rom 6:8; Col 2:20; 2 Tim 2:11), and have been planted/buried with Him (Rom 6:4–5; Col 2:12). They have also been raised with Him (Eph 2:6; Col 2:12; 3:1), been made alive with Him in His resurrection (Eph 2:5; Col 2:13), and have been seated and hidden with Him in His ascension (Eph 2:6; Col 3:3), just as if they were present in His crucifixion, resurrection, and ascension as once-for-all-time events of salvation history. In addition, Paul views those "in Christ" as being associated "with Christ" in His present-time living and His inheritance (Phil 3:10; Eph 2:5–6; Col 2:13; Rom 8:17). In the future, all believers shall be associated with Christ in the impending actions of His return (2 Cor 4:14; Col 3:4; 1 Thess 4:14), at which time they shall be glorified with Him (Rom 8:17) and shall be conformed with Him (Rom 8:29; Phil 3:21). Then, they shall reign with Him (2 Tim 2:12), being with Him and all His saints (1 Thess 4:17), having been given all things with Christ (Rom 8:32).[2] This chapter will demonstrate that these associative concepts are distinguished by Paul's own particular vocabulary, namely, in his use of the preposition σύν and related συ-compound words when he employs them to describe the association shared by the people of Christ with the "Man Christ Jesus" and with one another. Furthermore, it will be argued that

---

1. The gist of this chapter is culled from a New Testament Greek Linguistics seminar paper presented by the author to Dr David Allen Black at Southeastern Baptist Theological Seminary on November 13, 2007, "A Linguistic Analysis of Σύν and Συ-Compounds in the Pauline Epistles."

2. See Appendix 2, "A Synthesis of the Pauline References to Association With Christ."

THE "MAN CHRIST JESUS"

Paul utilizes this distinctive vocabulary to differentiate association *with* Christ from his better known concept of union *in* Christ, showing that the latter relates to positional and dynamic realities of salvation whereas the association motif consistently refers to events of the history of redemption enacted by the "Man Christ Jesus" with which Paul views the church as being associated with Christ.[3]

Believers can generally understand how they shall "be with Christ" in His future return and reign, but those incidents with a past or present reference raise a very crucial question: how can Paul consider the entire church to be associating with these essential events of salvation? Quite obviously, all believers were not physically present at the crucifixion, burial, resurrection, and ascension of Jesus—although Paul seems to insist they were—nor are believers presently living on earth actually seated with Christ in His heavenly reign—although Paul declares they are. Is the apostle describing some sort of mystical experience, as Schweitzer contends?[4] Has Paul embraced these ideas from contemporary Jewish Apocalyptic legends or borrowed concepts from Gnostic redemption myths, as Bultmann maintains?[5] Is this yet another irresolvable tension within Paul's thinking,[6] providing fuel for those who have accepted the premises of biblical deconstructionism, that what matters is a "reader-response" to Paul's literary compositions—meaning that there is no meaning at all in Paul's terminology?[7] This study contends quite the opposite, that Paul

---

3. Hooker, *From Adam to Christ: Essays on Paul*, 26–27, prefers the term "interchange" to describe the relationship of "reciprocal exchange" between Christ and His people. "Interchange" has some advantages, but it fails to capture the associative aspect of Christ's people in their relationship with Christ. As noted in Chapter 1, ftnt 49, other terms such as "partnership and alliance" were considered to describe this Pauline idea, but the term "association" was chosen as reflecting the basic meaning of the preposition Paul uses to convey this concept, σύν, which LN § 89.107 defines as "a marker of an associative relation, often involving joint participation in some activity." By use of σύν, Paul elicits an associative idea of a group of people—the church—associating with Christ in His historical actions as the "Man Christ Jesus;" thus, this study suggests that the phrase "association with Christ" portrays a distinctive Pauline concept while also distinguishing it from his more common idea of "union in Christ."

4. Schweitzer, *The Mysticism of Paul the Apostle*, 101–140. Schweitzer even describes union in Christ as physical (ibid., 127), effected by sharing in the physical elements of the Last Supper (ibid., 29). While Paul certainly teaches a concept of "mystery" (Rom 11:25; 16:25; 1 Cor 2:7; 15:51; Eph 1:9; 3:3–4, 9; 5:32; 6:19; Col 1:26–27; 2:2; 4:3; 2 Thess 2:7; 1 Tim 3:9, 16), this is a far cry from an mystical, irrational experience. Certainly, there are great mysteries surrounding the use of "Christ in you" (Col 1:27) and the indwelling of the Holy Spirit, but Paul roots these realities in the historical acts of Christ as applied supernaturally in regeneration.

5. Bultmann, "New Testament and Mythology," 3. Bultmann argues that the only way modern man can make sense of the NT is to demythologize it and understand the *kerygma* in an existential encounter (ibid., 16).

6. Gager, *Reinventing Paul*, surveys the approaches to the tensions in Paul: (1) "The psychological technique holds that Paul was lost in a hopeless, if understandable, quagmire of intellectual and emotional inconsistency" (ibid., 7); (2) "The resigned technique simply leaves the contradictions as they stand, a position especially prominent in the recent work of Räisänen" (ibid., 8); (3) "By far the most radical technique is to remove the offending passages altogether" as in the works on Romans and Galatians by J. C. O'Neill, (ibid., 8); and (4) "The fourth and final technique, also the dominant one, is to subordinate one set of passages to another" (ibid., 9). But there *is* a fifth method, one employed in this book, and that is to understand each tension in context and attempt to reconcile them. The earliest editors of Paul's letters could have "corrected" these tensions, but they let them remain as if expecting later readers to resolve the differences.

7. The influences of deconstructionism can be seen in the statement of Hauerwas, *Unleashing the Scripture: Freeing the Bible from Captivity to America*, 20, who writes, "There simply is no 'real meaning' of

places a deliberative significance in viewing the entire church as historically present with the "Man Christ Jesus" in the fundamental events of salvation. By this perspective, Paul addresses what Barrett keenly observes, "The basic problem of Paul's theology, perhaps in all theology, is that of the relation between the One and the Many."[8] The thrust of this chapter will be to explore the question: how is it that the historical experiences of the One, the "Man Christ Jesus," affect the Many so that all believers are considered to be associated with these events?

THE ASSOCIATION OF THE MANY WITH THE ONE

How indeed? The issue was raised by the initial question posed by the risen Lord to Saul on the Damascus Road when Jesus asked, "Saul, why are you persecuting Me?" This inquiry apparently pricked Paul's conscience, as he repeats that question whenever he retells that experience (Acts 9:4; 22:7; 26:14) and when throughout his letters he ruefully recalls his persecution of the church (1 Cor 15:9; Gal 1:13, 23; Phil 3:6; 1 Tim 1:13). As Paul stumbled blindly into Damascus, he may well have asked, "How have I been persecuting Jesus the Nazarene?" There could be only one answer: in persecuting the followers of Jesus, Saul had also been persecuting the One whom they were following. Even so, how could there be such a close connection between the heavenly Lord and His earthly followers?[9] This connection was further suggested when Ananias identified the disciples of Jesus as His saints (Acts 9:13), a description of believers Paul employs in his own recounting of his conversion (Acts 26:10) and many times in his letters.[10] This solidarity between Jesus and His people opened a new awareness for Paul that he later developed in his concept of Christ as Head of His church (Col 1:18), in which His people are the members of His Body (1 Cor 12:27). Thus, the demand of Jesus to Saul, "Why are you persecuting Me?" reveals an association more fully developed in Paul's letters, whereby the apostle indicates that Jesus not only acted on behalf of His people to purchase salvation for them, but *he also views these same people as participating with Jesus in the historical events of His saving acts*. From Paul's perspective, the One acts for the Many, and the Many associate with the One in those actions.

Paul's letters to the Corinthians once we understand they are no longer Paul's letters but rather the church's Scripture;" that is, the NT means whatever current reading is imposed on the text by "the church," whoever that may be. This reflects the views of such linguistic philosophers as Jacques Derrida, *Of Grammatology* (1976), and Stanley Fish, *Is There a Text in This Class? The Authority of Interpretive Communities* (1980), whose deconstruction ideas posit that no original meaning can ever be ascertained, since every text is necessarily understood differently each time it is read by each reader. See the analysis by Vanhoozer, *Is there a Meaning in This Text?*, 56, who notes this shift in hermeneutics from discovering what the original author intended on meaning to finding what the text means existentially to the contemporary reader.

8. Barrett, *Paul: An Introduction to His Thought*, 119.

9. Callen, *Dying and Rising with Christ: The Theology of Paul the Apostle*, 9, makes this observation: "It would be very natural for Paul to conclude from this (reply) that Jesus identified Himself with those who followed Him, that in some sense his followers were Jesus. And Paul could have inferred from this identification that Christians die and rise with Christ as part of the body of Christ."

10. Paul designates Christians as "saints" forty times (Rom 1:7; 8:27; 12:13; 15:25–26, 31; 16:2, 15; 1 Cor 1:2; 6:1–2; 14:33; 16:1, 15; 2 Cor 1:1; 8:4; 9:1,12; 13:13; Eph 1:1, 15, 18; 2:19; 3:8, 18; 4:12; 5:3; 6:18; Phil 1:1; 4:21–22; Col 1:2, 4, 12, 26; 1 Thess 3:13; 2 Thess 1:10; 1 Tim 5:10; Phlm 1:5, 7).

THE "MAN CHRIST JESUS"

Because of his acquaintance with the Hebrew Scriptures, Paul would already know before his encounter with the ascended Jesus of Nazareth that the idea of One acting on behalf of Many was an established biblical concept.[11] Supremely, God as One acts on behalf of His people ("I Myself do establish My covenant with you, and with your descendants after you," Gen 9:9), and the same representative principle also applies to the human mediators of God's covenant; for example, Abraham's obedience in offering Isaac assured that in his seed "all the nations—the many—of the earth shall be blessed, because you—the one—have obeyed My voice" (Gen 22:18). Likewise, the many of Israel were so closely associated with the one man Moses that Paul describes the nation as being "baptized into Moses in the cloud and in the sea" (1 Cor 10:2). While David ruled on behalf of many people as God's anointed one ("He gives great deliverance to His king, and shows lovingkindness to His anointed, to David *and his descendants* forever," Ps 18:50), all the tribes of Israel said to David, "Behold we are your bone and flesh," so intimate was their association with him (2 Sam 5:1). Thus, when one king such as Hezekiah "did right in the sight of the Lord according to all his father David had done" (2 Chr 29:2), the entire nation prospered by association with Him (2 Chr 30:20).

Of course, the principle also cuts in the opposite direction: the infamous standard is that of Jeroboam son of Nabat, who did evil in the sight of the Lord and made Israel to sin so that the entire nation suffered God's wrath because of the king's failures (1 Kgs 15:26). Paul takes this dark side of the One and the Many back to the "one man" Adam, whose one sin brought ruin to more than to many but to all (Rom 5:12, 15, 16, 17, 18, 19). By this act, all who are connected to Adam as their mediatorial head suffer the consequences of his disobedience in that "in Adam all die" (1 Cor 15:22). In contrast to Adam's disobedience bringing death to all, the obedience of the one Man Jesus brings life and righteousness to many (Rom 5:15, 19), who are defined as "those who receive the abundance of grace and of the gift of righteousness" (Rom 5:17). Paul expands the many to all in Rom 5:18, "so through one act of righteousness there resulted justification of life to all men," but he reverts back to "many" in the next verse ("through the obedience of the One the many will be made righteous," Rom 5:19), indicating that he is using "many" and "all" synonymously. The same interplay is noted in 1 Cor 15:22, "For as in Adam all die, so also in Christ all shall be made alive." On the surface, this analogy would seem to mean that since all without exception died in Adam, so all without exception are made alive in Christ, lending support for a universalistic salvation; however, Paul defines the "all" of 1 Cor 15:22 in the next verse, "But each in his own order: Christ the first fruits, after that those who are Christ's (οἱ τοῦ Χριστοῦ) at His coming" (1 Cor 15:23). "All" must be defined contextually as all whom God considered to be associated with Christ: they are the elect from the divine perspective (Rom 8:33; 2 Tim 2:10) and believers from the

---

11. Ridderbos, *Paul: An Outline of His Theology*, 38, observes that the OT idea of the 'all-in-one,' is "frequently denoted with the term 'corporate personality.' . . . It is that of the representation by Christ of those who belong to Him, the inclusion of the 'man' in the One and on this ground the application to these many of what has taken place, or will yet take place, in and with the One, Christ."

human perspective (Eph 1:13; 1:19).[12] These are the Many for whom the One has acted in His saving events.

Paul may well have found applications of the association of the Many with the One in the Messianic pictures in the OT, including the "Righteous One, the Lord's Servant" who "will justify many" in that "He Himself bore the sin of many" (Isa 53:11–12, echoed in Rom 4:25). Another OT picture is that of the one Son of Man who represents the many "saints of the Most High" (Dan 7:13–14). These many saints in turn escort the Son of Man to the Ancient of Days, so intimate is the association between these parties (Dan 7:18, 21, 22, 27). Paul had heard Stephen address Jesus as the ascended Son of Man (Acts 7:56), so it is a natural step for the apostle to apply such an association of many saints to the One, Christ Jesus.

Actually, Jesus—who often identified Himself as the Son of Man—had previously taken that step of association with others, as He appointed twelve disciples for the primary purpose "that they might be _with Him_" (μετ' αὐτοῦ, Mark 3:14).[13] The association with these twelve men with Jesus characterized His ministry, as "He *began* going about from one city and village to another, proclaiming and preaching the kingdom of God; and the twelve were _with Him_" (σὺν αὐτῷ, Luke 8:1). Jesus often emphasized the importance of this association with Him, by declaring, "He who is not _with Me_ (μετ' ἐμοῦ) is against Me; and he who does not gather _with Me_ (ὁ μὴ συνάγων μετ' ἐμοῦ) scatters" (Matt 12:30). He predicted to those "who have been _with Me_ (μετ' ἐμοῦ) from the beginning" (John 15:27) that He in turn would associate with them by drinking the fruit of the vine "new _with you_ (μεθ' ὑμῶν) in My Father's kingdom" (Matt 26:29). While Jesus promises, "I am _with you_ (μεθ' ὑμῶν) always, even to the end of the age" (Matt 28:20), this association is reciprocal: not only will He be with His disciples, but He prays, "Father, I desire that they also, whom Thou hast given Me, be _with Me_ (μετ' ἐμοῦ) where I am" (John 17:24). This is the same promise Jesus made to the thief crucified with Him, "Truly I say to you, today you shall be _with Me_ (μετ' ἐμοῦ) in Paradise" (Luke 23:43). Since we have established (in chapter 3) that Paul often echoes the sayings of Jesus, it is entirely possible that he detected in this conversation between the dying thief and the dying Lord an association that he extends to the entire church as not only dying with Christ, but also living with Him (Rom 6:8; Phil 1:23).

What then is the nature of this association between Jesus and His own? It is obviously not a physical association, because the original disciples did not physically die with Christ, nor were they actually entombed with Him, nor were they present at the moment of His resurrection. Yet Paul writes as if the entire church was present in those events.

---

12. Paul combines these seemingly contradictory concepts of election and faith in Titus 1:1, when he identifies himself as an apostle according to the "_faith_ of the _elect_ of God" (κατὰ πίστιν ἐκλεκτῶν θεου). He does the same in 2 Thess 2:13, "God has _chosen_ you from the beginning for salvation through sanctification by the Spirit and _faith_ in the truth."

13. Note the wording in this verse: it is not that Jesus chose the twelve so that He might associate with them—the One with the Many—but that they, the many—although twelve hardly seems to be very many—might associate with Him. The relationship begins with the sovereign initiative of Jesus' choice and then becomes reciprocal: Jesus first associates with His disciples so that they may associate with Him. This concept is illustrated in the Gospels by use of both prepositions μετά and σύν while Paul tends to distinguish them, as will be shown.

THE "MAN CHRIST JESUS"

How can this be possible? The interpretations vary considerably: Beker suggests that Paul is using nothing more than a metaphorical literary devise;[14] Maccoby insists that Paul describes a mystical experience of deification;[15] Goppelt understands the "with Christ" motif sacramentally, as occurring in baptism;[16] Kramer pushes the whole concept to the future *eschaton*, ignoring any historical connections.[17] It even seems that most evangelical commentators merge association with Christ completely into the dynamic union in Christ, losing the separate concept of association entirely.[18] The fact is, none of these views sufficiently recognizes Paul's historical orientation when he views the entire church as corporately placed in association with Christ in the historical events of His redemptive work. Ridderbos comments, "This is not a question of dying to sin in a metaphorical sense (conversion or something like it), but of the participation of the church in the death and burial of Christ in the one-time, redemptive historical sense of the word."[19] As the Jesus of history was crucified once, died once, buried once, resurrected once, and ascended once, so Paul takes these one-time historical events and indicates that the association of the church with Christ was also a one-time divine action, concurrent with the one-time redemptive events that occurred during the ministry of Jesus.

Of special concern for this study is the observation that Paul establishes the association concept from his understanding of historical realities: as all humanity had once died in the historical transgression of the first man Adam and had become "aliens and strangers to the covenant" (Eph 2:19), so now by divine declaration "those who receive the abundance of grace" (Rom 5:17) have become associated in the historical acts of the last "Man Christ Jesus." Quek recognizes, "In 1 Corinthians 15 (v. 22, "For as in Adam all die, so also in Christ all shall be made alive.") the common factor between both representative figures is their essential humanity and the basic point of the analogy is that death came

---

14. Beker, *The Triumph of God: the Essence of Paul's Thought*, 169, states, "Are not both co-crucifixion and co-resurrection profound 'images' not to be taken literally?" While he concedes that Paul believed in a historical resurrection (ibid., 196), he contends that Paul adapts his explanation of resurrection to a Hellenistic mentality (ibid., 170). Beker's understanding of the apocalyptic apparently does not necessitate corporeality, but what is resurrection if not the raising of physical bodies?

15. Maccoby, *The Mythmaker: Paul and the Invention of Christianity*, 106, traces the source of Paul's union in Christ to his comment in Gal 1:16, "God revealed His Son in me," so that Paul came to believe he was "the incarnation of the Son of God," a "deification" he eventually claims for all believers. However, this phrase ἀποκαλύψαι τὸν υἱὸν αὐτοῦ ἐν ἐμοί may be translated, "God revealed His Son *to* me" (as in 1 Cor 4:11, "the one who speaks will be a barbarian to me," ὁ λαλῶν ἐν ἐμοὶ βάρβαρος), and it is argued here that Paul's concept of union first traces to Mediatorial Headship (either a person is in Adam or in Christ) which in turn rests on historical acts (disobedience or obedience) effecting the progeny of each of these men.

16. Goppelt, *Theology of the New Testament*, 2:102.

17. Kramer, *Christ, Lord, Son of God*, 38–39, devotes only two pages to the σύν phrases, and he understands the usage either sacramentally (in connection with baptism) or eschatologically (in connection with the parousia or the resurrection).

18. This seems evident even in the titles of two of the most important evangelical books on this topic, Smedes, *Union with Christ: A Biblical View of the New Life in Jesus Christ* (1983); and Douty, *Union with Christ* (1973). Neither author takes note of any distinction between union in Christ and association with Christ, but this study begs to differ by demonstrating that Paul uses distinct vocabulary for each concept.

19. Ridderbos, *Paul*, 206.

through Adam and life through Christ."[20] Paul weaves this historical solidarity between Jesus and all His people into the tapestry of his soteriology, in that the apostle views all those who are spiritually "in Christ" are also being in association "with Christ" in His death, resurrection, and ascension. The solidarity is therefore a mediatorial connection: the moment when the church moved from Adam to Christ occurred by divine assessment in the historical-redemptive events of "the one mediator between God and man, the Man Christ Jesus" (1 Tim 2:5). This transaction is subsequently experienced by the individual believer in regeneration and faith (when one becomes a new creation in Christ, 2 Cor 5:17), but the initial association of the entire church coincides with the historical events when Jesus died, resurrected, and ascended. In contrast to Akenson's contention that "Saul's faith and the construction of his own belief system begin where the earthly Yeshua leaves off,"[21] the opposite is the reality, that Paul rests his message of salvation squarely upon the foundation of the historical events of the humanity of the "Man Christ Jesus." In those incidents that happened on the stage of human history, the Many became associated with the One—or so Paul declares by use of his own distinctive vocabulary.

PAUL'S DISTINCTIVE ASSOCIATION TERMINOLOGY

Can this assertion be established textually? After all, much is being claimed here that Paul uses a distinctive vocabulary in his use of the preposition σύν and related συ-compound nouns and verbs when he discusses association with the "Man Christ Jesus" in His historical actions. Even though Best proposes that Paul as a creative thinker "may have hit on the use of the term ('with Christ') quite by himself,"[22] for the most part, scholars, commentators, and translators assume that the terminology of association with Christ is merely a stylistic variation of the larger Pauline concept of union in Christ, merging them so completely that often the distinguishing nomenclature is lost in translation.[23] Although the Pauline concept of union in Christ (the ἐν Χριστῷ motif) has been a much explored teaching of Pauline studies,[24] few scholars have observed any significant differentiation

---

20. Quek, "Adam and Christ According to Paul," 72.
21. Akenson, *Saint Saul: A Skeleton Key to the Historical Jesus*, 243.
22. Best, *One Body in Christ*, 94.
23. For example, the KJV loses the associative connotation of σύν by its translation in Rom 6:5, "For if we have been planted *together* in the likeness of His death;" in Rom 8:29, "For whom He did foreknow, He also did predestinate to be conformed *to* the image of His Son;" in 2 Cor 4:14, "Knowing that He which raised up the Lord Jesus shall raise up us also *by* Jesus;" in Eph 2:5, "And hath raised us up *together*, and made us sit *together* in heavenly *places* in Christ Jesus;" and in Phil 3:10; "being made conformable *unto* His death." One must wonder why English versions do not at least translate in such a way to let readers know Paul is using different and distinct prepositions.
24. For example, see Deissmann, *Die neutestamentliche Formel "In Christo Jesu"* (1892); Bousset, *Kyrios Christos* (1913), 154–60; Neugebauer, *In Christus: Eine Untersuchung zum paulinischen Glaubensverständnis* (1961); Bouttier, *En Christ: Etude d'Exegese et de Theologie Paulinienne* (1962), 5–22; and more recently, Son, *Corporate Elements in Pauline Anthropology: A Study of the Selected Terms, Idioms, and Concepts in the Light of Paul's Usage and Background* (2001), 7–38.

between ἐν Χριστῷ[25] and σὺν Χριστῷ[26] other than an interchange of prepositions.[27] For example, Ridderbos finds the uniqueness in the apostle's thought in "a single point, although for the understanding of Paul's preaching a very important one: the frequently occurring formula 'in Christ,' 'with Christ,' and what is related to it"[28]— as if the phrases are identical in meaning.

With all due respect to past scholarship, the fact is that the apostle actually employs a different vocabulary to distinguish association with Christ from union in Christ. This peculiarity is not forced upon Paul's writings: linguistic analysis of his letters uncovers the complexity of the vocabulary and grammar employed by the apostle, revealing how deliberate he is in the selection of his terminology. Moo notes the difference, as he observes Paul's use of the Adam-Christ analogy of key individuals acting on behalf of many and suggests, "Attention to this more collective way of thinking will help us do justice to two other sets of distinctively Pauline christological passages: those that use the phase 'with Christ' and those that use the phrase 'in Christ.' Both ideas, 'with Christ' and 'in Christ,' are probably corollaries of Paul's basic conviction that Christ is 'the last Adam,' a corporate figure."[29] The most obvious difference between the two phrases is the utilization of different prepositions (ἐν or σύν), but is this usage merely a stylistic variation, or does the apostle intend to convey a different nuance in meaning? Subsequent comparison of these two phrases reveals that Paul does in fact intend a different meaning between union in Christ and association with Christ, especially by the use of a crafted terminology to express association with Christ in distinction from language describing union in Christ. Paul may even have invented new grammatical forms by prefixing the preposition σύν to a number of verbs and nouns paralleling the historical events in the ministry of the "Man Christ Jesus" in order to express this association that believers share with Him.[30] By use of such vivid language, Paul writes as if his readers were actually present with Jesus in His

---

25. Of the 161 verses in which Paul mentions the "in Christ" motif, only four times do the references intersect with the "with Christ" concept (2 Cor 13:4; Eph 2:6; 3:6; and Col 2:11–12), lending support to the argument that "in Christ" and "with Christ" project distinct themes.

26. See Appendix 1, "A Complete Listing of the Preposition Σύν in The Pauline Epistles."

27. Harvey, "The 'With Christ' Motif in Paul's Thought," 329–40, surveys the previous research into this concept and finds it sparse. Lohmeyer, "ΣΥΝ ΧΡΙΣΤΩ," (1927), wrote a classic monograph on the topic but provides surprisingly little exegesis. Best, *One Body in Christ*, 44–45, gives a two-page overview of the pertinent texts. Schweizer, "Dying and Rising with Christ," 3–14, calls his own article a "scanty summary" (ibid., 8). Other than Harvey's 1992 article, the fullest treatment appears to be that of Tannehill, *Dying and Rising with Christ* (2006), who understands the concept eschatologically and sacramentally rather than historically (ibid., 39–43). Smedes, *Union with Christ*, 94, does not even list all the pertinent passages and explains "with Christ" dynamically rather than historically (ibid., 95–97). While Douty, *Union with Christ*, 192–96, links the concept to the historical aspects of Christ's work, he gives no particular discussion to the "with Christ" idea in Paul, despite the title of his book; instead, he merges the concept into participative sanctification. Likewise Son, *Corporate Elements in Pauline Anthropology*, 20, notes that σὺν Χριστῷ "has a special implication for Paul's understanding of the relationship between Christ and the believer," but then he discusses it for only one more page, apparently treating it as synonymous with ἐν Χριστῷ.

28. Ridderbos, *Paul*, 38.

29. Moo, "The Christology of the Early Pauline Epistles," 176.

30. See Appendix 2, "A Synthesis of the Pauline References to Association With Christ."

life, His suffering, His crucifixion, His resurrection, His ascension, His session, and shall be with Him in His return and reign.

It is this historical perspective that distinguishes the σὺν Χριστῷ motif from the ἐν Χριστῷ motif.[31] The two concepts are not identical, nor should they be confused with each other.[32] Union in Christ quite properly describes an experiential position effected by the Holy Spirit and should be related to the experiences of regeneration and sanctification; however, association with Christ views a redemptive-historical relationship established by divine assessment in which God deems the entire church to be associated with the "Man Christ Jesus;" accordingly, it should then be related to the declarations of election, imputation, and justification.[33]

Paul's Use of Prepositions to Denote Association

This distinction between association with (σύν) Christ and union in (ἐν) Christ can be established by a statistical analysis of the use of prepositions in the Pauline corpus (Romans–Philemon),[34] as a compilation of the prepositions located in the Pauline epistles reveals that the apostle extensively uses these little parts of adverbial speech.[35] Scarcely a sentence appears without the inclusion of one of the seventeen prepositions Paul employs, adding to the vividness and definition of his linguistic style.[36] An examination of these

---

31. In his discussion of what he calls Paul's "Christ mysticism and cultic mysticism" based on the ἐν Χριστῷ motif, Bousset, *Kyrios Christos*, 158–60, declares, "It can definitely be asserted that what we call the ethical-religious personal image of Jesus was of no influence or significance at all for the piety of Paul.... The picture which Paul actually sketches of the κύριος Ἰησοῦς is not taken from the earthly life of Jesus of Nazareth. The Jesus whom Paul knows is the preexistent supra-terrestrial Christ... not the 'historical Jesus.'" In his zeal to divorce the historical Jesus from the living Christ, Bousset takes no notice whatsoever of the σὺν Χριστῷ motif, which is intensely historical in perspective.

32. For example, Kim, *Origin of Paul's Gospel*, 325, connects dying with Christ to the believer's participative experience with Christ by sharing experientially in Christ's sufferings. This view overlooks the redemptive-historical nature of the association of the church with Christ in the time and events of His life, suffering, death, and resurrection, as this chapter argues.

33. This can be seen in the way the many were "made sinners" by Adam's disobedience, and "made righteous" through the obedience of the One, Christ Jesus (Rom 5:19), although καθίστημι is far better translated as "appointed" (BDAG § 3836), as it is in Titus 1:5, "For this reason I left you in Crete, that you might ... *appoint* (not, "make") elders in every city as I directed you." The "divine passive" voice in Rom 5:19 indicates that it is God who did the appointing. See Wallace, *Greek Grammar*, 437–8.

34. As stated in the introduction, this study accepts the authenticity of the thirteen autographed letters of Paul as giving a fully-orbed view of Paul's thought. While Trobisch, *The First Edition of the New Testament*, 25, 34, 59, observes that the epistle to the Hebrews was circulated in the parchment manuscripts as if it was a Pauline letter, its consideration in this study is eliminated in that it is not *specifically* signed by Paul. Although the preposition σύν is not found in Hebrews, a significant number of συ-compounds words do appear (Heb 2:4; 4:2, 15; 7:1, 10; 8:8; 9:9, 14, 26; 10:2, 22, 34; 11:9, 25, 31; 12:10; 13:3, 18), some having parallels in the Pauline letters and lending support to Pauline authorship, as defended by Black, "Who Wrote Hebrews? The Internal and External Evidence Reexamined," 3–26.

35. See the discussion of "Syntax of Prepositions," in BDB 110–25, which notes, "The line of demarcation between adverb and preposition is naturally difficult to draw" (ibid., 110).

36. According to the word count in the BGT of *BibleWorks 8*, Paul uses the following prepositions listed here in order of frequency: (1) ἐν (1029 times); (2) εἰς (443 times); (3) διά (217 times); (4) κατά (150 times); (5) πρός (146 times); (6) ἐκ (141 times); (7) ὑπέρ (101 times); (8) ἐπί (92 times); (10) μετά (73 times); (11) ὑπό (62 times); (12) περί (51 times); (13) σύν (39 times); (14) παρά (23 times); (15) πρό (12 times); (16) ἀντί

THE "MAN CHRIST JESUS"

applications shows that Paul tends to use consistent vocabularies when discussing various aspects of the believer's relationship to Christ: when mentioning the presence of God with believers, he prefers to use expressions employing the preposition μετά to remind his readers that God is with them.[37] When discussing the dynamic union believers share in Christ, Paul uses the widely studied motif ἐν Χριστῷ, a phrase easily observable in his letters.[38] Not as widely recognized, however, is his use of the preposition σύν when he considers the association of the church with the "Man Christ Jesus." In such contexts, believers are not discussed in their dynamic union (as in the "in Christ" motif) nor in a communicative relationship (as in the "God with us" idea), but rather they are mentioned in association with the acts of the "Man Christ Jesus" in His humanity

This distinction is borne out by a comparison of the two prepositions of concern, ἐν and σύν. What one immediately observes is that ἐν is Paul's favorite preposition, or at least his most frequently used, as it appears 1,029 times, nearly three times more than the next closest preposition (εἰς, 443 occurrences). On the other hand, σύν appears much more selectively, only thirty-nine times,[39] of which twelve bear particular christological significance;[40] however, another ninety-two compound words prefixed with σύν[41] are

---

(4 times); (17) ἀνά (twice).

37. Paul uses the preposition μετά seventy-three times in his letters, and he consistently employs it when discussing (1) associative virtues (2 Cor 7:15; 8:4; Eph 4:2; 6:5, 7; Phil 1:4; 2:12, 29; 4:6; Col 1:11; 1 Thess 1:6; 3:12; 1 Tim 1:14; 2:9, 15; 3:4; 4:3, 4, 14; 6:6; 2 Tim 2:10; Titus 2:15; 3:15a); (2) believers in association with others (Rom 12:15, 18; 15:10; 1 Cor 6:6–7; 7:12–13; 16:11–12; 2 Cor 6:15; 8:18; Gal 2:1,12; 4:25, 30; Eph 4:25; Phil 4:3; 1 Thess 3:13; 2 Thess 1:7; 2 Tim 2:22; 4:11); (3) the association of God with His people (2 Cor 6:16; Eph 6:23; Phil 4:9), and especially (4) in the closing benedictions of all his letters as his apostolic blessing and imprimatur, of God being with believers (Rom 15:33, "Now the God of peace be with you all. Amen;" Rom 16:20, "The grace of our Lord Jesus be with you;" 1 Cor 16:23, "The grace of the Lord Jesus be with you;" 1 Cor 16:24, "My love be with you all in Christ Jesus. Amen;" 2 Cor 13:11, "The God of love and peace shall be with you;" 2 Cor 13:14, "The grace of the Lord Jesus Christ, and the love of God, and the fellowship of the Holy Spirit, be with you all;" Gal 6:18, "The grace of our Lord Jesus Christ be with your spirit, brethren. Amen;" Eph 6:24, "Grace be with all those who love our Lord Jesus Christ with *a love* incorruptible;" Phil 4:23, "The grace of the Lord Jesus Christ be with your spirit;" Col 4:18, "Grace be with you;" 1 Thess 5:28, "The grace of our Lord Jesus Christ be with you;" 2 Thess 3:16, "The Lord be with you all;" 2 Thess 3:18, "The grace of our Lord Jesus Christ be with you all;" 1 Tim 6:21, "Grace be with you;" 2 Tim 4:22, "The Lord be with (μετὰ) your spirit. Grace be with you (μεθ' ὑμῶν);" Titus 3:15c, "Grace be with you all;" Philm 1:25, "The grace of the Lord Jesus Christ be with (μετὰ) your spirit.").

38. See Seifrid, "In Christ," in *Dictionary of Paul and His Letters*, 433–36.

39. See Appendix 1: "A Complete Listing of The Preposition Σύν in The Pauline Epistles [1] The Preposition Σύν is used in the Pauline Corpus 39 times in 37 verses." Goppelt, *Theology of the New Testament*, 2:98–99, groups the *syn*-expressions in four distinct statements: (1) being with, as being together with Christians; (2) eschatological being with Christ; (3) a spiritual participation (Rom 6:4, 6; Col 2:12; Gal 2:10); and (4) Paul's own being as an apostle.

40. These twelve verses are Rom 6:8; 8:32; 2 Cor 4:14; 13:4; Phil 1:23; Col 2:13, 20; 3:3, 4; 1 Thess 4:14, 17; 5:10. See Appendix 2: "A Synthesis of The Pauline References to Association With Christ."

41. According to a count in Moulton, and Geden, *A Concordance of the Greek New Testament* (1963), the Westcott and Hort *Greek New Testament* includes 186 different words prefixed by the preposition σύν. Paul seems especially enamoured with the semantic possibilities of these compounds, using 92 of them, or nearly 50 per cent of the total. Of these, 51 are found only in Paul's vocabulary or fifty-five percent of Paul's total usage of the σύν compounds. These are: συλαγωγῶν, ἐσύλησα, σύμβουλος, συμμορφιζόμενος, σύμμορφον, σύμφορον, συμφυλετῶν, σύμφυτοι, συμφώνησις, συμφώνου, συναγωνίσασθαί, συναθλοῦντες, συναιχμαλώτους,

The "Man Christ Jesus" in Association with His People

found in the Pauline corpus (twenty-seven nouns used seventy-eight times[42] and seventy-seven verbs[43] used 121 times), of which at least twenty-five references apply to the "with Christ" motif.[44] Although this literary style is quite distinctive, there is actually nothing mysterious about Paul's utilization of σύν: he uses it in conformity with the general koine and classical usage.[45] While the basic meaning of σύν when used with the dative case is "with,"[46] that is just the rudimentary idea, because Paul packs it with Christological significance when he notes that the church is associated with Christ in various aspects of His saving work.[47]

Compare this extensive usage of σύν to the fact that the apostle employs only fifteen compound words that are prefixed with the nearly synonymous preposition μετά, yet one observes that Paul does not use μετά of the believer or the church in historical association with Christ.[48] He reserves that designation for the preposition σύν and does

---

συναναμίγνυσθαι, συναναπαύσωμαι, συναπέστειλα, συναρμολογουμένη, συνδοξασθῶμεν, συμβασιλεύσομεν, συνηγέρθητε, συζήσομεν, συζητητής, σύζυγε, συνεζωοποίησεν, συνήδομαι, συνηλικιώτας, συνετάφημεν, συνθρύπτοντές, συγκακοπάθησον, σύγκαμψον, συγκατάθεσις, συμμαρτυρούσης, συμμερίζονται, συμμέτοχα, Συμμιμηταί, συνοικοδομεῖσθε, συμπαρακληθῆναι, συμπάσχομεν, συνεπέμψαμεν, συμπολῖται, σύσσωμα, συστενάζει, συστοιχεῖ, συστρατιώτην, συντέμνων, σύντριμμα, συνυπουργούντων, σύμφημι, σύμψυχοι, συνωδίνει, συστατικῶν. This novelty lends credence to the idea that Paul created his own vocabulary to describe the new association brought by the coming of Christ Jesus.

42. See Appendix 1: "A Complete Listing of The Preposition Σύν in The Pauline Epistles [2] Various Nouns Prefixed by the Preposition Συ-."

43. See Appendix 1: "A Complete Listing of The Preposition Σύν in The Pauline Epistles [3] Verbal Compounds Prefixed by the Preposition Συ-."

44. See Appendix 2: "A Synthesis of the Pauline References to Association With Christ." This synthesis reveals these twenty-five references pertinent for this study: Rom 6:4, 5, 6, 8; 8:17, 29; 2 Cor 6:1; 7:3; Gal 2:20; 2:19; Eph 2:5, 6; 3:6; Phil 1:23; 3:10, 21; Col 2:12a, 12b, 13; 3:1; 2 Tim 1:8; 2:3, 11a, 11b, 12. Add these to the twelve references to Christ using σύν (Rom 6:8; 8:32; 2 Cor 4:14; 13:4; Phil 1:23; Col 2:13, 20; 3:3, 4; 1 Thess 4:14, 17; 5:10), and that totals thirty-seven references to association with Christ. Other verses could be added to this list, since it is sometimes difficult to know if Paul refers to association with Christ or with other believers (such as Col 2:19). Due to the oneness between Christ and His Body, there may no distinction in Paul's mind, but this study shall limit the scope to these unmistakable instances.

45. Lohmeyer, "ΣΥΝ ΧΡΙΣΤΩ," 229, surveys the use of σύν in extra-biblical Greek and concludes that the Pauline motif "with Christ" has no discernable historical connection to any other particular literature. "With Christ" seems to be unique to Paul.

46. LN § 89.107 defines σύν as "a marker of an associative relation, often involving joint participation in some activity–'with, together with;' ὁ δὲ Λάζαρος εἷς ἦν ἐκ τῶν ἀνακειμένων σὺν αὐτῷ, 'and Lazarus was one of those with Him at the table;' Jn 12.2; ἐρχόμεθα καὶ ἡμεῖς σὺν σοί, 'we also will go with you,' Jn 21.3."

47. This is not to imply that σύν itself carries some intrinsic meaning, as Grundmann, σύν-μετά, TDNT 7:770, seems to suggest: "It (σύν) denotes the totality of persons who are together, or who come together, or who accompany one another, or who work together, sharing common tasks or a common destiny, aiding and supporting one another." The preposition σύν only gains Christological significance when it modifies Χριστῷ.

48. According to a count in Moulton and Geden, A Concordance of the Greek New Testament, the Westcott and Hort Greek NT includes twenty-eight different words prefixed by the preposition μετά, of which Paul employs fifteen, as follows: μεταδίδωμι (Rom 1:11, 12:8, Eph 4:28; 1 Thess 2:8); μετακινέω (Col 1:23); μεταλαμβάνω (2 Tim 2:6); μετάλημψις (1 Tim 4:3); μεταλλάσσω (Rom 1:25; 1:26); μεταμέλομαι (2 Cor 7:8); μεταμορφόω (Rom 12:2; 2 Cor 3:18); μετανοέω (2 Cor 12:21); μετάνοια (Rom 2:4; 2 Cor 7:9, 10; 2 Tim 2:25); μεταξύ (adverb, "between," Rom 2:15); μεταστρέφω (Gal 1:7); μετασχηματίζω (1 Cor 4:6; 2 Cor 11:13–15; Phil 3:21); μετατίθημι (Gal 1:6); μετέχω (1 Cor 9:10; 9:12; 1 Cor 10:17, 21, 30); μετοχή (2 Cor

not interchange the prepositions: μετά is used of the presence of God with the believer,[49] whereas σύν describes the believer in association with Christ.[50] Paul consistently uses μετά when describing existential associations but employs σύν when his emphasis centers on historical associations.[51]

Despite the fact that this survey reveals that the apostle uses an extensive diversity of prepositions as part of his grammar, commentators tend to view the concept of association with Christ as identical to Paul's better known concept of union with Christ (ἐν Χριστῷ),[52] yet the variety among his terminology raises the question whether Paul's choice of prepositions in any given context is arbitrary or deliberate; for example, in his fifty-four uses of the verb πιστεύω, Paul specifies the object of believing by the preposition

---

6:14). Although the prepositions σύν and μετά are often used interchangeably, it is apparent that only a few of these μετά compounds carry any soteriological significance (such as Rom 12:2; 2 Cor 3:18; Phil 3:21; and Col 1:13), but none of these relate directly to the idea of association with Christ. This further confirms the thesis that Paul intentionally and carefully selected his vocabulary when referring to association with Christ in His historical actions.

49. Grundmann, σύν-μετά, *TDNT*, 7:773, notes that the expression "with God" is a common recurring phrase found in Greek literature. There is nothing distinctly biblical about the phrase, as it expresses "the common religious spirit from antiquity" (Lohmeyer, "ΣΥΝ ΧΡΙΣΤΩ," 229). However, in Scripture, to be with God, obviously, is to be in a state of divine favor and grace, as Enoch and Noah walked with God (Gen 5:22, 24; 6:9). Conversely, God gives this promise of divine presence to His people, "I am with you" (found in variations of ἐγὼ μετὰ σοῦ εἰμι, Gen 26:24 [אִתְּךָ אָנֹכִי]; Gen 28:15 [אָנֹכִי עִמָּךְ]; Isa 41:10 [עִמְּךָ־אָנִי]; 43:5; Jer 1:8, 19; 15:20; 30:11; 42:11, 46:28; Hag 1:13, 2:4). In the LXX, this expression is translated by *meta*, but the idea is certainly similar, if not identical with the use of σὺν ὑμῖν. It reflects the Emmanuel principle, "God with us" (Isa 7:14; 8:8, 10; Matt 1:23, עִמָּנוּ אֵל), given by Jesus is His closing promise before His ascension, "I am with you always" (ἐγὼ μεθ᾽ ὑμῶν εἰμι, Matt 28:20).

50. The reciprocal relationship of the people of God is that of association with the Covenantal head: As He is with His own, so His own are placed with Him, although in the LXX, this motif uses the preposition μετά rather than σύν.

51. LN § 89.107, footnote 21 (I. 791) observes, "The semantic domain of σύν[a] (89.107) and μετά[a] (89.108) overlap considerably, for in a number of instances, essentially the same referential relationship can be expressed by either σύν[a] or by μετά. However, in contexts involving hostility and combat, opposing forces may be spoken of as fighting against one another with μετά[a]. In this type of context the preposition σύν[a] would not be appropriate, since it would suggest those fighting on the same side, not on opposite sides of the conflict." If Paul understood μετά as having any sort of hostile connotation, it is not surprising that he would select σύν when discussing the believer's association with Christ, since the parties, being reconciled, share the same sides in all matters.

52. For example, Persons, "'In Christ' in Paul," 25, makes no distinction between "in Christ" or "with Christ," calling them "various equivalents." Scholarship has generally assumed that Paul makes no difference between "in Christ" and "with Christ," but this study challenges that assumption, since Paul actually chose to use different prepositions. The interpreter's task is to explore why he might have done so.

ἐν only once;⁵³ instead, he customarily selects ἐπί⁵⁴ or εἰς.⁵⁵ Does he vary these prepositions interchangeably for no other reason than stylistic or rhetorical modification, or does he find a more specific nuance in one word over another in differing contexts?

Paul's usage of grammar would argue for the latter, as one notes that the apostle is careful regarding his use of precise words, as shown in Gal 3:16 ("Now the promises were spoken to Abraham and to his seed. He does not say, 'And to seeds,' as *referring* to many, but *rather* to one, 'And to your seed,' that is, Christ."). Since his argument in this passage rests on the use of the singular as opposed to the plural, one can suppose that he is equally deliberate in his choice of prepositions. For example, there is a rare intersection of ἐν and σύν observed in the parallel structure of 2 Cor 13:4b:

καὶ γὰρ ἡμεῖς ἀσθενοῦμεν ἐν αὐτῷ,
ἀλλὰ ζήσομεν σὺν αὐτῷ ἐκ δυνάμεως θεοῦ εἰς ὑμᾶς.

Is there any reason Paul would have changed from "we are being weak *in Him*" (ἐν αὐτῷ) to "we shall live *with Him*" (σὺν αὐτῷ) other than stylistic, since he could have written "we shall live *in* Christ," as he does elsewhere?⁵⁶ Or is there a relational distinction the apostle intends to make by changing the preposition?⁵⁷ This study shall proceed on the assumption that the reader at the least ought to ask if any significance can be determined from the selection of a particular preposition in each context.⁵⁸

This question is especially pertinent with regard to this research, since the phase "with Christ" (σὺν Χριστῷ) is generally assumed to carry the same meaning as the more frequent phrase "in Christ (ἐν Χριστῷ)." A compilation of the occurrences of the phrases 'in Christ/in Lord/in Jesus' in the Pauline Epistles reveals that Paul uses seven variations of this motif: "in the Lord" (ἐν κυρίῳ, forty-nine times),⁵⁹ "in Christ Jesus" (ἐν Χριστῷ

---

53. That exception is Rom 10:9 ["that if you confess with your mouth Jesus *as* Lord, and believe in your heart (καὶ πιστεύσῃς ἐν τῇ καρδίᾳ σου) that God raised Him from the dead, you shall be saved."], yet here Paul is not specifying an object of believing but the location of belief, in the heart, in parallel to the confessing mouth. Ephesians 1:13 appears to be a second exception, "in whom also having believed (ἐν ᾧ καὶ πιστεύσαντες), you were sealed with the Holy Spirit of promise," but due to the parallel structure in this section, the prepositional phrase is better understood as modifying the verb "sealed" rather than the participle "having believed," as translated in the NASB, "having also believed, you were sealed in Him with the Holy Spirit of promise."

54. As in Rom 4:5, 24; 9:33; 10:11; 1 Tim 1:16, πιστεύειν ἐπ' αὐτῷ εἰς ζωὴν αἰώνιον.

55. As in Gal 2:16, ἡμεῖς εἰς Χριστὸν Ἰησοῦν ἐπιστεύσαμεν; and Phil 1:29, εἰς αὐτὸν πιστεύειν. See the discussion on this usage by Harris, "Prepositions and Theology in the Greek New Testament," in *DNTT* 3:1211–14.

56. As in 2 Timothy 3:12, καὶ πάντες δὲ οἱ θέλοντες εὐσεβῶς ζῆν ἐν Χριστῷ Ἰησοῦ διωχθήσονται.

57. See the later exegetical observations on 2 Cor 13:4 where this distinction shall be argued.

58. Harris, "Prepositions," *DNTT* 3:1173, suggests the following: "In seeking to determine the meaning of a prep. phrase the NT exegete should (at least ideally) consider: (1) the primary meaning of the prep. in itself (i.e. the local relation) and then its range of meaning when used with a particular case; (2) the basic significance of the case that is used with the prep.; (3) the indications afforded by the context as to the meaning of the prep.; (4) the distinctive features of prep. usage in the NT which may account for the seeming irregularities."

59. "In the Lord" (ἐν κυρίῳ) appears in Rom 14:14; 16:2, 8, 11, 12, 13, 22; 1:31; 4:17; 7:22, 39; 9:1, 2; 11:11; 15:58; 16:19; 2 Cor 2:12; 10:17; Gal 5:10; Eph 2:21; 4:1, 17; 5:8; 6:1, 10, 21; Phil 1:14; 2:19, 24, 29; 3:1;

THE "MAN CHRIST JESUS"

Ἰησοῦ, forty-six times),[60] "in Christ" (ἐν Χριστῷ, twenty-eight times),[61] "in Him" (ἐν αὐ
τῷ, where the antecedent noun refers to Christ, appears twenty-one times),[62] "in whom" (ἐν ᾧ), referring to Christ (nine times),[63] "in the Christ" (ἐν τῷ Χριστῷ, six times),[64] "in the Lord" (ἐν τῷ κυρίῳ Ἰησοῦ, once in Eph 1:15), and "in Jesus" (ἐν τῷ Ἰησοῦ, once, in Eph 4:21). In one form or another, these phrases are found in every letter of the Pauline corpus with the exception of Titus, an omission deserving of its own attention.[65] Why one of these seven variations is chosen in any given context provides the subject of another study; for example, it appears that the phrase "in the Lord" is used when the apostle emphasizes the lordship of Jesus in authoritative matters (as in the *Haustafel* discussion of Eph 6:1–4). In such cases, the use of the term κύριος would be completely expected and appropriate. Also, when Paul discusses the dynamic position of believers, he tends to use the shortened phrase, "in Christ," whereas in contexts where the emphasis lies on the personal relationship of believers to the Savior, he tends to use the more personal form "in Christ Jesus."[66] Whether this difference is accidental or deliberate needs to be demonstrat-

---

4:1, 2, 4, 10; Col 3:18, 20; 4:7, 17; 1 Thess 1:1; 3:8; 4:1; 5:12; 2 Thess 1:1; 3:4, 12; Philm 16, 20.

60. "In Christ Jesus" (ἐν Χριστῷ Ἰησοῦ) appears in Rom 3:24; 6:11; 23; 8:1, 2, 39; 15:17; 16:3; 1 Cor 1:2, 4, 30; 1 Cor 15:31; 16:24; Gal 2:4; 3:14, 26, 28; Eph 1:1; 2:6, 7, 10, 13; 3:6, 21; Phil 1:1, 26; 2:5; 3:3, 14; 4:7, 19, 21; Col 1:4; 1 Thess 2:14; 5:1; 2 Thess 1:1; 1 Tim 1:14; 3:13; 2 Tim 1:1, 9, 13; 2:1, 10; 3:12, 15; Philm 23.

61. "In Christ" (ἐν Χριστῷ) appears in Rom 9:1; 12:5; 16:7, 9, 10; 1 Cor 3:1; 4:10, 15, 17; 15:18, 19; 2 Cor 2:17; 3:14; 5:17, 19; 12:2, 19; Gal 1:22; 2:17; Eph 1:3; 4:32; Phil 1:13; 2:1; Col 1:2, 28; 1 Thess 4:16; Philm 8, 20.

62. "In Him" (ἐν αὐτῷ), referring to Christ, appears in 1 Cor 1:5; 2 Cor 1:19, 20; 5:21; 13:4; Eph 1:4, 9, 10; 2:15, 16; 4:21; Phil 3:9; Col 1:16, 17, 19; Col 2:6, 7, 9, 10, 15; 2 Thess 1:12.

63. "In whom" (ἐν ᾧ), referring to Christ: Eph 1:7, 11, 13; 2:21, 22; 3:12; Col 1:14; 2:3, 11.

64. "In the Christ" (ἐν τῷ Χριστῷ) appears in 1 Cor 15:22; 2 Cor 2:14; Eph 1:10, 12, 20; 3:11.

65 See the selected Bibliography of related studies in Harris, *DNTT* 3:1214–15. Refer also to the analysis of texts in Best, *One Body in Christ*, 1–8.

66. Interestingly, Paul never uses the prepositional phrase with the word order "in Jesus Christ," although the NASB (mis)translates it that way in Rom 3:22 ["even *the* righteousness of God through faith *in* Jesus Christ (although the phrase is "through faith of Jesus Christ," διὰ πίστεως Ἰησοῦ Χριστοῦ) for all those who believe;"] and in Gal 3:22 ["But the Scripture has shut up all men under sin, that the promise by faith *in* Jesus Christ (the phrase is "out of faith of Jesus Christ," ἐκ πίστεως Ἰησοῦ Χριστοῦ) might be given to those who believe."], but oddly, it does not translate the same word order that way in Gal 2:16 ("nevertheless knowing that a man is not justified by the works of the Law but through faith *in Christ Jesus* (διὰ πίστεως Ἰησοῦ Χριστοῦ), even we have believed in Christ Jesus (καὶ ἡμεῖς εἰς Χριστὸν Ἰησοῦν ἐπιστεύσαμεν) that we may be justified by faith in Christ (ἵνα δικαιωθῶμεν ἐκ πίστεως Χριστοῦ)." What should be noted in these verses is that Paul uses the genitive διὰ/ἐκ πίστεως Ἰησοῦ Χριστοῦ, as he does also in Rom 3:26 [that "He (God) might be just and the justifier of the one who has faith in Jesus" (εἰς τὸ εἶναι αὐτὸν δίκαιον καὶ δικαιοῦντα τὸν ἐκ πίστεως Ἰησοῦ); Eph 3:12 ["in whom (Christ) we have boldness and confident access through faith in Him" (ἐν ᾧ ἔχομεν τὴν παρρησίαν καὶ προσαγωγὴν ἐν πεποιθήσει διὰ τῆς πίστεως αὐτοῦ; and Phil 3:9 ["and may (I) be found in Him, not having a righteousness of my own derived from *the* Law, but that which is through faith in Christ" (καὶ εὑρεθῶ ἐν αὐτῷ, μὴ ἔχων ἐμὴν δικαιοσύνην τὴν ἐκ νόμου ἀλλὰ τὴν διὰ πίστεως Χριστοῦ, τὴν ἐκ θεοῦ δικαιοσύνην ἐπὶ τῇ πίστει)]. These issues are discussed in Robinson, "'Faith of Jesus Christ'—a New Testament Debate," 71–81, whether Paul intends the phrase "faith of Christ" as an objective genitive (Jesus as the object of faith, as translated in the NASB) or as a subjective genitive [the faith(fulness) of Jesus, as generally translated in the KJV.]. Other appearances of similar construction argue for the subjective genitive: Rom 4:12 ["Those who also follow in the steps of the faith of our father Abraham (καὶ πατέρα περιτομῆς τοῖς οὐκ ἐκ περιτομῆς μόνον ἀλλὰ καὶ τοῖς στοιχοῦσιν τοῖς ἴχνεσιν τῆς ἐν ἀκροβυστίᾳ πίστεως τοῦ πατρὸς ἡμῶν Ἀβραάμ. "Faith *in* Abraham" is quite obviously what Paul does

ed by further investigation outside the scope of this study. A count of phrases, however, notes that the appearances of the ἐν Χριστῷ motif vastly outnumber the few appearances of the phrase σὺν Χριστῷ (161:12); furthermore, the two phrases appear together in only four passages (2 Cor 13:4; Eph 2:6; 3:6; Col 2:11–13), indicating a particular significance peculiar to each motif. Since ἐν can also be used to convey an associative sense,[67] why would Paul select ἐν in one context and σύν in another if his intention was identical for each preposition? It is certainly possible that these prepositions are merely serving as variations of the same idea, but why would Paul use such a different vocabulary to convey the same concept, especially since he otherwise chooses his words with great care?

The apostle provides an important literary parallel of his theological use of σύν in Gal 3:9, when he writes, "So then those who are of faith are blessed with Abraham, the believer" (ὥστε οἱ ἐκ πίστεως εὐλογοῦνται σὺν τῷ πιστῷ 'Αβραάμ). In the context of this statement, Paul asks if God responds to "works of law" or to "hearing of faith" (Gal 3:2, 5), and for an answer he cites Gen 15:6, "Even so Abraham believed God, and it was reckoned to him as righteousness." From this quotation Paul deduces, "Therefore, be sure that it is those who are of faith who are sons of Abraham" (Gal 3:7), since "the Scripture, foreseeing that God would justify the Gentiles by faith, preached the gospel beforehand to Abraham, *saying*, 'All the nations shall be blessed in you'" (quoting Gen 12:3; 18:8; 22:18). This inference leads to Paul's next deduction, "So then those who are of faith are blessed with Abraham, the believer" (Gal 3:9). Here Paul considers present believers to be blessed with Abraham not merely by the example of his faith, but as being included in God's promise "to Abraham and his seed," in fulfillment of the prophecy that all nations will be blessed by the Seed of Abraham (Gen 22:17–18), whom Paul identifies typologically as Jesus Himself (Gal 3:16).[68] Thus, in his carefully reasoned application of biblical theology, Paul shows how all who are of Christ are also the seed of Abraham (Gal 3:29)—by associa-

---

not mean: it must be "faith *of* Abraham," and that is how the English versions render it—inconsistently)]; 1 Timothy 1:5 ("the goal of our instruction is love from . . . πίστεως ἀνυποκρίτου) would be nonsense if rendered "faith *in* unhypocrisy;" it must be "unhypocritical faith." In Philemon 1:6, Paul surely did not mean "faith *in* you" by the phrase ἡ κοινωνία τῆς πίστεώς σου; it must be "the *fellowship of your faith* may become effective through the knowledge of every good thing which is in you for Christ's sake" (ὅπως ἡ κοινωνία τῆς πίστεώς σου ἐνεργὴς γένηται ἐν ἐπιγνώσει παντὸς ἀγαθοῦ τοῦ ἐν ἡμῖν εἰς Χριστόν). An identical construction is found in Mark 11:22 when "Jesus answered, saying to them, ἔχετε πίστιν θεοῦ." Unlike most modern versions, the Geneva Bible retains the genitive and translates it as subjective, "Haue [sic] the faith *of* God." Robinson argues—persuasively to this reviewer—that what Paul emphasizes in Rom 3:22, 26; Gal 2:16, 20; Eph 3:12; and Phil 3:9, is that the believer believes in the belief (or the faithfulness) of Jesus as the basis of justification. See also the articles pro and con in Bird and Sprinkle, eds., *The Faith of Jesus Christ: Exegetical, Biblical, and Theological Studies* (2010).

67. As in Rom 1:12, "that I may be encouraged together with you *while* among you," συμπαρακληθῆναι ἐν ὑμῖν διὰ τῆς ἐν ἀλλήλοις πίστεως ὑμῶν τε καὶ Ἐμοῦ.

68. Unfortunately, Paul's skillfully argued references to the seed motif of the Abrahamic Covenant in Gal 3:16 and Gal 3:19 are obscured by the NASB translations of σπέρμα and זֶרַע as "offspring" (Gen 15:3; Gal 3:29) or as "descendents" (Gen 12:7; 13:15, 16, 16; 15:5; 13; 18; 16:10; 17:7, 7, 8, 9, 10, 12, 19; 21:12; 24:7; see the corresponding quotes in Rom 4:13, 16, 18; 9:7, 8; 11:1). Rather inconsistently but more accurately, the NASB renders Gen 22:17–18, "Indeed I will greatly bless you, and I will greatly multiply *your seed* as the stars of the heavens, and as the sand which is on the seashore; and *your seed* shall possess the gate of their enemies. And in *your seed* all the nations of the earth shall be blessed, because you have obeyed My voice."

THE "MAN CHRIST JESUS"

tion with Abraham, as if they were all present with him in his initial act of faith when he believed God and it was reckoned to him as righteousness.

This prepositional phrase σὺν ’Αβραάμ raises the same question posed by the σὺν Χριστῷ motif: How can believers living thousands of years after the patriarch's death be blessed "with him"? The manner by which believers are blessed with Abraham must be identical with the way that they are blessed with Christ: the one acted on behalf of the many, and the many are divinely considered to have acted in the one by association with Him. Paul never teaches that believers are dynamically "in Abraham" as they are "in Christ," but he certainly considers believers to be "with Abraham" in his historical events that effected his seed, suggesting that the similar motifs "in Christ" and "with Christ" also describe two different aspects of salvation, both having an important place in the scheme of redemption. These different aspects are distinguished as Paul takes the very ordinary preposition σύν and baptizes it with his own peculiar connotation, as determined by his application of the historical Person and events of Jesus. Paul sees in these historical realities an association of all those belonging to Christ with Him: what He did for them, they also did with Him, and what He shall do for them, they shall also do with Him.

On the basis of this observation, this chapter now proceeds on the deduction that Paul uses particular vocabulary when he purposes a different emphasis: when the subject matter concerns a positional or dynamic relationship of believers to the ascended Christ, he expresses that with the "in Christ" motif,[69] but when he speaks of the association of believers to the "Man Christ Jesus" in His humanity, whether in His earthly or heavenly ministries, Paul uses the σὺν Χριστῷ motif, as this study shall now demonstrate.

Linguistic Analysis of Σύν and Συ-Compounds in the Pauline Epistles Expressing Association

While ἐν is translated variously in the NASB as a dative of instrument ("For *by* Him—ἐν αὐτῷ—all things were created," Col 1:16), as a dative of location ("the church of God which is *at* Corinth," ἐν Κορίνθῳ) or even as a dative of association ("that I may be encouraged together *with* you while *among* you;" συμπαρακληθῆναι ἐν ὑμῖν, Rom 1:12),[70] such diversity is not the case with the preposition σύν, shown in modern English versions that almost universally translate σύν by the word "with,"[71] in accordance with its general usage in *koine* literature.[72] Its lack of variation leads BDF to comment, "There is

---

69. This observation comes notwithstanding the comment in BDF § 118, "The phrase ἐν Χριστῷ (κυρίῳ), which is copiously appended by Paul to the most varied concepts, utterly defies definite interpretation." Instead, because Paul does use the phrase many times in various ways means that each instance ought to be definitely interpreted, assuming he had his reasons for writing each phrase the way he does.

70. Wallace, *Greek Grammar*, 372, provides ten categories of uses of ἐν, calling it "the workhorse of prepositions in the NT."

71. LN § 89.107 defines σύν as "a marker of an associative relation, often involving joint participation in some activity—'with, together with.'"

72. Walter Grundmann, σύν-μετά, *TDNT* 7:770 notes, "The basic meaning of the preposition σύν with the associative dative is 'with,' and the term has a personal character. It denotes the totality of persons who are together, who come together, or who accompany one another, or who work together, sharing a common task or a common destiny, aiding and supporting one another."

little to note regarding its use,"⁷³ and such dismissive attitude may account for the lack of exegetical precision among commentators toward the "with Christ" motif, as if it contains nothing distinctive from the "in Christ" motif.⁷⁴ This indifference also extends to the συ-compounds of both nouns and verbs, as translators regularly lose the prefix in translation.⁷⁵ This fact makes it difficult for the non-Greek reader to explore the rich emphases of association found in Paul's writings, which show a wide variety and great ingenuity of the apostle with his use of the preposition σύν. Although he employs the preposition only thirty-nine times, Paul uses another seventy-two nouns and 121 compound verbs prefixed with σύν, words described by Schattenmann as "new expressions that (Paul) coined," since many of these terms appear in Greek literature only in the Pauline corpus.⁷⁶ A list culled from this group reveals that the primary sources for association with Christ appears in the following verses: Rom 6:4, 5, 6, 8 (twice); 8:17, 29, 32; 2 Cor 4:14; 6:1; 7:3; 13:4; Gal 2:19–20; Eph 2:5–6; Phil 1:23; 3:10, 21; Col. 2:12 (twice), 13, 20; 3:1, 3, 4; 1 Thess 4:14, 17; 5:10; and 2 Tim 2:11–12.

A synthesizing of these verses reveals that they are bound together not only by means of mutual linguistic features—namely, the preposition σύν defining some reference with Christ—but also by mention to soteriological events in the past, present or future ministry of Jesus by which believers are associated corporately with Him and collectively with one another.⁷⁷ A synthesis of the Pauline references to association with Christ, when organized in chronological sequence, gives an *ordo historicis* to the *ordo salutis*. Regarding the past, these events associate believers with the historical Jesus in the nailing of His crucifixion,⁷⁸ in the succumbing of His physical death,⁷⁹ and in the entombing of His burial⁸⁰ (pictured

---

73. BDF § 110.

74. For example, Callen, *Dying and Rising with Christ*, 125, merges "in Christ" and "with Christ," although he acknowledges that "Paul frequently refers to believers as being 'with Christ.' More important than the prepositional phrase are the many words compounded with the preposition 'with;' these are characteristic of Paul's writing." Despite these observations, he apparently sees no differences between the two phrases, "in Christ" and "with Christ."

75. The associative element disappears entirely in the NASB translations of Rom 8:29 ("conformed to"), Col 2:19 ("supplied and held together by"), and Phil 3:10 ("conformed to His death").

76. Schattenmann, "κοινωνία," *NIDNTT* 1:643. He combines the entire concept into dynamic incorporation into Jesus' death, burial, resurrection, and glory, and he argues that these "mixed metaphors" guard against mystical misunderstanding or divinization.

77. All the references are plural, with the exception of Gal 2:20, "I am crucified with Christ" and Phil 3:10, "I am being conformed with His death" (2 Tim 1:8 and 2:3 involve the association of Paul with Timothy). Otherwise, Paul emphasizes the plurality and completeness of the entire Body of Christ as being associated with Christ—and with one another—in the great saving events that are—or shall be—accomplished by the historical Jesus.

78. As in Rom 6:6, "our old man was crucified with *Him*" (ὁ παλαιὸς ἡμῶν ἄνθρωπος συνεσταυρώθη Aor. Pass. Ind., 3ms); Gal 2:20, "With Christ I have been crucified" (Χριστῷ συνεσταύρωμαι Perf. Pass, Ind., 1s).

79. As in Rom 6:8, "we died with Christ" (ἀπεθάνομεν σὺν Χριστῷ; Aor. Act. Ind., 1p); Col 2:20, "if you died with Christ" (Εἰ ἀπεθάνετε σὺν Χριστῷ, Aor. Act. Ind. 2p); 2 Tim 2:11, "if we died with *Him*" (εἰ γὰρ συναπεθάνομεν; Aor. Act. Ind., 1p). In this list 2 Cor 7:3 shall also be considered, "I do not speak to condemn you; for I have said before that you are in our hearts to die together (συναποθανεῖν, aorist active infinitive) and to live together" (συζῆν, present active infinitive).

80. In Rom 6:4, "Therefore we were buried with Him" (συνετάφημεν οὖν αὐτῷ; Aor. Pass. Ind., 1p); Col

as a planting with Him⁸¹). Then, believers are considered to be associated with Jesus in the events of His vivification,⁸² His resurrection,⁸³ and His seating in ascension,⁸⁴ having now been hidden with Him in His heavenly status.⁸⁵ In the present, believers are viewed as being associated with Christ and with His Body⁸⁶ so they are now experiencing the status of being His fellow-heirs⁸⁷ by being conformed to His death⁸⁸ through current suffering.⁸⁹ In the future, believers shall be associated with Christ's life,⁹⁰ so that after their physical death they shall be with Him.⁹¹ At His *parousia*, believers shall be raised with Jesus⁹² and

---

2:12, "buried with Him in baptism" (συνταφέντες αὐτῷ ἐν τῷ βαπτισμῷ; Aor. Pass. Past., mas. nom. pl.).

81. In Rom 6:5, "For if we have been united together in the likeness of His death" (εἰ γὰρ σύμφυτοι γεγόναμεν τῷ ὁμοιώματι τοῦ θανάτου αὐτοῦ; Perf. act. Ind., 1p).

82. In Eph 2:5, "(He) made us alive together with Christ" (συνεζωοποίησεν τῷ Χριστῷ; Aor. Act. Ind., 3s); Col 2:13, "He has made (you) alive together with Him" (συνεζωοποίησεν ὑμᾶς σὺν αὐτῷ, Aor. Act. Ind., 3s).

83. In Eph 2:6, "and (He) raised *us* up together" (καὶ συνήγειρεν; Aor. Act. Ind., 3s); Col 2:12, "you also were raised with *Him* through faith in the working of God, who raised Him from the dead" (καὶ συνηγέρθητε διὰ τῆς πίστεως τῆς ἐνεργείας τοῦ θεοῦ τοῦ ἐγείραντος αὐτὸν ἐκ νεκρῶν; Aor. Pass. Ind., 2p); Col 3:1, "If then you were raised with Christ, seek those things which are above, where Christ is, sitting at the right hand of God" (Εἰ οὖν συνηγέρθητε [Aor. Pass. Ind., 2p] τῷ Χριστῷ, τὰ ἄνω ζητεῖτε, οὗ ὁ Χριστός ἐστιν ἐν δεξιᾷ τοῦ θεοῦ καθήμενος).

84. In Eph 2:6, "(He) made *us* sit together in the heavenly *places* in Christ Jesus" (συνεκάθισεν ἐν τοῖς ἐπουρανίοις ἐν Χριστῷ Ἰησοῦ; Aor. Act. Ind., 3s).

85. In Col 3:3, "your life is hidden with Christ in God" (ἡ ζωὴ ὑμῶν κέκρυπται σὺν τῷ Χριστῷ ἐν τῷ θεῷ; Perf. Pass. Ind. 3s).

86. In 1 Cor 12:26, "And if one member suffers, all the members suffer with *it*" (καὶ εἴτε πάσχει ἓν μέλος, συμπάσχει [Pres. Act. Ind., 3s] πάντα τὰ μέλη); 2 Cor 6:1, "We then, *as* workers together *with Him* (Συνεργοῦντες; Pres. Act. Part., mas. nom. sing.) also plead with *you* not to receive the grace of God in vain;" Col 2:19, "the Head, from whom all the body, nourished and knit together (συμβιβαζόμενον; Pres. Pass. Part., neut. nom. sing.) by joints and ligaments, grows with the increase *that is* from God."

87. In Rom 8:17, "and if children, then heirs—heirs of God and joint heirs with Christ" (εἰ δὲ τέκνα, καὶ κληρονόμοι· κληρονόμοι μὲν θεοῦ, συγκληρονόμοι δὲ Χριστοῦ); Eph 3:6, "the Gentiles should be fellow heirs, of the same body, and partakers of His promise in Christ through the gospel" (εἶναι τὰ ἔθνη συγκληρονόμα καὶ σύσσωμα καὶ συμμέτοχα τῆς ἐπαγγελίας ἐν Χριστῷ Ἰησοῦ διὰ τοῦ εὐαγγελίου).

88. In Phil 3:10, "being conformed to His death" (συμμορφιζόμενος τῷ θανάτῳ αὐτοῦ; Pres. Pass. Part., mas. nom. sing.).

89. In Rom 8:17, "if indeed we suffer with *Him*" (εἴπερ συμπάσχομεν; Pres. Act. Ind., 1 p); 2 Tim 1:8, "share with me in the sufferings for the gospel according to the power of God" (συγκακοπάθησον τῷ εὐαγγελίῳ κατὰ δύναμιν θεοῦ; Aor. Act. Impv., 2s); 2 Tim 2:3, "You therefore must endure hardship as a good soldier of Jesus Christ" (Συγκακοπάθησον ὡς καλὸς στρατιώτης Χριστοῦ Ἰησοῦ; Aor. Act. Impv., 2s).

90. In Rom 6:8, "we believe that we shall also live with Him" (πιστεύομεν ὅτι καὶ συζήσομεν αὐτῷ; Fut. Act. Ind., 1p); 2 Cor 13:4, "we shall live with Him by the power of God toward you" (ζήσομεν σὺν αὐτῷ ἐκ δυνάμεως θεοῦ εἰς ὑμᾶς; Fut. Act. Ind., 1p); 1 Thess 5:10, "we should live together with Him" (σὺν αὐτῷ ζήσωμεν; Aor. Act. Subj., 1p); 2 Tim 2:11, "*This is* a faithful saying: For if we died with *Him,* We shall also live with *Him*" (πιστὸς ὁ λόγος· εἰ γὰρ συναπεθάνομεν, καὶ συζήσομεν; Fut. Act. Ind., 1p).

91. In Phil 1:23, "having a desire to depart and be with Christ" (τὴν ἐπιθυμίαν ἔχων εἰς τὸ ἀναλῦσαι καὶ σὺν Χριστῷ εἶναι); 1 Thess 4:17, "thus we shall always be with the Lord" (καὶ οὕτως πάντοτε σὺν κυρίῳ ἐσόμεθα).

92. In 2 Cor 4:14, "knowing that He who raised up the Lord Jesus will also raise us up with Jesus" (εἰδότες ὅτι ὁ ἐγείρας τὸν κύριον Ἰησοῦν καὶ ἡμᾶς σὺν Ἰησοῦ ἐγερεῖ; Fut. Act. Ind., 3s).

The "Man Christ Jesus" in Association with His People

shall appear with Him,[93] being brought with Him.[94] They shall be conformed with Christ[95] and glorified with Him[96] so that they shall reign with Him.[97] Finally, they shall be given all things with Christ.[98] This synthesis shows that the distinctiveness of this motif is the relational association the entire church shares with the historical Jesus in the events of salvation. Moo observes, "Paul claims that believers participate 'with Christ' in the whole gamut of redemptive events. . . . We must avoid a wooden literalism in explaining these passages. But they seem, at minimum, to imply a conception of Christ according to which believers are in God's sight included in the redemptive actions of Christ. What he does, they do."[99] So while the "in Christ" motif emphasizes the positional and dynamic aspects of salvation, the concept of being "with Christ" is distinguished by a historical perspective of the entire church being in association with the "Man Christ Jesus."[100]

Exegetical Analysis of the Narrative Sections Mentioning Association with Christ

The references of the "with Christ" motif appear in eight of the Pauline epistles in seventeen related paragraphical contexts. A brief analysis of each narrative unit in its canonical order shall show how the συ- concept is used.

ANALYSIS OF ROMANS 6:3–10[101]

This section (Rom 6:3–10) appears immediately after the comparison in Rom 5:12–21 between the two historical representatives of mankind, Adam and Christ. Humanity ei-

---

93. In Col 3:4, "When Christ *who is* our life appears, then you also will appear with Him in glory" (ὅταν ὁ Χριστὸς φανερωθῇ, ἡ ζωὴ ὑμῶν, τότε καὶ ὑμεῖς σὺν αὐτῷ φανερωθήσεσθε ἐν δόξῃ; Fut. Pass. Ind., 2p).

94. In 1 Thess 4:14, "God will bring with Him those who sleep in Jesus" (ὁ θεὸς τοὺς κοιμηθέντας διὰ τοῦ Ἰησοῦ ἄξει σὺν αὐτῷ; Fut. Act. Ind., 3s).

95. In Rom 8:29, "For whom He foreknew, He also predestined *to be* conformed to the image of His Son" (ὅτι οὓς προέγνω, καὶ προώρισεν συμμόρφους τῆς εἰκόνος τοῦ υἱοῦ αὐτοῦ); Phil 3:21, "who will transform our lowly body that it may be conformed to His glorious body" (ὃς μετασχηματίσει τὸ σῶμα τῆς ταπεινώσεως ἡμῶν σύμμορφον τῷ σώματι τῆς δόξης αὐτοῦ).

96. In Rom 8:17, "that we may also be glorified together" (ἵνα καὶ συνδοξασθῶμεν; Aor. Pass. Subj., 1p).

97. In 2 Tim 2:12, "If we endure, we shall also reign with *Him*" (εἰ ὑπομένομεν, καὶ συμβασιλεύσομεν; Fut. Act. Ind., 1p).

98. In Rom 8:32, "how shall He not with Him also freely give us all things" (πῶς οὐχὶ καὶ σὺν αὐτῷ τὰ πάντα ἡμῖν χαρίσεται; Fut. Mid. Ind., 3s).

99. Moo, "The Christology of the Early Pauline Epistles," 177.

100. Grundmann, σύν-μετά, *TDNT* 7:781, writes a very helpful and thorough article on these prepositions, but he ignores any historical connection of σὺν Χριστῷ by instead linking the phrase to the eschatological promises of the OT ("I will be with you," Jer 1:8) and to the practices of the Hellenistic mystery religions (ibid., 782, ftnt. 79). Grundmann's glaring omission is that neither the phrases σὺν θεῷ nor μετὰ θεοῦ appear in the LXX (While μετὰ τοῦ θεοῦ appears in 2 Chr 24:16, Ps 46:10 and Ps 78:8, it is obvious these verses have no connection with Paul's concept). While Yahweh promises to be "with you" (μετὰ σοῦ, Exod 3:12), the idea of believers being with God appears only three times, with regard to Enoch and Noah (Gen 5:22, 24; 6:9), and none of these passages use σύν at all. Grundmann, however, insists that the "primary reference (of the 'with Christ' motif) is to the eschatological being with Christ as eternal, non-terrestrial being." While many of the "with Christ" associations do relate to the heavenly Christ, Grundmann does not explain how one can be crucified and buried in death with a non-terrestrial being. Instead, Paul emphasizes that the heavenly Christ is the same as the earthly Jesus of history.

101. The author's literal translation of Rom 6:3–10 reads, "Or are you not knowing that as many as

ther lives or dies through[102] one man or the other, and those who receive the gift of grace though Christ reign though Him (Rom 5:21). The argument is interrupted at this point by rhetorical questions concerning the relationship of sin to grace (Rom 6:1–2), and Paul asks if his readers are ignorant of the fact that "as many of us who were baptized into Christ Jesus, into His death we were baptized?" It is appropriate to inquire into the origin of Paul's connection between the death of Jesus and baptism, especially since he chides his readers for not knowing its source, and in this regard Cullman points to "the only two sayings of Jesus which contain the verb βαπτισθῆναι, Mark 10:38 and Luke 12:50."[103] In this latter saying, Jesus announces, "But I have a baptism to undergo (βάπτισμα δὲ ἔχω βαπτισθῆναι), and how distressed I am until it is accomplished!" Add to this His question directed to His disciples James and John in Mark 10:38, "Are you able to drink the cup that I drink, or to be baptized with the baptism with which I am baptized?" (δύνασθε πιεῖν τὸ ποτήριον ὃ ἐγὼ πίνω ἢ τὸ βάπτισμα ὃ ἐγὼ βαπτίζομαι βαπτισθῆναι;). Surely both of these oblique comments refer to His impending death, as indicated in the Markan context when he uses this subject to illustrate His dominical saying, "For even the Son of Man did not come to be served, but to serve, and to give His life a ransom for many" (Mark 10:45). This saying has already been established as lying behind the Christ-Creed of 1 Tim 2:5–6, so it seems reasonable that Paul had contemplated how the disciples could be included in the baptizing-death of Jesus. James and John obviously did not physically die with Him on the cross, so there must be a typological significance in baptism as pointing toward the death with Christ not just for those two disciples but for all believers, just as Paul teaches in Rom 6:3, "Do you not know that *all of us* who have been baptized into Christ Jesus have been baptized into His death?"[104]

This mention of baptism introduces a new concept in this epistle, for what does it mean to be baptized into the death of Christ? The answer unfolds in the following narrative, introduced by the first of five association concepts: the first is, "we were buried with Him" (συνετάφημεν αὐτῷ), stated as a completed action in which the preposition σύν is supplied from the compound verb συνθάπτω[105] and associates the church with the historical entombment of Jesus (Matt 27:59–60). This association with Christ's burial "through the baptism unto the death" has a purpose: "that just as Christ was raised out of

---

were baptized into Christ Jesus, into His death were baptized? (4) Therefore we were buried with Him (συνετάφημεν οὖν αὐτῷ) through the baptism into the death, in order just as Christ was raised out of dead (ones) through the glory of the Father, thus also we (ourselves) in newness of life should be walking. (5) For if we have become planted with *Him* (σύμφυτοι γεγόναμεν) in the likeness of His death, but also we shall be also *in the likeness* of the resurrection, (6) knowing this, that our old man was crucified with *Him* (συνεσταυρώθη), that the body of the sin might be nullified, that we should no longer be serving the sin; (7) for the one having died has been justified from the sin. (8) But if we died with Christ (εἰ δὲ ἀπεθάνομεν σὺν Χριστῷ), we are believing that also we shall live with Him (συζήσομεν αὐτῷ), (9) knowing that Christ, having been raised out of dead (ones), no longer is dying: death of Him is no longer ruling, (10), for that which He died, to the sin He died once-for-all-time; but that which He is living, He is living to God."

102. Διά is the predominant preposition in this context, appearing twelve times.

103. Cullmann, *Christology of the New Testament*, 67.

104. See also Robinson, "The One Baptism as a Category of New Testament Soteriology," 158–76.

105. BDAG § 7100, "συνθάπτω, bury *(together) with.*"

dead (ones) through the glory of the Father, thus also we ourselves (emphasized by the pronoun, ἡμεῖς) in newness of life should be walking" (author's translation of Rom 6:4). This verse explains who did the burying—the Father, who also did the raising, and how the past events of co-burial results in the present experience of newness.

Romans 6:5 uses the second term of association as Paul changes the image from burying to planting in the next conditional sentence, "if we have been planted with the likeness of His death." The adjective σύμφυτοι is a ηαπαξ λεγομενον in the NT (although it does appear in the LXX in Amos 9:13; Zech 11:2; 3 Macc 3:22), but it is formed by coupling σύν with the common verb φυτεύω, "to plant" (1 Cor 3:6–8),[106] thus meaning to be "planted with" something, or in this case, with someone. It is an unexpected use of this word, since one does not usually think of the burial of the dead as a planting (nor of planting a person with seeds), but Paul uses it to emphasize the emergence of new life, as given in the apodosis, "but also we shall be of the resurrection." It is also quite possible that Paul echoes here the saying of Jesus in John 12:24 of the wheat dying in the earth to bring forth much fruit. The similarity is too striking to be merely coincidental.[107]

This illustration of planting follows in verse 6 with another fact Paul assumes his readers knows, "that our old man was crucified with," providing the third association compound word, συνεσταυρώθη, and the immediate questions arise: what is this communal old man and with whom was he crucified, since an object of this verb is not identified? The last reference to ἄνθρωπος appears in Rom 5:19, the "one man" Adam, although the reference in Rom 6:6 appears to be more experiential than imputational, as the sentence concludes, "in order that the body of sin should be nullified, that we (should) no longer be serving the sin, for the one having died has been justified from the sin" (author's translation). For this nullification to happen, there must be association with a crucifixion, and that concept seems to appear from nowhere, for there is no hint of crucifixion anywhere else in this entire letter. But then, Paul has previously mentioned the historical death of Christ several times (Rom 5:10; 6:3, 4, 5), and he assumes that his readers knew what the Gospels report, that "the chief priests and our rulers delivered (Jesus) up to the sentence of death, and crucified Him" (Luke 24:20); thus, the assumed referent of συνεσταυρώθη must be Christ (as Paul states in Gal 2:20, "I have been crucified with Christ," Χριστῷ συνεσταύρωμαι). The passive voice of συνεσταυρώθη indicates this crucifying must be performed by another (it is impossible to crucify oneself), and again, the implied subject of this verb is God, who associated His own people with Christ in His crucifixion, in order that the church should no longer serve sin but receive justification (Rom 6:7).

The fourth and fifth association terms follow from this fact of co-crucifixion in another first-class conditional sentence, "If we died with Christ (ἀπεθάνομεν σὺν Χριστῷ), we believe that also we shall live with Him (συζήσομεν αὐτῷ), knowing that Christ having been raised out of dead (ones) is no longer dying: death is no longer lording of Him." Here, Paul refers to two historical events that makes future living for His people a certainty; first is Christ's death and secondly is His resurrection from death, which they

---

106. BDAG § 7853, "φυτεύω, to *plant*."
107. See Appendix 3, "Similarities Between the Johannine and Pauline Literature."

THE "MAN CHRIST JESUS"

have learned means He will never die again. Because believers have been associated with Christ's death (and, implied, in His resurrection), they shall also live with Him in all that His future living entails. Thus, in the entire context of Rom 6:3-9, the emphasis is not on union *in* Christ (ἐν Χριστῷ), a phrase that does not appear until Rom 6:11, but rather it is on association *with* the "Man Christ Jesus" in His historical crucifixion, death, burial, resurrection, and living. This emphasis is accomplished by use of these five words related by the preposition σύν (συνετάφημεν, σύμφυτοι; συνεσταυρώθη; ἀπεθάνομεν σὺν Χριστῷ; συζήσομεν αὐτῷ).

ANALYSIS OF ROMANS 8:16-17[108]

Immediately meeting the eye of the reader in Rom 8:16-17 is Paul's use of four συ-compound words that flow out of the discussion of the Spirit's ministry (Rom 8:12-16), which is described in Rom 8:16 as being His associative witness (συμμαρτυρεῖ) with the spirit of believers assuring that "we are children of God." This adoption as God's children initiates a conditional sentence, assumed to be true: "If (we are) children, (then) also heirs—indeed, heirs of God, and fellow-heirs of Christ," since those in association with Him receive a joint inheritance (συγκληρονόμοι).[109] The fact of this co-inheritance produces another conditional sentence, introduced by εἴπερ, an "emphatic marker of condition,"[110] "if indeed we are suffering with (συμπάσχομεν[111]) that also we should be glorified with (συνδοξασθῶμεν)."[112] The reader must supply an object for each of these verbs, asking if Paul means that believers suffer and shall be glorified with one another, affiliations he teaches elsewhere (1 Cor 12:26; 2 Cor 3:18). In the context of Rom 8:16, however, the object of these verbs is Christ, provided from the earlier phrase, "fellow-heirs of Christ." Supplying "Christ" means that Paul shows what kind of inheritance believers receive in their association with Him—it is His present suffering (a concept Paul mentions in Col 1:24) with an anticipated future glorification with Him (a concept to be mentioned next in Rom 8:30). Paul seems to echo here a question Jesus posed to His disciples, "Was it not necessary for the Christ to suffer (παθεῖν) these things and to enter into His glory?" (εἰσελθεῖν εἰς τὴν δόξαν αὐτοῦ, Luke 24:26). Now Paul takes these same historical realities experienced initially by Christ (His sufferings and His ascension as entrance into His glory) and places the church in association with Christ in His present sufferings and in anticipation of His future glorification with the inheritance His co-heirs shall share with the "Man Christ Jesus."

---

108. The author's literal translation of Rom 8:16-17 reads, "The Spirit Himself is witnessing with (συμμαρτυρεῖ) our spirit that we are children of God, (17) and if children, heirs also, heirs indeed of God, fellow-heirs with Christ (συγκληρονόμοι δὲ Χριστοῦ), if indeed we are suffering with *Him* (συμπάσχομεν) in order that also we may be glorified with *Him*" (συνδοξασθῶμεν).

109. BDAG § 6900, συγκληρονόμος, "inheriting together with."

110. LN §89.66.

111. BDAG § 6972.1, συμπάσχω, "to have the same thing happen to one, *suffer with*."

112. BDAG § 7046.2, συνδοξάζω, "to honor together with, pass. *be glorified with someone, share in someone's glory*."

Analysis of Romans 8:28–32[113]

In the preceding context of Rom 8:28–32, Paul has reminded his readers of that which they already know concerning their salvation (Rom 8:22, 26),[114] and he introduces this next section (Rom 8:28–32) with additional facts "we are knowing" concerning various concepts of association: first, that all things are working with (συνεργεῖ) the ones loving God unto good, and the early manuscript 𝔓46 supplies "God" (ὁ θεός) as the agent who is doing this working.[115] Even if this aforementioned reading ὁ θεός is not part of the original letter to the Romans, it is certainly Pauline to assume that God is the agent of association, particularly since He is clearly the implied subject of the following verbs, including the next association compound, "whom He foreknew, He also predestined (to be) *conformed with*[116] the image of Christ" (Rom 8:29). The genitive after a συ- compound word (συμμόρφους τῆς εἰκόνος) is unusual, but since this phrase expresses an associative relationship, it is appropriate to include it in the association motif.[117] Secondly, after outlining the progression of divine actions on behalf of believers, Paul asks the rhetorical question, "If God is for us, who (is) against us?" (Rom 8:31). He answers his own question in Rom 8:32 with a third associative concept found in this section: since God delivered His Son for us (which He did, according to Rom 4:25), how shall He not grant to us all things *with Him*? While God has already given to Jesus the Name above every name (Phil 2:9),[118] the final demonstration of His honor awaits the time when every knee bows to Him and confesses Him as Lord (Phil 2:10–11), at which time Rom 8:32 pictures the entire church standing alongside Jesus "with Him" (σὺν αὐτῷ) when He is designated as "heir of all things" (Heb 1:2). Although that accolade is still future, the emphases in association are upon events that happen to the "Man Christ Jesus" in His incarnational state with which believers share—with final inheritance being the capstone of those events.

---

113. The author's translation of Rom 8:28–32 reads, "But we are knowing that to the ones loving God all-things are working-together (συνεργεῖ) unto good, to the ones being called according to purpose; (29) because whom He foreknew, He also predestined *to become* conformed with (συμμόρφους) the image of His Son, that He might be first-born in many brethren; and whom He predestined, these also He called; and whom He called, these also He justified; and whom He justified, these also He glorified. What therefore shall we say to these things? If God *is* for us, who *is* against us? He who did not spare His own Son, but delivered Him up concerning us all, how shall He not also with Him (σὺν αὐτῷ) freely give us all things?"

114. When Paul reminds his readers of previous knowledge they share in common, he may refer to that which he had formerly taught them, but that reminder does not apply in the Epistle to the Romans, since he had not yet visited these believers in Rome to teach them personally. What they know, then, may refer to their knowledge of OT Scripture, but more likely Paul has in mind knowledge of the "form of doctrine" that also contained various sayings of Jesus (Rom 6:17).

115. See Metzger, *TCNT*, 458.

116. LN § 58.5 defines σύμμορφος: "pertaining to that which has a similar form or nature—'similar in form, of the same form.'" The word is found elsewhere only at Phil 3:21, "the Lord Jesus Christ . . . will transform the body of our humble state into *conformity* with the body of His glory."

117. BDF § 161.

118. The same verb, χαρίζομαι, which BDAG § 7893 defines as "to give graciously," is used both here in Rom 8:32, "He . . . also with Him shall freely give (χαρίσεται) us all things," and in Phil 2:9, "God . . . bestowed (ἐχαρίσατο) on Him the name which is above every name."

THE "MAN CHRIST JESUS"

ANALYSIS OF 2 CORINTHIANS 4:14[119]

2 Corinthians 4:14 ("knowing that He who raised the Lord Jesus will raise us also with Jesus and will present us with you") appears in a context where Paul discusses his ministry in relationship to his readers in terms of the living and dying of Jesus being revealed in the physical body at the present moment (2 Cor 4:8–12). This association among believers is linked by the "same spirit of faith" in what is written and spoken (2 Cor 4:13),[120] and it is once again based on objective knowledge (εἰδότες is also used in the association discussions found in Rom 6:9 and Rom 8:28) of historical realities learned from previous catechizing, that the One (the Father) who raised up the Lord Jesus (Rom 8:11) also shall raise believers in an association with Jesus (σὺν Ἰησου) and also in a presentation with others (σὺν ὑμῖν). These two prepositional phrases emphasize that this relationship displaying God's people as sharing with one another in the final eschatological presentation (found also at Eph 5:27 and Col 1:22) depends upon their association with Jesus at that future resurrection. Even though the perspective of this raising is future, it is a historical connection with the "Man Christ Jesus" in His resurrection that certifies the final association.

ANALYSIS OF 2 CORINTHIANS 6:1

Following on the heels of the great passage on the reconciling ministry of Christ in the flesh (2 Cor 5:16–21), Paul draws a present application in 2 Cor 6:1, "And working together with (συνεργοῦντες), we also urge you not to receive the grace of God in vain" (author's translation). Paul again omits an object of the present plural participle, συνεργοῦντες, "to engage in an activity together with someone else,"[121] meaning he could refer to one of the many fellow-workers (συνεργοί) with whom Paul had ministered, such as Titus and Timothy.[122] But the apostle has just stated that "God encourages through us" (2 Cor 5:20), showing divine participation in the ministry, as he does also in 1 Cor 3:9, "For we are fellow workers of God" (θεοῦ γάρ ἐσμεν συνεργοί). Also, since the closest referent is αὐτῷ found in the previous verse ("that we might become the righteousness of God in Him," 2 Cor 5:21), referring to Christ, this fact qualifies Him as the object of συνεργοῦντες, providing yet another aspect of association with Christ. As Jesus worked the works of God during His ministry (John 5:17), so now His messengers work with the "Man Christ Jesus" by encouraging others to receive the grace of God.

---

119. The author's translation of 2 Cor 4:14 reads. "Knowing that the One having raised the Lord Jesus also shall raise us with Jesus (σὺν Ἰησοῦ) and shall present (us) with you (σὺν ὑμῖν)." This is the only instance of the particular structure σὺν Ἰησοῦ in the NT, although Acts 4:13 is similar ("they began to recognize them as having been with Jesus" [ὅτι σὺν τῷ Ἰησοῦ ἦσαν]). It is possible that Paul used the personal name of Jesus rather than the title "Christ" due to the more intimate tone of this context, but this is mere conjecture.

120. This phrase, "the same spirit of faith," is unique in the Bible, and it is unclear if Paul refers to a faithful spirit he shares with the Corinthians, or to "the promise of the Spirit through faith" (Gal 3:14). The context indicates that Paul refers to the Holy Spirit, since he quotes from "what is written" in the Spirit-inspired text of the OT, and because he earlier refers to believers as "being written not with ink, but with the Spirit of the living God" (2 Cor 3:3).

121. LN §42.15.

122. Paul mentions co-workers in Rom 16:3, 9, 21; 2 Cor 1:24; 8:23; Phil 2:25; 4:3; Col 4:11; 1 Thess 3:2; Phlm 1:1, 24.

Analysis of 2 Corinthians 7:3

In the context of 2 Cor 7:3, Paul lays out an emotional appeal in an effort to gain back the confidence of his Corinthian converts. He pleads, "Make room for us *in your hearts*; we wronged no one, we corrupted no one, we took advantage of no one" (2 Cor 7:2); then he adds this verse of consideration: "I do not speak to condemn you; for I have said before that you are in our hearts to die together and to live together" (2 Cor 7:3). Unquestionably, Paul uses the language of association (εἰς τὸ συναποθανεῖν καὶ συζῆν), and the apparent reference is to an association Paul desires with his readers, to die and live together with them. But pushing beyond the emotional sentiment, one must ask if Paul actually expected to die together and to live together with the Corinthians? And why does he place these experiences out of natural order, of dying first and then living next? Furthermore, we have already observed how Paul habitually uses terminology of association with Christ but omits Him as the direct object of the verb (Rom 8:17): is it possible he does the same here?

That seems to be the case, for when viewed in the sequence of the history of redemption, 2 Cor 7:3 places dying and living in the correct order: Jesus first died on the cross and then He lived in His resurrection—and the same is true of believers, as outlined in Rom 8:13, "if by the Spirit you are (first) putting to death the deeds of the body, (then) you will live." Furthermore, how else would all believers die and live together except by common association with the "Man Christ Jesus" in the acts which Paul applies to the entire church in 2 Tim 2:11, "If we died with *Him*, we shall also live with *Him*"? Once again, then, Paul apparently uses association of the church with this historical events of the death and resurrection of Jesus in order to express his own heart's desire to die and live with his readers in Corinth.

Analysis of 2 Corinthians 13:4

In 2 Cor 13:4, Paul remarks, "For indeed He was crucified out of weakness, but (instead) He lives out of the power of God, for also we ourselves are being weak in Him, but (rather) we shall live with Him (σὺν αὐτῷ) out of the power of God toward you" (author's translation). This statement appears in a context where Paul defends his Apostolic credentials (2 Cor 13:1–3), not by boasting in his strengths but by appealing to his weaknesses (2 Cor 11:29; 12:10). In 2 Cor 13:4a, he patterns his own weakness to the historical example of Jesus when He was crucified out of weakness—an allusion to the physical abuse suffered by Jesus in His scourging and crucifixion—but now He is living out of the power of God (ἐκ δυνάμεως θεου), a reference to His miraculous resurrection from the dead in another event enacted within human history. Based on the historical realities of Jesus' weakness at His crucifixion and His living now in resurrection power, Paul makes a chiastic application of weakness/power toward believers, a structure clearly evident in an analysis of 2 Cor 13:4.[123] In this rare instance where both motifs of union in Christ and association

---

123. Note the linguistic parallels in 2 Cor 13:4:

καὶ γὰρ	ἡμεῖς	ἀσθενοῦμεν	ἐν αὐτῷ	
ἀλλὰ		ζήσομεν	σὺν αὐτῷ	ἐκ δυνάμεως θεοῦ εἰς ὑμᾶς.

with Christ appear in the same verse (ἐν αὐτῷ... σὺν αὐτῷ),[124] the former shows a present dynamic experience currently being shared by His people ("we are being weak in Him"), but the second anticipates what shall happen in the future association when "we shall live with Him" by virtue of the power of God. Because Paul refers to the resurrection of Jesus earlier in the verse, he undoubtedly has in mind the final resurrection as a future event to be enacted at the end of human history when those "in Him" in their present regenerational experience shall live "with Him" in their future living with the "Man Christ Jesus."

ANALYSIS OF GALATIANS 2:20

In Galatians 2, Paul discusses the proper means of justification, whether it is through works of Law or through faith of Christ (Gal 2:15–19), and he personalizes his own experience as having died to Law in order to live to God (Gal 2:19). This death occurred in association with Christ, as he reports, "with Christ I have been crucified" (Χριστῷ συνεσταύρωμαι). Paul uses the same compound verb in his parallel discussion in Rom 6:6 (ὁ παλαιὸς ἡμῶν ἄνθρωπος συνεσταυρώθη), and in both instances, the verb is defined by the historical event of salvation, notably Christ's crucifixion. Had there been no actual crucifixion, Paul could not have stated, "with Christ I have been crucified," yet in that event he finds his own co-crucifixion with Christ—although he certainly was not nailed with Jesus on the cross of Calvary. Instead, this perception involved some incisive thinking on Paul's part, for he identifies himself with the thieves who actually were crucified with Jesus; in fact, Paul uses nearly identical vocabulary as found in Matt 27:38, "At that time two robbers were crucified with Him (σταυροῦνται σὺν αὐτῷ), one on the right and one on the left." Is this similarity merely coincidental, or does Paul intentionally evoke a particular memory of the repentant thief to whom the Lord promised, "Truly I say to you, today you shall be *with Me* in Paradise" (Luke 23:43)? Since the verb συσταυρόω is used in the NT only of co-crucifixion with Christ,[125] it is a reasonable connection to make, for what is clear is that Paul considers himself as being crucified with Christ—as if he himself was the penitent thief. Flowing out of this historical association with Christ comes the dynamic relationship of Christ "living in me," indicating that the existential experience of union in Christ rests upon the prior association with Christ. Furthermore, both aspects rest on the former "faith(fulness) of the Son of God" (previously argued as a subjective genitive, as also used in Gal 2:16, πίστεως Ἰησοῦ Χριστοῦ), by which He loved Paul and delivered Himself for Him (and "for us all," Rom 8:32). Thus, the historical crucifixion of

---

124. Of the 162 verses in which Paul mentions the "in Christ" motif, only four times do the references intersect with the "with Christ" concept, here in 2 Cor 13:4; in Eph 2:6 ("raised us up with Him, and seated us with Him in the heavenly places, in Christ Jesus"); Eph 3:6 ("the Gentiles are fellow heirs and fellow members of the body, and fellow partakers of the promise in Christ Jesus through the gospel"); and Col 2:12–13, "in Him you were also circumcised with a circumcision made without hands, in the removal of the body of the flesh by the circumcision of Christ, having been buried with Him in baptism, in which you were also raised up with Him through faith in the working of God." This rarity lends support to the argument that the phrases "in Christ" and "with Christ" portray distinct themes.

125. Besides Gal 2:20, Rom 6:6 and Matt 27:38, the verb συσταυρόω appears only elsewhere in Mark 15:32, "And those who were crucified with Him (οἱ συνεσταυρωμένοι σὺν αὐτῷ) were casting the same insult at Him;" and in John 19:32, "The soldiers therefore came, and broke the legs of the first man, and of the other man who was crucified with Him" (τοῦ ἄλλου τοῦ συσταυρωθέντος αὐτῷ).

Christ is foundational to the entire scope of salvation. It is the basis of Paul's deliverance by Christ (via the forensic aspect of redemption), of his association with Christ, and of his union in Christ. None of these could be spiritual realities unless there had first been a historical crucifixion of the "Man Christ Jesus" with whom Paul considers himself to have been crucified.

ANALYSIS OF EPHESIANS 2:4–6[126]

The context of Eph 2:4–6 contrasts the unredeemed, unregenerate life (Eph 2:1–3) with God's loving acts of salvation to "us in Christ Jesus," as Paul presumes his readers' union ἐν Χριστῷ Ἰησοῦ (Eph 2:6). To explain this union, Paul uses three συ-compound verbs in succession to show how new life comes by divine action, with God as the implied subject of these verbs; first, "He made (us) alive with the Christ," referring to the vivification of Jesus (as the Father gives life [ζῳοποιεῖ] to the dead, John 5:21); then, "He raised (us) with and seated (us) with," where the object of both verbs must be supplied from the previous dative, τῷ Χριστῷ, referring to Christ. In each of these three colons, Paul refers to historical realities that happened to Christ: God made Him alive, raised Him from the dead and seated Him in the events of His resurrection, ascension, and heavenly session.[127] Yet Paul views believers as having been associated with these acts, apparently at the same time (the verbs in question are aorist, indicating completed action). To be sure, this association has become actual in the experience of the regenerate who have been "saved by grace," but it is important to distinguish between the dynamic union in Christ from the historical association with Christ. Both realities stem from the mercy and grace of God, but the believers' union in Christ depends on the prior association with Christ with the historical certainties effected by "the "Man Christ Jesus."

ANALYSIS OF PHILIPPIANS 1:21–24[128]

In the joyous letter to the Philippians, Paul queries his own situation in Phil 1:21–24, and, by use of graphic infinitives ("to be living, to die, to depart"), he wonders whether it is best to live in the flesh or to depart and "be with Christ" (σὺν χριστῷ εἶναι), which is the best of all alternatives. While Phil 1:23 is (correctly) used to show what happens to the believer at the moment of death, the immediate desire of Paul is the associative relationship he hopes to experience with Christ after his death. In this expectancy, he echoes the prayer of Jesus, "Father, I desire that they also, whom Thou hast given Me, be with Me (μετ' ἐμοῦ)

---

126. The author's translation of Eph 2:4–6 reads, "But God, being rich in mercy, because of His great love with which He loved us, even when we (were) being dead in transgressions, He made (us) alive together with Christ (συνεζωοποίησεν τῷ Χριστῷ) (by grace you have been saved), and raised up with *Him* (συνήγειρεν), and seated us with (συνεκάθισεν) *Him* in the heavenly *places*, in Christ Jesus. . . ."

127. Beker, *The Triumph of God: the Essence of Paul's Thought*, 169, insists that the co-resurrection image is not to be taken literally, since he thinks that the historical resurrection in Paul's estimation was not physical anyway (ibid., 170). Beker's understanding of apocalyptic life apparently does not necessitate corporeality, but what is resurrection if not the raising of physical bodies?

128. The author's translation of Phil 1:21–24 reads, "For to me, to live is Christ, and to die is gain. But if *I am* to live *on* in the flesh, this to me *will mean* fruit of work, and what I shall choose I am not knowing. But I am hard-pressed out of the two, having the desire to depart and to be with Christ (σὺν Χριστῷ), for *that* is very much better; yet to be remaining in the flesh is more necessary for your sake."

THE "MAN CHRIST JESUS"

where I am" (John 17:24). While the preposition differs, the concept is certainly the same: the final hope of the believer is to be in association with the "Man Christ Jesus."

ANALYSIS OF PHILIPPIANS 3:8–11[129]

Based on the righteousness of faith (Phil 3:8–9), Paul aspires to know Christ experientially in two areas: the power of His resurrection and the fellowship of His suffering. He gives here the order of regeneration (being united to the risen Christ) leading to sanctification ("filling up that which is lacking in Christ's afflictions," Col 1:24), but he places these effects of salvation in a sequence reversed from historical actuality, "that the Christ should suffer and rise again from the dead the third day" (Luke 24:46). As a result of those events, Paul explains what he expects to happen, that he would find himself "being conformed with His death" (Phil 3:10).[130] The present tense compound participle συμμορφιζόμενος expresses a profound dynamic experience, presumably effected by God Himself, as implied in the passive voice (Paul is not conforming himself to Christ's death, but he is being conformed to it by Another). This "*sunmorphisizing*" is likewise mentioned in Phil 3:21 and Rom 8:29 as another effect of salvation,[131] showing that the divine imputation of association with the person of Christ is transformational. Even so, it again must not be overlooked that Paul assumes here another historical reality, the death of Jesus. Thus, while the experience described here is dynamic, it could not be actually experienced apart from the historical suffering, death, and resurrection of Jesus. In his aspiration to know Christ, Paul bases his knowledge in the context of history, that Jesus was raised from the dead, but before that event He suffered and died. If these incidents did not happen to the "Man Christ Jesus," Paul's comments make no sense, but because they did occur in the scheme of human history, then Paul's desire to know Christ can become an experiential reality.

ANALYSIS OF PHILIPPIANS 3:20–21[132]

In contrast to those who mind earthly things (Phil 3:19), Paul reminds his readers in Philippi of their citizenship in heaven, out of which believers await a specific Savior, identified as the "Lord Jesus Christ." His future work shall be "to cause a change in the form of something,"[133] which in this case is what Paul identifies as "the body of our humility" (Phil 3:21). Without the use of another verb (although implying εἶναι), Paul shows this change

---

129. The author's translation of Phil 3:8d–11 reads, ". . . that I may gain Christ, and may be found in Him, not having my own righteousness that out of law But that through faith of Christ, the out-of-God righteousness upon the faith, that I may know Him, and the power of His resurrection and the fellowship of His sufferings, being conformed to His death (συμμορφιζόμενος τῷ θανάτῳ αὐτοῦ); if somehow I may attain unto the resurrection the one out of dead (ones)."

130. BDAG § 6960, defines συμμορφίζω, "to cause to be similar in form or style to someth. else."

131. See Phil 3:21, "The Lord Jesus Christ . . . will transform the body of our humble state into conformity (σύμμορφον) with the body of His glory;" Rom 8:29, "For whom He foreknew, He also predestined *to become* conformed (συμμόρφους) to the image of His Son."

132. The author's translation of Phil 3:20–21 reads, "For our citizenship exists in heaven, from which also we are eagerly waiting a Savior, Lord Jesus Christ, who shall transform the body of our humiliation (to) conformity (σύμμορφον) with the body of His glory, according to the energy of His ability even to subject to Himself all things."

133. LN § 58.18.

shall be the "with-form" (σύμμορφον, or "same-form;"[134] the identical word is used in Rom 8:29) as that of the body of Christ's glory. Again, it ought to be noted that Paul assumes here the physical resurrection of Christ occurring within history; otherwise, his analogy with the believer's body as being changed and conformed to Christ's body is absurd at the least. Once more, it is the believer's association with the "Man Christ Jesus" in His historical realities that shall bring actual transformation, this time in the physical body.

ANALYSIS OF COLOSSIANS 2:11–13[135]

In a pericope parallel to Rom 6:3–10 and Eph 2:4–6 (discussed above), Col 2:11–13 uses three aorist συ-compound verbs, as Paul mingles regenerative ideas (circumcised without hands) with associative concepts related to the history of Jesus. The OT had already taught that heart-circumcision was the reality behind physical circumcision (Deut 10:16; 30:6; Jer 4:4),[136] a point Paul argues in Rom 2:29 when he defines a Jew as one "who is one inwardly; and circumcision is that which is of the heart, by the Spirit," describing circumcision as a "sign and seal of righteousness" (Rom 4:11). Now he tells the Colossians that they have received this inward circumcision "in the circumcision of the Christ," and while it is common to understand this phrase as referring to some sort of spiritual operation performed by the heavenly Christ, the reference is clearly historical. Paul has in mind the circumcision required by the Abrahamic Covenant (Gen 17:12) dutifully practiced by the parents of Jesus when they also conferred upon their eight day old son the name given by the angel before He was conceived in the womb (Luke 2:21). In that ritual of circumcision, the Mediator of the New Covenant endured the symbolic "cutting-off" from the covenant that He would actually suffer when He, as God's Servant, was "cut off out of the land of the living for the transgression of my people to whom that stroke was due" (Isa 53:8). Now Paul explains here in Col 2:11 that it is this "circumcision of the Christ" that brings heart circumcision to all those who are "in Christ." It should not be overlooked that this argument would carry no weight if Jesus had not been physically circumcised: the spiritual application rests on the historical event.

Furthermore, Paul explains how the circumcision of Christ became effective by means of an attending aorist passive participial phrase, "having been buried with Him in baptism" (συνταφέντες αὐτῷ ἐν τῷ βαπτισμῷ). The importance of this statement for historical theology is momentous, because Paul implies that the circumcision required by the Old Covenant has now been replaced in the New Covenant by a more convenient and

---

134. LN § 58.5.

135. The author's translation of Col 2:11–13 reads, " . . . in Him also you were circumcised with a circumcision made without hands, in the removal of the body of the flesh by the circumcision of the Christ, having been buried with Him (συνταφέντες αὐτῷ) in the baptism, in which also you were raised up with *Him* (συνηγέρθητε) through the faith of the energy of the God the one having raised Him out of dead (ones). And you being dead in the transgressions and the uncircumcision of your flesh, He made you alive together with *Him* (συνεζωοποίησεν ὑμᾶς σὺν αὐτῷ), having forgiven us all the transgressions. . . .'"

136. "Circumcise then your heart, and stiffen your neck no more" (Deut 10:16); "Moreover the LORD your God will circumcise your heart and the heart of your descendants, to love the LORD your God with all your heart and with all your soul, in order that you may live" (Deut 30:6); "Circumcise yourselves to the LORD and remove the foreskins of your heart" (Jer 4:4).

THE "MAN CHRIST JESUS"

universal sign: the circumcising knife has been swallowed up by the baptismal water. Yet the appearance of the associative plural compound verb συνταφέντες signals that Paul is not referring primarily to the individual believer's experience of baptism; rather, he refers to the divine perception that all who are in Christ have been associated with Christ in two other historical episodes—His baptism and His burial, for if these events did not occur to Jesus, Paul's application to regeneration cannot be valid. Instead, Jesus explained His own baptism as necessary "to fulfill all righteousness" (Matt 3:15). In giving this reason for John to baptize Him, Jesus anticipated how He would bring righteousness by fulfilling its demands, suffering the cutting-off curse of the deluge (Gen 9:11) when He expired His last breath of life and died (Gen 7:22; Mark 15:37). The reality of Jesus' death was confirmed in the other episode mentioned by Paul, when the body of Jesus was laid in the tomb of Joseph of Arimathea (Luke 23:53), yet Paul pictures the entire church as being entombed with Jesus in His burial.

The church did not remain in that deadly place or morbid state, as Paul continues, "in whom (Christ) you were also raised with" (ἐν ᾧ καὶ συνηγέρθητε, Col 2:12b). Again, the object of this compound verb is implied from the previous reference to αὐτῷ, so that all "in Christ" are viewed as having been resurrected with Christ by "the energy of God, the one having raised Him out of dead (ones)" (Col 2:12c). While Paul's now-believing readers once lay "dead in transgression and the uncircumcision of your flesh" (Col 2:13a), God made them alive with Christ (συνεζωοποίησεν ὑμᾶς σὺν αὐτῷ) by associating them with Him in the historical moment when Jesus also came back to life. The repetition of the preposition (συν εζωοποίησεν ... σὺν αὐτῷ) seems redundant, but Paul apparently repeats σύν to emphasize the associative element of the church with Christ in each aspect of His burial, resuscitation, and resurrection. While the effecting of this association comes "through faith," the reality of the believers forgiveness of all transgressions depends upon the association of those "in Christ" with the past historical events of the burial, vivification, and resurrection of the "Man Christ Jesus."

Analysis of Colossians 2:20

In the context of Col 2:20, Paul asks his readers why they would compromise with legalism (Col 2:16)[137] and be defrauded by religious deception (Col 2:18);[138] then he supplies the answer on the basis of an associative reality, "If you have died with Christ (ἀπεθάνετε σὺν Χριστῷ) to the elementary principles of the world, why, as if you were living in the world, do you submit yourself to decrees, 'Do not handle, do not taste, do not touch!'" The verb ἀπεθάνετε appears as the protasis of the first-class conditional clause (Εἰ ἀπεθάνετε σὺν Χριστῷ), assuming the statement to be true not merely for the sake of argument,[139] but as a christological reality: Paul considers believers to have actually died (not physically but

---

137. Colossians 2:16 reads, "Therefore let no one act as your judge in regard to food or drink or in respect to a festival or a new moon or a Sabbath day."

138. Colossians 2:18 warns, "Let no one keep defrauding you of your prize by delighting in self-abasement and the worship of the angels, taking his stand on *visions* he has seen, inflated without cause by his fleshly mind."

139. Wallace, *Greek Grammar*, 690.

The "Man Christ Jesus" in Association with His People

declaratively) with Christ in the event of His death. Furthermore, Paul uses terminology very similar to the boast of Peter made just before Jesus' arrest, "Even if I have to die with You (σὺν σοὶ ἀποθανεῖν), I will not deny You" (Matt 26:35), raising the possibility that Peter informed Paul of his bravado. As it turns out, Peter—along with the entire church—did die in association with Christ's death, a teaching Paul mentions a few verses later in Col 3:3 (ἀπεθάνετε γὰρ), and also in Rom 6:8 (εἰ δὲ ἀπεθάνομεν σὺν Χριστῷ) and 2 Tim 2:11 (γὰρ συναπεθάνομεν). In Col 2:20-23, whatever spiritual reality Paul conveys by association with Christ's death not only influences Christian conduct (Col 2:20-23), but it also assumes the historical reality of the death of the "Man Christ Jesus," with whose death Paul's believing readers are associated.

ANALYSIS OF COLOSSIANS 3:1-4[140]

In the pericope of Col 3:1-4, Paul clusters three association ideas, the first dealing with the association of believers with the past reality of the resurrection of the Christ, "if you were raised with Christ" (the same compound verb συνεγείρω appears earlier in Col 2:12 and in Eph 2:6). This co-raising being the case (presumed to be so by the first-class conditional sentence), believers ought to keep seeking where Christ is now seated in His heavenly reign, for they have died (implied: with Christ, as stated in Col 2:20) and their life "has been hidden with the Christ" (the perfect passive κέκρυπται stresses continued association), who Himself is "in the God." By these associative concepts, Paul reminds his readers of the location of their real life: it is not with earthly things (Col 3:2) but it is with the ascended Christ, who has been taken "out of our sight," as Luke reported the ascension event (Acts 1:9). The reality of the time-and-place ascension anticipates the future aspect of association, when believers "with Christ shall be manifested in glory" (in Col 3:4, the prepositional phrase σὺν αὐτῷ precedes the verb φανερωθήσεσθε for emphasis). Thus, Paul sweeps over the entire scope of salvation as depending in the past, present, and future association with Christ in His resurrection, ascension, session, and manifestation. These are—or shall be—historical works of the "Man Christ Jesus" with which all believers are also associated, so that their own death, resurrection, ascension, session, and manifestation are indelibly linked with Him.

---

140. The author's translation of Col 3:1-4 reads, "If then you have been raised up with Christ (Εἰ οὖν συνηγέρθητε τῷ Χριστῷ), the above (things) keep seeking, where the Christ is, at the right hand of God being seated. (2) The above (things) be thinking, not the things upon the earth, (3) for you died and your life is has been hidden with the Christ in the God (κέκρυπται σὺν τῷ Χριστῷ ἐν τῷ θεῷ). (4) When the Christ should become visible—our life—then also your yourselves with Him shall become visible in glory (σὺν αὐτῷ φανερωθήσεσθε ἐν δόξῃ)."

THE "MAN CHRIST JESUS"

ANALYSIS OF 1 THESSALONIANS 4:13–17[141]

The question in the context of 1 Thess 4:13–17 is the destiny of believers who have "fallen asleep"[142] before the coming of the Lord (1 Thess 4:13), and for an answer, Paul first appeals to an accepted norm of beliefs, that Jesus died and arose (1 Thess 4:14). These items are not merely confessional statements of faith but events of history, and on the basis of their occurrence, Paul makes applications to the ones who have embraced them by faith. First, "God shall bring with Him (σὺν αὐτῷ) those who have fallen asleep in Jesus" (1 Thess 4:14). Although the English versions in general do not reflect it,[143] Paul stresses another aspect of the relationship between Jesus and believers by writing that they fall asleep "through" (διά) Jesus, using a preposition that expresses agency, thus emphasizing that even physical death—an experience compared to falling asleep—comes to the believer through the mediation of Jesus.[144] Those who have died in this life shall reappear at the end of the age when God shall bring them with Jesus at His return. In this climactic culmination of Jesus' return at the conclusion of present human history, "the Lord Himself will descend from heaven with a shout, with the voice of *the* archangel, and with the trumpet of God" (1 Thess 4:16). At that moment, believers who have already gone to be "with Christ" (Phil 1:23) shall accompany Him in return, only not merely in a declarative aspect (as with dying and rising with Him), but brought by God in actual association with Him in His victory.[145] Secondly, those believers who are alive (presumably on earth)

---

141. The author's translation of 1 Thess 4:13–17 reads, "But we are not willing (that) you to be ignorant, brethren, concerning the ones sleeping, that you should not be grieving just as also the rest, the ones not having hope. (14) For if we are believing that Jesus died and raised, thus also the ones who have fallen asleep though Jesus God shall bring with Him (σὺν αὐτῷ). (15) For this we are saying to you by a word of the Lord, that we (ourselves) the ones living, the ones being remaining unto the coming of the Lord shall not (at all) precede the ones having fallen-asleep, (16) because the Lord Himself with a shout, with a voice of (an) archangel and with (a) trumpet of God, shall descend from heaven, and the dead (ones) in Christ shall rise first; (17) then we (ourselves), the ones living, the ones remaining at the same time with them (σὺν αὐτοῖς) shall be snatched in clouds unto a meeting of the Lord into (the) air; and thus always with (the) Lord we shall be (σὺν κυρίῳ ἐσόμεθα)."

142. "Falling asleep" is a common biblical metaphor for death (1 Kgs 2:10; Dan 12:2; Matt 27:52; Luke 8:51–52; Acts 7:60; 1 Cor 15:18).

143. While the Greek of this sentence seems simple enough (οὕτως καὶ ὁ θεὸς τοὺς κοιμηθέντας διὰ τοῦ Ἰησοῦ ἄξει σὺν αὐτῷ), the English versions can be torturous; for example, the ESV moves phrases around to render it, "Through Jesus, God will bring with Him those who have fallen asleep." The NIV shuffles words around, "We believe that God will bring with Him those who are fallen asleep in Jesus." The NET interprets rather than translates, "We believe that God will bring with Him those who have fallen asleep as Christians." Young's *Literal NT* gives an unreadable translation, "so also God those asleep through Jesus He will bring with Him," but at least it correctly translates the prepositions. It does not seem so difficult to render this in readable English that reflects the Greek, as the NCSB has done, "but God will bring with Him those who have fallen asleep through Jesus."

144. Wallace *Greek Grammar*, 368–69. The prepositional διά with the genitive is clearly not the preposition ἐν with the dative (as in 1 Thess 4:16, οἱ νεκροὶ ἐν Χριστῷ), yet this phrase διὰ τοῦ Ἰησοῦ is regularly translated in the English versions as "*in* Jesus" when surely Paul has a reason for the variation. Paul often uses διά with a combination of "Jesus, Lord, Christ" to express the agency *through* Him in mediating salvation and its benefits (Rom 1:8; 2:16; 5:1, 11, 21; 7:25; 15:30; 16:27; 1 Cor 15:57; 2 Cor 1:5; 3:4; 5:18; Gal 1:1; Eph 1:5; Phil 1:11; 1 Thess 4:2; 5:9; Titus 3:6).

145. BDAG § 99.1 defines the verb ἄγω "to direct the movement of an object from one position to

at the descent of Christ shall participate in another associative experience: they shall be "caught up together *with them* (σὺν αὐτοῖς) in the clouds to meet the Lord in the air" (1 Thess 4:17a), for Paul views association with Christ as a corporate participation of the entire church "with all the saints" (1 Cor 1:1; Eph 3:18). The third aspect of association concludes the entire matter: "thus we shall always be with the Lord" (1 Thess 4:17b). In his declaration, Paul describes the essence of future existence as an eternal association of all the people of God with the Lord.[146] Thus, with these comforting words (1 Thess 4:18), Paul teaches that the primary relationship in the *eschaton* shall be the association of believers with the "Man Christ Jesus" in His final victory.

ANALYSIS OF 1 THESSALONIANS 5:9–10[147]

This section in 1 Thess 5:9–10 concludes the topic begun in 1 Thess 4:13–18 concerning the return of the Lord and continuing in 1 Thess 5:1–8 with a discussion of the impending day of the Lord. Regardless of the coming destruction, Paul assures his readers that "God has not destined us for wrath, but for obtaining salvation through our Lord Jesus Christ" (1 Thess 5:9), and the basis for this assurance rests in the historical death of His Son, who "died for us" (1 Thess 5:10a). Obviously, there would be no comfort in this christological statement if the death of Jesus was only a religious myth and if He had not died on behalf of others.[148] The resulting effect of His substitutionary death is "whether we are awake or asleep, we may live together with Him," an assertion in which Paul repeats the same associative concept found at Rom 6:8 (συζήσομεν αὐτῷ) and 2 Cor 13:4 (ζήσομεν σὺν αὐτῷ). In 1 Thess 5:10, the prepositional phrase precedes the verb (σὺν αὐτῷ ζήσωμεν) for emphasis, that whether believers are living on earth or have "fallen asleep through Jesus" (1 Thess 4:13), they always live with Him.[149] Significant to this passage is the revelation that the sacrificial work of Christ as the one "having died for us" was accomplished in human history "in order that" believers should live with Christ, showing that the associative relationship with the "Man Christ Jesus" is a result of the juridical act of salvation.[150]

---

another," and Paul uses it to mean either "to bring" (2 Tim 4:11, "Bring Mark with you.") but more often as "to lead" (Rom 2:4; 8:14; 1 Cor 12:2; Gal 5:18; 2 Tim 3:6). That may be the emphasis even in 1 Thess 4:14, that God will lead His people in procession with Jesus.

146. The phrase σὺν κυρίῳ is unique to Paul, and by it he may stress the final authority of Jesus as sovereign over all.

147. The author's translation of 1 Thess 5:9–10 reads, "Because God did not appoint us unto wrath, But unto (a) possession of salvation through the Lord of us, Jesus Christ, the One having died for us, that whether we should be awake or sleeping, at the same time with Him we may live (σὺν αὐτῷ ζήσωμεν)."

148. See Wallace, *Greek Grammar*, 383–89, where he observes that the evidence in the papyri is "overwhelmingly in favor of treating ὑπέρ as bearing a substitutionary force in the NT era" (ibid., 386).

149. Ibid., 554, describes the aorist as giving a "snap-shot" aspect, so here ζήσωμεν scans the entire span of life and death in one sweep.

150. Schweizer, "Dying and Rising with Christ," 1, observes this important "coincidence."

THE "MAN CHRIST JESUS"

ANALYSIS OF 2 TIMOTHY 2:11–13[151]

In the "faithful word" of 2 Tim 2:11–13, Paul may be citing an early hymn or catechism,[152] and significantly, it contains three συ-compound verbs, "died with, live with, and reign with." All these words lack direct objects and so raise the question: are they describing associations with other believers, or with Christ? The context favors Christ as the object, since Paul inserts this "faithful word" as an explanation of "the salvation which is in Christ Jesus *and* with *it* eternal glory," mentioned in the previous verse (2 Tim 2:10). Also, the language is explicitly Pauline in that it discusses the association of the church with Christ in His saving events. In a sense, this final appearance of the association motif in the Pauline corpus summarizes the apostle's doctrine: first, by use of the first-class conditional sentence εἰ γὰρ συναπεθάνομεν, he states an association based on the death of Christ, that the church was declared to have died with Christ at that time.[153] This co-death is not—contrary to common interpretation[154]—a reference to the conversion or baptism of the individual believer but rather to the declarative association of the entire church with Christ in the historical event of His death. As Jesus died on a cross, Paul considers the church to have been crucified there with Him also (Rom 6:6).

Secondly, if it is true that "we died with Christ" (and Paul assumes it is), then "we shall also live with Him," a statement implying the resurrection of Jesus, when God brought Him back to life and also declared that the church was associated with that event, so that "whether we are awake or asleep, we may live together with Him" (1 Thess 5:10). Thirdly, "If we endure (again, Paul assumes this endurance to be true), then we shall also reign with Him," a statement echoing a saying of Jesus in Matt 24:13, "the one who endures to the end shall be saved." In this third statement, Paul introduces a new term for association (συμβασιλεύω), although he also uses it (perhaps ironically) in 1 Cor 4:8[155] of reigning with other believers. The idea of reigning with Christ, however, originates with Jesus when He promised His disciples, "When the Son of Man will sit on His glorious throne, you also shall sit upon twelve thrones, judging the twelve tribes of Israel" (Matt 19:28). Paul now expands that reign to all believers, in anticipation of the coming age, when the servants of the Lamb shall reign forever and ever (Rev 22:5).

---

151. The author translates 2 Tim 2:11–13, "Faithful is the word: 'For if we died with *Him* (εἰ γὰρ συναπεθάνομεν), also we shall live with *Him* (καὶ συζήσομεν); If we endure, also we shall reign with *Him* (συμβασιλεύσομεν); If we deny *Him*, He also shall deny us; If we are faithless, He remains faithful; for to deny Himself He is not able."

152. Mounce, *Pastoral Epistles*, 515.

153. This particular compound verb συναποθνῄσκω is used by Paul elsewhere only at 2 Cor 7:3 in another associative context, "You are in our hearts to die together and to live together." At Rom 5:7, 1 Cor 9:5, and Phil 1:21, Paul does use the basic verb ἀποθανεῖν, which BDAG § 924 defines quite simply as "to die," and more fully, "to cease to have vital functions, whether at an earthly or transcendent level."

154. Mounce, *Pastoral Epistles*, 516, claims, "Most agree that this first line refers to a believer's baptism and the new life that follows." If this is the case, then of necessity Paul teaches regenerational baptism, a matter to be addressed in the theological applications of Association with Christ.

155. 1 Corinthians 4:8 reads, "Already you are full! Already you are rich! You have reigned as kings without us—and indeed I could wish you reigned, that also we might reign with you!" (ἤδη κεκορεσμένοι ἐστέ, ἤδη ἐπλουτήσατε, χωρὶς ἡμῶν ἐβασιλεύσατε· καὶ ὄφελόν γε ἐβασιλεύσατε, ἵνα καὶ ἡμεῖς ὑμῖν συμβασιλεύσωμεν).

The "Man Christ Jesus" in Association with His People

SUMMARY TO PAUL'S DISTINCTIVE ASSOCIATION TERMINOLOGY

Thus, this "faithful word" in 2 Tim 2:11–13 summarizes the Pauline idea of association as determined through the careful analysis of all the Pauline passages containing the "with Christ" linguistic motif. This search has revealed that the apostle uses this theme when establishing the association of the entire church with the "Man Christ Jesus," whether in the historical events of salvation (His past suffering, crucifixion, death, burial, resurrection, and ascension); or in His present experience as seated in His heavenly Session; or in future expectation of living, being, and reigning with Christ in His eternal rule. In each incident, the church is considered as being "with Christ" in those events, so that whatever happens in His actual experience by divine enactment, the church is considered as being present with the "Man Christ Jesus" at those same moments by divine assessment. Thus, the salvation of all believers depends entirely upon the divinely declared association with the "Man Christ Jesus" in the historical actions He undertakes to secure their redemption.

CHAPTER SUMMARY: THE MAN CHRIST JESUS ASSOCIATED WITH HIS PEOPLE

By analyzing the use of prepositions in the Pauline literature, the chapter has shown that the apostle employs linguistic particularities sufficient enough to suggest that whenever a reader encounters one of the many prepositional phrases regarding the saving work of Christ, he should inquire what particular aspect of salvation is in view. For example, Paul shows by intentional and consistent selection of various prepositions that the Father saved His people "according to His own purpose and grace which was granted us *in* Christ Jesus (ἐν Χριστῷ Ἰησοῦ) from all eternity" (2 Tim 1:9). God mediated this salvation *through* Christ Jesus (διὰ Χριστοῦ), who died vicariously *for* (ὑπέρ) the sins of His people, whom God considers to be associated *with* Jesus (σὺν Χριστῷ) in His death, resurrection, and ascension. Christ's historical accomplishments are then applied vitally to the members of His body when they are sealed *in* Christ (ἐν ᾧ) by the Holy Spirit and justified when they believe *into* Christ (εἰς αὐτὸν πιστεύειν) or *upon* Him (ἐπὶ τῇ πίστει). This chapter has especially argued that Paul uses the preposition σύν and συ-compounds in order to present a soteriological concept of the association of believers with Christ (σὺν Χριστῷ) as distinct from the more commonly known and studied motif of union in Christ (ἐν Χριστῷ). As this study established, association with Christ concerns the relationship of the church with the "Man Christ Jesus" in His historical acts of salvation and His present ascended ministry. While it is now an imputational association, it shall become actual association when believers shall live together with Christ at His return and reign with Him forever.

In concluding this chapter, the assertion is made that Paul's "with Christ" motif is not merely a literary device used to make the readers feel as if they were present with Jesus as He walked about Galilee and Judea. Instead, Paul uses the preposition σύν and various συ-compound words when he discusses a particular aspect of salvation in the setting of redemptive-history, whereby he deems the entire church to be associated with the "Man Christ Jesus" in the events of His ministry—with His life, with His suffering, with His crucifixion, with His resurrection, with His ascension, and eventually, with His *parousia*.

THE "MAN CHRIST JESUS"

Paul's carefully chosen and crafted vocabulary displays that the association of the church with Christ serves as a distinct and important aspect of Pauline doctrine and is designed to demonstrate the final accomplishment of the history of salvation, that the redeemed community shall "always be with the Lord."

So then, since Paul applies the salvation of the church to its association with the historical "Man Christ Jesus," the question arises: what are the implications of these findings regarding the humanity of Jesus to the broader concepts of Paul's theological thinking? It is to this endeavor that this study shall turn in conclusion in the following chapter.

6

Implications of the "Man Christ Jesus" in the Teaching of the Apostle Paul

THE SPECIFIC TASK OF this study has been to examine what the apostle Paul meant by the particular description he uses in 1 Tim 2:5, the "Man Christ Jesus" (*ánthropos Christòs Iēsoûs*) and to explore how it illustrates his understanding of the humanity of Jesus of Nazareth. The findings do not pretend to present a full-orbed Pauline Christology; therefore, such concerns as the deity of Christ and the nature of His saving work are treated as secondary matters even though they are fully deserving of the in-depth studies other authors have devoted to these topics.[1] Indeed, the history of Pauline studies (surveyed in Chapter 1) reveals a tendency toward minimizing (and sometimes even ignoring) issues not considered germane to the scholar's specific emphasis.[2] To avoid such myopia, this study has endeavored to maintain a balance with the entirety of Paul's Christology even while focusing on his use of the humanity of Jesus in order to determine the relationship existing between the apostle and the "Man Christ Jesus."

In furthering this pursuit, the exegetical research of 1 Tim 2:5–6 in Chapter 2 revealed that Paul establishes his teaching of redemption upon the "Man Christ Jesus" as a human who lived out His life within the framework of verifiable human history. Furthermore, Chapter 3 conducted an investigation in the autographed epistles of Paul and found that he often refers to the same historical Jesus as the one presented in the Gospels. Chapter 4 explored how these references to Jesus in Paul's writings find corroboration in the Book of Acts, which shows that Paul was not only personally converted by the "Man Christ Jesus" on the Damascus Road, but that he also preaches the significance of the earthly life events of the historical Jesus in his proclamation of the gospel.[3] Furthermore, Chapter 5

---

1. Such works include Andrews, *The Meaning of Christ for Paul* (1949); Cerfaux, *Christ in the Theology of St. Paul* (1959); Scroggs, *Christology in Paul and John: The Reality and Revelation of God* (1988); Hurtado, "Paul's Christology," (2003), 185–98; Fee, *Pauline Christology: An Exegetical-Theological Study* (2007).

2. For example, Sanders, *Paul*, 79, while recognizing that Paul employs sacrificial and forensic terminology to the death of Christ, essentially dismisses its importance by insisting that Paul has a more radical conception of sin than mere transgression but as an enslaving power. The fact is that Paul presents atonement from sin in the work of Christ not as an either/or, but a both/and, with justification addressing forensic matters and sanctification discussing dynamic transformation. For a broad overview of Pauline studies, see Zetterholm, *Approaches to Paul: A Student's Guide to Recent Scholarship* (2009).

3. Maccoby, *The Mythmaker: Paul and the Invention of Christianity*, 184, describes Paul not as a theologian or philosopher, but a mythologist who created a new story about a "fictional character" based on Jesus, and that myth is his descent as a divine savior. It is interesting that Maccoby, a Jewish scholar, observes what

THE "MAN CHRIST JESUS"

noted how it is not Paul's interest merely to prove events of history: his concern is to apply those events experienced by Jesus to the salvation of his hearers—especially His death for others and His resurrection as the verification of their salvation. Paul takes this historical perspective even further when he views the church as being associated with Jesus in the particular incidents of salvation-history, teaching throughout his epistles that the church lived, died, resurrected, and ascended with Christ in those events—and shall return with Him and reign with Him in His future kingdom. Paul incorporates all these experiences of the historical Jesus into His teaching and preaching, showing that the "Man Christ Jesus" is foundational to his entire gospel.

Based on these observations, this study now suggests several implications of the humanity of the "Man Christ Jesus" to some of the traditional departments of Systematic Theology, including Christology, the History of Salvation, Soteriology, Evangelism, and Pastoral Theology. These implications derive from the substructure of Paul's gospel—the historicity of the life, death, and exaltation of the "Man Christ Jesus."

IMPLICATIONS OF THE "MAN CHRIST JESUS" FOR CHRISTOLOGY

Moule questions if an "ultimacy" of Christ can ever be reached, or if our understanding of Christ must always continue to develop as we learn more of "man and his psychology, about his personality and his mutual relations, about society and the corporate character of human life, and about the universe. . . ."[4] These questions are pertinent to an ongoing understanding of the person of Jesus, especially since the NT presents the career of Jesus in a historical progression—from His prophetic expectation to His earthly ministry to His heavenly session. Yet, the NT betrays no trace of evolution regarding the person of Jesus, as if His initial followers gradually conferred divine honors upon a mere man. Instead, the claim of Jesus that He is the Son of God (John 10:36) became the initial proclamation of Paul, "Jesus . . . is the Son of God" (Acts 9:20). However, one should not infer from Paul's immediate comprehension of Jesus as God's Son that his understanding of Jesus never developed as his knowledge of Him increased; instead, he writes that the church should always strive to "grow up in all *aspects* into Him, who is the head, *even* Christ" (Eph 4:15), even though "to know the love of Christ . . . surpasses knowledge" (Eph 3:19). Paul leads the way in this perpetual pursuit by aiming to "know Him, and the power of His resurrection and the fellowship of His sufferings, being conformed to His death" (Phil 3:10).

In the continuing quest to learn more about Jesus, this study highlights an area of neglect amid evangelical quarters, and that has been in the matter of His humanity, even though orthodoxy confesses an incarnational Christology, that "He was revealed in the flesh" (1 Tim 3:16).[5] Despite this confession, it has long been presumed that the apostle

---

many Protestant scholars deny, that Paul believes Jesus to be divine, although Maccoby insists that Paul borrowed this idea from Gnosticism; instead, this study has shown that Paul's view rests primarily on his Damascus Road experience with the Risen Jesus of Nazareth, leading him to a very different reading of the OT than that of Maccoby and Judaism in general.

4. Moule, *The Origin of Christology*, 142.

5. For example, the *Westminster Confession of Faith* 8.2, states, "The Son of God, the second person in the Trinity, being very and eternal God, of one substance and equal with the Father, did, when the fulness

Implications of the "Man Christ Jesus" in the Teaching of the Apostle Paul

Paul has minimal use for the human Jesus in his rush to proclaim a divine Christ, a presumption which is stopped dead in its tracks by Paul's mention in 1 Tim 2:5 of the "Man Christ Jesus." This phrase shows that Paul's understanding of the human Jesus reveals quite the opposite of any neglect or minimizing; after all, the one who appeared to Paul on the Damascus Road identified Himself not with divine titles but simply as "Jesus of Nazareth" (Acts 26:9), so that ". . . the movement of Pauline christology, if so it may be called, progresses from humanity to divinity, not from divinity to humanity," as Goguel insightfully observed.[6]

While this study emphasizes the importance of the humanity of Jesus in Paul's thinking, in no way does it claim to have found in Jesus' manhood *the* key to the apostle's Christology—the person of Jesus is far too diverse to be squeezed into one mold;[7] however, by examining the letters and sermons of Paul (as recorded in Acts), this inquiry found that his presentation is quite comprehensive in mentioning many aspects of the life and character of the "Man Christ Jesus." Paul is particularly persistent that Jesus had lived as a very human man and that He accomplished His saving work as mediator between God and men in His humanity. Despite the contention of Bella that a historical study cannot presuppose the normative character of the Bible,[8] this research revealed that Paul repeatedly illustrates his doctrines with references to the Jesus of history—the same man presented in the Gospels. If the task of Biblical Theology is to "unify biblical themes" (as per the definition of Grant Osbourne in *The Hermeneutical Spiral*[9]), then this study has demonstrated that there is a historical unity between the Jesus portrayed by the Gospels and the Jesus preached by Paul—both present the same person.

Indeed, the assumption of Historical Theology since the earliest writings of the Church Fathers has been the united identity of Jesus in the NT, as Kelly contends, "Nevertheless the all but universal Christian conviction as in the preceding centuries had been that Jesus Christ was divine as well as human;"[10] indeed, it was the rise of higher critical assertions

---

of time was come, take upon Him man's nature, with all the essential properties and common infirmities thereof, yet without sin; being conceived by the power of the Holy Ghost, in the womb of the Virgin Mary, of her substance. So that two whole, perfect, and distinct natures, the Godhead and the manhood, were inseparably joined together in one person, without conversion, composition, or confusion. Which person is very God, and very man, yet one Christ, the only Mediator between God and man" (citing John 1:1, 14; 1 John 5:20; Phil 2:6; Gal 4:4; Heb 2:14, 16, 17; 4:15; Luke 1:27, 31, 35; Col 2:9; Rom 9:5; 1 Pet 3:18; 1 Tim 3:16; Rom 1:3, 4; and significantly for this study, 1 Tim 2:5).

6. Goguel, *Jesus the Nazarene: Myth or History?*, 143.

7. This is the argument of Cupitt, "One Jesus, Many Christs?", 131–44, although he reasons from a relativistic viewpoint, that ". . . the way he is Christ for me may be very different from the way he is Christ for some other persons, and (if I may speak crudely) he himself is not troubled by being many Christs, or Christ in many ways." The more biblical response is to recognize there is but one Jesus, that of history, and that He assumed many titles and positions, one being that He is the representative Man.

8. Bella, *Challenges to New Testament Theology: An Attempt to Justify the Enterprise*, 32. Bella wants to justify NT theology strictly as a historical endeavor without engaging in the debate whether or not "the claims of the bible concerning its normativeness are true" (ibid., 33). This will prove to be a futile endeavor, as Bella's own critique of Overbeck's thesis against NT Theology shows (ibid., 37–45). Once the historical nature of Christianity is denied, there remains no abiding doctrines worth maintaining.

9. Osbourne, *The Hermeneutical Spiral*, 265.

10. Kelly, *Early Christian Doctrines*, 131. A survey of "The Index of Texts" in Coxe, ed., *The Ante-Nicene*

THE "MAN CHRIST JESUS"

in the nineteenth century that led to the notion that the Christ of Paul was a construct of the apostle with little or no connection to the historical Jesus.[11] This study, however, shows that the apostle did not concoct a divine Christ but rather began his Christology with a Man, Jesus of Nazareth, whom he identified as Christ, Lord, Son,[12] and even as God.[13] Most assuredly, Paul considers this Man Jesus to possess divine attributes, in that "all things were created by Him . . . and He is before all things, and in Him all things hold together" (Col 1:16–17). Although endowed with miraculous characteristics (being resurrected, ascended, and enthroned in heaven), the Jesus of Paul is the same man presented in the Gospel records, one whom the apostle claims was born of a woman, raised under the Jewish Law, preached the Kingdom of God to Israel, yet was subsequently betrayed, condemned by Pontius Pilate and crucified (see Gal 4:4; Rom 15:8; 1 Cor 11:23; 1 Tim 6:3; 1 Cor 2:2). While there is a notable elaboration in the anthropology of Jesus between the Gospels and the Pauline Epistles, it is one of fluctuating geographical relocation (Jesus has migrated from earth to heaven) and of christological status (Jesus has moved from humbleness to exaltation, as developed in Phil 2:6–11). It is by the historical resurrection and ascension of Jesus that God designated Him as Lord, and for this reason Paul can insist that "we now know Christ according to the flesh no longer" (2 Cor 5:16).

But Jesus *had* been formerly "known according to the flesh," as the first part of 2 Cor 5:16 affirms. Paul not only assumes the humanity of Jesus, but he *starts* with the "Man Christ Jesus" in His incarnational appearance ("He was manifested in the flesh," 1 Tim 3:16) and develops his concept of salvation from the historical events surrounding the life and death of Jesus; namely, His betrayal, suffering, crucifixion, and burial. Should the official records of the Sanhedrin and the Praetorium of Pontius Pilate be discovered someday, they would verify these incidents as facts of the case. Paul even invites such inquiry by mentioning the interrogation of Jesus by this Roman procurator in 1 Tim 6:13—an audacious proposal if such a cross-examination never happened but quite a proper motion if indeed it did.

This study, then, affirms that Jesus is not merely a "divine man" (*theois aner*) but the *Theos-Anthropos* of the christological creeds, because the Church Fathers found in Scripture the profound mystery of the God-Man.[14] God the Son not only become a man,

---

Fathers, 10:212–266, shows that the early church writers appealed equally and indiscriminately to the Gospels and to Paul in support of their views on Jesus.

11. According to Baird, *History of New Testament Research*, 2:150, it was William Wrede's *Paul* (1907) that challenged the unity between Jesus and Paul by projecting a "broad chasm between Paul and Jesus."

12. As seen in Rom 1:4, "His Son, . . . who was declared the Son of God with power by the resurrection from the dead, according to the Spirit of holiness, Jesus Christ our Lord;" and 1 Cor 1:9, "you were called into fellowship with His Son, Jesus Christ our Lord."

13. As in Rom 9:5, "the Christ according to the flesh, who is over all, God blessed forever."

14. *The Athanasian Creed* 30 reads, "For the right faith is, that we believe and confess: that our Lord Jesus Christ, the Son of God, is God and Man" ("Est ergo fides recta, ut credamus et confiteamur: quod Dominus noster Jesus Christus Dei Filius, Deus et homo est."); *The Symbol of Chalcedon* confesses, "We, then, following the holy Fathers, all with one consent, teach men to confess one and the same Son, our Lord Jesus Christ, the same perfect in Godhead and also perfect in manhood; truly God and truly man, of a reasonable [rational] soul. . . ." (Επόμενοι τοίνυν τοῖς ἁγίοις πατράσιν ἕνα καιτὸν αὐτὸν ὁμολογεῖν υἱὸν κύριον ἡμῶν Ἰησοῦν Χριστὸν συμφώνως ἅπαντες ἐκδιδάσκομεν, τέλειον τὸν αὐτὸν ἐν θεότητι καὶτέλειον τὸν αὐτὸν ἐν

as Phil 2:6–8 teaches (Christ Jesus "existed in the form of God" but was "found in appearance as man."), but He has remained a man in His exalted status. To this end, Witherington observes, "While it has sometimes been stressed that the efficacy of salvation was due to Jesus' divinity, Paul in fact emphasizes the opposite. If Jesus had not been human, humans would not have ever received God's grace. . . . Thus, for Paul and the early Christians to proclaim 'Christ crucified,' there must also be an emphasis on Christ's humanity."[15] Evangelical theology, then, should dismiss all inadvertent dismissal of the humanity of Jesus and embrace anew the implications of its ancient biblical confession by confirming the intriguing motif of 1 Tim 2:5, "There is one God, *and* one mediator also between God and men, *the* man Christ Jesus."

IMPLICATIONS OF THE "MAN CHRIST JESUS" FOR SALVATION HISTORY

The idea of Jesus as a man of history, however, is not merely a matter of fact or of speculative curiosity for Paul; instead, he embeds the essential realities of salvation into events enacted by the "Man Christ Jesus" in human history. This concept of "salvation-history" (*Heilsgeschichte*) is often credited to the observations of Oscar Cullmann,[16] and more recently, Herman Ridderbos has explored the connection of Paul's terminology with the historical events of salvation, showing how a "redemptive historical interpretation . . . is marked by a strong accentuation of the element of fulfillment, in the preaching of Jesus as well as in that of Paul."[17] Likewise, Persons observes that the apostle's "primary implication is objective, related to the historical person of Christ."[18] This crucial perception for Pauline theology is confirmed in this study, as it demonstrates (Chapter 3) that Paul often alludes to historical events and sayings from the life of Jesus. It is therefore conspicuously unfair to Paul—not to mention poor scholarship—to claim that Paul has little or no use for the historical Jesus when the textual analysis in Chapter 5 concerning Paul's particular use of the "with Christ" (σὺν Χριστῷ) motif reveals that Paul's arguments make sense only if there is historical reality to the Christ-events he mentions.

By use of the prepositional phrase σὺν Χριστῷ and compound words prefixed with σύν, Paul intricately binds the believer's salvation with the events experienced by the historical Jesus in His humanity. In stating "we died with Christ" (Rom 6:8; Col 2:20; 2 Tim 2:11), Paul affirms the Gospel records that Jesus physically died; furthermore, by teaching that the church was "crucified with Christ" (Rom 6:6; Gal 2:20), Paul agrees that crucifixion was the stated means of Jesus' execution. Significantly, the same verb συσταυρόω is found in the Gospel accounts, reporting that thieves also were crucified with Jesus in that actual event (Matt 27:44; Mark 15:32; John 19:32). As the burial of Jesus confirmed the historical reality of His bodily death, so Paul affirms the record of all four Gospels in

---

ἀνθρωπότητι, θεὸν ἀληθῶς καὶ ἄνθρωπον ἀληθῶς τὸν αὐτόν, ἐκ ψυχῆς λογικῆς. . . .).

15. Witherington, "Jesus as the Alpha and Omega of New Testament Thought," 40.

16. Cullmann, *Christ and Time: The Primitive Christian Concept of Time and History* (1950); Cullmann, *Salvation in History* (1967).

17. Ridderbos, *Paul: An Outline of His Theology*, 42–43.

18. Michael Persons, "'In Christ' in Paul," 25.

THE "MAN CHRIST JESUS"

this event (Matt 27:59–60; Mark 15:46; Luke 23:53; John 19:40–42) when he pictures the church as being buried with Christ (Rom 6:4; Col 2:12). When Paul likens the new life of the church to being made alive with Christ's resuscitative experience (Eph 2:5; Col 2:13) and raising with Christ (Eph 2:6; Col 2:12; 3:1), he affirms the historical facts of Jesus' physical resurrection as reported in the Gospels.[19] Furthermore, as the historical accounts report that Jesus ascended to heaven (Luke 24:51; Acts 1:9), likewise Paul maintains that fact when he mentions the corporate association of the church with the seating of Jesus in heavenly places (Eph 2:6), so that the church is now hidden with Christ as He is hidden from the sight of humanity (Col 3:3).

Salvation history, however, not only has reference to the works of the "Man Christ Jesus" in past historical events, but by means of the present tense Paul shows how salvation applies in the association of believers with Christ in His present ministry of heavenly session. As Christ inherits all things, so the church is a fellow-heir with Him (Rom 8:17) and thus also with one another (Eph 3:6).[20] As Jesus closely aligned Himself with the sufferings of His people by asking Saul, "Why are you persecuting Me?" (Acts 9:4), so the church suffers with Him (Rom 8:17, perhaps also 2 Tim 1:8 and 2:3) in such a way that it brings co-conformity with His death (Phil 3:10).[21]

Nonetheless, most of Paul's references to the church's association with the Jesus of history have an eschatological perspective with an eye on yet-future actions of the same "Man Christ Jesus" who died, rose, and ascended. These verses generally use verbs in the future tense or the aorist tense with prospective intention to show what shall be expected in the future for those associated with Christ. The initial step is the association that takes place at death, when the believer goes to "be with Christ" (Phil 1:23). Perhaps Paul deduced such knowledge from the Lord's promise to the thief on the cross, "Today you will be with me (μετ' ἐμοῦ) in paradise" (Luke 23:43) or from the prayer of Jesus, "Father, I desire that they also, whom Thou hast given Me, be with Me (μετ' ἐμοῦ) where I am" (John 17:24). Although these statements use a different preposition,[22] the concept is the same, that the final association of the church is to be always "with the Lord" (σὺν κυρίῳ, 1 Thess 4:17).

---

19. Oddly, Ellinger, "σύν," *EDNT* 3:291, asserts that Paul always uses "with Christ" in "a context speaking of the future," although the apostle unmistakably places believers with Christ in His past death and resurrection.

20. Note the use of the συ-compound verbs in Eph 3:6, that the "Gentiles should be fellow heirs, of the same body, and partakers of His promise in Christ through the gospel" (εἶναι τὰ ἔθνη συγκληρονόμα καὶ σύσσωμα καὶ συμμέτοχα τῆς ἐπαγγελίας ἐν Χριστῷ Ἰησοῦ διὰ τοῦ εὐαγγελίου).

21. "Indeed we suffer with *Him* in order that we may also be glorified with *Him*" (Rom 8:17); "join with *me* in suffering for the gospel according to the power of God" (2 Tim 1:8); "Suffer hardship with *me*, as a good soldier of Christ Jesus" (2 Tim 2:3); "that I may know Him . . . and the fellowship of His sufferings" (Phil 3:10).

22. Μετά seems to be the preposition of choice when companionship is viewed from the divine perspective and from the promise of Christ, "I shall be with you" (Matt 28:20; see also Rom 16:20; 1 Cor 16:23; 2 Cor 13:11; Phil 4:9; Col 4:18; 1 Thess 5:28; 1 Tim 6:21; 2 Tim 4:22). For that matter, the phrase σὺν σοί is not found in Paul's writings at all. He reserves the preposition σύν when discussing the association of the church being with the human Jesus of history rather than the heavenly Lord being with (μετά) His people. This is a subtle distinction, but one borne out by the linguistic evidence.

Implications of the "Man Christ Jesus" in the Teaching of the Apostle Paul

Before that final *eschaton*, however, Paul sees the climax of human history in the return of Jesus and the final resurrection of the dead, information he had acquired "by the word of the Lord" (ἐν λόγῳ κυρίου, 1 Thess 4:17), an evident reference to the prophecies of Jesus now recorded in the Gospels (such as Mark 8:38; John 6:40; 14:3).[23] Those believers who are already with Him shall appear with Christ in glory (Col 3:4) and shall be brought with Him at His return (1 Thess 4:14). At that event, the church shall be raised bodily with Christ in resurrection (2 Cor 4:14), which is the likely meaning of Paul's repeated emphasis of living with Christ (Rom 6:8; 2 Cor 13:4; 1 Thess 5:10; 2 Tim 2:11). As Jesus requested His Father to glorify Him (John 17:5), likewise His co-heirs shall be glorified with Him (Rom 8:17). This process shall involve a two-fold association: the physical bodies of believers shall be "conformed with" the body of His glory (σύμμορφον τῷ σώματι τῆς δόξης αὐτοῦ, Phil 3:21) and their whole persons shall be "conformed with" the image of the Son (συμμόρφους τῆς εἰκόνος τοῦ υἱοῦ αὐτοῦ, Rom 8:29). As Jesus promised His people would "inherit the kingdom prepared for you from the foundation of the world" (Matt 25:34), so Paul foresees the church as associated with Christ in His reign (2 Tim 2:12). Because God "did not spare His own Son, but delivered Him up for us all," the final blessing bestowed upon the church is that the Father shall freely grant all things "with Him" (Rom 8:32).

Thus, by use of this selective vocabulary, Paul embraces the historical events of the life and ministry of Jesus and His predictions of future events as finding fulfillment among those whom God has associated with Christ in His past, present and future aspects of redemptive-history. To this end, a corporate confessional statement based on Paul's salvation-history could read,

> We believe that Christ came to live for us, and we live with Him;
> that He suffered for us, and we suffer with Him;
> that He was crucified for us, and we were crucified with Him;
> that He was buried for us, and we were buried with Him;
> that He was raised for us, and we were raised with Him;
> that He ascended to heaven, and we ascended with Him;
> that He is seated in glory, and we are seated with Him;
> that He shall return for us, and we shall return with Him;
> Then we shall live with Him forever as He promised to be with us forever.

This confession captures the associative aspect of redemptive history in Pauline thought not generally recognized by scholars and typically overlooked by translators, although this study has demonstrated that Paul intentionally chose his vocabulary in order to distinguish *association with* Christ from *union in* Christ.[24] When the apostle

---

23. "The Son of Man will ... come in the glory of His Father with the holy angels" (Mark 8:38); "I Myself will raise him up on the last day" (John 6:40); "I will come again, and receive you to Myself" (John 14:3).

24. Evidence of the general merging of association with Christ as a subset of the larger concept of union in Christ is illustrated in the title of two major evangelical works by Norman Douty, *Union with Christ* (1973) and Louis Smedes, *Union with Christ: A Biblical View of the New Life in Jesus Christ* (1983). Neither of the words "association" nor "union" appear in the NT: they are theological terms applied to biblical concepts, reflecting a general use of particular prepositions "with" and "in." It is the argument of this paper that the two concepts should be carefully distinguished and not be confused by describing them as "*union with* Christ"

discusses the positional/dynamic concept of salvation, he characteristically uses his well-known "in Christ" motif, but when he considers matters relating to redemptive history, he consistently uses the "with Christ" motif, showing how the church is associated with Christ in the historical events of salvation. If this implication is accurate, then this study calls on future Pauline studies to recognize that the entire structure of Paul's concept of redemptive-history rests on the historical Jesus—every mention of Jesus by the apostle assumes that the "Man Christ Jesus" effects salvation "in His own time" (1 Tim 2:5–6).

IMPLICATIONS OF THE "MAN CHRIST JESUS" FOR SOTERIOLOGY

This study has also shown that the humanity of the "Man Christ Jesus" merits a particular aspect of Paul's soteriology, especially in his teaching that the church is associated with Christ in the historical events of His humanity, although there has been only a smattering of research conducted in this area in the past century.[25] The analysis in Chapter 5 revealed that Paul's concept of the association of the church with Christ is a distinctive aspect of his understanding of the humanity of Jesus which deserves to stand on its own merit. Of course, it is tempting to claim more for this observation than it can reasonably support, in the way that Callen contends that Paul's theology finds its "central theme as dying and rising with Christ as part of the body of Christ."[26] Callen's assertion is somewhat eccentric, since Paul identifies his own central theme in Col 3:11, "Christ is all and in all." Every point of Paul's theology flows from his understanding of the person of Christ.

That having been said, this concept of association with Christ is certainly an important aspect of Paul's soteriology yet one that has been ignored, neglected, or misunderstood. In early twentieth century scholarship, the understanding of the "with Christ" motif was influenced by the *religionsgeschichte Schule* of Deissman,[27] Weiss,[28] and Bultmann,[29] as these scholars advocated that Paul borrowed his idea from Hellenistic mystic cults or Gnostic mythology, so that to one degree or another, Paul taught that the believer was absorbed into a pneumatic oneness with the heavenly Christ. Lohmeyer, however, noted as early as 1927, "It appears the Pauline formula 'to be with Christ' stands alone and without clear historical connection. It cannot be derived from either an original Israelite tradition nor of a Greek or Hellenistic religion, although perhaps the use of the ceremonial little word σύν also may be influenced from the use of σὺν θεῷ" (in previously cited sources).[30] Albert Schweitzer advanced a ceremonial connection by insisting that Paul's motif concerns the

---

or "*association in* Christ."

25. See the historical survey of this topic in Tannehill, *Dying and Rising with Christ*, 1–5, and Harvey, "The 'With Christ' Motif in Paul's Thought," 329–30.

26. Callen, *Dying and Rising with Christ: The Theology of Paul the Apostle*, 8.

27. Deissmann, *Paul: A Study in Social and Religious History* (1926).

28. Weiss, *The History of Primitive Christianity* (1937).

29. Bultmann, *Theology of the New Testament*, 1:141.

30. Lohmeyer, "ΣΥΝ ΧΡΙΣΤΩ," 229, translation by this reviewer. Significantly, he suggests that Paul's use of "with Christ" may depend on the traditional wordings of a "*Herrenwortes*," as echoed in 1 Thess 4:15, "This we say by the word of the Lord."

believer's mystical participation with Christ via the sacraments.[31] Eduard Schweizer next claimed that the experience was effected in baptism, but then he inconsistently stated that the motif is only eschatological, describing the "final being with (Christ) after His parousia."[32]

None of these explanations, however, focuses on the historical emphasis prevalent in Paul's arguments, as shown in the linguistic analysis of Paul's use of the preposition σύν in Chapter 5, which revealed that the apostle uses the σὺν Χριστῷ theme in ways grammatically distinct from the ἐν Χριστῷ motif, even when the two phrases appear in the same verse (2 Cor 13:4; Eph 2:6; 3:6; Col 2:11–13). While "in Christ" describes the positional, dynamic relationship experienced by the believer, "with Christ" has reference to events in history (past, present, and future) with which Paul deems that the power and working of God associates the entire church with Jesus in His humanity. Association with Christ, then, is an imputational aspect of salvation, a divine declaration of how God esteems His church in association with the "Man Christ Jesus" in His saving events. This observation leads to the consideration of some soteriological implications:

First, as previously noted above, Paul bases his saving message firmly on the historical actualities of the "Man Christ Jesus." His many references and extensive allusions to the person and ministry of Jesus prove that the apostle assumed the historical record of the life of Jesus. It is in the human actions of Jesus—notably, His suffering, crucifixion, burial, resurrection, and ascension—that Paul proclaims salvation, as he declares in 1 Cor 15:3–5, "that Christ died for our sins according to the Scriptures, and that He was buried, and that He was raised on the third day according to the Scriptures, and that He appeared. . . ."

The second implication is that Paul associates all believers in these saving events *as if the church actually accompanies Jesus in those incidents*.[33] This inference means that Paul's linguistic motif of being "with Christ" is a distinct aspect of his soteriology explaining how the church relates to Christ as the "Man from heaven" (1 Cor 15:47). All that Jesus did, is doing, and shall do is accomplished in association together with His church and His church in association with Him, so that the eventual goal of salvation is for the entire saved community to be in co-conformity with Christ's image (Rom 8:29) and to be associating with Christ for eternity.

This concept is further confirmed when one considers how often the Gospels report that Jesus associated with other people who in turn associated with Him. This detail may seem to be rather insignificant, but the text of Mark 3:14 especially notes that Jesus initially appointed His twelve apostles "that they might be *with Him*" (ὦσιν μετ' αὐτοῦ). Luke 9:1 further describes this appointment as a call to associate together with Jesus ("Then He called together His twelve disciples [Συγκαλεσάμενος δὲ τοὺς δώδεκα] and gave them

---

31. Schweitzer, *The Mysticism of Paul the Apostle* (1955), chapters 4 and 9.

32 Schweizer, "Dying and Rising with Christ," 2, claims, "Baptism brings the eschatological being with Christ" (ibid., 5).

33. Paul pictures the church as actually present with Jesus in the future incidents of association, such as His *parousia* (1 Thess 4:17) and eternal reign (2 Tim 2:12), but the events of past history—the crucifixion, resurrection, and ascension—must of necessity describe an association of divine imputation, since it is evident that that the entire church was not physically present at those events.

power and authority over all demons, and to cure diseases"). Previously, Luke 8:1 had noted that when Jesus was "going about from one city and village to another, proclaiming and preaching the kingdom of God, (that) the twelve were *with Him*" (σὺν αὐτῷ), learning from their association with Him. Even in those moments when Jesus was praying alone, "the disciples were *with Him*" (συν ἦσαν αὐτῷ οἱ μαθηταί, Luke 9:18). From these twelve disciples, Jesus selected an inner circle of three, so that occasionally "He permitted no one to follow together *with Him* (οὐδένα μετ' αὐτοῦ συνακολουθῆσαι) except Peter, James, and John the brother of James" (Mark 5:37). These three were with Jesus as witnesses when "Moses and Elijah appeared to them, talking *with Him*" (συλλαλοῦντες μετ' αὐτοῦ, Matt 17:3). Even in His final public appearance (albeit late in the night of His arrest), Jesus "went forth *with His disciples* (σὺν τοῖς μαθηταῖς αὐτοῦ) over the ravine of the Kidron, where there was a garden, into which He Himself entered, and His disciples" (John 18:1). Then, at His appearance to His disciples on the day of resurrection, Jesus announced to them, "These are My words which I spoke to you while I was still *with you* (σὺν ὑμῖν), that all things which are written about Me in the Law of Moses and the Prophets and the Psalms must be fulfilled" (Luke 24:44). Thus, from the beginning of His earthly ministry until its conclusion, there was scarcely a moment when Jesus was not physically associating with His disciples. Indeed, Peter states that a primary qualification for membership in the Apostolate is that of initial and continued association with the other twelve disciples in their mutual association with Jesus (Acts 1:21–22).[34]

Furthermore, the association of Jesus with others is particularly noted in table fellowships, such as the supper when "Martha was serving; but Lazarus was one of those reclining *with Him*" (ἀνακειμένων σὺν αὐτῷ, John 12:2), and when He told His disciples that He "earnestly desired to eat this Passover *with you* (μεθ' ὑμῶν) before I suffer" (Luke 22:15). More scandalously were those fellowships when Jesus "sat at the table in the house, that behold, many tax collectors and sinners came and *sat down with Him* (συν ἀνέκειντο τῷ Ἰησοῦ) and His disciples" (Matt 9:10 ‖ Mark 2:15). Such gatherings occurred frequently enough that "the Pharisees and scribes complained, saying, 'This Man receives sinners and *eats with them*'" (συνεσθίει αὐτοῖς, Luke 15:2). On the afternoon of His resurrection, Jesus appeared as a stranger to Cleopas and another disciple, and "they urged Him, saying, 'Stay *with us* (μεῖνον μεθ' ἡμῶν), for it is getting toward evening, and the day is now nearly over....' And He went in to stay *with them*" (σὺν αὐτοῖς, Luke 24:29). Table fellowship with the resurrected Lord is especially noted later by Peter, who reported that Jesus appeared "not to all the people, but to witnesses chosen before by God, *even to us who ate and drank with Him* (οἵτινες συν εφάγομεν καὶ συν επίομεν αὐτῷ) after He arose from the dead" (Acts 10:41).

Jesus stresses the importance of association with Him by stating, "He who is not *with Me* (μετ' ἐμοῦ) is against Me, and he who does not *gather with Me* (ὁ μὴ συνάγων μετ' ἐμοῦ) scatters abroad" (Matt 12:30 ‖ Luke 11:23). Conversely, He makes a promise of as-

---

34. "It is therefore necessary that of the men who have *accompanied us* (συνελθόντων ἡμῖν) all the time that the Lord Jesus went in and out among us—beginning with the baptism of John, until the day that He was taken up from us—one of these should become a witness *with us* (σὺν ἡμῖν) of His resurrection" (Acts 1:21–22).

sociation when He announces, "For where two or three are *gathered together* (συνηγμένοι) in My name, I am there in the midst of them" (Matt 18:20). Although it is a disputed passage, Mark 16:20 reports that the apostles "went out and preached everywhere, the Lord working *with them*" (συνεργοῦντος), indicating that the concept of the Lord's association with His own was a prevalent idea to describe His continuing ascension ministry.

Especially noteworthy is that the association vocabulary employed in these Gospel references is also found in Paul's epistles. This linguistic affinity suggests the likelihood that the apostle derived his idea of association with Christ from these sayings and examples of association with Jesus during His earthly ministry. No doubt when Paul had opportunity to ask those who had been with Jesus, he inquired, what did the Lord mean when He promised to be "with" His own until the end of the age (Matt 28:20)? How would the thief crucified with Jesus be "with Him" in Paradise (Luke 23:43)? Paul finds answers to these questions, in large part, in his concept of the believer's association with Christ by which the apostle places his message firmly on the historical actualities of the life of "the Man Christ Jesus" as reported by the Evangelists.

A third implication toward soteriology is that that the church participates savingly in the sacrificial events of the "Man Christ Jesus" on behalf of others, and it does so through representational association with Him in those events. Paul argues in Rom 5:17–18 that as the transgression of the one Adam brought condemnation "unto all men" (εἰς πάντας ἀνθρώπους), so the one act of righteousness of Christ brought life "unto all men" (εἰς πάντας ἀνθρώπους). The critical question, then, is how "all men" are either "in Adam" or "in Christ."[35] Paul provides the answer in 1 Cor 1:30, "Of Him are you in Christ Jesus," where the antecedent to ἐξ αὐτοῦ is God (1 Cor 1:29). In the initial sense, it is God who determined union in Christ by divine election, as He "chose us in Him (ἐν αὐτῷ) before the foundation of the world" (Eph 1:4). Divine pre-determination, however, issues forth in the actuality of death or life, as Paul shows in the same Adam/Christ parallel in 1 Cor 15:22, "For as in Adam all die, so also in Christ all shall be made alive" (ὥσπερ γὰρ ἐν τῷ Ἀδὰμ πάντες ἀποθνῄσκουσιν, οὕτως καὶ ἐν τῷ Χριστῷ πάντες ζωοποιηθήσονται). In Eph 2:6, Paul prefixes σύν to this same verb ζωοποιέω to display how God "made us alive together with Christ" (συνεζωοποίησεν), linking together association with Christ and union in Christ by showing that association results in the dynamic relationship of spiritual life. In both these concepts of salvation, the works are monergistic: God places His own people in union *in* Christ, and He also associates them *with* Christ through the salvation He accomplishes for them.

These divine actions, however, do not negate human response, as Paul shows that the dynamic shift from Adam to Christ occurs for "the ones receiving the abundance of grace" (Rom 5:17), who then also are "sealed in Him" by the Holy Spirit of promise (Eph

---

35. To answer the question how Paul connects the Christian with Christ, Best, *One Body in Christ*, 56–57, adopts the suggestion of Dodd, *The Epistle of Paul to the Romans*, 86, as follows: "Thus, since Christ is an inclusive personality, when he died those who are included in him died with him; so, when he rose (sic), they rose with him. This explanation thus preserves the full 'withness' of the σύν; it is Christians with Christ on the cross and in the tomb, not Christ with Christians (in a pneumatic experience); . . .what happens to him . . . happens to them; in this they are 'solid' with him."

THE "MAN CHRIST JESUS"

1:13). Thus, the narrative in Rom 5:12–21, which shows how all are either in Adam or in Christ imputationally, flows into the narrative of Rom 6:1–6, where Paul shows how the church comes to be in Christ—by prior association with Him in His saving events. What Christ accomplished sacrificially "for us," the church also experienced associatively "with Him" so that all believers shall be vitally "in Him."

Fourthly, this interplay Paul gives among the various saving works of Christ implies that association *with* the "Man Christ Jesus" provides the foundation for the dynamic saving union *in* Christ. Viewed historically, the redemptive acts of Christ with which God associates the believer precede the dynamic experience of union in Christ; in other words, one must be *with* Christ in the works of salvation before one can be *in* Christ in the experience of salvation.[36] Prior to these vital experiences of regeneration and conversion, Paul views the entire church as being associated with Christ in the historical, time-and-space saving events of His death, burial, resurrection, and ascension that He accomplished "for us" (ὑπὲρ ἡμῶν, Rom 5:8). Thus, as Ridderbos observes, association is "not an ethical or mystical reality";[37] nor is it "a question of dying to sin in a metaphorical sense (conversion or something like it), but of the participation of the church in the death and burial of Christ in the one-time, redemptive historical sense of the word."[38] For this reason, the soteriological emphasis implied by association with Christ sheds some light on the order of salvation (*ordo salutis*): it tends to follow the historical order (*ordo historicis*) in that the accomplishments of the "Man Christ Jesus" *for* His church in human history (redemption) are imputed by God to the church as if it experienced the same events *with* Christ (association). This imputation results in the union of the church *in* Christ (calling and regeneration), leading to the justification of the church by its faith *into* Christ, producing what Christ works *in* the church by His Spirit (sanctification) and concluding with what God shall do *to* the church (glorification).[39]

Fifthly, association with the "Man Christ Jesus" clarifies a contentious issue of soteriology in the relationship of baptism to regeneration. It is often assumed that Paul teaches in Rom 6:4[40] and Col 2:12[41] that water baptism as a ritual ceremony effects vital

---

36. Of course, every relationship between Christ and His own depends on the eternal decree mentioned in Eph 1:4, "just as He chose us in Him (ἐξελέξατο ἡμᾶς ἐν αὐτῷ) before the foundation of the world." This is a positional union that issues forth in redemption through the blood of Christ (διὰ τοῦ αἵματος αὐτοῦ, Eph 1:7), which in turn leads to the sealing in Christ by the Holy Spirit (Eph 1:13). Thus, the experiential union in Christ effected in regeneration assumes the historical work of redemption secured by Christ's atonement previously determined by election in Christ.

37. Ridderbos, *Paul: An Outline of His Theology*, 206.

38. Ibid.

39. Note how Paul follows a historical order in Rom 8:30, that those whom God predestined (eternally past), "these He also called (existentially present); and whom He called, these He also justified; and whom He justified, these He also glorified" (presumptively future).

40. Romans 6:4 reads, "Therefore we were buried with Him through baptism into death, in order that just as Christ was raised out of dead (ones) through the glory of the Father, thus also we should walk in newness of life."

41. Colossians 2:12 notes, ". . . having been buried with Him in the baptism, in which also you were raised with *Him* through faith in the energy of God, the one having raised Him out of the dead ones."

Implications of the "Man Christ Jesus" in the Teaching of the Apostle Paul

participation with Christ.[42] For example, Ridderbos argues that when Paul mentions the historical-redemptive events that happened to Jesus at Golgotha and in the garden of the resurrection, the participation of believers in these events comes "by means of the sacrament of baptism"[43]—although he acknowledges that Paul can simply say in 2 Cor 5:14 that if one died for all, then all died "without special reference to baptism."[44] It seems quite odd that Ridderbos, who stresses so emphatically the historical nature of redemption, seems convinced that Paul refers to water baptism as effecting association with Christ when the apostle writes that the entire church—not merely an individual believer—has been buried with Christ through "the" baptism. Paul cannot be referring to a ritual (how could the entire church participate in one water-ritual at the same time?), but rather to the historical burial of Jesus. It is in that event of entombment that the entire church was associated with Christ; in fact, Rom 6:3 ties this baptism not to water but rather to the divine assessment "that all of us . . . have been baptized *into Christ Jesus*."[45] Furthermore,

---

42. This is the general assumption of the doctrine of "regenerational baptism," that the water of baptism effects regeneration. While this has long been a dogma of the Roman Catholic Church (*Catechism* § 1215 states that baptism "actually brings about the birth of water and the Spirit."), Protestant scholarship has lent weight to the same view, as when Elliger declares that "participation in (Christ's) death and resurrection is effected, according to Pauline understanding, through baptism" (*EDNT* 3:292). He ties this to "the cultic events of the mystery religions and is expressed by the plethora of σύν- compounds" (ibid.). Even Smedes, a Reformed scholar who denies any mythical connections in baptism, insists, "Union with Christ occurs for us at the moment of baptism. We did not die with Him back in A.D. 30 at Calvary in Jerusalem, but rather in our own time at the baptismal font in our local church" (Smedes, *Union with Christ*, 99). Actually, this is precisely what Paul is *not* saying, but instead he asserts that the church *did* die with Christ at the time of His death at Calvary in Jerusalem. The grammar and context of Rom 6:3–4 show that the whole church died historically at the cross, not that individual believers died sacramentally at the baptismal.

43. Ridderbos, *Paul: An Outline of His Theology*, 207. This view would seem to place Ridderbos, as a minister ordained in the Reformed Church, out of accord with the *Belgic Confession* § 34, which credits regeneration not to the water of baptism but to the blood of Christ and the power of the Holy Spirit.

44. Ibid.

45. Note the grammatical parallels throughout the Pauline writings:

(Rom 6:3)	ὅσοι	εἰς Χριστὸν Ἰησοῦν	ἐβαπτίσθημεν
(Gal 3:27)	ὅσοι γὰρ	εἰς Χριστὸν	ἐβαπτίσθητε
(1 Cor 10:2)	πάντες	εἰς τὸν Μωϋσῆν	ἐβαπτίσθησαν
(1 Cor 12:13)	ἡμεῖς πάντες	εἰς ἓν σῶμα	ἐβαπτίσθημεν

In each instance, the subject matter is not water baptism (Exod 15:19 notes that Israel did not get wet with Moses in the Red Sea!) but a baptizing into a spiritual experience effected by a divine action. In such contexts, LN § 53.49 defines βαπτίζω as "a figurative extension of meaning of βαπτίζω 'to baptize,' 53.41; to cause someone to have a highly significant religious experience involving special manifestations of God's power and presence." This experience is pictured variously as the application of water upon the believer, including cleansing (Acts 10:15; 11:19; 15:9; 2 Cor 7:1; Eph 5:26; Titus 2:14; Heb 9:14; 1 John 1:7, 9); washing (John 13:10; Acts 22:16; 1 Cor 6:11; Heb 10:22); purifying (1 Pet 1:22); sprinkling (Heb 10:22; 1 Pet 1:2); and a bathing (Eph 5:26; Titus 3:5). While this baptism is administered ἐν ὕδατι (Matt 3:11; John 1:16, 31, 33; Acts 8:36–38; 10:47), 1 Pet 3:21 makes it clear that baptism is far more than the mere removal of dirt from the flesh but rather "an appeal to God for a good conscience—through the resurrection of Jesus Christ." Thus, the reality of water baptism is the baptism ἐν πνεύματι ἁγίω (Matt 3:11; Mark 1:8; Luke 3:16; John 1:33; Acts 1:5; 11:16; 1 Cor 12:13).

Paul specifies this co-burial as occurring διὰ τοῦ βαπτίσματος (Rom 6:4), which surely refers to the declarative act when "we were baptized into Christ Jesus" mentioned in the previous verse. Since Paul refers to the historical death of Jesus, perhaps he has in mind the statement of Jesus, when he likens His impending death to "the baptism with which I am baptized" (τὸ βάπτισμα ὃ ἐγὼ βαπτίζομαι; Mark 10:38–39). If this correlation is the case (and the grammatical similarity to Rom 6:3–4 is most striking), then the manner by which James and John were baptized into Jesus' death serves as the model for Paul's thinking in Romans 6.

Also, in Col 2:11–12, the attendant aorist participial phrase συνταφέντες αὐτῷ ἐν τῷ βαπτισμῷ ("having been buried with Him in the baptism") explains the main verb of the sentence, which is περιετμήθητε ("you were circumcised," Col 2:11). Paul cannot be referring to the ritual of baptism, since it is patently obvious that circumcision uses a knife, not water! Paul explains how "you were circumcised" by a series of instrumental dative phrases:

> περιτομῇ ἀχειροποιήτῳ
> ἐν τῇ ἀπεκδύσει τοῦ σώματος τῆς σαρκός,
> ἐν τῇ περιτομῇ τοῦ Χριστοῦ,
> συνταφέντες αὐτῷ ἐν τῷ βαπτισμῷ,

The grammatical structure of this verse shows that the time of the co-burial of the church with Christ coincides with the divine act of circumcision "without hands," which is defined by two instrumental prepositional phrases: first, "in (or, by) the removal of the body of the flesh"—a probable reference to heart regeneration—and second, "in/by the circumcision of the Christ," an allusion to the historical event when Jesus received the sign of the Abrahamic Covenant as an eight-day old male (Luke 2:21), picturing how He would be "cut off" on behalf of His own (Gen 17:15; Isa 53:8). If "the baptism" mentioned in Rom 6:4 (διὰ τοῦ βαπτίσματος) and Col 2:12 (ἐν τῷ βαπτισμῷ) refers to the association of the church in the historical burial of Christ via divine assessment—as the verbal clauses indicate—rather than the believer's experience of water baptism,[46] then this connection removes the entire debate about the sacramental or regenerative property of water baptism. Instead, it keeps the discussion on Paul's emphasis—on the association of the entire church with Christ in His historical acts of salvation, mediated not through water but "through faith in the working of God, who raised Him from the dead" (Col 2:12).

Sixthly, the humanity of the "Man Christ Jesus" serves as the culmination of salvation in that believers are predestined to be 'conformed with' the image of His Son (συμμόρφους τῆς εἰκόνος τοῦ υἱοῦ αὐτου), so that He who is titled the "first-born" becomes eternally associated with His "many brethren" (Rom 8:29). This statement indicates that the final glorification of these "brothers" consists in their conformity with Jesus in His status as the perfect Man rather than being a deification with His nature as the perfect God. While Paul affirms the deity of Jesus in Rom 9:5 ("The Christ according to the flesh, who is over

---

46. While Rom 6:3–4 and Col 2:11–12 certainly illustrate a theology of water baptism, the ritual ought to be predicated on the historical burial of Christ and not on the believer's conversion or a sacramental ritual; thus, it seems better to initiate a theology of water baptism from the historical examples of the baptism of Jesus as recorded in the Gospels and in the practice of the early church described in Acts.

all, God blessed forever."), his perspective in Rom 8:29 relates to the humanity of Jesus, shown by his mention to "the image of the Son," an expression echoing Gen 1:26–27 when Adam—who is the original son of God, according to Luke 3:38—was created in the image of God. It is to the incarnate "image of the Son" that the believer is being transformed from glory to glory (2 Cor 3:18) and made like the image of the heavenly Man whom Paul witnessed on the road to Damascus (1 Cor 15:49). Paul, therefore, concludes his soteriology when redeemed humanity is fully restored by its association with the "Man Christ Jesus."

IMPLICATIONS OF THE "MAN CHRIST JESUS" FOR EVANGELISM

Yet another implication of the humanity of Jesus for Paul appears in his proclamation of Jesus as the Savior of sinners. The book of Acts shows that from its inception, the church verbally communicated the message of salvation through Jesus by means of preaching (Acts 2:38–40), and those evangelizing needed to convey a certain amount of information to the hearers in order for them to make an informed confession of faith. As Paul wrote his letters, he assumed that his readers shared in common some basic knowledge of the historical Man Jesus; otherwise, Paul's many references to the character and work of Jesus would be "casting pearls before swine," as Stanley insists.[47] To the contrary, this study shows that Paul often refers to the Man Jesus to bolster his arguments even though the references are generally passing allusions to Jesus' life and teachings rather than exact citations to specific events. Paul's absence of a detailed account to the life of Jesus may be nothing more complicated than the expense or scarcity of writing material (possibly hinted at in 2 Tim 4:13), but a more likely explanation is that Paul assumes that the traditions regarding Jesus had already been circulated among his readers in both oral and written forms (2 Cor 8:9; 2 Thess 2:15). Such common information was eventually compiled into the written Gospels, as the prologue in Luke 1:1–4 indicates.[48]

Yet, in the few examples of Paul's evangelistic preaching preserved for posterity, he provides the historical context for his gospel message by supplying information that depends on the hearer's knowledge of Jesus. For example, in his synagogue sermon at Pisidian Antioch where knowledge of Jesus among the Jews of the Diaspora does not appear to be widespread (Acts 13:13–42), Paul furnishes the historical setting of Jesus' ministry in the days of John the Baptist (Acts 13:25). He also provides some geographical information by telling where Jesus ministered (eventually in Jerusalem, Acts 13:27), and he gives some political insight by explaining that Jesus had been unjustly executed by Pilate (Acts 13:28). Paul also mentions the crucifixion and entombment of Jesus (Acts 13:29), but the most significant historical facts he declares are the resurrection and appearances of Jesus to eyewitnesses (Acts 13:30–31). On the basis of these events, Paul proclaims the evangelistic offer of forgiveness of sins and justification to everyone who

---

47. Stanley, "Pearls before Swine": Did Paul's Audiences Understand His Biblical Quotations?", 124–44.

48. See the discussion of oral transmission of Jesus-traditions in the early church in Gerhardsson, *Memory and Manuscript: Oral Tradition in Rabbinic Judaism and Early Christianity* with *Tradition and Transmission in Early Christianity*, 208–25.

THE "MAN CHRIST JESUS"

believes (Acts 13:38–39). It is important to observe that the message of Paul's gospel roots in historical realities enacted by the "Man Christ Jesus" in His humanity.

This historical perspective is also seen in Paul's evangelistic preaching to Gentile audiences; for example, the fullest account (his message to the Areopagus, Acts 17:22–31) concludes when Paul refers to the humanity of Jesus: "God has fixed a day in which He will judge the world in righteousness through a Man whom He has appointed, having furnished proof to all men by raising Him from the dead" (Acts 17:31). It is quite evident that without this Man of history who was raised from the dead in human history Paul would have no gospel to preach.

Even these condensed sermons indicate that the scope of information about Jesus presented in Paul's preaching depended on the depth of knowledge attained by the audience, although the primary fact always included in an evangelistic appeal is the resurrection of Jesus, an event that obviously implies His death. If Jesus had not risen from the dead, Paul would have no reason to preach Him at all, for why should anyone place his or her hope of salvation on a crucified Jew? On the other hand, if Jesus had been raised from the dead as a matter of historical record, then every other detail about Him of necessity became important: where and how He fit into history, what He did during His ministry, what He taught, what sort of character He displayed—all matters taken up in the Gospels and explained in Paul's letters.

Thus, an implication for evangelism drawn from Paul's preaching is that the evangelist must know his audience: the less knowledge of Jesus his hearers possess, the more information is required, but since time is of the essence of any gospel presentation, the crucial facts to include must be the crucifixion of Jesus (1 Cor 1:23; 2:2; Gal 3:1) and His resurrection (Rom 10:9; 1 Cor 15:1–4, 12). "Hence," Stanton observes, "it is as necessary today as ever to sketch out the life and character of Jesus as an essential part of evangelism. The church must ensure ever anew that the scandal and the uniqueness of the life and character of Jesus are held together and that both are linked to the scandal and uniqueness of the cross and resurrection."[49] In the final analysis, a sinner is not saved by imitating the character of Jesus—as important as that is, as Paul exhorts in 1 Cor 11:1—nor by following His teachings—despite their preservation in the Four Gospels and their recommendation by Paul as "the sound words of our Lord Jesus Christ" in 1 Tim 6:3. Instead, the sinner is saved by believing in the Jesus of history who "died for our sins according to the Scriptures, and that He was buried, and that He was raised on the third day according to the Scriptures" (1 Cor 15:3–4). Yet it is still Jesus of Nazareth, a Man who went about doing good, a Man who was crucified unjustly by Pilate, and a Man whom God raised from the dead, who is the same Jesus of Nazareth who appeared to the Pharisee Saul and commissioned Him to preach as the Apostle Paul. It is this "Man Christ Jesus" of history that must be proclaimed in the work of evangelism.

---

49. Stanton, *Jesus of Nazareth in New Testament Preaching*, 191.

IMPLICATIONS OF THE "MAN CHRIST JESUS" FOR PASTORAL THEOLOGY

This study has also noted that Paul does not preach about Jesus as a historical curiosity or as an academic endeavor: he has a particular pastoral interest that the transformational knowledge of the "Man Christ Jesus" produces ethical implications for the conduct and community of believers. In Chapter 3, this study explored how Paul commonly commends the character of Jesus as a moral example to follow (Rom 5:18–19; 15:3; 2 Cor 10:1; Phil 1:8; 2:5; 2 Thess 3:5; 2 Tim 1:13), particularly when he exhorts his readers, "Be imitators of me, just as I also am of Christ" (1 Cor 11:1).[50] Paul must be pointing to the earthly life of Jesus as an example because he mentions specific teachings of Jesus later in this chapter (1 Cor 11:23–25) as part of the traditions he had delivered to them (1 Cor 11:2). In like manner, robust pastoral care will commend the humanity of Jesus to believers as the pattern of righteous obedience and conformity of character to His image.

Another way in which Paul uses the humanity of Jesus with implications toward the discipline of Pastoral Theology is in the observation that Paul generally applies the accomplishments of salvation to the entire Body of believers rather than merely to individual believers;[51] for example, in Phil 1:7, he extends an inclusive application of grace by noting to his readers, "You are all partakers of grace with me (συγκοινωνούς μου τῆς χάριτος πάντας ὑμᾶς ὄντας)."[52] This associative noun συγκοινωνούς is but one of many words Paul uses that assumes his concept of association with Jesus in His historical actions and that carries significant ramifications for the community of the church. Thus, Paul employs his same συ- vocabulary to show why and how believers ought to associate with one another as Christ associates with His people,[53] teaching that God "co-composed" the entire Body

---

50. See the same idea in Phil 3:17, "Brethren, join in following my example (Συμμιμηταί μου γίνεσθε)."

51. Exceptions to this general rule are noted in Rom 14:15 where Paul mentions "him for whom Christ died;" and in Gal 2:20, where he personalizes the gospel, saying, "I have been crucified with Christ; and it is no longer I who live, but Christ lives in me; and the *life* which I now live in the flesh I live by faith in the Son of God, who loved me, and delivered Himself up for me." Besides making an application of association with Christ to Timothy (in 2 Tim 1:8 and 2 Tim 2:3), all the other references to association with Christ are in the plural, addressed to the entire church.

52. Related verses to being a co-partaker include Rom 11:17, "And if some of the branches were broken off, and you, being a wild olive tree, were grafted in among them, and *with them became a partaker* of the root and fatness of the olive tree" (συγκοινωνὸς τῆς ῥίζης τῆς πιότητος τῆς ἐλαίας ἐγένου); and 1 Cor 9:23, "Now this I do for the gospel's sake, that I may be *partaker of it with you*" (πάντα δὲ ποιῶ διὰ τὸ εὐαγγέλιον, ἵνα συγκοινωνὸς αὐτοῦ γένωμαι).

53. The various phrases related to the σὺν ὑμῖν motif express associative relationships based on association with Christ: Rom 16:14, "the brethren with them;" Rom 16:15, "all the saints who are _with them;_" 1 Cor 1:2, "to the church of God which is at Corinth, to those who have been sanctified in Christ Jesus, saints by calling, _with all_ who in every place call upon the name of our Lord Jesus Christ, their *Lord* and ours;" 1 Cor 16:19, "Aquila and Prisca greet you heartily in the Lord, _with the church_ that is in their house;" 2 Cor 1:1, "to the church of God which is at Corinth _with all the saints_ who are throughout Achaia;" 2 Cor 1:21, "Now He who establishes us _with you_ in Christ and anointed us is God;" 2 Cor 8:19, ". . . he has also been appointed by the churches to travel _with us_ in this gracious work;" Gal 1:2, "all the brethren who are _with me_, to the churches of Galatia;" Eph 3:18, "you may be able to comprehend _with all the saints_ what is the breadth and length and height and depth;" Phil 1:1 (ESV), "Paul and Timothy, servants of Christ Jesus, to all the saints in Christ Jesus who are at Philippi, _with the overseers and deacons;_" Phil 2:22, "But you know of his

THE "MAN CHRIST JESUS"

of Christ[54] and brings every believer into association with one another.[55] This truth lays the foundation for personal association in community and fellowship with other believers; they are to "associate together" (Rom 12:16)[56] and to "gather together" with one another for worship (1 Cor 5:4; 11:33; 14:23, 26)[57] as well as to "labor together" as fellow-servants in the work of ministry, as Paul notes in 2 Cor 6:1, "And working together with *us*, we also urge you not to receive the grace of God in vain." As noted in Chapter 5, Paul does not supply an object for this present plural participle, συνεργοῦντες, "to engage in an activity together with someone else,"[58] so he could refer to one of his many fellow-workers (συνεργοί) with whom he had ministered, such as Titus and Timothy.[59] But since the closest referent is αὐτῷ located in the previous verse ("that we might become the righteousness of God

---

proven worth that he served <u>with me</u> in the furtherance of the gospel;" Phil 4:21, "The brethren who are <u>with me</u> greet you;" Col 2:5, "For even though I am absent in body, nevertheless I am <u>with you</u> in spirit;" Col 4:9, "and <u>with him</u> Onesimus, *our* faithful and beloved brother, who is one of yours."

54. Verses related to this positional association include: 1 Cor 12:24, "But God <u>composed</u> (συνεκέρασεν) the body, having given greater honor to that *part* which lacks it;" Eph 2:19, "Now, therefore, you are no longer strangers and foreigners, but *fellow citizens* (συμπολῖται) with the saints and members of the household of God;" Eph 2:22, "in whom you also are being <u>built together</u> for a dwelling place of God in the Spirit" (ἐν ᾧ καὶ ὑμεῖς <u>συνοικοδομεῖσθε</u> εἰς κατοικητήριον τοῦ θεοῦ ἐν πνεύματι.); Eph 3:6, "that the Gentiles should be <u>fellow heirs, of the same body, and partakers</u> of His promise in Christ through the gospel" (εἶναι τὰ ἔθνη <u>συγκληρονόμα καὶ σύσσωμα καὶ συμμέτοχα</u> τῆς ἐπαγγελίας ἐν Χριστῷ Ἰησοῦ διὰ τοῦ εὐαγγελίου); Eph 4:16, "from whom the whole body, *joined and knit together* (συναρμολογούμενον καὶ συμβιβαζόμενον) by what every joint supplies, according to the effective working by which every part does its share, causes growth of the body for the edifying of itself in love."

55. Colossians 2:2 reads, "that their hearts may be encouraged, *being knit together* (<u>συμβιβασθέντες</u>) in love, and *attaining* to all riches of the full assurance of understanding, to the knowledge of the mystery of God, both of the Father and of Christ;" and Col 2:19, "and not holding fast to the Head, from whom all the body, nourished and knit together (<u>συμβιβαζόμενον</u>) by joints and ligaments (συνδέσμων), grows with the increase *that is* from God."

56. Romans 12:16 commands, "Do not set your mind on high things, but <u>associate with</u> the humble" (μὴ τὰ ὑψηλὰ φρονοῦντες ἀλλὰ τοῖς ταπεινοῖς <u>συναπαγόμενοι</u>).

57. 1 Corinthians 5:4 notes, "In the name of our Lord Jesus Christ, when you are <u>gathered together</u> (συναχθέντων ὑμῶν), along with my spirit, with the power of our Lord Jesus Christ;" 1 Cor 11:33, "Therefore, my brethren, when you <u>come together</u> (συνερχόμενοι) to eat, wait for one another;" 1 Cor 14:23, "Therefore if the whole church <u>comes together</u> (συνέλθῃ) in one place, and all speak with tongues, and there come in *those who are* uninformed or unbelievers, will they not say that you are out of your mind?"; 1 Cor 14:26, "Whenever you <u>comes together</u> (συνέρχησθε), each of you has a psalm, has a teaching, has a tongue, has a revelation, has an interpretation. Let all things be done for edification." Conversely the church should end associations with detrimental company [1 Cor 5:9, "I wrote to you in my epistle not to <u>keep company with</u> sexually immoral people (Ἔγραψα ὑμῖν ἐν τῇ ἐπιστολῇ μὴ <u>συναναμίγνυσθαι</u> πόρνοις);" 1 Cor 5:11, "But now I have written to you not to <u>keep company with</u> (μὴ συναναμίγνυσθαι) anyone named a brother, who is sexually immoral, or covetous, or an idolater, or a reviler, or a drunkard, or a swindler—not even to <u>eat with</u> such a person" (τῷ τοιούτῳ μηδὲ <u>συνεσθίειν</u>).

58. LN § 42.15.

59. Paul mentions co-workers in Rom 16:3, 9, 21; 2 Cor 1:24; 8:23; Phil 2:25; 4:3; Col 4:11; 1 Thess 3:2; Phlm 1:1, 24. The verbal concept appears in Phil 4:3, "And I urge you also, true companion, <u>help these</u> women who <u>labored with me</u> in the gospel, with Clement also, and the rest of my fellow workers, whose names *are* in the Book of Life" (ναὶ ἐρωτῶ καὶ σέ, γνήσιε σύζυγε, <u>συλλαμβάνου</u> αὐταῖς, αἵτινες ἐν τῷ εὐαγγελίῳ <u>συνήθλησάν</u>μ οι μετὰ καὶ Κλήμεντος καὶ τῶν λοιπῶν <u>συνεργῶν</u> μου, ὧν τὰ ὀνόματα ἐν βίβλῳ ζωῆς.); 1 Cor 16:16, "you also be in subjection to such men and to everyone who helps in the work and labors" (ἵνα καὶ ὑμεῖς ὑποτάσσησθε τοῖς τοιούτοις καὶ παντὶ τῷ <u>συνεργοῦντι</u> καὶ κοπιῶντι).

in *Him*," 2 Cor 5:21), referring to Christ, this would seem to qualify Jesus as the object of συνεργοῦντες, providing yet another aspect of association with Christ. As Jesus worked the works of God during His ministry (John 5:17), so now His messengers work with the "Man Christ Jesus" by encouraging others to receive the grace of God.

Thus, based upon their common association with Christ in His historical-redemptive salvation, believers are also to be involved in associative activities with one another, which includes common encouragement with one another (Rom 1:12),[60] striving with and helping with one another in prayer (Rom 15:30; 2 Cor 1:11);[61] being refreshed with one another (Rom 15:32);[62] rejoicing with one another (Phil 2:17-18);[63] and even in suffering with one another (1 Cor 12:26; Phil 4:14).[64] Believers are also "with one soul (to be) labouring (sic) together in the same conflict with the faith of the glad tidings" (Phil 1:27, *The Darby Bible*),[65] and eventually they shall all reign with one another (1 Cor 4:8).[66] In Paul's mind, the church should operate as the Body of Christ on earth by holding fast to Christ the Head, by whom it is "supplied and held together by the joints and ligaments, (and) grows with a growth which is from God" (Col 2:19). Individualistic North American Christians often neglect this corporate nature of the church, but a renewed emphasis in Paul's associative concepts would contribute to a healthier Pastoral Theology and ecclesiastical practice.

SUMMARY TO THE IMPLICATIONS OF THE "MAN CHRIST JESUS"

The greatest pastoral implication of Paul's view of the associative nature of the church with Christ and with one another is that the pastor needs to preach these particular doctrines to the church. Paul certainly assumed that his readers in Rome knew these teachings of

---

60. Romans 1:12 reads, "that I may be *encouraged together with you* by the mutual faith both of you and me" (τοῦτο δέ ἐστιν συμπαρακληθῆναι ἐν ὑμῖν διὰ τῆς ἐν ἀλλήλοις πίστεως ὑμῶν τε καὶ ἐμοῦ).

61. Romans 15:30 urges, "Now I beg you, brethren, through the Lord Jesus Christ, and through the love of the Spirit, that you *strive together with me* in prayers to God for me" (Παρακαλῶ δὲ ὑμᾶς [ἀδελφοί] διὰ τοῦ κυρίου ἡμῶν Ἰησοῦ Χριστοῦ καὶ διὰ τῆς ἀγάπης τοῦ πνεύματος συναγωνίσασθαί μοι ἐν ταῖς προσευχαῖς ὑπὲρ ἐμοῦ πρὸς τὸν θεόν); 2 Cor 1:11, "you also *helping together* in prayer for us" (συνυπουργούντων καὶ ὑμῶν ὑπὲρ ἡμῶν τῇ δεήσει).

62. In Rom 15:32, Paul announces "that I may come to you with joy by the will of God, and may be *refreshed together with* you" (ἵνα ἐν χαρᾷ ἐλθὼν πρὸς ὑμᾶς διὰ θελήματος θεοῦ συναναπαύσωμαι ὑμῖν).

63. Philippians 2:17 reads, "Yes, and if I am being poured out *as a drink offering* on the sacrifice and service of your faith, I am glad and *rejoice with you* all" (συγχαίρω πᾶσιν ὑμῖν·); Phil 2:18, "For the same reason you also be glad and *rejoice with me*" (συγχαίρετέ μοι).

64. 1 Corinthians 12:26 notes, "And if one member suffers, all the members suffer with *it*; or if one member is honored, all the members rejoice with *it*" (καὶ εἴτε πάσχει ἓν μέλος, συμπάσχει πάντα τὰ μέλη· εἴτε δοξάζεται [ἓν] μέλος, συγχαίρει πάντα τὰ μέλη); also Phil 4:14, "Nevertheless you have done well that you *shared in* my distress" (πλὴν καλῶς ἐποιήσατε συγκοινωνήσαντέ μου τῇ θλίψει).

65. Philippians 1:27 urges, "Only let your conduct be worthy of the gospel of Christ, so that whether I come and see you or am absent, I may hear of your affairs, that you stand fast in one spirit, with one mind *striving together* (συναθλοῦντες) for the faith of the gospel."

66. 1 Corinthians 4:8 states, "You have reigned as kings without us—and indeed I could wish you did reign, that we also might *reign with you*!" (καὶ ὄφελόν γε ἐβασιλεύσατε, ἵνα καὶ ἡμεῖς ὑμῖν συμβασιλεύσωμεν). Paul may speak a bit sarcastically here, but his comment about reigning with Christ is validly prophetic (Rev 20:6).

THE "MAN CHRIST JESUS"

the association of the church with the historical Jesus ("knowing this, that our old self was crucified with *Him*," Rom 6:1), implying that a pastor should teach these same truths to his congregation. In this manner, all believers should recognize their association with the "Man Christ Jesus" in the various aspects of the history of redemption, knowledge that will lead them to live accordingly with Christ (Col 3:1, "If then you were raised with Christ, seek those things which are above.") and with one another in the body of Christ ("with one mind striving together for the faith of the gospel;" Phil 1:27).

7

Conclusion: The "Man Christ Jesus" in the Teaching of Paul

IN CONCLUSION, THIS STUDY has investigated the humanity of Jesus in the teachings of the Apostle Paul by using as the source of its thesis the particular phrase found in 1 Tim 2:5, the "Man Christ Jesus."[1] It has demonstrated that the Apostle Paul in his letters and sermons not only refers constantly to the "Man Christ Jesus" as the basis of his gospel message, but he also constructs the primary framework of salvation on the historical-redemptive association of the church with the "Man Christ Jesus" in His redeeming work accomplished in space-time historical events. The conclusive finding of this study refutes the opinion of critical scholarship as surveyed in Chapter 1, that a disparity exists between Jesus and Paul, and instead, it supports the common consensus of evangelical scholarship espousing a continuity existing from Jesus to Paul; however, this study criticizes evangelicalism for assuming this succession while failing to demonstrate sufficiently how Paul implicitly establishes his gospel in general and his Christology in particular upon the space-time redemptive events enacted by the "Man Christ Jesus."

Chapter 2 provided the exegetical proof for this thesis in the examination of the primary clause of this study, *ànthropos Christòs Iēsoūs* (ἄνθρωπος Χριστὸς Ἰησοῦς), as it appears in the liturgical context of 1 Tim 2:5–6. The soteriological description of the "Man Christ Jesus" as the "one mediator between God and men" and as the ransom given in "the testimony in its own times" (YLT) was explored to determine the reason why Paul would identify Christ Jesus as "Man" instead of using the many other titles attributed to Him that Paul had at his ready disposal. The suggested answer is that Paul alludes to the OT appearances of the divine "Man" whose expectations have now been fulfilled in the "proper (historical) times" by the mediatorial work of the "Man Christ Jesus" as the ransom who brought reconciliation between "God and men."

Chapter 3 investigated how Paul uses the humanity of Jesus throughout his letters, which provide the earliest extant sources of the historical Jesus, along with the epistle of James. Although Paul does not frame his gospel message about Jesus in the setting of a narrative biography, he does refer repeatedly to the human Jesus, thereby challenging the assertion of critical scholarship that Paul had little or no interest in the earthly Galilean rabbi except as the paradigm for a deified redeemer. Instead, this study substantiates that in his identification of the "Man Christ Jesus," Paul refers to the same historical Jesus of

---

1. 1 Timothy 2:5 reads, "For there is one God, *and* one mediator also between God and men, *the* man Christ Jesus, who gave Himself as a ransom for all, the testimony *borne* at the proper time." This precise designation ἄνθρωπος Χριστὸς Ἰησοῦς appears only here in the NT.

THE "MAN CHRIST JESUS"

Nazareth as the one presented in the written Gospels, a very real flesh-and-blood man of Jewish descent.[2] He was also well aware that Jesus had ministered among the Jews as a teacher and preacher, and that He had been assisted by a band of disciples whom Paul labeled as the Twelve.[3] Paul also understood the character of Jesus well enough to commend Him as an example of righteous behavior,[4] particularly with regard to His undeserved sufferings[5] that culminated in His crucifixion after a betrayal and unjust condemnation by both Jewish and Roman authorities.[6] Paul, however, was genuinely persuaded that Jesus had been vindicated in the events of His bodily resurrection and physical ascension "in glory" (1 Tim 3:16, final clause).[7] Paul's letters indicate that the apostle agrees with the life of Jesus as it is presented in the Gospels; however, even if no biographical narratives of Jesus had ever been written, a thumbnail sketch of His life, character, and work could be derived from Paul's letters alone, providing sufficient information for his readers to believe in the one whom Paul preached as "Savior, the Lord Jesus Christ" (Phil 3:20).[8]

Chapter 4 of this study surveyed the indirect testimony of Paul regarding the "Man Christ Jesus" as recorded in the Acts of the Apostles. The research conducted in that first compilation of Christian history revealed that the Jesus of Paul's conversion accounts (Acts 9:1–22; 22:1–16; 26:4–18) is the very same Jesus Paul preached in his first recorded sermon, which is significantly framed in a sketch of Jesus' historical ministry (Acts 13:16–

---

2. The verses under this topic find Paul presenting Jesus as a man (1 Cor 15:21, 47; Phil 2:8) of physical flesh (Rom 1:3; 8:3; 9:5; 2 Cor 5:16; 1 Tim 3:16; 1 Cor 10:16; 11:24, 27; Col 1:22; 2:9) and blood (Rom 3:25; 5:9; 1 Cor 10:16; 11:25; Eph 1:7; Col 1:20). He was an Israelite (Rom 9:5) born of a woman (Gal 4:4) with several siblings (1 Cor 9:5; Gal 1:19), and He had lived in poverty (2 Cor 8:9). His circumcision (Col 2:11), Abrahamic and Davidic lineage (Gal 3:16–17; Rom 1:3; 15:12; 2 Tim 2:8), and legal upbringing under *Torah* (Gal 4:4) prove Him to be a man of Jewish descent.

3. The references to the ministry of Jesus include His service to the Jews (Rom 15:18), beginning (presumably) with His baptism (Rom 6:3, Col 2:12). He conducted His ministry by preaching (Rom 16:25), evangelizing (Eph 2:7), and teaching on various topics (1 Tim 6:3; Rom 14:14; 1 Cor 7:10; 9:14; 11:23–24; 1 Thess 4:15–5:2), with the assistance of disciples (1 Cor 15:5; Gal 2:9) and vindication by angels (1 Tim 3:16).

4. Paul refers to the moral character of Jesus in Rom 3:22, 26; 5:18; 15:3; 1 Cor 11:1; 2 Cor 5:20; 10:1; Gal 2:16; 3:22; Phil 1:8; 2:8; 3:19; 2 Thess 3:5; 1 Tim 1:15; 3:16.

5. The question Jesus asked Paul, "Why are you persecuting me?"(Acts 9:9:4; 22:7–8; 26:14), apparently deeply influenced the apostle's perception of the continuing suffering of Jesus even as the risen Lord (2 Cor 1:5; Phil 3:10; Col 1:24).

6. The events of Jesus' suffering include the Last Supper of Jesus (1 Cor 11:23–25) on the night of His betrayal (1 Cor 11:23); His deliverance for trial (Rom 4:25); His testimony (2 Tim 1:8); His condemnation under Pontius Pilate (1 Tim 6:13); His bodily injuries (Gal 6:17); His crucifixion (1 Cor 1:23; 2:2; 2 Cor 13:4); His crucifiers (1 Cor 2:8); His murder at the hands of Jewish leadership (1 Thess 2:15); His cross (1 Cor 1:18; Gal 3:1; 5:11; 6:12, 14; Eph 2:16; Phil 2:8; 3:18; Col 1:20); His nailing to a cross (Col 2:14); His death (Rom 5:6, 8, 10; 6:3, 5, 10; 8:34; 14:9, 15; 1 Cor 8:11; 11:26; 15:3; 2 Cor 4:10; 5:14–15; Gal 2:21; Phil 2:8; 3:10; Col 1:22; 1 Thess 4:14; 5:10; 2 Tim 2:11); His sacrifice at Passover (1 Cor 5:7); His giving as a ransom (1 Tim 2:6), and His burial in a tomb (Rom 6:4; 1 Cor 15:4; Col 2:12).

7. These references include Jesus' resurrection on the third day (1 Cor 15:4); His raising from the dead (Rom 4:24–25; 6:4–5, 9; 7:4; 8:34; 10:9; 1 Cor 6:14; 15:12–17; 2 Cor 4:14; 5:15; Eph 1:20; Col 2:12; 1 Thess 1:10; 4:14; 2 Tim 2:8); His appearances (1 Cor 9:1; 15:5–9); and His ascension (Rom 8:34; Eph 1:20; 1 Tim 3:16).

8. It is important to note, however, that the unknown editors who compiled the NT intended for Paul's letters to be supplemented by the Gospels and the book of Acts. Furthermore, Paul assumes that his readers shared common information about Jesus received from prior tradition (1 Cor 11:2; 2 Thess 2:15) and from catechetical teachings (Rom 6:17).

Conclusion: The "Man Christ Jesus" in the Teaching of Paul

41). The Jesus of Paul's missionary preaching is clearly intended to refer to this same man of human history (Acts 17:1–3, 18–31; 18:5; 19:1–7; 20:17–35), so that a comparison of these accounts in Acts with the letters of Paul prove that both works describe the same Jesus, indicating that had there been no historical Jesus, Paul would have had no heavenly Lord to proclaim as Savior. As it is, these combined records reveal that Paul refers to at least seventy-one different details and incidents derived from the person and life of Jesus of Nazareth.[9] In the face of this evidence, it is patently disingenuous to claim that Paul had no interest in the Jesus of history when it is very clear that he proclaimed the Jesus of history. While Paul also explains Jesus as "the image of the invisible God . . . by whom all things were created" (Col 1:15–16), intellectual honesty demands a recognition that Paul's divine Jesus "in whom dwells all the fulness of Deity" also dwells in bodily form (Col 2:9) because this glorified Man is the same Jesus of human history who reconciled His people in the body of His flesh through death on a cross (Col 1:22; 2:14). In that same human body, Jesus was raised from the dead and seated at the right hand of God (Col 2:12; 3:1)—supernatural events, to be sure, but divine actions that happened to a very earthly human being, the "Man Christ Jesus."

Chapter 5 explored how Paul applies the historical events of the "Man Christ Jesus" to his doctrine of salvation. He does so with a carefully crafted vocabulary, using the preposition σύν and συ-compounds in order to present a soteriological concept of the association of believers "with Christ" (σὺν Χριστῷ), in distinction to his more commonly known and widely researched motif of union "in Christ" (ἐν Χριστῷ). By picturing the entire church in this associative relationship with Christ, Paul looks on the acts of Jesus in redemptive history from the divine perspective. First, God has associated all believers with the "Man Christ Jesus" in His past historical actions that secured their salvation, most notably His crucifixion and resurrection.[10] Second, God associates His people with the sufferings of the "Man Christ Jesus" in the present trials of human experience.[11] Third, God shall associate the church with the future exaltation and reign of the "Man Christ Jesus."[12] Paul's perspective is not merely his own theological innovation nor a christological imposition thrust upon the Jesus of history, because each aspect of association with Christ depends upon Jesus as a real man who associated with sinners and disciples alike

---

9. This list concludes Chapter 4 (see pages 189–91).

10. These references include the following: that the church was crucified with Christ (Rom 6:6; Gal 2:19); planted with Christ in His death (Rom 6:5, 8; Col 2:20); buried with Christ (Rom 6:4; Col 2:12); made alive with Christ (Eph 2:5; Col 2:13); raised with Christ (Eph 2:6; Col 2:12; 3:1); seated with Christ (Eph 2:6); and now hidden with Christ (Col 3:3).

11. The references to the present sufferings of Jesus include Rom 8:17; 2 Cor 1:5; Phil 3:10; Col 1:24; 2 Tim 2:3.

12. These references include the following: that the church shall live with Christ (Rom 6:8; 2 Cor 13:4; 1 Thess 5:10; 2 Tim 2:11), shall be with Christ (Phil 1:23; 1 Thess 4:17); shall appear with Christ (Col 3:4); shall be brought with Christ (1 Thess 4:14); shall reign with Christ (2 Tim 2:12; 1 Cor 4:8); shall be conformed with Christ (Rom 8:29; Phil 3:21); shall be glorified with Christ (Rom 8:17); shall be raised with Christ (2 Cor 4:14); shall be a fellow heir with Christ (Rom 8:17; Eph 3:6); and shall be given all things with Christ (Rom 8:32).

during His earthly lifetime and who continues to associate with His people during their earthly pilgrimage and their eventual heavenly habitation.

What exactly does it mean that the "Man Christ Jesus" associates with His people and they in turn associate with Him and with one another? Chapter 6 answers this question by suggesting several christological, theological, and pastoral implications regarding the "historical humanity" of Jesus. It notes that Paul's order of salvation (*ordo salutis*) follows the historical order (*ordo historicis*), in that Paul shows that the Father saved His people "according to His own purpose and grace which was granted us in Christ Jesus (ἐν Χριστῷ Ἰησοῦ) from all eternity" (2 Tim 1:9). This redemptive grace was mediated *through* Christ (διὰ Χριστοῦ) who died in human history *for* (ὑπέρ) others, whom God considers as being associated *with* Christ (σὺν Χριστῷ) in His death, resurrection, and ascension. The historical accomplishments of salvation by the "Man Christ Jesus" are then applied vitally when His people are sealed *in* Christ (ἐν Χριστῷ) by the Holy Spirit in regeneration, and they are justified before God when they believe *into* (εἰς αὐτὸν πιστεύειν) or *upon* Christ (ἐπὶ τῇ πίστει). God then energizes believers by His transforming work of sanctification until the final day of history when they shall live together with Christ at His return and reign with Him forever. In each aspect of salvation, Paul views believers in their respective relationship with Christ, not only in His divinity as Lord, as Son, and even as God, but also—and one might even assert, primarily—in His humanity as the "Man Christ Jesus."

Thus, the conclusion of this study proposes that there is sufficient evidence to prove its intended thesis—that the apostle Paul affirms the humanity of the "Man Christ Jesus" as a figure of historical times. The comparative documentation presented from both the epistles of Paul and his sermons as recorded in Acts defends the proposition that the "Man Christ Jesus" referred to in 1 Tim 2:5 is the same historical Jesus as portrayed in the four Gospels, a man who claimed to be both the Son of God and also the Son of Man who came to give His life as a ransom for many (Mark 10:45). Paul makes use of the historical events of the "Man Christ Jesus" to substantiate his theology of redemption, in that he considers the church to be associated with Christ in the acts He accomplished in past history (namely, His life, death, burial, resurrection, and ascension) and in the events He shall complete in future history (namely, His return and reign). This book rests its case, then, by verifying that the Jesus of Paul's letters and sermons is the same Jesus portrayed in the Gospels, the Son of God who became a true human of human history and the one mediator of God and men by giving Himself as a ransom for sinful humans. Even as the resurrected Lord, this Jesus forever remains the human entitled by Paul, the "Man Christ Jesus."

Appendix 1

A Complete Listing of the Preposition Σύν in the Pauline Epistles

1. THE PREPOSITION ΣΥΝ IS USED IN THE PAULINE CORPUS 39 TIMES IN 37 VERSES.[1]

1. Romans 6:8, "*But if we died with Christ, we believe that also we shall live with Him*" (εἰ δὲ ἀπεθάνομεν σὺν Χριστῷ, πιστεύομεν ὅτι καὶ συζήσομεν αὐτῷ).

2. Romans 8:32, "*He who did not spare His own Son, but delivered Him up concerning us all, how also shall He not with Him* (σὺν αὐτῷ) *freely give us all things?*"

3. Romans 16:14, "Greet Asyncritus, Phlegon, Hermas, Patrobas, Hermes, and the brothers with them" (ἀσπάσασθε Ἀσύγκριτον, Φλέγοντα, Ἑρμῆν, Πατροβᾶν, Ἑρμᾶν καὶ τοὺς σὺν αὐτοῖς ἀδελφούς).

4. Romans 16:15, "Greet Philologus and Julia, Nereus and his sister, and Olympas, and all the saints with them" (ἀσπάσασθε Φιλόλογον καὶ Ἰουλίαν, Νηρέα καὶ τὴν ἀδελφὴν αὐτοῦ, καὶ Ὀλυμπᾶν καὶ τοὺς σὺν αὐτοῖς πάντας ἁγίους).

5. 1 Corinthians 1:2, "the ones having been sanctified in Christ Jesus, called (to be) saints, with all (σὺν πᾶσιν) the ones calling upon the name of our Lord Jesus Christ in every place."

6. 1 Corinthians 5:4, "In the name of our Lord Jesus Christ, when you have assembled together, along with my spirit, with the power of our Lord Jesus Christ" (σὺν τῇ δυνάμει τοῦ κυρίου ἡμῶν Ἰησοῦ).

7. 1 Corinthians 10:13, "A temptation has not taken you except human-kind, but God is faithful, who shall not allow you to be tempted beyond what you are able, but he shall make with the temptation (σὺν τῷ πειρασμῷ) also the outcome, that you are able to endure it."

8. 1 Corinthians 11:32, "But when we are judged, we are disciplined by the Lord, that we not with the world should be condemned" (ἵνα μὴ σὺν τῷ κόσμῳ κατακριθῶμεν).

9. 1 Corinthians 15:10, "but by grace of God I am what I am, and his grace in me did not become vain, but beyond all of them I labored, but not I but the grace of God with me" (ἡ χάρις τοῦ θεοῦ [ἡ] σὺν ἐμοί)."

---

1. Those verses with Christological significance are underlined. The English translations of the Greek texts are those of the author.

Appendix 1

10. 1 Corinthians 16:4, "they will go with me" (ἐὰν δὲ ἄξιον ᾖ τοῦ κἀμὲ πορεύεσθαι, σὺν ἐμοὶ πορεύσονται).

11. 1 Corinthians 16:19, "Aquila and Priscilla greet you much in the Lord, with the church in their house" (ἀσπάζεται ὑμᾶς ἐν κυρίῳ πολλὰ Ἀκύλας καὶ Πρίσκα σὺν τῇ κατ' οἶκον αὐτῶν ἐκκλησίᾳ).

12. 2 Corinthians 1:1, "Paul apostle of Christ Jesus through the will of God and Timothy the brother to the church of God the one being in Corinth with all the saints (σὺν τοῖς ἁγίοις) the ones being in all of Achaia."

13. 2 Corinthians 1:21, "and the one establishing us with you unto Christ and has anointed us *is* God" (ὁ δὲ βεβαιῶν ἡμᾶς σὺν ὑμῖν εἰς Χριστὸν καὶ χρίσας ἡμᾶς θεός).

14. <u>2 Corinthians 4:14, "*knowing that the one having rasied the Lord Jesus also shall raise us with Jesus, and will present us with you*</u>" (εἰδότες ὅτι ὁ ἐγείρας τὸν κύριον Ἰησοῦν καὶ ἡμᾶς σὺν Ἰησοῦ ἐγερεῖ καὶ παραστήσει σὺν ὑμῖν).

15. 2 Corinthians 8:19, "(he) was chosen by the churches (as) as travel-companion with us with this gift" (χειροτονηθεὶς ὑπὸ τῶν ἐκκλησιῶν συνέκδημος ἡμῶν σὺν τῇ χάριτι ταύτῃ . . .).

16. 2 Corinthians 9:4, "should any Macedonians coming with me (σὺν ἐμοὶ) also find you unprepared."

17. <u>2 Corinthians 13:4, "*For also we are being weak in Him, but we shall live with Him by the power of God toward you*</u>" (καὶ γὰρ ἡμεῖς ἀσθενοῦμεν ἐν αὐτῷ ἀλλὰ ζήσομεν σὺν αὐτῷ ἐκ δυνάμεως θεοῦ εἰς ὑμᾶς).

18. Galatians 1:2, "all the brothers with me" (οἱ σὺν ἐμοὶ πάντες ἀδελφοὶ).

19. Galatians 2:3, "Yet not Titus with me, being a Greek, was compelled to be circumcised" (ἀλλ' οὐδὲ Τίτος ὁ σὺν ἐμοί, Ἕλλην ὤν, ἠναγκάσθη περιτμηθῆναι).

20. Galatians 3:9, "So then the ones out of faith are blessed with believing Abraham" (ὥστε οἱ ἐκ πίστεως εὐλογοῦνται σὺν τῷ πιστῷ Ἀβραάμ).

21. Galatians 5:24, "And those of Christ have crucified the flesh with its passions and desires." (οἱ δὲ τοῦ Χριστοῦ [Ἰησοῦ] τὴν σάρκα ἐσταύρωσαν σὺν τοῖς παθήμασιν καὶ ταῖς ἐπιθυμίαις).

22. Ephesians 3:18, "that (you) may be able to comprehend with all the saints (σὺν πᾶσιν τοῖς ἁγίοις) what (is) the width and length and depth and height. . . ."

23. Ephesians 4:31, "Let all bitterness and wrath and anger and clamor and blasphemy be taken away from you, with all evil (σὺν πάσῃ κακίᾳ)."

24. Philippians 1:1, "Paul and Timothy, servants of Christ Jesus to all the saints in Christ Jesus, to the ones being in Philippi with overseers and deacons (σὺν ἐπισκόποις καὶ διακόνοις)."

25. <u>Philippians 1:23, "*But I am hard-pressed out of the two, having the desire to depart and to be with Christ, for that is very much better; yet to be remaining in the flesh is more necessary for your sake.*</u>" (συνέχομαι δὲ ἐκ τῶν δύο, τὴν ἐπιθυμίαν ἔχων εἰς τὸ ἀναλῦσαι καὶ σὺν Χριστῷ εἶναι, πολλῷ [γὰρ] μᾶλλον κρεῖσσον . . ."

26. Philippians 2:22, "But you know his proven character, that as a son with *his* father he served with me (σὺν ἐμοὶ) in the gospel."

27. Philippians 4:21, "The brethren with me greet you (ἀσπάζονται ὑμᾶς οἱ σὺν ἐμοὶ ἀδελφοί)."

28. Colossians 2:5, "For though I am absent in the flesh, but I am with you in spirit (ἀλλὰ τῷ πνεύματι σὺν ὑμῖν εἰμι), rejoicing to see your order and the steadfastness of your faith in Christ."

29. Colossians 2:13, "*And you, being dead in trespasses and the uncircumcision of your flesh, He made you alive together with Him, having forgiven you all trespasses* (καὶ ὑμᾶς νεκροὺς ὄντας [ἐν] τοῖς παραπτώμασιν καὶ τῇ ἀκροβυστίᾳ τῆς σαρκὸς ὑμῶν, συνεζωοποίησεν ὑμᾶς σὺν αὐτῷ, χαρισάμενος ἡμῖν πάντα τὰ παραπτώματα.)."

30. Colossians 2:20, "*If you died with Christ from the elements of the world, why, as though living in the world, do you subject yourselves to dogmas* (Εἰ ἀπεθάνετε σὺν Χριστῷ ἀπὸ τῶν στοιχείων τοῦ κόσμου, τί ὡς ζῶντες ἐν κόσμῳ δογματίζεσθε)."

31. Colossians 3:3, "*For you died, and your life is hidden with Christ in God* (ἀπεθάνετε γὰρ καὶ ἡ ζωὴ ὑμῶν κέκρυπται σὺν τῷ Χριστῷ ἐν τῷ θεῷ.)."

32. Colossians 3:4, "*When Christ who is our life appears, then also you shall appear with Him in glory* (ὅταν ὁ Χριστὸς φανερωθῇ, ἡ ζωὴ ὑμῶν, τότε καὶ ὑμεῖς σὺν αὐτῷ φανερωθήσεσθε ἐν δόξῃ)."

33. Colossians 3:9, "Do not lie to one another, having put off the old man with his deeds (μὴ ψεύδεσθε εἰς ἀλλήλους, ἀπεκδυσάμενοι τὸν παλαιὸν ἄνθρωπον σὺν ταῖς πράξεσιν αὐτοῦ)."

34. Colossians 4:9, "with Onesimus, a faithful and beloved brother, who is of you (σὺν Ὀνησίμῳ τῷ πιστῷ καὶ ἀγαπητῷ ἀδελφῷ, ὅς ἐστιν ἐξ ὑμῶν)."

35. 1 Thessalonians 4:14, "*For if we believe that Jesus died and rose again, thus also God will bring with Him those having slept through Jesus* (εἰ γὰρ πιστεύομεν ὅτι Ἰησοῦς ἀπέθανεν καὶ ἀνέστη, οὕτως καὶ ὁ θεὸς τοὺς κοιμηθέντας διὰ τοῦ Ἰησοῦ ἄξει σὺν αὐτῷ)."

36. 1 Thessalonians 4:17, "*Then we the ones living and remaining shall be caught up together with them in the clouds to a meeting of the Lord in the air; And thus always with the Lord we shall be* (ἔπειτα ἡμεῖς οἱ ζῶντες οἱ περιλειπόμενοι ἅμα σὺν αὐτοῖς ἁρπαγησόμεθα ἐν νεφέλαις εἰς ἀπάντησιν τοῦ κυρίου εἰς ἀέρα· καὶ οὕτως πάντοτε σὺν κυρίῳ ἐσόμεθα.)."

37. 1 Thessalonians 5:10, "*the one having died for us, that whether we are waking or sleeping, then we should live with Him*" (τοῦ ἀποθανόντος ὑπὲρ ἡμῶν, ἵνα εἴτε γρηγορῶμεν εἴτε καθεύδωμεν ἅμα σὺν αὐτῷ ζήσωμεν.).

2. VARIOUS NOUNS PREFIXED BY THE PREPOSITION ΣΥ-[2]

1. Romans 2:15, "such show the work of the law written in their hearts, their conscience also bearing witness, and between themselves *their* thoughts accusing or else ex-

---

2. According to a count in W. F. Moulton, and A. S. Geden, *A Concordance of the Greek New Testament*, fourth ed., revised H. K. Moulton. (Edinburgh: T. & T. Clark, 1963), the Westcott and Hort *Greek New Testament* includes 186 different words prefixed by the preposition σύν. Paul seems especially enamoured with the semantic possibilities of these compounds, using 92 of them, or nearly 50 per cent of the total. Of these, 51 are found only in Paul's vocabulary or fifty-five percent of Paul's total usage of the σύν compounds (These are: συλαγωγῶν, ἐσύλησα, σύμβουλος, συμμορφιζόμενος, σύμμορφον, σύμφορον, συμφυλετῶν,

Appendix 1

cusing *them*" (οἵτινες ἐνδείκνυνται τὸ ἔργον τοῦ νόμου γραπτὸν ἐν ταῖς καρδίαις αὐτῶν, συμμαρτυρούσης αὐτῶν τῆς συνειδήσεως καὶ μεταξὺ ἀλλήλων τῶν λογισμῶν κατηγορούντων ἢ καὶ ἀπολογουμένων).

2. Romans 3:16, "Destruction and misery *are* in their ways" (σύντριμμα καὶ ταλαιπωρία ἐν ταῖς ὁδοῖς αὐτῶν).

3. Romans 6:5, "*For if we have been planted with Him in the likeness of His death, but also we shall be in the likeness of His resurrection*" (εἰ γὰρ σύμφυτοι γεγόναμεν τῷ ὁμοιώματι τοῦ θανάτου αὐτοῦ, ἀλλὰ καὶ τῆς ἀναστάσεως ἐσόμεθα·).

4. Romans 8:17, "*and if children, heirs also, heirs indeed of God, fellow-heirs with Christ, if indeed we are suffering with Him in order that also we may be glorified with Him*" (εἰ δὲ τέκνα, καὶ κληρονόμοι· κληρονόμοι μὲν θεοῦ, συγκληρονόμοι δὲ Χριστοῦ, εἴπερ συμπάσχομεν ἵνα καὶ συνδοξασθῶμεν).

5. Romans 8:29, "*because whom He foreknew, He also predestined to become conformed with the image of His Son, that He might be first-born in many brethren*" (ὅτι οὓς προέγνω, καὶ προώρισεν συμμόρφους τῆς εἰκόνος τοῦ υἱοῦ αὐτοῦ, εἰς τὸ εἶναι αὐτὸν πρωτότοκον ἐν πολλοῖς ἀδελφοῖς).

6. Romans 9:1, "I tell the truth in Christ, I am not lying, my conscience also witnessing with me in the Holy Spirit" (Ἀλήθειαν λέγω ἐν Χριστῷ, οὐ ψεύδομαι, συμμαρτυρούσης μοι τῆς συνειδήσεώς μου ἐν πνεύματι ἁγίῳ).

7. Romans 9:3, "For I could wish that I myself were accursed from Christ for my brothers, my fellow-countrymen according to the flesh" (ηὐχόμην γὰρ ἀνάθεμα εἶναι αὐτὸς ἐγὼ ἀπὸ τοῦ Χριστοῦ ὑπὲρ τῶν ἀδελφῶν μου τῶν συγγενῶν μου κατὰ σάρκα).

8. Romans 11:17, "But if some of the branches were broken off, and you, being a wild olive tree, having been grafted in among them, and a fellow-partaker of the root and fatness of the olive tree" (Εἰ δέ τινες τῶν κλάδων ἐξεκλάσθησαν, σὺ δὲ ἀγριέλαιος ὢν ἐνεκεντρίσθης ἐν αὐτοῖς καὶ συγκοινωνὸς τῆς ῥίζης τῆς πιότητος τῆς ἐλαίας ἐγένου).

9. Romans 11:34, "For who has known the mind of the LORD? Or who has become His counselor?" (τίς γὰρ ἔγνω νοῦν κυρίου; ἢ τίς σύμβουλος αὐτοῦ ἐγένετο).

10. Romans 13:5, "Therefore *you* must be subject, not only because of wrath but also though the conscience" (ἀλλὰ καὶ διὰ τὴν συνείδησιν).

11. Romans 16:3, "Greet Priscilla and Aquila, my fellow-workers in Christ Jesus" (τοὺς συνεργούς μου ἐν Χριστῷ Ἰησοῦ).

12, 13. Romans 16:7, "Greet Andronicus and Junia, my fellow-countrymen and my fellow-prisoners (τοὺς συγγενεῖς μου καὶ συναιχμαλώτους μου) who are of note among the apostles, who also were in Christ before me."

σύμφυτοι, συμφώνησις, συμφώνου, συναγωνίσασθαί, συναθλοῦντες, συναιχμαλώτους, συναναμίγνυσθαι, συναναπαύσωμαι, συναπέστειλα, συναρμολογουμένη, συνδοξασθῶμεν, συμβασιλεύσομεν, συνηγέρθητε, συζήσομεν, συζητητής, σύζυγε, συνεζωοποίησεν, συνήδομαι, συνηλικιώτας, συνετάφημεν, συνθρύποντές, συγκακοπάθησον, σύγκαμψον, συγκατάθεσις, συμμαρτυρούσης, συμμερίζονται, συμμέτοχα, Συμμιμηταί, συνοικοδομεῖσθε, συμπαρακληθῆναι, συμπάσχομεν, συνεπέμψαμεν, συμπολῖται, σύσσωμα, συστενάζει, συστοιχεῖ, συστρατιώτην, συντέμνων, σύντριμμα, συνυπουργούντων, σύμφημι, σύμψυχοι, συνωδίνει, συστατικῶν). This novelty lends credence to the idea that Paul created his own vocabulary to describe the new association brought by the coming of Christ Jesus.

Appendix 1

14. Romans 16:9, "Greet Urbanus, our fellow-worker in Christ" (τὸν συνεργὸν ἡμῶν ἐν Χριστῷ).

15. Romans 16:11, "Greet Herodion, my fellow-countryman" (ἀσπάσασθε Ἡρῳδίωνα τὸν συγγενῆ μου.).

16–17. Romans 16:21, "Greet Timothy, my fellow-worker (ὁ συνεργός μου), and Lucius, Jason, and Sosipater, my fellow-countrymen (οἱ συγγενεῖς μου) greet you."

18. 1 Corinthians 1:19, "For it is written: 'I will destroy the wisdom of the wise, And bring to nothing the understanding (τὴν σύνεσιν) of the prudent.'"

19. 1 Corinthians 1:20, "Where *is* the disputer of this age?" (ποῦ συζητητὴς τοῦ αἰῶνος τούτου).

20. 1 Corinthians 3:9, "For we are God's fellow-workers" (θεοῦ γάρ ἐσμεν συνεργοί).

21. 1 Corinthians 7:5, "Do not deprive one another except out of common-consent (ἐκ συμφώνου) for a time, that you may give yourselves to fasting and prayer."

22. 1 Corinthians 7:35, "And this I say for your common-benefit (σύμφορον)."

23–24. 1 Corinthians 8:7, "But, *there is* not in everyone this knowledge; for some, with consciousness of the idol, until now eat *it* as a thing offered to an idol; and their conscience, being weak, is defiled" ('Ἀλλ' οὐκ ἐν πᾶσιν ἡ γνῶσις· τινὲς δὲ τῇ συνηθείᾳ ἕως ἄρτι τοῦ εἰδώλου ὡς εἰδωλόθυτον ἐσθίουσιν, καὶ ἡ συνείδησις αὐτῶν ἀσθενὴς οὖσα μολύνεται).

25. 1 Corinthians 8:10, "For if anyone sees you the one having knowledge eating in an idol's temple, shall not the conscience of him (ἡ συνείδησις αὐτοῦ) who is weak be emboldened to eat those things offered to idols?"

26. 1 Corinthians 8:12, "But when you thus sin against the brothers, and wound their conscience (τὴν συνείδησιν), being weak, you sin against Christ."

27. 1 Corinthians 9:23, "Now this I do through the gospel that I may be partaker of it" (πάντα δὲ ποιῶ διὰ τὸ εὐαγγέλιον, ἵνα συγκοινωνὸς αὐτοῦ γένωμαι).

28. 1 Corinthians 10:25, "Eat whatever is sold in the meat market, asking no questions because of conscience" (διὰ τὴν συνείδησιν).

29. 1 Corinthians 10:27, "If any of those who do not believe invites you *to* dinner, and you desire to go, eat whatever is set before you, examining nothing because of conscience" (διὰ τὴν συνείδησιν).

30. 1 Corinthians 10:28, "But if anyone says to you, 'This was offered to idols,' do not eat it for the sake of the one who told you, and for conscience' sake" (τὴν συνείδησιν).

31–32. 1 Corinthians 10:29, "'Conscience,' (συνείδησιν) I say, not your own, but that of the other. For why is my liberty judged by another's conscience?" (ὑπὸ ἄλλης συνειδήσεως).

33. 1 Corinthians 10:33, "I also please all in all things, not seeking my own profit (τὸ ἐμαυτοῦ σύμφορον), but the *profit* of the many, that they may be saved."

34. 1 Corinthians 11:16, "But if anyone seems to be contentious, we have no such custom (συνήθειαν), nor *do* the churches of God."

35. 1 Corinthians 12:7, "But to each one is given the manifestation of the Spirit unto the common-profit (πρὸς τὸ συμφέρον)."

Appendix 1

36. 2 Corinthians 1:12, "The testimony of our conscience (τῆς συνειδήσεως ἡμῶν) (is) that we conducted ourselves in the world in simplicity and sincerity;"

37. 2 Corinthians 1:24, "Not that we have dominion over your faith, but are fellow-workers of your joy" (οὐχ ὅτι κυριεύομεν ὑμῶν τῆς πίστεως ἀλλὰ συνεργοί ἐσμεν τῆς χαρᾶς ὑμῶν).

38. 2 Corinthians 2:4, "For out of much tribulation and anguish (συνοχῆς) of heart I wrote to you."

39. 2 Corinthians 3:1, "Do we begin again to commend ourselves? Or do we need, as some, letters of commendation to you or of commendation from you?" ('Αρχόμεθα πάλιν ἑαυτοὺς συνιστάνειν; ἢ μὴ χρήζομεν ὥς τινες συστατικῶν ἐπιστολῶν πρὸς ὑμᾶς ἢ ἐξ ὑμῶν).

40. 2 Corinthians 4:2, "... by disclosure of the truth commending (συνιστάνοντες) ourselves to every man's conscience (συνείδησιν) in the sight of God."

41. 2 Corinthians 5:11, "Knowing, therefore, the terror of the Lord, we are persuading men; but we are manifest to God, and I also trust are manifest in your consciences" (ἐν ταῖς συνειδήσεσιν ὑμῶν πεφανερῶσθαι).

42. 2 Corinthians 6:15, "And what common-agreement has Christ with Belial?" (τίς δὲ συμφώνησις Χριστοῦ πρὸς Βελιάρ).

43. 2 Corinthians 6:16, "And what common-agreement has the temple of God with idols?" (τίς δὲ συγκατάθεσις ναῷ θεοῦ μετὰ εἰδώλων).

44. 2 Corinthians 8:19, "(he) was also chosen by the churches as our fellow-traveler (συνέκδημος ἡμῶν) with this gift."

45. 2 Corinthians 8:23, "Titus my partner and fellow-worker (συνεργός) concerning you."

46. Galatians 1:14, "And I advanced in Judaism beyond many of my contemporaries (ὑπὲρ πολλοὺς συνηλικιώτας)."

47. Ephesians 2:19, "You are no longer strangers and aliens, but fellow-citizens (συμπολῖται) with the saints and members of the household of God."

48. Ephesians 3:4, "when you read, you may understand my knowledge (σύνεσίν) in the mystery of Christ."

49, 50, 51. Ephesians 3:6, "that the Gentiles should be fellow-heirs, of the same-body, and partakers of His promise in Christ through the gospel" (εἶναι τὰ ἔθνη συγκληρονόμα καὶ σύσσωμα καὶ συμμέτοχα τῆς ἐπαγγελίας ἐν Χριστῷ Ἰησοῦ διὰ τοῦ εὐαγγελίου).

52. Ephesians 4:3, "keep the unity of the Spirit in the same-bond of peace" (ἐν τῷ συνδέσμῳ τῆς εἰρήνης).

53. Ephesians 5:7, "Therefore do not be partakers of them" (μὴ οὖν γίνεσθε συμμέτοχοι αὐτῶν).

54. Philippians 2:2, "fulfill my joy by being... of one accord (σύμψυχοι)."

55, 56. Philippians 2:25, "Epaphroditus, my brother, fellow-worker and fellow-soldier (συνεργὸν καὶ συστρατιώτην μου,) but your messenger and the one who ministered to my need."

57. <u>Philippians 3:21, *"who will transform our lowly body that it may be conformed (σύμμορφον) to the body of his glory, according to the energy by which He is able even to subdue all things to Himself."*</u>

58. Colossians 1:7, "Epaphras, our dear fellow-servant (τοῦ ἀγαπητοῦ συνδούλου ἡμῶν)."

59. Colossians 1:9, "We . . . ask that you may be filled with the knowledge of His will in all wisdom and spiritual understanding" (συνέσει πνευματικῇ).

60. Colossians 2:2, "that their hearts may be encouraged, being knit together (συμβιβασθέντες) in love, unto all riches of the full assurance of understanding, to the knowledge (τῆς συνέσεως) of the mystery of God, both of the Father and of Christ."

61. <u>Colossians 2:19, "*and not holding fast to the Head, from whom all the body, nourished and knit together* (συμβιβαζόμενον) *by joints and ligaments* (συνδέσμων), *grows with the increase that is from God*."</u>

62. Colossians 3:14, "But above all these things put on love, which is the same-bond (σύνδεσμος) of perfection."

63. Colossians 4:7, "Tychicus, a . . . fellow-servant (σύνδουλος) in the Lord, will tell you all the news about me."

64, 65. Colossians 4:10–11, "Aristarchus my fellow-prisoner (ὁ συναιχμάλωτός μου) greets you, and Jesus who is called Justus. These *are my* only fellow-workers (συνεργοί) for the kingdom of God who are of the circumcision."

66. 1 Thessalonians 2:14, "For you also suffered the same things from your own fellow-countrymen (ὑπὸ τῶν ἰδίων συμφυλετῶν), just as they *did* from the Judeans."

67. 1 Thessalonians 3:2, "Timothy, . . . our fellow-laborer (συνεργὸν) in the gospel of Christ."

68. 1 Timothy 1:5, "Now the purpose of the commandment is love from a pure heart, *from* a good conscience (συνειδήσεως) and *from* sincere faith."

69. 1 Timothy 1:19, "having faith and a good conscience" (συνείδησιν).

70. 1 Timothy 3:9, "holding the mystery of the faith with a pure conscience" (ἐν καθαρᾷ συνειδήσει).

71. 1 Timothy 4:2, "having their own conscience (τὴν ἰδίαν συνείδησιν) seared with a hot iron."

72. 2 Timothy 1:3, "I thank God, whom I serve with a pure conscience" (ἐν καθαρᾷ συνειδήσει).

73. 2 Timothy 2:7, "Consider what I say, and may the Lord give you understanding (σύνεσιν) in all things."

74. Titus 1:15, "To those who are defiled and unbelieving nothing is pure; but even their mind and conscience (ἡ συνείδησις) are defiled."

75. Philemon 1:1, "To Philemon our beloved *friend* and fellow-worker" (καὶ συνεργῷ ἡμῶν).

76. Philemon 1:2, "To Archippus our fellow-soldier" ('Αρχίππῳ τῷ συστρατιώτῃ ἡμῶν).

77–78. Philemon 1:23–24, "Epaphras, my fellow-prisoner in Christ Jesus, greets you ('Ασπάζεταί σε Ἐπαφρᾶς ὁ συναιχμάλωτός μου ἐν Χριστῷ Ἰησοῦ), *as do* Mark, Aristarchus, Demas, Luke, my fellow-workers" (οἱ συνεργοί μου)."

Appendix 1

3. VERBAL COMPOUNDS PREFIXED BY THE PREPOSITION ΣΥ-

1. Romans 1:12, "that I may be encouraged together with you through the same faith both of you and me" (τοῦτο δέ ἐστιν συμπαρακληθῆναι ἐν ὑμῖν διὰ τῆς ἐν ἀλλήλοις πίστεως ὑμῶν τε καὶ ἐμοῦ).

2. Romans 1:32, "who, knowing the righteous judgment of God, that those who practice such things are deserving of death, not only do the same but also approve with those who practice them" (οἵτινες τὸ δικαίωμα τοῦ θεοῦ ἐπιγνόντες ὅτι οἱ τὰ τοιαῦτα πράσσοντες ἄξιοι θανάτου εἰσίν, οὐ μόνον αὐτὰ ποιοῦσιν ἀλλὰ καὶ συνευδοκοῦσιν τοῖς πράσσουσιν.).

3. Romans 2:15, "such ones show the work of the law written in their hearts, their conscience also bearing witness, and between themselves *their* thoughts accusing or even excusing *them*" (οἵτινες ἐνδείκνυνται τὸ ἔργον τοῦ νόμου γραπτὸν ἐν ταῖς καρδίαις αὐτῶν, συμμαρτυρούσης αὐτῶν τῆς συνειδήσεως καὶ μεταξὺ ἀλλήλων τῶν λογισμῶν κατηγορούντων ἢ καὶ ἀπολογουμένων).

4. Romans 3:5, "But if our unrighteousness demonstrates the righteousness of God, what shall we say? *Is* the God the one inflicts wrath unjust? (I speak as a man.)" (εἰ δὲ ἡ ἀδικία ἡμῶν θεοῦ δικαιοσύνην συνίστησιν, τί ἐροῦμεν; μὴ ἄδικος ὁ θεὸς ὁ ἐπιφέρων τὴν ὀργήν; κατὰ ἄνθρωπον λέγω.).

5. Romans 3:11, "There is none who understands; There is none seeking God" (οὐκ ἔστιν ὁ συνίων, οὐκ ἔστιν ὁ ἐκζητῶν τὸν θεόν.).

6. Romans 5:8, "But God demonstrates His own love toward us, because while we were being sinners, Christ died for us" (συνίστησιν δὲ τὴν ἑαυτοῦ ἀγάπην εἰς ἡμᾶς ὁ θεός, ὅτι ἔτι ἁμαρτωλῶν ὄντων ἡμῶν Χριστὸς ὑπὲρ ἡμῶν ἀπέθανεν.).

7. Romans 6:4, "*Therefore we were buried with Him through baptism into death, that just as Christ was raised from the dead by the glory of the Father, even so we also should walk in newness of life*" (συνετάφημεν οὖν αὐτῷ διὰ τοῦ βαπτίσματος εἰς τὸν θάνατον, ἵνα ὥσπερ ἠγέρθη Χριστὸς ἐκ νεκρῶν διὰ τῆς δόξης τοῦ πατρός, οὕτως καὶ ἡμεῖς ἐν καινότητι ζωῆς περιπατήσωμεν.).

8. Romans 6:6, "*knowing this, that our old man was crucified with Him that the body of the sin might be nullified, that we should no longer be serving the sin*;" (τοῦτο γινώσκοντες ὅτι ὁ παλαιὸς ἡμῶν ἄνθρωπος συνεσταυρώθη, ἵνα καταργηθῇ τὸ σῶμα τῆς ἁμαρτίας, τοῦ μηκέτι δουλεύειν ἡμᾶς τῇ ἁμαρτίᾳ.).

9. Romans 6:8, "*But if we died with Christ, we believe that also we shall live with Him*" (εἰ δὲ ἀπεθάνομεν σὺν Χριστῷ, πιστεύομεν ὅτι καὶ συζήσομεν αὐτῷ).

10. Romans 7:16, "I agree with the law that *it is* good" (σύμφημι τῷ νόμῳ ὅτι καλός.).

11. Romans 7:22, "For I delight in the law of God according to the inward man" (συνήδομαι γὰρ τῷ νόμῳ τοῦ θεοῦ κατὰ τὸν ἔσω ἄνθρωπον).

12. Romans 8:16, "The Spirit himself is witnessing with our spirit that we are children of God (αὐτὸ τὸ πνεῦμα συμμαρτυρεῖ τῷ πνεύματι ἡμῶν ὅτι ἐσμὲν τέκνα θεοῦ.)."

13, 14. Romans 8:17, "*and if children, heirs also, heirs indeed of God, fellow-heirs with Christ* (συγκληρονόμοι δὲ Χριστοῦ), *if indeed we are suffering with Him* (συμπάσχομεν) *in order that also we may be glorified with Him*" (συνδοξασθῶμεν).

Appendix 1

15. Romans 8:22, "For we know that all the creation is groaning with and laboring with birth pangs until now (οἴδαμεν γὰρ ὅτι πᾶσα ἡ κτίσις συστενάζει καὶ συνωδίνει ἄχρι τοῦ νῦν.)."

16. Romans 8:26, "Likewise the Spirit also helps with our weaknesses (Ὡσαύτως δὲ καὶ τὸ πνεῦμα συναντιλαμβάνεται τῇ ἀσθενείᾳ ἡμῶν)."

17. Romans 8:28, "And we know that to the ones loving God all things are working with for good , to the ones being called according to *His* purpose (Οἴδαμεν δὲ ὅτι τοῖς ἀγαπῶσιν τὸν θεὸν πάντα συνεργεῖ εἰς ἀγαθόν, τοῖς κατὰ πρόθεσιν κλητοῖς οὖσιν.)."

18. Romans 9:1, "I tell the truth in Christ, I am not lying, my conscience also bearing me witness in the Holy Spirit (Ἀλήθειαν λέγω ἐν Χριστῷ, οὐ ψεύδομαι, συμμαρτυρούσης μοι τῆς συνειδήσεώς μου ἐν πνεύματι ἁγίῳ)."

19, 20. Romans 9:28, "For He will finish the matter and cut *it* short in righteousness, because the LORD will make a short work upon the earth" (λόγον γὰρ συντελῶν καὶ συντέμνων ποιήσει κύριος ἐπὶ τῆς γῆς.).

21. Romans 11:10, "Let their eyes be darkened, so that they do not see, and their back always (be) bowed down (σκοτισθήτωσαν οἱ ὀφθαλμοὶ αὐτῶν τοῦ μὴ βλέπειν καὶ τὸν νῶτον αὐτῶν διὰ παντὸς σύγκαμψον.)."

22. Romans 11:32, "For God committed them all to disobedience, that to all He might have mercy" (συνέκλεισεν γὰρ ὁ θεὸς τοὺς πάντας εἰς ἀπείθειαν, ἵνα τοὺς πάντας ἐλεήσῃ.).

23. Romans 12:2, "And do not be conformed with this world, but be transformed by the renewal of your mind (καὶ μὴ συσχηματίζεσθε τῷ αἰῶνι τούτῳ, ἀλλὰ μεταμορφοῦσθε τῇ ἀνακαινώσει τοῦ νοὸς)."

24. Romans 12:16, "Do not be minding high things, but associate with the humble" (μὴ τὰ ὑψηλὰ φρονοῦντες ἀλλὰ τοῖς ταπεινοῖς συναπαγόμενοι).

25. Romans 15:21, "as it is written: "To whom He was not announced, they shall see; And those who have not heard shall understand (καὶ οἱ οὐκ ἀκηκόασιν συνήσουσιν.)."

26. Romans 15:30, "strive together with me in prayers to God for me (συναγωνίσασθαί μοι ἐν ταῖς προσευχαῖς ὑπὲρ ἐμοῦ πρὸς τὸν θεόν)."

27. Romans 15:32, "that in joy coming to you though the will of God, I may be refreshed together with you (ἵνα ἐν χαρᾷ ἐλθὼν πρὸς ὑμᾶς διὰ θελήματος θεοῦ συναναπαύσωμαι ὑμῖν.)."

28. Romans 16:1, "I commend (Συνίστημι) to you Phoebe our sister, who is a servant of the church in Cenchrea."

29. Romans 16:20, "And the God of peace will crush (συντρίψει) Satan under your feet shortly."

30. 1 Corinthians 2:13, "These things we also speak, not in words which man's wisdom teaches but which the Holy Spirit teaches, comparing spiritual things with spiritual (πνευματικοῖς πνευματικὰ συγκρίνοντες.)."

31. 1 Corinthians 2:16, "For who has known the mind of the LORD, who may may instruct Him?" (τίς γὰρ ἔγνω νοῦν κυρίου, ὃς συμβιβάσει αὐτόν;).

Appendix 1

32. 1 Corinthians 4:4, "For I know (σύνοιδα) nothing against myself, yet I am not justified in this; but He who judges me is the Lord."

33. 1 Corinthians 4:8, "You have reigned as kings without us—and indeed I could wish you did reign, that we also with you might reign! (καὶ ὄφελόν γε ἐβασιλεύσατε, ἵνα καὶ ἡμεῖς ὑμῖν συμβασιλεύσωμεν.)."

34. 1 Corinthians 5:4, "In the name of our Lord Jesus Christ, when you are gathered together (συναχθέντων ὑμῶν), along with my spirit, with the power of our Lord Jesus Christ."

35. 1 Corinthians 5:9, "I wrote to you in the epistle not to keep company with immoral ("Ἔγραψα ὑμῖν ἐν τῇ ἐπιστολῇ μὴ συναναμίγνυσθαι πόρνοις)."

36, 37. 1 Corinthians 5:11, "But now I have written to you not to keep company with anyone named a brother, who is sexually immoral, or covetous, or an idolater, or a reviler, or a drunkard, or an extortioner—with such not even to being eating (νῦν δὲ ἔγραψα ὑμῖν μὴ συναναμίγνυσθαι ἐάν τις ἀδελφὸς ὀνομαζόμενος ᾖ πόρνος ἢ πλεονέκτης ἢ εἰδωλολάτρης ἢ λοίδορος ἢ μέθυσος ἢ ἅρπαξ, τῷ τοιούτῳ μηδὲ συνεσθίειν.)."

38. 1 Corinthians 6:12, "All things are lawful for me, but all things are not helpful (Πάντα μοι ἔξεστιν ἀλλ' οὐ πάντα συμφέρει)."

39. 1 Corinthians 7:6, "But I say this as a concession, not as a commandment (τοῦτο δὲ λέγω κατὰ συγγνώμην οὐ κατ' ἐπιταγήν.)."

40. 1 Corinthians 7:12, "But to the rest I, not the Lord, say: If any brother has a wife who does not believe, and she is willing to live with him (καὶ αὕτη συνευδοκεῖ οἰκεῖν μετ' αὐτου), let him not divorce her."

41. 1 Corinthians 7:13, "And a woman who has a husband who does not believe, if he is willing to live with her (καὶ οὗτος συνευδοκεῖ οἰκεῖν μετ' αὐτῆς), let her not divorce him."

42. 1 Corinthians 7:29, "But this I say, brothers, the time *is* short (Τοῦτο δέ φημι, ἀδελφοί, ὁ καιρὸς συνεσταλμένος ἐστίν·)."

43. 1 Corinthians 7:35, "And this I say for your own profit (τὸ ὑμῶν αὐτῶν σύμφορον)."

44. 1 Corinthians 9:13, "Do you not know that those who minister the holy things eat of the temple, and those who serve at the altar partake (συμμερίζονται) of the altar?"

45. 1 Corinthians 10:11, "Now all these things happened (συνέβαινεν) to them as examples, and they were written for our instruction, upon whom the ends of the ages have come."

46. 1 Corinthians 10:23, "All things are lawful, but not all things are helpful (Πάντα ἔξεστιν ἀλλ' οὐ πάντα συμφέρει)."

47. 1 Corinthians 10:33, "just as I also please all *men* in all *things,* not seeking my own profit (σύμφορον), but that of many, that they may be saved."

48. 1 Corinthians 11:17, "Now commanding this, I do not praise *you,* because you come together (συνέρχεσθε) not for the better but for the worse."

49. 1 Corinthians 11:18, "when you come together as a church (συνερχομένων ὑμῶν ἐν ἐκκλησίᾳ), I hear that there are divisions among you, and partly I believe it."

50. 1 Corinthians 11:20, "Therefore when you come together (Συνερχομένων) in one place, it is not to eat the Lord's Supper."

Appendix 1

51. 1 Corinthians 11:33, "Therefore, my brethren, when you come together (συνερχόμενοι) to eat, wait for one another."

52. 1 Corinthians 11:34, "But if anyone is hungry, let him eat at home, that you not come together for judgment (ἵνα μὴ εἰς κρίμα συνέρχησθε.)."

53. 1 Corinthians 12:7, "But the manifestation of the Spirit is given to each one unto the profit *of all* (πρὸς τὸ συμφέρον.)."

54. 1 Corinthians 12:24, "But God composed (συνεκέρασεν) the body, having given greater honor to that which lacks it."

55, 56. 1 Corinthians 12:26, "And if one member suffers, all the members suffer with *it*; or if one member is honored, all the members rejoice with *it* (καὶ εἴτε πάσχει ἓν μέλος, συμπάσχει πάντα τὰ μέλη· εἴτε δοξάζεται [ἓν] μέλος, συγχαίρει πάντα τὰ μέλη.)."

57. 1 Corinthians 13:6, "Love does not rejoice in iniquity, but rejoices (συγχαίρει) in the truth."

58. 1 Corinthians 14:23, "Therefore if the whole church comes together (συνέλθῃ) in one place, and all speak with tongues, and there come in the uninformed or unbelievers, will they not say that you are out of your mind?"

59. 1 Corinthians 14:26, "Whenever you come together (συνέρχησθε), each of you has a psalm, has a teaching, has a tongue, has a revelation, has an interpretation. Let all things be done unto edification."

60. 1 Corinthians 16:16, "that you also submit to such, and to everyone who works with (παντὶ τῷ συνεργοῦντι) and labors with *us*."

61. 2 Corinthians 1:11, "you also helping together in prayer concerning us (συνυπουργούντων καὶ ὑμῶν ὑπὲρ ἡμῶν τῇ δεήσει)."

62. 2 Corinthians 3:1, "Do we begin again to commend ourselves? Or do we need, as some, letters of commendation to you or *letters* of commendation from you?" (Ἀρχόμεθα πάλιν ἑαυτοὺς συνιστάνειν; ἢ μὴ χρῄζομεν ὥς τινες συστατικῶν ἐπιστολῶν πρὸς ὑμᾶς ἢ ἐξ ὑμῶν;)."

63. 2 Corinthians 4:2, "by disclosure of the truth commending (συνιστάνοντες) ourselves to every man's conscience (συνείδησιν) in the sight of God."

64. 2 Corinthians 5:12, "For we do not commend ourselves (ἑαυτοὺς συνιστάνομεν) again to you."

65. 2 Corinthians 5:14, "for the love of Christ compels us (ἡ γὰρ ἀγάπη τοῦ Χριστοῦ συνέχει ἡμᾶς), having judged this, that if One died for all, then all died."

66. <u>2 Corinthians 6:1, *"We then, as workers together with—(Συνεργοῦντες) also plead with you not to receive the grace of God in vain;"*</u>

67. 2 Corinthians 6:4, "But in all *things* we commend ourselves (συνιστάντες ἑαυτοὺς) as ministers of God."

68, 69. <u>2 Corinthians 7:3, *"I do not say this to condemn; for I have said before that you are in our hearts, to die with and to live with*</u> (πρὸς κατάκρισιν οὐ λέγω· προείρηκα γὰρ ὅτι ἐν ταῖς καρδίαις ἡμῶν ἐστε εἰς τὸ συναποθανεῖν καὶ συζῆν.)" [compare to 2 Tim 2:11].

Appendix 1

70. 2 Corinthians 7:11, "In all *things* you proved yourselves to be pure in this matter (ἐν παντὶ συνεστήσατε ἑαυτοὺς ἁγνοὺς εἶναι τῷ πράγματι.)."

71. 2 Corinthians 8:10, "for this is to your profit (συμφέρει), who were not only the first to begin a year ago but also to be willing."

72. 2 Corinthians 8:18, "And we have sent with him (συνεπέμψαμεν δὲ μετ' αὐτοῦ) the brother whose praise *is* in the gospel throughout all the churches."

73. 2 Corinthians 8:22, "And we have sent (συνεπέμψαμεν) with them our brother."

74, 75, 76, 77. 2 Corinthians 10:12, "for we dare not classify or compare (συγκρῖναι) ourselves with such of the ones comparing (συνιστανόντων) themselves, but they by themselves are measuring and comparing (συγκρίνοντες) themselves with themselves, they are not understanding (συνιᾶσιν)

78, 79. 2 Corinthians 10:18, "For not the one commending himself is this one approved, but whom the Lord commends (οὐ γὰρ ὁ ἑαυτὸν συνιστάνων, ἐκεῖνός ἐστιν δόκιμος, ἀλλὰ ὃν ὁ κύριος συνίστησιν.)."

80. 2 Corinthians 12:1, "to boast is necessary, but not profitable (συμφέρον)."

81. 2 Corinthians 12:11, "For I ought to have been commended by you (ἐγὼ γὰρ ὤφειλον ὑφ' ὑμῶν συνίστασθαι·)."

82. 2 Corinthians 12:18, "I urged Titus, and sent the brother with *him* (παρεκάλεσα Τίτον καὶ συναπέστειλα τὸν ἀδελφόν)."

83. Galatians 2:1, "Then after fourteen years I went up again unto Jerusalem with Barnabas, taking also Titus with *me*" ("Επειτα διὰ δεκατεσσάρων ἐτῶν πάλιν ἀνέβην εἰς Ἱεροσόλυμα μετὰ Βαρναβᾶ συμπαραλαβὼν καὶ Τίτον.)."

84. Galatians 2:12, "for before certain men came from James, he would eat with the Gentiles; (πρὸ τοῦ γὰρ ἐλθεῖν τινας ἀπὸ Ἰακώβου μετὰ τῶν ἐθνῶν συνήσθιεν)."

85. Galatians 2:13, "And the rest of the Jews also joined in hypocrisy with him (καὶ συνυπεκρίθησαν αὐτῷ [καὶ] οἱ λοιποὶ Ἰουδαῖοι), so that even Barnabas was led away in their hypocrisy."

86. Galatians 2:18, "For if I build again the things I destroyed, I make myself a transgressor (εἰ γὰρ ἃ κατέλυσα ταῦτα πάλιν οἰκοδομῶ, παραβάτην ἐμαυτὸν συνιστάνω.)."

87. <u>Galatians 2:19, "*I am crucified with Christ*</u> (Χριστῷ συνεσταύρωμαι)."

88. Galatians 3:22, "But the Scripture has confined (συνέκλεισεν) all under sin, that the promise out of the faith of Jesus Christ might be given to the ones believing."

89. Galatians 3:23, "But before faith came, we were kept under guard under law, enclosed unto the faith about to be revealed (Πρὸ τοῦ δὲ ἐλθεῖν τὴν πίστιν ὑπὸ νόμον ἐφρουρούμεθα συγκλειόμενοι εἰς τὴν μέλλουσαν πίστιν ἀποκαλυφθῆναι)."

90. Galatians 4:25, "for this Hagar is Mount Sinai in Arabia, and she corresponds to the now Jerusalem (τὸ δὲ Ἁγὰρ Σινᾶ ὄρος ἐστὶν ἐν τῇ Ἀραβίᾳ· συστοιχεῖ δὲ τῇ νῦν Ἱερουσαλήμ)."

91, 92, 93. <u>Ephesians 2:5-6, "*even when we were dead in trespasses, He made us alive together with Christ*</u> *(συνεζωοποίησεν τῷ Χριστῷ,), and raised us with (Him), and made us sit*

Appendix 1

with (Him) in the heavenly places in Christ Jesus (καὶ συνήγειρεν καὶ συνεκάθισεν ἐν τοῖς ἐπουρανίοις ἐν Χριστῷ Ἰησοῦ)."

94. Ephesians 2:21, "In whom the whole structure, being joined together, grows into a holy temple in the Lord (ἐν ᾧ πᾶσα οἰκοδομὴ συναρμολογουμένη αὔξει εἰς ναὸν ἅγιον ἐν κυρίῳ)."

95. Ephesians 2:22, "in whom also you are being built with unto a habitation of God in the Spirit (ἐν ᾧ καὶ ὑμεῖς συνοικοδομεῖσθε εἰς κατοικητήριον τοῦ θεοῦ ἐν πνεύματι.)."

96, 97. Ephesians 4:16, "from whom the whole body, being joined and knit together (συναρμολογούμενον καὶ συμβιβαζόμενον) by what every joint supplies, according to the energy by which every part does its share, causes growth of the body for the edifying of itself in love."

98. Ephesians 5:11, "And have no fellowship (μὴ συγκοινωνεῖτε) with the unfruitful works of darkness, but rather expose."

99. Ephesians 5:17, "Therefore do not be unwise, but understand (συνίετε) what the will of the Lord *is*."

100. Philippians 1:7, "in my chains and in the defense and confirmation of the gospel, you all are being partakers with me of grace (ἔν τε τοῖς δεσμοῖς μου καὶ ἐν τῇ ἀπολογίᾳ καὶ βεβαιώσει τοῦ εὐαγγελίου συγκοινωνούς μου τῆς χάριτος πάντας ὑμᾶς ὄντας.)."

101. Philippians 1:27, "with one mind striving together (συναθλοῦντες) for the faith of the gospel."

102. Philippians 2:17, " I am rejoicing with you all (συγχαίρω πᾶσιν ὑμῖν·)."

103. Philippians 2:18, "And you also in the same way be glad and rejoice with me (συγχαίρετέ μοι)."

104. <u>Philippians 3:10, "*that I may know Him and the power of His resurrection, and the fellowship of His sufferings, being conformed with his death* (συμμορφιζόμενος τῷ θανάτῳ αὐτοῦ)."</u>

105. Philippians 3:17, "Be fellow-imitators of me, brothers (Συμμιμηταί μου γίνεσθε, ἀδελφοί)."

106, 107. Philippians 4:3, "And I urge you also, true companion, help with these women who labored with me in the gospel, with Clement also, and the rest of my fellow-workers, whose names *are* in the Book of Life (ναὶ ἐρωτῶ καὶ σέ, γνήσιε σύζυγε, συλλαμβάνου αὐταῖς, αἵτινες ἐν τῷ εὐαγγελίῳ συνήθλησάν μοι μετὰ καὶ Κλήμεντος καὶ τῶν λοιπῶν συνεργῶν μου, ὧν τὰ ὀνόματα ἐν βίβλῳ ζωῆς.)."

108. Philippians 4:14, "Nevertheless you have done well, having shared in my distress (πλὴν καλῶς ἐποιήσατε συγκοινωνήσαντές μου τῇ θλίψει.)."

109. Colossians 1:17, "And He is before all things, and in Him all things consist (συνέστηκεν)."

110. Colossians 2:2, "that their hearts may be encouraged, being knit together (συμβιβασθέντες) in love, and *attaining* to all riches of the full assurance of understanding, to the knowledge (τῆς συνέσεως) of the mystery of God, both of the Father and of Christ."

111. Colossians 2:8, "Beware lest anyone cheat (ὁ συλαγωγῶν) you through philosophy and empty deceit, according to the tradition of men, according to the basic elements of the world, and not according to Christ."

Appendix 1

112, 113. Colossians 2:12, "*having been buried with Him in baptism, in which also you were raised with Him through faith in the energy of God, the one having raised him out of the dead ones* (συνταφέντες αὐτῷ ἐν τῷ βαπτισμῷ, ἐν ᾧ καὶ συνηγέρθητε διὰ τῆς πίστεως τῆς ἐνεργείας τοῦ θεοῦ τοῦ ἐγείραντος αὐτὸν ἐκ νεκρῶν.)."

114. Colossians 2:13, "*And you, being dead in your trespasses and the uncircumcision of your flesh, He made you alive with Him* (συνεζωοποίησεν ὑμᾶς σὺν αὐτω), having forgiven you all trespasses."

115. Colossians 2:19, "not holding fast to the Head, from whom all the body, nourished and knit together (συμβιβαζόμενον) by joints and ligaments (συνδέσμων), grows with the increase from God."

116. Colossians 3:1, "*If therefore you were raised with Christ, the above-things seek, where Christ is, sitting at the right hand of God.*" (Εἰ οὖν συνηγέρθητε τῷ Χριστῷ, τὰ ἄνω ζητεῖτε, οὗ ὁ Χριστός ἐστιν ἐν δεξιᾷ τοῦ θεοῦ καθήμενος).

117. 2 Thessalonians 3:14, "If anyone does not obey our word in this letter, note that person and do not share company with him (μὴ συναναμίγνυσθαι αὐτῷ), that he may be ashamed."

118. 2 Timothy 1:8, "Therefore do not be ashamed of the testimony of our Lord, nor of me his prisoner, but share [with me. in the sufferings for the gospel according to the power of God" (μὴ οὖν ἐπαισχυνθῇς τὸ μαρτύριον τοῦ κυρίου ἡμῶν μηδὲ ἐμὲ τὸν δέσμιον αὐτοῦ, ἀλλὰ συγκακοπάθησον τῷ εὐαγγελίῳ κατὰ δύναμιν θεοῦ).

119. 2 Timothy 2:3, "Endure suffering with as a good soldier of Jesus Christ" (Συγκακοπάθησον ὡς καλὸς στρατιώτης Χριστοῦ Ἰησοῦ).

120, 121. 2 Timothy 2:11, "*Faithful is the word: For if we died with, we shall also live with*" (πιστὸς ὁ λόγος· εἰ γὰρ συναπεθάνομεν, καὶ συζήσομεν).

122. 2 Timothy 2:12, "*If we endure, We shall also reign with*" (συμβασιλεύσομεν).

Appendix 2

A Synthesis of the Pauline References to Association With Christ

A. **Association with Christ With Past Reference:** Generally, this group uses the aorist or perfect tenses, but the common feature is the completed work of Christ in the events of salvation:

1. Crucified with Christ:[1]

    Romans 6:6, "this knowing, that our old man was crucified with *Him*, in order that the body of sin might be done away with, that we should no longer be slaving to sin" (τοῦτο γινώσκοντες ὅτι ὁ παλαιὸς ἡμῶν ἄνθρωπος συνεσταυρώθη, ἵνα καταργηθῇ τὸ σῶμα τῆς ἁμαρτίας, τοῦ μηκέτι δουλεύειν ἡμᾶς τῇ ἁμαρτίᾳ).

    Galatians 2:19–20, "With Christ I have been crucified" (Χριστῷ συνεσταύρωμαι);

2. Died with Christ:

    Romans 6:8, "But if we died with Christ, we are believing that also we shall live with Him" (εἰ δὲ ἀπεθάνομεν σὺν Χριστῷ, πιστεύομεν ὅτι καὶ συζήσομεν αὐτῷ,);

    Colossians 2:20, "If you died with Christ from the elementary principles of the world, why, as *though* living in the world, do you subject yourselves to its dogmas" (Εἰ ἀπεθάνετε σὺν Χριστῷ ἀπὸ τῶν στοιχείων τοῦ κόσμου, τί ὡς ζῶντες ἐν κόσμῳ δογματίζεσθε;);

    2 Timothy 2:11, "Faithful is the word: For if we died with *Him, also w*e shall live with *Him*" (πιστὸς ὁ λόγος· εἰ γὰρ συναπεθάνομεν, καὶ συζήσομεν·);

    2 Corinthians 7:3 provides an interesting parallel, "For I have said before that you are in our hearts, to die together and to live together" (προείρηκα γὰρ ὅτι ἐν ταῖς καρδίαις ἡμῶν ἐστε εἰς τὸ συναποθανεῖν καὶ συζῆν.);

3. Planted with Christ in His Death:

    Romans 6:5, "For if we have been planted with *Him* in the likeness of His death, but also we shall be *in the likeness* of *His* resurrection" (εἰ γὰρ σύμφυτοι γεγόναμεν τῷ ὁμοιώματι τοῦ θανάτου αὐτοῦ, ἀλλὰ καὶ τῆς ἀναστάσεως ἐσόμεθα·);

4. Buried with Christ:

    Romans 6:4, "Therefore we were buried with Him through baptism into death, in order that just as Christ was raised out of dead (ones) through the glory of the

---

1. The English translations of the Greek NT text are those of the author.

Appendix 2

Father, thus also we should walk in newness of life" (συνετάφημεν οὖν αὐτῷ διὰ τοῦ βαπτίσματος εἰς τὸν θάνατον, ἵνα ὥσπερ ἠγέρθη Χριστὸς ἐκ νεκρῶν διὰ τῆς δόξης τοῦ πατρός, οὕτως καὶ ἡμεῖς ἐν καινότητι ζωῆς περιπατήσωμεν);

Colossians 2:12, ". . . having been buried with Him in the baptism, in which also you were raised with *Him* through faith in the energy of God, the one having raised Him out of the dead ones" (συνταφέντες αὐτῷ ἐν τῷ βαπτισμῷ, ἐν ᾧ καὶ συνηγέρθητε διὰ τῆς πίστεως τῆς ἐνεργείας τοῦ θεοῦ τοῦ ἐγείραντος αὐτὸν ἐκ νεκρῶν);

5. Raised with Christ:

Ephesians 2:6, "and (He) raised *us* up together, and made *us* sit together in the heavenly *places* in Christ Jesus" (καὶ συνήγειρεν καὶ συνεκάθισεν ἐν τοῖς ἐπουρανίοις ἐν Χριστῷ Ἰησοῦ);

Colossians 2:12, ". . . having been buried with Him in the baptism, in which also you were raised with *Him* through faith in the energy of God, the one having raised Him out of the dead ones" (συνταφέντες αὐτῷ ἐν τῷ βαπτισμῷ, ἐν ᾧ καὶ συνηγέρθητε διὰ τῆς πίστεως τῆς ἐνεργείας τοῦ θεοῦ τοῦ ἐγείραντος αὐτὸν ἐκ νεκρῶν);

Colossians 3:1, "If therefore you were raised with Christ, the above-things be seeking, where Christ is, sitting at the right hand of God" (Εἰ οὖν συνηγέρθητε τῷ Χριστῷ, τὰ ἄνω ζητεῖτε, οὗ ὁ Χριστός ἐστιν ἐν δεξιᾷ τοῦ θεοῦ καθήμενος);

6. Made Alive with Christ:

Ephesians 2:5, "and when we were dead in trespasses, (He) made us alive together with Christ (by grace you have been saved), (καὶ ὄντας ἡμᾶς νεκροὺς τοῖς παραπτώμασιν συνεζωοποίησεν τῷ Χριστῷ, - χάριτί ἐστε σεσῳσμένοι-)."

Colossians 2:13, "And you, being dead in the trespasses and the uncircumcision of your flesh, He made you alive with Him, having forgiven you all trespasses" (καὶ ὑμᾶς νεκροὺς ὄντας [ἐν] τοῖς παραπτώμασιν καὶ τῇ ἀκροβυστίᾳ τῆς σαρκὸς ὑμῶν, συνεζωοποίησεν ὑμᾶς σὺν αὐτῷ, χαρισάμενος ἡμῖν πάντα τὰ παραπτώματα);

7. Seated with Christ:

Ephesians 2:6, "and (He) raised *us* up with *Christ*, and made *us* sit with *Him* in the heavenly *places* in Christ Jesus" (καὶ συνήγειρεν καὶ συνεκάθισεν ἐν τοῖς ἐπουρανίοις ἐν Χριστῷ Ἰησοῦ);

8. Hidden with Christ:

Colossians 3:3, "For you died, and your life has been hidden with Christ in God" (ἀπεθάνετε γάρ καὶ ἡ ζωὴ ὑμῶν κέκρυπται σὺν τῷ Χριστῷ ἐν τῷ θεῷ).

B. **Association With Christ with Present Reference:** These verses generally use the present tense and emphasize how believers associate with one another and with Christ in His present ministry of heavenly Session:

Appendix 2

1. Being Fellow Heirs with Christ:

    Romans 8:17, "and if children, also heirs—heirs indeed of God, and joint-heirs with Christ, if indeed we suffer with *Him,* that also we may be glorified together" (εἰ δὲ τέκνα, καὶ κληρονόμοι· κληρονόμοι μὲν θεοῦ, συγκληρονόμοι δὲ Χριστοῦ, εἴπερ συμπάσχομεν ἵνα καὶ συνδοξασθῶμεν);

    Ephesians 3:6, "that the Gentiles should heirs with *Him,* and same-body with *Him,* and same-partakers of the promise in Christ through the gospel" (εἶναι τὰ ἔθνη συγκληρονόμα καὶ σύσσωμα καὶ συμμέτοχα τῆς ἐπαγγελίας ἐν Χριστῷ Ἰησοῦ διὰ τοῦ εὐαγγελίου,);

2. Being Conformed with Christ:

    Philippians 3:10, "that I may know Him and the power of His resurrection, and the fellowship of His sufferings, being conformed to His death" (συμμορφιζόμενος τῷ θανάτῳ αὐτοῦ).

3. Suffering with Christ:

    Romans 8:17, "and if children, also heirs—heirs indeed of God, and joint-heirs with Christ, if indeed we suffer with *Him,* that also we may be glorified together" (εἰ δὲ τέκνα, καὶ κληρονόμοι· κληρονόμοι μὲν θεοῦ, συγκληρονόμοι δὲ Χριστοῦ, εἴπερ συμπάσχομεν ἵνα καὶ συνδοξασθῶμεν);

    2 Timothy 1:8, "Therefore do not be ashamed of the testimony of our Lord, nor of me his prisoner, but share [with me.in the sufferings for the gospel according to the power of God" (μὴ οὖν ἐπαισχυνθῇς τὸ μαρτύριον τοῦ κυρίου ἡμῶν μηδὲ ἐμὲ τὸν δέσμιον αὐτοῦ, ἀλλὰ συγκακοπάθησον τῷ εὐαγγελίῳ κατὰ δύναμιν θεοῦ);

    2 Timothy 2:3, "Share suffering with as a good soldier of Jesus Christ"(Συγκακοπάθησον ὡς καλὸς στρατιώτης Χριστοῦ Ἰησοῦ);

4. Association with Christ's Body:

    1 Corinthians 12:26, "And if one member suffers, all the members suffer with *it;* or if one member is honored, all the members rejoice with *it*" (καὶ εἴτε πάσχει ἓν μέλος, συμπάσχει πάντα τὰ μέλη· εἴτε δοξάζεται [ἓν] μέλος, συγχαίρει πάντα τὰ μέλη);

    2 Corinthians 6:1, "We then, *as* working *with Him* (Συνεργοῦντες) also plead with *you* not to receive the grace of God in vain."

    Colossians 2:19, "and not holding fast to the Head, from whom all the body, nourished and knit together (συμβιβαζόμενον) by joints and ligaments (συνδέσμων), grows with the increase *that is* from God."

C. Association with Christ with Future Reference: These verses generally use the future tense or the aorist tense with future intention.

1. Shall Live with Christ:

    Romans 6:8, "But if we died with Christ, we believe that also we shall live with Him" (εἰ δὲ ἀπεθάνομεν σὺν Χριστῷ, πιστεύομεν ὅτι καὶ συζήσομεν αὐτῷ);

Appendix 2

    2 Corinthians 7:3, "For I have said before that you are in our hearts, to die together and to live together" (προείρηκα γὰρ ὅτι ἐν ταῖς καρδίαις ἡμῶν ἐστε εἰς τὸ συναποθανεῖν καὶ συζῆν.);

    2 Corinthians 13:4, "For also He was crucified out of weakness, but He lives out of the power of God. And also we are weak in Him, but we shall live with Him out of the power of God toward you" (καὶ γὰρ ἐσταυρώθη ἐξ ἀσθενείας, ἀλλὰ ζῇ ἐκ δυνάμεως θεοῦ. καὶ γὰρ ἡμεῖς ἀσθενοῦμεν ἐν αὐτῷ, ἀλλὰ ζήσομεν σὺν αὐτῷ ἐκ δυνάμεως θεοῦ εἰς ὑμᾶς);

    1 Thessalonians 5:10, "the one having died for us, that whether we wake or sleep, we should live together with Him" (τοῦ ἀποθανόντος ὑπὲρ ἡμῶν, ἵνα εἴτε γρηγορῶμεν εἴτε καθεύδωμεν ἅμα σὺν αὐτῷ ζήσωμεν);

    2 Timothy 2:11, "Faithful is the word: For if we died with *Him*, also *w*e shall live with *Him*." (πιστὸς ὁ λόγος· εἰ γὰρ συναπεθάνομεν, καὶ συζήσομεν·);

2. Shall Be with Christ:

    Philippians 1:23, "but I am hard pressed between the two, having the desire to depart and be with Christ, *which is* much better" (συνέχομαι δὲ ἐκ τῶν δύο, τὴν ἐπιθυμίαν ἔχων εἰς τὸ ἀναλῦσαι καὶ σὺν Χριστῷ εἶναι, πολλῷ [γὰρ] μᾶλλον κρεῖσσον).

    1 Thessalonians 4:17, "then we (ourselves), the ones living, the ones remaining at the same time with them (σὺν αὐτοῖς) shall be snatched in clouds unto a meeting of the Lord into (the) air; and thus always with (the) Lord we shall be" (ἔπειτα ἡμεῖς οἱ ζῶντες οἱ περιλειπόμενοι ἅμα σὺν αὐτοῖς ἁρπαγησόμεθα ἐν νεφέλαις εἰς ἀπάντησιν τοῦ κυρίου εἰς ἀέρα· καὶ οὕτως πάντοτε σὺν κυρίῳ ἐσόμεθα.).

3. Shall Be Raised with Christ:

    2 Corinthians 4:14, "knowing that the one having raised up the Lord Jesus also shall raise us up with Jesus, and shall present *us* with you" (εἰδότες ὅτι ὁ ἐγείρας τὸν κύριον Ἰησοῦν καὶ ἡμᾶς σὺν Ἰησοῦ ἐγερεῖ καὶ παραστήσει σὺν ὑμῖν);

4. Shall Appear with Christ:

    Colossians 3:4, "When Christ *who is* our life appears, then also you shall appear with Him in glory" (ὅταν ὁ Χριστὸς φανερωθῇ, ἡ ζωὴ ὑμῶν, τότε καὶ ὑμεῖς σὺν αὐτῷ φανερωθήσεσθε ἐν δόξῃ.).

5. Shall be Brought with Christ:

    1 Thessalonians 4:14, "For if we are believing that Jesus died and raised, thus also the ones who have fallen asleep though Jesus God shall bring with Him" (εἰ γὰρ πιστεύομεν ὅτι Ἰησοῦς ἀπέθανεν καὶ ἀνέστη, οὕτως καὶ ὁ θεὸς τοὺς κοιμηθέντας διὰ τοῦ Ἰησοῦ ἄξει σὺν αὐτῷ).

6. Shall be Conformed with Christ:

    Romans 8:29, "For whom He foreknew, He also predestined *to be* conformed to the image of His Son, that He might be the firstborn among many brothers" (ὅτι οὓς προέγνω, καὶ προώρισεν συμμόρφους τῆς εἰκόνος τοῦ υἱοῦ αὐτοῦ, εἰς τὸ εἶναι αὐτὸν πρωτότοκον ἐν πολλοῖς ἀδελφοῖς);

Philippians 3:21, "who shall transform the body of our humiliation (to be) conformed with the body of hid glory according to the energy by which He is able even to subdue all things to Himself" (ὃς μετασχηματίσει τὸ σῶμα τῆς ταπεινώσεως ἡμῶν σύμμορφον τῷ σώματι τῆς δόξης αὐτοῦ κατὰ τὴν ἐνέργειαν τοῦ δύνασθαι αὐτὸν καὶ ὑποτάξαι αὐτῷ τὰ πάντα);

7. Shall be Glorified with Christ:

Romans 8:17, "and if children, also heirs—heirs indeed of God, and joint-heirs with Christ, if indeed we suffer with *Him,* that also we may be glorified together" (εἰ δὲ τέκνα, καὶ κληρονόμοι· κληρονόμοι μὲν θεοῦ, συγκληρονόμοι δὲ Χριστοῦ, εἴπερ συμπάσχομεν ἵνα καὶ συνδοξασθῶμεν);

8. Shall Reign with Christ:

2 Timothy 2:12, "If we endure, also we shall reign with *Him.* If we deny *Him,* He also will deny us" (εἰ ὑπομένομεν, καὶ συμβασιλεύσομεν· εἰ ἀρνησόμεθα, κἀκεῖνος ἀρνήσεται ἡμᾶς);

1 Corinthians 4:8 provides a related parallel: "Already you are full! Already you are rich! You have reigned as kings without us—and indeed I could wish you reigned, that also we might reign with you!" (ἤδη κεκορεσμένοι ἐστέ, ἤδη ἐπλουτήσατε, χωρὶς ἡμῶν ἐβασιλεύσατε· καὶ ὄφελόν γε ἐβασιλεύσατε, ἵνα καὶ ἡμεῖς ὑμῖν συμβασιλεύσωμεν);

9. Shall be Given all Things with Christ:

Romans 8:32, "He who did not spare His own Son, but delivered Him up concerning us all, how shall He not also with Him freely give us all things?" (ὅς γε τοῦ ἰδίου υἱοῦ οὐκ ἐφείσατο ἀλλὰ ὑπὲρ ἡμῶν πάντων παρέδωκεν αὐτόν, πῶς οὐχὶ καὶ σὺν αὐτῷ τὰ πάντα ἡμῖν χαρίσεται;).

Appendix 3

Similarities Between the Johannine and Pauline Literature

THERE HAS NOT BEEN much research conducted into the link between the Johannine and Pauline literature, perhaps because it is generally assumed that there can be no direct literary quotations or allusions to the Fourth Gospel in the Pauline corpus, since it is an accepted norm that this Gospel was written long after the composition of the letters written by Paul. Still, there are many recognizable similarities of vocabulary, grammar, and theology shared between the Gospel of John and the Epistles of Paul. For example, the *Nestle-Aland Greek NT*[1] lists in the marginal apparatus of the Gospel of John and the thirteen ascribed letters of Paul these common cross-references, which are here categorized:

1. Certain OT literary sources shared by both John and Paul (5 references): John 6:49 with 1 Cor 10:3 (a common reference to Exodus 16); John 7:22 with Rom 4:11 (a common reference to Abraham's circumcision); John 7:42 with Rom 1:3 (a common reference to Jesus as David's Son); John 8:39 with Rom 4:12 (a common allusion to Abraham as father); John 12:38 with Rom 10:16 (a common quotation of Isa 53:1);

2. Certain life-of-Jesus sources shared by both John and Paul (5 references): John 1:42 with 1 Cor 1:12 and 1 Cor 9:5 (a reference to Cephas); John 7:3 with 1 Cor 9:5 (the brothers of Jesus); 1 Cor 15:5 with John 21:15 (Jesus appears to Peter); 1 Tim 6:13 with John 18:36 (Jesus' confession before Pilate);

3. Grammatical similarity indicating a probable common source shared by both John and Paul (39 references): John 1:3 with 1 Cor 8:6 and Col 1:16 (πάντα δι' αὐτοῦ); John 1:10 with 1 Cor 2:8 (not knowing Christ); John 1:14 with Col 1:22 and 1 Tim 3:16 (Christ in flesh); John 1:16 with Col 1:19; 2:9; Eph 1:23; 4:13 (the concept of πλήρωμα); John 3:6 with Rom 8:5–8 and Gal 6:8 (a contrast of σάρξ and πνεῦμα); John 3:13 with Rom 10:6 and 1 Cor 15:47 (the topic of the ascension); John 3:17 with Gal 4:4 (God sending His Son); John 3:20 with Eph 5:11, 13 (reproving by light); John 3:27 with 1 Cor 4:7 (receiving from heaven); John 3:31 with 1 Cor 15:47 (Christ out of heaven); John 5:35 with 2 Cor 7:8 (light shining for an hour); John 5:44 with 1 Tim 1:17 (glory of the one God); John 8:34 with Rom 6:16, 20 (slaves to sin); John 8:36 with Rom 6:18 (and Rom 6:20; 1 Cor 7:22; 2 Cor 3:17; Gal 5:1 on the topic of freedom); John 8:43 with Rom 8:7 and 1 Cor 2:14 (spiritual inability); John 10:14 with 1 Cor 13:12 (being known by Christ); John 11:50 with 2 Cor 5:14 (Christ ἀποθάνῃ ὑπὲρ others); John 12:31 with 1 Cor 2:6 and Eph 2:2 (Satan as ruler);

---

1. Kurt and Barbara Aland, et. cel., editors, *Novum Testamentum Graece post Eberhard et Erwin Nestle* (editione vicesima septima revisa, n.p.: Deutsche Bibelgesellschaft, 2006).

Appendix 3

John 12:36 with Eph 5:8 and 1 Thess 5:5 ("sons of light"); John 13:35 with 1 Thess 4:9 ("love one another"); John 17:12 with 2 Thess 2:3 (ὁ υἱὸς τῆς ἀπωλείας); John 17:21 with Gal 3:28 (they are/you are one); John 20:17 with Rom 8:29 (believers as Christ's brothers); John 21:22 with Phil 1:25 (remaining rather than dying). The 27th *NA* NT lists these additional nine references in Paul's letters: Rom 5:1 with John 16:33 (having peace); Rom 4:25 with John 16:10 (righteousness); 1 Cor 1:30 with John 17:19 (holiness); Gal 4:4 with John 5:36 (God sending Son); Eph 1:4 with John 17:24 (foundation of the world); Phil 2:6 with John 5:18 (worthy of God); 2 Thess 1:12 with John 17:10 (Christ glorified in believers); 2 Tim 1:10 with John 1:14, and John 1:9 (the contrast of light and dark);

4. No grammatical similarity but a probable theological concept shared by both John and Paul (20 references): John 1:12 with Gal 3:26 and Eph 1:5 (adoption); John 3:13 with Phil 2:6–7 (Christ's descent as preexistent); John 3:29 with 2 Cor 11:2 (Christ as a bridegroom); John 4:23 with Rom 12:1 (true worship); John 7:19 with Rom 2:17–23 (Jews given the Law but break it); John 8:34 with Rom 8:2 and Gal 4:30 (slavery/freedom from sin); John 10:18 with Phil 2:7 (Christ lays down His life); John 12:31 with 2 Cor 4:4 (Satan as the god of this age/world); John 13:34 with Gal 6:2 (Christ's command to love); John 14:3 with 1 Thess 4:17 (believers with Christ); John 14:17 with 1 Cor 2:11 and 2:14 (the world not receiving the Spirit); John 14:23 with 2 Cor 6:16 and Eph 3:17 (Christ dwelling in believers); John 15:4 with 2 Cor 3:5 (inability apart from Christ); John 15:5 with Rom 12:4 (branches/members of Christ); John 15:22 with Rom 1:20 (sinners without excuse); John 16:2 with Gal 1:13 (persecuting the church); John 20:9 with 1 Cor 15:4 (Christ rising again). The 27th *NA* NT lists these additional six references in Paul's letters as probable: Rom 10:17 with John 17:8 (the word of Christ); Rom 11:25 with John 10:16 (fullness of Gentiles/bring other sheep); 1 Cor 2:12 with John 16:13 (The Spirit reveals the things of God); Phil 2:6 with John 17:5 (Christ's preexistence); Phil 4:13 with John 15:5 (strength/ability in Christ); 1 Thess 4:17 with John 12:26 (being with the Lord).

5. Feasible semantic similarity showing incidental grammatical commonality but a possible similarity of theological concept shared by both John and Paul (47 references): John 1:1 with Phil 2:6 (the preexistence of Christ); John 1:17 with Rom 6:14 and 10:4 (law and grace); John 1:18 with 1 Tim 1:17 and 6:16 (no one has seen God); John 2:21 with 1 Cor 6:19 (body as the Temple); John 3:5 with Titus 3:5 (Spirit and water); John 3:10 with Rom 2:20 (teachers of the Law); John 3:16 with Rom 5:8 and 8:32 (God's love giving the Son); John 3:19 with Col 1:21 (evil deeds); John 3:31 with Rom 9:5 (Christ over all); John 3:36 with Rom 2:8 (wrath of God); John 4:2 with 1 Cor 1:17 (baptizing); John 4:23 with Eph 2:18 (Spirit and worship); John 5:24 with Rom 8:1 (judgment); John 5:29 with 1 Thess 1:16 (resurrection); John 5:39 with Rom 2:17–20 and 2 Tim 3:15–16 (common Scripture); John 5:41 with 1 Thess 2:6 (glory from men); John 5:42 with 2 Thess 3:5 (love of God); John 5:44 with Rom 2:29 and 1 Thess 2:6 (glory from God); John 6:45 with 1 Thess 4:9 (taught by God); John 6:63 with Gal 6:8 (God/Spirit gives life); John 8:12 with Phil 2:15 and 1 Thess 5:5 (darkness/light); John 8:39 with Gal 3:14 (Abraham); John 8:45–46 with 2 Cor 5:21 (not reproved of sin); John 10:16 with Eph 2:14 (one flock/one body); John 12:24 with 1 Cor 15:36 (grain dying and living); John 13:14 with 1 Tim 5:10 (washing feet); John 13:18 with Eph 1:4 (election); John 13:34 with 1 Thess 4:9 (command to love another); John 14:2 with 2 Cor 5:1 (dwelling of God); John 14:6 with Rom 5:2 and Eph 3:12 (coming to the Father/access to the Father); John 14:26 with 1 Cor 2:13 (taught by the Spirit); John 14:27

Appendix 3

with Rom 5:1, Col 3:15, 2 Thess 3:16, and 2 Tim 1:7 (peace); John 15:16 with Rom 1:13 and Phil 1:22 (fruit-bearing); John 16:3 with 1 Cor 2:8 (not knowing God); John 17:3 with 1 Thess 1:9 (the true God); John 17:23 with Rom 8:10 (Christ in us); John 19:11 with Rom 13:1 (authority).

6. The 27th *NA* NT lists these additional six references in Paul's letters showing incidental grammatical commonality expressing a possible similarity of theological concept: Rom 7:14 with John 3:6 (flesh); Rom 8:37 with John 16:33 (conquering); Rom 8:39 with John 17:26 (love of God); Rom 11:22 with John 15:2 and 15:4 (abiding); Gal 2:20 with John 13:1 (Christ's love for us).

The combination of these similarities suggests a common source–and that would be no one other than Jesus Himself.

Scripture Index

THE OLD TESTAMENT

Genesis

Ref	Pages
1:26–27	27, 27, 174, 243
1:26	33, 35, 40, 71, 154
2:7	27, 34, 37
2:17	32
2:23	40
2:24	99, 101
3:3–4	32
3:6	35
3:15	38, 82
3:19	32
4:1	37, 38
4:25	25
4:26	38
5:1–4	25
5:2	40
5:22	204, 211
6:9	204, 211
7:22	222
9:9	196
9:11	222
12:3	207
13:15	83
15:3	207
15:6	207
16:10	45
17:1	135
17:11	85
17:12	135
17:15	242
18:1	44
18:2	44
18:14	44
18:22	44
18:33	44
22:1	153, 160
22:9	126
22:17–18	207
22:18	196
26:24	204
28:15	204
31:11	160
31:13	48
32:24.	44
32:29	47
32:30	44
44:33	59
46:2	160

Exodus

Ref	Pages
3:2	33, 132, 159
3:6	14, 158
3:12	211
4:20	49
4:22	165
12:12	47
15:2	39
15:3	44
15:19	241
17:6	99
17:10	51
24:8	79
25:17–22	52
25:17	79
33:20	159
34:28	38

Leviticus

Ref	Pages
4:3	47

Scripture Index

4:20	20	13:6	44, 45
5:11	86	13:10	45
6:15	47		
6:26	101	**Ruth**	
12:8	86		
14:12–14	53	4:12	74
16:13–15	52	4:17	83
16:15	79		
18:5	244, 100	**1 Samuel**	
19:18	85, 97		
19:20	55	2:10	47, 67
21:10, 12	67	2:26	38
23:11–15	133	3:4	160
25:29	54	13:14	40
25:48	55	14:45	186
		16:13	48

Numbers

12:8	47	**2 Samuel**	
23:19	41, 47	2:5	48
24:7	49, 50	5:1	196
24:17	49, 50	7:11–15	48
27:16	40	7:12–13	83
27:18	40	7:14	40, 83, 165, 178
		14:11	186
		22:3	15

Deuteronomy

1:11	161	22:7	48
3:23	38	22:51	67
4:12–16	45, 47	23:1	39
5:5	20		
5:17–21	97	**1 Kings**	
6:4	17, 18, 85	2:10	178, 224
10:16	221	3:5	135
19:15	99, 100	8:46	116
21:23	147, 183	15:26	196
25:4	94	19:10	101
30:6	221		
32:2	22	**2 Kings**	
33:5	49	3:14	14
		9:3	38

Joshua

1:11	161	**1 Chronicles**	
5:13–15	44, 47, 158	5:29	80
		16:22	47
Judges		17:7–14	74
6:12	135	17:13	165, 178

2 Chronicles

22:10	165, 178
28:6	165
3:1	135
6:36	41
6:42	47, 67
29:2	196
30:5	105
30:20	196

Job

1:6	165
9:2	20
9:33	20
11:2	81
11:12	81
14:1	81
15:7	34, 81
15:14	81
25:4	81
25:6	41
35:8	41
38:7	165

Psalms

2:2	47, 67, 84
2:7	163, 165, 173, 178
2:12	165, 178
8:4	25, 26, 42
8:6	33, 36, 137, 173
8:7	33, 138
16:10	178
18:15	186
46:10	211
49:7–8	55
18:50	196
40:12	58
68:17	22
69:4	186
69:9	1 19, 128
71:23	54
77:35	55
78:8	211
80:15	42, 137
80:17/18	41, 42, 137
89:26	165, 178
103:14	34
106:30	20
110:1	26, 33, 36, 43, 136 137, 138, 156, 159
115:3	15
118:22	107
118:26	29, 106
130:7	38
144:3	42

Proverbs

3:13	41
8:22–31	161
8:34	41
9:3	105
28:14	41

Ecclesiastes

3:20	34

Isaiah

2:11	40
6:1–9	156, 158
7:14	204
8:14	107, 108
11:10	83
19:20	50, 51
28:16	107
29:13	93
41:10	204
43:25	158
44:3	162
45:1	47, 67
45:13	55
45:15	51
45:21	51
49:4	38
51:12	41
52:7	106
52:13–53:12	58
53:1	41, 272
53:3	41
53:6	58, 126
53:8	221, 242
53:10	53, 58
53:11	89, 117, 147, 162, 197

Scripture Index

Isaiah–continued

53:12	52, 58, 126
55:3	177, 178
56:2	41, 42
57:19	106
59:16	4
61:1	48, 49, 8, 102, 106

Jeremiah

1:8	221
4:4	221
5:1	41
17:7	41
22:14	48
23:5	48, 162
31:31–33	79
33:15	162
33:17	41
49:18	42

Ezekiel

1:26	45, 72
1:28	45, 154
2:3	45, 154
2:4	45
8:2	45, 47, 72
18:23	15
36:26–17	162
37:14	162
43:6–7	45

Daniel

2:34–35	108
2:44 45	48
3:24–26	15
3:25	45, 46
4:25	46
4:34	55
5:5	45
5:24	45
7:12	49, 115
7:13–14	42, 43, 197
7:13	25, 36, 41, 42, 43, 63, 72, 158, 181
7:16	59
7:18	2, 197

8:1–14	45
8:15	45
8:17	41
9:19	46
9:24	48, 49
9:25	47, 84
9:26	67
10:5	46, 47
10:16	46
10:18	46
12:2	224
12:6	47

Hosea

6:2	14, 133
11:1	165
13:4	15, 39
13:14	36

Joel

2:32	15, 156, 160

Amos

4:13	48
6:6	48, 188
9:13	213

Jonah

2:9	39
3:2	105

Micah

4:10	55
6:4	80

Habakkuk

1:5	178
3:13	47, 67

Zephaniah

3:9	160
3:15	55

Haggai

1:13	204

Zechariah

6:12	4
9:9	162
9:11	79
10:8	55
11:2	213
11:5	180
12:10	162
13:7	49
13:9	160

Malachi

3:2	177
3:16	14

THE NEW TESTAMENT

Matthew

1:6	83
1:16	80, 81
1:20	37, 108, 153
1:21	67
1:23	185, 20
3:1	179
3:11	29, 177, 179, 181, 241
3:15	117, 222
3:17	120, 166
4:12	125
4:17	106
5:6	98
5:17	85
5:20	102
5:37	99
5:39	97
5:42	52. 184
5:44	97
7:6	102
8:17	58
8:29	199
9:10	238
9:36	112
10:5	94
10:6	88
10:10	94
10:16	96
10:26	98
10:28	55
11:27	164, 166
11:29	111, 115
12:28	98, 119
12:30	197, 238
12:41	105
13:11	99
13:16	99
13:55	80, 83, 84
14:13	192
14:19	52
14:33	166
15:4	100
15:11	93
15:22	179
15:24	88
15:27	88
12:32	112
16:1	147
16:8	56
16:13	43
16:16	68, 88, 165, 166, 175
16:18	87
16:21	130, 180
17:1–8	89
17:2	90
17:3	238
17:5	89, 166
17:12	190
17:20	99
18:6	104
18:16	99, 100
18:20	100, 239
19:5	99
19:10–12	93
19:18–20	97, 100
19:21	99, 184
19:28	102, 226
20:19	128, 134
20:28	1, 53, 54, 58, 89, 150
21:11	178
21:42	107, 150
21:43	179
22:35	148
22:37–40	85
22:42	165, 178

Scripture Index

Matthew–continued

22:44	138
23:10	150, 166
23:11	89
23:13	101
23:23	100
24:8	101
24:13	226
24:27	95
24:30	95
24:39–40	95
24:43	100
25:6	95
25:31	25
25:34	102, 235
25:41	102
26:4	125
26:12	78, 130
26:19	123
26:26–28.	94, 124
26:28	79, 100, 179
26:29	197
26:35	223
26:39	116
26:56	192
26:61	149
26:63	48, 68, 165
26:64	43, 138, 147, 150
26:65	117, 126
27:12	58
27:16	51
27:19	117
27:23	179
27:38	218
27:43	119
27:52	160, 224
27:59–60.	130, 212, 234
28:1	133
28:2	108
28:9	134, 135
28:16	134
28:19	19
28:20	197, 204, 234, 239

Mark

1:1	165
1:7	177
1:8	241
1:11	166
1:15	62
1:35	192
1:38	106
1:41	112
2:15	238
3:14	192, 197, 237
3:31	80
4:22	98
5:37	238
6:3	80, 83, 84
6:34	112
7:7	93
7:16	100
7:19	93
7:27	179
8:2	112
8:15	102
8:23–25	162
8:31	43, 104, 189
8:38	235
9:2	90, 192
9:7	166
9:12	58, 180
9:33	101
9:35	89
9:42	98
9:50	97
10:7	99
10:9	93
10:12	93
10:19	97
10:20	116
10:21	112, 113
10:28	192
10:34	128
10:38	212, 242
10:44	89
10:45	1, 25, 53, 54, 55, 58, 89, 124, 183, 212, 252
11:9	29, 106
11:22	207
12:17	91, 97
12:29	18
12:35	157
12:46	138
13:33–37	97
14:1	125
14:8	130
14:10	125
14:24	58, 79

280

Scripture Index

14:33	87	4:22	84, 90
14:36	82, 96	4:41	163, 165
14:41	62	4:43	107
14:61	68	4:44	106
14:62	3, 138	6:13	87
14:71	187	6:27	97
15:1	126	6:28	97
15:27	58, 129	6:35	97
15:32	84, 128, 167, 218, 233	6:37	98
15:37	222	6:38	184
15:39	175, 187	7:13	112
15:41	192	7:16	150
15:46	130, 234	7:20	182
16:2	133	7:22	106, 107
16:6	133, 135	7:27	179
16:8	105	7:50	179
16:19	136	8:1	192, 197, 238
16:20	239	8:2–3	86
		8:17	98
Luke		8:51–52	224
		9:1	237
1:1–4	94, 104, 110, 141, 243	9:18	238
1:11	135	9:22	180
1:26	108, 185	9:28	87, 89
1:27	80, 82, 231	9:31	61, 90
1:32–33	42	9:35	163
1:35	163, 166	9:51	114
1:41	80	9:58	86
1:43	81	10:1	94
1:68	54, 55, 84	10:7	2, 94
2:11	150	10:16	101
2:13	108	10:22	163
2:21	84, 221, 242	10:25	148
2:22	85	10:27	99
2:23	73, 86	10:28	100
2:27	85	11:23	238
2:38	55	11:32	105, 106
2:39	85	11:41	184
2:51	116	12:23	99
3:1	127, 192	12:33	184
3:9	14	12:50	212
3:16	106, 177, 179, 181, 241	13:32	134
3:22	163, 166	13:33	150
3:23	26, 83, 84	13:35	106
3:31	83	15:2	238
3:38	25, 26, 30, 44, 83, 163, 165, 243	16:15	179
		16:18	93
4:1–13	25	17:2	98
4:3	163	17:25	180
4:18	48, 106	18:14	179

Scripture Index

Luke–continued

18:19	14
18:20	97
18:31–32	126
18:33	128
19:10	14, 114
19:38	106
19:42	106
20:18	108
20:42	138
20:44	150
21:5	14
21:12–17	186
21:18	186
21:23	100
21:28	55
21:34	101
22:4	124
22:14	87
22:15	180
22:17–20	94
22:19	54, 123, 183
22:20	79
22:21	124
22:30	102
22:37	179
22:43	108, 135
22:48	124, 125
22:63	128
22:69	138, 148
22:70	121, 163
23:4	120
23:6	187
24:7	134
23:14	120, 187
23:22	120
23:24	179
23:33	129
23:43	197, 218, 234, 239
23:46	134, 148
23:47	117, 150, 187
23:53	130, 179. 222, 234
23:55	179
24:1	133
24:3	135
24:6	133, 179
24:7	126
24:19	187
24:20	126, 213
24:21	30, 55
24:24	135
24:25–27	180
24:26	50, 180, 214
24:29	238
24:33	134
24:34	133, 135
24:36	134
24:39	78, 135
24:44	172, 177, 180, 238
24:46	53, 180, 220
24:50	179
24:51	136, 234

John

1:1	231, 273
1:9	273
1:10	272
1:12	185, 273
1:14	72, 81, 231, 272, 273
1:15	181
1:17	273
1:18	159, 273
1:29	58
1:30	187
1:33	241
1:41	48, 84
1:42	272
1:46	37
2:17	119, 128
2:18	119
2:19	79, 101, 19
2:21	79, 273
3:5	58, 98, 120, 273
3:6	272, 274
3:10	273
3:13	36, 137, 272, 273
3:14	58
3:16	57, 273
3:17	272
3:19	273
3:20	272
3:27	272
3:29	273
3:31	272, 273
3:34	166
3:36	273
4:2	273
4:9	84
4:10	99

4:19	150	11:27	165, 175
4:23	273	11:49	30
4:25	67, 106	11:50	187, 272
4:29	73, 187	12:2	238
4:32	150	12:3	78
4:48	109	12:7	130
5:17	216, 247	12:13	30, 106
5:18	273	12:24	213, 273
5:21	164, 219	12:26	273
5:24	273	12:27	62
5:27	43	12:28	120
5:35	272	12:31	272, 273
5:36	52, 273	12:36	273
5:39	273	12:38	58, 272
5:41	273	12:47	114
5:42	273	13:1	113, 274
5:44	272, 273	13:2	124
6:14	106	13:10	241
6:31	99	13:13	150, 157
6:37	37	13:14	273
6:40	235	13:34	85, 273
6:42	84	13:35	273
6:45	273	13:37	56
6:49	272	14:3	235, 273
6:51	52, 58	14:6	19, 150, 273
6:62	137	14:7	77
7:3	272	14:9	77
7:6	62	14:17	273
7:18	117, 121	14:23	272
7:19	273	14:26	273
7:22	272	14:27	106, 273
7:27	106	15:4	273
7:40	150	15:5	273
7:42	272	15:22	273
7:46	187	15:27	197
8:12	273	16:2	273
8:29	116, 119	16:3	274
8:34	272, 273	16:10	273
8:39	272, 273	16:13	273
8:40	73, 187	16:33	106, 273, 274
8:46	121	17:1	62
9:16	187	17:3	167, 274
10:11	58	17:5	235, 273
10:14	272	17:8	273
10:16	273	17:10	273
10:17	54	17:12	273
10:18	273	17:19	273
10:33	5, 187	17:21	273
10:36	164, 230	17:23	274
11:13	95	17:24	197, 220, 235, 273

Scripture Index

John–continued

17:25	95	1:6	84, 147, 149, 156, 169
17:26	274	1:9–12	136
18:1	238	1:9	136, 137, 144.224, 234
18:2	125	1:11	136
18:14	30, 187	1:14	80, 81, 83
18:17	187	1:21	147, 149, 156, 159, 169, 238
18:23	128	1:22	136, 169, 238, 156
18:36	272	1:24	147, 149, 156
18:37	60, 126	2:4	162
18:38	120, 127	2:21	15, 150, 156, 160
19:1	128	2:22	109, 149, 187
19:2	128	2:23	125
19:4	120, 127	2:30	149
19:5	148, 187	2:31	147, 149, 167
19:6	129, 127	2:32	145, 172
19:9	127	2:33	137, 147
19:11	274	2:34	147
19:14	123	2:36	147, 149
19:17	130	2:36	159
19:18	129	2:42	17, 95, 105, 114, 123
19:19	158, 169	2:44	146
19:25	81	3:6	149
19:32	218, 233	3:13	58, 126, 127, 147, 149, 162
19:34	80, 123	3:14	117, 147, 149
19:40	234	3:15	145, 147, 162
20:1	133	3:16	118, 146
20:9	273	3:18	147, 180
20:11	134	3:20	147
20:15	156	3:26	147
20:17	137, 273	4:2	146
20:19	133, 134	4:4	146
20:24	124	4:10	149, 167
20:25	129	4:11	108, 147, 149
20:26	134	4:12	19
20:28	175	4:13	216
20:30	184	4:26	167
20:31	163, 165, 175	4:27	149
21:1–25	124	4:30	147, 149
21:14	133	4:33	126, 149
21:15	272	4:36	144
21:22	272	5:19–20	153
21:25	91, 188	5:30	146, 147, 162, 183
		5:31	138, 147, 149
		5:32	145
Acts		5:42	146, 167
		6:1	147
1:1	134, 143, 144, 184	6:2	124, 170
1:2	136	6:7	146
1:5	241	6:9	149

6:13	146, 158, 179	13:7	176
6:14	147, 149	13:9	176
7:2	135	13:11	109
7:30	135	13:16–41	xv, 176, 250
7:32	162	13:16	179
7:35	55	13:17–22	176
7:52	22, 117, 147, 149, 162	13:23–31	86, 179
7:55–56	138, 144, 147	13:23	83, 177, 188, 189
7:56	25, 43, 137, 149, 197	13:24–25	87, 187, 189
7:58	144, 148, 149	13:24	177
7:59	148, 149, 159	13:25	243
8:1	145, 151	13:27	177, 178, 179, 188, 190, 243
8:12	107	13:28	127, 177, 179, 188, 190, 243
8:16	149, 159	13:29	129, 130, 177, 183, 188, 190, 191, 243
8:32	41, 58		
8:37	163	13:30	178, 179, 188, 191, 243
9:1–25	xv, 145, 153, 161, 250, 278	13:31	135, 145, 178, 179, 191, 192,
9:1	32, 146, 149, 150, 155, 170	13:33	163, 173, 179, 189
9:2	144, 160, 172	13:34	132, 177, 178
9:3	37, 134, 150	13:35	178
9:4	154, 156, 176, 195, 234	13:36	178
9:5	144, 151, 154, 158, 159, 184	13:38–39	176, 178, 179, 244
9:6	151, 155	13:39	59, 179, 191
9:7	151, 152	13:40–41	178
9:8–9	151	14:3	170
9:10	156, 159	14:11	47
9:13	159, 195	14:22	90
9:14	147, 160	15:9	241
9:15	153, 159, 160, 161	15:19–29	169
9:17	135, 147, 157, 159, 162, 168, 173	15:23	172
9:20	145, 163, 164, 166, 187, 188, 230	15:26	167
9:22	50, 68, 150, 163, 166, 167, 188	16:9	153
9:26	169, 170,	16:18	109, 167
9:27	170, 173	16:31	188
9:32	160	17:1–3	xv, 179, 251
9:41	160	17:3	132, 167, 180, 190
10:15	241	17:7	187
10:28	153	17:11	179
10:38	48, 185	17:18–31	xv, 181, 251
10:39–41	145	17:19	105
10:39	183	17:25–26	28
10:40	134	17:27	14
10:41	153, 238	17:30	15, 181, 188, 189
11:16	241	17:31	132, 181, 24
11:19	147, 241	17:32	131, 181
11:20	107	17:34	181
11:25–26	176	18:5	xv, 167, 180, 187, 251
12:2	87	18:9–10	92
12:17	87	18:18	170
13:3	188	18:28	167

Scripture Index

Acts–continued

19:1–7	xv, 251
19:3	181
19:4	87, 181, 187, 189
19:8	90, 107
19:13	283
19:15	187
20:5	95
20:7	133
20:17–35	xv, 182, 251
20:21	118, 182
20:24	182
20:25	90
20:28	55, 182, 183, 188, 189
20:35	55, 92, 103, 173, 183, 186, 187
21:13	185, 189
21:17	141
22:1–16	xv, 250
22:2	151
22:3	129, 148, 150, 152, 158
22:4–5	146
22:6	37, 150
22:7	151, 154, 195
22:8	147, 151, 154, 156, 158, 176, 184, 187
22:9	151, 152, 154
22:10	151, 152, 157, 158
22:11	90, 151, 154, 174
22:12	156, 159
22:14	53, 117, 153, 161, 162, 168, 188
22:16	160, 162, 173, 183, 241
23:1–6	184
23:7	21
23:8	108
24:4	111
24:10–21	184
24:15	184
25:19	184, 250
26:4–18	xv, 158
26:4	148
26:9	82, 146, 147, 150, 184, 187, 189, 231
26:13	90, 150, 154
26:14	151, 154, 155, 156, 185, 187, 189, 195
26:15	154, 157
26:16	151
26:18	182, 185
26:19	153
26:22–23	185, 188
26:24	152
26:25	152
27:1	141
27:18	185
27:21–26	185
27:22	186
27:33–34	185
27:34	186, 187
28:17	125, 186
28:23	107, 186
28:30	186
28:31	107, 167, 186

Romans

1:1	89
1:3	xv, 74, 81, 83, 86, 163, 166, 173, 174, 188, 189, 231, 250, 272
1:4	75, 109, 120, 131, 132, 163, 165, 188, 232
1:5	115, 169
1:8	118, 224
1:11	203
1:12	207, 208, 247
1:13	274
1:18	26, 69
1:20	273
1:23	69, 72
1:25	203
1:26	203
2:1	69
2:5	59
2:12	100
2:13	100, 116, 117
2:15	203
2:16	105
2:20	273
2:29	119, 221, 273
3:3	118
3:4	24
3:20	14
3:22	xv, 117, 118, 190, 206, 207, 250
3:23	120, 188
3:24	55, 173, 176, 206
3:25	xv, 51, 52, 79, 118, 182, 189, 250
3:26	1, 61, 117, 190, 206, 207, 250
3:30	18
4:1	74, 77
4:5	118, 205
4:6	69

4:11	221, 272	6:22	185
4:12	206, 272	7:1	101
4:13	185, 207	7:4	132
4:15	118	7:7–25	155
4:17	34	7:12	116
4:24	xv, 57, 58, 132, 173, 188, 190, 250	7:14	274
		7:24	24
4:25	xv, 30, 52, 58, 113, 124, 125, 126, 132, 197, 215, 250, 273	8:1	273
		8:2	273
5:1	58, 273, 274	8:3	xv, 26, 75
5:2	273	8:4	74, 116
5:5	162	8:5	272
5:6	xv, 1, 61, 130, 250	8:7	272
5:7	56, 226	8:10	135, 274
5:8	57, 182, 240, 273	8:11	34, 51, 132, 216
5:9	xv, 189, 250	8:15	82, 92, 96, 173
5:10	80, 140, 213	8:16–17	214
5:12–21	26, 27, 28, 30, 31, 32, 34, 70, 140, 211, 240	8:16	94, 216
		8:17	xvi, 11, 185, 193, 210, 211, 217, 234, 235, 251
5:12	29, 30, 31, 196,		
5:14	29, 30, 63	8:23	55
5:15	8, 29, 30, 31, 55, 63, 69, 70, 73, 162, 188, 189, 196	8:28–32	215
		8:28	216
5:16	30, 196	8:29	xvi, 11, 193, 199, 209, 211, 215, 220, 221, 235, 237, 242, 243, 251, 273
5:17	30, 58, 69, 116, 117, 196, 198, 239		
5:18	xv, 30, 31, 69, 115, 116, 127, 190, 196, 245	8:30	214, 240
		8:31	215
5:19	30, 31, 32, 39, 58, 63, 69, 196	8:32	xvi, 12, 52, 57, 124, 126, 193, 211, 215, 218, 235, 251
5:20	30, 31, 39, 85, 116, 190, 196, 201, 213		
		8:34	xv, 130, 132, 136, 138, 191, 250
5:21	221		
6:1	212. 240, 248	8:38	108
6:3–10	214, 221	9:1	92, 206
6:3	xv, 87, 101, 183, 189, 212, 213, 241, 242, 250	9:3	74, 77, 152
		9:4	84, 86
6:4	xv, 11, 131, 132, 191, 193, 202, 203, 209, 213, 234, 242, 250, 251	9:5	xv, 5, 9, 74, 77, 82, 189, 231, 232, 242, 250, 273
6:5	xv, 11, 131, 199, 210, 251	9:14	120
6:6	xv, 11, 24, 193, 209, 213, 218, 226, 233, 251	9:18	15
		9:30	107
6:7	213	9:33	107, 108, 190
6:8	xvi, 11, 193, 197, 202, 203, 209, 210, 223, 225, 233, 235, 251	10:5	24, 117
		10:6–8	164, 272
6:9	132, 216	10:9	109, 132, 157, 182, 188, 191, 205, 244
6:14	273		
6:16	115, 272	10:12	21, 183
6:17	16, 92, 104, 106, 142, 173, 215, 250	10:13	15, 169, 193
		10:16	41, 58, 272
6:19	185	10:17	273
6:20	272	11:14	74

Scripture Index

287

Scripture Index

Romans–continued

11:22	274
11:25	194, 273
12:1	91, 273
12:2	90, 203, 204
12:4	273
12:5	78, 79, 206
12:14	97, 103, 273
12:15	202
12:16	246
12:17	97, 103
12:18	97
12:19–21	97
12:21	103
13:1	115, 273
13:5	115
13:7	91, 97, 103, 173
13:9	97
13:14	48, 110
14:4	98
14:9	130, 191
14:10	98, 103
14:13	98
14:14	xv, 93, 96, 98, 189, 205, 250
14:15	57, 130, 245
14:17	90, 92, 98, 107
14:18	69
15:1	69, 92, 110, 119
15:3	88, 119, 128, 245
15:6	88
15:8	55, 82, 86, 88, 89, 232
15:12	xv, 86, 189, 250
15:13	83, 162
15:18	xv, 109, 250
15:19	3, 93
15:20	202
15:30	247
15:32	247
15:33	202
16:7	206
16:14	245
16:15	245
16:19	96, 173
16:20	38, 208, 234
16:25	xv, 105, 106, 194, 195, 250
16:26	169

1 Corinthians

1:1	225
1:2	160, 169, 185, 195, 206, 245
1:5	206
1:6	60
1:9	163, 232
1:11	110
1:12	78, 87, 272
1:17	129, 273
1:18	xv, 129, 250
1:21	105, 114
1:23	xv, 9, 49, 106, 129, 167, 190, 244, 250
1:24	109, 164, 174
1:29	14, 74, 239
1:30	55, 116, 164, 174, 239, 273
2:2	xv, 48, 65, 129, 167, 190, 232, 244, 250
2:5	109, 118
2:6–8	127
2:6	272
2:7	194
2:8	xv, 77, 127, 129, 154, 157, 159, 190, 250, 272, 274
2:9	58
2:11	273
2:12	77, 273
2:13	273
2:14	24, 272, 273
3:1	206
3:9	216
3:11	12, 67
3:16	101
4:1	24
4:5	61, 98
4:6	203
4:7	272
4:8	xvi, 247, 251
4:11–13	98, 198
5:4	100, 246
5:6	101, 102
5:7	xv, 58, 79, 120, 123, 161, 191, 250
5:9	246
5:11	246
6:2	102
6:3	102
6:5	19
6:9	96, 102, 107, 116, 185
6:11	162, 183, 241
6:14	xv, 109, 132. 191, 250

6:15	102	11:25	xv, 79, 250
6:16	99, 101	11:26	123, 130
6:19	79, 101, 273	11:27	78, 189, 250
7:10	xv, 64, 65, 91, 92, 93, 103, 173, 189	11:29–30	125
		11:33	246
7:12	92, 93	12:2	225
7:15	115	12:13	8, 78, 87, 241
7:22	55, 272	12:24	246
7:28	74	12:26	210, 214, 247
7:31	72	12:27	78, 195
8:1	77	13:1	69
8:2	77	13:2–3	99, 173
8:4–6	18	13:7	114
8:6	18, 19, 48, 157, 1665, 272	13:9	77
8:11	xv, 130, 250	13:12	272
9:1	xv, 86, 134, 152, 153, 155, 158, 191, 250	13:13	173
		14:11	164
9:5	xv, 65, 83, 87, 189, 226, 250, 272	14:23	246
9:10	27, 203	14:25	98
9:14	xv, 65, 66, 91, 93, 94, 03, 109, 173, 189, 250	14:26	246
		14:37	93, 103
9:18	94	15:1–3	32, 50, 57, 66, 171, 173, 244
9:21	97	15:1	107
9:22	15	15:3–4	53, 55, 63, 180, 188, 237, 244
9:23	245	15:3	53, 57, 58, 95, 124, 130, 141, 171, 172, 183, 191
10:1–2	29, 99, 164, 176		
10:2	196, 241	15:4	xv, 130, 132, 133, 134, 178, 188, 191, 250, 273
10:3	29, 272		
10:4	29, 99, 165	15:5	xv, 53, 65, 87, 124, 134, 135, 250, 272
10:6	29		
10:7	29	15:8	32, 37, 134, 135, 136, 145, 150, 152
10:8	29		
10:9–10	29	15:9	146, 195
10:16	xv, 78, 79, 189, 250	15:12–17	xv
10:17	78, 203	15:12	32, 71, 131, 132
10:18	74	15:13	32, 131, 132
10:27	99	15:14	62, 106, 132
11:1	xv, 110, 111, 121, 142, 156, 244, 245, 250	15:17	132
		15:19	132
11:2	16, 55, 95, 104, 110, 121, 124, 141, 142, 245, 250	15:20	32, 132, 167
		15:21	xv, 21, 27, 32, 35, 71, 73, 189, 250, 131
11:7	26, 27, 154		
11:20	123	15:22	26, 27, 32, 34, 36, 39, 165, 196, 206, 239
11:23–25	xv, 57, 64, 65, 66, 91, 93, 94, 95, 102, 123, 124, 141, 173, 183, 189, 190, 245, 250		
		15:25	25, 33, 136, 137,
		15:28	33, 163
11:23	xv, 52, 65, 123, 124, 171, 190, 232, 250	15:36	34, 273
		15:40–44	37, 133
11:24	xv, 78, 123, 189, 250	15:42	131

Scripture Index

1 Corinthians–continued

15:44	134
15:45	24, 25, 26, 27, 31, 34, 36, 37, 63, 73, 137, 164, 165
15:46	34, 36, 71, 135
15:47	xv, 24, 34, 36, 37, 38, 63, 69, 71, 73, 137, 154, 189, 237, 250, 272,
15:48	34, 37
15:49	34, 35, 246 72, 174, 243
15:50	135, 185
15:53	135
16:2	133
16:16	246
16:19	245
16:22	156
16:23	202, 234
16:24	202

2 Corinthians

1:1	160, 195, 245
1:5	122, 190, 224, 250, 251
1:6	114
1:11	247
1:13	102
1:17	10, 74, 99
1:18	99
1:19	163, 165, 173, 206
1:21	48, 245
1:22.	162
2:12	205
2:13	3
2:14	206
2:17	206
3:1	157
3:3	216
3:4	158
3:5	273
3:6	89
3:14	18
3:16	154
3:17	272
3:18	26, 90, 110, 154, 174, 203, 204, 214, 243
4:1–2	67
4:2	17
4:3	114
4:4	37, 164, 273
4:5	48, 51
4:7	161
4:10	xv, 80, 130, 190, 250
4:13	216
4:14	xv, xvi, 12, 132, 193, 199, 202, 203, 209, 210, 216, 235, 250, 251
4:16	24, 69
5:1	77, 273
5:14	xv, 59, 71, 112, 130, 190, 191, 241, 250, 272
5:15	xv, 132, 250
5:16	xiii, xv, 8, 68, 75, 76, 77, 78, 139, 148, 173, 189, 192, 232, 250
5:17	76, 78, 199
5:20	xv, 120, 215, 250
5:21	25, 57, 116, 120, 121, 190, 216, 247, 273
6:1	203, 209
6:2	61
6:6	119
6:16	202, 273
7:1	241
7:2	14
7:3	203, 209, 210, 216, 217, 226, 246
7:8	203, 272
7:9	203
7:10	221
7:15	202
8:4	86
8:9	xv, 69, 85, 86, 165, 190, 243, 250
8:14	61
8:19	245
9:2	169
10:1	xv, 250
10:4	116
10:16	107
11:2	73, 273
11:3	26
11:4	xiv, 2, 12, 51, 67
11:22	152, 170
11:23–25	128
11:23	89
11:29	217
11:31	92, 178
12:1–5	78, 176
12:2	69
12:9	92, 103
12:12	109
12:21	203
13:1	99, 100, 217

13:4	xv, xvi, 12, 129, 190, 200, 202, 203, 205, 207, 209, 210, 217, 218, 225, 235, 237, 250, 251	3:16–17	xv, 82, 250
		3:16	22, 82, 83, 205, 207
		3:17	189
13:11	202, 234	3:18	185
13:14	19, 202	3:19	20, 21, 22, 207
		3:20	18, 22, 23
		3:21	118, 206
		3:23	85

Galatians

1:1	69, 132, 163, 224	3:26	87, 118, 273
1:2	245	3:27	241
1:4	53, 55, 182	3:28	71, 273
1:6	203	3:29	207
1:7	3, 203	4:4	xv, 26, 65, 68, 72, 80, 81, 82, 85, 86, 189, 231, 232, 250, 272, 273
1:8	105, 108		
1:9	16		
1:10	89	4:5	85
1:11	69, 173	4:6	82, 92, 96, 162
1:12	4, 94, 145, 171	4:17	101
1:13	18, 25, 125, 146, 150, 155, 158, 160, 195, 273	4:23	74, 81
		4:29	74
1:14	146, 150, 155	4:30	272
1:16	107, 152, 157, 158, 163, 164, 168, 170, 198	5:1	272
		5:10	205
1:17	87, 164, 170	5:11	129
1:18	37, 170	5:14	85, 91, 97
1:19	189	5:18	225
1:22	148, 206	5:21	90, 107
2:1	144	5:23	111
2:6	87, 169	6:1	24, 119
2:7	88, 170	6:2	85, 97, 101, 273
2:8	87	6:7	24
2:9	xv, 87, 88, 189, 250	6:8	272, 273
2:10	202	6:13	74
2:15	218	6:14	129, 190
2:16	2, 74, 117, 190, 205, 206, 207, 218, 250	6:17	xv, 51, 128, 190, 250
		6:18	202
2:17–21	55		
2:19	15, 52, 209, 218, 251	## Ephesians	
2:20	11, 113, 118, 124, 165, 189, 203, 209, 213, 218, 233, 245, 274		
		1:1	160, 195, 206
		1:2	163
2:21	xv, 130, 230	1:3	206
3:1	xv, 48, 122, 129, 149, 167, 190, 249, 250	1:4	206, 239, 240, 273
		1:5	224, 273
3:2	207	1:7	xv, 55, 97, 100, 185, 189, 206, 240, 250
3:7	207		
3:9	207	1:13	15, 17, 182, 197, 240
3:12	24, 100	1:14	80
3:13	57, 188, 191	1:15	115, 206
3:14	216, 273	1:20–22	33, 132

Scripture Index

Ephesians–continued

1:20	xv, 33, 132, 136, 137, 191, 250
1:22	46
1:23	78, 272
2:1–3	219
2:2	127, 272
2:4–6	219, 221,
2:5–6	193, 209
2:5	xv, 11, 34, 193, 199, 203, 210, 234, 251
2:6	xv, 11, 193, 200, 207, 210, 218, 219, 223, 234, 237, 239, 251
2:7	xv, 189, 250
2:13	79, 106
2:14	74, 273
2:15	69, 71
2:16	xv, 129, 250
2:17	106
2:18	273
2:19	198, 246
2:20	108, 190
2:22	119, 246
3:5	69
3:6	xvi, 210, 218, 234, 246, 251
3:12	118, 206, 207, 273
3:16	69
3:17	273
3:18	225, 245
3:19	112, 230
4:2	111, 202
4:6	18
4:8–10	136
4:12	79
4:13	163
4:15	230
4:16	26
4:30	80
5:1–2	182
5:2	52, 53, 28, 113, 124
5:5	90, 107
5:6	59
5:11	272
5:13	272
5:18	162
5:20	59, 169
5:25	52, 71, 113
5:29	74
5:31	24, 99
6:1–4	206
6:2–3	100
6:5	74, 77
6:7	69
6:23	202
6:24	38, 202

Philippians

1:1	89, 160, 195, 206, 245
1:2	163
1:4	59, 202
1:7	245
1:8	xv, 112, 190, 245, 250
1:11	224
1:13	206
1:14	205
1:21–24	219
1:21	110. 226
1:22	292
1:23	xvi, 12, 197, 202, 203, 209, 210, 219, 224, 234, 251
1:25	273
1:27	3, 118, 247, 248
1:29	205
2:1–8	121
2:1	112
2:5–11	71, 110, 115, 286
2:5	2, 72, 115
2:6–7	273
2:6–8	26, 72, 233
2:6–11	27, 73, 232
2:6–12	173
2:6	63, 69, 165, 231, 273,
2:7–8	53
2:7	24, 55, 58, 69, 71, 72, 81, 89, 164, 189, 273
2:8	xv, 24, 69, 71, 72, 73, 115, 116, 129, 130, 189, 190, 250
2:9	169, 215
2:10	51, 215
2:11	48, 215
2:12	115
2:15	273
2:17–18	247
2:18	247
2:22	245
2:25	216, 245
3:3–5	150
3:3–6	160
3:4–6	18
3:5	145, 152

Scripture Index

3:6	71, 116, 117, 146, 155, 195	2:1	116
3:8–9	152, 220	2:2	194
3:9	71, 118, 206, 207	2:3	174
3:10	122, 130, 131, 139, 193, 199, 209, 210, 220, 230, 234, 250, 251	2:5	118, 246
		2:6	206
3:11	131	2:7	17, 206
3:12	145	2:8	69
3:17	17, 245	2:9	xv, 71, 78, 206, 231, 250, 251, 272
3:19	190, 220		
3:20–21	220	2:10	206
3:20	48, 250	2:11–12	242
3:21	xvi, 11, 71, 133, 135, 193, 203, 204, 211, 215, 220, 235, 251	2:11–13	207, 221, 237
		2:11	xv, 9, 84, 86, 189, 221, 242, 250
		2:12–13	218
4:3	202, 246	2:12	xv, 11, 87, 131, 132, 189, 191, 193, 209, 212, 223, 234, 242, 250, 251
4:6	173		
4:9	202, 234		
4:13	273	2:13	xv, 11, 34, 193, 202, 203, 209, 210, 234, 251
4:14	247		
4:21	246	2:14	xv, 190, 250, 272
4:23	202	2:15	129, 206
		2:16	222
		2:18	108, 222
Colossians		2:19	203, 209, 210, 246, 247
1:2	160, 195, 206	2:20–23	223
1:3	163	2:20	xv, 11, 193, 202, 203, 209, 222, 223, 233, 251
1:4	118, 206		
1:5–6	100	2:21–22	93
1:8	11:9	2:22	69
1:11	114, 202	3:1–4	223
1:12	185	3:1	xv, 11, 136, 138, 193, 209, 210, 234, 248
1:13–14	55		
1:13	90, 107, 163, 204	3:2	223
1:14	55, 185, 206	3:3	xvi, 11, 193, 202, 203, 209, 210, 223, 234, 251
1:15–20	173		
1:15–21	147	3:4	xvi, 12, 193, 202, 203, 209, 211, 223, 235, 251
1:15	37, 157, 164, 174, 251		
1:16–17	232	3:6	59
1:16	206, 208, 272	3:9	69
1:17	206	3:10	26
1:18	78, 195	3:11	236
1:19	206, 272	3:12	111
1:20	xv, 79, 129, 189, 250	3:13	173
1:21	273	3:15	274
1:22	xv, 75, 78, 130, 189, 216, 250, 251, 272	3:17	169
		3:18	115, 206
1:23	189, 203	3:20	206
1:24	78, 122, 190, 214, 220, 250, 231	3:22	74, 77, 115
1:26–27	194	3:23	69
1:27	194	4:1	51

Scripture Index

Colossians–continued

4:3	190
4:5	61
4:9	246
2:11	216, 246
4:13	116
4:14	10, 82
4:16	116
4:18	202, 234

1 Thessalonians

1:1	48, 163, 206
1:3	114
1:5	119
1:6	100, 110, 202
1:7	59
1:8	103
1:9	173, 274
1:10	xv, 51, 132, 163, 250
2:4	69
2:6	69, 273
2:8	203
2:12	90, 107
2:13	69, 95
2:14	188, 206
2:15	xv, 69, 125, 190, 250
2:16	100
2:17	61
2:19	61
3:2	3, 216, 246
3:8	206
3:12	202
3:13	61, 160, 185, 195, 202, 2216, 26
4:1	95, 173, 206
4:2	17, 103, 188, 224
4:3	185
4:4	185
4:7	185
4:8	69, 101, 103
4:9	103, 273
4:13–14	103
4:13–17	224, 225
4:13	224, 225
4:14	xv, xvi, 12, 51, 83, 130, 132, 189, 193, 202, 203, 209, 211, 224, 225, 235, 250, 251
4:15–16	64
4:15–17	95, 103
4:15–5:2	xv, 250
4:15	6195, 173, 236
4:16	206, 224
4:17	xvi, 12, 103, 193, 202, 203, 209, 210, 234, 235, 237, 251, 273
4:18	225
5:1–8	225
5:1	61, 206
5:2	100, 103
5:3	59, 100, 101
5:5	273
5:6	101
5:9–10	225
5:10	xv, xvi, 12, 57, 130, 182, 202, 203, 209, 210, 225, 226, 235, 250, 251
5:12	206
5:23	61, 185

2 Thessalonians

1:1	48, 163, 206
1:3	118
1:4	114
1:5	90, 107
1:7	108, 202
1:8–9	15
1:8	115
1:9	59
1:10	59, 60, 126, 160, 195
1:12	169, 206, 273
2:1	61
2:2	2
2:3	24, 69, 273
2:5	101, 105, 141
2:6	61
2:7	194
2:8	61
2:13	185, 197
2:15	17, 95, 141, 171, 243, 250
2:16	48, 113
3:2	69
3:3	173
3:5	xv, 114, 190, 145, 250, 273
3:6	95, 169, 171, 173
3:14	115
3:16	202, 274
3:18	202

Scripture Index

1 Timothy

1:1	2, 13, 15
1:2	1, 2, 13, 14, 163
1:4	13
1:5	118
1:8	77
1:10	13, 16
1:11	13
1:12	1, 2, 161
1:13	113, 146, 152, 195
1:14	2, 14, 202, 206
1:15	xv, 14, 16, 113, 114, 190, 250
1:16	2, 14, 156, 205
1:17	2, 13, 272, 273
2:1–2	14
2:1–5	69
2:1	23, 59, 69
2:2	15, 59
2:3–4	1, 13, 15, 63
2:4	14, 15, 23, 32, 59
2:5–6	1, 12, 13, 15, 16, 17, 25, 26, 31, 55, 63, 171, 212, 229, 236, 249
2:5	14, 69, 70, 71, 73, 148, 159, 171, 189, 199, 229, 231, 233, 249, 252, 284
2:6	xv, 1, 2, 53, 54, 55, 56, 58, 59, 60, 61, 126, 250
2:7	2, 60, 92, 152
2:8	17, 59
2:11	59, 115
2:12–14	26
2:13-14	26, 27
3:1	16, 113
3:4	61, 115
3:5`	13, 61
3:9	194
3:12	61
3:13	118
3:14–15	2
3:15	13
3:16	xv, 14, 16, 73, 74, 108, 119, 136, 189, 190, 191, 194, 230, 231, 232, 250, 272
4:2	61
4:3	203
4:3–4	13
4:5	185
4:6	16
4:9	16, 113
4:10	13, 15
4:11–16	13
4:12	121
4:13	2
5:4	13, 61
5:8	61
5:10	13, 160, 195, 273
5:11	14
5:18	2, 93, 94
5:19	100
5:21	2, 13, 108
5:23	2
6:1	13, 61
6:3	xv, 13, 14, 90, 103, 184, 189, 232, 244, 250
6:6–7	16
6:9	69
6:11–12	16
6:11	13, 69, 70, 114
6:13	xv, 1, 2, 14, 53, 60, 120, 127, 148, 188, 190, 232, 250, 272
6:14–15	61
6:14	14, 61, 159
6:15–16	16
6:15	14
6:16	273
6:21	202, 234

2 Timothy

1:1	206
1:2	163
1:7	274
1:8	xv, 11, 60, 128, 126, 203, 209, 210, 234, 245, 250
1:9–10	60, 206
1:9	227, 252
1:10	61, 273
1:11	152
1:13	112, 184, 206, 245
2:1	206
2:2	69
2:3	11, 203, 209, 210, 234, 245, 251
2:6	203
2:8	xv, 48, 74, 83, 86, 104, 105, 132, 188, 189, 190, 191, 250
2:10	114, 196, 202, 206, 226
2:11–13	113, 209, 226, 227

Scripture Index

2 Timothy–continued

2:11	xv, xvi, 11, 130, 193, 203, 209, 210, 217, 223, 233, 235, 250, 251, 263
2:12	xvi, 11, 114, 193, 203, 211, 235, 237, 251
2:13	119
2:14	14
2:15	ix
2:18	131
2:19	169
2:20–21	160
2:21	185
2:22	202
2:25	111, 203, 215
3:1	61, 206
3:2	69
3:6	225
3:7	15
3:8	69
3:10	114, 121
3:13	69
3:15	118, 206, 273
3:16–17	3
3:17	24, 69
4:1	14, 61, 90, 107
4:3	61
4:6	61
4:8	61, 188
4:11	82, 202, 225
4:13	243
2:17	105
4:18	90, 107
4:22	234

Titus

1:1	15, 89, 197
1:2–3	61
1:3	1, 15, 61, 88, 105
1:4	62
1:5	30, 201
1:9	118
1:14	15, 69
1:15	251
2:2	114
2:5	115
2:9	115
2:10	15
2:11	60, 69
2:13	188
2:14	53, 55, 57, 182, 241
2:15	202
3:1	115
3:2	69, 111
3:4	15, 60
3:5	162, 241, 273
3:6	224
3:8	185
3:15	202

Philemon

1:1	259
1:2	259
1:6	207
1:8	206
1:16	206
1:20	206
1:21	115
1:23–24	259
1:25	202

Hebrews

1:2	215
1:3	138
1:5	178
2:2	22
2:4	201
2:6	25, 43
2:8	33
2:9	42, 57
2:14–17	231
2:18	180
3:6	119, 165
4:2	202
4:13	14
4:15	75, 76, 120, 121, 202, 231
5:5	178, 179
5:8	180
6:17	20
6:18	120, 121
7:1	202
7:10	202
7:14	83, 84
7:22	20
7:27	53
7:28	30
8:1	138, 139

8:6	20	3:18	57, 180, 231
8:8	202	3:21	241
9:9	202	3:22	33, 138
9:12	55	4:1	180
9:14	53, 202		
9:15	20, 55	**2 Peter**	
9:20	79, 80		
9:22	80, 81	1:16–19	90
9:25	53		
9:26	180, 202	**1 John**	
9:28	58		
10:2	202	1:3	165
10:12	57, 139	1:7	241
10:20	76	1:9	241
10:22	202, 241, 242	3:5	58, 120
10:26	15	3:11	38
10:29	80	3:16	57
10:34	202	3:22	14
10:37	29, 108	3:23	163, 165
11:4	38	4:2	23, 29
11:9	202	5:6	29
11:25	202	5:10	185
11:31	202	5:20	165, 166, 231
11:35	55		
12:2	114, 116, 138, 139	**2 John**	
12:3	112		
12:10	202	7	23, 29, 70
12:24	20	9	163
13:3	202		
13:12	181	**Jude**	
13:18	202		
13:20	14	1:11	38
		1:25	15
James			
2:1	118	**Revelation**	
		1:4	29
1 Peter		1:8	29
		1:11–18	154
1:2	241	1:12	154
1:18	55	1:13	43
1:19	120	1:15	154
1:22	241	1:16	154
2:7–8	108	1:17	154
2:21	57, 110, 180	5:6	58
2:22	41, 58, 120	5:7	138
2:23	180	12:7	25, 82
2:24	58	12:17	82
2:25	58	14:5	58
3:4	14	14:12	118

Scripture Index

Revelation–continued

20:6	247
22:3	138
22:5	226

JEWISH APOCRYPHA AND PSEUDEPIGRAPHA

Apocalypse of Adam

1:712–19	26

Epistle of Jeremiah

1:33	180
2Q246	42
4Q246	42, 165

1 Enoch

46:2–4	150
48:2	150
60:10	150
62:5, 7, 9, 14	150
63:11	150
69:26–27, 29	150
70:1	150
71:14, 17	150

Life of Adam and Eve

2:258–95	26

2 Maccabees

6:30	180
7:18	180
9:28	180

3 Maccabees

3:22	213

4 Maccabees

4:25	180
9:8	180
10:10	180
14:9	180

Pseudo-Jonathan Targum

Gen 4:1	37

Sirach

24:3–12	164
38:16	180

Testament of Adam

1:993–95	26

Testament of Dan

6:2	21

Wisdom

10:17	164
11:4	164
12:27	180
18:1, 11	180
19:13	180

Author Index

Addley, W. P., 91
Akenson, D. H., 7, 47,48, 49, 66, 68, 71, 81, 86, 93, 95, 133, 134, 135, 153, 162, 165, 167, 199
Allison, D. C., 103
Andrews, E., 36, 76, 168, 229
Archer, G. L., 83, 177
Augustine, 23, 56, 155
Baird, W., 232
Barclay, W., 111, 178
Barnett, P., 65, 66, 82, 90, 143, 148, 173
Barrett, C. K., 30, 35, 36, 63, 108, 161, 195
Barth, K., 28
Bauckham, R., 5, 18, 51
Bauer, B., 5
Bauer, W., 4
Baur, F. C., 6, 10, 75, 87, 144
Beare, F. W., 5
Becker, J., 20
Bedard, S. J., 91
Behm, J., 79
Beker, J. C., 67, 198, 219
Bella, P., 10, 231
Bénétreau, S., 5
Bentham, J., 64
Bernard, J. H., 20
Best, E., 8, 199, 200, 206, 239
Bird, M. F., 3, 19, 28, 42, 43, 59, 92, 110, 147, 150, 171, 207
Black, D. A., 193, 201
Black, M., 36, 73
Blaiklock, E. M., 144
Bornkamm, G., 75
Bousset, W., 3, 4, 5, 6, 10, 27, 30, 31, 118, 130, 156, 159, 164, 199, 201
Bouttier, M., 199
Brandenburger, E., 26, 28
Brenton, H., 158
Bockmuehl, M., 102, 173
Bouttier, M., 199

Bruce, F. F., 3, 4, 6, 76, 91, 94, 97, 99,122, 130, 14, 156, 172, 173, 176
Brückner, M., 6
Buitenwerf, R., 144, 145, 153, 161
Bultmann, R., xi, 3, 4, 5, 6, 9, 10, 26, 27, 28, 36, 55, 68, 69, 75, 86, 18, 164, 194, 236,
Callen, T., 195, 209, 236
Calvert, D., 91
Carrington, P., 17
Case, S. J., 6
Cerfaux, L., 229
Charlesworth, J. H., 26
Chester, A., 47
Chilton, B., 148
Chirichigno, G., 83, 177
Chrisope, T., 157
Ciampa. R., 33
Collinwood, R., 7
Conzelmann, H., 16
Corley, B., 154, 155
Cousins, P. E., 149
Creed, J. M., 35
Cullmann, O., 5, 10, 27, 42, 47, 212, 233
Cupitt, D., 231
Cutton, G., 154
Danielou, J., 149
Danizier, D. D., 3
Davies, W. D., 9, 25, 34, 148
Deissmann, A., 6, 8, 199, 236
de Lacey, D. R., 19
Dibelius, M., 16, 47, 54, 56, 59, 60, 101
Dodd, C. H., 8, 17, 66, 93, 100, 111, 140, 172, 180, 239
Douty, N., 8, 198, 200, 235
Duling, D. C., 83
Duncan, G. S., 5
Dungan, D. L., 6, 91, 92, 93, 96
Dunn, J. D. G., 4, 5, 6, 26, 30, 33, 35, 36, 64, 72, 91, 92, 93, 94, 105, 129, 131, 146, 160, 168

Author Index

Dupont, J., 146
Eadie, J., 22
Ehrman, B. D., 4, 64, 65, 82, 91, 103, 104, 124, 143, 151, 176, 183, 188
Ellinger, W., 234
Ellis, E. E., 25, 29, 97, 99, 102, 103, 108, 180
Epiphanius, 94
Evans, C., 21, 35
Fee, G. D., 4, 5, 9, 18, 19, 23, 31, 32, 37, 47, 63, 73, 83, 94, 103, 115, 120, 122, 164, 165, 229
Fitzmyer, J. A., 170, 172
Foerster, W., 15
Fraser, J. W., 10, 75, 76
Fredriksen, P., 76, 143
Fuchs, E., 7
Furnish, V. P., 5, 66, 91
Gager, J. G., 146, 152, 160, 179, 194
Gaventa, B. R., 126, 127
Gerhardsson, B., 91, 243
Giles, H., 19
Goguel, M., 6, 18, 50, 51, 81, 99, 100, 101, 129, 142, 231
Goppelt, L., 29, 42, 79, 198, 202
Grundmann, W., 48, 203, 204, 208, 211
Gundry, R, 155
Guthrie, D., 7, 53
Hagner, D., 18
Hahn, F., 147
Harris, J. R., 172
Harris, M. J., 205, 206
Harvey, J., 8, 11, 200, 236
Hatch, E., 172
Hauerwas, S., 194
Hays, R. B., 47, 91, 141
Heitmüller, W., 5, 75, 147
Hengel, M., 5, 18 33, 42, 47, 48, 49, 52, 53, 54, 66, 129, 137, 138, 143, 144, 147, 149, 152, 159, 163, 164, 167, 171, 172, 173, 183
Higgins, A. J. B., 143
Hooker, M., 71, 73, 199, 194
Horbury, W., 40, 49, 50
Hultgren, S., 32
Hunter, A. M., 4, 61, 72, 73, 169, 173
Hurtado, L., 5, 18, 43, 48, 145, 163, 166, 229
Irenaeus, 4, 23, 163
Janowski, B., 55
Jeremias, J., 123
Johnson, L .T., 1, 7, 66, 67, 121, 123, 125, 128
Jones, E., 3
Jülicher, A., 5
Jüngel, E., 5
Käsemann, E., 9, 26, 28, 31, 52, 57, 62, 72, 136, 137, 155

Kelly, J. N. D., 53, 56, 78, 231
Kim, S., 4, 5, 27, 33, 35, 37, 39, 45, 46, 76, 83, 90, 91, 95, 102, 103, 105, 109, 111, 147, 154, 157, 158, 160, 164, 165, 166, 167, 168, 174, 183, 201
Kittel, G., 5
Klausner, J., 3, 6, 152, 153, 164, 175
Knight, R., 5
Köstenberger, A., ix, xi, xiii, 3, 4, 90, 144, 161, 179
Kramer, W., 5, 167, 198
Kuhn, A. B., 3
Kümmel, W., 4, 10, 75
Ladd, G., 7, 124
Lattey, C., 5
Lau, A., 1, 16, 19, 21, 54, 171
Lewis, C. S., 176
Liddon, H., 74
Lightfoot, J. B., 3, 22, 23, 144
Lindemann, A., 6, 91
Lloyd, R. R., 5
Loflin, L., 3
Lohmeyer, E., 8, 72, 200, 203, 204, 236
Longenecker, B., 184
Longenecker, R., 17, 75, 93, 149, 150, 162, 168
Lüdemann, G., 3, 11, 64, 104, 144, 155, 162, 175
Lyttleton, G., 176
McCready, D., 71, 72
Maccoby, H., 3, 64, 94, 145, 147, 148, 152, 155, 157, 162, 164, 169, 176, 198, 229, 230
MacDonald, W., 45
Machen, J. G., 3, 5, 6, 8, 76, 78, 95, 97, 121, 140, 141, 145, 150, 155, 156, 171, 174, 175,
Manson, T. W., 52
Marshall, I. H., 44, 48, 150, 157, 165, 166, 180
Martin, R. P., 71, 72, 89, 115
Matheson, G., 5
Meeks, W., 6
Metzger, B. M., 35, 74, 163, 215
Meyer, A., 6, 103, 104
Moo, D., 39, 64, 136, 200, 211
Morgan, W., 75
Morris, L., 7, 52, 56, 70, 79
Moule, C., 43, 47, 48, 56, 109, 156, 164, 230
Mounce, W. D., 1, 2, 16, 18, 53, 54, 108, 226
Mowinckel, S., 42, 43, 46, 47, 48, 49
Murphy-O'Connor, J. 5
Nazariah, B., 3
Neill, S., 4
Neirynck, F., 91
Neugebauer, F., 199
Neusner, J., 148
Newman, C., 18
Nietzsche, F., 57, 153

Author Index

Noack, B., 2
O'Connor, J. M., 5
Osbourne, G., 231
Paret, H., 6
Persons, M., 204, 233
Pfleiderer, O., 36, 75
Philo, 26, 35, 42
Picirilli, R. E., 155
Porter, S. E., 1, 144
Pullman, P., 4
Quek, S., 28, 30, 32, 33, 198, 199
Räisänen, H., 10, 54, 148, 149, 194
Ramsey, W., 143, 151, 181
Rawlinson, A., 3, 149
Regner, F., 5
Reitzenstein, R., 10, 164
Renan, E., 6
Resch, A., 5, 91, 96, 101, 141, 179, 180
Ridderbos, H., 1, 5, 6, 7, 9, 26, 39, 54, 61, 62, 69,
    71, 77, 164, 168, 170, 172, 173, 180, 196,
    198, 200, 233, 240, 241
Riesner, R., 55, 170
Robinson, D., 118, 206, 207
Robinson, J., 1, 17, 55, 65
Rostron, S. N., 26, 140, 155, 175
Sanders, Ed , 9, 64, 148, 191, 229
Sandmel, S., 31
Schattenmann, J., 209
Schmoller, O., 5
Schreiner, T. R., 26, 35
Schweitzer, A., 4, 9, 10, 194, 236, 237
Schweizer, E., 8, 200, 225, 237
Scroggs, R., 37, 229
Segal, A. F., 154, 155, 159, 176
Seifrid, M. A., 83, 202
Shaw, G. B., 90, 152
Sherwin-White, A. N., 143
Shriner, S., 3
Singer, I., 5
Smedes, L., 8, 198, 200, 235, 241
Stanley, C., 243, 17, 27, 37, 38, 102, 179
Stanley, D., 5, 91
Stanton, G., 75, 85, 89, 110, 121, 148, 174, 244
Stendahl, K., 155
Stevens, G., 2
Still, T. D., 5, 6
Stonehouse, N., 181
Stout, S. O., 57, 95, 123, 171, 173
Strum, W., 6
Stuhlmacher, P., 58, 91
Tannehill, R., 8, 200, 236
Taylor, V., 149
Thielman, F., 7

Thompson, M., 91, 93, 95, 97, 98
Thrall, M. E., 154
Towner, P., 2, 14, 19, 21, 50, 51, 63, 108
Trobisch, D., 105, 201
Turlington, H., 5
Usteri, L., 10
Vanhoozer, K., 195
Vos, G., 60, 132, 135, 156
Wallace, D., 14, 21, 24, 52, 56, 61, 69, 77, 88, 117,
    118, 119, 201, 208, 222, 224, 225
Walter, N., 91, 98
Watson, F., 51, 56, 94
Warfield, B. B., 74
Wedderburn, A., 5, 6, 28
Weinel, H., 6, 75
Weiss, J., , 6, 77, 78, 110, 122, 149, 236
Weizsäcker, K., 6, 75
Wendt, H. H., 6, 75
Wenham, D., xi, 5, 6, 81, 85, 87, 88, 90, 94, 95, 96,
    98, 99, 100, 101, 103, 107, 128, 129, 140,
    142, 157, 171, 191
Westerholm, S., 146
Wilder, T. L., 2, 92
Wiles, M. F., 28,
Wilson, A. N., 94, 147, 152
Windisch, H., 6
Witherington, B., 23, 49, 75, 120, 123, 170, 233
Wrede, W., 3, 5, 6, 10, 31, 64, 66, 75, 232
Wright, N. T., 3, 4, 9, 12, 18, 19, 60, 62
Yamauchi, E., 31
Zawadi, B., 3
Zetterholm, M., 229
Ziesler, J., 16, 48, 64, 103, 166, 176
Zeoli, R., 3

Subject Index

Abba, 82, 92, 96, 97, 140
Abraham, 22, 44, 61, 65, 71, 82, 83, 86, 118, 160, 162, 171, 189, 205, 206, 207, 208, 272, 273
Adam, 24–40, 43, 44, 59, 61, 63, 69–73, 83, 115, 117, 119, 140, 154, 164, 194, 196, 198, 200, 211, 213, 239, 240
   Jesus as second Adam, 25, 35, 36, 59, 140
   Second Man, 24, 34, 36, 37, 38, 69, 71, 73, 154
   Jesus as last Adam, 26, 27, 30, 33, 34, 63, 71, 72, 73, 154, 200
Adoptionist Christology, 5, 166
Allusions, xv, 7, 11, 22, 43, 54, 55, 58, 65, 66, 73, 87, 91, 92, 95–105, 110, 111, 120, 126, 128, 133, 139, 140–142, 158, 17, 179, 191, 193, 237, 243, 272
Ananias, 117, 153, 159–162, 168, 172, 173, 183, 188, 195
Angel(s), 21, 22, 44, 46, 47, 95, 102, 108, 109, 131, 129, 161, 165, 186, 190, 221, 235
   of God/of the Lord, 4, 21, 38, 44, 45, 46, 159, 160
Apostles, 23, 47, 87, 108, 127, 130, 134, 137, 146, 162, 164, 169, 170, 173, 192, 237, 239
Apollonarianism, 9
Appearances of Jesus, 1, 14, 21, 24, 32, 40, 61, 72, 73, 74, 77, 90, 133, 134, 135, 136, 144, 145, 149, 153, 154, 155, 158, 168, 169, 177, 178, 182, 191, 232, 233, 243
Ascension of Jesus, 3, 7, 8, 42, 108, 136–38, 169, 191, 193, 194, 210, 219, 223, 240, 250
Association with Christ, xv, 8, 9, 194–203, 207, 236–243, 245–247
   Alive with Christ, xv, 11, 26, 32–34, 193, 196, 210, 219, 222, 239, 251
   Appear with Christ, xvi, 211, 235, 250
   Be with Christ, xvi, 96, 192, 194, 197, 202, 210, 218, 219, 225, 228, 234, 237
   Brought with Christ, xvi, 211, 224, 235
   Buried with Christ, xv, 87, 131, 212, 218, 221, 234, 235, 241, 242
   Conformed with Christ, xvi, 122, 139, 193, 199, 210, 211, 215, 220, 221, 235, 242
   Crucified with Christ, xv, 128, 197, 213, 218, 233, 235, 239
   Died with Christ, 11, 197, 213, 217, 222, 226, 233, 241
   Glorified with Christ, xvi, 193, 211, 214, 235
   Heirs with Christ, 210, 214
   Hidden with Christ, xvi, 193, 210, 223, 234, 251
   Live with Christ, 217, 218, 219, 222, 225, 226, 235
   Made alive with Christ, xv, 193, 219, 222, 234, 251
   Planted with Christ, xv, 11, 212, 213, 251, 267
   Raised with Christ, xvi, 210, 222, 223, 235, 251
   Reign with Christ, xvi, 193, 211, 226, 227, 247, 252
   Return with Christ, 230, 235
   Seated with Christ, xv, 11, 194, 235, 251
   Suffer with Christ, 210, 214, 234, 235, 247
   Working with Christ, 216, 239, 247
Atonement, 20, 49, 52, 53, 57, 176, 183, 229, 240
Authority, 2, 3, 17, 26, 44, 46, 94, 95, 98, 105, 144, 146, 151, 156, 161, 173
Baptism
   of believers, 101, 181, 183, 212, 241, 242
   of Jesus, 84, 87, 89, 108, 117, 119, 163, 187, 242
Barnabas, 144, 169, 170, 173, 176
Belief, Believing, 104, 109, 118, 185, 204, 244
Betrayal of Jesus, xv, 52, 62, 124, 125, 190, 250
Biblical Theology, 10, 207, 231
Birth of Jesus, 82, 84, 108, 189
Blood of Jesus, 58, 79, 80, 120, 123, 129, 182, 183, 189, 240, 250
Body of Jesus, 78, 79, 133, 135, 222
Branch, 41, 49, 162

Subject Index

Brand marks of Jesus, 128
Burial of Jesus, xvi, 78, 130, 131, 140, 191, 209, 213, 233, 240, 241, 242
Cain, 37, 38
Catholicism, 84, 172, 241
Cephas, 66, 87, 134, 170, 173, 189
Christos, 47, 67, 68
Christology, 3, 4, 9, 10, 19, 33, 35, 62, 104, 136, 142, 149, 162, 164, 175, 182, 230, 231, 232
Church, xvi, 79, 107, 108, 172, 192, 195, 227, 245–247
Circumcision of Jesus, 84, 189, 221–222, 242
Coming One, 29, 281, 182
Compassion of Jesus, 112, 190
Communion (see Lord's Supper)
Covenant, 18, 20, 39, 39, 58, 79, 94, 183, 196, 198, 221
Creed(s), 13, 16–17, 63, 89, 173, 192, 232
Critical method, xiv, 3, 4, 6, 9, 10, 49, 66, 135, 156, 231, 249
Cross, of Jesus, xv, 79, 115–116, 129–130, 177, 190
Crucifixion of Jesus, xv, 53, 64, 122, 128–130, 167, 190, 213, 218, 233, 250
Curse, 57, 97, 222
Damascus, 159, 162, 163, 166, 168, 170
David, 39–41, 49, 74, 83, 165, 177, 196
Death; of Jesus, xv, 52–54, 64–65, 72, 115, 125, 130, 183, 212, 223, 250–51
Deity of Jesus, 5, 9, 20, 33, 74, 78, 157, 174, 182, 242, 251
Deliverance of Jesus, xv, 113, 126, 188, 190, 250
Devil(s), 25, 102
Didachē, 17, 104
Disciples of Jesus, xv, 87, 124, 134–135, 238, 250
Discourse Analysis, 17, 88
Doceticism, 23, 71, 72, 78, 72
Doctrine, 3, 4, 13, 16, 74, 106, 172, 189, 191, 231, 247
Ebionites, 94
Epiphany, 14, 61, 154, 158, 159
Eschatology, 4, 61, 173
Eternal life, 61, 100
Ethics, 13, 93, 110
Ethnicity of Jesus, 82
Eucharist (see Lord's Supper), 78, 94, 102, 123–24, 183, 189
Evangelism, 176, 243–245
Evangelizing by Jesus, xv, 106–107, 189
Eve, 26, 27, 38
Eyewitnesses of Jesus, 39, 110, 115, 117, 124, 129, 134, 136, 156, 171
Faith of Jesus, 117, 118, 141, 206, 207
Fall of Adam, 23, 25, 27, 28, 32

Flesh, 8, 9, 73–78, 82–83, 173, 189, 232
Fulfillment, 51, 60, 117, 167, 177, 233
Gamaliel, 148
Gentleness of Jesus, 111, 112, 150, 190
Glory of God, 27, 42, 45, 90, 136, 154, 214, 235, 243
Gnosticism, 21, 26, 31, 35, 36, 164, 194, 230, 236
God
   As Father, 18, 89, 96, 116, 117, 120, 132, 163, 165, 178, 219, 252
   As Savior, 1, 13, 14, 15, 63, 69
   Oneness, 22, 23, 70
   Image of, 27, 33, 34, 37, 47, 90, 154, 215, 235, 242–43
Holy One, 147, 149, 150, 178
Holy Spirit, 79, 101, 119, 162, 176, 201, 239, 240, 241
   Humanity of Jesus, xiii, 2, 3, 6, 7, 9, 12, 23, 31, 62, 69, 77, 80, 192, 231–233, 245
   Humbleness of Jesus, 115, 190, 232
   Incarnation, 26, 74, 75, 81, 86, 114, 115, 230, 232
   Innocence of Jesus, 127, 188, 290
   Israel, Jesus of, 47, 74, 82, 84, 177, 189
   James, 81, 83, 87, 134, 170, 189
Jesus (see individual entries)
   Appearances of, 1, 14, 21, 24, 32, 40, 61, 72, 73, 74, 77, 90, 133, 134, 135, 136, 144, 145, 149, 153, 154, 155, 158, 168, 169, 177, 178, 182, 191, 232, 233, 243
   Ascension of, 3, 7, 8, 42, 108, 136–38, 169, 191, 193, 194, 210, 219, 223, 240, 250
   Baptism of, 84, 87, 89, 108, 117, 119, 163, 187, 242
   Betrayal of, xv, 52, 62, 124, 125, 190, 250
   Birth of, 82, 84, 108, 189
   Blood of, 58, 79, 80, 120, 123, 129, 182, 183, 189, 240, 250
   Body of, 78, 79, 133, 135, 222
   Brand marks of, 128
   Brothers of, 81, 83, 87, 170, 189
   Burial of, xvi, 78, 130, 131, 140, 191, 209, 213, 233, 240, 241, 242
   Circumcision of, 84, 189, 221–222, 242
   Compassion of, 112, 190
   Cross of, xv, 79, 115–116, 12–130, 177, 190
   Crucifixion of, xv, 53, 64, 122, 128–130, 167, 190, 213, 218, 233, 250
   Death of, xv, 52–54, 64–65, 72, 115, 125, 130, 183, 212, 223, 250–51
   Deity of, 5, 9, 20, 33, 74, 78, 157, 174, 182, 242, 251
   Deliverance of, xv, 113, 126, 188, 190, 250

Subject Index

Dialect of, 82, 152, 156, 185, 187
Ethnicity of, 82
Faith of, 117, 118, 141, 206, 207
Gentleness of, 111, 112, 150, 190
Humanity of, xiii, 2, 3, 6, 7, 9, 12, 23, 31, 62, 69, 77, 80, 192, 231–233, 245
Humbleness of, 115, 121, 190, 232
Innocence of, 127, 188, 290
Jewishness of, 44
as Lord, 15, 138, 157, 158, 159, 160, 164, 176, 183, 206
Love of, 85, 112, 113, 114, 189,
Meekness of, 111, 112, 190
Miracles of, 110–111, 132, 146, 192
Nailing of, xv, 130, 191, 210, 219
from Nazareth, 37, 82, 167, 178, 185, 187, 189, 244
Obedience of, 27, 28, 29, 30, 112, 116, 117, 122, 128, 191, 197
as Passover, xv, 58, 79, 121, 124, 162, 239
Poverty of, 65, 85, 86, 190
Preaching of, xv, 90, 98, 105–106, 108, 189, 192, 197, 238
Pre-existence of, 36, 37, 42, 3, 71, 72, 80, 121, 164, 165
as Prophet, 147, 149, 150, 178, 187
Reproaches of, 119, 128, 190
Raised third day, 53, 133, 134, 220, 237, 244
as Ransom, 1, 25, 53, 54–56, 58–60, 62, 63, 183, 212
Resurrection of, 3, 11, 32, 63, 78, 109, 131–135, 167, 175, 178, 181, 184, 191, 213, 218, 221, 224, 244
as Righteous/Just One, 53, 89, 117, 147, 149, 150, 153, 161, 162, 188, 197
Righteousness of, 30, 29, 115, 116–118, 120, 127, 190, 196, 239
as Sacrifice, xv, 52, 53, 57, 58, 78, 122, 161, 182, 183, 191
as Savior, 14, 50–51, 149, 150, 117, 188, 206, 220, 250
as Servant, 72, 73, 88, 89, 117, 126, 149, 162, 189, 197, 221
as Seed of Abraham, 22, 189, 205, 207
as Seed of David, 74, 83, 104, 177
Sinlessness of, 75, 120–121
As Son of God, 26, 43, 80, 121, 138, 163–168, 174, 175, 188, 230, 243, 252
As Son of Man, 1, 25, 36, 41–44, 53, 54, 76. 89, 104, 124, 126, 138, 147, 150, 182, 197, 226, 235, 252
Steadfastness of, 114
Stone, Jesus as, 107–108, 149, 150, 190
Sufferings of, 41, 53, 54, 58, 122, 127, 128, 161, 180, 192, 214, 220, 250
Teachings of, 11, 65, 90–97, 101–105, 140, 187, 245
Testimony of, xiii, 59, 60, 66, 126–127, 131
Transfiguration of, 89–90, 166, 190
Weakness of Jesus, 74, 129, 217
Johannine Literature, 272–274
John the Baptist, 87, 178, 189, 243
Judgment, 29, 30, 116, 117, 127
Judas, 52, 124, 125
Justice, 116, 117
Justification, 115–119, 125, 132, 196, 207, 229, 243
kairoīs idíois, 60, 61
Kingdom, 62, 90, 98, 107, 165, 186, 197, 232
Law of God, 21, 22, 75, 85, 97, 100, 104, 116, 117, 156, 179
Linguistics, xiv, 11, 17, 25, 31, 54, 103, 195, 209, 217, 237, 239
Lord, Jesus as, 15, 138, 157, 158, 159, 160, 164, 176, 183, 206
Lord's Supper, 65, 79, 123, 171, 173
Love, of Jesus, 85, 112, 113, 114, 189
Maranatha, 156, 157, 173
Marriage, 189
Mary Magdelene, 134, 158
Mary, mother of Jesus, 84, 85, 116
Mediator, 18, 19–32, 31, 47, 50, 59, 63, 70, 231
Meekness of Jesus, 111, 112, 190
Messiah, 39, 42, 43, 47–51, 53, 67, 68, 89, 148–150, 167, 178
Miracles of Jesus, 110–111, 132, 146, 192
Moses, 20, 22, 23, 29, 47, 196, 238, 241
Myth, 6, 26, 27, 36, 137, 164, 225
Nazareth, 37, 82, 167, 178, 185, 187, 189, 244
New Covenant, 20, 58, 80, 95, 184, 222
New Creation, 25, 200
Obedience of Jesus, 27, 28, 29, 30, 112, 116, 117, 122, 128, 191, 197
One and Many, 59, 116, 163, 196–198, 200, 202, 209
Paradosis, 55, 67, 141, 167
Parousia, 9, 61, 96, 111, 174, 211, 228, 238
Passover, 53, 124, 125, 134, 192
  Jesus as, xv, 58, 80, 121, 124, 162, 239
Pastoral Theology, 12, 246–248
Paul, as apostle, 95, 157, 161, 162, 176
  As Saul, 118, 126, 145, 146, 148, 156, 158, 163, 169, 177
  As an author, 1, 2, 3, 26, 102, 201
  Baptism of, 117, 164, 173
  Choosing of, 161, 194

Subject Index

conversion, 50, 146–148, 150–153, 155, 156, 158, 159, 161, 168–171, 173, 177
commission, 147, 161, 162, 163, 167,172, 186
Pharisee, 18, 109, 117, 126, 128, 146, 149, 150, 156, 159
Peter, 6, 55, 87, 88, 108, 144, 167, 169, 173, 223, 238
Pharisees, 117, 149, 188, 239
Pontius Pilate, xv, 2, 60, 120, 127, 129, 148, 158, 177, 178, 190, 192, 232, 243
poverty of Jesus, 65, 85, 86, 190
Prayer, 92, 98, 114, 116, 156, 234
Preaching of Jesus, xv, 90, 98, 105–106, 108, 189, 192, 197, 238
Election, 197, 201, 239, 273
Pre-existence of Jesus, 36, 37, 42, 3, 71, 72, 80, 121, 164, 165
Prince, Jesus as, 138, 147, 149
Prophet, Jesus as, 147, 149, 150, 178, 187
Propitiation, 52, 79
Pseudonymity, 2, 92
Quotations of Jesus, 90, 92, 94, 99, 103, 124, 141, 274
Ransom, 1, 25, 53, 54–56, 58–60, 62, 63, 183, 212
Reconciliation, 75, 78, 129, 171, 249
Regeneration, 8, 132, 199, 220, 222, 240–242, 252
Redeemed, redemption, 23, 26, 54, 56, 58, 59, 79, 219, 240, 241
Religionsgeschichte Schule, 6, 10
Reproaches of Jesus, 119, 128, 190
Resurrection of Christ, 3, 11, 32, 63, 78, 109, 131–135, 167, 175, 178, 181, 184, 191, 213, 218, 221, 224, 244
of the dead, 32, 71, 95, 131, 132, 135, 218, 235
of believers, 32, 218, 226
Righteous One /Just One, 53, 89, 117, 147, 149, 150, 153, 161, 162, 188, 197
Righteousness of Jesus, 30, 29, 115, 116–118, 120, 127, 190, 196, 239, Right Hand, 25, 33, 41–44, 136, 137–139, 147–151
Roman Catholicism, 84, 172, 241
Sabbath, 123, 133, 135
Sacrifice of Christ, xv, 52, 53, 57, 58, 78, 122, 161, 182, 183, 191
Salvation-history, 7, 60, 228, 230, 233, 235
heilsgeschichte, 61, 233
Sanctification, 8, 183, 185, 200, 201, 220, 240, 252
Satan, 25, 38, 56, 82, 127, 182
Saul, 118, 126, 145, 146, 148, 156, 158, 163, 169, 177
Savior, Jesus as, 14, 50–51, 149, 150, 117, 188, 206, 220, 250

Seed, 21, 22, 25, 38, 50, 53, 74, 82, 83, 177, 189, 205, 207, 208
Servant of the Lord, 41, 43, 58, 117, 126, 162, 197, 221
Jesus as, 72, 73, 88, 89, 117, 126, 149, 162, 189, 197, 221
Sin, 28–30, 38, 57, 120, 213
Sinlessness of Jesus, 75, 120–121, 190
Son of David, 83, 138, 157
Son of God, 26, 43, 80, 121, 138, 163–168, 174, 175, 188, 230, 243, 252
Son of Man, 1, 25, 36, 41–44, 53, 54, 76. 89, 104, 124, 126, 138, 147, 150, 182, 197, 226, 235, 252
Soteriology, 1, 3, 8, 39, 70, 130, 146, 199, 236–243
Steadfastness of Jesus, 114
Stephen, 25, 43, 138, 144, 146–149, 158, 197
Stone, Jesus as, 107–108, 149, 150, 190
Suffering of Jesus, 41, 53, 54, 58, 122, 127, 128, 161, 180, 192, 214, 220, 250
sún (σύν), xv, 11, 193, 194, 199, 200–205, 207–209, 212, 227, 234, 251
Symbol, 48, 79, 128, 137, 183, 221
Teachings of Jesus, 11, 65, 90–97, 101–105, 140, 187, 245
Testimony of Jesus, xiii, 59, 60, 66, 126–127, 131
Third Day, 53, 133, 134, 220, 237, 244
Tradition, 95, 96, 105, 110, 115, 123, 141, 171–173, 243
Transfiguration of Jesus, 89–90, 166, 190
Tree, 147, 177, 183, 188, 191
Typology, 27, 29, 30, 35, 82, 99, 108, 120
Union In Christ, xv, 8, 9, 76, 112, 194, 198–201, 217–119, 235, 239–240
Unitarianism, 19
Universalism, 15, 32, 59, 196
Weakness of Jesus, 74, 129, 217
Witness, 60, 62, 110, 126

Bibliography

with Annotations

Abbot, Harold Charles. "Jesus, the Historic Source of Paul's Gospel." S. T. D. Diss., Gordon College of Theology and Missions, 1932.
Addley, W. P. "The Sayings of Jesus in the Epistles of Paul." Th. M. thesis. University of Edinburgh, 1971.
Akenson, Donald Harmon. *Saint Saul: A Skeleton Key to the Historical Jesus.* Oxford: University Press, 2000.
Aldwinckle, Russell Foster. *More Than Man: A Study in Christology.* Grand Rapids: Eerdmans, 1976.
Allen, J. A. "The 'In Christ' Formula in Ephesians." *New Testament Studies* 5 (1958– 59) 54–62.
Allen, Charlotte. *The Human Christ: The Search for the Historical Jesus.* New York: Free Press, 1998.
Allison, Dale C. "The Pauline Epistles and the Synoptic Gospels: The Pattern of the Parallels." *New Testament Studies* (1982) 1–32.
Anderson, Janice Capel, Philip Harl Sellew, and Claudia Setzer, eds. *Pauline Conversations in Context: Essays in Honor of Calvin J. Roetzel.* London; New York: Sheffield Academic, 2002.
Andrews, Elias. *The Meaning of Christ for Paul.* New York: Abingdon-Cokesbury, 1949.
Archer, Gleason L. and Gregory Chirichigno. *Old Testament Quotations in the New Testament.* Chicago: Moody, 1983.
Ayres, S. G. *Jesus Christ Our Lord: An English Bibliography of Christology Comprising over Five Thousand Titles Annotated and Classified.* New York: A. C. Armstrong, 1906.
Bacon, Benjamin W. *Jesus and Paul: Lectures Given at Manchester College Oxford for the Winter Term 1920.* London: Hodder and Stoughton, 1921.
Baird, William. *History of New Testament Research.* 2 vols. Minneapolis: Fortress, 1992.
Balla, Peter. *Challenges to New Testament Theology: An Attempt to Justify the Enterprise.* Peabody, Mass.: Hendrickson, 1998.
Balz, Horst, and Gerhard Schneider, eds.. *Exegetical Dictionary of the New Testament.* 3 vols. Grand Rapids: Eerdmans, 1993.
Barber, Gerald Wayne. "The Contribution of the Concept '*Upo Nomon*' in Romans 6:14–15 to the Theology of Romans 5–8 and Paul's View of Salvation History." Ph.D. Diss., Trinity Evangelical Divinity School, 1996.
Barclay, J. M. G. "Jesus and Paul." Pages 492–503 in *Dictionary of Paul and His Letters.* Edited by Gerald F. Hawthorne and Ralph P. Martin. Downer's Grove, Ill.: InterVarsity, 1993.
Barclay, William. "A Comparison of Paul's Missionary Preaching and Preaching in the Church." Pages 165–75 in *Apostolic History and the Gospel.* Edited by W. Ward Gasque and Ralph P. Martin. Grand Rapids: Eerdmans, 1970.
Barnett, Paul. *Jesus and the Logic of History.* New Studies in Biblical Theology. Edited by D. A. Carson. Grand Rapids: Eerdmans, 1997.
———. *Paul: Missionary of Jesus.* Grand Rapids: Eerdmans, 2008.
Barrett, Charles Kingsley. *Essays on Paul.* London: SPCK, 1982.
———. *From First Adam to Last: A Study in Pauline Theology.* London: Adam & Charles Black, 1962.
———. *Paul: An Introduction to His Thought.* Louisville: Westminster John Knox, 1994.
Barth, Karl. *Christ and Adam: Man and Humanity in Romans 5.* Translated by T. A. Smail. New York: Harper, 1957.
Bassler, Jouette, M., ed. *Pauline Theology: Volume I: Thessalonians, Philippians, Galatians, Philemon.* Minneapolis: Fortress, 1994.

Bibliography

Bauckham, Richard. *God Crucified: Monotheism and Christology in the New Testament.* Grand Rapids: Eerdmans, 1999.

———. *Jesus and the Eyewitnesses: The Gospels as Eyewitness Testimony.* Grand Rapids: Eerdmans, 2006.

———. *Jesus and the God of Israel: God Crucified and Other Studies on the New Testament's Christology of Divine Identity.* Grand Rapids: Eerdmans, 2008.

Bauer, Bruno. *Kritik der Evangelien und Geschichte ihres Ursprungs.* 2 Vols. Berlin: Hempel, 1850. [Declares there never was any historical Jesus.]

Bauer, Walter. *Orthodoxy and Heresy in Earliest Christianity.* Translated by a team from the Philadelphia Seminar on Christian Origins. Edited by Robert Kraft and Gerhard Krodel. Philadelphia: Fortress Press, 1971.

———, Frederick W. Danker, W. F. Arndt, and F. W. Gingrich. *Greek-English Lexicon of the New Testament and Other Early Christian Literature.* 3rd ed. Chicago: University of Chicago Press, 2000.

Baur, Ferdinand Christian. *The Church History of the First Three Centuries.* Translated and edited by the Rev. Allan Menzies. London, Edinburgh, Williams and Norgate, 1878-79. Translated from the 3rd German edition of *Das Christenthum und die christiche Kirche der drei ersten Jahrhunderte* (1853-63).

———. "Die Christuspartie in der corintheschen Gemeinde, der Gegensatz des peterinischen und paulinischen Christenthums in der alten Kirche, der Apostel Petrus in Rom." *Tüberinger Zeitschrift für Theologie* (1831) 61–206. [Applies Hegelian dialectic to apostolic Christianity.]

———. *Paulus der Apostel Jesus Christi.* Leipzig: Fues's Verlag (L.W. Reisland), 1845, 1866-67. *Paul, The Apostle of Jesus Christ, His Life and Work, His Epistles and His Doctrine. A Contribution to the Critical History of Primitive Christianity.* 2 Vols. 2nd ed. Translated from the second German by Eduard Zeller. Revised by Allan Menzies. London, Edinburgh, Williams and Norgate, 1876. [Questions why Paul seem indifferent to the historical facts of the life of Jesus.]

Beale, G. K., and D. A. Carson, eds. *Commentary on the New Testament Use of the Old Testament.* Grand Rapids: Baker Academic, 2007.

Beare, Francis Wright. *The Earliest Records of Jesus.* 1st ed. New York: Abingdon, 1962.

———. "Jesus and Paul." *Canadian Journal of Theology* 5 (1959) 79–86.

———, Peter Richardson; John Coolidge Hurd, eds.. *From Jesus to Paul: Studies in Honour of Francis Wright Beare.* Waterloo, Ontario, Canada: Wilfrid Laurier University Press, 1984.

Becker, Jurgen. *Paul, Apostle to the Gentiles.* Translated by O. C. Dean. Louisville: Westminster/John Knox, 1993.

Bedard, Stephen J. "Paul and the Historical Jesus: A Case Study in First Corinthians." *McMaster Journal of Theology and Ministry* 7 (2006) 9–22.

Behm, Johannes. "κλάω." In *TDNT* 3:726–43.

Beker, J. Christian. *The Triumph of God: the Essence of Paul's Thought.* Translated by Loren Stuckenbruck. Minneapolis: Fortress, 1990. Translation of *Der Seig Gottes: eine Untersuchung zur Structur des paulinischen Denkens.* Stuttgart: Verlag Katholisches Bibelwerk, 1988.

Bella, Peter. *Challenges to New Testament Theology: An Attempt to Justify the Enterprise.* Peabody, Mass.: Hendrickson, 1998.

Bénétreau, Samuel. "Jésus ou Paul? Qui et le fondateur du christianisme?" Online at http://www.unpoisson dansle.net/rr/9809/benetreau.htm. [He suggest in Paul there is from Jesus "nouveauté dans la continuité."]

Bentham, Jeremy, nee Gamaliel Smith. *Not Paul But Jesus.* London: John Hunt, 1823.

Bernard, J. H. *The Pastoral Epistles.* Cambridge: University Press, 1899; rpt. Grand Rapids: Baker Book House, 1980.

Best, Ernest. *One Body in Christ.* London: SPCK, 1955.

———. *Paul and His Converts.* Edinburgh: T&T Clark, 1988.

Betz, Hans Deiter. "The Birth of Christianity as a Hellenistic Religion: Three Theories of Origin." *Journal of Religion,* 74 (Jan 1994) 15–24.

"Bibliography on Paul." *Journal for the Study of the New Testament* 27 (2005) 85–93; also *Journal for the Study of the New Testament* 28 (2006) 73–84; *Journal for the Study of the New Testament* 29 (2007) 79–88.

Bird, Michael F. *Are You the One Who Is To Come? The Historical Jesus and the Messianic Question.* Foreword by Stanley E. Porter. Grand Rapids: Baker Academic, 2009.

———. *Introducing Paul: The Man, His Mission, and His Message.* Downer's Grove: IVP Academic, 2008.

———. "The Purpose and Preservation of the Jesus Tradition: Moderate Evidence for a Conserving Force in its Transmission." *Bulletin for Biblical Research* 15 (2005) 161–185.

———, and Preston M. Sprinkle. *The Faith of Jesus Christ: Exegetical, Biblical, and Theological Studies*. Peabody, Mass.: Hendrickson, 2010.

Black, David Allen. "Who Wrote Hebrews? The Internal and External Evidence Reexamined." *Faith and Mission* 18 (2001) 3–26.

Black, Matthew. "Jesus and the Son of Man." *Journal for the Study of the New Testament* 1 (1978) 4–18.

———. "The Pauline Doctrine of the Second Adam." *Scottish Journal of Theology* 7 (1954) 170–79.

———. "The Son of Man Problem in Recent Research and Debate," *Bulletin of the John Rylands Library Manchester* 45.2 (March 1963) 305–18.

Blaiklock, E. M. "The Acts of the Apostles as a Document of First Century History." Pages 41–54 in *Apostolic History and the Gospel*. Edited by W. Ward Gasque and Ralph P. Martin. Grand Rapids: Eerdmans, 1970.

Blank, Josef. *Paulus und Jesus: Eine theologische Grundlegung*. Studien zum Alten und Neuen Testament. Herausgegeben von Vinzenz Hamp und Josef Schmid unter Mitarbeit von Paul Neuenzeit. Book 18. München: Kösel-Verlag, 1968.

Blass, F., and Debrunner, A. *A Greek Grammar of the New Testament and other Early Christian Literature*. Translated and revised from the ninth-tenth German edition incorporating supplementary notes of A. Debrunner by Robert W. Funk. Chicago: University of Chicago Press, 1961.

Boers, Hendrikus. *Christ in the Letters of Paul: In Place of a Christology*. Berlin; New York: Walter de Gruyter, 2006.

Bornkamm, Günther. *Paul*. Translated by D. M. G. Stalker. New York: Harper and Row, 1971.

Bousset, Wilhelm. *Kyrios Christos: A History of the Belief in Christ from the Beginnings of Christianity to Irenaeus*. Translated by John E. Steely. Nashville: Abingdon, 1970. Translation of *Kyrios Christos: Geschichte des Christusglaubens von den Anfangen Des Christentums bis Irenaeus*. Göttingen: Vandenhoeck and Ruprecht, 1913; rev. ed. 1921. [He claims to find the origin of Paul's Christology in Hellenistic mystery religions.]

Bouttier, Michel. *En Christ: Etude d'Exegese et de Theologie Paulinienne*. Paris: Presses Universitaires de France, 1962.

Boyarin, Daniel. *A Radical Jew: Paul and the Politics of Identity*. Berkeley: University of California Press, 1994.

Brandenburger, Egon. *Adam und Christus: Exegetisch-religiongeschichtliche Untersuching zu Röm. 5, 12–21 (1. Kor 15)*. Wissenschaftliche Monographien zum Alten und Neuen Testament 7. Neukirkchen-Vluyn: Neukirchener Verlag, 1962.

Bratton, Fred Gladstone. *Divergence and Continuity in Jesus and Paul*. Boston:Boston University, 1927.

Brenton, Howard. *Paul*. N. P.: Nick Hern Books, 2006. [Paul was tricked into converting]

Brinsley, John. *Mesites, or, The One and Onely Mediatour betwixt God and Men, the Man Christ Jesus, wherein the Doctrine of Christs Mediatorship is Largely Handled, and the Great Gospel-Mystery of Reconciliation betwixt God and Man Is Opened, Vindicated, and Applied*. London: Tho. Maxcy for Ralph Smith, 1651.

Bockmuehl, Marcus. "Peter Between Jesus and Paul: The 'Third Quest' and the 'New Perspective' on the First Disciple. Pages 67–102 in *Jesus and Paul Reconnected: Fresh Pathways into an Old Debate*. Edited by Todd D. Still. Grand Rapids: Eerdmans, 2007.

———. *Seeing the Word: Refocusing New Testament Study*. Grand Rapids: Baker, 2006.

Bouttier, Michel. *En Christ: Etude d'Exegese et de Theologie Paulinienne*. Paris: Presses Universitaires de France, 1962.

Brown, Colin, ed. *New International Dictionary of the New Testament*. 3 vols. Grand Rapids: Zondervan, 1975–1985.

Brown, Francis, S. R. Driver, and Charles Briggs. *Hebrew-Aramaic and English Lexicon of the Old Testament*. Complete and unabridged. Oxford: Clarendon, 1906. Electronic edition is Copyright © 2001 by BibleWorks, LLC. All rights reserved. Significant Hebrew formatting modifications and improvements made by Michael S. Bushell, 2001, to conform to lemma and inflected Hebrew forms and typeface.

Bruce, Frederick Fyvie. "Further Thoughts on Paul's Autobiography: Galatians 1:11–2:14." Pages 21–29 in *Jesus und Paulus: Festschrift für Werner Georg Kümmell zum 70, Geburstag*. Earl. E. Ellis and Erich Grässer, editors. Göttingen: Vandenhoeck and Ruprecht, 1975.

Bibliography

———. "Jesus and Paul." *Theological Students Fellowship Bulletin* 46 (Autumn 1966) 21–26.
———. *Paul and Jesus*. Grand Rapids, Baker, 1974.
———. *Paul: Apostle of the Heart Set Free*. Grand Rapids: Eerdmans, 1977.
———. "Salvation History in the New Testament." Page 75–90 in *Man and His Salvation: Studies in Memory of Samuel George Frederick Brandon*. Edited by Eric John Sharpe and John R. Hinnells. Manchester: University Press; Totowa, N.J.: Rowman and Littlefield, 1974.
Brückner, Martin. "Zum Theme Jesus und Paulus." *Zeitschrift für die neutestamenliche Wissenschaft* 7 (1906) 112–19. [Poses the question, How has Paul presented Jesus? He concludes that Paul reveals no influence of Jesus on his Christology: their only commonality is found in Judaism.]
Buck, C. H., and Greer M. Taylor. *St. Paul: A Study in the Development of His Thought*. New York: Scribner's, 1969.
Buitenwerf, Rieuward. "Acts 9:1–25. Narrative History Based on the Letters of Paul." Pages 61–88 in *Jesus, Paul and Early Christianity: Studies in Honour of Henk Jan De Jonge*. Edited by Rieuward Buitenwerf, Harm Hollander, and Johannes Tromp. Leiden: Brill Academic, 2008.
Bultmann, Rudolph. "Adam and Christ according to Romans 5." *Zeitschrift für die neutestamenliche Wissenschaft* 50 (1969) 145–60.
———. *Das Verhältnis der urchristlichen Christusbotscaft zum historischen Jesus*. Heidelberg: C. Winter, 1960. [The Christ of the kerygma replaces the historical Jesus.]
———. "Die Bedeutung des geschichtlichen Jesus für die Theologie des Paulus." Pages 220–46 in *Faith and Understanding: Collected Essays*. London: SCM, 1969. Reprinted pages 220–46 as "The Significance of the Historical Jesus for the Theology of Paul." *Faith and Understanding*. Edited with an introduction by Robert W. Funk. Translated by Louise Pettibone Smith. Philadelphia: Fortress, 1987. [Jesus' preaching is irrelevant for Paul: the apostle centers not on the *Was* of Jesus as a *historische* person but the *Dass* of the *kerygma*.]
———. "Jesus Christus im Zeugnis der Heiligen Schrift und der Kirche." Pages 183–201 in *Existence and Faith*. Translated by S. M. Ogden. New York: Living Age Books, 1960.
———. "New Testament and Mythology." Pages 1-44 in *Kerygma and Myth: A Theological Debate*. Edited by Hans Werner Bartsch. Translated by Reginald H. Fuller. New York: Harper and Brothers, 1961.
———. *Theology of the New Testament*. Two volumes in one. Translated by Kendrick Grobel. New York: Scribner's, 1951, 1955.
Burgess, Robert Gerald. "The Earthly Jesus, Paul and the Tradition." M.A. Thesis. Abilene Christian College, 1973.
Bushell, Michael S., Michael D. Tan, and Glenn L. Weaver, programmers. *BibleWorks*™ Copyright © 1992-2008 BibleWorks, LLC. All rights reserved.
Callen, Terrance. *Dying and Rising with Christ: The Theology of Paul the Apostle*. New York: Paulist, 2006.
Calvert, D. "An Examination of the Criteria for Distinguishing the Authentic Words of Jesus," *New Testament Studies* 18 (1971–72) 209–19.
Carrington, Philip. *The Primitive Christian Catechism: A Study in the Epistles*. Cambridge: University Press, 1940.
Carson, D. A., Peter O'Brien, and Mark Seifrid, eds. *Justification and Variegated Nomism*. 2 Vols. Grand Rapids: Baker, 2001, 2004. [Essays reappraising Ed Sander's views on Paul.]
Case, Shirley Jackson. *Jesus: A New Biography*. Chicago: University Press, 1927. [Insists that Paul had no interest in the traditions of the life and teaching of Jesus.]
Casey, Maurice. *From Jewish Prophet To Gentile God: The Origins and Development of New Testament Christology*. Cambridge: J. Clarke & Co.; Louisville: Westminster/John Knox, 1991.
———. *Son of Man The Interpretation and Influence of Daniel 7*. London: SPCK, 1979.
Castledine, Edwin. *Jesus or Paul*. Berkeley: Pacific School of Religion, 1925.
Catechism of the Catholic Church. New York: Image Books, 1995.
Cerfaux, Lucien. *Christ in the Theology of St. Paul*. Translated by G. Webb and A. Walker. New York: Herder and Herder, 1959. Translation of *Le Christ dans la Theologie de S. Paul*. Paris: de Cerf, 1951.
Charlesworth, James H., Editor. *The Old Testament Pseudepigrapha*. 2 vols. Garden City, New York., Doubleday, 1983. 1985.

Bibliography

Chester, A. "Jewish Messianic Expectations and Mediatorial Figures and Pauline Christianity." Pages 17-89 in *Paulus und antlike Judentum*. Edited by Martin Hengel and U. Henkel. Wissenchaftliche Untersuchungen zum Neuen Testament 58. Tübingen: Mohr Siebeck, 1991.

Chilton, Bruce D. and Jacob Neusner. "Paul and Gamaliel." *Bulletin for Biblical Research* 14.1 (2004) 1-43.

Chrisope, T. Alan, *Jesus is Lord: A Study in the Unity of Confessing Jesus as Lord and Saviour in the New Testament*. Hertfordshire: Evangelical Press, 1982.

Ciampa. Roy E., and Brian S. Rosner. "1 Corinthians." Pages 695-752 in *Commentary on the New Testament Use of the Old Testament*. Edited by G. K. Beale and D. A. Carson. Grand Rapids: Baker Academic, 2007.

Clayton, John Powell, and Stephen Sykes. *Christ, Faith and History: Cambridge Studies in Christology*. London, Cambridge University Press, 1972.

Collinwood, R. G. *The Idea of History*. Oxford: University Press, 1961.

Cook, Michael L. *The Jesus of Faith: A Study in Christology*. New York: Paulist, 1981.

Corley, Bruce. "Interpreting Paul's Conversion—Then and Now." Pages 1-17 in *The Road from Damascus: The Impact of Paul's Conversion on His Life, Thought, and Ministry*. Edited by Richard N. Longenecker. Grand Rapids: Eerdmans, 1997.

Couser, G. A. "'The Testimony about the Lord', 'Borne by the Lord', or Both?: An Insight into Paul and Jesus in the Pastoral Epistles Source." *Tyndale Bulletin*, 55, no. 2, (2004) 295-316.

Cousins, P. E. "Stephen and Paul." *Evangelical Quarterly* 33 (1961) 157-62.

Creed, J. M. "The Heavenly Man." *Journal of Theological Studies* 26 (1925) 113-36.

Crossan, John Dominic, and Jonathan L. Reed. *In Search of Paul: How Jesus' Apostle Opposed Rome's Empire with God's Kingdom: A New Vision of Paul's Words and World*. 1st ed. San Francisco: HarperSanFrancisco, 2004.

Cullmann, Oscar. *Christ and Time: The Primitive Christian Concept of Time and History*. Translated by Floyd V. Wilson. Philadelphia: Westminster, 1950.

———. *Salvation in History*. Translated by Sidney G. Sowers et al. New York: Harper and Row, 1967.

———. *The Christology of the New Testament*. Translated by Shirley C. Guthrie and Charles A. M. Hall. Philadelphia: Westminster, 1959.

Cupitt, Don. "One Jesus, many Christs?" Pages 131-44 in *Christ, Faith and History: Cambridge Studies in Christology*. Edited by S. W. Sykes and J. P. Clayton. Cambridge: University Press, 1972.

Cutton, George. *The Psychological Phenomena of Christianity*. New York: Scribner's, 1908.

Dahl, Nils. A. *Studies in Paul*. Minneapolis: Augsburg, 1977.

———. "The Messiahship of Jesus in Paul." Pages 15-25 in *Jesus the Christ: The Historical Origins of Christological Doctrine*. Edited by Donald. H. Juel. Minneapolis: Fortress, 1991.

Danielou, Jean. *The Theology of Jewish Christianity*. Philadelphia: Westminster John Knox, 1977.

Danizier, Davis D. "Paul vs. Jesus." No pages. Online: http://www.Wordwiz72.com/paul.hyml;

Danker, Frederick William, editor. *A Greek-English Lexicon of the New Testament and Other Early Christian Literature*. Based on Walter Bauer's *Griechisch-deutsches Wörterbuch zu den Schriften des Neuen Testaments und für frühchristlichen Literatur*. 6th ed. Edited by Kurt Aland and Barbara Aland, with Viktor Reichmann and on previous English Editions by W. F. Arndt, F. W. Gingrich, and F. W. Danker. Chicago, Ill.: University of Chicago Press, 2000. The edition cited is an electronic version of the print edition published by the University of Chicago Press accessed on BibleWorks™ Copyright © 1992-2008 BibleWorks, LLC.

Davies, W. D. *Paul and Rabbinic Judaism*. Rev. ed. New York: Harper, 1967.

Davis, G. M. "The Humanity of Jesus." *Journal of Biblical Literature* 70 (1951) 105-12.

Davis, Stephen T. *Encountering Jesus: A Debate on Christology*. Atlanta: John Knox, 1988.

Deissmann, Adolf. *Die neutestamentliche Formel "In Christo Jesu."* Marburg: N. G. Elwart, 1892.

———. *Paul: A Study in Social and Religious History*. Translated by W. E. Wilson. New York: Doran, 1926.

———. *The Religion of Jesus and the Faith of Paul*. Translated by W. E. Wilson. London: Hodder and Stoughton, 1923. [To Paul, Jesus is not a historical figure but a present reality.]

de Lacey, D. R. "Jesus as Mediator." *Journal for the Study of the New Testament* (1987) 101-121.

Delos, Andrew C. *Myths We Live By: From the Life and Times of Jesus and Paul*. N.P.: Booksurge, 2005.

Desmond, Shaw. *Jesus Or Paul?* London: Skeffington and Son, 1945.

Bibliography

Dibelius, Martin, and Hans Conzelmann. *The Pastoral Epistles*. Translated by Philip Buttolph and Adela Yarbro. Edited by Helmut Koester. Philadelphia: Fortress, 1972.

———, and Werner Georg Kümmel. *Paul*. Translated by Frank Clarke. London: Longmans, 1953.

Dodd, Charles H. *According to the Scriptures: the Substructure of New Testament Theology*. London, Nesbit, 1953.

———. *The Apostolic Preaching and its Developments*. London: Hodder & Stoughton, 1950.

———. "*Ennomos Christou*." Pages 134-48 in *More New Testament Studies*. Manchester: University Press, 1968.

———. *History and the Gospel*. London: Nesbitt and Co., 1938.

———. *The Epistle of Paul to the Romans*. New York: Harper, 1932.

———. *The Meaning of Paul for Today*. London: Allen and Unwin, 1949.

Douty, Norman. *Union with Christ*. Swengel, Pa.: Reiner, 1973.

Duling, D. C. "The Promises of David and Their Entrance into Christianity—Nailing Down a Likely Hypothesis." *New Testament Studies* 19 (1974) 55-77.

Duncan, George. S. "From Jesus to Paul." *Scottish Journal of Theology* 2 (1949) 1-12.

———. *Jesus, Son of Man: Studies contributory to a Modern Portrait*. New York: Macmillan, 1948.

Dungan, David L. *The Sayings of Jesus in the Churches of Paul: The Use of the Synoptic Tradition in the Regulation of Early Church Life*. Philadelphia: Fortress, 1971.

Dunn, James D. G. *Christology in the Making: A New Testament Inquiry into the Origins of the Doctrine of the Incarnation*. 2d ed. Grand Rapids: Eerdmans, 1996.

———. *Jesus Remembered*. Christianity in the Making. Volume 1. Grand Rapids: Eerdmans, 2003.

———. "Jesus Tradition in Paul." Pages 155-78 in *Studying the Historical Jesus: Evaluations of the State of Current Research*. Edited by Bruce Chilton, and Craig A. Evans. Leiden: Brill, 1994.

———, ed. *The Cambridge Companion to Paul*. Cambridge: University Press, 2003.

———. *The New Perspective on Paul: Collected Essays*. Tübingen: Mohr Siebeck, 2005.

———. *The Theology of Paul the Apostle*. Grand Rapids: Eerdmans, 1998.

Dupont, Jacques. "The Conversion of Paul and its Influence on His Understanding of Salvation by Faith." Pages 176-94 in *Apostolic History and the Gospel*. Edited by W. Ward Gasque and Ralph P. Martin. Grand Rapids: Eerdmans, 1970.

Eadie, John. *A Commentary on the Greek Text of the Epistle of Paul to the Galatians*. Edinburgh: T. & T. Clark, 1869. Reprint, Grand Rapids: Baker, 1979.

Eckardt, A. Roy. *Reclaiming the Jesus of History: Christology Today*. Minneapolis: Fortress, 1992.

Ehrman, Bart D. *Jesus: Apocalyptic Prophet of the New Millennium*. Oxford: University Press, 1999.

———. *Jesus, Interrupted: Revealing the Hidden Contradictions in the Bible (and Why We Don't know About Them)*. N.Y.: HarperCollins, 2009.

———. *Lost Christianities: The Battle for Scripture and The Faith We Never Knew*. Oxford: University Press, 2003.

———. *Misquoting Jesus: The Story Behind Who Changed the Bible and Why*. N.Y.: HarperCollins, 2005.

———. *Peter, Paul, and Mary Magdalene: The Followers of Jesus in History and Legend*. Oxford: University Press, 2006.

———. *The Lost Gospel of Judas Iscariot: A New Look at Betrayer and Betrayed*. Oxford: University Press, 2006.

———. *The New Testament: A Historical Introduction*. Oxford: University Press, 2000.

Ellinger, Winfried. "σύν." *EDNT* 3:291-92.

Ellis, Earl. E., and Erich Grässer, eds.. *Jesus und Paulus: Festschrift für Werner Georg Kümmell zum 70, Geburstag*. Göttingen: Vandenhoeck and Ruprecht, 1975.

Ellis, Earl. E. *Paul's Use of the Old Testament*. Grand Rapids: Baker, 1957.

English, John. "Christ and 'the Second-Last Adam' Theme." L. S. T. Thesis, Immaculate Conception of Montreal, 1965.

Epiphanius of Salamis. *Panarion (Refutation of all Heresies)*. 2 Vols. Leiden: Brill Academic, 1987.

Evans, Craig. *Ancient Texts for New Testament Studies*. Peabody, Mass.: Hendrickson, 2006.

Fee, Gordon D. *Pauline Christology: An Exegetical-Theological Study*. Peabody, Mass.: Hendrickson, 2007.

———. "Philippians 2:5-11: Hymn or Exalted Pauline Prose?" *Bulletin for Biblical Research* 2 (1992) 29-46.

Feine, Paul. *Jesus Christus und Paulus*. Leipzig: J. C. Heinrich, 1902.

———. *Paul as a Theologian*. New York: Eaton & Mains; Cincinnati: Jennings & Graham, 1908. Translated from *Paulus als Theologe*. Edwin Runge, 1906. [Refutes Hellenistic influences on Paul and understands Paul in Jewish apocalyptic].

Fitzmyer, Joseph A. *Paul and His Theology: A Brief Sketch*. 2d ed. Englewood Cliffs, N.J.: Prentice Hall, 1989.

Flusser, David, and R. Steven Notley. *The Sage from Galilee: Rediscovering Jesus' Genius*. 4th exp. Ed. Grand Rapids: Eerdmans, 2007.

Foerster, Werner. "σωτήρ." *TDNT* 7:1010–12.

Fraser, John W. *Jesus and Paul: Paul as Interpreter of Jesus from Harnack to Kümmel*. Abingdon: Marcham Books, 1974.

Fredriksen, Paula. *From Jesus to Paul: The Origins of the New Testament Images of Jesus*. New Haven: Yale University Press, 1988.

Frei, Hans W. *The Eclipse of Biblical Narrative: A Study in Eighteenth and Nineteenth Century Hermeneutics*. New Haven: Yale University Press, 1974.

Freyne, S. "The Jesus-Paul Debate Revisited and Re-Imaging Christian Origins." Pages 143–63 in *Journal for the Study of the New Testament*. Supplement series. No. 241 (2003). Sheffield: University of Sheffield, 2003.

Fuchs, Ernst. "The Theology of the New Testament and the Historical Jesus." Pages 167–90 in *Studies of the Historical Jesus*. Translated by Andrew Scobie. London: SCM, 1964.

Fuller, Reginald H. *The Foundations of New Testament Christology*. New York: Scribners, 1965. [Seeks to establish a historical christology on the basis of higher-critical and history-of-religion assumptions.]

———. *Who Is This Christ? Gospel Christology and Contemporary Faith*. Philadelphia: Fortress, 1983.

Furnish, Victor P. *Jesus According to Paul*. Cambridge: University Press, 1993.

———. "The Jesus-Paul Debate." In *Paul and Jesus: Collected Essays*. Edited by A. J. M. Wedderburn. Journal for the Study of the New Testament. Supplement Series 37. Sheffield: Academic, 1989.

———. "On Putting Paul in His Place." *Journal of Biblical Literature* (1994), 7.

Fusselle, Warner Earle. "The Historical Jesus in the Thinking of Paul." Th. D. Dissertation. Southern Baptist Theological Seminary, 1950.

Gager, John G. *Reinventing Paul*. Oxford: University Press, 2002.

Garner, Paul. *The New Creationism: Building Scientific Theory on a Biblical Foundation*. Webster, New York: Evangelical Press, 2009.

Gasque, W. Ward and Ralph P. Martin, eds. *Apostolic History and the Gospel: Biblical and Historical Essays presented to F. F. Bruce on his 60th Birthday*. Grand Rapids: Eerdmans, 1970.

Gaventa, Beverly Roberts, "Interpreting the Death of Jesus Apocalyptically: Reconsidering Romans 8:32." Pages 125–145 in *Jesus and Paul Reconnected: Fresh Pathways into an Old Debate*. Edited by Todd D. Still. Grand Rapids: Eerdmans, 2007.

Gerhardsson, Birger. *Memory and Manuscript: Oral Tradition in Rabbinic Judaism and Early Christianity* with *Tradition and Transmission in Early Christianity*. Foreword by Jacob Neusner. Translated by Eric J. Sharpe. Grand Rapids: Eerdmans, 1998.

Giles, Henry. *There is one God, and one Mediator between God and men, the Man Christ Jesus: a Lecture, Delivered in Paradise Street Chapel, Liverpool, on Tuesday, March 5, 1839*. Liverpool: Willmer and Smith; London: J. Green, 1839. [Defends Unitarianism]

Goguel, Maurice. *Jesus the Nazarene: Myth or History?* Translated by Frederick Stephens. Introduction by R. Joseph Hoffmann. Amherst, New York.: Prometheus Books, 2006.

———. *L'Apôtre Paul et Jésus-Christ*. Paris: Fischbacher, 1904. [Thèse présentée à la Faculté de théologie protestante de Paris, pour obtenir le grade de licencié en théologie. "Paul constitué une christologie; . . . dans sa théologie, une théorie du salut a remplacé la prédication du Royaume" (p. 167).]

Golike, Robert Raymond. "The Significance of the Manhood of Jesus Christ to the Apostle Paul." M. A. Thesis. Wheaton College, 1955.

Goppelt, Leonhard. *Jesus, Paul, and Judaism: An Introduction to New Testament Theology*. Translated and edited by Edward Schroeder. New York: Thomas Nelson, 1964.

———. *Theology of the New Testament*. Translated by John E. Alsup. Edited by Jürgen Roloff. 2 vols. Grand Rapids: Eerdmans, 1982.

———. *Tupos: The Typological Interpretation of the Old Testament in the New*. Translated by Donald Madvig. Foreword by E. Earle Ellis. Grand Rapids: Eerdmans, 1982.

Bibliography

Grant, Michael. *Saint Paul.* New York: Scribner's, 1976.

Grässer, Erich. "Der mensch Jesus als Thema der Theologie." Pages 129-150 in *Jesus und Paulus: Festschrist für Werner Georg Küzum 70, Geburtstag.* Herausgegeben von E. Earl Ellis, und Erich Grässer. Göttingen: Vandenhoeck & Ruprecht, 1975. [Surveys how the humanity of Jesus has been used in Theology.]

Green, Joel B., and Max Turner. *Jesus of Nazareth: Lord and Christ: Essays on the Historical Jesus and New Testament Christology.* Grand Rapids: Eerdmans; Carlisle, UK: Paternoster, 1994.

Griffith-Jones, Robin. *The Gospel According to Paul: The Creative Genius who Brought Jesus to the World.* San Francisco: HarperCollins, 2005.

Grundmann, Walter. "σύν-μετά." In *TDNT* 7:766-97.

Gu, David Qi Wei. "An Analytical Study of Linguistic Similarities between the Teachings of Jesus and Paul." M. T. S. Thesis, Southeastern Baptist Theological Seminary, 2001.

Guelich, Robert A., ed. *Unity and Diversity in New Testament Theology: Essays in Honor of George E. Ladd.* Grand Rapids: Eerdmans, 1978.

Gundry, Robert. "The Moral Frustration of Paul before His Conversion." Pages 228-45 in *Pauline Studies: Essays Presented to Professor F. F. Bruce on his 70th Birthday.* Edited by Donald A. Hagner and Murray J. Harris. Exeter: Paternoster, 1980.

Guthrie, Donald. *New Testament Theology.* Downer's Grove, Ill.: InterVarsity, 1981.

Hagner, Donald A. "Paul's Christology and Jewish Montheism." Pages 19-38 in *Perspectives on Christology.* Edited by Marguerite Shuster and Richard A. Muller. Grand Rapids: Zondervan, 1991.

———, and Murray J. Harris, eds. *Pauline Studies: Essays Presented to Professor F. F. Bruce on his 70th Birthday.* Exeter: Paternoster, 1980.

Hahn, Ferdinand. *The Titles of Jesus in Christology: Their History in Early Christianity.* Translated by Harold Knight and George Ogg. New York: World Publishing, 1969.

Haines, Perry F. *The Jesus Paul Preached.* Boston: W. A. Wilde, 1949.

Harrington, Wilfrid J. *Jesus and Paul: Signs of Contradiction.* Wilmington, Del.: M. Glazier, 1987.

Harris, James Rendel. *Testimonies.* Cambridge: University Press, 1916, 1920.

Harris, Murray. J. "Prepositions and Theology in the Greek New Testament." Pages 1211-14 in vol. 3 of *The New International Dictionary of New Testament Theology.* Edited by Colin Brown. 3 vols. Grand Rapids: Zondervan, 1978.

Harris, R. Laird, Gleason L. Archer, Bruce K, Waltke. *Theological Wordbook of the Old Testament.* 2 Vols. Chicago: Moody Press, 1980.

Hart, Trevor A. and Daniel P. Thimell. *Christ in Our Place: The Humanity of God in Christ for the Reconciliation of the World: Essays Presented to Professor James Torrance.* Exeter, GB: Paternoster; Allison Park, Pa.: Pickwick Publications, 1989.

Harvey, John D. "The 'With Christ' Motif in Paul's Thought." *Journal of the Evangelical Theological Society* 35 (Sept 1992) 329-40.

Hatch, Edwin. "On Composite Quotations from the Septuagint." Pages 203-14 in *Essays in Biblical Greek.* Oxford: Clarendon, 1889

Hauerwas, Stanley. *Unleashing the Scripture: Freeing the Bible from Captivity to America.* Nashville: Abington, 1993.

Hay, David, editor. *Pauline Theology: Volume II: 1 & 2 Corinthians.* Minneapolis: Fortress, 1993.

———, and E. Elizabeth Johnson. *Pauline Theology. Volume III: Romans.* Minneapolis: Fortress, 1995.

Hays, Richard B. *Echoes of Scripture in the Letters of Paul.* New Haven: Yale University Press, 1989.

———. *The Faith of Jesus Christ: The Substructure of Galatians 3:1—4:11.* 2d ed. Grand Rapids: Eerdmans, 2001.

Hawthorne, Gerald F. and Otto Betz, eds. *Tradition and Interpretation in the New Testament: Essays in Honor of E. Earle Ellis for his 60th birthday.* Grand Rapids: Eerdmans, 1987.

Heitmüller, Wilhelm. "Hellenistic Christianity Before Paul." Pages 308-19 in *The Writings of St. Paul: A Norton Critical Edition.* Edited by Wayne A. Meeks. New York: Norton, 1972. Repr. of "Zum Problem Paulus und Jesus." *Zeitschrift für die neutestamenliche Wissenschaft* 13 (1912) 320-37. [Paul depends on Jesus as defined by Hellenistic Christianity.]

Hengel, Martin. *Acts and the History of Earliest Christianity.* Translated by John Bowden. Philadelphia: Fortress, 1980.

———. *Between Jesus and Paul: Studies in the Earliest History of Christianity*. Translated by John Bowden. Philadelphia: Fortress, 1983.

———. *Crucifixion: In the Ancient World and the Folly of the Message of the Cross*. Translated by John Bowden. Philadelphia: Fortress, 1977.

———. "'Sit at My Right Hand!' The Enthronement of Christ at the Right Hand of God and Psalm 110:1." Pages 119–225 in *Studies in Early Christology*. Edinburgh: T & T Clark, 1995.

———. *Studies in Early Christology*. Edinburgh: T & T Clark, 1995.

———. *The Atonement: Origins of the Doctrine in the New Testament*. Translated by John Bowen. Philadelphia: Fortress, 1981.

———. *The Pre-Christian Paul*. London: SCM, 1991.

———. *The Son of God: The Origin of Christology and the History of Jewish-Hellenistic Religion*. Translated by John Bowden. Philadelphia: Fortress, 1976.

———, and Anna Maria Schwemer. *Paul: Between Damascus and Antioch: The Unknown Years*. Louisville: Westminster/John Knox, 1997.

Higgins, A. J. B. "The Preface to Luke and the Kerygma in Acts." Pages 78–91 in *Apostolic History and the Gospel*. Edited by W. Ward Gasque and Ralph P. Martin. Grand Rapids: Eerdmans, 1970.

Hollander, Harm. "The Words of Jesus: From Oral Traditions to Written Record in Paul Q." Pages 340–57 in *Novum Testamentum* 42, no. 4 (2000). Leiden: Brill Academic Publishers, 2000.

Hooker, Morna Dorothy. *From Adam to Christ: Essays on Paul*. Cambridge; New York: University Press, 1990.

———. "Philippians 2:6–11." Pages 151–164 in *Jesus und Paulus: Festschrift für Werner Georg Küzum 70, Geburtstag*. Herausgegeben von E. Earl Ellis, und Erich Grässer. Göttingen: Vandenhoeck & Ruprecht, 1975.

———. *The Son of Man in Mark: A Study of the Background of the Term 'Son of Man' and its use in St. Mark's Gospel*. Montreal: McGill University Press, 1967.

Hoppe, Rudolf, and Ulrich Busse, eds.. *Von Jesus Zum Christus: Christologische Studien: Festgabe Für Paul Hoffmann Zum 65. Geburtstag*. Berlin; New York: W. de Gruyter, 1998.

Horbury, William. *Jewish Messianism and the Cult of Christ*. London: SCM, 1998.

———. "Jewish Messianism and Early Christianity." Pages 3–24 in *Contours of Christology in the New Testament*. Edited by Richard Longenecker. Grand Rapids: Eerdmans, 2005.

Hultgren, Arland J., and G. E. Gorman. *New Testament Christology: A Critical Assessment and Annotated Bibliography*. New York: Greenwood, 1988.

Hultgren, Stephen. "The Origin of Paul's Doctrine of the Two Adams in 1 Corinthians 15.45–49." *Journal for the Study of the New Testament* 25 (2003) 343–70.

Hunter, Archibald M. *The Gospel According to Paul*. Revised edition of *Interpreting Paul's Gospel*. Philadelphia: Westminster, 1978.

———. *Paul and His Predecessors*. New rev. ed. London: SCM, 1961.

Hurd, John C. "The Jesus Whom Paul Preaches (Acts 19:13)." Pages 73–90 in *From Jesus to Paul: Studies in Honour of Francis Wright Beare*. Edited by P. Richardson and J. C. Hurd. Waterloo, Ont: Laurier University, 1984.

Hurtado, Larry W. "Convert, Apostate, or Apostle to the Nations? The 'Conversion of Paul in Recent Scholarship." *Studies in Religion* 22 (1993) 273–84.

———. *Lord Jesus Christ: Devotion to Jesus in Earliest Christianity*. Grand Rapids: Eerdmans, 2003.

———. *One God, one Lord: Early Christian Devotion and Ancient Jewish Monotheism*. Philadelphia: Fortress, 1988.

———. "Paul's Christology." Pages 185–98 in *The Cambridge Companion to St. Paul*. Edited by James D. G. Dunn. Cambridge: University Press, 2003.

Jaegher, Paul de. *Vie d'identification au Christ Jésus*. Translated, *One with Jesus: the Life of Identification with Christ*. Translator unknown. Westminster, Md.: Christian Classics, Year: 1993.

Janowski, Bernd, and Peter Stuhlmacher. *Suffering Servant: Isaiah 53 in Jewish and Christian Sources*. Translated by Daniel P. Bailey. Grand Rapids: Eerdmans, 2004.

Jenni, Ernst, and Claus Westermann. *Theological Lexicon of the Old Testament*. 3 Vols. Translated by Mark E. Biddle. Peabody, Mass.; Hendrickson, 1997.

Jeremias, Joachim. *The Eucharistic Words of Jesus*. Translated by Norman Perrin. London: SCM, 1966.

Bibliography

Jervell, Jacob. *Imago Deo: Gen 1.26f. im Spätjudentum, in der Gnosis und in den paulinischen Briefen.* Göttingen, Vandenhoeck & Ruprecht, 1960.

Jewett, Robert. *A Chronology of Paul's Life.* Philadelphia: Fortress, 1979.

Johnson, E. Elizabeth, and David M. Hay, eds. *Pauline Theology: Volume IV: Looking Back, Pressing On.* Atlanta: Scholars Press, 1997.

Johnson, Luke Timothy. *The Real Jesus: the Misguided Quest for the Historical Jesus and the Truth of the Traditional Gospels.* San Francisco: Harper Collins, 1996.

———. *The Writings of the New Testament: An Interpretation.* Rev. ed. Minneapolis: Fortress, 1999.

Jones, Edgar. "Paul vs. Jesus: a List." No pages. Online: http:// www.truthseekers.co.za/content/view/84/59.

Jones, Rees. Jenkins. *Iesu neu Crist: y dyn Crist Iesu (1 Tim. 2:5).* Llandyssul, Wales: Cymdeithas Undodaidd Gymreig, 1909.

Juel, Donald. *Messianic Exegesis Christological Interpretation of the Old Testament in Early Christianity.* New ed. Philadelphia: Fortress, 1987.

Jülicher, Adolf. *Paulus und Jesus.* Tübingen: Mohr, 1907.

Jüngel, Eberhard. *Paulus und Jesus; eine Untersuchung zur Präzisierung der Frage nach dem Ursprung der Christologie.* Tübingen, J. C. B. Mohr (P. Siebeck) 1967.

Kärkkäinen, Veli-Matti. *Christology: A Global Introduction.* Grand Rapids: Baker Academic, 2003.

Käsemann, Ernst. *Commentary on Romans.* Translated and edited by Geoffrey W. Bromiley. Grand Rapids: Eerdmans, 1980.

———. "A Critical Analysis of Philippians 2:5-11." Pages 45–88 in *God and Christ: Existence and Province.* Edited by Robert W. Funk. Translated by A. F. Carse. New York: Harper & Row, 1968.

———. "Justification and Salvation History in the Epistle to the Romans." Pages 60–78 in *Perspectives on Paul.* Translated by Margaret Kohl. Philadelphia: Fortress, 1971.

———. "The Saving Significance of the Death of Jesus in Paul." Pages 32–59 in *Perspectives on Paul.* Translated by Margaret Kohl. Philadelphia: Fortress, 1971.

Keegan, Stephen J. "Paul's Use of the Sayings of Jesus and His Interest in the Historical Jesus." Thesis, Romae: Pontificia Universitas S. Thomae, 1976.

Kelly, J. N. D. *Early Christian Doctrines.* Rev. ed. Peabody, Mass.: Prince Press, 2003.

Kephart, Jeffrey. "Paul and the Human Jesus." M. Div. Thesis, Ashland Theological Seminary, 1987.

Kim, Seyoon. "*Imitatio Christi* (1 Corinthians 11:1): How Paul Imitates Jesus Christ in Dealing with Idol Food (1 Corinthians 8–10)." *Bulletin of Biblical Research* 13.2 (2003) 193–226.

———. "Jesus, Sayings of." Pages 474–92 in *Dictionary of Paul and His Letters.* Edited by Gerald F. Hawthorne and Ralph P. Martin. Downer's Grove, Ill.: InterVarsity, 1993.

———. "The Jesus Tradition in I Thess 4.13–5:11." *New Testament Studies* 48 (2002) 225–42.

———. *Origin of Paul's Gospel.* Eugene: Wipf and Stock, 2007.

———. *Paul and the New Perspective: Second Thoughts on the Origin of Paul's Gospel.* Grand Rapids: Eerdmans, 2002.

Kittel, Gerhard. "Jesus bei Paulus." *Theologische Studien und Kritiken* 85 (1912) 366–402. [Finds historical Jesus in the foreground of Paul.]

———, and Gerhard Friedrich, eds. *Theological Dictionary of the New Testament.* 10 vols. Translated by Geoffrey W. Bromiley. Grand Rapids: Eerdmans, 1964–76.

Klausner, Joseph. *From Jesus to Paul.* Translated by William F. Stinespring. New York, Macmillan, 1943. [Paul founded Christianity on Hellenistic Judaism]

Knight, R. "Jesus or Paul? In Continuation of Gospels and Epistles." *Hibbert Journal* 47 (1948) 41–9.

Knowling, R. J. *The Testimony of St. Paul to Christ Viewed in Some of its Aspects.* London; New York: Hodder and Stoughton, 1911.

Knox, John. *Chapters in a Life of Paul.* Nashville: Abingdon, 1950.

———. *Jesus: Lord and Christ; a Trilogy Comprising: The Man Christ Jesus, Christ the Lord, On the Meaning of Christ.* New York: Harper, 1958.

Knox, R. A. *St. Paul's Gospel.* London: Sheed and Ward, 1953.

Koehler, Ludwig, and Walter Baumgartner. *The Hebrew and Aramaic Lexicon of the Old Testament.* Revised by Walter Baumgartner and Johann Jakob Stamm. Translated and edited under the supervision of M. E. J. Richardson. Leiden, The Netherlands: Koninklijke Brill NV, 1994–2000.

Koester, Helmut. *Paul and His World.* Philadelphia: Fortress, 2007.

Köstenberger, Andreas J. "Diversity and Unity in the New Testament." Pages 144–158 in *Biblical Theology: Retrospect and Prospect*. Edited by Scott Hafemann. Downer's Grove, Ill.: InterVarsity, 2002.

———, and L. Scott Kellum, and Charles Quarles. *The Cradle, the Cross, and the Crown: An Introduction to the New Testament*. Grand Rapids: B&H Academic, 2009.

———, and Michael J. Kruger. *The Heresy of Orthodoxy: How Contemporary Culture's Fascination and Diversity Has Reshaped Our Understanding of Early Christianity*. Wheaton: Crossway, 2010.

———, and Peter T. O'Brien. *Salvation to the Ends of the Earth: A Biblical Theology of Mission*. New Studies in Biblical Theology 11. Edited by D. A. Carson. Downer's Grove, Ill.: InterVarsity, 2001.

———, Thomas R. Schreiner, and H. Scott Baldwin. *Women in the Church: A Fresh Analysis of 1 Timothy 2:9-15*. 2d ed. Grand Rapids: Baker Academic, 2005.

Kramer, Werner. *Christ, Lord, Son of God*. Translated by Brian Hardy. Naperville, Ill.: A. R. Allenson, 1966.

Kuhn, H. W. "Der irdische Jesus bei Paulus als traditionsgeschichtliches und theologisches Problem." *Zeitschrift für Theologie und Kirche* 67 (1971) 295–320.

Kuhn, Alvin Boyd. *Paul Knows Not Jesus*. Whitefish, Mont.: Kessinger Publishing, 2005.

Kümmel, Werner Georg. "Jesus und Paulus." Pages 439–56 in *Helisgeschichte und Geschichte; gesammelte Aufsätze, 1933–1964*. Hrsg. von Erich Grässer, Otto Merk und Adolf Fritz. Marburg: N. G. Elwart, 1965.

———. *The New Testament: The History of the Investigation of Its Problems*. Translated by S. McLean Gilmour and Howard C. Kee. Nashville: Abingdon, 1972.

———. *The Theology of the New Testament According to its Major Witnesses: Jesus-Paul-John*. Translated by John E. Steely. Nashville, Abingdon, 1973.

Kuss, Otto. *Paulus: Die Rolle des Apostels in der theologischen Entwicklung der Urkirche*. Regensburg: Verlag Friedrich Pustet, 1971.

Ladd, George Eldon. *A Theology of the New Testament*. Grand Rapids: Eerdmans, 1974.

———. "Revelation and Tradition in Paul." Pages 223–30 in *Apostolic History and the Gospel*. Edited by W. Ward Gasque and Ralph P. Martin. Grand Rapids: Eerdmans, 1970.

Läger, Karoline. *Die Christologie der Pastoralbriefe*. Hamburger theologische Studien 12. Münster: LIT, 1996.

Lategan, B. C. *Die Aardse Jesus in die Prediking van Paulus. Volgens sy briewe*. Rotterdam: Bronder-Offset, 1967. [Dissertation: Proefschrift—Theologische Hoogschool, Kampen.].

Lattey, C. "Quotations of Christ's Sayings in St. Paul's Epistles." *Scripture* 4 (1949) 22–4.

Lau, Andrew Y. *Manifest in Flesh: The Epiphany Christology of the Pastoral Epistles*. Wissenschaftliche Untersuchungen zum Neuen Testament, 86. Hersausgegeben von Martin Hengel und Otfried Hofius. Tübingen: J. C. B. Mohr, 1996.

Leary, T. J. "Paul's Improper Name." *New Testament Studies* 38 (1992) 467–9.

Leathes, Stanley. *The Witness of St. Paul to Christ: Being the Boyle Lectures for 1869*. London: Rivingtons, 1869.

Leipoldt, Johannes. *Jesus und Paulus—Jesus oder Paulus? Ein wort an Paulus' gegner*. Leipzig: Dörffling & Franke, 1936.

Lentz, John C. *Luke's Portrait of Paul*. Cambridge: University Press, 1993.

Lewis, C. S. *Surprised by Joy: the Shape of My Early Life*. New York: Harcourt, 1956.

Liddon, Henry Parry. *The Divinity of Our Lord and Saviour Jesus Christ*. London: Longmans, Green, and Co., 1897. [Brampton Lectures at Oxford, 1866].

Lietzmann, Hans. *Paulus*. Berlin: Leipzig, W. de Gruyter, 1934.

Lightfoot, J. B. "St. Paul and the Three." Pages 292–374 in *The Epistle of St. Paul to the Galatians*. Grand Rapids: Zondervan, 1957.

Linhart, G. W. "Paul's Doctrinal Use of Verbs Compounded with *Sun*." Th. M. thesis, Dallas Theological Seminary, 1949.

Lindemann, Andreas. "Paulus und die JesusTradition." Pages 281–316 in *Jesus, Paul and Early Christianity: Studies in Honour of Henk Jan De Jonge*. Edited by Rieuward Buitenwerf, Harm Hollander, and Johannes Tromp. Leiden: Brill Academic, 2008. [Contains a bibliography of twentieth century German works on Jesus and Paul.]

Linnemann, Eta. *Biblical Criticism on Trial: How Scientific Is "Scientific Theology"?* Translated by Robert Yarbrough. Grand Rapids: Kregel, 2001.

Lloyd, R. R. "The Historic Christ in the Letters of Paul." *Bibliotheca sacra* 58 (1901) 270–93.

Bibliography

Loflin, Lewis. "The Apostle Paul Founder of Christianity." No pages. Online: http://www.sullivan-county.com/news /paul/ paul.htm.

Lohmeyer, Ernst. *Kyrios Jesus: Eine Untersuchung zu Philipper 2,5–11*.unveränderte Auflage. Sitzungsberichten der Heidelberger: Akadamie der Wissenschaften, 1927. [First to apply *formgeschichte* to Paul, in Phil 2:5–11].

———. *Grundlagen paulinischer Theologie*. Tübingen, Mohr, 1929; Liechtenstein, Kraus Reprint, 1966.

———. "ΣὺΝ ΧΡΙΣΤῼ,"*Festgabe für Adolph Deissmann*. Edited by K. L. Schmidt. Tubingen: Mohr, 1927.

Longenecker, Bruce W. "Good New to the Poor: Jesus, Paul and Jerusalem." Pages 37–65 in *Jesus and Paul Reconnected: Fresh Pathways into an Old Debate*. Edited by Todd D. Still. Grand Rapids: Eerdmans, 2007.

Longenecker, Richard N. "A Realized Hope, a New Commitment, and a Developed Proclamation: Paul and Jesus." Pages 18–41 in *The Road from Damascus: The Impact of Paul's Conversion on His Life, Thought, and Ministry*. Edited by Richard Longenecker. Grand Rapids: Eerdmans, 1997.

———. "Christological Materials in Early Christian Communities." Pages 47–78 in *Contours of Christology in the New Testament*. Richard N. Longenecker, editor. Grand Rapids: Eerdmans, 2005.

———, editor. *Contours of Christology in the New Testament*. Grand Rapids: Eerdmans, 2005.

———. *The Christology of Early Jewish Christianity*. Studies in Biblical Theology. A. R. Allenson, Naperville, Ill., 1970.

———. *Studies in Paul, Exegetical and Theological*. Sheffield: Pheonox Press, 2004.

Lopez, Divina. C. *Apostle to the Conquered: Reimagining Paul's Mission*. Minneapolis: Fortress, 2008.

Louw, Johannes, and Eugene Nida, eds. *Greek-English Lexicon of the New Testament: Based on Semantic Domains*. 2 vols. 2d ed. New York: United Bible Societies, 1988.

Lüdemann, Gerd. *Early Christianity According to the Traditions in Acts: A Commentary*. Minneapolis: Fortress, 1984.

———. *Heretics: The Other Side of Early Christianity*. Louisville: Westminster John Knox, 1996.

———. *Opposition to Paul in Jewish Christianity*. Translated by M. Eugene Boring. Minneapolis: Fortress, 1989.

———. *Paul, Apostle to the Gentiles: Studies in Chronology*. Foreword by John Knox. Translated by F. Stanley Jones. Philadelphia: Fortress, 1984.

———. *Paul: The Founder of Christianity*. Amherst, New York.: Proetheus Books, 2002.

Lüdemann, Herrmann. *Die Anthropologie des Apostles Paulus*. Kiel, 1872. [Claims Paul uses Hellenistic dualism of flesh/spirit].

Lyttleton, George. *Observations on the Conversion and Apostleship of St. Paul*. Burlington, N. J.: S. C. Ustick, 1805.

McCasland, S. V. "The 'Image of God' according to Paul.'" *Journal of Biblical Literature* 69 (1950) 85–100.

McCready, Douglas. *He Came Down from Heaven: the Preexistence of Christ and the Christian Faith*. Downer's Grove, Ill.: InterVarsity, 2005.

Maccoby, Hyam. *The Mythmaker: Paul and the Invention of Christianity*. New York: Harper & Row, 1986.

———. *Paul and Hellenism*. Philadelphia: Trinity Press International, 1991.

MacDonald, William G. "Christology and 'The Angel of the Lord.'" Pages 324–35 in *Current Issues in Biblical and Patristic Interpretation: Studies in Honor of Merrill C. Tenney Presented by His Former Students*. Edited by G. F. Hawthorne. Grand Rapids: Eerdmans, 1975.

MacEwen, Robert. K. "Paul's Encounter with Christ on the Road to Damascus: A Comparison of Acts and Paul's Letters." Th. D. Dissertation, Dallas Theological Seminary, 2004.

Machen, J. Gresham. "Jesus and Paul." Pages 547–78 in *Biblical and Theological Studies*. New York: Scribner, 1912. [Observes that liberals created a liberal Jesus and then accused Paul of denying this Jesus.]

———. *The Origin of Paul's Religion: The James Sprunt Lectures Delivered at Union Theological Seminary (1925)*. Grand Rapids: Eerdmans, 1970.

Mackintosh, H. R. *The Doctrine of the Person of Jesus Christ*. Edinburgh: T & T Clark, 1912.

Macleod, Donald. *Jesus Is Lord: Christology Yesterday and Today*. Fearn, Ross-shire: Mentor, 2000.

———. *The Person of Christ*. Downer's Grove, Ill.: InterVarsity, 1998.

Manson, T. W. " ἹΛΑΣΤΗΡΙΟΝ." *Journal of Theological Studies* 46 (1945) 1–10.

Marshall, I. Howard. *The Origins of New Testament Christology*. Updated ed. Downer's Grove, Ill.: InterVarsity, 1990.

———. "The Resurrection in the Acts of the Apostles." Pages 92–107 in *Apostolic History and the Gospel*. Edited by W. Ward Gasque and Ralph P. Martin. Grand Rapids: Eerdmans, 1970.
Martin, Ralph P. *A Hymn of Christ: Philippians 2:5-11 in Recent Interpretation and in the Setting of Early Christian Worship*. Downer's Grove, Ill.: InterVarsity, 1997.
———. "The Christology of the Prison Epistles." Pages 193–218 in *Contours of Christology in the New Testament*. Richard N. Longenecker, editor. Grand Rapids: Eerdmans, 2005.
Matheson, George. "The Historical Christ of St Paul." Pages 1: 43–62; 125–38; 193–208; 264–75; 352–71; 432–43; 2: 27–47; 137–54; 287–301; 357–71; in The *Expositor*. 2nd series. Edited by W. Robertson Nicoll. London: Hodder and Stoughton, 1881. [Confirms agreement of Paul with Synoptics.]
Meeks, Wayne A., ed. *The Writings of St. Paul: A Norton Critical Edition*. New York: Norton, 1972.
Metzger, Bruce M. *A Textual Commentary on the Greek New Testament*. 2d ed. Stuttgart: Deutsche Bibelgesellschaft, 2002.
Meyer, Arnold. *Jesus or Paul?* Translated J. R. Wilkinson. New York: Harper and Brothers, 1909.
Meyer, Marvin W, and Charles Hughes. *Jesus Then and Now: Images of Jesus in History and Christology*. Harrisburg, Pa.: Trinity Press International, 2001.
Montefiore, Claude G. *Judaism and St. Paul: Two Essays*. London, Goshen Press, 1914.
Moo, Douglas. "The Christology of the Early Pauline Epistles." Pages 169–192 in *Contours of Christology in the New Testament*. Edited by Richard Longenecker. Grand Rapids: Eerdmans, 2005.
Morgan, William. *The Religion and Theology of Paul: The Kerr Lectures Delivered in the United Free Church College, Glasgow (1914-15)*. Edinburgh, T. & T. Clark, 1917. Reprint, Philadelphia: Fortress, 1950.
Morris, Henry M. ed. *Scientific Creationism*. 2d ed. El Cajon, Calif.: Master Books, 1985.
Morris, Leon. *The Apostolic Preaching of the Cross*. 3d ed. Grand Rapids: Eerdmans, 1965.
———. *New Testament Theology*. Grand Rapids: Zondervan, 1986.
Moule, C. F. D. "Further Reflections on Philippians 2:5–11." Pages 264–76 in *Apostolic History and the Gospel*. Edited by W. Ward Gasque and Ralph P. Martin. Grand Rapids: Eerdmans, 1970.
———. "Jesus, Judaism and Paul." Pages 43–52 in *Tradition and Interpretation in the New Testament: Essays in Honor of E. Earle Ellis for His 60th Birthday*. Edited by Gerald F. Hawthorne with Otto Betz. Grand Rapids: Eerdmans, 1987.
———. *The Origin of Christology*. Cambridge; New York: Cambridge University Press, 1977.
———. "The Manhood of Jesus in the New Testament." Pages 95–110 in *Christ, Faith and History: Cambridge Studies in Christology*. Edited by S. W. Sykes and J. P. Clayton. Cambridge: University Press, 1972.
Moulton, James Hope, and George Milligan. *The Vocabulary of the Greek Testament: Illustrated from the Papyri and Other Non-Literary Sources*. 1930. Reprinted, Peabody, Mass.: Hendrickson, 1997.
Moulton, W. F., and A. S. Geden. *A Concordance of the Greek New Testament*. 4th ed. Revised by H. K. Moulton. Edinburgh: T. & T. Clark, 1963.
Mounce, William D. *Pastoral Epistles*. Vol. 46 of the *Word Biblical Commentary*. Edited by Bruce M. Metzger, et al. N. p.: Thomas Nelson, 2000.
Mowinckel, Sigmund. *He That Cometh: The Messiah Concept in the Old Testament and Later Judaism*. Translated by G. W. Anderson. Foreword by John J. Collins. Grand Rapids: Eerdmans, 2005.
Murphy-O'Connor, Jerome. *Paul: A Critical Life*. Oxford: University Press, 1996.
Nazariah, Brother. "Yahshua or Paul? Essene Christianity Versus Paulinity: An Exposé and Call to Action." No pages. Online: http://www.essene.org/ Yahowshua_or_Paul.htm.
Neill, Stephen, and Tom Wright. *The Interpretation of the New Testament: 1861-1986*. 2d ed. Oxford: University Press, 1988.
Neirynck, Franz. "Paul and the Sayings of Jesus." Pages 265–321 in *L'Apôtre Paul: Personnalité, Style et Conception du Ministère*. Edited by Albert Vanhoye. Leuven, Peeters/ Leuven University Press, 1986.
Nelson, Scott. "Yahshua (Jesus) and Judaism Versus Paul and Christianity." No pages. Online: http: // judaismvschristianity.com/.
Neugebauer, Fritz. "Das paulinische 'in christo' *New Testament Studies* (Jan 1958), 124-138.
———. *In Christus: Eine Untersuchung zum paulinischen Glaubensverständnis*. Göttingen: Vandenhoeck and Ruprecht, 1961.
Newman, Carey C., James R. Davila, and Gladys S. Lewis, editors. *The Jewish Roots of Christological Monotheism: Papers from the St. Andrews Conference on the Historical Origins of the Worship of Jesus*. Journal for the Study of Judaism Supplement 63. Leiden: Brill, 1999.

Bibliography

Nietzsche, Friedrich. "The First Christian." Pages 288–91 in *The Writings of St. Paul: A Norton Critical Edition*. Edited by Wayne A. Meeks. New York: Norton, 1972.

———. "The Jewish Dysangelist." Pages 291–96 in *The Writings of St. Paul: A Norton Critical Edition*. Edited by Wayne A. Meeks. New York: Norton, 1972.

Noack, Bent. "Teste Paulo: Paul as the Principal Witness to Jesus and the Primitive Christianity." Pages 9–28 in *Die Paulinische Literatur und Theologie*. Edited by Sigfred Pederen. Göttingen: Vanderhoeck & Ruprecht, 1980.

Nock, Arthur Darby. *St. Paul*. London: Butterworth, 1938.

Norten, Eduard. *Agnostos Theos: Untersuchungen zur Formengeschichte religiöser Rede*. 1913; Stuttgart: Teubner, 1956. [Studies in the form-history of the religious addresses in Acts]

O'Collins, Gerald. *Christology: A Biblical, Historical, and Systematic Study of Jesus Christ*. Oxford; New York: Oxford University Press, 1995.

O'Connor, Jerome Murphy. *Paul: A Critical Life*. Oxford: Clarendon Press, 1996.

———. *Paul the Letter Writer: His World, His Options, His Skills*. Collegeville: Liturgical Press, 1995.

Olford, David Lindsay. "The Knowledge and Use of Information Concerning the Historical Jesus by the Apostle Paul as Evidenced in the Epistles: An Evaluation of the Evidence for the Significant Effect of the Life and Teachings of the Historical Jesus Upon the Structure of Paul's Thought." Thesis, Wheaton College, 1980.

Osbourne, Grant. *The Hermeneutical Spiral*. Downer's Grove, Ill,: InterVarsity, 1991.

Pagels, Elaine. *The Gnostic Paul: Gnostic Exegesis of the Pauline Letters*. 1st ed. Minneapolis: Fortress, 1975.

Paret, Heinrich. "Paulus und Jesus, Einige Bemerkungen über das Verhältnis des Apostels Paulus und seiner Lehre zu der Person, dem Leben und der Lehre des geschichtlichen Christus." *Jahrbücher für deutsche Theologie* 3 (1858) 1–85. [Apart from the Geschichte Jesus, the Geschichte des Herrn cannot be discerned.]

Pate, C. Marvin. *The End of the Age Has Come: The Theology of Paul*. Grand Rapids: Zondervan, 1995.

Persons, Michael. "'In Christ' in Paul." *Vox Evangelica* 18 (1987) 25–44.

Pfleiderer, Otto. *Paulinism: A Contribution to the History of Primitive Christian Theology*. Translated by Edward Peters. 2 vols. London: Williams and Norgate, 1877. [Insists on a hellenizing influence of Paul]

Picirilli, Robert E. *Paul the Apostle*. Chicago: Moody, 1986.

Pokorný, Petr. *The Genesis of Christology: Foundations for a Theology of the New Testament*. Translated by Marcus Lefébure. Edinburgh: T. & T. Clark, 1987.

Porter, Stanley E. "Pauline Authorship and the Pastoral Epistles: Implications for Canon." *Bulletin for Biblical Research* 5 (1995) 105–23.

———. *The Paul of Acts: Essays in Literary Criticism, Rhetoric, and Theology*. Tübingen: J. C. B. Mohr (Paul Siebeck), 1999.

Presbyter of the Church of England. *A Defence of the Doctrine of the Man-Christ Jesus: His Descent from Heaven, as it is Laid Down and Prov'd in the Bishop of Gloucester's Discourse*. London: printed for John Wyat, 1707. Also reproduced on microfilm, Woodbridge, Conn.: Research Publications, Inc., 1986. / The Eighteenth Century; reel 2624, no. 4.

Pullman, Philip. *The Good Man Jesus and the Scoundrel Christ*. Edinburgh: Canongate, 2010.

Quek, See-Hwa. "Adam and Christ according to Paul." Pages 67–79 in *Pauline Studies: Essays Presented to Professor F. F. Bruce on his 70th Birthday*. Edited by Donald A. Hagner, and Murray J. Harris. Exeter: Paternoster, 1980.

Räisänen, Heikki. "'The Hellenists': A Bridge Between Jesus and Paul?" Pages 149–202 in *Jesus, Paul and Torah: Collected Essays*. Translated by David Orten. Sheffield: JSOT, 1992.

———. *Paul and the Law*. Philadelphia: Fortress, 1986.

Ramsey, William. *St. Paul the Traveler and Roman Citizen*. 1897. Revised and updated by Mark Wilson. Grand Rapids: Kregel, 2001. [Affirms historicity of Acts]

Rawlinson, A. E. J. *The New Testament Doctrine of the Christ: The Brampton Lectures for 1926*. London: Longmans and Green, 1926.

Regner, Friedmann. *"Paulus und Jesus" im neunsehnten Jahrhundert: Beiträge zue Geschichte des Themas "Paulus und Jesus" in der neutestamentlichen Theologie*. Göttingen: Vandenhoeck & Ruprecht, 1977.

Reitzenstein, Richard. *Hellenistic Mystery-Religions: Their Basic Ideas and Significance*. Translated by John E. Steely. Pittsburgh: Pickwick, 1978. Translated from *Die hellenistischen Mysterienreligionen nach Ihren Grundgedanken und Wirkungen*. Berlin: B.G. Teubner, 1910.

Bibliography

Renan, Ernest. *St. Paul*. Translated by Ingersoll Lockwood. New York: Carleton, 1889. http://www.archive.org/stream/saintpaul00renarich [Paul transformed Jesus into the divine Christ].

Resch, Alfred. *Die Logia Jesu nach dem griechischen und hebräischen Text wiederhergesestellt: ein Versuch*. Leipzig: J. C. Hinrichs, 1898.

——. *Der Paulinismus und die Logia Jesu in ihrem gegenseitigen Verhaltnis untersucht*. Leipzig: J. C. Hinrichs, 1904.

Richardson, Peter and John C. Hurd, editors. *From Jesus to Paul: Studies in Honour of Francis Wright Beare*. Waterloo, Ont: Laurier University, 1984.

Ridderbos, Hermann. *Paul and Jesus: Origin and General Character of Paul's Preaching of Christ*. Translated by David. H. Freeman. Philadelphia: Presbyterian and Reformed, 1974.

——. *Paul: An Outline of His Theology*. Translated by Richard De Witt. Grand Rapids: Eerdmans, 1975.

——. *When the Time Had Fully Come*. Grand Rapids, Eerdmans, 1957.

Ridgeway, Don. "A Study of Paul's Understanding of Jesus Christ." M. A. Thesis. Butler University, 1960.

Riesner, Rainer. "Back To The Historical Jesus Through Paul and His School (The Ransom Logion—Mark 10.45; Matthew 20.28)." *Journal for the Study of the Historical Jesus* (June, 2003) 171-199.

——. *Paul's Early Period: Chronology, Mission Strategy, Theology*. Translated by Doug Stott. Grand Rapids: Eerdmans, 1998.

Robinson, D. W. B. "Faith of Jesus Christ'—a New Testament Debate." *Reformed Theological Review* 29 (1970) 71-81.

Robinson, John A. T. *Redating the New Testament*. Philadelphia: Westminster, 1976.

——. *Twelve New Testament Studies*. Alec R. Allenson: Naperville, Ill., 1962.

Robinson, Maurice A., and William G. Pierpoint. *The New Testament in the Original Greek: Byzantine Textform (2005)*. Southborough, Mass.: Chilton, 2005.

Roetzel, Calvin J. *Paul: The Man and Myth*. Columbia: University of South Carolina Press, 1998.

Rostron, S. Nowell. *The Christology of St. Paul; Hulsean Prize Essay, With an Additional Chapter*. London: Robert Scott, 1912. [Generally presents a conservative overview of Paul's views].

Rowden, H. H., ed. *Christ the Lord: Studies in Christology Presented to Donald Guthrie*. Leister: InterVarsity, 1982.

Sanders, Ed P. *The Historical Figure of Jesus*. London: Allen Lane: Penguin, 1993.

——. *Paul*. Oxford: University Press, 1991.

——. *Paul and Palestinian Judaism: A Comparison of Patterns of Religion*. Philadelphia: Fortress, 1977.

Sandmel, Samuel. "Parallelomania." *Journal of Biblical Literature* 81 (1962) 1-13.

——. *The Genius of Paul*. New York: Schocken Books, 1970.

Sapp, David A. "An Introduction to Adam Christology in Paul: A History of Interpretation, The Jewish Background, and an Exegesis of Romans 5:12-21." Ph. D. Diss., Southwestern Baptist Theological Seminary, 1990.

Schattenmann, Johannes. κοινωνία. Pages 639-44 in *The Dictionary of New Testament Theology*. Edited by Colin Brown. Vol. 1. Grand Rapids: Zondervans, 1975.

Schillebeeckx, Edward. *Jesus: An Experiment in Christology*. New York: Seabury, 1979.

Schmithals, Walter. *Paulus, die Evangelien, und das Urchristentum: Beiträge von und zu Walter Schmithals zu seinem 80. Geburtstag*. Herausgegeben von Cilliers Breytenbach. Leiden and Boston: Brill Academic, 2004.

——. "Paulus und der historische Jesus." *Zeitschrift für die neutestamentliche Wissenschaft und die Kunde der ältern Kirche* 53 (1962) 145-60.

Schmoller, Otto. "Die geschichtliche Person Jesu nach den paulinischen Schriften." *Theologische Studien und Kritiken* 67 (1894) 656-705. [Answers B. Bauer, that Paul contributes to knowledge of Jesus.]

Schnackenburg, Rudolph. *Baptism in the Thought of St. Paul*. Oxford: Blackwell, 1964.

Schnelle, Udo. *Apostle Paul: His Life and Theology*. Grand Rapids: Baker Academic, 2005.

Schoeps, Hans Joachim. *Paul: The Theology of the Apostle in the Light of Jewish Religious History*. Translated by Harold Knight. London: Lutterworth, 1961.

Schreiner, Thomas R. "An Interpretation of 1Timothy 2:9-15: A Dialogue with Scholarship." Pages 85-120 in *Women in the Church: A Fresh Analysis of 1 Timothy 2:9-15*. Edited by Andreas Köstenberger, Thomas R. Schreiner, and H. Scott Baldwin. 2d ed. Grand Rapids: Baker Academic, 2005.

——. *Paul: Apostle of God's Glory in Christ*. Downer's Grove, Ill.: InterVarsity, 2006.

Bibliography

Schwarz, Hans. *Christology*. Grand Rapids: Eerdmans, 1998.

Schweitzer, Albert. *The Mysticism of Paul the Apostle*. Translated by William Montgomery. Prefaced by F. C. Burkitt. New York: Macmillan, 1955. Translation of *Die Mystik des Apostels Paulus* (1931).

———. *Paul and His Interpreters: A Critical History*. Translated by William Montgomery. London: Adam and Charles Black, 1948. Translated from the first German edition of *Geschichte der paulinischen Forschung*. Tübingen: Mohr, 1912

Schweizer, Eduard. "Concerning the Speeches in Acts." Pages 208–16 in *Studies in Luke-Act.: Essays Presented in Honour of Paul Schubert*. Edited by L. E. Keck, and J. L. Martyn. Nashville: Abingdon, 1966.

———. "Dying and Rising with Christ." *New Testament Studies* 14 (1967–68) 1–14.

———. *Jesus Christ: The Man from Nazareth and the Exalted Lord*. Edited by Hulitt Gloer. London: SCM, 1989.

Scroggs, Robin. *Christology in Paul and John: The Reality and Revelation of God*. Philadelphia: Fortress, 1988.

———. *The Last Adam: A Study in Pauline Anthropology*. Philadelphia: Fortress, 1966.

Seeberg, D. Alfred. *Der Katechismus der Urchristenheit*. Leipzig: A. Deichert'sche Verlagsbuchlandlung Nachf. (Georg Böhme), 1903.

Segal, Alan F. "Paul's Jewish Presuppositions." Pages 159–72 in *The Cambridge Companion to St. Paul*. Edited by James D. G. Dunn. Cambridge: University Press, 2003.

———. *Paul the Convert: the Apostolate and Apostasy of Saul the Pharisee*. New Haven: Yale University Press, 1990.

Segundo, Juan Luis. *The Humanist Christology of Paul*. Edited and translated by John Drury. Maryknoll, New York: Orbis, 1986.

Seifrid, Mark A. "Romans." Pages 607–94 in the *Commentary on the New Testament Use of the Old Testament*. G. K. Beale and D. A. Carson, eds.; Grand Rapids: Baker Academic, 2007.

Sharpe, Eric John, and John R. Hinnells, editors. *Man and His Salvation: Studies in Memory of Samuel George Frederick Brandon*. Manchester: University Press, 1973.

Shaw, George Benard. "The Monstrous Imposition upon Jesus." Pages 296–302 in *The Writings of St. Paul: A Norton Critical Edition*. Edited by Wayne A. Meeks. New York: Norton, 1972.

Sherwin-White, A. N. *Roman Society and Roman Law in the New Testament*. Oxford: University Press, 1963.

Shriner, Sherry. "The Apostle Paul Was a Deceiver!" No pages. Online: http://www.justgivemethetruth.com/paul_was_a_deceiver.htm;

Sinclair, Scott Gambrill. *Jesus Christ According to Paul: The Christologies of Paul's Undisputed Epistles and the Christology of Paul*. Berkeley, Calif.: Bibal, 1988.

Singer, Ignatius. *The Rival Philosophies of Jesus and of Paul: Being an Explanation of the Failures of Organized Christianity and a Vindication of the Teachings of Jesus, which are Shown to Contain a Religion for all Men and for All Times*. London: George Allen, 1919. Reprint, Whitefish, Mont.: Kessinger, 2008.

Smedes, Louis. *Union with Christ: A Biblical View of the New Life in Jesus Christ*. Rev. ed. Grand Rapids: Eerdmans, 1983.

Son, Sang-Won. *Corporate Elements in Pauline Anthropology: A Study of the Selected Terms, Idioms, and Concepts in the Light of Paul's Usage and Background*. Rome: Pontificium Institutum Biblicum, 2001.

Speer, Robert E. *Studies of the Man Christ Jesus*. New York: Fleming H. Revell, 1896.

Sporken, Paul. *Jesus, Mensch für andere Menschen*. Edition: 1. Aufl. Mit einem Beitrag von Curt M. Genewein. Düsseldorf: Patmos-Verlag, 1978.

Stanley, Christopher D. *Arguing with Scripture: The Rhetoric of Quotations in the Letters of Paul*. New York: T & T Clark, 2004.

———. "Pearls before Swine": Did Paul's Audiences Understand His Biblical Quotations?" *Novum testamentum* 41.2 (April 1999), 124–44.

Stanley, David M. "Pauline Allusions to the Sayings of Jesus." *Catholic Biblical Quarterly* 23 (1961) 26–39.

Stanton, Graham N. "Paul's Gospel." Pages 173–84 in *The Cambridge Companion to St. Paul*. Edited by James D. G. Dunn. Cambridge: University Press, 2003.

———. *Jesus of Nazareth in New Testament Preaching*. Cambridge: University Press, 1974.

Stauffer, Ethelbert. *Jesus, Paulus, und Wir: Antwort auf einen Offenen Brief*. Hamburg, F. Wittig Verlag, 1961.

Bibliography

Stendahl, Krister. *Paul Among Jews and Gentiles and other Essays*. Philadelphia: Fortress, 1976. [Develops Paul's theology as a "call rather than conversion; justification rather than forgiveness; weakness rather than sin; love rather than integrity; unique rather than universal."]

———. "The Apostle Paul and the Introspective Conscience of the West." Pages 78–96 in *Paul Among Jews and Gentiles*. Philadelphia: Fortress, 1976.

Stevens, George Barker. *The Pauline Theology: A Study of the Origin and Correlation of the Doctrinal Teachings of the Apostle Paul*. Rev. ed. New York: Scribners' Sons, 1911.

Stewart, James Stuart. *A Man in Christ: The Vital Elements of St. Paul's Religion*. New York: Harper and Brothers, 1935.

Still, Todd, D., ed. *Jesus and Paul Reconnected: Fresh Pathways into an Old Debate*. Grand Rapids: Eerdmans, 2007.

Stonehouse, Ned. B. *Paul Before the Areopagus and Other New Testament Studies*. London: Tyndale, 1957.

Strauss, David Friedrich. *The Life of Jesus Critically Examined*. Translated from the Fourth German Edition by George Eliot. New York: Macmillan, 1892.

Stout, Stephen O. "The Man Christ Jesus: The Humanity of Jesus in the Teachings of Paul." Ph.D. Dissertation, Southeastern Baptist Theological Seminary, 2010.

———. "The New Testament Concept of Tradition." Th.M. thesis, Westminster Theological Seminary, Philadelphia, Pa., 1977.

Strum, W. *Der Apostel Paulus und die evangelische Ueberlieferung*. Berlin: Gaertner, 1900. [Compares "salvation words" of Jesus and Paul to demonstrate similarities.]

Stuhlmacher, Peter. *Das paulinische Evangelium*. I. Vorgeschichte. Göttingen: Vandenhoeck and Ruprecht, 1968.

———. "Jesustradition im Römerbrief: Eine Skizze?" *Theologische Beiträge* 14 (1983) 240–50.

Suzuki, Shigeru. "The Nature of the Believer's Co-crucifixion with Christ according to the Apostle Paul." Th.M. Thesis. Western Conservative Baptist Seminary, 1992.

Swidler, Leonard J. *Bursting the Bonds? A Jewish-Christian Dialogue on Jesus and Paul*. Maryknoll, N.Y.: Orbis Books, 1990.

Sykes, S. W. "The Theology of the Humanity of Christ." Pages 53–72 in *Christ, Faith and History: Cambridge Studies in Christology*. Edited by S. W. Sykes and J. P. Clayton. Cambridge: University Press, 1972.

Tannehill, Robert C. *Dying and Rising with Christ*. Berlin: Topelmann, 1967. Rpt., Eugene, Oregon: Wipf and Stock, 2006.

Taylor, Vincent. *The Names of Jesus*. New York: Macmillan, 1953.

———. *The Person of Christ in New Testament Teaching*. London: Macmillan, 1963.

Theissen, Gerd, and Annette Merz. *The Historical Jesus: A Comprehensive Guide*. Translated by John Bowden. Minneapolis: Fortress, 1998.

Thielman, Frank. *Theology of the New Testament*. Grand Rapids: Zondervan, 2005.

Thompson, Bert. *The Scientific Case for Creation*. 2d rev. ed. Montgomery, Alabama: Apologetics Press, 2002.

Thompson, Michael. *Clothed with Christ: The Example and Teaching of Jesus in Romans 12.1–15.13*. Journal for the Study of the New Testament. Supplement Series 59. Sheffield: Academic, 1991.

Thrall, Margaret E. "The Origin of Pauline Christology." Pages 304–18 in *Apostolic History and the Gospel*. Edited by W. Ward Gasque and Ralph P. Martin. Grand Rapids: Eerdmans, 1970.

Tichy, L. "Christ in Paul: The Apostle Paul's Relation to Christ Viewed Through Gal. 2.20A." Pages 40–48 in *Journal for the Study of the New Testament*. Supplement series. no. 272. Sheffield: University of Sheffield, 2004.

Towner, Philip. "Christology in the Letters to Timothy and Titus." Pages 219–244 in *Contours of Christology in the New Testament*. Edited by Richard Longenecker. Grand Rapids: Eerdmans, 2005.

———. "1–2 Timothy and Titus." Pages 891–918 in *Commentary on the New Testament Use of the Old Testament*. Edited by G. K. Beale and D. A. Carson. Grand Rapids: Baker Academic, 2007.

Trench, John Alfred. *Our Association with Christ: John XII, 24*. 2nd ed. London: The Central Bible Truth Depot, 1900–1920.

Trobisch, David. *The First Edition of the New Testament*. Oxford: University Press, 2000.

Tuckett, C. M. *Christology and the New Testament: Jesus and His Earliest Followers*. Louisville, Ky.: Westminster John Knox, 2001.

Bibliography

Turlington, H. E. "The Apostle Paul and the Gospel History." *Review and Expositor* 38 (1951) 35–66.
Usteri, Leonhard. *Entwicklung des Paulinischen Lehrbegriffs.* Zürich, Orell, Füssli und Compagnie, 1824. [First systematic study of Paul]
Vanhoozer, Kevin J. *Is there a Meaning in This Text? The Bible, the Reader, and the Morality of Literary Knowledge.* Grand Rapids: Zondervan, 1998.
VanHoye, Albert., ed. *L'Apôtre Paul. Personnalité, style et conception du ministère.* Leuven, Peeters/ Leuven University Press, 1986.
Vawter, Bruce. *This Man Jesus: An Essay toward a New Testament Christology.* Garden City, N.Y., Doubleday, 1973.
Vermes, Geza. "The 'Son of Man' Debate." *Journal for the Study of the New Testament* (1978) 1: 19–32.
Vielhauer, Philip. "On the 'Paulinisms of Acts.'" Pages 33–50 in *Studies in Luke-Acts: Essays Presented in Honor of Paul Schubert.* Edited by L. E. Keek and J. L. Martyn. Philadelphia: Fortress, 1980.
Vos, Geerhardus. "The Kyrios Christos Controversy." *Princeton Theological Review* 15 (1917) 21–89.
———. *The Pauline Eschatology.* Phillipsburg, N.J.: Presbyterian and Reformed, 1991.
Wallace, Daniel B. *Greek Grammar Beyond the Basics: An Exegetical Syntax of the New Testament.* Grand Rapids: Zondervan, 1996.
Walter, Nicolas. "Paul and the Early Christian Jesus-Tradition." Pages 51–80 in *Paul and Jesus: Collected Essays.* Edited by Alexander Wedderburn. Journal for the Study of the New Testament. Supplement Series 37. Sheffield: Academic, 1989.
Watson, Francis. "'I Received from the Lord . . . :' Paul, Jesus and the Last Supper." Pages 103–124 in *Jesus and Paul Reconnected: Fresh Pathways into an Old Debate.* Edited by Todd D. Still. Grand Rapids: Eerdmans, 2007.
———. *Paul and the Hermeneutics of Faith.* Edinburgh: T & T Clark, 2004. [Studies how Paul and his fellow-Jews read the same texts of the OT, yet read them very differently. "The difference (is) summed up in the Christian invocation of Jesus as Lord." (p. 533).]
———. *Paul, Judaism, and the Gentiles: A Sociological Approach.* Cambridge: University Press, 1986.
———. *Paul, Judaism, and the Gentiles: Beyond the New Perspective.* Rev. and exp. ed. Grand Rapids: Eerdmans, 2007.
———. "Toward a Literal Reading of the Gospels." Pages 195–217 in *The Gospel for All Christians.* Edited by Richard Bauckham. Grand Rapids: Eerdmans, 1998.
Warfield, Benjamin Breckinridge. "The Christ that Paul Preached." Pages 73–90 in *The Person and Work of Christ.* Edited by Samuel Craig. Philadelphia: Presbyterian and Reformed, 1970.
———. "The Divine Messiah in the Old Testament." Pages 79–126 in *Biblical and Theological Studies.* Edited by Samuel Craig. Philadelphia: Presbyterian and Reformed, 1968.
Wedderburn, Alexander J. M. *Adam and Christ: An Investigation into the Background of 1 Corinthians XV and Romans V 12–21.* Ph.D. Diss., Cambridge University, 1970.
———, editor. *Paul and Jesus: Collected Essays.* Journal for the Study of the New Testament. Supplement Series 37. Sheffield: Academic Press, 1989.
———. "Some Observations on Paul's Use of the Phrases 'In Christ' and 'With Christ.'" *Journal for the Study of the New Testament* 25 (1985) 83–97.
Weinel, Heinrich. *St. Paul: The Man and His Work.* Translated by G. A. Bienemann. Edited by W. D. Morrison. New York: Putnam's, 1906. Translation of *Paulus: Der Mensch und sein Werk: Die Anfänge des Christentums, der Kirche und des Dogmas.* Tübingen, Verlag von J. C. B. Mohr (Paul Siebeck), 1904. [Uses history-of-religion method to support liberal theology].
Weiss, Johannes. *Paul and Jesus.* Translated by H. J. Chaytor. London: Harper, 1909. [Paul is influenced by Jesus' personality rather than his teaching, but contends Paul had witnessed the historical Jesus.]
———. *The History of Primitive Christianity.* Translated by F. C. Grant. New York: Wilson-Erickson, 1937.
Weizsäcker, Karl von. *The Apostolic Age.* Translated by J. Millar. London: Williams and Norgate, 1894. [Paul's theology derives from his own intuitions rather than the teachings of Jesus.]
Wells, George Albert. *The Jesus of the Early Christians: A Study in Christian Origins.* 1st ed. London: Pemberton, 1971.
Wendt, Hans Hinrich, "Die Lehre des Paulus verglichen mit der Lehre Jesu." *Zeitschrift fur die neutestamenliche Wissenschaft* 4 (1984) 1–78. [Paul recast the teaching of Jesus in terms of salvation.]
Wenham, David. *Did St. Paul Get Jesus Right?* Oxford: Lion Hill, 2010.

———. *Paul and Jesus: The True Story*. Grand Rapids: Eerdmans, 2002.

———. *Paul and the Historical Jesus*. Cambridge: Grove Books, 1998.

———. *Paul: Follower of Jesus or Founder of Christianity?* Grand Rapids: Eerdmans, 1995.

———, ed. *The Jesus Tradition Outside the Gospels*. Gospel Perspectives. Vol. 5. Sheffield: JSOT, 1984.

Westerholm, Stephen. *Perspectives Old and New on Paul*. Grand Rapids: Eerdmans, 2003.

Wilder, Terry L. *Pseudonymity, the New Testament, and Deception: An Inquiry into Intention and Reception*. Lantham, Md.: University Press of America, 2004.

Wiles, Maurice F. "Does Christology Rest on a Mistake?" Pages 3–12 in *Christ and History: Cambridge Studies in Christology*. Edited by S. W. Sykes and J. P. Clayton. Cambridge: University Press, 1972.

———. *The Divine Apostle: The Interpretation of St Paul's Epistles in the Early Church*. Cambridge University Press, 1967.

Wills, Garry. *What Paul Meant*. Penguin Books, 2007.

Wilson, A. N. *Paul: The Mind of the Apostle*. New York: Norton, 1997.

Wilson, Barrie. *How Jesus Became Christian: St. Paul, the Early Church and the Jesus Cover-up*. Random House of Canada, Limited, 2008.

Wilson, S. G. "From Jesus to Paul: The Contours and Consequences of a Debate." Pages 1–22 in *From Jesus to Paul: Studies in Honour of Francis Wright Beare*. Edited by Peter Richardson and John C. Hurd. Waterloo, Ont: Laurier University, 1984.

Wilson, Walter T. *Pauline Parallels: A Comprehensive Guide*. Louisville: Westminster/ John Knox, 2009.

Windisch, Hans. "Paulus und Jesus." *Theologische Studien und Kritiken* 106 (1936) 432–68.

Winter, Bruce M., and Andrew D. Clarke. *The Book of Acts in Ancient Literary Setting*. Grand Rapids: Eerdmans, 1994.

Winter, Bruce M. *The Book of Acts in its Theological Setting*. Grand Rapids: Eerdmans, 2007.

Witherington, Ben. "Contemporary Perspectives on Paul." Pages 256–69 in *The Cambridge Companion to St. Paul*. Edited by James D. G. Dunn. Cambridge: University Press, 2003.

———. "Jesus as the Alpha and Omega of New Testament Thought." Pages 25–46 in *Contours of Christology in the New Testament*. Richard N. Longenecker, editor. Grand Rapids: Eerdmans, 2005.

———. *Paul's Narrative Thought World: The Tapestry of Tragedy and Triumph*. Louisville: Westminster/John Knox, 1994.

———. *The Christology of Jesus*. Minneapolis: Fortress, 1990.

———. *The Paul Quest: The Renewed Search for the Jew of Tarsus*. New York: InterVarsity, 1998.

Wrede, William. *Paulus*. Translated by E. Lummis. London: Green, 1907. [Paul identified Jesus with his pre-conversion idea of a divine Christ, making Paul the "second founder of Christianity."]

Wright, N. T. "Adam in Pauline Christology." Pages 359–89 in *The Society of Biblical Literature* 22 (1983). Edited by K. H. Richards. Chico, Calif.: Scholars Press, 1983.

———. *Paul in Fresh Perspective*. Philadelphia: Fortress, 2006. [Frames Paul around Jewish symbols]

———. *What Saint Paul Really Said*. Grand Rapids: Eerdmans, 1997.

———. "Who Founded Christianity: Jesus or Paul?" No pages. Online: http://www.beliefnet,com /Faiths / Christianity/ 2004/04/Who-Founded-Christianity-Jesus-Or Paul.aspx.

Wright, Richard. *A Plain View of the Unitarian Christian Doctrine: In a Series of Essays on the one God, the Father, and the Mediator between God and Men, the Man Christ Jesus*. London: F. B. Wright, 1815. [Defends Unitarianism]

Yamauchi, Edwin M. *Pre-Christian Gnosticism: A Survey of the Proposed Evidence*. Grand Rapids: Eerdmans, 1973.

Yeung, Maureen. *Faith in Jesus and Paul*. Tubingen: Mohr Siebeck, 2002.

Young, Brad. *Paul the Jewish Theologian: A Pharisee among Christians, Jews, and Gentiles*. Peabody, Mass.: Hendrickson, 1997.

Zawadi, Bassam. "What Did Paul Want To Know About Jesus?" No pages. Online: http://www.answering-Christianity.com/bassam_zawadi/paul_Jesus.htm.

Zetterholm, Magnus. *Approaches to Paul: A Student's Guide to Recent Scholarship*. Minneapolis: Fortress, 2009.

Ziesler, John. *Pauline Christianity*. Rev. ed. Oxford Bible Series. Oxford: University Press, 1990.

Zeoli, Ronda. "Paul or Jesus?" No pages. Online: http://sherryshriner.com/zeoli.htm.

www.ingramcontent.com/pod-product-compliance
Lightning Source LLC
Chambersburg PA
CBHW080934300426
44115CB00017B/2815